HINDUISM AND BUDDHISM

HINDUISM AND BUDDHISM

AN HISTORICAL SKETCH

SIR CHARLES ELIOT

IN THREE VOLUMES

VOLUME III

GYAN

Published by

GYAN

Gyan Publishing House
5, Ansari Road
Daryaganj, New Delhi-110002
Phone: 011-47034999, 9811692060
E-mail: books@gyanbooks.com

Distribution Network
gyanbooks.com
India, USA, Canada, UK, Australia, France

ISBN: 978-81-212-8865-1 (SET)
ISBN: 978-81-212-8862-0 (PB)
First Published, 1921

2nd Impression 2023

Printed at: Gyan Press, Delhi.

HINDUISM AND BUDHISM (VOL. III)

AUTHOR: CHARLES ELIOT

HINDUISM AND BUDDHISM

VOLUME III

HINDUISM AND BUDDHISM

AN HISTORICAL SKETCH

BY

SIR CHARLES ELIOT

In three volumes

VOLUME III

ROUTLEDGE & KEGAN PAUL LTD

Broadway House, 68-74 Carter Lane,

London, E.C.4.

CONTENTS

BOOK VI

BUDDHISM OUTSIDE INDIA

BOOK VII

MUTUAL INFLUENCE OF EASTERN AND WESTERN RELIGIONS

BOOK VI

BUDDHISM OUTSIDE INDIA

CHAPTER XXXIV

EXPANSION OF INDIAN INFLUENCE

Introductory

The subject of this Book is the expansion of Indian influence throughout Eastern Asia and the neighbouring islands. That influence is clear and wide-spread, nay almost universal, and it is with justice that we speak of Further India and the Dutch call their colonies Neerlands Indië. For some early chapters in the story of this expansion the dates and details are meagre, but on the whole the investigator's chief difficulty is to grasp and marshal the mass of facts relating to the development of religion and civilization in this great region.

The spread of Hindu thought was an intellectual conquest, not an exchange of ideas. On the north-western frontier there was some reciprocity, but otherwise the part played by India was consistently active and not receptive. The Far East counted for nothing in her internal history, doubtless because China was too distant and the other countries had no special culture of their own. Still it is remarkable that whereas many Hindu missionaries preached Buddhism in China, the idea of making Confucianism known in India seems never to have entered the head of any Chinese.

It is correct to say that the sphere of India's intellectual conquests was the East and North, not the West, but still Buddhism spread considerably to the west of its original home and entered Persia. Stein discovered a Buddhist monastery in "the terminal marshes of the Helmund" in Seistan[1] and Bamian is a good distance from our frontier. But in Persia and its border lands there were powerful state religions, first Zoroastrianism and then Islam, which disliked and hindered the importation of foreign creeds and though we may see some resemblance between Sufis and Vedantists, it does not appear that the Moslim civilization of Iran owed much to Hinduism.

[1] *Geog. Jour.* Aug., 1916, p. 362.

But in all Asia north and east of India, excluding most of Siberia but including the Malay Archipelago, Indian influence is obvious. Though primarily connected with religion it includes much more, such as architecture, painting and other arts, an Indian alphabet, a vocabulary of Indian words borrowed or translated, legends and customs. The whole life of such diverse countries as Tibet, Burma, and Java would have been different had they had no connection with India.

In these and many other regions the Hindus must have found a low state of civilization, but in the Far East they encountered a culture comparable with their own. There was no question of colonizing or civilizing rude races. India and China met as equals, not hostile but also not congenial, a priest and a statesman, and the statesman made large concessions to the priest. Buddhism produced a great fermentation and controversy in Chinese thought, but though its fortunes varied it hardly ever became as in Burma and Ceylon the national religion. It was, as a Chinese Emperor once said, one of the two wings of a bird. The Chinese characters did not give way to an Indian alphabet nor did the Confucian Classics fall into desuetude. The subjects of Chinese and Japanese pictures may be Buddhist, the plan and ornaments of their temples Indian, yet judged as works of art the pictures and temples are indigenous. But for all that one has only to compare the China of the Hans with the China of the T'angs to see how great was the change wrought by India.

This outgrowing of Indian influence, so long continued and so wide in extent, was naturally not the result of any one impulse. At no time can we see in India any passion of discovery, any fever of conquest such as possessed Europe when the New World and the route to the East round the Cape were discovered. India's expansion was slow, generally peaceful and attracted little attention at home. Partly it was due to the natural permeation and infiltration of a superior culture beyond its own borders, but it is equally natural that this gradual process should have been sometimes accelerated by force of arms. The Hindus produced no Tamerlanes or Babers, but a series of expeditions, spread over long ages, but still not few in number, carried them to such distant goals as Ceylon, Java and Camboja.

But the diffusion of Indian influence, especially in China, was also due to another agency, namely religious propaganda and the deliberate despatch of missions. These missions seem to have been exclusively Buddhist for wherever we find records of Hinduism outside India, for instance in Java and Camboja, the presence of Hindu conquerors or colonists is also recorded[1]. Hinduism accompanied Hindus and sometimes spread round their settlements, but it never attempted to convert distant and alien lands. But the Buddhists had from the beginning the true evangelistic temper: they preached to all the world and in singleness of purpose: they had no political support from India. Many as were the charges brought against them by hostile Confucians, it was never suggested that they sought political or commercial privileges for their native land. It was this simple disinterested attitude which enabled Buddhism, though in many ways antipathetic to the Far East, to win its confidence.

Ceylon is the first place where we have a record of the introduction of Indian civilization and its entry there illustrates all the phenomena mentioned above, infiltration, colonization and propaganda. The island is close to the continent and communication with the Tamil country easy, but though there has long been a large Tamil population with its own language, religion and temples, the fundamental civilization is not Tamil. A Hindu called Vijaya who apparently started from the region of Broach about 500 B.C. led an expedition to Ceylon and introduced a western Hindu language. Intercourse with the north was doubtless maintained, for in the reign of Asoka we find the King of Ceylon making overtures to him and receiving with enthusiasm the missionaries whom he sent. It is possible that southern India played a greater part in this conversion than the accepted legend indicates, for we hear of a monastery built by Mahinda near Tanjore[2]. But still language, monuments and tradition attest the reality of the connection with northern India.

It is in Asoka's reign too that we first hear of Indian influence spreading northwards. His Empire included Nepal and Kashmir,

[1] The presence of Brahmans at the Courts of Burma and Siam is a different matter. They were expressly invited as more skilled in astrology and state ceremonies than Buddhists.

[2] Watters, *Yüan Chuang*, vol. II. p. 228.

he sent missionaries to the region of Himavanta, meaning apparently the southern slopes of the Himalayas, and to the Kambojas, an ambiguous race who were perhaps the inhabitants of Tibet or its border lands. The Hindu Kush seems to have been the limit of his dominions but tradition ascribes to this period the joint colonization of Khotan from India and China.

Sinhalese and Burmese traditions also credit him with the despatch of missionaries who converted Suvarṇabhûmi or Pegu. No mention of this has been found in his own inscriptions, and European critics have treated it with not unnatural scepticism for there is little indication that Asoka paid much attention to the eastern frontiers of his Empire. Still I think the question should be regarded as being *sub judice* rather than as answered in the negative.

Indian expeditions to the East probably commenced, if not in the reign of Asoka, at least before our era. The Chinese Annals[1] state that Indian Embassies reached China by sea about 50 B.C. and the Questions of Milinda allude to trade by this route: the Ramayaṇa mentions Java and an inscription seems to testify that a Hindu king was reigning in Champa (Annam) about 150 A.D. These dates are not so precise as one could wish, but if there was a Hindu kingdom in that distant region in the second century it was probably preceded by settlements in nearer halting places, such as the Isthmus of Kra[2] or Java, at a considerably anterior date, although the inscriptions discovered there are not earlier than the fifth century A.D.

Java seems to have left some trace in Indian tradition, for instance the proverb that those who go to Java do not come back, and it may have been an early distributing centre for men and merchandize in those seas. But Ligor probably marks a still earlier halting place. It is on the same coast as the Mon kingdom of Thaton, which had connection with Conjevaram by sea and was a centre of Pali Buddhism. At any rate there was a movement of conquest and colonization in these regions which brought with it Hinduism and Mahayanism, and established Hindu kingdoms in Java, Camboja, Champa and Borneo, and another movement of Hinayanist propaganda, apparently

[1] But not contemporary Annals. The Liang Annals make the statement about the reign of Hsüan Li 73–49 B.C.

[2] Especially at Ligor or Dharmaraja.

earlier, but of which we know less[1]. Though these expeditions both secular and religious probably took ship on the east coast of India, *e.g.* at Masulipatam or the Seven Pagodas, yet their original starting point may have been in the west, such as the district of Badami or even Gujarat, for there were trade routes across the Indian Peninsula at an early date[2].

It is curious that the early history of Burma should be so obscure and in order not to repeat details and hypotheses I refer the reader to the chapter dealing specially with this country. From an early epoch Upper Burma had connection with China and Bengal by land and Lower Burma with Orissa and Conjevaram by sea. We know too that Pali Buddhism existed there in the sixth century, that it gained greatly in power in the reign of Anawrata (*c.* 1060) and that in subsequent centuries there was a close ecclesiastical connection with Ceylon.

Siam as a kingdom is relatively modern but like Burma it has been subject to several influences. The Siamese probably brought some form of Buddhism with them when they descended from the north to their present territories. From the Cambojans, their neighbours and at one time their suzerains, they must have acquired some Hinduism and Mahayanism, but they ended by adopting Hinayanism. The source was probably Pegu but learned men from Ligor were also welcomed and the ecclesiastical pre-eminence of Ceylon was accepted.

We thus see how Indian influence conquered Further India and the Malay Archipelago and we must now trace its flow across Central Asia to China and Japan, as well as the separate and later stream which irrigated Tibet and Mongolia.

Tradition as mentioned ascribes to Asoka some connection with Khotan and it is probable that by the beginning of our era the lands of the Oxus and Tarim had become Buddhist and acquired a mixed civilization in which the Indian factor was large. As usual it is difficult to give precise dates, but Buddhism probably reached China by land a little before rather than after our era and the prevalence of Gandharan art in the cities of the Tarim basin makes it likely that their efflorescence was not far removed in time from the Gandharan epoch of India.

[1] The statement of I-Ching that a wicked king destroyed Buddhism in Funan is important.

[2] See Fleet in *J.R.A.S.* 1901, p. 548.

The discovery near Khotan of official documents written in Prakrit makes colonization as well as religious missions probable. Further, although the movements of Central Asian tribes commonly took the form of invading India, yet the current of culture was, on the whole, in the opposite direction. The Kushans and others brought with them a certain amount of Zoroastrian theology and Hellenistic art, but the compound resulting from the mixture of these elements with Buddhism was re-exported to the north and to China.

I shall discuss below the grounds for believing that Buddhism was known in China before A.D. 62, the date when the Emperor Ming Ti is said to have despatched a mission to enquire about it. For some time many of its chief luminaries were immigrants from Central Asia and it made its most rapid progress in that disturbed period of the third and fourth centuries when North China was split up into contending Tartar states which both in race and politics were closely connected with Central Asia. Communication with India by land became frequent and there was also communication *viâ* the Malay Archipelago, especially after the fifth century, when a double stream of Buddhist teachers began to pour into China by sea as well as by land. A third tributary joined them later when Khubilai, the Mongol conqueror of China, made Lamaism, or Tibetan Buddhism, the state religion.

Tibetan Buddhism is a form of late Indian Mahayanism with a considerable admixture of Hinduism, exported from Bengal to Tibet and there modified not so much in doctrine as by the creation of a powerful hierarchy, curiously analogous to the Roman Church. It is unknown in southern China and not much favoured by the educated classes in the north, but the Lamaist priesthood enjoys great authority in Tibet and Mongolia, and both the Ming and Ch'ing dynasties did their best to conciliate it for political reasons. Lamaism has borrowed little from China and must be regarded as an invasion into northern Asia and even Europe[1] of late Indian religion and art, somewhat modified by the strong idiosyncrasy of the Tibetan people. This northern movement was started by the desire of imitation, not of conquest. At the beginning of the seventh century the King

[1] There are settlements of Kalmuks near Astrakhan who have Lama temples and maintain a connection with Tibet.

of Tibet, who had dealings with both India and China, sent a mission to the former to enquire about Buddhism and in the eighth and eleventh centuries eminent doctors were summoned from India to establish the faith and then to restore it after a temporary eclipse.

In Korea, Annam, and especially in Japan, Buddhism has been a great ethical, religious and artistic force and in this sense those countries owe much to India. Yet there was little direct communication and what they received came to them almost entirely through China. The ancient Champa was a Hindu kingdom analogous to Camboja, but modern Annam represents not a continuation of this civilization but a later descent of Chinese culture from the north. Japan was in close touch with the Chinese just at the period when Buddhism was fermenting their whole intellectual life and Japanese thought and art grew up in the glow of this new inspiration, which was more intense than in China because there was no native antagonist of the same strength as Confucianism.

In the following chapters I propose to discuss the history of Indian influence in the various countries of Eastern Asia, taking Ceylon first, followed by Burma and Siam. Whatever may have been the origin of Buddhism in these two latter they have had for many centuries a close ecclesiastical connection with Ceylon. Pali Buddhism prevails in all, as well as in modern Camboja.

The Indian religion which prevailed in ancient Camboja was however of a different type and similar to that of Champa and Java. In treating of these Hindu kingdoms I have wondered whether I should not begin with Java and adopt the hypothesis that the settlements established there sent expeditions to the mainland and Borneo[1]. But the history of Java is curiously fragmentary whereas the copious inscriptions of Camboja and Champa combined with Chinese notices give a fairly continuous chronicle. And a glance at the map will show that if there were Hindu colonists at Ligor it would have been much easier for

[1] The existence of a Hindu kingdom on the *East* Coast of Borneo in 400 A.D. or earlier is a strong argument in favour of colonization from Java. Expeditions from any other quarter would naturally have gone to the *West* Coast. Also there is some knowledge of Java in India, but apparently none of Camboja or Champa. This suggests that Java may have been the first halting place and kept up some slight connection with the mother country.

them to go across the Gulf of Siam to Camboja than *viâ* Java. I have therefore not adopted the hypothesis of expansion from Java (while also not rejecting it) nor followed any chronological method but have treated of Camboja first, as being the Hindu state of which on the whole we know most and then of Champa and Java in comparison with it.

In the later sections of the book I consider the expansion of Indian influence in the north. A chapter on Central Asia endeavours to summarize our rapidly increasing knowledge of this meeting place of nations. Its history is closely connected with China and naturally leads me to a somewhat extended review of the fortunes and achievements of Buddhism in that great land, and also to a special study of Tibet and of Lamaism. I have treated of Nepal elsewhere. For the history of religion it is not a new province, but simply the extreme north of the Indian region where the last phase of decadent Indian Buddhism which practically disappeared in Bengal still retains a nominal existence.

CHAPTER XXXV

CEYLON

1

THE island of Ceylon, perhaps the most beautiful tropical country in the world, lies near the end of the Indian peninsula but a little to the east. At one point a chain of smaller islands and rocks said to have been built by Rama as a passage for his army of monkeys leads to the mainland. It is therefore natural that the population should have relations with southern India. Sinhalese art, religion and language show traces of Tamil influence but it is somewhat surprising to find that in these and in all departments of civilization the influence of northern India is stronger. The traditions which explain the connection of Ceylon with this distant region seem credible and the Sinhalese, who were often at war with the Tamils, were not disposed to imitate their usages, although juxtaposition and invasion brought about much involuntary resemblance.

The school of Buddhism now professed in Ceylon, Burma and Siam is often called Sinhalese and (provided it is not implied that its doctrines originated in Ceylon) the epithet is correct. For the school ceased to exist in India and in the middle ages both Burma and Siam accepted the authority of the Sinhalese Sangha[1]. This Sinhalese school seems to be founded on the doctrines and scriptures accepted in the time of Asoka in Magadha and though the faith may have been codified and supplemented in its new home, I see no evidence that it underwent much corruption or even development. One is inclined at first to think that the Hindus, having a continuous living tradition connecting them with Gotama who was himself a Hindu, were more likely than these distant islanders to preserve the spirit of his teaching. But there is another side to

[1] *E.g.* Burma in the reign of Anawrata and later in the time of Chapaṭa about 1200, and Siam in the time of Sûryavaṃsa Râma, 1361. On the other hand in 1752 the Sinhalese succession was validated by obtaining monks from Burma.

the question. The Hindus being addicted to theological and metaphysical studies produced original thinkers who, if not able to found new religions, at least modified what their predecessors had laid down. If certain old texts were held in too high esteem to be neglected, the ingenuity of the commentator rarely failed to reinterpret them as favourable to the views popular in his time. But the Sinhalese had not this passion for theology. So far as we can judge of them in earlier periods they were endowed with an amiable and receptive but somewhat indolent temperament, moderate gifts in art and literature and a moderate love and understanding of theology. Also their chiefs claimed to have come from northern India and were inclined to accept favourably anything which had the same origin. These are exactly the surroundings in which a religion can flourish without change for many centuries and Buddhism in Ceylon acquired stability because it also acquired a certain national and patriotic flavour: it was the faith of the Sinhalese and not of the invading Tamils. Such Sinhalese kings as had the power protected the Church and erected magnificent buildings for its service.

If Sinhalese tradition may be believed, the first historical contact with northern India was the expedition of Vijaya, who with 700 followers settled in the island about the time of the Buddha's death. Many details of the story are obviously invented. Thus in order to explain why Ceylon is called Sinhala, Vijaya is made the grandson of an Indian princess who lived with a lion. But though these legends inspire mistrust, it is a fact that the language of Ceylon in its earliest known form is a dialect closely connected with Pali (or rather with the spoken dialect from which ecclesiastical Pali was derived) and still more closely with the Mahârâshtri Prakrit of western India. It is not however a derivative of this Prakrit but parallel to it and in some words presents older forms[1]. It does not seem possible to ascribe the introduction of this language to the later mission of Mahinda, for, though Buddhist monks have in many countries influenced literature and the literary vocabulary, no instance is recorded of their changing the popular speech[2]. But Vijaya is said to have conquered Ceylon and to have slaughtered many

[1] Geiger, *Literatur und Sprache der Singhalesen*, p. 91.

[2] Compare the history of Khotan. The first Indian colonists seem to have introduced a Prakrit dialect. Buddhism and Sanskrit came afterwards.

of its ancient inhabitants, called Yakkhas[1], of whom we know little except that Sinhalese contains some un-Aryan words probably borrowed from them. According to the Dîpavaṃsa[2], Vijaya started from Bharukaccha or Broach and both language and such historical facts as we know confirm the tradition that some time before the third century B.C. Ceylon was conquered by Indian immigrants from the west coast.

It would not be unreasonable to suppose that Vijaya introduced into Ceylon the elements of Buddhism, but there is little evidence to indicate that it was a conspicuous form of religion in India in his time. Sinhalese tradition maintains that not only Gotama himself but also the three preceding Buddhas were miraculously transported to Ceylon and made arrangements for its conversion. Gotama is said to have paid no less than three visits[3]: all are obviously impossible and were invented to enhance the glory of the island. But the legends which relate how Paṇḍuvâsudeva came from India to succeed Vijaya, how he subsequently had a Sakya princess brought over from India to be his wife and how her brothers established cities in Ceylon[4], if not true in detail, are probably true in spirit in so far as they imply that the Sinhalese kept up intercourse with India and were familiar with the principal forms of Indian religion. Thus we are told[5] that King Paṇḍukâbhaya built religious edifices for Nigaṇṭhas (Jains), Brahmans, Paribbâjakas (possibly Buddhists) and Âjîvikas. When Devânampiya Tissa ascended the throne (*circ.* 245 B.C.) he sent a complimentary mission bearing wonderful treasures to Asoka with whom he was on friendly terms, although they had never met. This implies that the kingdom of Magadha was known and respected in Ceylon, and we hear that the mission included a Brahman. The answer attributed to Asoka will surprise no one acquainted with the inscriptions of that pious monarch. He said that he had taken

[1] Literally demons, that is wild uncanny men. I refrain from discussing the origin and ethnological position of the Vaeddas for it hardly affects the history of Buddhism in Ceylon. For Vijaya's conquests see Mahâvaṃsa VII.

[2] IX. 26.

[3] Dîpavaṃsa I. 45–81, II. 1–69. Mahâvaṃsa I. 19–83. The legend that the Buddha visited Ceylon and left his footprint on Adam's peak is at least as old as Buddhaghosa. See Samanta-pâsâdikâ in Oldenburg's *Vinaya Pitaka*, vol. III, p. 332 and the quotations in Skeen's *Adam's Peak*, p. 50.

[4] Dîpa. V. X. 1–9. Mahâvaṃsa VIII. 1–27, IX. 1–12.

[5] Mahâvaṃsa X. 96, 102.

refuge in the law of Buddha and advised the King of Ceylon to find salvation in the same way. He also sent magnificent presents consisting chiefly of royal insignia and Tissa was crowned for the second time, which probably means that he became not only the disciple but the vassal of Asoka.

In any case the records declare that the Indian Emperor showed the greatest solicitude for the spiritual welfare of Ceylon and, though they are obviously embellished, there is no reason to doubt their substantial accuracy[1]. The Sinhalese tradition agrees on the whole with the data supplied by Indian inscriptions and Chinese pilgrims. The names of missionaries mentioned in the Dîpa and Mahâvamsas recur on urns found at Sanchi and on its gateways are pictures in relief which appear to represent the transfer of a branch of the Bo-tree in solemn procession to some destination which, though unnamed, may be conjectured to be Ceylon[2]. The absence of Mahinda's name in Asoka's inscriptions is certainly suspicious, but the Sinhalese chronicles give the names of other missionaries correctly and a mere *argumentum ex silentio* cannot disprove their testimony on this important point.

The principal repositories of Sinhalese tradition are the Dîpavamsa, the Mahâvamsa, and the historical preface of Buddhaghosa's Samanta-pâsâdikâ[3]. All later works are founded on these three, so far as concerns the conversion of Ceylon and the immediately subsequent period, and the three works appear to be rearrangements of a single source known as the Aṭṭhakathâ, Sihalaṭṭhakathâ, or the words of the Porâṇa (ancients). These names were given to commentaries on the Tipiṭaka written in Sinhalese prose interspersed with Pali verse and several of the greater monasteries had their own editions of them, including a definite historical section[4]. It is probable that at the beginning of the fifth century A.D. and perhaps in the fourth century the old Sinhalese in which the prose parts of the Atthakathâ were

[1] For the credibility of the Sinhalese traditions see Geiger introd. to translation of Mahâvaṃsa 1912 and Norman in *J.R.A.S.* 1908, pp. 1 ff. and on the other side R. O. Franke in *W.Z.K.M.* 21, pp. 203 ff., 317 ff. and *Z.D.M.G.* 63, pp. 540 ff.

[2] Grünwedel, *Buddhist art in India*, pp. 69–72. Rhys Davids, *Buddhist India*, p. 302.

[3] The Jâtaka-nidâna-kathâ is also closely allied to these works in those parts where the subject matter is the same.

[4] This section was probably called Mahâvaṃsa in a general sense long before the name was specially applied to the work which now bears it.

written was growing unintelligible, and that it was becoming more and more the fashion to use Pali as the language of ecclesiastical literature, for at least three writers set themselves to turn part of the traditions not into the vernacular but into Pali. The earliest and least artistic is the unknown author of the short chronicle called Dîpavamsa, who wrote between 302 A.D. and 430 A.D.[1] His work is weak both as a specimen of Pali and as a narrative and he probably did little but patch together the Pali verses occurring from time to time in the Sinhalese prose of the Atthakathâ. Somewhat later, towards the end of the fifth century, a certain Mahânâma arranged the materials out of which the Dîpavamsa had been formed in a more consecutive and artistic form, combining ecclesiastical and popular legends[2]. His work, known as the Mahâvamsa, does not end with the reign of Eḷâra, like the Dîpavamsa, but describes in 15 more chapters the exploits of Duṭṭhagâmaṇi and his successors ending with Mahâsena[3]. The third writer, Buddhaghosa, apparently lived between the authors of the two chronicles. His voluminous literary activity will demand our attention later but so far as history is concerned his narrative is closely parallel to the Mahâvamsa[4].

The historical narrative is similar in all three works. After the Council of Pataliputra, Moggaliputta, who had presided over it, came to the conclusion that the time had come to despatch missionaries to convert foreign countries. Sinhalese tradition represents this decision as emanating from Moggaliputta whereas the inscriptions of Asoka imply that the king himself initiated the momentous project. But the difference is small. We cannot now tell to whom the great idea first occurred but it must have been carried out by the clergy with the assistance of Asoka, the apostle selected for Ceylon was his[5]

[1] See introduction to Oldenburg's edition, pp. 8, 9.

[2] Perhaps this is alluded to at the beginning of the Mahâvaṃsa itself, "The book made by the ancients (porvâṇehi kato) was in some places too diffuse and in others too condensed and contained many repetitions."

[3] The Mahâvaṃsa was continued by later writers and brought down to about 1780 A.D.

[4] The Mahâvaṃsatîkâ, a commentary written between 1000 and 1250 A.D., has also some independent value because the old Aṭṭhakathâ-Mahâvaṃsa was still extant and used by the writer.

[5] Son according to the Sinhalese sources but according to Hsüan Chuang and others, younger brother. In favour of the latter it may be said that the younger brothers of kings often became monks in order to avoid political complications.

near relative Mahinda who according to the traditions of the Sinhalese made his way to their island through the air with six companions. The account of Hsüan Chuang hints at a less miraculous mode of progression for he speaks of a monastery built by Mahinda somewhere near Tanjore.

The legend tells how Mahinda and his following alighted on the Missaka mountain[1] whither King Devânampiya Tissa had gone in the course of a hunt. The monks and the royal cortege met: Mahinda, after testing the king's intellectual capacity by some curious dialectical puzzles, had no difficulty in converting him[2]. Next morning he proceeded to Anuradhapura and was received with all honour and enthusiasm. He preached first in the palace and then to enthusiastic audiences of the general public. In these discourses he dwelt chiefly on the terrible punishment awaiting sinners in future existences[3].

We need not follow in detail the picturesque account of the rapid conversion of the capital. The king made over to the Church the Mahâmegha garden and proceeded to construct a series of religious edifices in Anuradhapura and its neighbourhood. The catalogue of them is given in the Mahâvamsa[4] and the most important was the Mahâvihâra monastery, which became specially famous and influential in the history of Buddhism. It was situated in the Mahâmegha garden close to the Bo-tree and was regarded as the citadel of orthodoxy. Its subsequent conflicts with the later Abhayagiri monastery are the chief theme of Sinhalese ecclesiastical history and our version of the Pali Piṭakas is the one which received its imprimatur.

Tissa is represented as having sent two further missions to India. The first went in quest of relics and made its way not only to Pataliputra but to the court of Indra, king of the gods, and the relics obtained, of which the principal was the Buddha's alms-bowl[5], were deposited in Anuradhapura. The king then built the Thuparâma dagoba over them and there is no reason

[1] The modern Mahintale.

[2] The Mahâvaṃsa implies that he had already some acquaintance with Buddhism. It represents him as knowing that monks do not eat in the afternoon and as suggesting that it would be better to ordain the layman Bhandu.

[3] The chronicles give with some slight divergences the names of the texts on which his preaching was based. It is doubtless meant that he recited the Sutta with a running exposition.

[4] Mahâvaṃ. xx. 17.

[5] Many other places claimed to possess this relic.

to doubt that the building which now bears this name is genuine. The story may therefore be true to the extent that relics were brought from India at this early period.

The second mission was despatched to bring a branch of the tree[1] under which the Buddha had sat when he obtained enlightenment. This narrative[2] is perhaps based on a more solid substratum of fact. The chronicles connect the event with the desire of the Princess Anulâ to become a nun. Women could receive ordination only from ordained nuns and as these were not to be found on the island it was decided to ask Asoka to send a branch of the sacred tree and also Mahinda's sister Sanghamittâ, a religieuse of eminence. The mission was successful. A branch from the Bo-tree was detached, conveyed by Asoka to the coast with much ceremony and received in Ceylon by Tissa with equal respect. The princess accompanied it. The Bo-tree was planted in the Meghavana garden. It may still be seen and attracts pilgrims not only from Ceylon but from Burma and Siam. Unlike the buildings of Anuradhapura it has never been entirely neglected and it is clear that it has been venerated as the Bo-tree from an early period of Sinhalese history. Botanists consider its long life, though remarkable, not impossible since trees of this species throw up fresh shoots from the roots near the parent stem. The sculptures at Sanchi represent a branch of a sacred tree being carried in procession, though no inscription attests its destination, and Fa-Hsien says that he saw the tree[3]. The author of the first part of the Mahâvamsa clearly regards it as already ancient, and throughout the history of Ceylon there are references to the construction of railings and terraces to protect it.

Devânampiya Tissa probably died in 207 B.C. In 177 the kingdom passed into the hands of Tamil monarchs who were not Buddhists, although the chroniclers praise their justice and the respect which they showed to the Church. The most important of them, Eḷâra, reigned for forty-four years and was dethroned by a descendant of Tissa, called Duṭṭhagâmaṇi[4].

[1] Of course the antiquity of the Sinhalese Bo-tree is a different question from the identity of the parent tree with the tree under which the Buddha sat.

[2] Mahâvaṃ. XVIII.; Dîpavaṃ. XV. and XVI.

[3] But he says nothing about Mahinda or Sanghamittâ and does not support the Mahâvaṃsa in details.

[4] Duṭṭha, meaning bad, angry or violent, apparently refers to the ferocity shown in his struggle with the Tamils.

The exploits of this prince are recorded at such length in the Mahâvamsa (XXII.–XXXII.) as to suggest that they formed the subject of a separate popular epic, in which he figured as the champion of Sinhalese against the Tamils, and therefore as a devout Buddhist. On ascending the throne he felt, like Asoka, remorse for the bloodshed which had attended his early life and strove to atone for it by good works, especially the construction of sacred edifices. The most important of these were the Lohapasâda or Copper Palace and the Mahâthûpa or Ruwanweli Dagoba. The former[1] was a monastery roofed or covered with copper plates. Its numerous rooms were richly decorated and it consisted of nine storeys, of which the four uppermost were set apart for Arhats, and the lower assigned to the inferior grades of monks. Perhaps the nine storeys are an exaggeration: at any rate the building suffered from fire and underwent numerous reconstructions and modifications. King Mahâsena (301 A.D.) destroyed it and then repenting of his errors rebuilt it, but the ruins now representing it at Anuradhapura, which consist of stone pillars only, date from the reign of Parâkrama Bâhu I (about A.D. 1150). The immense pile known as the Ruwanweli Dagoba, though often injured by invaders in search of treasure, still exists. The somewhat dilapidated exterior is merely an outer shell, enclosing a smaller dagoba[2]. This is possibly the structure erected by Duṭṭhagâmaṇi, though tradition says that there is a still smaller edifice inside. The foundation and building of the original structure are related at great length[3]. Crowds of distinguished monks came to see the first stone laid, even from Kashmir and Alasanda. Some have identified the latter name with Alexandria in Egypt, but it probably denotes a Greek city on the Indus[4]. But in any case tradition represents Buddhists from all parts of India as taking part in the ceremony and thus recognizing the unity of Indian and Sinhalese Buddhism.

[1] Dîpavaṃsa XIX. 1. Mahâvaṃsa XXVII. 1–48. See Fergusson, *Hist. Ind. Architecture*, 1910, pp. 238, 246. I find it hard to picture such a building raised on pillars. Perhaps it was something like the Sat-mahal-prasâda at Pollanarua.

[2] Parker, *Ancient Ceylon*, p. 282. The restoration of the Ruwanweli Dagoba was undertaken by Buddhists in 1873.

[3] Mahâvaṃsa XXVIII.–XXXI. Duṭṭhagâmaṇi died before it was finished.

[4] Mahâvaṃsa XXIX. 37. Yonanâgarâlasanda. The town is also mentioned as situated on an Island in the Indus: Mil. Pan. III. 7. 4.

Of great importance for the history of the Sinhalese Church is the reign of Vaṭṭagâmaṇi Abhaya who after being dethroned by Tamils recovered his kingdom and reigned for twelve years[1]. He built a new monastery and dagoba known as Abhayagiri[2], which soon became the enemy of the Mahâvihâra and heterodox, if the latter is to be considered orthodox. The account of the schism given in the Mahâvaṃsa[3] is obscure, but the dispute resulted in the Piṭakas, which had hitherto been preserved orally, being committed to writing. The council which defined and edited the scriptures was not attended by all the monasteries of Ceylon, but only by the monks of the Mahâvihâra, and the text which they wrote down was their special version and not universally accepted. It included the Parivâra, which was apparently a recent manual composed in Ceylon. The Mahâvaṃsa says no more about this schism, but the Nikâya-Sangrahawa[4] says that the monks of the Abhayagiri monastery now embraced the doctrines of the Vajjiputta school (one of the seventeen branches of the Mahâsanghikas) which was known in Ceylon as the Dhammaruci school from an eminent teacher of that name. Many pious kings followed who built or repaired sacred edifices and Buddhism evidently flourished, but we also hear of heresy. In the third century A.D.[5] King Voharaka Tissa suppressed[6] the Vetulyas. This sect was connected with the Abhayagiri monastery, but, though it lasted until the twelfth century, I have found no Sinhalese account of its tenets. It is represented as the worst of heresies, which was suppressed by

[1] According to the common reckoning B.C. 88–76: according to Geiger B.C. 29–17. It seems probable that in the early dates of Sinhalese history there is an error of about 62 years. See Geiger, *Trans. Mahâvaṃsa*, pp. xxx ff. and Fleet, *J.R.A.S.* 1909, pp. 323–356.

[2] For the site see Parker's *Ancient Ceylon*, pp. 299 ff. The Mahâvaṃsa (XXXIII. 79 and X. 98–100) says it was built on the site of an ancient Jain establishment and Kern thinks that this tradition hints at circumstances which account for the heretical and contentious spirit of the Abhaya monks.

[3] Mahâv. XXXIII. 100–104. See too the Ṭikâ quote by Turnour in his introduction, p. liii.

[4] A work on ecclesiastical history written about 1395. Ed. and Trans. Colombo Record Office.

[5] The probable error in Sinhalese dates mentioned in a previous note continues till the twelfth century A.D. though gradually decreasing. For the early centuries of the Christian era it is probable that the accepted dates should be put half a century later

[6] Mahâvaṃsa XXXVI. 41. Vetulyavâdam madditvâ. According to the Nikâya Sang. he burnt their Piṭaka.

all orthodox kings but again and again revived, or was re-introduced from India. Though it always found a footing at the Abhayagiri it was not officially recognized as the creed of that Monastery which since the time of Vaṭṭagâmaṇi seems to have professed the relatively orthodox doctrine called Dhammaruci.

Mention is made in the Kathâ-vatthu of heretics who held that the Buddha remained in the Tusita heaven and that the law was preached on earth not by him but by Ânanda and the commentary[1] ascribes these views to the Vetulyakas. The reticence of the Sinhalese chronicles makes it doubtful whether the Vetulyakas of Ceylon and these heretics are identical but probably the monks of the Abhayagiri, if not strictly speaking Mahayanist, were an off-shoot of an ancient sect which contained some germs of the Mahayana. Hsüan Chuang in his narrative[2] states (probably from hearsay) that the monks of the Mahâvihâra were Hinayanists but that both vehicles were studied at the Abhayagiri. I-Ching on the contrary says expressly that all the Sinhalese belonged to the Âryasthavira Nikâya. Fa-Hsien describes the Buddhism of Ceylon as he saw it about 412 A.D., but does not apply to it the terms Hina or Mahayana. He evidently regarded the Abhayagiri as the principal religious centre and says it had 5000 monks as against 3000 in the Mahâvihâra, but though he dwells on the gorgeous ceremonial, the veneration of the sacred tooth, the representations of Gotama's previous lives, and the images of Maitreya, he does not allude to the worship of Avalokita and Mañjusrî or to anything that can be called definitely Mahayanist. He describes a florid and somewhat superstitious worship which may have tended to regard the Buddha as superhuman, but the relics of Gotama's body were its chief visible symbols and we have no ground for assuming that such teaching as is found in the Lotus sûtra was its theological basis. Yet we may legitimately suspect that the traditions of the Abhayagiri remount to early prototypes of that teaching.

In the second and third centuries the Court seems to have favoured the Mahâvihâra and King Goṭhâbhaya banished

[1] On Kathâ-vat. XVIII. 1 and 2. Printed in the *Journal of the Pali Text Soc.* for 1889.

[2] Watters, II. 234. Cf. *Hsüan Chuang's life*, chap. IV.

monks belonging to the Vetulya sect[1], but in spite of this a monk of the Abhayagiri named Sanghamitta obtained his confidence and that of his son, Mahâsena, who occupied the throne from 275 to 302 A.D. The Mahâvihâra was destroyed and its occupants persecuted at Sanghamitta's instigation but he was murdered and after his death the great Monastery was rebuilt. The triumph however was not complete for Mahâsena built a new monastery called Jetavana on ground belonging to the Mahâvihâra and asked the monks to abandon this portion of their territory. They refused and according to the Mahâvamsa ultimately succeeded in proving their rights before a court of law. But the Jetavana remained as the headquarters of a sect known as Sagaliyas. They appear to have been moderately orthodox, but to have had their own text of the Vinaya for according to the Commentary[2] on the Mahâvamsa they "separated the two Vibhangas of the Bhagavâ[3] from the Vinaya... altering their meaning and misquoting their contents." In the opinion of the Mahâvihâra both the Abhayagiri and Jetavana were schismatical, but the laity appear to have given their respect and offerings to all three impartially and the Mahâvamsa several times records how the same individual honoured the three Confraternities.

With the death of Mahâsena ends the first and oldest part of the Mahâvamsa, and also in native opinion the grand period of Sinhalese history, the subsequent kings being known as the Cûlavaṃsa or minor dynasty. A continuation[4] of the chronicle takes up the story and tells of the doings of Mahâsena's son Sirimeghavaṇṇa[5]. Judged by the standard of the Mahâvihâra, he was fairly satisfactory. He rebuilt the Lohapasâda and caused a golden image of Mahinda to be made and carried in

[1] Mahâvaṃ. XXXVI. iii. ff. Goṭhâbhaya's date was probably 302–315 and Mahâsena's 325–352. The common chronology makes Goṭhâbhaya reign from 244 to 257 and Mahâsena from 269 to 296 A.D.

[2] Quoted by Turnour, Introd. p. liii. The Mahâvaṃ. v. 13, expressly states that the Dhammaruci and Sâgaliya sects originated in Ceylon.

[3] *I.e.* as I understand, the two divisions of the Sutta Vibhanga.

[4] It was written up to date at various periods. The chapters which take up the history after the death of Mahâsena are said to be the work of Dhammakitti, who lived about 1250.

[5] He was a contemporary of the Gupta King Samudragupta who reigned approximately 330–375 A.D. See S. Lévi in *J.A.* 1900, pp. 316 ff, 401 ff. This synchronism is a striking confirmation of Fleet and Geiger's chronology.

procession. This veneration of the founder of a local church reminds one of the respect shown to the images of half-deified abbots in Tibet, China and Japan. But the king did not neglect the Abhayagiri or assign it a lower position than the Mahâvihâra for he gave it partial custody of the celebrated relic known as the Buddha's tooth which was brought to Ceylon from Kalinga in the ninth year of his reign and has ever since been considered the palladium of the island.

2

It may not be amiss to consider here briefly what is known of the history of the Buddha's relics and especially of this tooth. Of the minor distinctions between Buddhism and Hinduism one of the sharpest is this cultus. Hindu temples are often erected over natural objects supposed to resemble the footprint or some member of a deity and sometimes tombs receive veneration[1]. But no case appears to be known in which either Hindus or Jains show reverence to the bones or other fragments of a human body. It is hence remarkable that relic-worship should be so wide-spread in Buddhism and appear so early in its history. The earliest Buddhist monuments depict figures worshipping at a stupa, which was probably a reliquary, and there is no reason to distrust the traditions which carry the practice back at least to the reign of Asoka. The principal cause for its prevalence was no doubt that Buddhism, while creating a powerful religious current, provided hardly any objects of worship for the faithful[2]. It is also probable that the rudiments of relic worship existed in the districts frequented by the Buddha. The account of his death states that after the cremation of his body the Mallas placed his bones in their council hall and honoured them with songs and dances. Then eight communities or individuals demanded a portion of the relics and over each portion a cairn was built. These proceedings are mentioned as if they were the usual ceremonial observed on the death of a great man and in

[1] *E.g.* the tomb of Râmânuja at Srîrangam.

[2] For a somewhat similar reason the veneration of relics is prevalent among Moslims. Islam indeed provides an object of worship but its ceremonies are so austere and monotonous that any devotional practices which are not forbidden as idolatrous are welcome to the devout.

the same Sutta[1] the Buddha himself mentions four classes of men worthy of a cairn or dagoba[2]. We may perhaps conclude that in the earliest ages of Buddhism it was usual in north-eastern India to honour the bones of a distinguished man after cremation and inter them under a monument. This is not exactly relic worship but it has in it the root of the later tree. The Piṭakas contain little about the practice but the Milinda Pañha discusses the question at length and in one passage[3] endeavours to reconcile two sayings of the Buddha, "Hinder not yourselves by honouring the remains of the Tathâgatha" and "Honour that relic of him who is worthy of honour." It is the first utterance rather than the second that seems to have the genuine ring of Gotama.

The earliest known relics are those discovered in the stupa of Piprâvâ on the borders of Nepal in 1898. Their precise nature and the date of the inscription describing them have been the subject of much discussion. Some authorities think that this stupa may be one of those erected over a portion of the Buddha's ashes after his funeral. Even Barth, a most cautious and sceptical scholar, admitted[4] first that the inscription is not later than Asoka, secondly that the vase is a reliquary containing what were believed to be bones of the Buddha. Thus in the time of Asoka the worship of the Buddha's relics was well known and I see no reason why the inscription should not be anterior to that time.

According to Buddhaghosa's *Sumangalavilâsinî* and Sinhalese texts which though late are based on early material[5], Mahâkassapa instigated Ajâtasattu to collect the relics of the Buddha, and to place them in a stupa, there to await the advent of Asoka. In Asoka's time the stupa had become overgrown and hidden by jungle but when the king was in search of relics, its position was revealed to him. He found inside it an inscription authorizing him to disperse the contents and pro-

[1] Dig. Nik. XVI. v. 27.

[2] Plutarch mentions a story that the relics of King Menander were similarly divided into eight portions but the story may be merely a replica of the obsequies of the Buddha.

[3] IV. 3, 24. The first text is from Mahâparinibbâna Sutta, v. 24. The second has not been identified.

[4] *Journal des Savants*, Oct. 1906.

[5] See Norman, "Buddhist legends of Asoka and his times," in *J.A.S.* Beng. 1910.

ceeded to distribute them among the 84,000 monasteries which he is said to have constructed.

In its main outlines this account is probable. Ajâtasattu conquered the Licchavis and other small states to the north of Magadha and if he was convinced of the importance of the Buddha's relics it would be natural that he should transport them to his capital, regarding them perhaps as talismans[1]. Here they were neglected, though not damaged, in the reigns of Brahmanical kings and were rescued from oblivion by Asoka, who being sovereign of all India and anxious to spread Buddhism throughout his dominions would be likely to distribute the relics as widely as he distributed his pillars and inscriptions. But later Buddhist kings could not emulate this imperial impartiality and we may surmise that such a monarch as Kanishka would see to it that all the principal relics in northern India found their way to his capital. The bones discovered at Peshawar are doubtless those considered most authentic in his reign.

Next to the tooth, the most interesting relic of the Buddha was his *patra* or alms-bowl, which plays a part somewhat similar to that of the Holy Grail in Christian romance. The Mahâvamsa states that Asoka sent it to Ceylon, but the Chinese pilgrim Fa-Hsien[2] saw it at Peshawar about 405 A.D. It was shown to the people daily at the midday and evening services. The pilgrim thought it contained about two pecks yet such were its miraculous properties that the poor could fill it with a gift of a few flowers, whereas the rich cast in myriads of bushels and found there was still room for more. A few years later Fa-Hsien heard a sermon in Ceylon[3] in which the preacher predicted that the bowl would be taken in the course of centuries to Central Asia, China, Ceylon and Central India whence it would ultimately ascend to the Tusita heaven for the use of the future Buddha. Later accounts to some extent record the fulfilment of these predictions inasmuch as they relate how the bowl (or bowls) passed from land to land but the story of its wandering may have little foundation since it is combined with the idea that it is wafted from shrine to shrine according as the faith is flourishing or decadent. Hsüan Chuang says that it "had gone

[1] Just as the Tooth was considered to be the palladium of Sinhalese kings.

[2] Record of Buddhist kingdoms. Legge, pp. 34, 35. Fa-Hsien speaks of the country not the town of Péshawar (Purûshapura).

[3] *Ibid.* p. 109. Fa-Hsien does not indicate that at this time there was a rival bowl in Ceylon but represents the preacher as saying it was then in Gandhara.

on from Peshawar to several countries and was now in Persia[1]." A Mohammedan legend relates that it is at Kandahar and will contain any quantity of liquid without overflowing. Marco Polo says Kublai Khan sent an embassy in 1284 to bring it from Ceylon to China[2].

The wanderings of the tooth, though almost as surprising as those of the bowl, rest on better historical evidence, but there is probably more continuity in the story than in the holy object of which it is related, for the piece of bone which is credited with being the left canine tooth of the Blessed One may have been changed on more than one occasion. The Sinhalese chronicles[3], as mentioned, say that it was brought to Ceylon in the ninth year of Sirimeghavaṇṇa[4]. This date may be approximately correct for about 413 or later Fa-Hsien described the annual festival of the tooth, during which it was exposed for veneration at the Abhayagiri monastery, without indicating that the usage was recent.

The tooth did not, according to Sinhalese tradition, form part of the relics distributed after the cremation of the Buddha. Seven bones, including four teeth[5], were excepted from that distribution and the Sage Khema taking the left canine tooth direct from the funeral pyre gave it to the king of Kalinga, who enshrined it in a gorgeous temple at Dantapura[6] where it is supposed to have remained 800 years. At the end of that period

[1] Watters, I. pp. 202, 203. But the life of Hsüan Chuang says Benares not Persia.

[2] Marco Polo trans. Yule, II. pp. 320, 330.

[3] For the history of the tooth see *Mahâvaṃsa*, p. 241, in Turnour's edition: the Dathavaṃsa in Pali written by Dhammakitti in 1211 A.D.: and the Sinhalese poems Daladapujavali and Dhatuvansaya. See also Da Cunha, *Memoir on the History of the Tooth Relic of Ceylon*, 1875, and Yule's notes on Marco Polo, II. pp. 328–330.

[4] *I.e.* about 361 or 310, according to which chronology is adopted, but neither Fa-Hsien or Hsüan Chuang says anything about its arrival from India and this part of the story might be dismissed as a legend. But seeing how extraordinary were the adventures of the tooth in historical times, it would be unreasonable to deny that it may have been smuggled out of India for safety.

[5] Various accounts are given of the disposal of these teeth, but more than enough relics were preserved in various shrines to account for all. Hsüan Chuang saw or heard of sacred teeth in Balkh, Nagar, Kashmir, Kanauj and Ceylon. Another tooth is said to be kept near Foo-chow.

[6] Plausibly supposed to be Puri. The ceremonies still observed in the temple of Jagannath are suspected of being based on Buddhist rites. Dantapura of the Kâlingas is however mentioned in some verses quoted in Dîgha Nikâya XIX. 36. This looks as if the name might be pre-Buddhist.

a pious king named Guhasiva became involved in disastrous wars on account of the relic, and, as the best means of preserving it, bade his daughter fly with her husband[1] and take it to Ceylon. This, after some miraculous adventures, they were able to do. The tooth was received with great ceremony and lodged in an edifice called the Dhammacakka from which it was taken every year for a temporary sojourn[2] in the Abhayagiri monastery.

The cultus of the tooth flourished exceedingly in the next few centuries and it came to be regarded as the talisman of the king and nation. Hence when the court moved from Anuradhapura to Pollunaruwa it was installed in the new capital. In the troubled times which followed it changed its residence some fifteen times. Early in the fourteenth century it was carried off by the Tamils to southern India but was recovered by Parâkrama Bâhu III and during the commotion created by the invasions of the Tamils, Chinese and Portuguese it was hidden in various cities. In 1560 Dom Constantino de Bragança, Portuguese Viceroy of Goa, led a crusade against Jaffna to avenge the alleged persecution of Christians, and when the town was sacked a relic, described as the tooth of an ape mounted in gold, was found in a temple and carried off to Goa. On this Bayin Naung, King of Pegu, offered an enormous ransom to redeem it, which the secular government wished to accept, but the clergy and inquisition put such pressure on the Viceroy that he rejected the proposal. The archbishop of Goa pounded the tooth in a mortar before the viceregal court, burned the fragments and scattered the ashes over the sea[3].

But the singular result of this bigotry was not to destroy one sacred tooth but to create two. The king of Pegu, who wished to marry a Sinhalese princess, sent an embassy to Ceylon to arrange the match. They were received by the king of Cotta, who bore the curiously combined name of Don Juan Dharmapâla. He had no daughter of his own but palmed off the daughter of a chamberlain. At the same time he informed the king

[1] They are called Ranmali and Danta in the Râjâvaliya.

[2] There is a striking similarity between this rite and the ceremonies observed at Puri, where the images of Jagannâtha and his relatives are conveyed every summer with great pomp to a country residence where they remain during some weeks.

[3] See Tennent's *Ceylon*, vol. II. pp. 29, 30 and 199 ff. and the Portuguese uthorities quoted.

of Pegu that the tooth destroyed at Goa was not the real relic and that this still remained in his possession. Bayin Naung was induced to marry the lady and received the tooth with appropriate ceremonies. But when the king of Kandy heard of these doings, he apprized the king of Pegu of the double trick that had been played on him. He offered him his own daughter, a veritable princess, in marriage and as her dowry the true tooth which, he said, was neither that destroyed at Goa nor yet that sent to Pegu, but one in his own possession. Bayin Naung received the Kandyan embassy politely but rejected its proposals, thinking no doubt that it would be awkward to declare the first tooth spurious after it had been solemnly installed as a sacred relic. The second tooth therefore remained in Kandy and appears to be that now venerated there. When Vimala Dharma re-established the original line of kings, about 1592, it was accepted as authentic.

As to its authenticity, it appears to be beyond doubt that it is a piece of discoloured bone about two inches long, which could never have been the tooth of an ordinary human being, so that even the faithful can only contend that the Buddha was of superhuman stature. Whether it is the relic which was venerated in Ceylon before the arrival of the Portuguese is a more difficult question, for it may be argued with equal plausibility that the Sinhalese had good reasons for hiding the real tooth and good reasons for duplicating it. The strongest argument against the authenticity of the relic destroyed by the Portuguese is that it was found in Jaffna, which had long been a Tamil town, whereas there is no reason to believe that the real tooth was at this time in Tamil custody. But, although the native literature always speaks of it as unique, the Sinhalese appear to have produced replicas more than once, for we hear of such being sent to Burma and China[1]. Again, the offer to ransom the tooth came not from Ceylon but from the king of Pegu, who, as the sequel shows, was gullible in such matters: the Portuguese clearly thought that they had acquired a relic of primary importance; on any hypothesis one of the kings of Ceylon must have deceived the king of Pegu, and finally Vimala Dharma had the strongest political reasons for accepting as

[1] Fortune in *Two Visits to Tea Countries of China*, vol. II. pp. 107–8, describes one of these teeth preserved in the Ku-shan monastery near Foo-chow.

genuine the relic kept at Kandy, since the possession of the true tooth went far to substantiate a Sinhalese monarch's right to the throne.

The tooth is now preserved in a temple at Kandy. The visitor looking through a screen of bars can see on a silver table a large jewelled case shaped like a bell. Flowers scattered on the floor or piled on other tables fill the chamber with their heavy perfume. Inside the bell are six other bells of diminishing size, the innermost of which covers a golden lotus containing the sacred tooth. But it is only on rare occasions that the outer caskets are removed. Worshippers as a rule have to content themselves with offering flowers[1] and bowing but I was informed that the priests celebrate *puja* daily before the relic. The ceremony comprises the consecration and distribution of rice and is interesting as connecting the veneration of the tooth with the ritual observed in Hindu temples. But we must return to the general history of Buddhism in Ceylon.

3

The kings who ruled in the fifth century were devout Buddhists and builders of vihâras but the most important event of this period, not merely for the island but for the whole Buddhist church in the south, was the literary activity of Buddhaghosa who is said to have resided in Ceylon during the reign of Mahânâma. The chief authorities for his life are a passage in the continuation of the Mahâvamsa[2] and the Buddhaghosuppatti, a late Burmese text of about 1550, which, while adding many anecdotes, appears not to come from an independent source[3]. The gist of their account is that he was born in a Brahman family near Gaya and early obtained renown as a disputant. He was converted to Buddhism by a monk named Revata and began to write theological treatises[4]. Revata observing his

[1] This practice must be very old. The Vinaya of the Mûlasarvâstivâdins and similar texts speak of offering flowers to a tooth of the Buddha. See *J.A.* 1914, II. pp. 523, 543. The Pali Canon too tells us that the relics of the Buddha were honoured with garlands and perfumes.

[2] Chap. XXXVII.

[3] Both probably represent the tradition current at the Mahâvihâra, but according to the Talaing tradition Buddhaghosa was a Brahman born at Thaton.

[4] The Mahâvaṃsa says he composed the Jñânodaya and Atthasâlinî at this time before starting for Ceylon.

intention to compose a commentary on the Piṭakas, told him that only the text (pâlimattam) of the scriptures was to be found in India, not the ancient commentaries, but that the Sinhalese commentaries were genuine, having been composed in that language by Mahinda. He therefore bade Buddhaghosa repair to Ceylon and translate these Sinhalese works into the idiom of Magadha, by which Pali must be meant. Buddhaghosa took this advice and there is no reason to distrust the statement of the Mahâvamsa that he arrived in the reign of Mahânâma, who ruled according to Geiger from 458 to 480, though the usual reckoning places him about fifty years earlier. The fact that Fa-Hsien, who visited Ceylon about 412, does not mention Buddhaghosa is in favour of Geiger's chronology[1].

He first studied in the Mahâvihâra and eventually requested permission to translate the Sinhalese commentaries. To prove his competence for the task he composed the celebrated Visuddhi-magga, and, this being considered satisfactory, he took up his residence in the Ganthâkara Vihâra and proceeded to the work of translation. When it was finished he returned to India or according to the Talaing tradition to Thaton. The Buddhaghosuppatti adds two stories of which the truth and meaning are equally doubtful. They are that Buddhaghosa burnt the works written by Mahinda and that his knowledge of Sanskrit was called in question but triumphantly proved. Can there be here any allusion to a Sanskrit canon supported by the opponents of the Mahâvihâra?

Even in its main outline the story is not very coherent for one would imagine that, if a Buddhist from Magadha went to Ceylon to translate the Sinhalese commentaries, his object must have been to introduce them among Indian Buddhists. But there is no evidence that Buddhaghosa did this and he is for us simply a great figure in the literary and religious history of Ceylon. Burmese tradition maintains that he was a native of Thaton and returned thither, when his labours in Ceylon were completed, to spread the scriptures in his native language. This version of his activity is intelligible, though the evidence for it is weak.

[1] Fa-Hsien is chary of mentioning contemporary celebrities but he refers to a well-known monk called Ta-mo-kiu-ti (? Dhammakathi) and had Buddhaghosa been already celebrated he would hardly have omitted him.

He composed a great corpus of exegetical literature which has been preserved, but, since much of it is still unedited, the precise extent of his labours is uncertain. There is however little doubt of the authenticity of his commentaries on the four great Nikâyas, on the Abhidhamma and on the Vinaya (called Samanta-pâsâdikâ) and in them[1] he refers to the Visuddhi-magga as his own work. He says expressly that his explanations are founded on Sinhalese materials, which he frequently cites as the opinion of the ancients (porânâ). By this word he probably means traditions recorded in Sinhalese and attributed to Mahinda, but it is in any case clear that the works which he consulted were considered old in the fifth century A.D. Some of their names are preserved in the Samanta-pâsâdikâ where he mentions the great commentary (Mahâ-Aṭṭhakathâ), the Raft commentary (Paccari, so called because written on a raft), the Kurundi commentary composed at Kurunda-Velu and others[2]. All this literature has disappeared and we can only judge of it by Buddhaghosa's reproduction which is probably not a translation but a selection and rearrangement. Indeed his occasional direct quotations from the ancients or from an Aṭṭhakathâ imply that the rest of the work is merely based on the Sinhalese commentaries.

Buddhaghosa was not an independent thinker but he makes amends for his want of originality not only by his industry and learning but by his power of grasping and expounding the whole of an intricate subject. His Visuddhi-magga has not yet been edited in Europe, but the extracts and copious analysis[3] which have been published indicate that it is a comprehensive restatement of Buddhist doctrine made with as free a hand as orthodoxy permitted. The Mahâvamsa observes that the Theras held his works in the same estimation as the Piṭakas. They are in no way coloured by the Mahayanist tenets which were already prevalent in India, but state in its severest form the Hinayanist creed, of which he is the most authoritative exponent. The Visuddhi-magga is divided into three parts treating of conduct (sîlam), meditation (samâdhi) and knowledge

[1] In the Coms. on the Dîgha and Dhammasangani.

[2] See Rhys Davids and Carpenter's introduction to *Sumangalavi*, I. p. x.

[3] In the *Journal of Pali Text Soc.* 1891, pp. 76–164. Since the above was written the first volume of the text of the Visuddhi magga, edited by Mrs Rhys Davids, has been published by the Pali Text Society, 1920.

(paññâ), the first being the necessary substratum for the religious life of which the others are the two principal branches. But though he intersperses his exposition with miraculous stories and treats exhaustively of superhuman powers, no trace of the worship of Mahayanist Bodhisattvas is found in his works and, as for literature, he himself is the chief authority for the genuineness and completeness of the Pali Canon as we know it.

When we find it said that his works were esteemed as highly as the Piṭakas, or that the documents which he translated into Pali were the words of the Buddha[1], the suspicion naturally arises that the Pali Canon may be in part his composition and it may be well to review briefly its history in Ceylon. Our knowledge appears to be derived entirely from the traditions of the Mahâvihâra which represent Mahinda as teaching the text of the Piṭakas orally, accompanied by a commentary. If we admit the general truth of the narrative concerning Mahinda's mission, there is nothing improbable in these statements, for it would be natural that an Indian teacher should know by heart his sacred texts and the commentaries on them. We cannot of course assume that the Piṭakas of Mahinda were the Pali Canon as we know it, but the inscriptions of Asoka refer to passages which can be found in that canon and therefore parts of it at any rate must have been accepted as scripture in the third century B.C. But it is probable that considerable variation was permitted in the text, although the sense and a certain terminology were carefully guarded. It was not till the reign of Vaṭṭagâmaṇi, probably about 20 B.C., that the canon was committed to writing and the Parivâra, composed in Ceylon[2], was included in it.

In the reign of Buddhadâsa[3] a learned monk named Mahâdhammakathi is said to have translated the Suttas into Sinhalese, which at this time was esteemed the proper language for letters and theology, but in the next century a contrary tendency, probably initiated by Buddhaghosa, becomes apparent and Sinhalese works are rewritten in Pali[4]. But nothing indicates that

[1] Bhagavato Sâsanam. See Buddhaghosuppatti, cap. I.

[2] It appears to be unknown to the Chinese Tripitaka. For some further remarks on the Sinhalese Canon see Book III. chap. XIII. § 3.

[3] That is according to Geiger 386–416 A.D. Perhaps he was the Ta-mo-kiu-ti mentioned by Fa-Hsien.

[4] The tendency seems odd but it can be paralleled in India where it is not uncommon to rewrite vernacular works in Sanskrit. See Grierson, *J.R.A.S.* 1913,

any part of what we call the Pali Canon underwent this process. Buddhaghosa distinguishes clearly between text and comment, between Pali and Sinhalese documents. He has a coherent history of the text, beginning with the Council of Râjagaha; he discusses various readings, he explains difficult words. He treated the ancient commentaries with freedom, but there is no reason to think that he allowed himself any discretion or right of selection in dealing with the sacred texts accepted by the Mahâvihâra, though it might be prudent to await the publication of his commentaries on all the Nikâyas before asserting this unreservedly.

To sum up, the available evidence points to the conclusion that in the time of Asoka texts and commentaries preserved orally were brought to Ceylon. The former, though in a somewhat fluid condition, were sufficiently sacred to be kept unchanged in the original Indian language, the latter were translated into the kindred but still distinct vernacular of the island. In the next century and a half some additions to the Pali texts were made and about 20 B.C. the Mahâvihâra, which proved as superior to the other communities in vitality as it was in antiquity, caused written copies to be made of what it considered as the canon, including some recent works. There is no evidence that Buddhaghosa or anyone else enlarged or curtailed the canon, but the curious tradition that he collected and burned all the books written by Mahinda in Sinhalese[1] may allude to the existence of other works which he (presumably in agreement with the Mahâvihâra) considered spurious.

Soon after the departure of Buddhaghosa Dhâtusena came to the throne and "held like Dhammasoka a convocation about the three Piṭakas[2]." This implies that there was still some doubt as to what was scripture and that the canon of the Mahâvihâra was not universally accepted. The Vetulyas, of

p. 133. Even in England in the seventeenth century Bacon seems to have been doubtful of the immortality of his works in English and prepared a Latin translation of his *Essays*.

[1] It is reported with some emphasis as the tradition of the Ancients in Buddhaghosuppatti, cap. VII. If the works were merely those which Buddhaghosa himself had translated the procedure seems somewhat drastic.

[2] Mahâv. XXXIII. Dhammasokova so kasi Piṭakattaye Saṅgahan. Dhâtusena reigned from 459–477 according to the common chronology or 509–527 according to Geiger.

whom we heard in the third century A.D., reappear in the seventh when they are said to have been supported by a provincial governor but not by the king Aggabodhi[1] and still more explicitly in the reign of Parâkrama Bâhu (*c.* 1160). He endeavoured to reconcile to the Mahâvihâra "the Abhayagiri brethren who separated themselves from the time of king Vaṭṭagâmaṇi Abhaya and the Jetavana brethren that had parted since the days of Mahâsena and taught the Vetulla Piṭaka and other writings as the words of Buddha, which indeed were not the words of Buddha[2]." So it appears that another recension of the canon was in existence for many centuries.

Dhâtusena, though depicted in the Mahâvaṃsa as a most orthodox monarch, embellished the Abhayagiri monastery and was addicted to sumptuous ceremonies in honour of images and relics. Thus he made an image of Mahinda, dedicated a shrine and statue to Metteyya and ornamented the effigies of Buddha with the royal jewels. In an image chamber (apparently at the Abhayagiri) he set up figures of Bodhisattvas[3], by which we should perhaps understand the previous births of Gotama. He was killed by his son and Sinhalese history degenerated into a complicated story of crime and discord, in which the weaker faction generally sought the aid of the Tamils. These latter became more and more powerful and with their advance Buddhism tended to give place to Hinduism. In the eighth century the court removed from Anuradhapura to Pollannaruwa, in order to escape from the pressure of the Tamils, but the picture of anarchy and decadence grows more and more gloomy until the accession of Vijaya Bâhu in 1071 who succeeded in making himself king of all Ceylon. Though he recovered Anuradhapura it was not made the royal residence either by himself or by his greater successor, Parâkrama Bâhu[4]. This monarch, the most eminent in the long list of Ceylon's sovereigns, after he had consolidated his power, devoted himself, in the words of Tennent, "to the two grand objects of royal solicitude, religion and agriculture." He was lavish in building monasteries, temples and libraries, but not less generous in constructing or repairing

[1] Mahâv. XLII. 35 ff.

[2] Mahâv. LXXVIII. 21–23.

[3] Mahâv. XXXVIII. Akâsi patimâgehe bahumangalacetiye boddhisatte ca tathâsun. Cf. Fa-Hsien, chap. XXVIII. *ad fin.*

[4] Or Parakkama Bâhu. Probably 1153–1186.

tanks and works of irrigation. In the reign of Vijaya Bâhu hardly any duly ordained monks were to be found[1], the succession having been interrupted, and the deficiency was supplied by bringing qualified Theras from Burma. But by the time of Parâkrama Bâhu the old quarrels of the monasteries revived, and, as he was anxious to secure unity, he summoned a synod at Anuradhapura. It appears to have attained its object by recognizing the Mahâvihâra as the standard of orthodoxy and dealing summarily with dissentients[2]. The secular side of monastic life also received liberal attention. Lands, revenues and guest-houses were provided for the monasteries as well as hospitals. As in Burma and Siam Brahmans were respected and the king erected a building for their use in the capital. Like Asoka, he forbade the killing of animals.

But the glory of Parâkrama Bâhu stands up in the later history of Ceylon like an isolated peak and thirty years after his death the country had fallen almost to its previous low level of prosperity. The Tamils again occupied many districts and were never entirely dislodged as long as the Sinhalese kingdom lasted. Buddhism tended to decline but was always the religion of the national party and was honoured with as much magnificence as their means allowed. Parâkrama Bâhu II (*c.* 1240), who recovered the sacred tooth from the Tamils, is said to have celebrated splendid festivals and to have imported learned monks from the country of the Colas[3]. Towards the end of the fifteenth century the inscriptions of Kalyani indicate that Sinhalese religion enjoyed a great reputation in Burma[4].

A further change adverse to Buddhism was occasioned by the arrival of the Portuguese in 1505. A long and horrible struggle ensued between them and the various kings among whom the distracted island was divided until at the end of the sixteenth century only Kandy remained independent, the whole coast being in the hands of the Portuguese. The singular barbarities which they perpetrated throughout this struggle are vouched for by their own historians[5], but it does not appear

[1] Mahâvaṃsa LX. 4–7.

[2] Mahâvaṃsa LXXVIII. 21–27.

[3] Mahâv. LXXXIV. If this means the region of Madras, the obvious question is what learned Buddhist can there have been there at this period.

[4] *J. Ant.* 1893, pp. 40, 41.

[5] I take this statement from Tennent who gives references.

that the Sinhalese degraded themselves by similar atrocities. Since the Portuguese wished to propagate Roman Catholicism as well as to extend their political rule and used for this purpose (according to the Mahâvaṃsa) the persuasions of gold as well as the terrors of torture, it is not surprising if many Sinhalese professed allegiance to Christianity, but when in 1597 the greater part of Ceylon formally accepted Portuguese sovereignty, the chiefs insisted that they should be allowed to retain their own religion and customs.

The Dutch first appeared in 1602 and were welcomed by the Court of Kandy as allies capable of expelling the Portuguese. This they succeeded in doing by a series of victories between 1638 and 1658, and remained masters of a great part of the island until their possessions were taken by the British in 1795. Kandy however continued independent until 1815. At first the Dutch tried to enforce Christianity and to prohibit Buddhism within their territory[1] but ultimately hatred of the Roman Catholic church made them favourable to Buddhism and they were ready to assist those kings who desired to restore the national religion to its former splendour.

4

In spite of this assistance the centuries when the Sinhalese were contending with Europeans were not a prosperous time for Buddhism. Hinduism spread in the north[2], Christianity in the coast belt, but still it was a point of honour with most native sovereigns to protect the national religion so far as their distressed condition allowed. For the seventeenth century we have an interesting account of the state of the country called *An Historical Relation of the Island of Ceylon* by an Englishman, Robert Knox, who was detained by the king of Kandy from 1660 to 1680. He does not seem to have been aware that there was any distinction between Buddhism and Hinduism. Though he describes the Sinhalese as idolaters, he also emphasizes the fact that Buddou (as he writes the name) is the God "unto whom the salvation of souls belongs," and for whom "above all others they have a high respect and devotion." He also describes

[1] See *Ceylon Antiquary*, I. 3, pp. 148, 197.

[2] Râjasinha I (1581) is said to have made Śivaism the Court religion.

the ceremonies of pirit and bana, the perahera procession, and two classes of Buddhist monks, the elders and the ordinary members of the Sangha. His narrative indicates that Buddhism was accepted as the higher religion, though men were prone to pray to deities who would save from temporal danger.

About this time Vimala Dharma II[1] made great efforts to improve the religious condition of the island and finding that the true succession had again failed, arranged with the Dutch to send an embassy to Arakan and bring back qualified Theras. But apparently the steps taken were not sufficient, for when king Kittisiri Râjasiha (1747–81), whose piety forms the theme of the last two chapters of the Mahâvaṃsa, set about reforming the Sangha, he found that duly ordained monks were extinct and that many so-called monks had families. He therefore decided to apply to Dhammika, king of Ayuthia in Siam, and like his predecessor despatched an embassy on a Dutch ship. Dhammika sent back a company of "more than ten monks" (that is more than sufficient for the performance of all ecclesiastical acts) under the Abbot Upâli in 1752 and another to relieve it in 1755[2]. They were received by the king of Ceylon with great honour and subsequently by the ordination which they conferred placed the succession beyond dispute. But the order thus reconstituted was aristocratic and exclusive: only members of the highest caste were admitted to it and the wealthy middle classes found themselves excluded from a community which they were expected to honour and maintain. This led to the despatch of an embassy to Burma in 1802 and to the foundation of another branch of the Sangha, known as the Amarapura school, distinct in so far as its validity depended on Burmese not Siamese ordination.

Since ordination is for Buddhists merely self-dedication to a higher life and does not confer any sacramental or sacerdotal

[1] His reign is dated as 1679–1701, also as 1687–1706. It is remarkable that the Mahâvaṃsa makes *both* the kings called Vimala Dharma send religious embassies to Arakan. See XCIV. 15, 16 and XCVII. 10, 11.

[2] See for some details Lorgeou: Notice sur un Manuscrit Siamois contenant la relation de deux missions religieuses envoyées de Siam à Ceylon au milieu du xviii Siècle. *Jour. Asiat.* 1906, pp. 533 ff. The king called Dhammika by the Mahâvaṃsa appears to have been known as Phra Song Tham in Siam. The interest felt by the Siamese in Ceylon at this period is shown by the Siamese translation of the Mahâvaṃsa made in 1796.

powers, the importance assigned to it may seem strange. But the idea goes back to the oldest records in the Vinaya and has its root in the privileges accorded to the order. A Bhikkhu had a right to expect much from the laity, but he also had to prove his worth and Gotama's early legislation was largely concerned with excluding unsuitable candidates. The solicitude for valid ordination was only the ecclesiastical form of the popular feeling that the honours and immunities of the order were conditional on its maintaining a certain standard of conduct. Other methods of reform might have been devised, but the old injunction that a monk could be admitted only by other duly ordained monks was fairly efficacious and could not be disputed. But the curious result is that though Ceylon was in early times the second home of Buddhism, almost all (if indeed not all) the monks found there now derive their right to the title of Bhikkhu from foreign countries.

The Sinhalese Sangha is generally described as divided into four schools, those of Siam, Kelani, Amarapura and Ramanya, of which the first two are practically identical, Kelani being simply a separate province of the Siamese school, which otherwise has its headquarters in the inland districts. This school, founded as mentioned above by priests who arrived in 1750, comprises about half of the whole Sangha and has some pretensions to represent the hierarchy of Ceylon, since the last kings of Kandy gave to the heads of the two great monasteries in the capital, Asgiri and Malwatte, jurisdiction over the north and south of the island respectively. It differs in some particulars from the Amarapura school. It only admits members of the highest caste and prescribes that monks are to wear the upper robe over one shoulder only, whereas the Amarapurans admit members of the first three castes (but not those lower in the social scale) and require both shoulders to be covered. There are other minor differences among which it is interesting to note that the Siamese school object to the use of the formula "I dedicate this gift to the Buddha" which is used in the other schools when anything is presented to the order for the use of the monks. It is held that this expression was correct in the lifetime of the Buddha but not after his death. The two schools are not mutually hostile, and members of each find a hospitable reception in the monasteries of the other. The laity patronize both indifferently and both frequent the same places of pilgrimage, though all of these and the majority of the temple lands belong to the sect of Siam. It is wealthy, aristocratic and has inherited the ancient traditions of Ceylon, whereas the Amarapurans are more active and inclined to propaganda. It is said they are the chief allies of the Theosophists and European Buddhists. The Ramanya[1] school is more recent and distinct than the others, being in some ways a reformed community. It aims at greater strictness of life, forbidding monasteries to hold property and insisting on genuine poverty. It also totally rejects the worship of Hindu deities and its lay members do not recognize the monks of other schools. It is not large but its influence is considerable.

It has been said that Buddhism flourished in Ceylon only when it was able to secure the royal favour. There is some truth in this, for the Sangha does not struggle on its own behalf but expects the laity to provide for its material needs, making a return in educational and religious services. Such a body if not absolutely dependent on royal patronage has at least much to gain from it. Yet this admission must not blind us to the fact that during its long and often distinguished history Sinhalese Buddhism has been truly the national faith, as opposed to the beliefs of various invaders, and has also ministered to the spiritual aspirations of the nation. As Knox said in a period when it was not particularly flourishing, the Hindu gods look after worldly affairs but Buddha after the soul. When the island passed under British rule and all religions received impartial recognition, the result was not disastrous to Buddhism: the number of Bhikkhus greatly increased, especially in the latter half of the nineteenth century. And if in earlier periods there was an interval in which technically speaking the Sangha did not exist, this did not mean that interest in it ceased, for as soon as the kingdom became prosperous the first care of the kings was to set the Church in order. This zeal can be attributed to nothing but conviction and affection, for Buddhism is not a faith politically useful to an energetic and warlike prince.

[1] Râmañña is the part of Burma between Arakan and Siam.

5

Sinhalese Buddhism is often styled primitive or original and it may fairly be said to preserve in substance both the doctrine and practice inculcated in the earliest Pali literature. In calling this primitive we must remember the possibility that some of this literature was elaborated in Ceylon itself. But, putting the text of the Piṭakas aside, it would seem that the early Sinhalese Buddhism was the same as that of Asoka, and that it never underwent any important change. It is true that mediæval Sinhalese literature is full of supernatural legends respecting the Buddha[1], but still he does not become a god (for he has attained Nirvana) and the great Bodhisattvas, Avalokita and Manjuśrî, are practically unknown. The *Abhidhammattha-sangaha*[2], which is still the text-book most in use among the Bhikkhus, adheres rigidly to the methods of the Abhidhamma[3]. It contains neither devotional nor magical matter but prescribes a course of austere mental training, based on psychological analysis and culminating in the rapture of meditation. Such studies and exercises are beyond the capacity of the majority, but no other road to salvation is officially sanctioned for the Bhikkhu. It is admitted that there are no Arhats now—just as Christianity has no contemporary saints—but no other ideal, such as the Boddhisattva of the Mahayanists, is held up for imitation.

Mediæval images of Avalokita and of goddesses have however been found in Ceylon[4]. This is hardly surprising for the island was on the main road to China, Java, and Camboja[5] and Mahayanist teachers and pilgrims must have continually passed through it. The Chinese biographies of that eminent tantrist, Amogha, say that he went to Ceylon in 741 and elaborated his system there before returning to China. It is said that in 1408 the Chinese being angry at the ill-treatment of envoys whom they had sent to the shrine of the tooth, conquered Ceylon and

[1] See Spence Hardy, *Manual of Buddhism*, chap. VII.

[2] A translation by S. Z. Aung and Mrs Rhys Davids has been published by the Pali Text Society. The author Anuruddha appears to have lived between the eighth and twelfth centuries.

[3] The Sinhalese had a special respect for the Abhidhamma. Kassapa V (c. A.D. 930) caused it to be engraved on plates of gold. *Ep. Zeyl.* I. p. 52.

[4] See Coomaraswamy in *J.R.A.S.* 1909, pp. 283–297.

[5] For intercourse with Camboja see *Epigr. Zeylanica*, II. p. 74.

made it pay tribute for fifty years. By conquest no doubt is meant merely a military success and not occupation, but the whole story implies possibilities of acquaintance with Chinese Buddhism.

It is clear that, though the Hinayanist church was predominant throughout the history of the island, there were up to the twelfth century heretical sects called Vaitulya or Vetulyaka and Vâjira which though hardly rivals of orthodoxy were a thorn in its side. A party at the Abhayagiri monastery were favourably disposed to the Vaitulya sect which, though often suppressed, recovered and reappeared, being apparently reinforced from India. This need not mean from southern India, for Ceylon had regular intercourse with the north and perhaps the Vaitulyas were Mahayanists from Bengal. The Nikâya-Sangrahawa also mentions that in the ninth century there was a sect called Nîlapatadarśana[1], who wore blue robes and preached indulgence in wine and love. They were possibly Tantrists from the north but were persecuted in southern India and never influential in Ceylon.

The Mahâvaṃsa is inclined to minimize the importance of all sects compared with the Mahâvihâra, but the picture given by the Nikâya-Sangrahawa may be more correct. It says that the Vaitulyas, described as infidel Brahmans who had composed a Piṭaka of their own, made four attempts to obtain a footing at the Abhayagiri monastery[2]. In the ninth century it represents king Matvalasen as having to fly because he had embraced the false doctrine of the Vâjiras. These are mentioned in another passage in connection with the Vaitulyas: they are said to have composed the Gûḍha Vinaya[3] and many Tantras. They perhaps were connected with the Vajrayâna, a phase of Tantric Buddhism. But a few years later king Mungayinsen set the church in order. He recognized the three orthodox schools or nikâyas called Theriya, Dhammaruci and Sâgaliya but proscribed the others and set guards on the coast to prevent the importation of heresy. Nevertheless the Vâjiriya and Vaitulya doctrines

[1] A dubious legend relates that they were known in the north and suppressed by Harsha. See Ettinghausen, *Harsha Vardhana*, 1906, p. 86. Nil Sâdhana appears to be a name for tantric practices. See Avalon, *Principles of Tantra*, preface, p. xix.

[2] In the reigns of Vohâratissa, Goṭhâbhaya, Mahâsena and Ambaherana Salamevan. The kings Matvalasen and Mungayinsen are also known as Sena I and II.

[3] Secret Vinaya.

were secretly practised. An inscription in Sanskrit found at the Jetavana and attributed to the ninth century[1] records the foundation of a Vihâra for a hundred resident monks, 25 from each of the four nikâyas, which it appears to regard as equivalent. But in 1165 the great Parâkrama Bâhu held a synod to restore unity in the church. As a result, all Nikâyas (even the Dhammaruci) which did not conform to the Mahâvihâra were suppressed[2] and we hear no more of the Vaitulyas and Vâjiriyas.

Thus there was once a Mahayanist faction in Ceylon, but it was recruited from abroad, intermittent in activity and was finally defeated, whereas the Hinayanist tradition was national and continuous.

Considering the long lapse of time, the monastic life of Ceylon has not deviated much in practice from the injunctions of the Vinaya. Monasteries like those of Anuradhapura, which are said to have contained thousands of monks, no longer exist. The largest now to be found—those at Kandy—do not contain more than fifty but as a rule a pansala (as these institutions are now called) has not more than five residents and more often only two or three. Some pansalas have villages assigned to them and some let their lands and do not scruple to receive the rent. The monks still follow the ancient routine of making a daily round with the begging bowl, but the food thus collected is often given to the poor or even to animals and the inmates of the pansala eat a meal which has been cooked there. The Pâtimokkha is recited (at least in part) twice a month and ordinations are held annually[3].

The duties of the Bhikkhus are partly educational, partly clerical. In most villages the children receive elementary education gratis in the pansala, and the preservation of the ancient texts, together with the long list of Pali and Sinhalese works produced until recent times almost exclusively by members of the Sangha[4], is a proof that it has not neglected literature. The

[1] *Epigraphia Zeylan.* I. p. 4.

[2] One of the king's inscriptions says that he reconciled the clergy of the three Nikâyas. *Ep. Zeyl.* I. p. 134.

[3] See Bowden in *J.R.A.S.* 1893, pp. 159 ff. The account refers to the Malwatte Monastery. But it would appear that the Pâtimokkha is recited in country places when a sufficient number of monks meet on Uposatha days.

[4] Even the poets were mostly Bhikkhus. Sinhalese literature contains a fair number of historical and philosophical works but curiously little about law. See Jolly, *Recht und Sitte*, p. 44.

chief public religious observances are preaching and reading the scriptures. This latter, known as Bana, is usually accompanied by a word for word translation made by the reciter or an assistant. Such recitations may form part of the ordinary ceremonial of Uposatha days and most religious establishments have a room where they can be held, but often monks are invited to reside in a village during Was (July to October) and read Bana, and often a layman performs a pinkama or act of merit by entertaining monks for several days and inviting his neighbours to hear them recite. The recitation of the Jâtakas is particularly popular but the suttas of the Dîgha Nikâya are also often read. On special occasions such as entry into a new house, an eclipse or any incident which suggests that it might be well to ward off the enmity of supernatural powers, it is usual to recite a collection of texts taken largely from the Suttanipâta and called Pirit. The word appears to be derived from the Pali *paritta*, a defence, and though the Pali scriptures do not sanction this use of the Buddha's discourses they countenance the idea that evil may be averted by the use of formulæ[1].

Although Sinhalese Buddhism has not diverged much from the Pali scriptures in its main doctrines and discipline, yet it tolerates a superstructure of Indian beliefs and ceremonies which forbid us to call it pure except in a restricted sense. At present there may be said to be three religions in Ceylon; local animism, Hinduism and Buddhism are all inextricably mixed together. By local animism I mean the worship of native spirits who do not belong to the ordinary Hindu pantheon though they may be identified with its members. The priests of this worship are called Kapuralas and one of their principal ceremonies consists in dancing until they are supposed to be possessed by a spirit—the devil dancing of Europeans. Though this religion is distinct from ordinary Hinduism, its deities and ceremonies find parallels in the southern Tamil country. In Ceylon it is not merely a village superstition but possesses

[1] *E.g.* in the Âṭânâṭiya sutta (Dig. Nik. XXXII.) friendly spirits teach a spell by which members of the order may protect themselves against evil ones and in Jâtaka 159 the Peacock escapes danger by reciting every day a hymn to the sun and the praises of past Buddhas. See also Bunyiu, *Nanjios Catalogue*, Nos. 487 and 800.

temples of considerable size[1], for instance at Badulla and near Ratnapura. In the latter there is a Buddhist shrine in the court yard, so that the Blessed One may countenance the worship, much as the Piṭakas represent him as patronizing and instructing the deities of ancient Magadha, but the structure and observances of the temple itself are not Buddhist. The chief spirit worshipped at Ratnapura and in most of these temples is Mahâ Saman, the god of Adam's Peak. He is sometimes identified with Lakshmana, the brother of Râma, and sometimes with Indra.

About a quarter of the population are Tamils professing Hinduism. Hindu temples of the ordinary Dravidian type are especially frequent in the northern districts, but they are found in most parts and at Kandy two may be seen close to the shrine of the Tooth[2]. Buddhists feel no scruple in frequenting them and the images of Hindu deities are habitually introduced into Buddhist temples. These often contain a hall, at the end of which are one or more sitting figures of the Buddha, on the right hand side a recumbent figure of him, but on the left a row of four statues representing Mahâbrahmâ, Vishṇu, Kârttikeya and Mahâsâman. Of these Vishṇu generally receives marked attention, shown by the number of prayers written on slips of paper which are attached to his hand. Nor is this worship found merely as a survival in the older temples. The four figures appear in the newest edifices and the image of Vishṇu never fails to attract votaries. Yet though a rigid Buddhist may regard such devotion as dangerous, it is not treasonable, for Vishṇu is regarded not as a competitor but as a very reverent admirer of the Buddha and anxious to befriend good Buddhists.

Even more insidious is the pageantry which since the days of King Tissa has been the outward sign of religion. It may be justified as being merely an edifying method of venerating the memory of a great man but when images and relics are treated with profound reverence or carried in solemn procession it is hard for the ignorant, especially if they are accustomed to the ceremonial of Hindu temples, not to think that these symbols are divine. This ornate ritualism is not authorized in any

[1] See for an account of the Maha Saman Devale, *Ceylon Ant.* July, 1916.

[2] So a mediæval inscription at Mahintale of Mahinda IV records the foundation of Buddhist edifices and a temple to a goddess. *Ep. Zeyl.* I. p. 103.

known canonical text, but it is thoroughly Indian. Asoka records in his inscriptions the institution of religious processions and Hsüan Chuang relates how King Harsha organized a festival during which an image of the Buddha was carried on an elephant while the monarch and his ally the king of Assam, dressed as Indra and Brahmâ respectively, waited on it like servants[1]. Such festivities were congenial to the Sinhalese, as is attested by the long series of descriptions which fill the Mahâvaṃsa down to the very last book, by what Fa-Hsien saw about 412 and by the Perahera festival celebrated to-day.

6

The Buddhism of southern India resembled that of Ceylon in character though not in history. It was introduced under the auspices of Asoka, who mentions in his inscriptions the Colas, Pândyas and Keralaputras[2]. Hsüan Chuang says that in the Malakûta country, somewhere near Madura or Tanjore, there was a stupa erected by Asoka's orders and also a monastery founded by Mahinda. It is possible that this apostle and others laboured less in Ceylon and more in south India than is generally supposed. The pre-eminence and continuity of Sinhalese Buddhism are due to the conservative temper of the natives who were relatively little moved by the winds of religion which blew strong on the mainland, bearing with them now Jainism, now the worship of Vishṇu or Śiva.

In the Tamil country Buddhism of an Asokan type appears to have been prevalent about the time of our era. The poem Manimegalei, which by general consent was composed in an early century A.D., is Buddhist but shows no leanings to Mahayanism. It speaks of Śivaism and many other systems[3] as flourishing, but contains no hint that Buddhism was persecuted. But persecution or at least very unfavourable conditions set in. Since at the time of Hsüan Chuang's visit Buddhism

[1] Similarly in a religious procession described in the Mahâvaṃsa (XCIX. 52; about 1750 A.D.) there were "men in the dress of Brahmâs."

[2] Rock Edicts, II. and XIII. Three inscriptions of Asoka have been found in Mysore.

[3] The Manimegalei even mentions six systems of philosophy which are not the ordinary Darśanas but Lokâyatam, Bauddham, Sâṅkhyam, Naiyâyikam, Vaiśeshikam, Mîmâmsakam.

was in an advanced stage of decadence, it seems probable that the triumph of Śivaism began in the third or fourth century and that Buddhism offered slight resistance, Jainism being the only serious competitor for the first place. But for a long while, perhaps even until the sixteenth century, monasteries were kept up in special centres, and one of these is of peculiar importance, namely Kancîpuram or Conjeveram[1]. Hsüan Chuang found there 100 monasteries with more than 10,000 brethren, all Sthaviras, and mentions that it was the birthplace of Dharmapâla[2]. We have some further information from the Talaing chronicles[3] which suggests the interesting hypothesis that the Buddhism of Burma was introduced or refreshed by missionaries from southern India. They give a list of teachers who flourished in that country, including Kaccâyana and the philosopher Anuruddha[4]. Of Dharmapâla they say that he lived at the monastery of Bhadratittha near Kancipura and wrote fourteen commentaries in Pali[5]. One was on the Visuddhi-magga of Buddhaghosa and it is probable that he lived shortly after that great writer and like him studied in Ceylon.

I shall recur to this question of south Indian Buddhism in treating of Burma, but the data now available are very meagre.

[1] Kan-chih-pu-lo. Watters, *Yüan Chuang*, II. 226. The identification is not without difficulties and it has been suggested that the town is really Negapatam. The Life of the pilgrim says that it was on the coast, but he does not say so himself and his biographer may have been mistaken.

[2] See art. by Rhys Davids in *E.R.E.*

[3] See Forchhammer, *Jardine Prize Essay*, 1885, pp. 24 ff.

[4] Author of the *Abhidhammattha-sangaha*.

[5] Some have been published by the P.T. Society.

CHAPTER XXXVI

BURMA

1

UNTIL recent times Burma remained somewhat isolated and connected with foreign countries by few ties. The chronicles contain a record of long and generally peaceful intercourse with Ceylon, but this though important for religion and literature had little political effect. The Chinese occasionally invaded Upper Burma and demanded tribute but the invasions were brief and led to no permanent occupation. On the west Arakan was worried by the Viceroys of the Mogul Emperors and on the east the Burmese frequently invaded Siam. But otherwise from the beginning of authentic history until the British annexation Burma was left to itself and had not, like so many Asiatic states, to submit to foreign conquest and the imposition of foreign institutions. Yet let it not be supposed that its annals are peaceful and uneventful. The land supplied its own complications, for of the many races inhabiting it, three, the Burmese, Talaings and Shans, had rival aspirations and founded dynasties. Of these three races, the Burmese proper appear to have come from the north west, for a chain of tribes speaking cognate languages is said to extend from Burma to Nepal. The Mōns or Talaings are allied linguistically to the Khmers of Camboja. Their country (sometimes called Râmaññadesa) was in Lower Burma and its principal cities were Pegu and Thaton. The identity of the name Talaing with Telingana or Kalinga is not admitted by all scholars, but native tradition connects the foundation of the kingdom with the east coast of India and it seems certain that such a connection existed in historical times and kept alive Hinayanist Buddhism which may have been originally introduced by this route.

The Shan States lie in the east of Burma on the borders of Yünnan and Laos. Their traditions carry their foundation back to the fourth and fifth centuries B.C. There is no confirmation of this, but bodies of Shans, a race allied to the Siamese, may have migrated into this region at any date, perhaps bringing Buddhism with them or receiving it direct from China. Recent investigations have shown that there was also a fourth race, designated as Pyus, who occupied territory between the Burmese and Talaings in the eleventh century. They will probably prove of considerable importance for philology and early history, perhaps even for the history of some phases of Burmese Buddhism, for the religious terms found in their inscriptions are Sanskrit rather than Pali and this suggests direct communication with India. But until more information is available any discussion of this interesting but mysterious people involves so many hypotheses and arguments of detail that it is impossible in a work like the present. Prome was one of their principal cities, their name reappears in P'iao, the old Chinese designation of Burma, and perhaps also in Pagan, one form of which is Pugâma[1].

Throughout the historical period the pre-eminence both in individual kings and dynastic strength rested with the Burmese but their contests with the Shans and Talaings form an intricate story which can be related here only in outline. Though the three races are distinct and still preserve their languages, yet they conquered one another, lived in each other's capitals and shared the same ambitions so that in more recent centuries no great change occurred when new dynasties came to power or territory was redistributed. The long chronicle of bloodstained but ineffectual quarrels is relieved by the exploits of three great kings, Anawrata, Bayin Naung and Alompra.

Historically, Arakan may be detached from the other provinces. The inhabitants represent an early migration from Tagaung and were not annexed by any kingdom in Burma until 1784 A.D. Tagaung, situated on the Upper Irrawaddy in the Ruby Mines district, was the oldest capital of the Burmese and has a scanty history apparently going back to the early centuries of our era. Much the same may be said of the Talaing kingdom in Lower Burma. The kings of Tagaung were succeeded by another dynasty connected with them which reigned at Prome. No dates can be given for these events, nor is the part which the Pyus played in them clear, but it is said that the Talaings

[1] For the Pyus see Blagden in *J.R.A.S.* pp. 365–388. *Ibid.* in *Epigr. Indica,* 1913, pp. 127–133. Also reports of *Burma Arch. Survey,* 1916, 1917.

destroyed the kingdom of Prome in 742 A.D.[1] According to tradition the centre of power moved about this time to Pagan[2] on the bank of the Irrawaddy somewhat south of Mandalay. But the silence of early Chinese accounts[3] as to Pagan, which is not mentioned before the Sung dynasty, makes it probable that later writers exaggerated its early importance and it is only when Anawrata, King of Pagan and the first great name in Burmese history, ascended the throne that the course of events becomes clear and coherent. He conquered Thaton in 1057 and transported many of the inhabitants to his own capital. He also subdued the nearer Shan states and was master of nearly all Burma as we understand the term. The chief work of his successors was to construct the multitude of pagodas which still ornament the site of Pagan. It would seem that the dynasty gradually degenerated and that the Shans and Talaings acquired strength at its expense. Its end came in 1298 and was hastened by the invasion of Khubilai Khan. There then arose two simultaneous Shan dynasties at Panya and Sagaing which lasted from 1298 till 1364. They were overthrown by King Thadominpaya who is believed to have been a Shan. He founded Ava which, whether it was held by Burmese or Shans, was regarded as the chief city of Burma until 1752, although throughout this period the kings of Pegu and other districts were frequently independent. During the fourteenth century another kingdom grew up at Toungoo[4] in Lower Burma. Its rulers were originally Shan governors sent from Ava but ultimately they claimed to be descendants of the last king of Pagan and, in this character, Bureng or Bayin Naung (1551–1581), the second great ruler of Burma, conquered Prome, Pegu and Ava. His kingdom began to break up immediately after his death but his dynasty ruled in Ava until the middle of the eighteenth century.

During this period Europeans first made their appearance and quarrels with Portuguese adventurers were added to native

[1] So C. C. Lowis in the *Gazetteer of Burma*, vol. I. p. 292, but according to others the Burmese chronicles place the event at the beginning of the Christian era.

[2] Sometimes called New Pagan to distinguish it from Old Pagan which was a name of Tagaung. Also called Pagan or Pugâma and in Pali Arimaddanapura.

[3] See the travels of Kia Tan described by Pelliot in *B.E.F.E.O.* 1904, pp. 131–414.

[4] More correctly Taung-ngu.

dissensions. The Shans and Talaings became turbulent and after a tumultuous interval the third great national hero, Alaungpaya or Alompra, came to the front. In the short space of eight years (1752–1760), he gained possession of Ava, made the Burmese masters of both the northern and southern provinces, founded Rangoon and invaded both Manipur and Siam. While on the latter expedition he died. Some of his successors held their court at Ava but Bodawpaya built a new capital at Amarapura (1783) and Mindon Min another at Mandalay (1857). The dynasty came to an end in 1886 when King Thibaw was deposed by the Government of India and his dominions annexed.

2

The early history of Buddhism in Burma is obscure, as in most other countries, and different writers have maintained that it was introduced from northern India, the east coast of India, Ceylon, China or Camboja[1]. All these views may be in a measure true, for there is reason to believe that it was not introduced at one epoch or from one source or in one form.

It is not remarkable that Indian influence should be strong among the Burmese. The wonder rather is that they have preserved such strong individuality in art, institutions and everyday life, that no one can pass from India into Burma without feeling that he has entered a new country. This is because the mountains which separate it from Eastern Bengal and run right down to the sea form a barrier still sufficient to prevent com-

[1] For the history and present condition of Buddhism in Burma the following may be consulted besides other works referred to in the course of this chapter.

M. Bode, *Edition of the Sâsanavaṃsa* with valuable dissertations, 1897. This work is a modern Burmese ecclesiastical history written in 1861 by Paññâsâmi.

M. Bode, *The Pali Literature of Burma*, 1909.

The Gandhavaṃsa: containing accounts of many Pali works written in Burma. Edited by Minayeff in *Jour. Pali Text Soc.* for 1886, pp. 54 ff. and indexed by M. Bode, *ibid.* 1896, 53 ff.

Bigandet, *Vie ou Légende de Gautama*, 1878.

Yoe, *The Burman, his life and notions.*

J. G. Scott, *Burma, a handbook of practical information*, 1906.

Reports of the Superintendent, Archaeological Survey, Burma, 1916–1920.

Various articles (especially by Duroiselle, Taw-Sein-Ko and R. C. Temple) in the *Indian Antiquary, Buddhism*, and *Bulletin de l'École Française de l'Extrême Orient.*

munication by rail. But from the earliest times Indian immigrants and Indian ideas have been able to find their way both by land and sea. According to the Burmese chronicles Tagaung was founded by the Hindu prince Abhirâja in the ninth century B.C. and the kingdom of Arakan claims as its first ruler an ancient prince of Benares. The legends have not much more historical value than the Kshattriya genealogies which Brahmans have invented for the kings of Manipur, but they show that the Burmese knew of India and wished to connect themselves with it. This spirit led not only to the invention of legends but to the application of Indian names to Burmese localities. For instance Aparantaka, which really designates a district of western India, is identified by native scholars with Upper Burma[1]. The two merchants Tapussa and Bhallika who were the first to salute the Buddha after his enlightenment are said to have come from Ukkala. This is usually identified with Orissa but Burmese tradition locates it in Burma. A system of mythical geography has thus arisen.

The Buddha himself is supposed to have visited Burma, as well as Ceylon, in his lifetime[2] and even to have imparted some of his power to the celebrated image which is now in the Arakan Pagoda at Mandalay. Another resemblance to the Sinhalese story is the evangelization of lower Burma by Asoka's missionaries. The Dîpavamsa states[3] that Sona and Uttara were despatched to Suvarṇabhûmi. This is identified with Râmaññadesa or the district of Thaton, which appears to be a corruption of Saddhammapura[4] and the tradition is accepted in Burma. The scepticism with which modern scholars have received it is perhaps unmerited, but the preaching of these missionaries, if it ever took place, cannot at present be connected with other historical events. Nevertheless the statement of the Dîpavaṃsa is significant. The work was composed in the fourth century A.D. and taken from older chronicles. It may therefore be con-

[1] So too Prome is called Śrîkshetra and the name Irrawaddy represents Irâvatî (the modern Ravi). The ancient town of Śrâvastî or Sâvatthi is said to reappear in the three forms Tharawaddy, Tharawaw and Thawutti.

[2] See *Indian Antiquary*, 1893, p. 6, and Forchhammer on the Mahamuni Pagoda in *Burmese Archaeological Report* (? 1890).

[3] Dîpav. VIII. 12, and in a more embellished form in Mahâvaṃsa XII. 44–54. See also the Kalyani Inscriptions in *Indian Ant.* 1893, p. 16.

[4] Through the form Saton representing Saddhan. Early European travellers called it Satan or Xatan.

cluded that in the early centuries of our era lower Burma had the reputation of being a Buddhist country[1]. It also appears certain that in the eleventh century, when the Talaings were conquered by Anawrata, Buddhist monks and copies of the Tipiṭaka were found there. But we know little about the country in the preceding centuries. The Kalyani inscription says that before Anawrata's conquest it was divided and decadent and during this period there is no proof of intercourse with Ceylon but also no disproof. One result of Anawrata's conquest of Thaton was that he exchanged religious embassies with the king of Ceylon, and it is natural to suppose that the two monarchs were moved to this step by traditions of previous communications. Intercourse with the east coast of India may be assumed as natural, and is confirmed by the presence of Sanskrit words in old Talaing and the information about southern India in Talaing records, in which the city of Conjevaram, the great commentator Dharmapâla and other men of learning are often mentioned. Analogies have also been traced between the architecture of Pagan and southern India[2]. It will be seen that such communication by sea may have brought not only Hinayanist Buddhism but also Mahayanist and Tantric Buddhism as well as Brahmanism from Bengal and Orissa, so that it is not surprising if all these influences can be detected in the ancient buildings and sculptures of the country[3]. Still the most important evidence as to the character of early Burmese Buddhism is Hinayanist and furnished by inscriptions on thin golden plates and tiles, found near the ancient site of Prome and deciphered by Finot[4]. They consist of Hinayanist religious formulæ: the language is Pali: the alphabet is of a south Indian type and is said to resemble closely that used in the inscriptions of the Kadamba dynasty which ruled in Kanara from the third to the

[1] The Burmese identify Aparantaka and Yona to which Asoka also sent missionaries with Upper Burma and the Shan country. But this seems to be merely a misapplication of Indian names.

[2] See Forchhammer, *Jardine Prize Essay*, 1885, pp. 23–27. He also says that the earliest Talaing alphabet is identical with the Vengi alphabet of the fourth century A.D. *Burma Archaeol. Report*, 1917, p. 29.

[3] See R. C. Temple, "Notes on Antiquities of Râmaññadesa," *Ind. Antiq.* 1893, pp. 327 ff. Though I admit the possibility that Mahâyânism and Tantrism may have flourished in lower Burma, it does not seem to me that the few Hindu figures reproduced in this article prove very much.

[4] *J.A.* 1912, II. pp. 121–136.

sixth century. It is to the latter part of this period that the inscriptions are to be attributed. They show that a form of the Hinayana, comparable, so far as the brief documents permit us to judge, with the church of Ceylon, was then known in lower Burma and was probably the state church. The character of the writing, taken together with the knowledge of southern India shown by the Talaing chronicles and the opinion of the Dîpavamsa that Burma was a Buddhist country, is good evidence that lower Burma had accepted Hinayanism before the sixth century and had intercourse with southern India. More than that it would perhaps be rash to say.

The Burmese tradition that Buddhaghosa was a native of Thaton and returned thither from Ceylon merits more attention than it has received. It can be easily explained away as patriotic fancy. On the other hand, if Buddhaghosa's object was to invigorate Hinayanism in India, the result of his really stupendous labours was singularly small, for in India his name is connected with no religious movement. But if we suppose that he went to Ceylon by way of the holy places in Magadha and returned from the Coromandel Coast to Burma where Hinayanism afterwards flourished, we have at least a coherent narrative[1].

It is noticeable that Târanâtha states[2] that in the Koki countries, among which he expressly mentions Pukham (Pagan) and Haṃsavatî (Pegu), Hinayanism was preached from the days of Asoka onwards, but that the Mahayana was not known until the pupils of Vasubandhu introduced it.

The presence of Hinayanism in Lower Burma naturally did not prevent the arrival of Mahayanism. It has not left many certain traces but Atîśa (*c.* 1000), a great figure in the history of Tibetan Buddhism, is reported to have studied both in Magadha and in Suvarnadvîpa by which Thaton must be meant. He would hardly have done this, had the clergy of Thaton been unfriendly to Tantric learning. This mediæval Buddhism was also, as in other countries, mixed with Hinduism

[1] It is remarkable that Buddhaghosa commenting on Ang. Nik. 1.14. 6 (quoted by Forchhammer) describes the merchants of Ukkala as inhabiting Asitañjana in the region of Haṃsavatî or Pegu. This identification of Ukkala with Burmese territory is a mistake but accepted in Burma and it is more likely that a Burmese would have made it than a Hindu.

[2] Chap. XXXIX.

but whereas in Camboja and Champa Śivaism, especially the worship of the lingam, was long the official and popular cult and penetrated to Siam, few Śivaite emblems but numerous statues of Vishṇuite deities have hitherto been discovered in Burma.

The above refers chiefly to Lower Burma. The history of Burmese Buddhism becomes clearer in the eleventh century but before passing to this new period we must enquire what was the religious condition of Upper Burma in the centuries preceding it. It is clear that any variety of Buddhism or Brahmanism may have entered this region from India by land at any epoch. According to both Hsüan Chuang and I-Ching Buddhism flourished in Samaṭata and the latter mentions images of Avalokita and the reading of the Prajñâ-pâramitâ. The precise position of Samaṭata has not been fixed but in any case it was in the east of Bengal and not far from the modern Burmese frontier. The existence of early Sanskrit inscriptions at Taungu and elsewhere has been recorded but not with as much detail as could be wished[1]. Figures of Bodhisattvas and Indian deities are reported from Prome[2], and in the Lower Chindwin district are rock-cut temples resembling the caves of Barabar in Bengal. Inscriptions also show that at Prome there were kings, perhaps in the seventh century, who used the Pyu language but bore Sanskrit titles. According to Burmese tradition the Buddha himself visited the site of Pagan and prophesied that a king called Sammutiraya would found a city there and establish the faith. This prediction is said to have been fulfilled in 108 A.D. but the notices quoted from the Burmese chronicles are concerned less with the progress of true religion than with the prevalence of heretics known as Aris[3]. It has been conjectured that this name is a corruption of Ârya but it appears that the correct orthography is *arañ* representing an original *araṇyaka*, that is forest priests. It is hard to say whether they were degraded Buddhists or an indigenous priesthood who in some

[1] See however *Epig. Indica*, vol. v. part iv. Oct. 1898, pp. 101–102. For the prevalence of forms which must be derived from Sanskrit not Pali see *Burma Arch. Rep.* 1916, p. 14, and 1917, p. 39.

[2] *Report of Supt. Arch. Survey Burma*, 1909, p. 10, 1910, p. 13, and 1916, pp. 33, 38. Finot, *Notes d'Epigraphie*, p. 357.

[3] See especially Finot in *J.A.* 1912, II. p. 123, and Huber in *B.E.F.E.O.* 1909 p. 584.

ways imitated what they knew of Brahmanic and Buddhist institutions. They wore black robes, let their hair grow, worshipped serpents, hung up in their temples the heads of animals that had been sacrificed, and once a year they assisted the king to immolate a victim to the Nats on a mountain top. They claimed power to expiate all sins, even parricide. They lived in convents (which is their only real resemblance to Buddhist monks) but were not celibate[1]. Anawrata is said to have suppressed the Aris but he certainly did not extirpate them for an inscription dated 1468 records their existence in the Myingyan district. Also in a village near Pagan are preserved Tantric frescoes representing Bodhisattvas with their Śaktis. In one temple is an inscription dated 1248 and requiring the people to supply the priests morning and evening with rice, beef, betel, and a jar of spirits[2]. It is not clear whether these priests were Aris or not, but they evidently professed an extreme form of Buddhist Śaktism.

Chinese influences in Upper Burma must also be taken into account. Burmese kings were perhaps among the many potentates who sent religious embassies to the Emperor Wu-ti about 525 A.D. and the T'ang[3] annals show an acquaintance with Burma. They describe the inhabitants as devout Buddhists, reluctant to take life or even to wear silk, since its manufacture involves the death of the silk worms. There were a hundred monasteries into which the youth entered at the age of seven, leaving at the age of twenty, if they did not intend to become monks. The Chinese writer does not seem to have regarded the religion of Burma as differing materially from Buddhism as he knew it and some similarities in ecclesiastical terminology shown by Chinese and Burmese may indicate the presence of Chinese

[1] The Aris are further credited with having practised a sort of *jus primæ noctis*. See on this question the chapter on Camboja and alleged similar customs there.

[2] See *Burma Arch. Rep.* 1916, pp. 12, 13. They seem to have been similar to the Nīlapatanadarśana of Ceylon. The Prabodhacandrodaya (about 1100 A.D.) represents Buddhist monks as drunken and licentious.

[3] See Parker, *Burma*, 1892. The annalist says "There is a huge white elephant (or image) 100 feet high. Litigants burn incense and kneel before it, reflecting within themselves whether they are right or wrong....When there is any disaster or plague the king also kneels in front of it and blames himself." The Chinese character means either image or elephant, but surely the former must be the meaning here.

influence[1]. But this influence, though possibly strong between the sixth and tenth centuries A.D., and again about the time of the Chinese invasion of 1284[2], cannot be held to exclude Indian influence.

Thus when Anawrata came to the throne[3] several forms of religion probably co-existed at Pagan, and probably most of them were corrupt, though it is a mistake to think of his dominions as barbarous. The reformation which followed is described by Burmese authors in considerable detail and as usual in such accounts is ascribed to the activity of one personality, the Thera Arahanta who came from Thaton and enjoyed Anawrata's confidence. The story implies that there was a party in Pagan which knew that the prevalent creed was corrupt and also looked upon Thaton and Ceylon as religious centres. As Anawrata was a man of arms rather than a theologian, we may conjecture that his motive was to concentrate in his capital the flower of learning as known in his time—a motive which has often animated successful princes in Asia and led to the unceremonious seizure of living saints. According to the story he broke up the communities of Aris at the instigation of Arahanta and then sent a mission to Manohari, king of Pegu, asking for a copy of the Tipiṭaka and for relics. He received a contemptuous reply intimating that he was not to be trusted with such sacred objects. Anawrata in indignation collected an army, marched against the Talaings and ended by carrying off to Pagan not only elephant loads of scriptures and relics, but also all the Talaing monks and nobles with the king himself[4]. The Piṭakas were stored in a splendid pagoda and Anawrata

[1] See Taw-Sein-Ko, in *Ind. Antiquary*, 1906, p. 211. But I must confess that I have not been able to follow or confirm all the etymologies suggested by him.

[2] See for Chinese remains at Pagan, *Report of the Superintendent, Arch. Survey, Burma, for year ending* 31*st March*, 1910, pp. 20, 21. An inscription at Pagan records that in 1285 Khubilai's troops were accompanied by monks sent to evangelize Burma. Both troops and monks halted at Tagaung and both were subsequently withdrawn. See *Arch. Survey*, 1917, p. 38.

[3] The date of Anawrata's conquest of Thaton seems to be now fixed by inscriptions as 1057 A.D., though formerly supposed to be earlier. See *Burma Arch. Rep.* 1916. For Anawrata's religious reforms see *Sâsanavaṃsa*, pp. 17 ff. and 57 ff.

[4] It has been noted that many of the inscriptions explanatory of the scenes depicted on the walls of the Ânanda temple at Pagan are in Talaing, showing that it was some time before the Burmans were able to assimilate the culture of the conquered country.

sent to Ceylon[1] for others which were compared with the copies obtained from Thaton in order to settle the text[2].

For 200 years, that is from about 1060 A.D. until the later decades of the thirteenth century, Pagan was a great centre of Buddhist culture not only for Burma but for the whole east, renowned alike for its architecture and its scholarship. The former can still be studied in the magnificent pagodas which mark its site. Towards the end of his reign Anawrata made not very successful attempts to obtain relics from China and Ceylon and commenced the construction of the Shwe Zigon pagoda. He died before it was completed but his successors, who enjoyed fairly peaceful reigns, finished the work and constructed about a thousand other buildings among which the most celebrated is the Ananda temple erected by King Kyansithâ[3].

Pali literature in Burma begins with a little grammatical treatise known as Kârikâ and composed in 1064 A.D. by the monk Dhammasenâpati who lived in the monastery attached to this temple. A number of other works followed. Of these the most celebrated was the Saddanîti of Aggavaṃsa (1154), a treatise on the language of the Tipiṭaka which became a classic not only in Burma but in Ceylon. A singular enthusiasm for linguistic studies prevailed especially in the reign of Kyocvâ (*c.* 1230), when even women are said to have been distinguished for the skill and ardour which they displayed in conquering the difficulties of Pali grammar. Some treatises on the Abhidhamma were also produced.

Like Mohammedanism, Hinayanist Buddhism is too simple and definite to admit much variation in doctrine, but its clergy are prone to violent disputes about apparently trivial questions. In the thirteenth century such disputes assumed grave proportions in Burma. About 1175 A.D. a celebrated elder named

[1] So the *Sâsanavaṃsa*, p. 64 and p. 20. See also Bode, *Pali Literature of Burma*, p. 15. But the Mahâvaṃsa, LX. 4–7, while recording the communications between Vijaya Bahu and Aniruddha (=Anawrata) represents Ceylon as asking for monks from Râmañña, which implies that lower Burma was even then regarded as a Buddhist country with a fine tradition.

[2] The Burmese canon adds four works to the Khuddaka-Nikâya, namely: (*a*) Milinda Pañha, (*b*) Netti-Pakaraṇa, (*c*) Suttasaṅgaha, (*d*) Peṭakopadesa.

[3] Inscriptions give his reign as 1084–1112 A.D. See *Burma Arch. Rep.* 1916, p. 24. Among many other remarkable edifices may be mentioned the Thapinyu or Thabbannu (1100), the Gaudapalin (1160) and the Bodhi (*c.* 1200) which is a copy of the temple at Bodhgaya.

Uttarâjîva accompanied by his pupil Chapaṭa left for Ceylon. They spent some years in study at the Mahâvihâra and Chapaṭa received ordination there. He returned to Pagan with four other monks and maintained that valid ordination could be conferred only through the monks of the Mahâvihâra, who alone had kept the succession unbroken. He with his four companions, having received this ordination, claimed power to transmit it, but he declined to recognize Burmese orders. This pretension aroused a storm of opposition, especially from the Talaing monks. They maintained that Arahanta who had reformed Buddhism under Anawrata was spiritually descended from the missionaries sent by Asoka, who were as well qualified to administer ordination as Mahinda. But Chapaṭa was not only a man of learning and an author[1] but also a vigorous personality and in favour at Court. He had the best of the contest and succeeded in making the Talaing school appear as seceders from orthodoxy. There thus arose a distinction between the Sinhalese or later school and the old Burmese school, who regarded one another as schismatics. A scandal was caused in the Sinhalese community by Râhula, the ablest of Chapaṭa's disciples, who fell in love with an actress and wished to become a layman. His colleagues induced him to leave the country for decency's sake and peace was restored but subsequently, after Chapaṭa's death, the remaining three disciples[2] fell out on questions of discipline rather than doctrine and founded three factions, which can hardly be called schools, although they refused to keep the Uposatha days together. The light of religion shone brightest at Pagan early in the thirteenth century while these three brethren were alive and the Sâsanavaṃsa states that at least three Arhats lived in the city. But the power of Pagan collapsed under attacks from both Chinese and Shans at the end of the century

[1] The best known of his works are the Sutta-niddesa on grammar and the Sankhepavaṇṇanâ. The latter is a commentary on the Abhidhammattha-sangaha, but it is not certain if Chapaṭa composed it or merely translated it from the Sinhalese.

[2] Some authorities speak as if the four disciples of Chapaṭa had founded four sects, but the reprobate Râhula can hardly have done this. The above account is taken from the Kalyani inscription, *Ind. Ant.* 1893, pp. 30, 31. It says very distinctly "There were in Pugama (Pagan) 4 sects. 1. The successors of the priests who introduced the religion from Sudhammanâgara (*i.e.* the Mramma Sangha). 2. The disciples of Sîvalimahâthera. 3. The disciples of Tâmalindamahâthera. 4. The disciples of Ânanda Mahâthera."

and the last king became a monk under the compulsion of Shan chiefs. The deserted city appears to have lost its importance as a religious centre, for the ecclesiastical chronicles shift the scene elsewhere.

The two Shan states which arose from the ruin of Pagan, namely Panya (Vijayapura) and Sagaing (Jeyyapura), encouraged religion and learning. Their existence probably explains the claim made in Siamese inscriptions of about 1300 that the territory of Siam extended to Haṃsavatî or Pegu and this contact of Burma and Siam was of great importance for it must be the origin of Pali Buddhism in Siam which otherwise remains unexplained.

After the fall of the two Shan states in 1364, Ava (or Ratnapura) which was founded in the same year gradually became the religious centre of Upper Burma and remained so during several centuries. But it did not at first supersede older towns inasmuch as the loss of political independence did not always involve the destruction of monasteries. Buddhism also flourished in Pegu and the Talaing country where the vicissitudes of the northern kingdoms did not affect its fortunes.

Anawrata had transported the most eminent Theras of Thaton to Pagan and the old Talaing school probably suffered temporarily. Somewhat later we hear that the Sinhalese school was introduced into these regions by Sâriputta[1], who had been ordained at Pagan. About the same time two Theras of Martaban, preceptors of the Queen, visited Ceylon and on returning to their own land after being ordained at the Mahâvihâra considered themselves superior to other monks. But the old Burmese school continued to exist. Not much literature was produced in the south. Sâriputta was the author of a Dhammathat or code, the first of a long series of law books based upon Manu. Somewhat later Mahâyasa of Thaton (*c.* 1370) wrote several grammatical works.

The most prosperous period for Buddhism in Pegu was the reign of Dhammacceti, also called Râmâdhipati (1460–1491). He was not of the royal family, but a simple monk who helped a princess of Pegu to escape from the Burmese court where she was detained. In 1453 this princess became Queen of Pegu and Dhammaceti left his monastery to become her prime minister,

[1] Also known by the title of Dhammavitasa. He was active in 1246.

son-in-law and ultimately her successor. But though he had returned to the world his heart was with the Church. He was renowned for his piety no less than for his magnificence and is known to modern scholars as the author of the Kalyani inscriptions[1], which assume the proportions of a treatise on ecclesiastical laws and history. Their chief purpose is to settle an intricate and highly technical question, namely the proper method of defining and consecrating a *sîmâ*. This word, which means literally *boundary*, signifies a plot of ground within which Uposatha meetings, ordinations and other ceremonies can take place. The expression occurs in the Vinaya Piṭaka[2], but the area there contemplated seems to be an ecclesiastical district within which the Bhikkhus were obliged to meet for Uposatha. The modern *sîmâ* is much smaller[3], but more important since it is maintained that valid ordination can be conferred only within its limits. To Dhammaceti the question seemed momentous, for as he explains, there were in southern Burma six schools who would not meet for Uposatha. These were, first the Camboja[4] school (identical with the Arahanta school) who claimed spiritual descent from the missionaries sent by Asoka to Suvarṇabhûmi, and then five divisions of the Sinhalese school, namely the three founded by Chapata's disciples as already related and two more founded by the theras of Martaban. Dhammaceti accordingly sent a mission to Ceylon charged to obtain an authoritative ruling as to the proper method of consecrating a *sîmâ* and conferring ordination. On their return a locality known as the Kalyanisîmâ was consecrated in the manner prescribed by the Mahâvihâra and during three years all the Bhikkhus of Dhammaceti's kingdom were reordained there. The total number reached 15,666, and the king boasts that he had thus purified religion and made the school of the Mahâvihâra the only sect, all other distinctions being obliterated.

[1] Found in Zaingganaing, a suburb of Pegu. The text, translation and notes are contained in various articles by Taw-Sein-Ko in the *Indian Antiquary* for 1893–4.

[2] Mahâvagga, II. 11, 12, 13.

[3] According to Taw-Sein-Ko (*Ind. Ant.* 1893, p. 11) "about 105 or 126 feet in perimeter."

[4] No contact with Cambojan religion is implied. The sect was so called because its chief monastery was near the Camboja market and this derived its name from the fact that many Cambojan (probably meaning Shan) prisoners were confined near it.

There can be little doubt that in the fifteenth century Burmese Buddhism had assumed the form which it still has, but was this form due to indigenous tradition or to imitation of Ceylon? Five periods merit attention. (*a*) In the sixth century, and probably several centuries earlier, Hinayanism was known in Lower Burma. The inscriptions attesting its existence are written in Pali and in a south Indian alphabet. (*b*) Anawrata (1010–1052) purified the Buddhism of Upper Burma with the help of scriptures obtained from the Talaing country, which were compared with other scriptures brought from Ceylon. (*c*) About 1200 Chapata and his pupils who had studied in Ceylon and received ordination there refused to recognize the Talaing monks and two hostile schools were founded, predominant at first in Upper and Lower Burma respectively. (*d*) About 1250 the Sinhalese school, led by Sâriputta and others, began to make conquests in Lower Burma at the expense of the Talaing school. (*e*) Two centuries later, about 1460, Dhammaceti of Pegu boasts that he has purified religion and made the school of the Mahâvihâra, that is the most orthodox form of the Sinhalese school, the only sect.

In connection with these data must be taken the important statement that the celebrated Tantrist Atîśa studied in Lower Burma about 1000 A.D. Up to a certain point the conclusion seems clear. Pali Hinayanism in Burma was old: intercourse with southern India and Ceylon tended to keep it pure, whereas intercourse with Bengal and Orissa, which must have been equally frequent, tended to import Mahayanism. In the time of Anawrata the religion of Upper Burma probably did not deserve the name of Buddhism. He introduced in its place the Buddhism of Lower Burma, tempered by reference to Ceylon. After 1200 if not earlier the idea prevailed that the Mahâvihâra was the standard of orthodoxy and that the Talaing church (which probably retained some Mahayanist features) fell below it. In the fifteenth century this view was universally accepted, the opposition and indeed the separate existence of the Talaing church having come to an end.

But it still remains uncertain whether the earliest Burmese Buddhism came direct from Magadha or from the south. The story of Asoka's missionaries cannot be summarily rejected but it also cannot be accepted without hesitation[1]. It is the Ceylon chronicle which knows of them and communication between Burma and southern India was old and persistent. It may have existed even before the Christian era.

After the fall of Pagan, Upper Burma, of which we must now speak, passed through troubled times and we hear little of religion or literature. Though Ava was founded in 1364 it did not become an intellectual centre for another century. But the reign of Narapati (1442–1468) was ornamented by several writers of eminence among whom may be mentioned the monk poet Sîlavaṃsa and Ariyavaṃsa, an exponent of the Abhidhamma. They are noticeable as being the first writers to publish religious works, either original or translated, in the vernacular and this practice steadily increased. In the early part of the sixteenth century[2] occurred the only persecution of Buddhism known in Burma. Thohanbwâ, a Shan who had become king of Ava, endeavoured to exterminate the order by deliberate massacre and delivered temples, monasteries and libraries to the flames. The persecution did not last long nor extend to other districts but it created great indignation among the Burmese and was perhaps one of the reasons why the Shan dynasty of Ava was overthrown in 1555.

Bayin (or Bureng) Naung stands out as one of the greatest personalities in Burmese history. As a Buddhist he was zealous even to intolerance, since he forced the Shans and Moslims of the northern districts, and indeed all his subjects, to make a formal profession of Buddhism. He also, as related elsewhere, made not very successful attempts to obtain the tooth relic from Ceylon. But it is probable that his active patronage of the faith, as shown in the construction and endowment of religious buildings, was exercised chiefly in Pegu and this must be the reason why the Sâsanavaṃsa (which is interested chiefly in Upper Burma) says little about him.

His successors showed little political capacity but encouraged religion and literature. The study of the Abhidhamma was

[1] In favour of it, it may be said that the Dîpavaṃsa and the earlier traditions on which the Dîpavaṃsa is based are ancient and impartial witnesses: against it, that Asoka's attention seems to have been directed westwards, not towards Bengal and Burma, and that no very early proof of the existence of Buddhism in Burma has been found.

[2] Apparently about 1525–1530.

specially flourishing in the districts of Ava and Sagaing from about 1600 to 1650 and found many illustrious exponents. Besides works in Pali, the writers of this time produced numerous Burmese translations and paraphrases of Abhidhamma works, as well as edifying stories.

In the latter part of the seventeenth century Burma was in a disturbed condition and the Sâsanavaṃsa says that religion was dimmed as the moon by clouds. A national and religious revival came with the victories of Alompra (1752 onwards), but the eighteenth century also witnessed the rise of a curious and not very edifying controversy which divided the Sangha for about a hundred years and spread to Ceylon[1]. It concerned the manner in which the upper robe of a monk, consisting of a long piece of cloth, should be worn. The old practice in Burma was to wrap this cloth round the lower body from the loins to the ankles, and draw the end from the back over the left shoulder and thence across the breast over the right shoulder so that it finally hung loose behind. But about 1698 began the custom of walking with the right shoulder bare, that is to say letting the end of the robe fall down in front on the left side. The Sangha became divided into two factions known as *Ekaṃsika* (one-shouldered) and *Pârupana* (fully clad). The bitterness of the seemingly trivial controversy was increased by the fact that the Ekaṃsikas could produce little scriptural warrant and appealed to late authorities or the practice in Ceylon, thus neglecting sound learning. For the Vinaya frequently[2] prescribes that the robe is to be adjusted so as to fall over only one shoulder as a mark of special respect, which implies that it was usually worn over both shoulders. In 1712 and again about twenty years later arbitrators were appointed by the king to hear both sides, but they had not sufficient authority or learning

[1] See *Sâsanavaṃsa*, pp. 118 ff.

[2] *E.g.* Mahâvagga, I. 29, 2; IV. 3, 3. Ekaṃsam uttarâsangam karitvâ. But both arrangements of drapery are found in the oldest images of the Buddha and perhaps the Ekaṃsika fashion is the commoner. See Grünwedel, *Buddhist Art in India*, 1901, p. 172. Though these images are considerably later than the Mahâvagga and prove nothing as to the *original* practice of the Saṅgha, yet they show that the Ekaṃsika fashion prevailed at a relatively early period. It now prevails in Siam and partly in Ceylon. I-Ching (chap. XI.) has a discussion on the way robes were worn in India (*c.* 680 A.D.) which is very obscure but seems to say that monks may keep their shoulders covered while in a monastery but should uncover one when they go out.

to give a decided opinion. The stirring political events of 1740 and the following years naturally threw ecclesiastical quarrels into the shade but when the great Alompra had disposed of his enemies he appeared as a modern Asoka. The court religiously observed Uposatha days and the king was popularly believed to be a Bodhisattva[1]. He was not however sound on the great question of ecclesiastical dress. His chaplain, Atula, belonged to the Ekaṃsika party and the king, saying that he wished to go into the whole matter himself but had not for the moment leisure, provisionally ordered the Saṅgha to obey Atula's ruling. But some champions of the other side stood firm. Alompra dealt leniently with them, but died during his Siamese campaign before he had time to unravel the intricacies of the Vinaya.

The influence of Atula, who must have been an astute if not learned man, continued after the king's death and no measures were taken against the Ekaṃsikas, although King Hsin-byu-shin (1763–1776) persecuted an heretical sect called Paramats[2]. His youthful successor, Sing-gu-sa, was induced to hold a public disputation. The Ekaṃsikas were defeated in this contest and a royal decree was issued making the Pârupana discipline obligatory. But the vexed question was not settled for it came up again in the long reign (1781–1819) of Bodôpayâ. This king has won an evil reputation for cruelty and insensate conceit[3], but he was a man of vigour and kept together his great empire. His megalomania naturally detracted from the esteem won by his piety. His benefactions to religion were lavish, the shrines and monasteries which he built innumerable. But he desired to build a pagoda larger than any in the world and during some twenty years wasted an incalculable amount of labour and money on this project, still commemorated by a gigantic but unfinished mass of brickwork now in ruins. In order to supervise its erection he left his palace and lived at Mingun, where he

[1] *Sâsanav.* p. 123. Sakala-Maramma-raṭṭhavâsino ca: ayaṃ amhakâṃ râjâ bodhisatto ti vohârimsu. In the Po-U-Daung inscription, Alompra's son, Hsin-byu-shin. says twice "In virtue of this my good deed, may I become a Buddha,... an omniscient one." *Indian Antiquary,* 1893, pp. 2 and 5. There is something Mahâyânist in this aspiration. Cf. too the inscriptions of the Siamese King Śrî-Sûryavaṃsa Râma mentioned below.

[2] They were Puritans who objected to shrines and images and are said to be represented to-day by the Sawti sect.

[3] See *The Burmese Empire* by the Italian Father Sangermano, who went to Burma in 1783 and lived there about 20 years.

conceived the idea that he was a Buddha, an idea which had not been entirely absent from the minds of Alompra and Hsin-byu-shin. It is to the credit of the Theras that, despite the danger of opposing an autocrat as cruel as he was crazy, they refused to countenance these pretensions and the king returned to his palace as an ordinary monarch.

If he could not make himself a Buddha, he at least disposed of the Ekaṃsika dispute, and was probably influenced in his views by Ñânâbhivaṃsa, a monk of the Pârupana school whom he made his chaplain, although Atula was still alive. At first he named a commission of enquiry, the result of which was that the Ekaṃsikas admitted that their practice could not be justified from the scriptures but only by tradition. A royal decree was issued enjoining the observance of the Pârupana discipline, but two years later Atula addressed a letter to the king in which he maintained that the Ekaṃsika costume was approved in a work called Cûlaganṭhipada, composed by Moggalâna, the immediate disciple of the Buddha. The king ordered representatives of both parties to examine this contention and the debate between them is dramatically described in the Sâsanavaṃsa. It was demonstrated that the text on which Atula relied was composed in Ceylon by a thera named Moggalâna who lived in the twelfth century and that it quoted mediæval Sinhalese commentaries. After this exposure the Ekaṃsika party collapsed. The king commanded (1784) the Pârupana discipline to be observed and at last the royal order received obedience.

It will be observed that throughout this controversy both sides appealed to the king, as if he had the right to decide the point in dispute, but that his decision had no compelling power as long as it was not supported by evidence. He could ensure toleration for views regarded by many as heretical, but was unable to force the views of one party on the other until the winning cause had publicly disproved the contentions of its opponents. On the other hand the king had practical control of the hierarchy, for his chaplain was *de facto* head of the Church and the appointment was strictly personal. It was not the practice for a king to take on his predecessor's chaplain and the latter could not, like a Lamaist or Catholic ecclesiastic, claim any permanent supernatural powers. Bodôpayâ did something towards organizing the hierarchy for he appointed four elders of repute to be Saṅgharâjas or, so to speak, Bishops, with four more as assistants and over them all his chaplain Ñâṇa as Archbishop. Ñâṇa was a man of energy and lived in turn in various monasteries supervising the discipline and studies.

In spite of the extravagances of Bodôpayâ, the Church was flourishing and respected in his reign. The celebrated image called Mahâmuni was transferred from Arakan to his capital together with a Sanskrit library, and Burma sent to Ceylon not only the monks who founded the Amarapura school but also numerous Pali texts. This prosperity continued in the reigns of Bagyidaw, Tharrawadi and Pagan-min, who were of little personal account. The first ordered the compilation of the Yazawin, a chronicle which was not original but incorporated and superseded other works of the same kind. In his reign arose a question as to the validity of grants of land, etc., for religious purposes. It was decided in the sense most favourable to the order, *viz.* that such grants are perpetual and are not invalidated by the lapse of time. About 1845 there was a considerable output of vernacular literature. The Dîgha, Samyutta and Anguttara Nikâyas with their commentaries were translated into Burmese but no compositions in Pali are recorded.

From 1852 till 1877 Burma was ruled by Mindon-min, who if not a national hero was at least a pious, peace-loving, capable king. His chaplain, Paññâsâmi, composed the Sâsanavaṃsa, or ecclesiastical history of Burma, and the king himself was ambitious to figure as a great Buddhist monarch, though with more sanity than Bodôpayâ, for his chief desire was to be known as the Convener of the Fifth Buddhist Council. The body so styled met from 1868 to 1871 and, like the ancient Saṅgîtis, proceeded to recite the Tipiṭaka in order to establish the correct text. The result may still be seen at Mandalay in the collection of buildings commonly known as the four hundred and fifty Pagodas: a central Stupa surrounded by hundreds of small shrines each sheltering a perpendicular tablet on which a portion of this veritable bible in stone is inscribed. Mindon-min also corrected the growing laxity of the Bhikkhus, and the esteem in which the Burmese church was held at this time is shown by the fact that the monks of Ceylon sent a deputation to the Saṅgharâja of Mandalay referring to his decision a dispute about a *sîmâ* or ecclesiastical boundary.

Mindon-min was succeeded by Thibaw, who was deposed by the British. The Saṅgharâja maintained his office until he died in 1895. An interregnum then occurred for the appointment had always been made by the king, not by the Sangha. But when Lord Curzon visited Burma in 1901 he made arrangements for the election by the monks themselves of a superior of the whole order and Taunggwin Sayâdaw was solemnly installed in this office by the British authorities in 1903 with the title of Thathanabaing[1].

3

We may now examine briefly some sides of popular religion and institutions which are not Buddhist. It is an interesting fact that the Burmese law books or Dhammathats[2], which are still accepted as regulating inheritance and other domestic matters, are Indian in origin and show no traces of Sinhalese influence although since 1750 there has been a decided tendency to bring them into connection with authorities accepted by Buddhism. The earliest of these codes are those of Dhammavilâsa (1174 A.D.) and of Waguru, king of Martaban in 1280. They professedly base themselves on the authority of Manu and, so far as purely legal topics are concerned, correspond pretty closely with the rules of the Mânava-dharmaśâstra. But they omit all prescriptions which involve Brahmanic religious observances such as penance and sacrifice. Also the theory of punishment is different and inspired by the doctrine of Karma, namely, that every evil deed will bring its own retribution. Hence the Burmese codes ordain for every crime not penalties to be suffered by the criminal but merely the payment of compensation to the party aggrieved, proportionate to the damage suffered[3]. It is probable that the law-books on which these codes were based were brought from the east coast of India and

[1] Thathana is the Pali Sâsana. In Burmese pronunciation the s of Indian words regularly appears as th ($=\theta$), r as y and j as z. Thus Thagya for Sakra, Yazawin for Râjavaṃśa.

[2] See E. Forchhammer, *Jardine Prize Essay* (on the sources and development of Burmese Law), 1885. J. Jolly, "Recht und Sitte" in *Grundriss der Ind. Ar. Phil.* 1896, pp. 41–44. M. H. Bode, *Pali Lit. of Burma*, pp. 83 ff. Dhammathat is the Burmese pronunciation of Dhammasattha, Sanskrit Dharmaśâstra.

[3] This theory did not prevent the kings of Burma and their subordinates from inflicting atrociously cruel punishments.

were of the same type as the code of Nârada, which, though of unquestioned Brahmanic orthodoxy, is almost purely legal and has little to say about religion. A subsidiary literature embodying local decisions naturally grew up, and about 1640 was summarized by a Burmese nobleman called Kaing-zâ in the Mahârâjadhammathat. He received from the king the title of Manurâja and the name of Manu became connected with his code, though it is really based on local custom. It appears to have superseded older law-books until the reign of Alompra who remodelled the administration and caused several codes to be compiled[1]. These also preserve the name of Manu, but he and Kaing-zâ are treated as the same personage. The rules of the older law-books are in the main retained but are made to depend on Buddhist texts. Later Dhammathats become more and more decidedly Buddhist. Thus the Mohavicchedanî (1832) does not mention Manu but presents the substance of the Manu Dhammathats as the law preached by the Buddha.

Direct Indian influence may be seen in another department not unimportant in an oriental country. The court astrologers, soothsayers and professors of kindred sciences were even in recent times Brahmans, known as Pônnâ and mostly from Manipur. An inscription found at Pagan and dated 1442 mentions the gift of 295 books[2] to the Sangha among which several have Sanskrit titles and about 1600 we hear of Pandits learned in the Vedaśâstras, meaning not Vedic learning in the strict sense but combinations of science and magic described as medicine, astronomy, Kâmaśâstras, etc. Hindu tradition was sufficiently strong at the Court to make the presence of experts in the Atharva Veda seem desirable and in the capital they were in request for such services as drawing up horoscopes[3] and

[1] Forchhammer gives a list of 39 Dhammathats compiled between 1753 and 1882.

[2] They seem to have included tantric works of the Mahâkâlacakra type. See Bode, *Pali Lit. of Burma*, p. 108, Nos. 270, 271. But the name is given in the Pali form cakka.

[3] Among usages borrowed from Hinduism may be mentioned the daily washing in holy water of the image in the Arakan temple at Mandalay. Formerly court festivities, such as the New Year's feast and the festival of ploughing, were performed by Pônnâs and with Indian rites. On the other hand the Râmâyana does not seem to have the same influence on art and literature that it has had in Siam and Java, though scenes from it are sometimes depicted. See *Report, Supt. Archaeolog. Survey, Burma*, 1908, p. 22.

invoking good luck at weddings whereas monks will not attend social gatherings.

More important as a non-Buddhist element in Burmese religion is the worship of Nats[1] or spirits of various kinds. Of the prevalence of such worship there is no doubt, but I cannot agree with the authorities who say that it is the practical religion of the Burmese. No passing tourist can fail to see that in the literal as well as figurative sense Burma takes its colour from Buddhism, from the gilded and vermilion pagodas and the yellow robed priests. It is impossible that so much money should be given, so many lives dedicated to a religion which had not a real hold on the hearts of the people. The worship of Nats, wide-spread though it be, is humble in its outward signs and is a superstition rather than a creed. On several occasions the kings of Burma have suppressed its manifestations when they became too conspicuous. Thus Anawrata destroyed the Nat houses of Pagan and recent kings forbade the practice of firing guns at funerals to scare the evil spirits.

Nats are of at least three classes, or rather have three origins. Firstly they are nature spirits, similar to those revered in China and Tibet. They inhabit noticeable natural features of every kind, particularly trees, rivers and mountains; they may be specially connected with villages, houses or individuals. Though not essentially evil they are touchy and vindictive, punishing neglect or discourtesy with misfortune and ill-luck. No explanation is offered as to the origin of many Nats, but others, who may be regarded as forming the second category, are ghosts or ancestral spirits. In northern Burma Chinese influence encouraged ancestor worship, but apart from this there is a disposition (equally evident in India) to believe that violent and uncanny persons and those who meet with a tragic death become powerful ghosts requiring propitiation. Thirdly, there are Nats who are at least in part identified with the Indian deities recognized by early Buddhism. It would seem that the Thirty Seven Nats, described in a work called the Mahâgîtâ Medânigyân, correspond to the Thirty Three Gods of Buddhist mythology, but that the number has been raised for unknown

[1] See especially *The Thirty Seven Nats* by Sir R. C. Temple, 1906, and *Burma* by Sir J. G. Scott, 1906, pp. 380 ff. The best authorities seem agreed that Nat is not the Sanskrit Nâtha but an indigenous word of unknown derivation.

reasons to 37[1]. They are spirits of deceased heroes, and there is nothing unbuddhist in this conception, for the Piṭakas frequently represent deserving persons as being reborn in the Heaven of the Thirty Three. The chief is Thagyâ, the Śakra or Indra of Hindu mythology[2], but the others are heroes, connected with five cycles of legends based on a popular and often inaccurate version of Burmese history[3].

Besides Thagyâ Nat we find other Indian figures such as Man Nat (Mâra) and Byammâ Nat (Brahmâ). In diagrams illustrating the Buddhist cosmology of the Burmans[4] a series of heavens is depicted, ascending from those of the Four Kings and Thirty Three Gods up to the Brahmâ worlds, and each inhabited by Nats according to their degree. Here the spirits of Burma are marshalled and classified according to Buddhist system just as were the spirits of India some centuries before. But neither in ancient India nor in modern Burma have the devas or Nats anything to do with the serious business of religion. They have their place in temples as guardian genii and the whole band may be seen in a shrine adjoining the Shwe-zigon Pagoda at Pagan, but this interferes no more with the supremacy of the Buddha than did the deputations of spirits who according to the scriptures waited on him.

4

Buddhism is a real force in Burmese life and the pride of the Burmese people. Every male Burman enters a monastery when he is about 15 for a short stay. Devout parents send their sons for the four months of *Was* (or even for this season during three successive years), but by the majority a period of from one month to one week is considered sufficient. To omit this stay in a monastery altogether would not be respectable: it is in common esteem the only way to become a human being, for without it a boy is a mere animal. The praises of the Buddha

[1] Possibly in order to include four female spirits: or possibly because it was fel that sundry later heroes had as strong a claim to membership of this distinguished body as the original 33.

[2] It is noticeable that Thagyâ comes from the Sanskrit Śakra not the Pali Sakka. Th = Sk. s: y = Sk. r.

[3] See R. C. Temple, *The Thirty Seven Nats*, chaps. X.–XIII., for these cycles.

[4] *E.g.* R. C. Temple, *l.c.* p. 36.

and vows to lead a good life are commonly recited by the laity[1] every morning and evening. It is the greatest ambition of most Burmans to build a pagoda and those who are able to do so (a large percentage of the population to judge from the number of buildings) are not only sure of their reward in another birth but even now enjoy respect and receive the title of pagoda-builder. Another proof of devotion is the existence of thousands of monasteries[2]—perhaps on an average more than two for each large village and town—built and supported by voluntary contributions. The provision of food and domicile for their numerous inmates is no small charge on the nation, but observers are agreed that it is cheerfully paid and that the monks are worthy of what they receive. In energy and morality they seem, as a class, superior to their brethren in Ceylon and Siam, and their services to education and learning have been considerable. Every monastery is also a school, where instruction is given to both day boys and boarders. The vast majority of Burmans enter such a school at the age of eight or nine and learn there reading, writing, and arithmetic. They also receive religious instruction and moral training. They commit to memory various works in Pali and Burmese, and are taught the duties which they owe to themselves, society and the state. Sir J. G. Scott, who is certainly not disposed to exaggerate the influence of Buddhism in Burma, says that "the education of the monasteries far surpasses the instruction of the Anglo-vernacular schools from every point of view except that of immediate success in life and the obtaining of a post under Government[3]." The more studious monks are not merely schoolmasters but can point to a considerable body of literature which they have produced in the past and are still producing[4]. Indeed among the Hinayanist churches that of Burma has in recent centuries held the first place for learning. The age and continuity of Sinhalese traditions have given the Sangha of Ceylon a correspondingly great prestige but it has more than

[1] According to Sir J. G. Scott much more commonly than prayers among Christians. *Burma*, p. 366.

[2] 15,371 according to the census of 1891. The figures in the last census are not conveniently arranged for Buddhist statistics.

[3] Hastings' *Encycl. of Religion and Ethics*, art. "Burma (Buddhism)."

[4] See Bode, *Pali Literature in Burma*, pp. 95 ff.

once been recruited from Burma and in literary output it can hardly rival the Burmese clergy.

Though many disquisitions on the Vinaya have been produced in Burma, and though the Jâtakas and portions of the Sutta Piṭaka (especially those called Parittam) are known to everybody, yet the favourite study of theologians appears to be the Abhidhamma, concerning which a multitude of handbooks and commentaries have been written, but it is worth mentioning that the Abhidhammattha-sangaha, composed in Ceylon about the twelfth century A.D., is still the standard manual[1]. Yet it would be a mistake to think of the Burmese monks as absorbed in these recondite studies: they have on the contrary produced a long series of works dealing with the practical things of the world, such as chronicles, law-books, ethical and political treatises, and even poetry, for Sîlavamsa and Ratthapâla whose verses are still learned by the youth of Burma were both of them Bhikkhus. The Sangha has always shown a laudable reserve in interfering directly with politics, but in former times the king's private chaplain was a councillor of importance and occasionally matters involving both political and religious questions were submitted to a chapter of the order. In all cases the influence of the monks in secular matters made for justice and peace: they sometimes interceded on behalf of the condemned or represented that taxation was too heavy. In 1886, when the British annexed Burma, the Head of the Sangha forbade monks to take part in the political strife, a prohibition which was all the more remarkable because King Thibaw had issued proclamations saying that the object of the invasion was to destroy Buddhism.

In essentials monastic life is much the same in Burma and Ceylon but the Burmese standard is higher, and any monk known to misconduct himself would be driven out by the laity. The monasteries are numerous but not large and much space is wasted, for, though the exterior suggests that they are built in several stories the interior usually is a single hall, although it may be divided by partitions. To the eastern side is attached a chapel containing images of Gotama before which daily devotions

[1] No less than 22 translations of it have been made into Burmese. See S. Z. Aung in *J.P.T.S.* 1912, p. 129. He also mentions that night lectures on the Abhidhamma in Burmese are given in monasteries.

are performed. It is surmounted by a steeple culminating in a *hti*, a sort of baldachino or sacred umbrella placed also on the top of dagobas, and made of open metal work hung with little bells. Monasteries are always built outside towns and, though many of them become subsequently enclosed by the growth of the larger cities, they retain spacious grounds in which there may be separate buildings, such as a library, dormitories for pupils and a hall for performing the ordination service. The average number of inmates is six. A large establishment may house a superior, four monks, some novices and besides them several lay scholars. The grades are *Sahin* or novice, *Pyit-shin* or fully ordained monk and *Pôngyi*, literally great glory, a monk of at least ten years' standing. Rank depends on seniority—that is to say the greatest respect is shown to the monk who has observed his vows for the longest period, but there are some simple hierarchical arrangements. At the head of each monastery is a Sayâ or superior, and all the monasteries of a large town or a country district are under the supervision of a Provincial called Gaing-Ok. At the head of the whole church is the Thathanabaing, already mentioned. All these higher officials must be Pôngyîs.

Although all monks must take part in the daily round to collect alms yet in most monasteries it is the custom (as in Ceylon and Siam) not to eat the food collected, or at least not all of it, and though no solid nourishment is taken after midday, three morning meals are allowed, namely, one taken very early, the next served on the return from the begging round and a third about 11.30. Two or three services are intoned before the image of the Buddha each day. At the morning ceremony, which takes place about 5.30, all the inmates of the monastery prostrate themselves before the superior and vow to observe the precepts during the day. At the conclusion of the evening service a novice announces that a day has passed away and in a loud voice proclaims the hour, the day of the week, the day of the month and the year. The laity do not usually attend these services, but near large monasteries there are rest houses for the entertainment of visitors and Uposatha days are often celebrated by a pious picnic. A family or party of friends take a rest-house for a day, bring a goodly store of cheroots and betel nut, which are not regarded as out of place during divine service[1], and listen at their ease to the exposition of the law delivered by a yellow-robed monk. When the congregation includes women he holds a large fan-leaf palm before his face lest his eyes should behold vanity. A custom which might not be to the taste of western ecclesiastics is that the congregation ask questions and, if they do not understand, request the preacher to be clearer.

There is little sectarianism in Burma proper, but the Sawtis, an anti-clerical sect, are found in some numbers in the Shan States and similar communities called Man are still met with in Pegu and Tenasserim, though said to be disappearing. Both refuse to recognize the Sangha, monasteries or temples and perform their devotions in the open fields. Otherwise their mode of thought is Buddhist, for they hold that every man can work out his own salvation by conquering Mâra[2], as the Buddha did, and they use the ordinary formulæ of worship, except that they omit all expressions of reverence to the Sangha. The orthodox Sangha is divided into two schools known as Mahâgandi and Sûlagandi. The former are the moderate easy-going majority who maintain a decent discipline but undeniably deviate somewhat from the letter of the Vinaya. The latter are a strict and somewhat militant Puritan minority who protest against such concessions to the flesh. They insist for instance that a monk should eat out of his begging bowl exactly as it is at the end of the morning round and they forbid the use of silk robes, sunshades and sandals. The Sûlagandi also believe in free will and attach more value to the intention than the action in estimating the value of good deeds, whereas the Mahâgandi accept good actions without enquiring into the motive and believe that all deeds are the result of karma.

5

In Burma all the higher branches of architecture are almost exclusively dedicated to religion. Except the Palace at Mandalay there is hardly a native building of note which is not connected with a shrine or monastery. Burmese architectural

[1] But on such occasions the laity usually fast after midday.

[2] Man is the Burmese form of Mâra.

forms show most analogy to those of Nepal and perhaps[1] both preserve what was once the common style for wooden buildings in ancient India. In recent centuries the Burmese have shown little inclination to build anything that can be called a temple, that is a chamber containing images and the paraphernalia of worship. The commonest form of religious edifice is the dagoba or zedi[2]: images are placed in niches or shrines, which shelter them, but only rarely, as on the platform of the Shwe Dagon at Rangoon, assume the proportions of rooms. This does not apply to the great temples of Pagan, built from about 1050 to 1200, but that style was not continued and except the Arakan Pagoda at Mandalay has perhaps no modern representative. Details of these buildings may be found in the works of Forchhammer, Fergusson, de Beylié and various archæological reports. Their construction is remarkably solid. They do not, like most large buildings in India or Europe, contain halls of some size but are rather pyramids traversed by passages. But this curious disinclination to build temples of the usual kind is not due to any dislike of images. In no Buddhist country are they more common and their numbers are more noticeable because there is here no pantheon as in China and Tibet, but images of Gotama are multiplied, merely in order to obtain merit. Some slight variety in these figures is produced by the fact that the Burmese venerate not only Gotama but the three Buddhas who preceded him[3]. The Shwe Dagon Pagoda is reputed to contain relics of all four; statues of them all stand in the beautiful Ânanda Pagoda at Pagan and not infrequently they are represented by four sitting figures facing the four quarters. A gigantic group of this kind composed of statues nearly 90 feet high

[1] Among the most striking characteristics of the Nepalese style are buildings of many stories each with a projecting roof. No examples of similar buildings from ancient India have survived, perhaps because they were made of wood, but representations of two-storied buildings have come down to us, for instance on the Sohgaura copper plate which dates probably from the time of Asoka (see Bühler, *W.Z.K.M.* 1896, p. 138). See also the figures in Foucher's *Art Gréco-bouddhique du Gandhâra*, on pp. 121, 122. The monuments at Mâmallapuram known as Raths (see Fergusson, *Indian and Eastern Architecture*, I. p. 172) appear to be representations of many storied Vihâras. There are several references to seven storied buildings in the Jâtakas.

[2] =cetiya.

[3] Occasionally groups of five Buddhas, that is, these four Buddhas together with Metteyya, are found. See *Report of the Supt. Arch. Survey (Burma) for the year ending March 31st*, 1910, p. 16.

stands in the outskirts of Pegu, and in the same neighbourhood is a still larger recumbent figure 180 feet long. It had been forgotten since the capture of Pegu by the Burmans in 1757 and was rediscovered by the engineers surveying the route for the railway. It lies almost in sight of the line and is surprising by its mere size, as one comes upon it suddenly in the jungle. As a work of art it can hardly be praised. It does not suggest the Buddha on his death bed, as is intended, but rather some huge spirit of the jungle waking up and watching the railway with indolent amusement.

In Upper Burma there are not so many large images but as one approaches Mandalay the pagodas add more and more to the landscape. Many are golden and the rest are mostly white and conspicuous. They crown the hills and punctuate the windings of the valleys. Perhaps Burmese art and nature are seen at their best near Sagaing on the bank of the Irrawaddy, a mighty flood of yellow water, sweeping down smooth and steady, but here and there showing whirlpools that look like molten metal. From the shore rise hills of moderate height studded with monasteries and shrines. Flights of white steps lead to the principal summits where golden spires gleam and everywhere are pagodas of all ages, shapes and sizes. Like most Asiatics the Burmese rarely repair, but build new pagodas instead of renovating the old ones. The instinct is not altogether unjust. A pagoda does not collapse like a hollow building but understands the art of growing old. Like a tree it may become cleft or overgrown with moss but it remains picturesque. In the neighbourhood of Sagaing there is a veritable forest of pagodas; humble seedlings built by widows' mites, mature golden domes reared by devout prosperity and venerable ruins decomposing as all compound things must do.

The pagoda slaves are a curious institution connected with temples. Under the Burmese kings persons could be dedicated to pagodas and by this process not only became slaves for life themselves but involved in the same servitude all their posterity, none of whom could by any method become free. They formed a low caste like the Indian Pariahs and though the British Government has abolished the legal status of slavery, the social stigma which clings to them is said to be undiminished.

Art and architecture make the picture of Burma as it

remains in memory and they are the faithful reflection of the character and ways of its inhabitants, their cheerful but religious temper, their love of what is fanciful and graceful, their moderate aspirations towards what is arduous and sublime. The most striking feature of this architecture is its free use of gold and colour. In no country of the world is gilding and plating with gold so lavishly employed on the exterior of buildings. The larger Pagodas such as the Shwe Dagon are veritable pyramids of gold, and the roofs of the Arakan temple as they rise above Mandalay show tier upon tier of golden beams and plates. The brilliancy is increased by the equally lavish use of vermilion, sometimes diversified by glass mosaic. I remember once in an East African jungle seeing a clump of flowers of such brilliant red and yellow that for a moment I thought it was a fire. Somewhat similar is the surprise with which one first gazes on these edifices. I do not know whether the epithet flamboyant can be correctly applied to them as architecture but both in colour and shape they imitate a pile of flame, for the outlines of monasteries and shrines are fanciful in the extreme; gabled roofs with finials like tongues of fire and panels rich with carvings and fret-work. The buildings of Hindus and Burmans are as different as their characters. When a Hindu temple is imposing it is usually because of its bulk and mystery, whereas these buildings are lighthearted and fairy-like: heaps of red and yellow fruit with twining leaves and tendrils that have grown by magic. Nor is there much resemblance to Japanese architecture. There also, lacquer and gold are employed to an unusual extent but the flourishes, horns and finials which in Burma spring from every corner and projection are wanting and both Japanese and Chinese artists are more sparing and reticent. They distribute ornament so as to emphasize and lead up to the more important parts of their buildings, whereas the open-handed, splendour-loving Burman puts on every panel and pillar as much decoration as it will hold.

The result must be looked at as a whole and not too minutely. The best work is the wood carving which has a freedom and boldness often missing in the minute and crowded designs of Indian art. Still as a rule it is at the risk of breaking the spell that you examine the details of Burmese ornamentation. Better rest content with your first amazement on beholding these carved and pinnacled piles of gold and vermilion, where the fantastic animals and plants seem about to break into life.

The most celebrated shrine in Burma is the Shwe Dagon Pagoda which attracts pilgrims from all the Buddhist world. No descriptions of it gave me any idea of its real appearance nor can I hope that I shall be more successful in giving the reader my own impressions. The pagoda itself is a gilt bell-shaped mass rather higher than the Dome of St Paul's and terminating in a spire. It is set in the centre of a raised mound or platform, approached by lofty flights of steps. The platform, which is paved and level, is of imposing dimensions, some nine hundred feet long and seven hundred wide. Round the base of the central pagoda is a row of shrines and another row runs round the edge of the platform so that one moves, as it were, in a street of these edifices, leading here and there into side squares where are quiet retreats with palm trees and gigantic images. But when after climbing the long staircase one first emerges on the platform one does not realize the topography at once and seems to have entered suddenly into Jerusalem the Golden. Right and left are rows of gorgeous, fantastic sanctuaries, all gold, vermilion and glass mosaic, and within them sit marble figures, bland, enigmatic personages who seem to invite approach but offer no explanation of the singular scene or the part they play in it. If analyzed in detail the artistic merits of these shrines might be found small but the total impression is unique. The Shwe Dagon has not the qualities which usually distinguish great religious buildings. It is not specially impressive by its majesty or holiness; it is certainly wanting in order and arrangement. But on entering the platform one feels that one has suddenly passed from this life into another and different world. It is not perhaps a very elevated world; certainly not the final repose of the just or the steps of the throne of God, but it is as if you were walking in the bazaars of Paradise—one of those Buddhist Paradises where the souls of the moderately pure find temporary rest from the whirl of transmigration, where the very lotus flowers are golden and the leaves of the trees are golden bells that tinkle in the perfumed breeze.

CHAPTER XXXVII

SIAM[1]

1

THE Buddhism of Siam does not differ materially from that of Burma and Ceylon but merits separate mention, since it has features of its own due in some measure to the fact that Siam is still an independent kingdom ruled by a monarch who is also head of the Church. But whereas for the last few centuries this kingdom may be regarded as a political and religious unit, its condition in earlier times was different and Siamese history tells us nothing of the introduction and first diffusion of Indian religions in the countries between India and China.

[1] The principal sources for information about Siamese Buddhism are: *Journal of Siam Society*, 1904, and onwards.

L. Fournereau, *Le Siam Ancien*, 2 vols. 1895 and 1908 in *Annales du Musée Guimet*. Cited here as Fournereau.

Mission Pavie II, *Histoire du Laos, du Cambodge et du Siam*, 1898.

Gerini, *Researches on Ptolemy's Geography of Eastern Asia*, 1909. Cited here as Gerini, *Ptolemy*.

Gerini, *Chŭlâkantamangala or Tonsure Ceremony*, 1893.

H. Alabaster, *The Wheel of the Law*, 1871.

P. A. Thompson, *Lotus Land*, 1906.

W. A. Graham, *Siam*, 1912.

Petithuguenin, "Notes critiques pour servir à l'histoire du Siam," *B.E.F.E.O.* 1916, No. 3.

Coedès, "Documents sur la Dynastie de Sukhodaya," *ib.* 1917, No. 2.

Much curious information may be found in the *Directory for Bangkok and Siam*, a most interesting book. I have only the issue for 1907.

I have adopted the conventional European spelling for such words as may be said to have one. For other words I have followed Pallegoix's dictionary (1896) for rendering the vowels and tones in Roman characters, but have departed in some respects from his system of transliterating consonants as I think it unnecessary and misleading to write j and x for sounds which apparently correspond to y and ch as pronounced in English.

The King of Siam has published a work on the spelling of His Majesty's own language in Latin letters which ought to be authoritative, but it came into my hands too late for me to modify the orthography here adopted.

As Pallegoix's spelling involves the use of a great many accents I have sometimes begun by using the strictly correct orthography and afterwards a simpler but intelligible form. It should be noted that in this orthography ":" is not a colon but a sign that the vowel before it is very short.

The people commonly known as Siamese call themselves Thăi which (in the form Tai) appears to be the racial name of several tribes who can be traced to the southern provinces of China. They spread thence, in fanlike fashion, from Laos to Assam, and the middle section ultimately descended the Menam to the sea. The Siamese claim to have assumed the name Thăi (free) after they threw off the yoke of the Cambojans, but this derivation is more acceptable to politics than to ethnology. The territories which they inhabited were known as Siem, Syâm or Syâma, which is commonly identified with the Sanskrit Śyâma, dark or brown[1]. But the names Shan and A-hom seem to be variants of the same word and Śyâma is possibly not its origin but a learned and artificial distortion[2]. The Lao were another division of the same race who occupied the country now called Laos before the Tai had moved into Siam. This movement was gradual and until the beginning of the twelfth century they merely established small principalities, the principal of which was Lamphun[3], on the western arm of the Mekong. They gradually penetrated into the kingdoms of Svankalok, Sukhothai[4] and Lavo (Lophburi) which then were vassals of Camboja, and they were reinforced by another body of Tais which moved southwards early in the twelfth century. For some time the Cambojan Empire made a successful effort to control these immigrants but in the latter part of the thirteenth century the Siamese definitely shook off its yoke and founded an independent state with its capital at Sukhothai. There was probably some connection between these events and the southern expeditions of Khubilai Khan who in 1254 conquered Talifu and set the Tai tribes in motion.

The history of their rule in Siam may be briefly described as a succession of three kingdoms with capitals at Sukhothai, Ayuthia and Bangkok respectively. Like the Burmese, the Siamese have annals or chronicles. They fall into two divisions,

[1] The name is found on Champan inscriptions of 1050 A.D. and according to Gerini appears in Ptolemy's *Samarade* = Sâmaraṭṭha. See Gerini, *Ptolemy*, p. 170. But Samarade is located near Bangkok and there can hardly have been Tais there in Ptolemy's time.

[2] So too in Central Asia Kustana appears to be a learned distortion of the name Khotan, made to give it a meaning in Sanskrit.

[3] Gerini states (*Ptolemy*, p. 107) that there are Pali manuscript chronicles of Lamphun apparently going back to 924 A.D.

[4] Strictly Sŭkhŏthăi.

the chronicles[1] of the northern kingdom in three volumes which go down to the foundation of Ayuthia and are admitted even by the Siamese to be mostly fabulous, and the later annals in 40 volumes which were rearranged after the sack of Ayuthia in 1767 but claim to begin with the foundation of the city. Various opinions have been expressed as to their trustworthiness[2], but it is allowed by all that they must be used with caution. More authoritative but not very early are the inscriptions set up by various kings, of which a considerable number have been published and translated[3].

The early history of Sukhothai and its kings is not yet beyond dispute but a monarch called Râmarâja or Râma Khomhĕng played a considerable part in it. His identity with Phăya Rùang, who is said to have founded the dynasty and city, has been both affirmed and denied. Sukhothai, at least as the designation of a kingdom, seems to be much older than his reign[4]. It was undoubtedly understood as the equivalent of the Sanskrit Sukhodaya, but like Śyâma it may be an adaptation of some native word. In an important inscription found at Sukhothai and now preserved at Bangkok[5], which was probably composed about 1300 A.D., Râma Khomhĕng gives an account of his kingdom. On the east it extended to the banks of the Mekhong and beyond it to Chavâ (perhaps a name of Luang-Prabang): on the south to the sea, as far as Śrî Dharmarâja or Ligor: on the west to Haṃsavatî or Pegu. This last statement is important for it enables us to understand how at this period, and no doubt considerably earlier, the Siamese were acquainted with Pali Buddhism. The king states that hitherto his people had no alphabet but that he invented one[6]. This script subse-

[1] Phongsá va: dan or Vaṃsavâda. See for Siamese chronicles, *B.E.F.E.O.* 1914, No. 3, "Recension palie des annales d'Ayuthia," and *ibid.* 1916, pp. 5–7.

[2] *E.g.* Aymonier in *J.A.* 1903, p. 186, and Gerini in *Journal of Siam Society*, vol. II. part 1, 1905.

[3] See especially Fournereau and the publications of the Mission Pavie and *B.E.F.E.O.*

[4] Gerini, *Ptolemy*, p. 176.

[5] See Fournereau, I. p. 225. *B.E.F.E.O.* 1916, III. pp. 8–13, and especially Bradley in *J. Siam Society*, 1909, pp. 1–68.

[6] This alphabet appears to be borrowed from Cambojan but some of the letters particularly in their later shapes show the influence of the Môn or Talaing script. The modern Cambojan alphabet, which is commonly used for ecclesiastical purposes in Siam, is little more than an elaborate form of Siamese.

quently developed into the modern Siamese writing which, though it presents many difficulties, is an ingenious attempt to express a language with tones in an alphabet. The vocabulary of Siamese is not homogeneous: it comprises (*a*) a foundation of Thai, (*b*) a considerable admixture of Khmer words, (*c*) an element borrowed from Malay and other languages, (*d*) numerous ecclesiastical and learned terms taken from Pali and Sanskrit. There are five tones which must be distinguished, if either written or spoken speech is to be intelligible. This is done partly by accents and partly by dividing the forty-four consonants (many of which are superfluous for other purposes) into three groups, the high, middle and deep.

The king also speaks of religion. The court and the inhabitants of Sukhothai were devout Buddhists: they observed the season of Vassa and celebrated the festival of Kaṭhina with processions, concerts and reading of the scriptures. In the city were to be seen statues of the Buddha and scenes carved in relief, as well as large monasteries. To the west of the city was the Forest Monastery, presented to a distinguished elder who came from Śrî Dharmarâja and had studied the whole Tripitaka. The mention of this official and others suggests that there was a regular hierarchy and the king relates how he exhumed certain sacred relics and built a pagoda over them. Though there is no direct allusion to Brahmanism, stress is laid on the worship of spirits and devas on which the prosperity of the kingdom depends.

The form of Buddhism described seems to have differed little from the Hinayanism found in Siam to-day. Whence did the Siamese obtain it? For some centuries before they were known as a nation, they probably professed some form of Indian religion. They came from the border lands, if not from the actual territory of China, and must have been acquainted with Chinese Buddhism. Also Burmese influence probably reached Yünnan in the eighth century[1], but it is not easy to say what form of religion it brought with it. Still when the Thai entered what is now Siam, it is likely that their religion was some form of Buddhism. While they were subject to Camboja they must have felt the influence of Śivaism and possibly

[1] See *B.E.F.E.O.* 1904, p. 161.

of Mahayanist Sanskrit Buddhism but no Pali Buddhism can have come from this quarter[1].

Southern Siam was however to some extent affected by another wave of Buddhism. From early times the eastern coast of India (and perhaps Ceylon) had intercourse not only with Burma but with the Malay Peninsula. It is proved by inscriptions that the region of Ligor, formerly known as Śrî Dharmarâja, was occupied by Hindus (who were probably Buddhists) at least as early as the fourth century A.D.[2], and Buddhist inscriptions have been found on the mainland opposite Penang. The Chinese annals allude to a change in the customs of Camboja and I-Ching says plainly that Buddhism once flourished there but was exterminated by a wicked king, which may mean that Hinayanist Buddhism had spread thither from Ligor but was suppressed by a dynasty of Śivaites. He also says that at the end of the seventh century Hinayanism was prevalent in the islands of the Southern Sea. An inscription of about the fourth century found in Kedah and another of the seventh or eighth from Phra Pathom both contain the formula *Ye dharmâ*, etc. The latter inscription and also one from Mergui ascribed to the eleventh century seem to be in mixed Sanskrit and Pali. The Sukhothai inscription summarized above tells how a learned monk was brought thither from Ligor and clearly the Pali Buddhism of northern Siam may have followed the same route. But it probably had also another more important if not exclusive source, namely Burma. After the reign of Anawrata Pali Buddhism was accepted in Burma and in what we now call the Shan States as the religion of civilized mankind and this conviction found its way to the not very distant kingdom of Sukhothai. Subsequently the Siamese recognized the seniority and authority of the Sinhalese Church by inviting an instructor to come from Ceylon, but in earlier times they can hardly have had direct relation with the island.

[1] Bradley, *J. Siam Society*, 1913, p. 10, seems to think that Pali Buddhism may have come thence but the objection is that we know a good deal about the religion of Camboja and that there is no trace of Pali Buddhism there until it was imported from Siam. The fact that the Siamese alphabet was borrowed from Camboja does not prove that religion was borrowed in the same way. The Mongol alphabet can be traced to a Nestorian source.

[2] See for these inscriptions papers on the Malay Peninsula and Siam by Finot and Lajonquière in *Bull. de la Comm. Archéol. de l'Indo-Chine*, 1909, 1910 and 1912.

We have another picture of religious life in a Khmer inscription[1] of Lidaiya or Śrî Sûryavaṃsa Râma composed in 1361 or a little later. This monarch, who is also known by many lengthy titles, appears to have been a man of learning who had studied the Tipiṭaka, the Vedas, the Śâstrâgama and Dharmañâya and erected images of Maheśvara and Vishnu as well as of the Buddha. In 1361 he sent a messenger to Ceylon charged with the task of bringing back a Metropolitan or head of the Saṅgha learned in the Pitakas. This ecclesiastic, who is known only by his title, was duly sent and on arriving in Siam was received with the greatest honour and made a triumphal progress to Sukhothai. He is not represented as introducing a new religion: the impression left by the inscription is rather that the king and his people being already well-instructed in Buddhism desired ampler edification from an authentic source. The arrival of the Saṅgharâja coincided with the beginning of Vassa and at the end of the sacred season the king dedicated a golden image of the Buddha, which stood in the midst of the city, and then entered the order. In doing so he solemnly declared his hope that the merit thus acquired might make him in future lives not an Emperor, an Indra or a Brahmâ but a Buddha able to save mankind. He pursued his religious career with a gratifying accompaniment of miracles and many of the nobility and learned professions followed his example. But after a while a deputation waited on his Majesty begging him to return to the business of his kingdom[2]. An edifying contest ensued. The monks besought him to stay as their preceptor and guide: the laity pointed out that government was at an end and claimed his attention. The matter was referred to the Saṅgharâja who decided that the king ought to return to his secular duties. He appears to have found little difficulty in resuming lay habits for he proceeded to chastise the people of Luang-Prabang.

Two other inscriptions[3], apparently dating from this epoch,

[1] Fournereau, pp. 157 ff. and Coedès in *B.E.F.E.O.* 1917, No. 2. Besides the inscription itself, which is badly defaced in parts, we have (1) a similar inscription in Thăi, which is not however a translation, (2) a modern Siamese translation, used by Schmitt but severely criticized by Coedès and Petithuguenin.

[2] This portion of the narrative is found only in Schmitt's version of the Siamese translation. The part of the stone where it would have occurred is defaced.

[3] See Fournereau, vol. II. inscriptions XV and XVI and the account of the Jâtakas, p. 43.

relate that a cutting of the Bo-tree was brought from Ceylon and that certain relics (perhaps from Patna) were also installed with great solemnity. To the same time are referred a series of engravings on stone (not reliefs) found in the Vat-si-jum at Sukhothai. They illustrate about 100 Jatakas, arranged for the most part according to the order followed in the Pali Canon.

The facts that King Śrî Sûryavaṃsa sent to Ceylon for his Metropolitan and that some of the inscriptions which extol his merits are in Pali[1] make it probable that the religion which he professed differed little from the Pali Buddhism which flourishes in Siam to-day and this supposition is confirmed by the general tone of his inscriptions. But still several phrases in them have a Mahayanist flavour. He takes as his model the conduct of the Bodhisattvas, described as ten headed by Metteyya, and his vow to become a Buddha and save all creatures is at least twice mentioned. The Buddhas are said to be innumerable and the feet of Bhikkhus are called Buddha feet[2]. There is no difficulty in accounting for the presence of such ideas: the only question is from what quarter this Mahayanist influence came. The king is said to have been a student of Indian literature: his country, like Burma, was in touch with China and his use of the Khmer language indicates contact with Camboja.

Another inscription engraved by order of Dharmâsokarâja[3] and apparently dating from the fourteenth century is remarkable for its clear statement of the doctrine (generally considered as Mahayanist) that merit acquired by devotion to the Buddha can be transferred. The king states that a woman called Bunrak has transferred all her merit to the Queen and that he himself makes over all his merit to his teacher, to his relations and to all beings in unhappy states of existence.

At some time in this period the centre of the Thai empire

[1] Fournereau, I. pp. 247, 273. *B.E.F.E.O.* 1917, No. 2, p. 29.

[2] See the texts in *B.E.F.E.O.* *l.c.* The Bodhisattvas are described as Ariyametteyâdînam dasannam Bodhisattânam. The vow to become a Buddha should it seems be placed in the mouth of the King, not of the Metropolitan as in Schmitt's translation.

[3] See Fournereau, pp. 209 ff. Dharmâsokarâja may perhaps be the same as Mahâdharmarâja who reigned 1388–1415. But the word may also be a mere title applied to all kings of this dynasty, so that this may be another inscription of Śrî Sûryavaṃsa Râma.

changed but divergent views have been held as to the date[1] and character of this event. It would appear that in 1350 a Siamese subsequently known as King Râmâdhipati, a descendant of an ancient line of Thai princes, founded Ayuthia as a rival to Sukhothai. The site was not new, for it had long been known as Dvâravatî and seems to be mentioned under that name by I-Ching (*c.* 680), but a new city was apparently constructed. The evidence of inscriptions indicates that Sukhothai was not immediately subdued by the new kingdom and did not cease to be a royal residence for some time. But still Ayuthia gradually became predominant and in the fifteenth century merited the title of capital of Siam.

Its rise did not affect the esteem in which Buddhism was held, and it must have contained many great religious monuments. The jungles which now cover the site of the city surround the remnants of the Wăt Somarokot, in which is a gigantic bronze Buddha facing with scornful calm the ruin which threatens him. The Wăt Chern, which lies at some distance, contains another gigantic image. A curious inscription[2] engraved on an image of Śiva found at Sukhothai and dated 1510 A.D. asserts the identity of Buddhism and Brahmanism, but the popular feeling was in favour of the former. At Ayuthia the temples appear to be exclusively Buddhist and at Lophburi ancient buildings originally constructed for the Brahmanic cult have been adapted to Buddhist uses. It was in 1602 that the mark known as the footprint of Buddha was discovered at the place now called Phra-bat.

Ayuthia was captured by the Burmese in 1568 and the king was carried into captivity but the disaster was not permanent, for at the end of the century the power of the Siamese reached its highest point and their foreign relations were extensive. We hear that five hundred Japanese assisted them to repulse a Burmese attack and that there was a large Japanese colony in Ayuthia. On the other hand when Hideyoshi invaded Korea in 1592, the Siamese offered to assist the Chinese. Europeans appeared first in 1511 when the Portuguese took Malacca. But on the whole

[1] 1350 is the accepted date but M. Aymonier, *J.A.* 1903, pp. 185 ff. argues in favour of about 1460. See Fournereau, *Ancien Siam*, p. 242, inscription of 1426 A.D. and p. 186, inscription of 1510 described as Groupe de Sajjanalaya et Sukhodaya.

[2] Fournereau, vol. I. pp. 186 ff.

the dealings of Siam with Europe were peaceful and both traders and missionaries were welcomed. The most singular episode in this international intercourse was the career of the Greek adventurer Constantine Phaulcon who in the reign of King Nărai was practically Foreign Minister. In concert with the French missionaries he arranged an exchange of embassies (1682 and 1685) between Nărai and Louis XIV, the latter having been led to suppose that the king and people of Siam were ready to embrace Christianity. But when the French envoys broached the subject of conversion, the king replied that he saw no reason to change the religion which his countrymen had professed for two thousand years, a chronological statement which it might be hard to substantiate. Still, great facilities were given to missionaries and further negotiations ensued, in the course of which the French received almost a monopoly of foreign trade and the right to maintain garrisons. But the death of Nărai was followed by a reaction. Phaulcon died in prison and the French garrisons were expelled. Buddhism probably flourished at this period for the Mahâvaṃsa tells us that the king of Ceylon sent to Ayuthia for monks in 1750 because religion there was pure and undefiled.

Ayuthia continued to be the capital until 1767 when it was laid in ruins by the Burmese who, though Buddhists, did not scruple to destroy or deface the temples and statues with which it was ornamented. But the collapse of the Siamese was only local and temporary. A leader of Chinese origin named Phăya Tāk Sin rallied their forces, cleared the Burmese out of the country and made Bangkok, officially described as the Capital of the Angels, the seat of Government. But he was deposed in 1782 and one of the reasons for his fall seems to have been a too zealous reformation of Buddhism. In the troublous times following the collapse of Ayuthia the Church had become disorganized and corrupt, but even those who desired improvement would not assent to the powers which the king claimed over monks. A new dynasty (of which the sixth monarch is now on the throne) was founded in 1782 by Chao Phăya Chakkri. One of his first acts was to convoke a council for the revision of the Tipiṭaka and to build a special hall in which the text thus agreed on was preserved. His successor Phra: Buddha Löt La is considered the best poet that Siam has produced and it is probably the only country in the world where this distinction has fallen to the lot of a sovereign. The poet king had two sons, Phra: Nang: Klao, who ascended the throne after his death, and Mongkut, who during his brother's reign remained in a monastery strictly observing the duties of a monk. He then became king and during his reign (1851–1868) Siam "may be said to have passed from the middle ages to modern times[1]." It is a tribute to the excellence of Buddhist discipline that a prince who spent twenty-six years as a monk should have emerged as neither a bigot nor an impractical mystic but as an active, enlightened and progressive monarch. The equality and simplicity of monastic life disposed him to come into direct touch with his subjects and to adopt straightforward measures which might not have occurred to one who had always been surrounded by a wall of ministers. While still a monk he founded a stricter sect which aimed at reviving the practice of the Buddha, but at the same time he studied foreign creeds and took pleasure in conversing with missionaries. He wrote several historical pamphlets and an English Grammar, and was so good a mathematician that he could calculate the occurrence of an eclipse. When he became king he regulated the international position of Siam by concluding treaties of friendship and commerce with the principal European powers, thus showing the broad and liberal spirit in which he regarded politics, though a better acquaintance with the ways of Europeans might have made him refuse them extraterritorial privileges. He abolished the custom which obliged every one to keep indoors when the king went out and he publicly received petitions on every Uposatha day. He legislated against slavery[2], gambling, drinking spirits and smoking opium and considerably improved the status of women. He also published edicts ordering the laity to inform the ecclesiastical authorities if they noticed any abuses in the monasteries. He caused the annals of Siam to be edited and issued numerous orders on archaeological and literary questions, in which, though a good Pali scholar, he deprecated the affected use of Pali words and enjoined the use of a terse and simple Siamese style, which he certainly wrote himself. He appears to

[1] O. Frankfürter, "King Mongkut," *Journal of Siam Society*, vol. I. 1904.

[2] But it was his son who first decreed in 1868 that no Siamese could be born a slave. Slavery for debt, though illegal, is said not to be practically extinct.

have died of scientific zeal for he caught a fatal fever on a trip which he took to witness a total eclipse of the sun.

He was succeeded by his son Chulalongkorn[1] (1868–1911), a liberal and enlightened ruler, who had the misfortune to lose much territory to the French on one side and the English on the other. For religion, his chief interest is that he published an edition of the Tipiṭaka. The volumes are of European style and printed in Siamese type, whereas Cambojan characters were previously employed for religious works.

2

As I have already observed, there is not much difference between Buddhism in Burma and Siam. In mediæval times a mixed form of religion prevailed in both countries and Siam was influenced by the Brahmanism and Mahayanism of Camboja. Both seem to have derived a purer form of the faith from Pegu, which was conquered by Anawrata in the eleventh century and was the neighbour of Sukhothai so long as that kingdom lasted. Both had relations with Ceylon and while venerating her as the metropolis of the faith also sent monks to her in the days of her spiritual decadence. But even in externals some differences are visible. The gold and vermilion of Burma are replaced in Siam by more sober but artistic tints—olive, dull purple and dark orange—and the change in the colour scheme is accompanied by other changes in the buildings.

A religious establishment in Siam consists of several edifices and is generally known as Wăt[2], followed by some special designation such as Wăt Chang. Bangkok is full of such establishments mostly constructed on the banks of the river or canals. The entrance is usually guarded by gigantic and grotesque figures which are often lions, but at the Wăt Phô in Bangkok the tutelary demons are represented by curious caricatures of Europeans wearing tall hats. The gate leads into several courts opening out of one another and not arranged on any fixed plan. The first is sometimes surrounded by a colonnade in which are set a long line of the Buddha's eighty disciples. The most

[1] =Cûlâlaṅkâra.

[2] The word has been derived from Vâta, a grove, but may it not be the Pali Vatthu, Sanskrit Vâstu, a site or building?

important building in a Wăt is known as Bŏ̃t[1]. It has a colonnade of pillars outside and is surmounted by three or four roofs, not much raised one above the other, and bearing finials of a curious shape, said to represent a snake's head[2]. It is also marked off by a circuit of eight stones, cut in the shape of Bo-tree leaves, which constitute a sîmâ or boundary. It is in the Bŏ̃t that ordinations and other acts of the Sangha are performed. Internally it is a hall: the walls are often covered with paintings and at the end there is always a sitting figure of the Buddha[3] forming the apex of a pyramid, the lower steps of which are decorated with smaller images and curious ornaments, such as clocks under glass cases.

Siamese images of the Buddha generally represent him as crowned by a long flame-like ornament called Sĭrô rồt[4], probably representing the light supposed to issue from the prominence on his head. But the ornament sometimes becomes a veritable crown terminating in a spire, as do those worn by the kings of Camboja and Siam. On the left and right of the Buddha often stand figures of Phra: Môkha: la (Moggalâna) and Phra: Sárîbŭt (Sâriputta). It is stated that the Siamese pray to them as saints and that the former is invoked to heal broken limbs[5]. The Buddha when represented in frescoes is robed in red but his face and hands are of gold. Besides the Bŏ̃t a Wăt contains one or more wĭháns. The word is derived from *Vihâra* but has come to mean an image-house. The wĭháns are halls not unlike the Bŏ̃ts but smaller. In a large Wăt there is usually one containing a gigantic recumbent image of the Buddha and they sometimes shelter Indian deities such as Yama.

In most if not in all Wăts there are structures known as Phra: chedi and Phra: prang. The former are simply the ancient cetiyas, called dagobas in Ceylon and zedis in Burma. They do not depart materially from the shape usual in other countries

[1] =Uposatha.

[2] These finials are very common on the roof ends of Siamese temples and palaces. It is strange that they also are found in conjunction with multiple roofs in Norwegian Churches of eleventh century. See de Beylié, *Architecture hindoue dans l'extrême Orient*, pp. 47, 48.

[3] The Buddha is generally known as Phra: Khodom (=Gotama).

[4] In an old Siamese bronze from Kampeng Pet, figured in Grünwedel's *Buddhist Art in India*, p. 179, fig. 127, the Sirô rồt seems to be in process of evolution.

[5] P. A. Thompson, *Lotus Land*, 1906, p. 100.

and sometimes, for instance in the gigantic chedi at Pra Pratom, the part below the spire is a solid bell-shaped dome. But Siamese taste tends to make such buildings slender and elongate and they generally consist of stone discs of decreasing size, set one on the other in a pile, which assumes in its upper parts the proportions of a flagstaff rather than of a stone building. The Phra: prangs though often larger than the Phra: chedis are proportionally thicker and less elongate. They appear to be derived from the Brahmanic temple towers of Camboja which consist of a shrine crowned by a dome. But in Siam the shrine is often at some height above the ground and is reduced to small dimensions, sometimes becoming a mere niche. In large Phra: prangs it is approached by a flight of steps outside and above it rises the tower, terminating in a metal spire. But whereas in the Phra: chedis these spires are simple, in the Phra: prangs they bear three crescents representing the trident of Śiva and appear like barbed arrows. A large Wat is sure to contain a number of these structures and may also comprise halls for preaching, a pavilion covering a model of Buddha's foot print, tanks for ablution and a bell tower. It is said that only royal Wats contain libraries and buildings called chătta mŭkh, which shelter a four-faced image of Brahmâ[1].

The monks are often housed in single chambers arranged round the courts of a Wat but sometimes in larger buildings outside it. The number of monks and novices living in one monastery is larger than in Burma, and according to the Bangkok Directory (1907) works out at an average of about 12. In the larger Wats this figure is considerably exceeded. Altogether there were 50,764 monks and 10,411 novices in 1907[2], the province of Ayuthia being decidedly the best provided with clergy. As in Burma, it is customary for every male to spend some time in a monastery, usually at the age of about 20, and two months is considered the minimum which is respectable. It is also common to enter a monastery for a short stay on the day when a parent is cremated. During the season of Vassa all

[1] Four images facing the four quarters are considered in Burma to represent the last four Buddhas and among the Jains some of the Tirthankaras are so represented, the legend being that whenever they preached they seemed to face their hearers on every side.

[2] These figures only take account of twelve out of the seventeen provinces.

monks go out to collect alms but at other seasons only a few make the daily round and the food collected, as in Burma and Ceylon, is generally not eaten. But during the dry season it is considered meritorious for monks to make a pilgrimage to Phra Bât and while on the way to live on charity. They engage to some extent in manual work and occupy themselves with carpentering[1]. As in Burma, education is in their hands, and they also act as doctors, though their treatment has more to do with charms and faith cures than with medicine.

As in Burma there are two sects, the ordinary unreformed body, and the rigorous and select communion founded by Mongkut and called Dhammayut. It aims at a more austere and useful life but in outward observances the only distinction seems to be that the Dhammayuts hold the alms-bowl in front of them in both hands, whereas the others hold it against the left hip with the left hand only. The hierarchy is well developed but somewhat secularized, though probably not more so than it was in India under Asoka. In the official directory where the departments of the Ministry of Public Instruction are enumerated, the Ecclesiastical Department comes immediately after the Bacteriological, the two being clearly regarded as different methods of expelling evil spirits. The higher clerical appointments are made by the king. He names four Primates[2], one of whom is selected as chief. The Primates with nineteen superior monks form the highest governing body of the Church. Below them are twelve dignitaries called Gurus, who are often heads of large Wats. There are also prelates who bear the Cambojan title of Burien equivalent to Mahâcârya. They must have passed an examination in Pali and are chiefly consulted on matters of ceremonial.

It will thus be seen that the differences between the churches of Burma, Ceylon and Siam are slight; hardly more than the local peculiarities which mark the Roman church in Italy, Spain, and England. Different opinions have been expressed as to the moral tone and conduct of Siamese monks and most critics state that they are somewhat inferior to their Burmese

[1] Thompson, *Lotus Land*, p. 120.

[2] They bear the title of Sŏmdĕt Phra: Chào Ràjagama and have authority respectively over (*a*) ordinary Buddhists in northern Siam, (*b*) ordinary Buddhists in the south, (*c*) hermits, (*d*) the Dhammayut sect.

brethren. The system by which a village undertakes to support a monk, provided that he is a reasonably competent schoolmaster and of good character, works well. But in the larger monasteries it is admitted that there are inmates who have entered in the hope of leading a lazy life and even fugitives from justice. Still the penalty for any grave offence is immediate expulsion by the ecclesiastical authorities and the offender is treated with extreme severity by the civil courts to which he then becomes amenable.

The religious festivals of Siam are numerous and characteristic. Many are Buddhist, some are Brahmanic, and some are royal. Uposatha days (wăn phra:) are observed much as in Burma. The birth, enlightenment and death of the Buddha (which are all supposed to have taken place on the 15th day of the 6th waxing moon) are celebrated during a three days festival. These three days are of peculiar solemnity and are spent in the discharge of religious duties, such as hearing sermons and giving alms. But at most festivals religious observances are mingled with much picturesque but secular gaiety. In the morning the monks do not go their usual round[1] and the alms-bowls are arranged in a line within the temple grounds. The laity (mostly women) arrive bearing wicker trays on which are vessels containing rice and delicacies. They place a selection of these in each bowl and then proceed to the Bŏ̃t where they hear the commandments recited and often vow to observe for that day some which are usually binding only on monks. While the monks are eating their meal the people repair to a river, which is rarely far distant in Siam, and pour water drop by drop saying "May the food which we have given for the use of the holy ones be of benefit to our fathers and mothers and to all of our relatives who have passed away." This rite is curiously in harmony with the injunctions of the Tirokuḍḍasuttam in the Khuddakapâtha, which is probably an ancient work[2]. The rest of the day is usually devoted to pious merrymaking, such as processions by day and illuminations by night. On some feasts

[1] For this and many other details I am indebted to P. A. Thompson, *Lotus Land*, p. 123.

[2] When gifts of food are made to monks on ceremonial occasions, they usually acknowledge the receipt by reciting verses 7 and 8 of this Sutta, commonly known as *Yathâ* from the first word.

the laws against gambling are suspended and various games of chance are freely indulged in. Thus the New Year festival called Trŭt (or Krŭt) Thăi lasts three days. On the first two days, especially the second, crowds fill the temples to offer flowers before the statues of Buddha and more substantial presents of food, clothes, etc., to the clergy. Well-to-do families invite monks to their houses and pass the day in listening to their sermons and recitations. Companies of priests are posted round the city walls to scare away evil spirits and with the same object guns are fired throughout the night. But the third day is devoted to gambling by almost the whole population except the monks. Not dissimilar is the celebration of the Sŏngkran holidays, at the beginning of the official year. The special religious observance at this feast consists in bathing the images of Buddha and in theory the same form of watery respect is extended to aged relatives and monks. In practice its place is taken by gifts of perfumes and other presents.

The rainy season is preceded and ended by holidays. During this period both monks and pious laymen observe their religious duties more strictly. Thus monks eat only once a day and then only what is put into their bowls and laymen observe some of the minor vows. At the end of the rains come the important holidays known as Thòt Kăthin[1], when robes are presented to monks. This festival has long had a special importance in Siam. Thus Râma Khomhĕng in his inscription of A.D. 1292[2] describes the feast of Kaṭhina which lasts a month. At the present day many thousands of robes are prepared in the capital alone so as to be ready for distribution in October and November, when the king or some deputy of high rank visits every temple and makes the offering in person. During this season Bangkok witnesses a series of brilliant processions.

These festivals mentioned may be called Buddhist though their light-hearted and splendour-loving gaiety, their processions and gambling are far removed from the spirit of Gotama. Others however are definitely Brahmanic and in Bangkok are superintended by the Brahmans attached to the Court. Since the time of Mongkut Buddhist priests are also present as a sign that the rites, if not ordered by Buddhism, at least have its

[1] Kaṭhina in Pali. See Mahâvag. cap. VII.

[2] Fournereau, p. 225.

countenance. Such is the Rȅk Na[1], or ploughing festival. The king is represented by the Minister of Agriculture who formerly had the right to exact from all shops found open such taxes as he might claim for his temporary sovereignty. At present he is escorted in procession to Dusit[2], a royal park outside Bangkok, where he breaks ground with a plough drawn by two white oxen.

Somewhat similar is the Thĩb-Chĭng-Cha, or Swinging holidays, a two days' festival which seems to be a harvest thanksgiving. Under the supervision of a high official, four Brahmans wearing tall conical hats swing on a board suspended from a huge frame about 100 ft high. Their object is to catch with their teeth a bag of money hanging at a little distance from the swing. When three or four sets of swingers have obtained a prize in this way, they conclude the ceremony by sprinkling the ground with holy water contained in bullock horns. Swinging is one of the earliest Indian rites[3] and as part of the worship of Krishna it has lasted to the present day. Yet another Brahmanic festival is the Loi Kăthŏng[4], when miniature rafts and ships bearing lights and offerings are sent down the Menam to the sea.

Another class of ceremonies may be described as royal, inasmuch as they are religious only in so far as they invoke religion to protect royalty. Such are the anniversaries of the birth and coronation of the king and the Thŭ Năm or drinking of the water of allegiance which takes place twice a year. At Bangkok all officials assemble at the Palace and there drink and sprinkle on their heads water in which swords and other weapons have been dipped thus invoking vengeance on themselves should they prove disloyal. Jars of this water are despatched to Governors who superintend the performance of the same ceremony in the

[1] The ploughing festival is a recognized imperial ceremony in China. In India ceremonies for private landowners are prescribed in the Gṛihya Sûtras but I do not know if their performance by kings is anywhere definitely ordered. However in the Nidâna Kathâ 270 the Buddha's father celebrates an imposing ploughing ceremony.

[2] *I.e.* Tusita. Compare such English names descriptive of beautiful scenery as Heaven's Gate.

[3] See Keith, *Aitereya Âranyaka*, pp. 174–178. The ceremony there described undoubtedly originated in a very ancient popular festival.

[4] *I.e.* float-raft. Most authors give the word as Krathong, but Pallegoix prefers Kathong.

provincial capitals. It is only after the water has been drunk that officials receive their half yearly salary. Monks are excused from drinking it but the chief ecclesiastics of Bangkok meet in the Palace temple and perform a service in honour of the occasion.

Besides these public solemnities there are a number of domestic festivals derived from the twelve Saṃskâras of the Hindus. Of these only three or four are kept up by the nations of Indo-China, namely the shaving of the first hair of a child a month after birth, the giving of a name, and the piercing of the ears for earrings. This last is observed in Burma and Laos, but not in Siam and Camboja where is substituted for it the Kôn Chũk or shaving of the topknot, which is allowed to grow until the eleventh or thirteenth year. This ceremony, which is performed on boys and girls alike, is the most important event in the life of a young Siamese and is celebrated by well-to-do parents with lavish expenditure. Those who are indigent often avail themselves of the royal bounty, for each year a public ceremony is performed in one of the temples of Bangkok at which poor children receive the tonsure gratis. An elaborate description of the tonsure rites has been published by Gerini[1]. They are of considerable interest as showing how closely Buddhist and Brahmanic rites are intertwined in Siamese family life.

Marriages are celebrated with a feast to which monks are invited but are not regarded as religious ceremonies. The dead are usually disposed of by cremation, but are often kept some time, being either embalmed or simply buried and exhumed subsequently. Before cremation the coffin is usually placed within the grounds of a temple. The monks read Suttas over it and it is said[2] that they hold ribbons which enter into the coffin and are supposed to communicate to the corpse the merit acquired by the recitations and prayers.

3

In the preceding pages mention has often been made not only of Brahmanic rites but of Brahman priests[3]. These are

[1] *Chulakantamangalam*, Bangkok, 1893.

[2] P. A. Thompson, *Lotus Land*, p. 134.

[3] For the Brahmans of Siam see Frankfürter, *Oriental. Archiv.* 1913, pp. 196–7.

still to be found in Bangkok attached to the Court and possibly in other cities. They dress in white and have preserved many Hindu usages but are said to be poor Sanskrit scholars. Indeed Gerini[1] seems to say that they use Pali in some of their recitations. Their principal duty is to officiate at Court functions, but wealthy families invite them to take part in domestic rites, and also to cast horoscopes and fix lucky days. It is clear that the presence of these Brahmans is no innovation. Brahmanism must have been strong in Siam when it was a province of Camboja, but in both countries gave way before Buddhism. Many rites, however, connected with securing luck or predicting the future were too firmly established to be abolished, and, as Buddhist monks were unwilling to perform them[2] or not thought very competent, the Brahmans remained and were perhaps reinforced from time to time by new importations, for there are still Brahman colonies in Ligor and other Malay towns. Siamese lawbooks, like those of Burma, seem to be mainly adaptations of Indian Dharmaśâstras.

On a cursory inspection, Siamese Buddhism, especially as seen in villages, seems remarkably free from alien additions. But an examination of ancient buildings, of royal temples in Bangkok and royal ceremonial, suggests on the contrary that it is a mixed faith in which the Brahmanic element is strong. Yet though this element appeals to the superstition of the Siamese and their love of pageantry, I think that as in Burma it has not invaded the sphere of religion and ethics more than the Piṭakas themselves allow. In art and literature its influence has been considerable. The story of the Ramayana is illustrated on the cloister walls of the royal temple at Bangkok and Indian mythology has supplied a multitude of types to the painter and sculptor; such as Yŏmma: ràt (Yâma), Phăya Man (Mâra), Phra: In (Indra). These are all deities known to the Piṭakas but the sculptures or images[3] in Siamese temples also

[1] *Chulakantamangala*, p. 56.

[2] They are mostly observances such as Gotama would have classed among "low arts" (tîracchânavijjâ). At present the monks of Siam deal freely in charms and exorcisms but on important occasions public opinion seems to have greater confidence in the skill and power of Brahmans.

[3] King Śrî Sûryavaṃsa Râma relates in an inscription of about 1365 how he set up statues of Parameśvara and Vishṇukarma (?) and appointed Brahmans to serve them.

include Ganeśa, Phra: Nărai (Nârâyana or Vishṇu) riding on the Garuda and Phra: Isuén (Śiva) riding on a bull. There is a legend that the Buddha and Śiva tried which could make himself invisible to the other. At last the Buddha sat on Śiva's head and the god being unable to see him acknowledged his defeat. This story is told to explain a small figure which Śiva bears on his head and recalls the legend found in the Piṭakas[1] that the Buddha made himself invisible to Brahmâ but that Brahmâ had not the corresponding power. Lingas are still venerated in a few temples, for instance at Wăt Phô in Bangkok, but it would appear that the majority (*e.g.* those found at Pra Pratom and Lophburi) are survivals of ancient Brahmanic worship and have a purely antiquarian importance. The Brahmanic cosmology which makes Mt Meru the centre of this Universe is generally accepted in ecclesiastical treatises and paintings, though the educated Siamese may smile at it, and when the topknot of a Siamese prince is cut off, part of the ceremony consists in his being received by the king dressed as Śiva on the summit of a mound cut in the traditional shape of Mt Kailâśa.

Like the Nâts of Burma, Siam has a spirit population known as Phís[2]. The name is occasionally applied to Indian deities, but the great majority of Phís fall into two classes, namely, ghosts of the dead and nature spirits which, though dangerous, do not rise above the position of good or bad fairies. In the first class are included the Phí Prĕt, who have the characteristics as well as the name of the Indian Pretas, and also a multitude of beings who like European ghosts, haunt houses and behave in a mysterious but generally disagreeable manner. The Phí ăm is apparently our nightmare. The ghosts of children dying soon after birth are apt to kill their mothers and in general women are liable to be possessed by Phís. The ghosts of those who have died a violent death are dangerous but it would seem that Siamese magicians know how to utilize them as familiar spirits. The better sort of ghosts are known as Chào Phí and shrines called San Chào are set up in their honour. It does not however appear that there is any hierarchy of Phís like the thirty-seven Náts of Burma.

[1] Maj. Nik. 47.

[2] *Siam Society*, vol. IV. part ii. 1907. *Some Siamese ghost-lore* by A. J. Irwin.

Among those Phís who are not ghosts of the dead the most important is the Phí rüen or guardian spirit of each house. Frequently a little shrine is erected for him at the top of a pole. There are also innumerable Phís in the jungle mostly malevolent and capable of appearing either in human form or as a dangerous animal. But the tree spirits are generally benevolent and when their trees are cut down they protect the houses that are made of them.

Thus the Buddhism of Siam, like that of Burma, has a certain admixture of Brahmanism and animism. The Brahmanism is perhaps more striking than in Burma on account of the Court ceremonies: the belief in spirits, though almost universal, seems to be more retiring and less conspicuous. Yet the inscription of Râma Komhĕng mentioned above asserts emphatically that the prosperity of the Empire depends on due honour being shown to a certain mountain spirit[1].

It is pretty clear that the first introduction of Hinayanist Buddhism into Siam was from Southern Burma and Pegu, but that somewhat later Ceylon was accepted as the standard of orthodoxy. A learned thera who knew the Sinhalese Tipitaka was imported thence, as well as a branch of the Bo-tree. But Siamese patriotism flattered itself by imagining that the national religion was due to personal contact with the Buddha, although not even early legends can be cited in support of such traditions. In 1602 a mark in the rocks, now known as the Phra: Bãt, was discovered in the hills north of Ayuthia and identified as a footprint of the Buddha similar to that found on Adam's Peak and in other places. Burma and Ceylon both claim the honour of a visit from the Buddha but the Siamese go further, for it is popularly believed that he died at Praten, a little to the north of Phra Pathom, on a spot marked by a slab of rock under great trees[2]. For this reason when the Government of India presented

[1] *Jour. Siam Soc.* 1909, p. 28. "In yonder mountain is a demon spirit Phră Khăphŭng that is greater than every other spirit in this realm. If any Prince ruling this realm reverences him well with proper offerings, this realm stands firm, this realm prospers. If the spirit be not reverenced well, if the offerings be not right, the spirit in the mountain does not protect, does not regard:—this realm perishes."

[2] The most popular life of the Buddha in Siamese is called Pa:thómma Sóm-phôthiyan, translated by Alabaster in *The Wheel of the Law*. But like the Lalita vistara and other Indian lives on which it is modelled it stops short at the enlighten-

the king of Siam with the relics found in the Piprava vase, the gift though received with honour, aroused little enthusiasm and was placed in a somewhat secluded shrine[1].

ment. Another well-known religious book is the Traiphûm (=Tribhûmi), an account of the universe according to Hindu principles, compiled in 1776 from various ancient works.

The Pali literature of Siam is not very large. Some account of it is given by Coedès in *B.E.F.E.O.* 1915, III. pp. 39–46.

[1] When in Bangkok in 1907 I saw in a photographer's shop a photograph of the procession which escorted these relics to their destination. It was inscribed "Arrival of Buddha's tooth from Kandy." This shows how deceptive historical evidence may be. The inscription was the testimony of an eye-witness and yet it was entirely wrong.

CHAPTER XXXVIII

CAMBOJA[1]

1

THE French Protectorate of Camboja corresponds roughly to the nucleus, though by no means to the whole extent of the former Empire of the Khmers. The affinities of this race have given rise to considerable discussion and it has been proposed to connect them with the Muṇḍa tribes of India on one side and with the Malays and Polynesians on the other[2]. They are allied linguistically to the Mons or Talaings of Lower Burma and to the Khasias of Assam, but it is not proved that they are similarly related to the Annamites, and recent investigators are not disposed to maintain the Mon-Annam family of languages

[1] See among other authorities:

(a) E. Aymonier, *Le Cambodge*, Paris, 3 vols. 1900, 1904 (cited as Aymonier).

(b) A. Barth, *Inscriptions Sanscrites du Cambodge* (*Notices et extraits des MSS. de la Bibliot. Nat.*), Paris, 1885 (cited as *Corpus*, I.).

(c) A. Bergaigne, *Inscriptions Sanscrites de Campâ et du Cambodge* (in same series), 1893 (cited as *Corpus*, II.).

(d) L. Finot, "Buddhism in Indo-China," *Buddhist Review*, Oct. 1909.

(e) G. Maspéro, *L'Empire Khmèr, Phnom Penh*, 1904 (cited as Maspéro).

(f) P. Pelliot, "Mémoires sur les Coutumes de Cambodge par Tcheou Ta-kouan, traduits et annotés," *B.E.F.E.O.* 1902, pp. 123–177 (cited as Pelliot, *Tcheou Ta-kouan*).

(g) *Id.* "Le Founan," *B.E.F.E.O.* 1903, pp. 248–303 (cited as Pelliot, *Founan*).

(h) Articles on various inscriptions by G. Coedès in *J.A.* 1908, XI. p. 203, XII. p. 213; 1909, XIII. p. 467 and p. 511.

(i) *Bulletin de la Commission Archéologique de l'Indochine*, 1908 onwards.

(j) *Le Bayon d'Angkor Thom, Mission Henri Dufour*, 1910–1914.

Besides the articles cited above the *Bulletin de l'École Française d'Extrême Orient* (quoted as *B.E.F.E.O.*) contains many others dealing with the religion and archaeology of Camboja.

(k) L. Finot, *Notes d'Épigraphie Indo-Chinoise*, 1916.

See for literature up to 1909, G. Coedès, *Bibliothèque raisonnée des travaux relatifs à l'Archéologie du Cambodge et du Champa*. Paris, Imprimerie Nationale, 1909.

[2] See especially P. W. Schmitt, *Die Mon-Khmer Völker. Ein Bindeglied zwischen Völkern Zentral-Asiens und Austronesiens.* Braunschweig, 1906.

proposed by Logan and others. But the undoubted similarity of the Mon and Khmer languages suggests that the ancestors of those who now speak them were at one time spread over the central and western parts of Indo-China but were subsequently divided and deprived of much territory by the southward invasions of the Thais in the middle ages.

The Khmers also called themselves Kambuja or Kamvuja and their name for the country is still either Srŏk Kâmpûchéa or Sṛŏk Khmer[1]. Attempts have been made to find a Malay origin for this name Kambuja but native tradition regards it as a link with India and affirms that the race is descended from Kambu Svayambhuva and Merâ or Perâ who was given to him by Śiva as wife[2]. This legend hardly proves that the Khmer people came from India but they undoubtedly received thence their civilization, their royal family and a considerable number of Hindu immigrants, so that the mythical ancestor of their kings naturally came to be regarded as the progenitor of the race. The Chinese traveller Chou Ta-kuan (1296 A.D.) says that the country known to the Chinese as Chên-la is called by the natives Kan-po-chih but that the present dynasty call it Kan-p'u-chih on the authority of Sanskrit (Hsi-fan) works. The origin of the name Chên-la is unknown.

There has been much discussion respecting the relation of Chên-la to the older kingdom of Fu-nan which is the name given by Chinese historians until the early part of the seventh century to a state occupying the south-eastern and perhaps central portions of Indo-China. It has been argued that Chên-la is simply the older name of Fu-nan and on the other hand that Fu-nan is a wider designation including several states, one of which, Chên-la or Camboja, became paramount at the expense of the others[3]. But the point seems unimportant for their

[1] Cambodge is the accepted French spelling of this country's name. In English Kamboja, Kambodia, Camboja and Cambodia are all found. The last is the most usual but *di* is not a good way of representing the sound of *j* as usually heard in this name. I have therefore preferred Camboja.

[2] See the inscription of Bàksĕ, Càṃkrŏṅ, *J.A.* XIII. 1909, pp. 468, 469, 497.

[3] The Sui annals (Pelliot, *Founan*, p. 272) state that "Chên-la lies to the west of Lin-yi: it was originally a vassal state of Fu-nan....The name of the king's family was Kshatriya: his personal name was Citrasena: his ancestors progressively acquired the sovereignty of the country: Citrasena seized Fu-nan and reduced it to submission." This seems perfectly clear and we know from Cambojan inscriptions that Citrasena was the personal name of the king who reigned as

religious history with which we have to deal. In religion and general civilization both were subject to Indian influence and it is not recorded that the political circumstances which turned Fu-nan into Chên-la were attended by any religious revolution.

The most important fact in the history of these countries, as in Champa and Java, is the presence from early times of Indian influence as a result of commerce, colonization, or conquest. Orientalists have only recently freed themselves from the idea that the ancient Hindus, and especially their religion, were restricted to the limits of India. In mediæval times this was true. Emigration was rare and it was only in the nineteenth century that the travelling Hindu became a familiar and in some British colonies not very welcome visitor. Even now Hindus of the higher caste evade rather than deny the rule which forbids them to cross the ocean[1]. But for a long while Hindus have frequented the coast of East Africa[2] and in earlier

Mahendravarman, c. 600 A.D. But it would appear from the inscriptions that it was his predecessor Bhavavarman who made whatever change occurred in the relations of Camboja to Fu-nan and in any case it is not clear who were the inhabitants of Fu-nan if not Cambojans. Perhaps Maspéro is right in suggesting that Fu-nan was something like imperial Germany (p. 25), "Si le roi de Bavière s'emparait de la couronne impériale, rien ne serait changé en Allemagne que la famille régnante."

[1] It is remarkable that the Baudhâyana-dharma-sûtra enumerates going to sea among the customs peculiar to the North (I. 1, 2, 4) and then (II. 1, 2, 2) classes making voyages by sea as the first of the offences which cause loss of caste. This seems to indicate that the emigrants from India came mainly from the North, but it would be rash to conclude that in times of stress or enthusiasm the Southerners did not follow their practice. A passage in the second chapter of the Kauṭilîya Arthaśâstra has been interpreted as referring to the despatch of colonists to foreign countries, but it probably contemplates nothing more than the transfer of population from one part of India to another. See Finot, *B.E.F.E.O.* 1912, No. 8. But the passage at any rate shows that the idea of the King being able to transport a considerable mass of population was familiar in ancient India. Jâtaka 466 contains a curious story of a village of carpenters who being unsuccessful in trade built a ship and emigrated to an island in the ocean. It is clear that there must have been a considerable seafaring population in India in early times for the Rig Veda (II. 48, 3; I. 56, 2; I. 116, 3), the Mahabharata and the Jâtakas allude to the love of gain which sends merchants across the sea and to shipwrecks. Sculptures at Salsette ascribed to about 150 A.D. represent a shipwreck. Ships were depicted in the paintings of Ajanta and also occur on the coins of the Andhra King Yajñaśrî (c. 200 A.D.) and in the sculptures of Boroboedoer. The Dîgha Nikâya (XI. 85) speaks of sea-going ships which when lost let loose a land sighting bird. Much information is collected in Radhakumud Mookerji's *History of Indian Shipping*, 1912.

[2] Voyages are still regularly made in dhows between the west coast of India and Zanzibar or Mombasa and the trade appears to be old.

centuries their traders, soldiers and missionaries covered considerable distances by sea. The Jâtakas[1] mention voyages to Babylon: Vijaya and Mahinda reached Ceylon in the fifth and third centuries B.C. respectively. There is no certain evidence as to the epoch when Hindus first penetrated beyond the Malay peninsula, but Java is mentioned in the Ramayana[2]: the earliest Sanskrit inscriptions of Champa date from our third or perhaps second century, and the Chinese Annals of the Tsin indicate that at a period considerably anterior to that dynasty there were Hindus in Fu-nan[3]. It is therefore safe to conclude that they must have reached these regions about the beginning of the Christian era and, should any evidence be forthcoming, there is no reason why this date should not be put further back. At present we can only say that the establishment of Hindu kingdoms probably implies earlier visits of Hindu traders and that voyages to the south coast of Indo-China and the Archipelago were probably preceded by settlements on the Isthmus of Kra, for instance at Ligor.

The motives which prompted this eastward movement have been variously connected with religious persecution in India, missionary enterprise, commerce and political adventure. The first is the least probable. There is little evidence for the systematic persecution of Buddhists in India and still less for the persecution of Brahmans by Buddhists. Nor can these Indian settlements be regarded as primarily religious missions. The Brahmans have always been willing to follow and supervise the progress of Hindu civilization, but they have never shown any disposition to evangelize foreign countries apart from Hindu settlements in them. The Buddhists had this evangelistic temper and the journeys of their missionaries doubtless stimulated other classes to go abroad, but still no inscriptions or annals suggest that the Hindu migrations to Java and Camboja were parallel to Mahinda's mission to Ceylon. Nor is there any reason to think that they were commanded or encouraged by

[1] See Jâtaka 339 for the voyage to Baveru or Babylon. Jâtakas 360 and 442 mention voyages to Suvaṇṇabhûmi or Lower Burma from Bharukaccha and from Benares down the river. The Milinda Pañha (VI. 21) alludes to traffic with China by sea.

[2] Râm. IV. 40, 30.

[3] Pelliot, *Founan*, p. 254. The Western and Eastern Tsin reigned from 265 to 419 A.D.

Indian Rajas, for no mention of their despatch has been found in India, and no Indian state is recorded to have claimed suzerainty over these colonies. It therefore seems likely that they were founded by traders and also by adventurers who followed existing trade routes and had their own reasons for leaving India. In a country where dynastic quarrels were frequent and the younger sons of Rajas had a precarious tenure of life, such reasons can be easily imagined. In Camboja we find an Indian dynasty established after a short struggle, but in other countries, such as Java and Sumatra, Indian civilization endured because it was freely adopted by native chiefs and not because it was forced on them as a result of conquest.

The inscriptions discovered in Camboja and deciphered by the labours of French savants offer with one lacuna (about 650–800 A.D.) a fairly continuous history of the country from the sixth to the thirteenth centuries. For earlier periods we depend almost entirely on Chinese accounts which are fragmentary and not interested in anything but the occasional relations of China with Fu-nan. The annals of the Tsin dynasty[1] already cited say that from 265 A.D. onwards the kings of Fu-nan sent several embassies to the Chinese Court, adding that the people have books and that their writing resembles that of the Hu. The Hu are properly speaking a tribe of Central Asia, but the expression doubtless means no more than alphabetic writing as opposed to Chinese characters and such an alphabet can hardly have had other than an Indian origin. Originally, adds the Annalist, the sovereign was a woman, but there came a stranger called Hun-Hui who worshipped the Devas and had had a dream in which one of them gave him a bow[2] and ordered him to sail for Fu-nan. He conquered the country and married the Queen but his descendants deteriorated and one Fan-Hsün founded another dynasty. The annals of the Ch'i dynasty (479–501) give substantially the same story but say that the stranger was called Hun-T'ien (which is probably the correct form of the name) and that he came from Chi or Chiao, an unknown locality. The same annals state that towards the end

[1] Pelliot, *Founan*, p. 254. Most of the references to Chinese annals are taken from this valuable paper.

[2] The inscription of Mi-son relates how Kauṇḍinya planted at Bharapura (? in Camboja) a javelin given to him by Aśvatthâman.

of the fifth century the king of Fu-nan who bore the family name of Ch'iao-ch'ên-ju[1] or Kauṇḍinya and the personal name of Shê-yeh-po-mo (Jayavarman) traded with Canton. A Buddhist monk named Nâgasena returned thence with some Cambojan merchants and so impressed this king with his account of China that he was sent back in 484 to beg for the protection of the Emperor. The king's petition and a supplementary paper by Nâgasena are preserved in the annals. They seem to be an attempt to represent the country as Buddhist, while explaining that Maheśvara is its tutelary deity.

The Liang annals also state that during the Wu dynasty (222–280) Fan Chan, then king of Fu-nan, sent a relative named Su-Wu on an embassy to India, to a king called Mao-lun, which probably represents Muruṇḍa, a people of the Ganges valley mentioned by the Purâṇas and by Ptolemy. This king despatched a return embassy to Fu-nan and his ambassadors met there an official sent by the Emperor of China[2]. The early date ascribed to these events is noticeable.

The Liang annals contain also the following statements. Between the years 357 and 424 A.D. named as the dates of embassies sent to China, an Indian Brahman called Ch'iao-ch'ên-ju (Kauṇḍinya) heard a supernatural voice bidding him go and reign in Fu-nan. He met with a good reception and was elected king. He changed the customs of the country and made them conform to those of India. One of his successors, Jayavarman, sent a coral image of Buddha in 503 to the Emperor Wu-ti (502–550). The inhabitants of Fu-nan are said to make bronze images of the heavenly genii with two or four heads and four or eight arms. Jayavarman was succeeded by a usurper named Liu-t'o-pa-mo (Rudravarman) who sent an image made of sandal wood to the Emperor in 519 and in 539 offered him a hair of the Buddha twelve feet long. The Sui annals (589–618) state that Citrasena, king of Chên-la, conquered Fu-nan and was succeeded by his son Îśânasena.

Two monks of Fu-nan are mentioned among the translators of the Chinese scriptures[3], namely, Saṅghapâla and Mandra.

[1] This is the modern reading of the characters in Peking, but Julien's *Méthode* justifies the transcription Kau-ḍi-nya.

[2] See S. Lévi in *Mélanges Charles de Harlez*, p. 176. Deux peuples méconnus. i. Les Muruṇḍas.

[3] *Nanjio Catalogue*, p. 422.

Both arrived in China during the first years of the sixth century and their works are extant. The pilgrim I-Ching who returned from India in 695 says[1] that to the S.W. of Champa lies the country Po-nan, formerly called Fu-nan, which is the southern corner of Jambudvîpa. He says that "of old it was a country the inhabitants of which lived naked; the people were mostly worshippers of devas and later on Buddhism flourished there, but a wicked king has now expelled and exterminated them all and there are no members of the Buddhist brotherhood at all."

These data from Chinese authorities are on the whole confirmed by the Cambojan inscriptions. Rudravarman is mentioned[2] and the kings claim to belong to the race of Kauṇḍinya[3]. This is the name of a Brahman gotra, but such designations were often borne by Kshatriyas and the conqueror of Camboja probably belonged to that caste. It may be affirmed with some certainty that he started from south-eastern India and possibly he sailed from Mahâbalipûr (also called the Seven Pagodas). Masulipatam was also a port of embarcation for the East and was connected with Broach by a trade route running through Tagara, now Têr in the Nizam's dominions. By using this road, it was possible to avoid the west coast, which was infested by pirates.

The earliest Cambojan inscriptions date from the beginning of the seventh century and are written in an alphabet closely resembling that of the inscriptions in the temple of Pâpanâtha at Paṭṭadkal in the Bîjapur district[4]. They are composed in

[1] I-Tsing, trans. Takakusu, p. 12.

[2] *Corpus*, I. p. 65.

[3] *Corpus*, I. pp. 84, 89, 90, and *Jour. Asiatique*, 1882, p. 152.

[4] When visiting Badami, Paṭṭadkal and Aihole in 1912 I noted the following resemblances between the temples of that district and those of Camboja. (*a*) The chief figures are Harihara, Vâmana and Nrisiṃha. At Paṭṭadkal, as at Angkor Wat, the reliefs on the temple wall represent the Churning of the Sea and scenes from the Râmâyana. (*b*) Large blocks of stone were used for building and after being put in their positions were carved *in situ*, as is shown by unfinished work in places. (*c*) Medallions containing faces are frequent. (*d*) The architectural scheme is not as in Dravidian temples, that is to say larger outside and becoming smaller as one proceeds towards the interior. There is generally a central tower attached to a hall. (*e*) The temples are often raised on a basement. (*f*) Mukhalingas and koshas are still used in worship. (*g*) There are verandahs resembling those at Angkor Wat. They have sloping stone roofs, sculptures in relief on the inside wall and a series of windows in the outside wall. (*h*) The doors of the Linga shrines have a serpentine ornamentation and are very like those of the Bayon. (*i*) A native gentleman told me that he had seen temples with five towers in this neighbourhood, but I have not seen them myself.

Sanskrit verse of a somewhat exuberant style, which revels in the commonplaces of Indian poetry. The deities most frequently mentioned are Śiva by himself and Śiva united with Vishṇu in the form Hari-Hara. The names of the kings end in Varman and this termination is also specially frequent in names of the Pallava dynasty[1]. The magnificent monuments still extant attest a taste for architecture on a large scale similar to that found among the Dravidians. These and many other indications justify the conclusion that the Indian civilization and religion which became predominant in Camboja were imported from the Deccan.

The Chinese accounts distinctly mention two invasions, one under Ch'iao-ch'ên-ju (Kauṇḍinya) about 400 A.D. and one considerably anterior to 265 under Hun-T'ien. It might be supposed that this name also represents Kauṇḍinya and that there is a confusion of dates. But the available evidence is certainly in favour of the establishment of Hindu civilization in Fu-nan long before 400 A.D. and there is nothing improbable in the story of the two invasions and even of two Kauṇḍinyas. Maspéro suggests that the first invasion came from Java and formed part of the same movement which founded the kingdom of Champa. It is remarkable that an inscription in Sanskrit found on the east coast of Borneo and apparently dating from the fifth century mentions Kuṇḍagga as the grandfather of the reigning king, and the Liang annals say that the king of Poli (probably in Borneo but according to some in Sumatra) was called Ch'iao-ch'ên-ju. It seems likely that the Indian family of Kauṇḍinya was established somewhere in the South Seas (perhaps in Java) at an early period and thence invaded various countries at various times. But Fu-nan is a vague geographical term and it may be that Hun-T'ien founded a Hindu dynasty in Champa.

[1] *E.g.* Mahendravarman, Narasinhavarman, Parameśvaravarman, etc. It may be noticed that Paṭṭadkal is considerably to the N.W. of Madras and that the Pallavas are supposed to have come from the northern part of the present Madras Presidency. Though the Hindus who emigrated to Camboja probably embarked in the neighbourhood of Madras, they may have come from countries much further to the north. Varman is recognized as a proper termination of Kshatriya names, but it is remarkable that it is found in *all* the Sanskrit names of Cambojan kings and is very common in Pallava names. The name of Aśvatthâman figures in the mythical genealogies of both the Pallavas and the kings of Champa or perhaps of Camboja, see *B.E.F.E.O.* 1904, p. 923.

It is clear that during the period of the inscriptions the religion of Camboja was a mixture of Brahmanism and Buddhism, the only change noticeable being the preponderance of one or other element in different centuries. But it would be interesting to know the value of I-Ching's statement that Buddhism flourished in Fu-nan in early times and was then subverted by a wicked king, by whom Bhavavarman[1] may be meant. *Primâ facie* the statement is not improbable, for there is no reason why the first immigrants should not have been Buddhists, but the traditions connecting these countries with early Hinayanist missionaries are vague. Târanâtha[2] states that the disciples of Vasubandhu introduced Buddhism into the country of Koki (Indo-China) but his authority does not count for much in such a matter. The statement of I-Ching however has considerable weight, especially as the earliest inscription found in Champa (that of Vocan) appears to be inspired by Buddhism.

2

It may be well to state briefly the chief facts of Cambojan history[3] before considering the phases through which religion passed. Until the thirteenth century our chief authorities are the Sanskrit and Khmer inscriptions, supplemented by notices in the Chinese annals. The Khmer inscriptions are often only a translation or paraphrase of Sanskrit texts found in the same locality and, as a rule, are more popular, having little literary pretension. They frequently contain lists of donations or of articles to be supplied by the population for the upkeep of pious foundations. After the fourteenth century we have Cambojan annals of dubious value and we also find inscriptions in Pali or in modern Cambojan. The earliest Sanskrit inscriptions date from the beginning of the seventh century and mention works undertaken in 604 and 624.

The first important king is Bhavavarman (*c.* 500 A.D.), a

[1] Some authorities think that Kaundinya is meant by the wicked king, but he lived about 300 years before I-Ching's visit and the language seems to refer to more recent events. Although Bhavavarman is not known to have been a religious innovator he appears to have established a new order of things in Camboja and his inscriptions show that he was a zealous worshipper of Śiva and other Indian deities. It would be even more natural if I-Ching referred to Îśânavarman (*c.* 615) or Jayavarman I (*c.* 650), but there is no proof that these kings were anti-buddhist.

[2] Schiefner, p. 262.

[3] See Maspéro, *L'Empire Khmèr*, pp. 24 ff.

conqueror and probably a usurper, who extended his kingdom considerably towards the west. His career of conquest was continued by Mahâvarman (also called Citrasena), by Îśânavarman and by Jayavarman[1]. This last prince was on the throne in 667, but his reign is followed by a lacuna of more than a century. Notices in the Chinese annals, confirmed by the double genealogies given for this period in later inscriptions, indicate that Camboja was divided for some time into two states, one littoral and the other inland.

Clear history begins again with the reign of Jayavarman II (802–869). Later sovereigns evidently regard him as the great national hero and he lives in popular legend as the builder of a magnificent palace, Beng Mealea, whose ruins still exist[2] and as the recipient of the sacred sword of Indra which is preserved at Phnom-penh to this day. We are told that he "came from Javâ," which is more likely to be some locality in the Malay Peninsula or Laos than the island of that name. It is possible that Jayavarman was carried away captive to this region but returned to found a dynasty independent of it[3].

The ancient city of Angkor has probably done more to make Camboja known in Europe than any recent achievements of the Khmer race. In the centre of it stands the temple now called Bayon and outside its walls are many other edifices of which the majestic Angkor Wat is the largest and best preserved.

[1] Perhaps a second Bhavavarman came between these last two kings; see Coedès in *B.E.F.E.O.* 1904, p 691.

[2] See Mecquenem in *B.E.F.E.O.* 1913, No. 2.

[3] But the captivity is only an inference and not a necessary one. Finot suggests that the ancient royal house of Fu-nan may have resided at Javâ and have claimed suzerain rights over Camboja which Jayavarman somehow abolished. The only clear statements on the question are those in the Sdok Kak Thom inscription, Khmer text c. 72, which tell us that Camboja had been dependent on Javâ and that Jayavarman II instituted a special state cult as a sign that this dependence had come to an end.

It is true that the Hindu colonists of Camboja may have come from the island of Java, yet no evidence supports the idea that Camboja was a dependency of the island about 800 A.D. and the inscriptions of Champa seem to distinguish clearly between Yavadvîpa (the island) and the unknown country called Javâ. See Finot, *Notes d'Épig.* pp. 48 and 240. Hence it seems unlikely that the barbarous pirates (called the armies of Java) who invaded Champa in 787 (see the inscription of Yang Tikuh) were from the island. The Siamese inscription of Râma Khomhĕng, c. 1300 A.D., speaks of a place called Chavâ, which may be Luang Prabang. On the other hand it does not seem likely that pirates, expressly described as using ships, would have come from the interior.

King Indravarman (877–899) seems responsible for the selection of the site but he merely commenced the construction of the Bayon. The edifice was completed by his son Yaśovarman (889–908) who also built a town round it, called Yaśodharapura, Kambupuri or Mahânagara. Angkor Thom is the Cambojan translation of this last name, Angkor being a corruption of Nokor (= Nagara). Yaśovarman's empire comprised nearly all Indo-China between Burma and Champa and he has been identified with the Leper king of Cambojan legend. His successors continued to embellish Angkor Thom, but Jayavarman IV abandoned it and it was deserted for several years until Rajendravarman II (944–968) made it the capital again. The Chinese Annals, supported by allusions in the inscriptions, state that this prince conquered Champa. The long reigns of Jayavarman V, Sûryavarman I, and Udayâdityavarman, which cover more than a century (968–1079) seem to mark a prosperous period when architecture flourished, although Udayâdityavarman had to contend with two rebellions. Another great king, Sûryavarman II (1112–1162) followed shortly after them, and for a time succeeded in uniting Camboja and Champa under his sway. Some authorities credit him with a successful expedition to Ceylon. There is not sufficient evidence for this, but he was a great prince and, in spite of his foreign wars, maintained peace and order at home.

Jayavarman VII, who appears to have reigned from 1162 to 1201, reduced to obedience his unruly vassals of the north and successfully invaded Champa which remained for thirty years, though not without rebellion, the vassal of Camboja. It was evacuated by his successor Indravarman in 1220.

After this date there is again a gap of more than a century in Cambojan history, and when the sequence of events becomes clear again, we find that Siam has grown to be a dangerous and aggressive enemy. But though the vigour of the kingdom may have declined, the account of the Chinese traveller Chou Ta-kuan who visited Angkor Thom in 1296 shows that it was not in a state of anarchy nor conquered by Siam. There had however been a recent war with Siam and he mentions that the country was devastated. He unfortunately does not tell us the name of the reigning king and the list of sovereigns begins again only in 1340 when the Annals of Camboja take up the history. They are not of great value. The custom of recording all events of importance prevailed at the Cambojan Court in earlier times but these chronicles were lost in the eighteenth century. King Ang Chan (1796–1834) ordered that they should be re-written with the aid of the Siamese chronicles and such other materials as were available and fixed 1340 as the point of departure, apparently because the Siamese chronicles start from that date[1]. Although the period of the annals offers little but a narrative of dissensions at home and abroad, of the interference of Annam on one side and of Siam on the other, yet it does not seem that the sudden cessation of inscriptions and of the ancient style of architecture in the thirteenth century was due to the collapse of Camboja, for even in the sixteenth century it offered a valiant, and often successful, resistance to aggressions from the west. But Angkor Thom and the principal monuments were situated near the Siamese frontier and felt the shock of every collision. The sense of security, essential for the construction of great architectural works, had disappeared and the population became less submissive and less willing to supply forced labour without which such monuments could not be erected.

The Siamese captured Angkor Thom in 1313, 1351 and 1420 but did not on any occasion hold it for long. Again in 1473 they occupied Chantaboun, Korat and Angkor but had to retire and conclude peace. King Ang Chan I successfully disputed the right of Siam to treat him as a vassal and established his capital at Lovek, which he fortified and ornamented. He reigned from 1505 to 1555 and both he and his son, Barom Racha, seem entitled to rank among the great kings of Camboja. But the situation was clearly precarious and when a minor succeeded to the throne in 1574 the Siamese seized the opportunity and recaptured Lovek and Chantaboun. Though this capture was the death blow to the power of the Khmers, the kingdom of Camboja did not cease to exist but for nearly three centuries continued to have an eventful but uninteresting history as the

[1] For these annals see F. Garnier, "La Chronique royale du Cambodje," *J.A.* 1871 and 1872. A. de Villemereuil, *Explorations et Missions de Doudard de Lagrée*, 1882. J. Moura, *Le Royaume de Cambodje*, vol. II. 1883. E. Aymonier, *Chronique des Anciens rois du Cambodje.* (*Excursions et reconnaissances.* Saigon, 1881.)

vassal of Siam or Annam or even of both[1], until in the middle of the nineteenth century the intervention of France substituted a European Protectorate for these Asiatic rivalries.

The provinces of Siem-reap and Battambang, in which Angkor Thom and the principal ancient monuments are situated, were annexed by Siam at the end of the eighteenth century, but in virtue of an arrangement negotiated by the French Government they were restored to Camboja in 1907, Krat and certain territories being at the same time ceded to Siam[2].

3

The religious history of Camboja may be divided into two periods, exclusive of the possible existence there of Hinayanist Buddhism in the early centuries of our era. In the first period, which witnessed the construction of the great monuments and the reigns of the great kings, both Brahmanism and Mahayanist Buddhism flourished, but as in Java and Champa without mutual hostility. This period extends certainly from the sixth to the thirteenth centuries and perhaps its limits should be stretched to 400–1400 A.D. In any case it passed without abrupt transition into the second period in which, under Siamese influence, Hinayanist Buddhism supplanted the older faiths, although the ceremonies of the Cambojan court still preserve a good deal of Brahmanic ritual.

During the first period, Brahmanism and Mahayanism were professed by the Court and nobility. The multitude of great temples and opulent endowments, the knowledge of Sanskrit literature and the use of Indian names, leave no doubt about this, but it is highly probable that the mass of the people had their own humbler forms of worship. Still there is no record of anything that can be called Khmer—as opposed to Indian—religion. As in Siam, the veneration of nature spirits is universal in Camboja and little shrines elevated on poles are erected in their honour in the neighbourhood of almost every house.

[1] *E.g.* Ang Chan (1796–1834) received his crown from the King of Siam and paid tribute to the King of Annam; Ang Duong (1846–1859) was crowned by representatives of Annam and Siam and his territory was occupied by the troops of both countries.

[2] The later history of Camboja is treated in considerable detail by A. Leclerc, *Histoire de Cambodge*, 1914.

Possibly the more important of these spirits were identified in early times with Indian deities or received Sanskrit names. Thus we hear of a pious foundation in honour of Brahmarakshas[1], perhaps a local mountain spirit. Śiva is adored under the name of Śrî Śikhareśvara, the Lord of the Peak and Kṛishṇa appears to be identified with a local god called Śrî Champeśvara who was worshipped by Jayavarman VI[2].

The practice of accepting and hinduizing strange gods with whom they came in contact was so familiar to the Brahmans that it would be odd if no examples of it occurred in Camboja. Still the Brahmanic religion which has left such clear records there was in the main not a hinduized form of any local cult but a direct importation of Indian thought, ritual and literature. The Indian invaders or colonists were accompanied by Brahmans: their descendants continued to bear Indian names and to give them to all places of importance: Sanskrit was the ecclesiastical and official language, for the inscriptions written in Khmer are clearly half-contemptuous notifications to the common people, respecting such details as specially concerned them: *Âśramas* and castes (*varṇa*) are mentioned[3] and it is probable that natives were only gradually and grudgingly admitted to the higher castes. There is also reason to believe that this Hindu civilization was from time to time vivified by direct contact with India. The embassy of Su-Wu has already been mentioned[4] and an inscription records the marriage of a Cambojan princess with a Brahman called Divâkara who came from the banks of the Yamunâ, "where Kṛishṇa sported in his infancy."

During the whole period of the inscriptions the worship of Śiva seems to have been the principal cultus and to some extent the state religion, for even kings who express themselves in their inscriptions as devout Buddhists do not fail to invoke him. But there is no trace of hostility to Vishnuism and the earlier inscriptions constantly celebrate the praises of the compound deity Vishṇu-Śiva, known under such names as

[1] Inscrip. of Moroun, *Corpus*, II. 387.

[2] Other local deities may be alluded to, under the names of Śrî Jayakshetra, "the field of victory" adored at Bassêt Simâdamataka, Śrî Mandareśvara, and Śrî Jalangeśvara. Aymonier, II. p. 297; I. pp. 305, 306 and 327.

[3] Inscrip. of Lovek.

[4] Prea Eynkosey, 970 A.D. See *Corpus*, I. pp. 77 ff.

Hari-Hara[1], Śambhu-Vishṇu, Śaṅkara-Narâyaṇa, etc. Thus an inscription of Ang-Pou dating from Îśânavarman's reign says "Victorious are Hara and Acyuta become one for the good of the world, though as the spouses of Parvatî and Śrî they have different forms[2]." But the worship of this double being is accompanied by pure Śivaism and by the adoration of other deities. In the earliest inscriptions Bhavavarman invokes Śiva and dedicates a linga. He also celebrates the compound deity under the name of Śambhu-Vishṇu and mentions Umâ, Lakshmî, Bhâratî, Dharma, the Maruts, and Vishṇu under the names of Caturbhuja and Trailokyasâra. There appears to be no allusion to the worship of Vishṇu-Śiva as two in one after the seventh century, but though Śiva became exalted at the expense of his partner, Vishṇu must have had adorers for two kings, Jayavarman III and Sûryavarman II, were known after their death by the names of Vishṇu-loka and Parama-Vishṇu-loka.

Śiva became generally recognized as the supreme deity, in a comprehensive but not an exclusive sense. He is the universal spirit from whom emanate Brahmâ and Vishṇu. His character as the Destroyer is not much emphasized: he is the God of change, and therefore of reproduction, whose symbol is the Linga. It is remarkable to find that a pantheistic form of Śivaism is clearly enunciated in one of the earliest inscriptions[3]. Śiva is there styled Vibhu, the omnipresent, Paramvrahmâ (= Brahmâ), Jagatpati, Paśupati. An inscription found at Angkor[4] mentions an Âcârya of the Pâśupatas as well as an Âcârya of the Śaivas and Chou Ta-kuan seems to allude to the worshippers of Paśupati under the name of Pa-ssŭ-wei. It would therefore appear that the Pâśupatas existed in Camboja as a distinct sect and there are some indications[5] that ideas which prevailed among the Lingayats also found their way thither.

[1] This compound deity is celebrated in the Harivamsa and is represented in the sculptures of the rock temple at Badami, which is dated 578 A.D. Thus his worship may easily have reached Camboja in the sixth or seventh century.

[2] Jayato jagatâm bhûtyai Kṛitasandhî Harâcyutau, Parvatîśripatitvena Bhinnamûrttidharâvapi. See also the Inscrip. of Ang Chumnik (667 A.D.), verses 11 and 12 in *Corpus*, I. p. 67.

[3] The Bayang Inscription, *Corpus*, I. pp. 31 ff. which mentions the dates 604 and 626 as recent.

[4] *Corpus*, II. p. 422 Śaivapaśupatâcâryyau. The inscription fixes the relative rank of various Acâryas.

[5] See *B.E.F.E.O.* 1906, p. 70.

The most interesting and original aspect of Cambojan religion is its connection with the state and the worship of deities somehow identified with the king or with prominent personages[1]. These features are also found in Champa and Java. In all these countries it was usual that when a king founded a temple, the god worshipped in it should be called by his name or by something like it. Thus when Bhadravarman dedicated a temple to Śiva, the god was styled Bhadreśvara. More than this, when a king or any distinguished person died, he was commemorated by a statue which reproduced his features but represented him with the attributes of his favourite god. Thus Indravarman and Yaśovarman dedicated at Bakô and Lolei shrines in which deceased members of the royal family were commemorated in the form of images of Śiva and Devî bearing names similar to their own. Another form of apotheosis was to describe a king by a posthumous title, indicating that he had gone to the heaven of his divine patron such as Paramavishṇuloka or Buddhaloka. The temple of Bayon was a truly national fane, almost a Westminster abbey, in whose many shrines all the gods and great men of the country were commemorated. The French archæologists recognize four classes of these shrines dedicated respectively to (*a*) Indian deities, mostly special forms of Śiva, Devî and Vishṇu; (*b*) Mahayanist Buddhas, especially Buddhas of healing, who were regarded as the patron saints of various towns and mountains; (*c*) similar local deities apparently of Cambojan origin and perhaps corresponding to the God of the City worshipped in every Chinese town; (*d*) deified kings and notables, who appear to have been represented in two forms, the human and divine, bearing slightly different names. Thus one inscription speaks of Śrî Mahendreśvarî who is the divine form (vraḥ rûpa) of the lady Śrî Mahendralakshmî.

The presiding deity of the Bayon was Śiva, adored under the form of the linga. The principal external ornaments of the building are forty towers each surmounted by four heads. These were formerly thought to represent Brahmâ but there is little doubt that they are meant for lingas bearing four faces of Śiva,

[1] See specially on this subject, Coedès in *Bull. Comm. Archéol. de l'Indochine*, 1911, p. 38, and 1913, p. 81, and the letterpress of *Le Bayon d'Angkor Thom*, 1914.

since each head has three eyes. Such lingas are occasionally seen in India[1] and many metal cases bearing faces and made to be fitted on lingas have been discovered in Champâ. These four-headed columns are found on the gates of Angkor Thom as well as in the Bayon and are singularly impressive. The emblem adored in the central shrine of the Bayon was probably a linga but its title was *Kamrateṅ jagat ta râja* or *Devarâja*, the king-god. More explicitly still it is styled *Kamrateṅ jagat ta râjya*, the god who is the kingdom. It typified and contained the royal essence present in the living king of Camboja and in all her kings. Several inscriptions make it clear that not only dead but living people could be represented by statue-portraits which identified them with a deity, and in one very remarkable record a general offers to the king the booty he has captured, asking him to present it "to your subtle ego who is Îśvara dwelling in a golden linga[2]." Thus this subtle ego dwells in a linga, is identical with Śiva, and manifests itself in the successive kings of the royal house.

The practices described have some analogies in India. The custom of describing the god of a temple by the name of the founder was known there[3]. The veneration of ancestors is universal; there are some mausolea (for instance at Ahar near Udeypore) and the notion that in life the soul can reside elsewhere than in the body is an occasional popular superstition. Still these ideas and practices are not conspicuous features of Hinduism and the Cambojans had probably come within the sphere of another influence. In all eastern Asia the veneration of the dead is the fundamental and ubiquitous form of religion and in China we find fully developed such ideas as that the great should be buried in monumental tombs, that a spirit can be made to reside in a tablet or image, and that the human soul is compound so that portions of it can be in different places. These beliefs combined with the Indian doctrine that the deity

[1] I have seen myself a stone lingam carved with four faces in a tank belonging to a temple at Maḥakut not far from Badami.

[2] Suvarṇamayalingagateśvare te sûkshmântarâtmani. Inscrip. of Prea Ngouk, *Corpus*, I. p. 157.

[3] *E.g.* see *Epig. Indica*, vol. III. pp. 1 ff. At Paṭṭadkal (which region offers so many points of resemblance to Camboja) King Vijayâditya founded a temple of Vijayeśvara and two Queens, Lokamahâdevî and Trailokyamahâdevî founded temples of Lokeśvara and Trailokyeśvara.

is manifested in incarnations, in the human soul and in images afford a good theoretical basis for the worship of the Devarâja. It was also agreeable to far-eastern ideas that religion and the state should be closely associated and the Cambojan kings would be glad to imitate the glories of the Son of Heaven. But probably a simpler cause tended to unite church and state in all these Hindu colonies. In mediæval India the Brahmans became so powerful that they could claim to represent religion and civilization apart from the state. But in Camboja and Champa Brahmanic religion and civilization were bound up with the state. Both were attacked by and ultimately succumbed to the same enemies.

The Brahmanism of Camboja, as we know it from the inscriptions, was so largely concerned with the worship of this "Royal God" that it might almost be considered a department of the court. It seems to have been thought essential to the dignity of a Sovereign who aspired to be more than a local prince, that his Chaplain or preceptor should have a pontifical position. A curious parallel to this is shown by those mediæval princes of eastern Europe who claimed for their chief bishops the title of patriarch as a complement to their own imperial pretensions. In its ultimate form the Cambojan hierarchy was the work of Jayavarman II, who, it will be remembered, re-established the kingdom after an obscure but apparently disastrous interregnum. He made the priesthood of the Royal God hereditary in the family of Śivakaivalya and the sacerdotal dynasty thus founded enjoyed during some centuries a power inferior only to that of the kings.

In the inscriptions of Sdok Kâk Thom[1] the history of this family is traced from the reign of Jayavarman II to 1052. The beginning of the story as related in both the Sanskrit and Khmer texts is interesting but obscure. It is to the effect that Jayavarman, anxious to assure his position as an Emperor (Cakravartin) independent of Javâ[2], summoned from Janapada a Brahman called Hiranyadâma, learned in magic (siddhividyâ), who arranged the rules (viddhi) for the worship of the Royal God and taught the king's Chaplain, Śivakaivalya, four treatises called Vrah Vinâśikha, Nayottara, Sammoha and

[1] Aymonier, II. pp. 257 ff. and especially Finot in *B.E.F.E.O.* 1915, xv. 2, p. 53.

[2] See above.

Śiraścheda. These works are not otherwise known[1]. The king made a solemn compact that "only the members of his (Śiva-kaivalya's) maternal[2] family, men and women, should be Yâjakas (sacrificers or officiants) to the exclusion of all others." The restriction refers no doubt only to the cult of the Royal God and the office of court chaplain, called Purohita, Guru or Hotri, of whom there were at least two.

The outline of this narrative, that a learned Brahman was imported and charged with the instruction of the royal chaplain, is simple and probable but the details are perplexing. The Sanskrit treatises mentioned are unknown and the names singular. Janapada as the name of a definite locality is also strange[3], but it is conceivable that the word may have been used in Khmer as a designation of India or a part of it.

The inscription goes on to relate the gratifying history of the priestly family, the grants of land made to them, the honours they received. We gather that it was usual for an estate to be given to a priest with the right to claim forced labour from the population. He then proceeded to erect a town or village embellished with temples and tanks. The hold of Brahmanism on the country probably depended more on such priestly towns than on the convictions of the people. The inscriptions often speak of religious establishments being restored and sometimes say that they had become deserted and overgrown. We may conclude that if the Brahman lords of a village ceased for any reason to give it their attention, the labour and contributions requisite for the upkeep of the temples were not forthcoming and the jungle was allowed to grow over the buildings.

Numerous inscriptions testify to the grandeur of the Śiva-kaivalya family. The monotonous lists of their properties and slaves, of the statues erected in their honour and the number of parasols borne before them show that their position was almost regal, even when the king was a Buddhist. They prudently refrained from attempting to occupy the throne, but

[1] Sammohana and Niruttara are given as names of Tantras. The former word may perhaps be the beginning of a compound. There are Pali works called Sammohavinodinî and S. vinâśinî. The inscription calls the four treatises the four faces of Tumburu.

[2] This shows that matriarchy must have been in force in Camboja.

[3] Jânapada as the name of a locality is cited by Böthlingck and Roth from the Gaṇa to Pâṇini, 4. 2. 82.

probably no king could succeed unless consecrated by them. Sadaśiva, Śaṅkarapaṇḍita and Divâkarapaṇḍita formed an ecclesiastical dynasty from about 1000 to 1100 A.D. parallel to the long reigns of the kings in the same period[1]. The last-named mentions in an inscription that he had consecrated three kings and Śaṅkarapaṇḍita, a man of great learning, was *de facto* sovereign during the minority of his pupil Udayâdityavarman nor did he lose his influence when the young king attained his majority.

The shrine of the Royal God was first near Mt Mahendra and was then moved to Hariharâlaya[2]. Its location was definitely fixed in the reign of Indravarman, about 877 A.D. Two Śivakaivalya Brahmans, Śivasoma and his pupil Vâmaśiva, chaplain of the king, built a temple called the Śivâśrama and erected a linga therein. It is agreed that this building is the Bayon, which formed the centre of the later city of Angkor. Indravarman also illustrated another characteristic of the court religion by placing in the temple now called Prah Kou three statues of Śiva with the features of his father, grandfather and Jayavarman II together with corresponding statues of Śakti in the likeness of their wives. The next king, Yaśovarman, who founded the town of Angkor round the Bayon, built near his palace another linga temple, now known as Ba-puon. He also erected two convents, one Brahmanic and one Buddhist. An inscription[3] gives several interesting particulars respecting the former. It fixes the provisions to be supplied to priests and students and the honours to be rendered to distinguished visitors. The right of sanctuary is accorded and the sick and helpless are to receive food and medicine. Also funeral rites are to be celebrated within its precincts for the repose of the friendless and those who have died in war. The royal residence was moved from Angkor in 928, but about twenty years later the court returned thither and the inscriptions record that the Royal God accompanied it.

The cultus was probably similar to what may be seen in the

[1] Possibly others may have held office during this long period, but evidently all three priests lived to be very old men and each may have been Guru for forty years.

[2] This place which means merely "the abode of Hari and Hara" has not been identified.

[3] *Corpus*, II. Inscrip. lvi. especially pp. 248–251.

Sivaite temples of India to-day. The principal lingam was placed in a shrine approached through other chambers and accessible only to privileged persons. Libations were poured over the emblem and sacred books were recited. An interesting inscription[1] of about 600 A.D. relates how Śrîsomasarman (probably a Brahman) presented to a temple "the Râmâyaṇa, the Purâṇa and complete Bhârata" and made arrangements for their recitation. Sanskrit literature was held in esteem. We are told that Sûryavarman I was versed in the Atharva-Veda and also in the Bhâshya, Kâvyas, the six Darśanas, and the Dharmaśâstras[2]. Sacrifices are also frequently mentioned and one inscription records the performance of a Koṭihoma[3]. The old Vedic ritual remained to some extent in practice, for no circumstances are more favourable to its survival than a wealthy court dominated by a powerful hierarchy. Such ceremonies were probably performed in the ample enclosures surrounding the temples[4].

4

Mahayanist Buddhism existed in Camboja during the whole of the period covered by the inscriptions, but it remained in such close alliance with Brahmanism that it is hard to say whether it should be regarded as a separate religion. The idea that the two systems were incompatible obviously never occurred to the writers of the inscriptions and Buddhism was not regarded as more distinct from Śivaism and Vishnuism than these from one another. It had nevertheless many fervent and generous, if not exclusive, admirers. The earliest record of its existence is a short inscription dating from the end of the sixth or beginning of the seventh century[5], which relates how a person called Pon Prajnâ Candra dedicated male and female slaves to the three Bodhisattvas, Śâstâ[6], Maitreya and Avalo-

[1] Veal Kantel, *Corpus*, I. p. 28.

[2] Inscr. of Prah Khan, *B.E.F.E.O.* 1904, p. 675.

[3] *B.E.F.E.O.* 1904, p. 677.

[4] Just as a Vedic sacrifice was performed in the court of the temple of Chidambaram about 1908.

[5] Aymonier, *Cambodja*, I. p. 442.

[6] Śâstâ sounds like a title of Śâkyamuni, but, if Aymonier is correct, the personage is described as a Bodhisattva. There were pagoda slaves even in modern Burma.

kiteśvara. The title given to the Bodhisattvas (Vrah Kamratâ añ) which is also borne by Indian deities shows that this Buddhism was not very different from the Brahmanic cult of Camboja.

It is interesting to find that Yaśovarman founded in Angkor Thom a Saugatâśrama or Buddhist monastery parallel to his Brâhmaṇâśrama already described. Its inmates enjoyed the same privileges and had nearly the same rules and duties, being bound to afford sanctuary, maintain the destitute and perform funeral masses. It is laid down that an Âcârya versed in Buddhist lore corresponds in rank to the Âcâryas of the Śaivas and Pâsupatas and that in both institutions greater honour is to be shown to such Âcâryas as also are learned in grammar. A Buddhist Âcârya ought to be honoured a little less than a learned Brahman. Even in form the inscriptions recording the foundation of the two Âśramas show a remarkable parallelism. Both begin with two stanzas addressed to Śiva: then the Buddhist inscription inserts a stanza in honour of the Buddha who delivers from transmigration and gives nirvâṇa, and then the two texts are identical for several stanzas[1].

Mahayanism appears to have flourished here especially from the tenth to the thirteenth centuries and throughout the greater part of this period we find the same feature that its principal devotees were not the kings but their ministers. Sûryavarman I († 1049) and Jayavarman VII († 1221) in some sense deserved the name of Buddhists since the posthumous title of the former was Nirvâṇapada and the latter left a long inscription[2] beginning with a definitely Buddhist invocation. Yet an inscription of Sûryavarman which states in its second verse that only the word of the Buddha is true, opens by singing the praises of Śiva, and Jayavarman certainly did not neglect the Brahmanic gods. But for about a hundred years there was a series of great ministers who specially encouraged Buddhism. Such were Satyavarman (*c.* 900 A.D.), who was charged with the erection of the building in Angkor known as Phimeanakas; Kavindrârimathana, minister under Râjendravarman II and Jayavarman V, who erected many Buddhist statues and Kîrtipaṇḍita, minister of Jayavarman V. Kîrtipaṇḍita was the

[1] See Coedès, "La Stèle de Tép Praṇaṃ," in *J.A.* XI. 1908, p. 203.
[2] Inscrip. of Ta Prohm, *B.E.F.E.O.* 1906, p. 44.

author[1] of the inscription found at Srey Santhor, which states that thanks to his efforts the pure doctrine of the Buddha re-appeared like the moon from behind the clouds or the sun at dawn.

It may be easily imagined that the power enjoyed by the court chaplain would dispose the intelligent classes to revolt against this hierarchy and to favour liberty and variety in religion, so far as was safe. Possibly the kings, while co-operating with a priesthood which recognized them as semi-divine, were glad enough to let other religious elements form some sort of counterpoise to a priestly family which threatened to be omnipotent. Though the identification of Śivaism and Buddhism became so complete that we actually find a Trinity composed of Padmodbhava (Brahmâ), Ambhojanetra (Vishṇu) and the Buddha[2], the inscriptions of the Buddhist ministers are marked by a certain diplomacy and self-congratulation on the success of their efforts, as if they felt that their position was meritorious, yet delicate.

Thus in an inscription, the object of which seems to be to record the erection of a statue of Prajñâ-pâramitâ by Kavindrârimathana we are told that the king charged him with the embellishment of Yaśodharapura because "though an eminent Buddhist" his loyalty was above suspicion[3]. The same minister erected three towers at Bàṭ Čuṃ with inscriptions[4] which record the dedication of a tank. The first invokes the Buddha, Vajrapâni[5] and Lokeśvara. In the others Lokeśvara is replaced by Prajñâ-pâramitâ who here, as elsewhere, is treated as a goddess or Śakti and referred to as Devî in another stanza[6]. The three inscriptions commemorate the construction of a sacred tank

[1] See Senart in *Revue Archéologique*, 1883. As in many inscriptions it is not always plain who is speaking but in most parts it is apparently the minister promulgating the instructions of the king.

[2] Inscript. of Prasat Prah Khse, *Corpus*, I. p. 173.

[3] Buddhânâm agraṇîr api, *J.A.* XX. 1882, p. 164.

[4] See Coedès, "Inscriptions de Bàt Cuṃ." in *J.A.* XII. 1908, pp. 230, 241.

[5] The Bodhisattva corresponding to the Buddha Akshobhya. He is green or blue and carries a thunderbolt. It seems probable that he is a metamorphosis of Indra.

[6] An exceedingly curious stanza eulogizes the doctrine of the non-existence of the soul taught by the Buddha which leads to identification with the universal soul although contrary to it. Vuddho vodhîm vidaddhyâd vo yena nairâtmyadarśanaṁ viruddhasyâpi sâdhûktaṃ sâdhanaṃ paramâtmanaḥ.

but, though the author was a Buddhist, he expressly restricts the use of it to Brahmanic functionaries.

The inscription of Srey Santhor[1] (*c.* 975 A.D.) describes the successful efforts of Kîrtipaṇḍita to restore Buddhism and gives the instructions of the king (Jayavarman V) as to its status. The royal chaplain is by no means to abandon the worship of Śiva but he is to be well versed in Buddhist learning and on feast days he will bathe the statue of the Buddha with due ceremony.

A point of interest in this inscription is the statement that Kîrtipaṇḍita introduced Buddhist books from abroad, including the Śâstra Madhyavibhâga and the commentary on the Tattvasangraha. The first of these is probably the Mâdhyântavibhâga śâstra[2] by Vasubandhu and the authorship is worth attention as supporting Târanâtha's statement that the disciples of Vasubandhu introduced Buddhism into Indo-China.

In the time of Jayavarman VII (*c.* 1185 A.D.), although Hindu mythology is not discarded and though the king's chaplain (presumably a Śivaite) receives every honour, yet Mahayanist Buddhism seems to be frankly professed as the royal religion. It is noteworthy that about the same time it becomes more prominent in Java and Champa. Probably the flourishing condition of the faith in Ceylon and Burma increased the prestige of all forms of Buddhism throughout south-eastern Asia. A long inscription of Jayavarman in 145 stanzas has been preserved in the temple of Ta Prohm near Angkor. It opens with an invocation to the Buddha, in which are mentioned the three bodies, Lokeśvara[3], and the Mother of the Jinas, by whom Prajñâ-pâramitâ must be meant. Śiva is not invoked but allusion is made to many Brahmanic deities and Bhikkhus and Brahmans are mentioned together. The inscription contains a curious list of the materials supplied daily for the temple services and of the personnel. Ample provision is made for both, but it is not clear how far a purely Buddhist ritual is contemplated and it seems probable that an extensive Brahmanic cultus existed side by side with the Buddhist ceremonial.

[1] Aymonier, I pp. 261 ff. Senart, *Revue Archéologique*, Mars-Avril, 1883.

[2] Nanjio, 1244 and 1248.

[3] The common designation of Avalokita in Camboja and Java. For the inscription see *B.E.F.E.O.* 1906, pp. 44 ff.

We learn that there were clothes for the deities and forty-five mosquito nets of Chinese material to protect their statues. The Uposatha days seem to be alluded to[1] and the spring festival is described, when "Bhagavat and Bhagavatî" are to be escorted in solemn procession with parasols, music, banners and dancing girls. The whole staff, including Burmese and Chams (probably slaves), is put down at the enormous figure of 79,365, which perhaps includes all the neighbouring inhabitants who could be called on to render any service to the temple. The more sacerdotal part of the establishment consisted of 18 principal priests (adhikâriṇaḥ), 2740 priests and 2232 assistants, including 615 dancing girls. But even these figures seem very large[2].

The inscription comes to a gratifying conclusion by announcing that there are 102 hospitals in the kingdom[3]. These institutions, which are alluded to in other inscriptions, were probably not all founded by Jayavarman VII and he seems to treat them as being, like temples, a natural part of a well-ordered state. But he evidently expended much care and money on them and in the present inscription he makes over the fruit of these good deeds to his mother. The most detailed description of these hospitals occurs in another of his inscriptions found at Say-fong in Laos. It is, like the one just cited, definitely Buddhist and it is permissible to suppose that Buddhism took a more active part than Brahmanism in such works of charity. It opens with an invocation first to the Buddha who in his three bodies transcends the distinction between existence and non-existence, and then to the healing Buddha and the two Bodhisattvas who drive away darkness and disease. These divinities, who are the lords of a heaven in the east, analogous to the paradise of Amitâbha, are still worshipped in China and Japan and were evidently gods of light[4]. The hospital erected

[1] Stanza XLVI.

[2] The inscription only says "There are here (atra)." Can this mean in the various religious establishments maintained by the king?

[3] See also Finot, *Notes d'Epig.* pp. 332–335. The Mahâvaṃsa repeatedly mentions that kings founded hospitals and distributed medicines. See too, Yule, *Marco Polo*, I. p. 446. The care of the sick was recognized as a duty and a meritorious act in all Buddhist countries and is recommended by the example of the Buddha himself.

[4] Their somewhat lengthy titles are Bhaishajyaguruvaidûryaprabharâja, Sûryavairocanacaṇḍaroci and Candravairocanarohiṇîśa. See for an account of them and the texts on which their worship is founded the learned article of M. Pelliot, "Le Bhaiṣajyaguru," *B.E.F.E.O.* 1903, p. 33.

under their auspices by the Cambojan king was open to all the four castes and had a staff of 98 persons, besides an astrologer and two sacrificers (yâjaka).

5

These inscriptions of Jayavarman are the last which tell us anything about the religion of mediæval Camboja but we have a somewhat later account from the pen of Chou Ta-kuan, a Chinese who visited Angkor in 1296[1]. He describes the temple in the centre of the city, which must be the Bayon, and says that it had a tower of gold and that the eastern (or principal) entrance was approached by a golden bridge flanked by two lions and eight statues, all of the same metal. The chapter of his work entitled "The Three Religions," runs as follows, slightly abridged from M. Pelliot's version.

"The literati are called Pan-ch'i, the bonzes Ch'u-ku and the Taoists Pa-ssŭ-wei. I do not know whom the Pan-ch'i worship. They have no schools and it is difficult to say what books they read. They dress like other people except that they wear a white thread round their necks, which is their distinctive mark. They attain to very high positions. The Ch'u-ku shave their heads and wear yellow clothes. They uncover the right shoulder, but the lower part of their body is draped with a skirt of yellow cloth and they go bare foot. Their temples are sometimes roofed with tiles. Inside there is only one image, exactly like the Buddha Śâkya, which they call Po-lai (= Prah), ornamented with vermilion and blue, and clothed in red. The Buddhas of the towers (? images in the towers of the temples) are different and cast in bronze. There are no bells, drums, cymbals, or flags in their temples. They eat only one meal a day, prepared by someone who entertains them, for they do not cook in their temples. They eat fish and meat and also use them in their offerings to Buddha, but they do not drink wine. They recite numerous texts written on strips of palm-leaf. Some bonzes have a right to have the shafts of their palanquins and the handles of their parasols in gold or silver. The prince consults them on serious matters. There are no Buddhist nuns.

"The Pa-ssŭ-wei dress like everyone else, except that they wear on their heads a piece of red or white stuff like the Ku-ku

[1] His narrative is translated by M. Pelliot in *B.E.F.E.O.* 1902, pp. 123–177.

worn by Tartar women but lower. Their temples are smaller than those of the Buddhists, for Taoism is less prosperous than Buddhism. They worship nothing but a block of stone, somewhat like the stone on the altar of the God of the Sun in China. I do not know what god they adore. There are also Taoist nuns. The Pa-ssŭ-wei do not partake of the food of other people or eat in public. They do not drink wine.

"Such children of the laity as go to school frequent the bonzes, who give them instruction. When grown up they return to a lay life.

"I have not been able to make an exhaustive investigation."

Elsewhere he says "All worship the Buddha" and he describes some popular festivals which resemble those now celebrated in Siam. In every village there was a temple or a Stûpa. He also mentions that in eating they use leaves as spoons and adds "It is the same in their sacrifices to the spirits and to Buddha."

Chou Ta-kuan confesses that his account is superficial and he was perhaps influenced by the idea that it was natural there should be three religions in Camboja, as in China. Buddhists were found in both countries: Pan-ch'i no doubt represents Paṇḍita and he saw an analogy between the Brahmans of the Cambojan Court and Confucian mandarins: a third and less known sect he identified with the Taoists. The most important point in his description is the prominence given to the Buddhists. His account of their temples, of the dress and life of their monks[1] leaves no doubt that he is describing Hinayanist Buddhism such as still flourishes in Camboja. It probably found its way from Siam, with which Camboja had already close, but not always peaceful, relations. Probably the name by which the bonzes are designated is Siamese[2]. With Chou Ta-kuan's statements may be compared the inscription of the Siamese King Râma Khomhĕng[3] which dwells on the flourishing condition of Pali Buddhism in Siam about 1300 A.D. The contrast indicated by Chou Ta-kuan is significant. The Brahmans held

[1] Pelliot (*B.E.F.E.O.* 1902, p. 148) cites a statement from the Ling Wai Tai Ta that there were two classes of bonzes in Camboja, those who wore yellow robes and married and those who wore red robes and lived in convents.

[2] M. Finot conjectures that it represents the Siamese Chao (Lord) and a corruption of Guru.

[3] See chapter on Siam, sect. 1.

high office but had no schools. Those of the laity who desired education spent some portion of their youth in a Buddhist monastery (as they still do) and then returned to the world. Such a state of things naturally resulted in the diffusion of Buddhism among the people, while the Brahmans dwindled to a Court hierarchy. When Chou Ta-kuan says that all the Cambojans adored Buddha, he probably makes a mistake, as he does in saying that the sculptures above the gates of Angkor are heads of Buddha. But the general impression which he evidently received that everyone frequented Buddhist temples and monasteries speaks for itself. His statement about sacrifices to Buddha is remarkable and, since the inscriptions of Jayavarman VII speak of sacrificers, it cannot be rejected as a mere mistake. But if Hinayanist Buddhism countenanced such practices in an age of transition, it did not adopt them permanently for, so far as I have seen, no offerings are made to-day in Cambojan temples, except flowers and sticks of incense.

The Pa-ssŭ-wei have given rise to many conjectures and have been identified with the Basaih or sacerdotal class of the Chams. But there seems to be little doubt that the word really represents Pâśupata and Chou Ta-kuan's account clearly points to a sect of linga worshippers, although no information is forthcoming about the "stone on the altar of the Sun God in China" to which he compares their emblem. His idea that they represented the Taoists in Camboja may have led him to exaggerate their importance but his statement that they were a separate body is confirmed, for an inscription of Angkor[1] defines the order of hierarchical precedence as "the Brahman, the Śaiva Âcârya, the Pâśupata Âcârya[2]."

From the time of Chou Ta-kuan to the present day I have

[1] *Corpus*, II. p. 422.

[2] The strange statement of Chou Ta-kuan (pp. 153–155) that the Buddhist and Taoist priests enjoyed a species of *jus primæ noctis* has been much discussed. Taken by itself it might be merely a queer story founded on a misunderstanding of Cambojan customs, for he candidly says that his information is untrustworthy. But taking it in connection with the stories about the Aris in Burma (see especially Finot, *J.A.* 1912, p. 121) and the customs attributed by Chinese and Europeans to the Siamese and Philippinos, we can hardly come to any conclusion except that this strange usage was an aboriginal custom in Indo-China and the Archipelago, prior to the introductions of Indian civilization, but not suppressed for some time. At the present day there seems to be no trace or even tradition of such a custom. For Siamese and Philippine customs see *B.E.F.E.O.* 1902, p. 153, note 4.

found few notices about the religion of Camboja. Hinayanist Buddhism became supreme and though we have few details of the conquest we can hardly go wrong in tracing its general lines. Brahmanism was exclusive and tyrannical. It made no appeal to the masses but a severe levy of forced labour must have been necessary to erect and maintain the numerous great shrines which, though in ruins, are still the glory of Camboja[1]. In many of them are seen the remains of inscriptions which have been deliberately erased. These probably prescribed certain onerous services which the proletariat was bound to render to the established church. When Siamese Buddhism invaded Camboja it had a double advantage. It was the creed of an aggressive and successful neighbour but, while thus armed with the weapons of this world, it also appealed to the poor and oppressed. If it enjoyed the favour of princes, it had no desire to defend the rights of a privileged caste: it offered salvation and education to the average townsman and villager. If it invited the support and alms of the laity, it was at least modest in its demands. Brahmanism on the other hand lost strength as the prestige of the court declined. Its greatest shrines were in the provinces most exposed to Siamese attacks. The first Portuguese writers speak of them as already deserted at the end of the sixteenth century. The connection with India was not kept up and if any immigrants came from the west, after the twelfth century they are more likely to have been Moslims than Hindus. Thus driven from its temples, with no roots among the people, whose affections it had never tried to win, Brahmanism in Camboja became what it now is, a court ritual without a creed and hardly noticed except at royal functions.

It is remarkable that Mohammedanism remained almost unknown to Camboja, Siam and Burma. The tide of Moslim invasion swept across the Malay Peninsula southwards. Its effect was strongest in Sumatra and Java, feebler on the coasts of Borneo and the Philippines. From the islands it reached Champa, where it had some success, but Siam and Camboja lay on one side of its main route, and also showed no sympathy

[1] The French Archæological Commission states that exclusive of Angkor and the neighbouring buildings there are remains of 600 temples in Camboja, and probably many have entirely disappeared.

for it. King Rama Thuppdey Chan[1] who reigned in Camboja from 1642–1659 became a Mohammedan and surrounded himself with Malays and Javanese. But he alienated the affections of his subjects and was deposed by the intervention of Annam. After this we hear no more of Mohammedanism. An unusual incident, which must be counted among the few cases in which Buddhism has encouraged violence, is recorded in the year 1730, when a Laotian who claimed to be inspired, collected a band of fanatics and proceeded to massacre in the name of Buddha all the Annamites resident in Camboja. This seems to show that Buddhism was regarded as the religion of the country and could be used as a national cry against strangers.

As already mentioned Brahmanism still survives in the court ceremonial though this by no means prevents the king from being a devout Buddhist. The priests are known as Bakus. They wear a top-knot and the sacred thread after the Indian fashion, and enjoy certain privileges. Within the precincts of the palace at Phnom Penh is a modest building where they still guard the sword of Indra. About two inches of the blade are shown to visitors, but except at certain festivals it is never taken out of its sheath.

The official programme of the coronation of King Sisowath (April 23–28, 1906), published in French and Cambojan, gives a curious account of the ceremonies performed, which were mainly Brahmanic, although prayers were recited by the Bonzes and offerings made to Buddha. Four special Brahmanic shrines were erected and the essential part of the rite consisted in a lustral bath, in which the Bakus poured water over the king. Invocations were addressed to beings described as "Anges qui êtes au paradis des six séjours célestes, qui habitez auprès d'Indra, de Brahmâ et de l'archange Sahabodey," to the spirits of mountains, valleys and rivers and to the spirits who guard the palace. When the king has been duly bathed the programme prescribes that "le Directeur des Bakous remettra la couronne à M. le Gouverneur Général qui la portera sur la tête de Sa Majesté au nom du Gouvernement de la République Française." Equally curious is the "Programme des fêtes royales à l'occasion de la crémation de S.M. Norodom" (January 2–16, 1906). The lengthy ceremonial consisted of a strange mixture of prayers,

[1] Maspéro, pp. 62–3.

sermons, pageants and amusements. The definitely religious exercises were Buddhist and the amusements which accompanied them, though according to our notions curiously out of place, clearly correspond to the funeral games of antiquity. Thus we read not only of "offrande d'un repas aux urnes royales" but of "illuminations générales...lancement de ballons...luttes et assauts de boxe et de l'escrime...danses et soirée de gala....Après la crémation, Sa Majesté distribuera des billets de tombola."

The ordinary Buddhism of Camboja at the present day resembles that of Siam and is not mixed with Brahmanic observances. Monasteries are numerous: the monks enjoy general respect and their conduct is said to be beyond reproach. They act as schoolmasters and, as in Siam and Burma, all young men spend some time in a monastery. A monastery generally contains from thirty to fifty monks and consists of a number of wooden houses raised on piles and arranged round a square. Each monk has a room and often a house to himself. Besides the dwelling houses there are also stores and two halls called Salâ and Vihéar (vihâra). In both the Buddha is represented by a single gigantic sitting image, before which are set flowers and incense. As a rule there are no other images but the walls are often ornamented with frescoes of Jâtaka stories or the early life of Gotama. Meals are taken in the Salâ at about 7 and 11 a.m.[1], and prayers are recited there on ordinary days in the morning and evening. The eleven o'clock meal is followed by a rather long grace. The prayers consist mostly of Pali formulæ, such as the Three Refuges, but they are sometimes in Cambojan and contain definite petitions or at least wishes formulated before the image of the Buddha. Thus I have heard prayers for peace and against war. The more solemn ceremonies, such as the Uposatha and ordinations, are performed in the Vihear. The recitation of the Pâtimokkha is regularly performed and I have several times witnessed it. All but ordained monks have to withdraw outside the Sîmâ stones during the service. The ceremony begins about 6 p.m.: the Bhikkhus kneel down in pairs face to face and rubbing their foreheads in the dust ask for mutual forgiveness if they have inadvertently offended.

[1] The food is prepared in the monasteries, and, as in other countries, the begging round is a mere formality.

This ceremony is also performed on other occasions. It is followed by singing or intoning lauds, after which comes the recitation of the Pâtimokkha itself which is marked by great solemnity. The reader sits in a large chair on the arms of which are fixed many lighted tapers. He repeats the text by heart but near him sits a prompter with a palm-leaf manuscript who, if necessary, corrects the words recited. I have never seen a monk confess in public, and I believe that the usual practice is for sinful brethren to abstain from attending the ceremony and then to confess privately to the Abbot, who assigns them a penance. As soon as the Pâtimokkha is concluded all the Bhikkhus smoke large cigarettes. In most Buddhist countries it is not considered irreverent to smoke[1], chew betel or drink tea in the intervals of religious exercises. When the cigarettes are finished there follows a service of prayer and praise in Cambojan. During the season of Wassa there are usually several Bhikkhus in each monastery who practise meditation for three or four days consecutively in tents or enclosures made of yellow cloth, open above but closed all round. The four stages of meditation described in the Piṭakas are said to be commonly attained by devout monks[2].

The Abbot has considerable authority in disciplinary matters. He eats apart from the other monks and at religious ceremonies wears a sort of red cope, whereas the dress of the other brethren is entirely yellow. Novices prostrate themselves when they speak to him.

Above the Abbots are Provincial Superiors and the government of the whole Church is in the hands of the Somdec prâh sanghrâc. There is, or was, also a second prelate called Lòk prâh sòkŏn, or Braḥ Sugandha, and the two, somewhat after the manner of the two primates of the English Church, supervise the clergy in different parts of the kingdom, the second being inferior to the first in rank, but not dependent on him. But it is said that no successor has been appointed to the last Braḥ Sugandha who died in 1894. He was a distinguished scholar and introduced the Dhammayut sect from Siam into Camboja.

[1] But in Chinese temples notices forbidding smoking are often posted on the doors.

[2] The word dhyâna is known, but the exercise is more commonly called Vipassanâ or Kammathâna.

The king is recognized as head of the Church, but cannot alter its doctrine or confiscate ecclesiastical property.

6

No account of Cambojan religion would be complete without some reference to the splendid monuments in which it found expression and which still remain in a great measure intact. The colonists who established themselves in these regions brought with them the Dravidian taste for great buildings, but either their travels enlarged their artistic powers or they modified the Indian style by assimilating successfully some architectural features found in their new home. What pre-Indian architecture there may have been among the Khmers we do not know, but the fact that the earliest known monuments are Hindu makes it improbable that stone buildings on a large scale existed before their arrival. The feature which most clearly distinguishes Cambojan from Indian architecture is its pyramidal structure. India has stupas and gopurams of pyramidal appearance but still Hindu temples of the normal type, both in the north and south, consist of a number of buildings erected on the same level. In Camboja on the contrary many buildings, such as Ta-Keo, Ba-phuong and the Phimeanakas, are shrines on the top of pyramids, which consist of three storeys or large steps, ascended by flights of relatively small steps. In other buildings, notably Angkor Wat, the pyramidal form is obscured by the slight elevation of the storeys compared with their breadth and by the elaboration of the colonnades and other edifices, which they bear. But still the general plan is that of a series of courts each rising within and above the last and this gradual rise, by which the pilgrim is led, not only through colonnade after colonnade, but up flight after flight of stairs, each leading to something higher but invisible from the base, imparts to Cambojan temples a sublimity and aspiring grandeur which is absent from the mysterious halls of Dravidian shrines.

One might almost suppose that the Cambojan architects had deliberately set themselves to rectify the chief faults of Indian architecture. One of these is the profusion of external ornament in high relief which by its very multiplicity ceases to produce any effect proportionate to its elaboration, with the result that the general view is disappointing and majestic outlines are wanting. In Cambojan buildings on the contrary the general effect is not sacrificed to detail: the artists knew how to make air and space give dignity to their work. Another peculiar defect of many Dravidian buildings is that they were gradually erected round some ancient and originally humble shrine with the unfortunate result that the outermost courts and gateways are the most magnificent and that progress to the holy of holies is a series of artistic disappointments. But at Angkor Wat this fault is carefully avoided. The long paved road which starts from the first gateway isolates the great central mass of buildings without dwarfing it and even in the last court, when one looks up the vast staircases leading to the five towers which crown the pyramid, all that has led up to the central shrine seems, as it should, merely an introduction.

The solidity of Cambojan architecture is connected with the prevalence of inundations. With such dangers it was of primary importance to have a massive substructure which could not be washed away and the style which was necessary in building a firm stone platform inspired the rest of the work. Some unfinished temples reveal the interesting fact that they were erected first as piles of plain masonry. Then came the decorator and carved the stones as they stood in their places, so that instead of carving separate blocks he was able to contemplate his design as a whole and to spread it over many stones. Hence most Cambojan buildings have a peculiar air of unity. They have not had ornaments affixed to them but have grown into an ornamental whole. Yet if an unfavourable criticism is to be made on these edifices—especially Angkor Wat—it is that the sculptures are wanting in meaning and importance. They cannot be compared to the reliefs of Boroboedoer, a veritable catechism in stone where every clause teaches the believer something new, or even to the piles of figures in Dravidian temples which, though of small artistic merit, seem to represent the whirl of the world with all its men and monsters, struggling from life into death and back to life again. The reliefs in the great corridors of Angkor are purely decorative. The artist justly felt that so long a stretch of plain stone would be wearisome, and as decoration, his work is successful. Looking outwards the eye is satisfied with such variety as the trees and houses in the temple courts afford: looking inwards it finds similar variety in the warriors and deities portrayed on the walls. Some of the scenes have an historical interest, but the attempt to follow the battles of the Ramayana or the Churning of the Sea soon becomes a tedious task, for there is little individuality or inspiration in the figures.

This want of any obvious correspondence between the decoration and cult of the Cambojan temples often makes it difficult to say to what deities they were dedicated. The Bayon, or Śivâśrama, was presumably a linga temple, yet the conjecture is not confirmed as one would expect by any indubitable evidence in the decoration or arrangements. In its general plan the building seems more Indian than others and, like the temple of Jagannâtha at Puri, consists of three successive chambers, each surmounted by a tower. The most remarkable feature in the decoration is the repetition of the four-headed figure at the top of every tower, a striking and effective motive, which is also found above the gates of the town. Chou Ta-kuan says that there were golden statues of Buddhas at the entrance to the Bayon. It is impossible to say whether this statement is accurate or not. He may have simply made a mistake, but it is equally possible that the fusion of the two creeds may have ended in images of the Buddha being placed outside the shrine of the linga.

Strange as it may seem, there is no clear evidence as to the character of the worship performed in Camboja's greatest temple, Angkor Wat. Since the prince who commenced it was known by the posthumous title of Paramavishṇuloka, we may presume that he intended to dedicate it to Vishṇu and some of the sculptures appear to represent Vishṇu slaying a demon. But it was not finished until after his death and his intentions may not have been respected by his successors. An authoritative statement[1] warns us that it is not safe to say more about the date of Angkor Wat than that its extreme limits are 1050 and 1170. Jayavarman VII (who came to the throne at about this latter date) was a Buddhist, and may possibly have used the great temple for his own worship. The sculptures are hardly

[1] M. G. Coedès in *Bull. Comm. Archéol.* 1911, p. 220.

Brahmanic in the theological sense, and those which represent the pleasures of paradise and the pains of hell recall Buddhist delineations of the same theme[1]. The four images of the Buddha which are now found in the central tower are modern and all who have seen them will, I think, agree that the figure of the great teacher which seems so appropriate in the neighbouring monasteries is strangely out of place in this aerial shrine. But what the designer of the building intended to place there remains a mystery. Perhaps an empty throne such as is seen in the temples of Annam and Bali would have been the best symbol[2].

Though the monuments of Camboja are well preserved the grey and massive severity which marks them at present is probably very different from the appearance that they wore when used for worship. From Chou Ta-kuan and other sources[3] we gather that the towers and porches were gilded, the bas-reliefs and perhaps the whole surface of the walls were painted, and the building was ornamented with flags. Music and dances were performed in the courtyards and, as in many Indian temples, the intention was to create a scene which by its animation and brilliancy might amuse the deity and rival the pleasures of paradise.

It is remarkable that ancient Camboja which has left us so many monuments, produced no books[4]. Though the inscriptions and Chou Ta-kuan testify to the knowledge of literature (especially religious), both Brahmanic and Buddhist, diffused among the upper classes, no original works or even adaptations of Indian originals have come down to us. The length and

[1] Although there is no reason why these pictures of the future life should not be Brahmanic as well as Buddhist, I do not remember having seen them in any purely Brahmanic temple.

[2] After spending some time at Angkor Wat I find it hard to believe the theory that it was a palace. The King of Camboja was doubtless regarded as a living God, but so is the Grand Lama, and it does not appear that the Potala where he lives is anything but a large residential building containing halls and chapels much like the Vatican. But at Angkor Wat everything leads up to a central shrine. It is quite probable however that the deity of this shrine was a deified king, identified with Vishṇu after his death. This would account for the remarks of Chou Ta-kuan who seems to have regarded it as a tomb.

[3] See especially the inscription of Bassac. Kern, *Annales de l'Extrême Orient*, t. III. 1880, p. 65.

[4] Pali books are common in monasteries. For the literature of Laos see Finot, *B.E.F.E.O.* 1917, No. 5.

ambitious character of many inscriptions give an idea of what the Cambojans could do in the way of writing, but the result is disappointing. These poems in stone show a knowledge of Sanskrit, of Indian poetry and theology, which is surprising if we consider how far from India they were composed, but they are almost without exception artificial, frigid and devoid of vigour or inspiration.

CHAPTER XXXIX

CHAMPA[1]

1

The kingdom of Champa, though a considerable power from about the third century until the end of the fifteenth, has attracted less attention than Camboja or Java. Its name is a thing of the past and known only to students: its monuments are inferior in size and artistic merit to those of the other Hindu kingdoms in the Far East and perhaps its chief interest is that it furnishes the oldest Sanskrit inscription yet known from these regions.

Champa occupied the south-eastern corner of Asia beyond the Malay Peninsula, if the word corner can be properly applied to such rounded outlines. Its extent varied at different epochs, but it may be roughly defined in the language of modern geography as the southern portion of Annam, comprising the provinces of Quãng-nam in the north and Bînh-Thuan in the south with the intervening country. It was divided into three provinces, which respectively became the seat of empire at different periods. They were (i) in the north Amarâvatî (the modern Quãng-nam) with the towns of Indrapura and Sinhapura;

[1] Also spelt Campâ and Tchampa. It seems safer to use Ch for C in names which though of Indian origin are used outside India. The final *a* though strictly speaking long is usually written without an accent. The following are the principal works which I have consulted about Champa.

(*a*) G. Maspéro, *Le Royaume de Champa*. Published in *T'oung Pao*, 1910–1912. Cited as Maspéro.

(*b*) A. Bergaigne, "Inscriptions Sanskrites de Champa" in *Notices et Extraits des Manuscrits de la Bibliothèque Nationale*, tome XXVII. 1re partie. 2e fascicule, 1893, pp. 181–292. Cited as *Corpus*, II.

(*c*) H. Parmentier, *Inventaire descriptif des Monuments Čams de l'Annam*. 1899.

(*d*) L. Finot, "La Religion des Chams," *B.E.F.E.O.* 1901, and *Notes d'Épigraphie*. "Les Inscriptions de Mi-son," *ib.* 1904. Numerous other papers by this author, Durand, Parmentier and others in the same periodical can be consulted with advantage.

(*e*) *Id.*, *Notes d'Épigraphie Indo-Chinoise*, 1916.

(ii) in the middle Vijaya (the modern Bing-Dinh) with the town of Vijaya and the port of Śrî-Vinaya; (iii) in the south Pâṇḍurânga or Panran (the modern provinces of Phanrang and Binh-Thuan) with the town of Vîrapura or Râjapura. A section of Pâṇḍurânga called Kauthâra (the modern Kanh hoa) was a separate province at certain times. Like the modern Annam, Champa appears to have been mainly a littoral kingdom and not to have extended far into the mountains of the interior.

Champa was the ancient name of a town in western Bengal near Bhagalpur, but its application to these regions does not seem due to any connection with north-eastern India. The conquerors of the country, who were called Chams, had a certain amount of Indian culture and considered the classical name Champa as an elegant expression for the land of the Chams. Judging by their language these Chams belonged to the Malay-Polynesian group and their distribution along the littoral suggests that they were invaders from the sea like the Malay pirates from whom they themselves subsequently suffered. The earliest inscription in the Cham language dates from the beginning of the ninth century but it is preceded by a long series of Sanskrit inscriptions the oldest of which, that of Vo-can[1], is attributed at latest to the third century, and refers to an earlier king. It therefore seems probable that the Hindu dynasty of Champa was founded between 150 and 200 A.D. but there is no evidence to show whether a Malay race already settled in Champa was conquered and hinduized by Indian invaders, or whether the Chams were already hinduized when they arrived, possibly from Java.

The inferiority of the Chams to the Khmers in civilization was the result of their more troubled history. Both countries had to contend against the same difficulty—a powerful and aggressive neighbour on either side. Camboja between Siam and Annam in 1800 was in very much the same position as Champa had been between Camboja and Annam five hundred years earlier. But between 950 and 1150 A.D. when Champa by no means enjoyed stability and peace, the history of Camboja, if not altogether tranquil, at least records several long reigns of powerful kings who were able to embellish their capital and assure its security. The Chams were exposed to attacks not only

[1] *Corpus*, II. p. 11, and Finot, *Notes d'Épig.* pp. 227 ff.

from Annam but also from the more formidable if distant Chinese and their capital, instead of remaining stationary through several centuries like Angkor Thom, was frequently moved as one or other of the three provinces became more important.

The inscription of Vo-can is in correct Sanskrit prose and contains a fragmentary address from a king who seems to have been a Buddhist and writes somewhat in the style of Asoka. He boasts that he is of the family of Śrîmâraràja. The letters closely resemble those of Rudradaman's inscription at Girnar and contemporary inscriptions at Kanheri. The text is much mutilated so that we know neither the name of the writer nor his relationship to Śrîmâra. But the latter was evidently the founder of the dynasty and may have been separated from his descendant by several generations. It is noticeable that his name does not end in Varman, like those of later kings. If he lived at the end of the second century this would harmonize with the oldest Chinese notices which fix the rise of Lin-I (their name for Champa) about 192 A.D.[1] Agreeably to this we also hear that Hun T'ien founded an Indian kingdom in Fu-nan considerably before 265 A.D. and that some time between 220 and 280 a king of Fu-nan sent an embassy to India. The name Fu-nan may include Champa. But though we hear of Hindu kingdoms in these districts at an early date we know nothing of their civilization or history, nor do we obtain much information from those Cham legends which represent the dynasties of Champa as descended from two clans, those of the cabbage palm (aréquier) and cocoanut.

Chinese sources also state that a king called Fan-yi sent an embassy to China in 284 and give the names of several kings who reigned between 336 and 440. One of these, Fan-hu-ta, is apparently the Bhadravarman who has left some Sanskrit inscriptions dating from about 400 and who built the first temple at Mĩ-so'n. This became the national sanctuary of Champa: it was burnt down about 575 A.D. but rebuilt. Bhadravarman's son Gangarâja appears to have abdicated and to have gone on a pilgrimage to the Ganges[2]—another instance of the intercourse prevailing between these regions and India.

[1] See authorities quoted by Maspéro, *T'oung Pao*, 1910, p. 329.

[2] Finot in *B.E.F.E.O.* 1904, pp. 918 and 922.

It would be useless to follow in detail the long chronicle of the kings of Champa but a few events merit mention. In 446 and again in 605 the Chinese invaded the country and severely chastised the inhabitants. But the second invasion was followed by a period of peace and prosperity. Śambhuvarman († 629) restored the temples of Mi-so'n and two of his successors, both called Vikrântavarman, were also great builders. The kings who reigned from 758 to 859, reckoned as the fifth dynasty, belonged to the south and had their capital at Vîrapura. The change seems to have been important, for the Chinese who had previously called the country Lin-I, henceforth call it Huan-wang. The natives continued to use the name Champa but Satyavarman and the other kings of the dynasty do not mention Mi-so'n though they adorned and endowed Po-nagar and other sanctuaries in the south. It was during this period (A.D. 774 and 787) that the province of Kauthâra was invaded by pirates, described as thin black barbarians and cannibals, and also as the armies of Java[1]. They pillaged the temples but were eventually expelled. They were probably Malays but it is difficult to believe that the Javanese could be seriously accused of cannibalism at this period[2].

The capital continued to be transferred under subsequent dynasties. Under the sixth (860–900) it was at Indrapura in the north: under the seventh (900–986) it returned to the south: under the eighth (989–1044) it was in Vijaya, the central province. These internal changes were accompanied by foreign attacks. The Khmers invaded the southern province in 945. On the north an Annamite Prince founded the kingdom of Dai-cô-viêt, which became a thorn in the side of Champa. In 982 its armies destroyed Indrapura, and in 1044 they captured Vijaya. In 1069 King Rudravarman was taken prisoner but was released in return for the cession of the three northernmost provinces. Indrapura however was rebuilt and for a time successful wars were waged against Camboja, but though the kings of Champa did not acquiesce in the loss of the northern provinces, and

[1] *Corpus*, II. *Stêle de Po Nagar*, pp. 252 ff. and *Stêle de Yang Tikuh*, p. 208, etc.

[2] The statements that they came from Java and were cannibals occur in different inscriptions and may conceivably refer to two bodies of invaders. But the dates are very near. Probably Java is not the island now so called. See the chapter on Camboja, sec. 2. The undoubted references in the inscriptions of Champa to the island of Java call it Yavadvîpa.

though Harivarman III (1074–80) was temporarily victorious, no real progress was made in the contest with Annam, whither the Chams had to send embassies practically admitting that they were a vassal state. In the next century further disastrous quarrels with Camboja ensued and in 1192 Champa was split into two kingdoms, Vijaya in the north under a Cambojan prince and Panran in the south governed by a Cham prince but under the suzerainty of Camboja. This arrangement was not successful and after much fighting Champa became a Khmer province though a very unruly one from 1203 till 1220. Subsequently the aggressive vigour of the Khmers was tempered by their own wars with Siam. But it was not the fate of Champa to be left in peace. The invasion of Khubilai lasted from 1278 to 1285 and in 1306 the provinces of Ô and Ly were ceded to Annam.

Champa now became for practical purposes an Annamite province and in 1318 the king fled to Java for refuge. This connection with Java is interesting and there are other instances of it. King Jaya Simhavarman III († 1307) of Champa married a Javanese princess called Tapasi. Later we hear in Javanese records that in the fifteenth century the princess Darawati of Champa married the king of Madjapahit and her sister married Raden Radmat, a prominent Moslim teacher in Java[1].

The power of the Chams was crushed by Annam in 1470. After this date they had little political importance but continued to exist as a nationality under their own rulers. In 1650 they revolted against Annam without success and the king was captured. But his widow was accorded a titular position and the Cham chronicle[2] continues the list of nominal kings down to 1822.

In Champa, as in Camboja, no books dating from the Hindu period have been preserved and probably there were not many. The Cham language appears not to have been used for literary purposes and whatever culture existed was exclusively Sanskrit. The kings are credited with an extensive knowledge of Sanskrit literature. An inscription at Po-nagar[3] (918 A.D.) says that Śrî Indravarman was acquainted with the Mîmâṃsâ and other

[1] *Veth. Java*, I. p. 233.

[2] See "La Chronique Royale," *B.E.F.E.O.* 1905, p. 377.

[3] *Corpus*, II. p. 259. Jinendra may be a name either of the Buddha or of a grammarian. The mention of the Kâśikâ vṛitti is important as showing that this work must be anterior to the ninth century. The Uttara Kalpa is quoted in the Tantras (see Bergaigne's note), but nothing is known of it.

systems of philosophy, Jinendra, and grammar together with the Kâśikâ (vṛitti) and the Śaivottara-Kalpa. Again an inscription of Mi-son[1] ascribes to Jaya Indravarmadeva (*c.* 1175 A.D.) proficiency in all the sciences as well as a knowledge of the Mahâyâna and the Dharmaśâstras, particularly the Nâradîya and Bhârgavîya. To some extent original compositions in Sanskrit must have been produced, for several of the inscriptions are of considerable length and one[2] gives a quotation from a work called the Purâṇârtha or Arthapurâṇaśâstra which appears to have been a chronicle of Champa. But the language of the inscriptions is often careless and incorrect and indicates that the study of Sanskrit was less flourishing than in Camboja.

2

The monuments of Champa, though considerable in size and number, are inferior to those of Camboja. The individual buildings are smaller and simpler and the groups into which they are combined lack unity. Brick was the chief material, stone being used only when brick would not serve, as for statues and lintels. The commonest type of edifice is a square pyramidal structure called by the Chams Kalan. A Kalan is as a rule erected on a hill or rising ground: its lowest storey has on the east a porch and vestibule, on the other three sides false doors. The same shape is repeated in four upper storeys of decreasing size which however serve merely for external decoration and correspond to nothing in the interior. This is a single windowless pyramidal cell lighted by the door and probably also by lamps placed in niches on the inner walls. In the centre stood a pedestal for a linga or an image, with a channel to carry off libations, leading to a spout in the wall. The outline of the tower is often varied by projecting figures or ornaments, but the sculpture is less lavish than in Camboja and Java.

In the greater religious sites several structures are grouped together. A square wall surrounds an enclosure entered by a gateway and containing one or more Kalans, as well as smaller buildings, probably for the use of priests. Before the gateway there is frequently a hall supported by columns but open at the sides.

[1] *B.E.F E.O.* 1904, p. 973.

[2] From Mi-son, date 1157 A.D. See *B.E.F.E.O.* 1904, pp. 961 and 963.

All known specimens of Cham architecture are temples; palaces and other secular buildings were made of wood and have disappeared. Of the many sanctuaries which have been discovered, the most remarkable are those of Mi-son, and Dong Duong, both in the neighbourhood of Tourane, and Po Nagar close to Nhatrang.

Mi-son[1] is an undulating amphitheatre among mountains and contains eight or nine groups of temples, founded at different times. The earliest structures, erected by Bhadravarman I about 400, have disappeared[2] and were probably of wood, since we hear that they were burnt (apparently by an accident) in 575 A.D. New temples were constructed by Śambhuvarman about twenty-five years later and were dedicated to Śambhubhadreśvara, in which title the names of the founder, restorer and the deity are combined. These buildings, of which portions remain, represent the oldest and best period of Cham art. Another style begins under Vikrântavarman I between 657 and 679 A.D. This reign marks a period of decadence and though several buildings were erected at Mi-son during the eighth and ninth centuries, the locality was comparatively neglected[3] until the reign of Harivarman III (1074–1080). The temples had been ravaged by the Annamites but this king, being a successful warrior, was able to restore them and dedicated to them the booty which he had captured. Though his reign marks a period of temporary prosperity in the annals of Champa, the style which he inaugurated in architecture has little originality. It reverts to the ancient forms but shows conscious archaism rather than fresh vigour. The position of Mi-son, however, did not decline and about 1155 Jaya Harivarman I repaired the buildings, dedicated the booty taken in battle and erected a new temple in fulfilment of a vow. But after this period the princes of Champa had no authority in the district of Mi-son, and the Annamites, who seem to have disliked the religion of the Chams, plundered the temples.

[1] =Chinese Mei shan, beautiful mountain. For an account of the temples and their history see the articles by Parmentier and Finot, *B.E.F.E.O.* 1904, pp. 805–977.

[2] But contemporary inscriptions have been discovered. *B.E.F.E.O.* 1902, pp. 185 ff.

[3] Doubtless because the capital was transferred to the south where the shrine of Po-nagar had rival claims.

Po-nagar[1] is near the port of Nha-trang and overlooks the sea. Being smaller that Mi-son it has more unity but still shows little attempt to combine in one architectural whole the buildings of which it is composed.

An inscription[2] states with curious precision that the shrine was first erected in the year 5911 of the Dvâpara age and this fantastic chronology shows that in our tenth century it was regarded as ancient. As at Mi-son, the original buildings were probably of wood for in 774 they were sacked and burnt by pirates who carried off the image[3]. Shortly afterwards they were rebuilt in brick by King Satyavarman and the existing southern tower probably dates from his reign, but the great central tower was built by Harivarman I (817 A.D.) and the other edifices are later.

Po Nagar or Yang Po Nagar means the Lady or Goddess of the city. She was commonly called Bhagavatî in Sanskrit[4] and appears to have been the chief object of worship at Nha-trang, although Śiva was associated with her under the name of Bhagavatîśvara. In 1050 an ardhanarî image representing Śiva and Bhagavatî combined in one figure was presented to the temple by King Parameśvara and a dedicatory inscription describes this double deity as the cosmic principle.

When Champa was finally conquered the temple was sold to the Annamites, who admitted that they could not acquire it except by some special and peaceful arrangement. Even now they still continue the worship of the goddess though they no longer know who she is[5].

Dong Duong, about twenty kilometres to the south of Mi-son, marks the site of the ancient capital Indrapura. The monument which has made its name known differs from those already described. Compared with them it has some pretensions to be a whole, laid out on a definite plan and it is Buddhist. It consists of three courts[6] surrounded by walls and entered by massive porticoes. In the third there are about twenty buildings

[1] See especially the article by Parmentier, *B.E.F.E.O.* 1902, pp. 17–54.

[2] XXVI *Corpus*, II. pp. 244, 256; date 918 A.D.

[3] Śivamukham: probably a mukhalinga.

[4] Also Yāpunagara even in Sanskrit inscriptions.

[5] Parmentier, *l.c.* p. 49.

[6] This is only a very rough description of a rather complicated structure. For details see Parmentier, *Monuments Čams*, planche XCVIII.

and perhaps it did not escape the fault common to Cham architecture of presenting a collection of disconnected and unrelated edifices, but still there is clearly an attempt to lead up from the outermost portico through halls and gateways to the principal shrine. From an inscription dated 875 A.D. we learn that the ruins are those of a temple and vihâra erected by King Indravarman and dedicated to Avalokita under the name of Lakshmîndra Lokeśvara.

3

The religion of Champa was practically identical with that of Camboja. If the inscriptions of the former tell us more about mukhalingas and koshas and those of the latter have more allusions to the worship of the compound deity Hari-hara, this is probably a matter of chance. But even supposing that different cults were specially prominent at different places, it seems clear that all the gods and ceremonies known in Camboja were also known in Champa and *vice versa*. In both countries the national religion was Hinduism, mainly of the Śivaite type, accompanied by Mahayanist Buddhism which occasionally came to the front under royal patronage. In both any indigenous beliefs which may have existed did not form a separate system. It is probable however that the goddess known at Po-nagar as Bhagavatî was an ancient local deity worshipped before the Hindu immigration and an inscription found at Mi-son recommends those whose eyes are diseased to propitiate Kuvera and thus secure protection against Ekâkshapingalâ, "the tawny one-eyed (spirit)." Though this goddess or demon was probably a creation of local fancy, similar identifications of Kâlî with the spirits presiding over cholera, smallpox, etc., take place in India.

The social system was theoretically based on the four castes, but Chinese accounts indicate that in questions of marriage and inheritance older ideas connected with matriarchy and a division into clans still had weight. But the language of the inscriptions is most orthodox. King Vikrântavarman[1] quotes with approval the saying that the horse sacrifice is the best of good deeds and the murder of a Brahman the worst of sins. Brahmans, chaplains (purohita), pandits and ascetics are frequently mentioned

[1] Inscrip. at Mi-son of 658 A.D. See *B.E.F.E.O.* 1904, p. 921.

as worthy of honour and gifts. The high priest or royal chaplain is styled Śrîparamapurohita but it does not appear that there was a sacerdotal family enjoying the unique position held by the Śivakaivalyas in Camboja. The frequent changes of capital and dynasty in Champa were unfavourable to continuity in either Church or State.

Śivaism, without any hostility to Vishṇuism or Buddhism, was the dominant creed. The earliest known inscription, that of Vo-can, contains indications of Buddhism, but three others believed to date from about 400 A.D. invoke Śiva under some such title as Bhadreśvara, indicating that a temple had been dedicated to him by King Bhadravarman. Thus the practice of combining the names of a king and his patron deity in one appellation existed in Champa at this early date[1]. It is also recorded from southern India, Camboja and Java. Besides Śiva one of the inscriptions venerates, though in a rather perfunctory manner, Umâ, Brahmâ, Vishṇu and the five elements. Several inscriptions[2] give details of Śivaite theology which agree with what we know of it in Camboja. The world animate and inanimate is an emanation from Śiva, but he delivers from the world those who think of him. Meditation, the practice of Yoga, and devotion to Śiva are several times mentioned with approval[3]. He abides in eight forms corresponding to his eight names Śarva, Bhava, Paśupati, Îśâna, Bhîma, Rudra, Mahâdeva, and Ugra. He is also, as in Java, Guru or the teacher and he has the usual mythological epithets. He dances in lonely places, he rides on the bull Nandi, is the slayer of Kâma, etc. Though represented by figures embodying such legends he was most commonly adored under the form of the linga which in Champa more than elsewhere came to be regarded as not merely symbolic but as a personal god. To mark this individuality it was commonly enclosed in a metal case (kosha) bearing one or more human faces[4]. It was then called mukhalinga and the

[1] Other examples are Indrabhadreśvara, *Corpus*, II. p. 208. Harivarmeśvara, *B.E.F.E.O.* 1904, p. 961.

[2] *E.g.* *B.E.F.E.O.* pp. 918 ff. Dates 658 A.D. onwards.

[3] Yogaddhyâna, Śivârâdha, Śivabhakti. See *B.E.F.E.O.* 1904, pp. 933–950. Harivarman III abdicated in 1080 and gave himself up to contemplation and devotion to Śiva.

[4] See *B.E.F.E.O.* 1904, pp. 912 ff. and esp. p. 970. I have seen a kosha which is still in use in the neighbourhood of Badami. It is kept in a village called Nandike-

faces were probably intended as portraits of royal donors, identified with the god in form as well as in name. An inscription of 1163 A.D. records the dedication of such a kosha, adorned with five royal faces, to Śrîśânabhadreśvara. The god, it is said, will now be able to give his blessing to all regions through his five mouths which he could not do before, and being enclosed in the kosha, like an embryo in the matrix, he becomes Hiraṇyagarbha. The linga, with or without these ornaments, was set on a *snânadroṇi* or stone table arranged for receiving libations, and sometimes (as in Java and Camboja) four or more lingas were set upon a single slab. From A.D. 400 onwards, the cult of Śiva seems to have maintained its paramount position during the whole history of Champa, for the last recorded Sanskrit inscription is dedicated to him. From first to last it was the state religion. Śiva is said to have sent Uroja to be the first king and is even styled the root of the state of Champa.

An inscription[1] of 811 A.D. celebrates the dual deity Śankara-Nârâyaṇa. It is noticeable that Nârâyaṇa is said to have held up Mt Govardhana and is apparently identified with Kṛishṇa. Râma and Kṛishṇa are both mentioned in an inscription of 1157 which states that the whole divinity of Vishṇu was incarnate in King Jaya Harivarman I[2]. But neither allusions to Vishṇu nor figures of him[3] are numerous and he plays the part of an accessory though respected personage. Garuḍa, on whom he rides, was better known than the god himself and is frequently represented in sculpture.

The Śakti of Śiva, amalgamated as mentioned with a native goddess, received great honour (especially at Nhatrang) under the names of Umâ, Bhagavatî, the Lady of the city (Yang Po Nagar) and the goddess of Kauthâra. In another form or aspect

śvara, but on certain festivals it is put on a linga at the temple of Mahakut. It is about 2 feet high and 10 inches broad; a silver case with a rounded and ornamented top. On one side is a single face in bold embossed work and bearing fine moustaches exactly as in the mukhalingas of Champa. In the tank of the temple of Mahakut is a half submerged shrine, from which rises a stone linga on which are carved four faces bearing moustaches. There is said to be a gold kosha set with jewels at Śringeri. See *J. Mythic. Society* (Bangalore), vol. VIII. p. 27. According to Gopinatha Rao, *Indian Iconography*, vol. II. p. 63, the oldest known lingas have figures carved on them.

[1] *Corpus*, II. pp. 229, 230.

[2] *B.E.F.E.O.* 1904, pp. 959, 960.

[3] See for an account of same *B.E.F.E.O.* 1901, p. 18.

she was called Maladâkuṭhâra[1]. There was also a temple of Ganeśa (Śrî-Vinâyaka) at Nhatrang but statues of this deity and of Skanda are rare.

The Chinese pilgrim I-Ching, writing in the last year of the seventh century, includes Champa (Lin-I) in the list of countries which "greatly reverence the three jewels" and contrasts it with Fu-nan where a wicked king had recently almost exterminated Buddhism. He says "In this country Buddhists generally belong to the Ârya-sammiti school, and there are also a few followers of the Âryasarvâstivâdin school." The statement is remarkable, for he also tells us that the Sarvâstivâdins were the predominant sect in the Malay Archipelago and flourished in southern China. The headquarters of the Sammitîyas were, according to the accounts of both Hsüan Chuang and I-Ching, in western India though, like the three other schools, they were also found in Magadha and eastern India. We also hear that the brother and sister of the Emperor Harsha belonged to this sect and it was probably influential. How it spread to Champa we do not know, nor do the inscriptions mention its name or indicate that the Buddhism which they knew was anything but the mixture of the Mahayana with Śivaism[2] which prevailed in Camboja.

I-Ching's statements can hardly be interpreted to mean that Buddhism was the official religion of Champa at any rate after 400 A.D., for the inscriptions abundantly prove that the Śivaite shrines of Mi-son and Po-nagar were so to speak national cathedrals where the kings worshipped on behalf of the country. But the Vo-can inscription (? 250 A.D.), though it does not mention Buddhism, appears to be Buddhist, and it would be quite natural that a dynasty founded about 150 A.D. should be Buddhist but that intercourse with Camboja and probably with India should strengthen Śivaism. The Chinese annals mention[3] that 1350 Buddhist books were carried off during a Chinese invasion in 605 A.D. and this allusion implies the existence of Buddhism and monasteries with libraries. As in Camboja it was

[1] *Corpus*, II. p. 282.

[2] In several passages Hsüan Chuang notes that there were Pâśupatas or other Śivaites in the same towns of India where Sammitiyas were found. See Watters, *Yüan Chwang*, I. 331, 333; II. 47, 242, 256, 258, 259.

[3] Maspéro, *T'oung Pao*, 1910, p. 514.

perhaps followed by ministers rather than by kings. An inscription found[1] in southern Champa and dated as 829 A.D. records how a sthavira named Buddhanirvâṇa erected two vihâras and two temples (devakula) to Jina and Śankara (Buddha and Śiva) in honour of his deceased father. Shortly afterwards there came to the throne Indravarman II (860–890 A.D.), the only king of Champa who is known to have been a fervent Buddhist. He did not fail to honour Śiva as the patron of his kingdom but like Asoka he was an enthusiast for the Dharma[2]. He desires the knowledge of the Dharma: he builds monasteries for the sake of the Dharma: he wishes to propagate it: he even says that the king of the gods governs heaven by the principles of Dharma. He wishes to lead all his subjects to the "yoke and abode of Buddha," to "the city of deliverance."

To this end he founded the vihâra of Dong Duong, already described, and dedicated it to Śri Lakshmîndra Lokeśvara[3]. This last word is a synonym of Avalokita, which also occurs in the dedicatory inscription but in a fragmentary passage. Lakshmîndra is explained by other passages in the inscription from which we learn that the king's name before he ascended the throne was Lakshmîndra Bhûmîśvara, so that the Bodhisattva is here adored under the name of the king who erected the vihâra according to the custom prevalent in Śivaite temples. Like those temples this vihâra received an endowment of land and slaves of both sexes, as well as gold, silver and other metals[4].

A king who reigned from 1080 to 1086 was called Paramabodhisattva, but no further epigraphic records of Buddhism are known until the reigns of Jaya Indravarmadeva (1167–1192) and his successor Sûryavarmadeva[5]. Both of these monarchs, while worshipping Śiva, are described as knowing or practising the jñâna or dharma of the Mahayana. Little emphasis seems to be laid on these expressions but still they imply that the

[1] At Yang Kur. See *Corpus*, II. pp. 237–241.

[2] For his views see his inscriptions in *B.E.F.E.O.* 1904, pp. 85 ff. But kings who are not known to have been Buddhists also speak of Dharma. *B.E.F.E.O.* 1904, pp. 922, 945.

[3] Apparently special forms of deities such as Śrîśânabhadreśvara or Lakshmînda Lokeśvara were regarded as to some extent separate existences. Thus the former is called a portion of Śiva, *B.E.F.E.O.* 1904, p. 973.

[4] Presumably in the form of vessels.

[5] *B.E.F.E.O.* 1904, pp. 973–975.

Mahayana was respected and considered part of the royal religion. Sûryavarmadeva erected a building called Śrî Heruka-harmya[1]. The title is interesting for it contains the name of the Tantric Buddha Heruka.

The grotto of Phong-nha[2] in the extreme north of Champa (province of Quang Binh) must have been a Buddhist shrine. Numerous medallions in clay bearing representations of Buddhas, Bodhisattvas and Dagobas have been found there but dates are wanting.

It does not appear that the Hinayanist influence which became predominant in Camboja extended to Champa. That influence came from Siam and before it had time to traverse Camboja, Champa was already in the grip of the Annamites, whose religion with the rest of their civilization came from China rather than India. Chinese culture and writing spread to the Cambojan frontier and after the decay of Champa, Camboja marks the permanent limit within which an Indian alphabet and a form of Buddhism not derived through China have maintained themselves.

A large number of the Chams were converted to Mohammedanism but the time and circumstances of the event are unknown. When Friar Gabriel visited the country at the end of the sixteenth century a form of Hinduism seems to have been still prevalent[3]. It would be of interest to know how the change of religion was effected, for history repeats itself and it is likely that the Moslims arrived in Champa by the route followed centuries before by the Hindu invaders.

There are still about 130,000 Chams in the south of Annam and Camboja. In the latter country they are all Mohammedans. In Annam some traces of Hinduism remain, such as mantras in broken Sanskrit and hereditary priests called Baśaih. Both religions have become unusually corrupt but are interesting as showing how beliefs which are radically distinct become distorted and combined in Eastern Asia[4].

[1] *B.E.F.E.O.* 1904, p. 975.

[2] *Ib.* 1901, p. 23, and Parmentier, *Inventaire des Monuments Chams*, p. 542.

[3] Gabriel de San Antonio, *Breve y verdadera relation de los successos de Reyno de Camboxa*, 1604.

[4] See for the modern Chams the article "Chams" in *E.R.E. and Ethics*, and Durand, "Les Chams Bani," *B.E.F.E.O.* 1903, and "Notes sur les Chams," *ib.* 1905–7.

CHAPTER XL

JAVA AND THE MALAY ARCHIPELAGO

1

In most of the countries which we have been considering, the native civilization of the present day is still Indian in origin, although in the former territories of Champa this Indian phase has been superseded by Chinese culture with a little Mohammedanism. But in another area we find three successive stages of culture, indigenous, Indian and Mohammedan. This area includes the Malay Peninsula with a large part of the Malay Archipelago, and the earliest stratum with which we need concern ourselves is Malay. The people who bear this name are remarkable for their extraordinary powers of migration by sea, as shown by the fact that languages connected with Malay are spoken in Formosa and New Zealand, in Easter Island and Madagascar, but their originality both in thought and in the arts of life is small. The three stages are seen most clearly in Java where the population was receptive and the interior accessible. Sumatra and Borneo also passed through them in a fashion but the indigenous element is still predominant and no foreign influence has been able to affect either island as a whole. Islam gained no footing in Bali which remains curiously Hindu but it reached Celebes and the southern Philippines, in both of which Indian influence was slight[1]. The destiny of south-eastern Asia with its islands depends on the fact that the tide of trade and conquest whether Hindu, Moslim or European, flowed from India or Ceylon to the Malay Peninsula and Java and thence northwards towards China with a reflux westwards in Champa and Camboja. Burma and Siam lay outside this track. They received their culture from India mainly by land and were untouched by Mohammedanism. But the Mohammedan current

[1] I have not been able to find anything more than casual and second-hand statements to the effect that Indian antiquities have been found in these islands.

which affected the Malays was old and continuous. It started from Arabia in the early days of the Hijra and had nothing to do with the Moslim invasions which entered India by land.

2

Indian civilization appears to have existed in Java from at least the fifth century of our era[1]. Much light has been thrown on its history of late by the examination of inscriptions and of fairly ancient literature but the record still remains fragmentary. There are considerable gaps: the seat of power shifted from one district to another and at most epochs the whole island was not subject to one ruler, so that the title king of Java merely indicates a prince pre-eminent among others doubtfully subordinate to him.

The name Java is probably the Sanskrit *Yava* used in the sense of grain, especially millet. In the Ramayana[2] the monkeys of Hanuman are bidden to seek for Sîtâ in various places including Yava-dvîpa, which contains seven kingdoms and produces gold and silver. Others translate these last words as referring to another or two other islands known as Gold and Silver Land. It is probable that the poet did not distinguish clearly between Java and Sumatra. He goes on to say that beyond Java is the peak called Śiśira. This is possibly the same as the Yavakoṭi mentioned in 499 A.D. by the Indian astronomer Âryabhaṭṭa.

[1] There is no lack of scholarly and scientific works about Java, but they are mostly written in Dutch and dissertations on special points are more numerous than general surveys of Javanese history, literature and architecture. Perhaps the best general account of the Hindu period in Java will be found in the chapter contributed by Kern to the publication called *Neerlands Indië* (Amsterdam, 1911, chap. VI. II. pp. 219–242). The abundant publications of the Bataviaasch Genootschap van Kunsten en Wetenschappen comprise *Verhandelingen*, *Notulen*, and the *Tijdschrift voor Indische Taal-, Land-, en Volkenkunde* (cited here as *Tijdschrift*), all of which contain numerous and important articles on history, philology, religion and archæology. The last is treated specially in the publications called *Archaeologisch Onderzoek op Java en Madura*. Veth's *Java*, vols. I. and IV. and various articles in the *Encyclopaedie van Nederlandsch-Indië* may also be consulted. I have endeavoured to mention the more important editions of Javanese books as well as works dealing specially with the old religion in the notes to these chapters.

Although Dutch orthography is neither convenient nor familiar to most readers I have thought it better to preserve it in transcribing Javanese. In this system of transcription j = y; tj = ch; dj = j; sj = sh; w = v; oe = u.

[2] Râm. IV. 40, 30. Yavadvipam saptarâjyopaśobhitam Suvarṇarûpyakadvipam suvarṇakaramaṇḍitam.

Since the Ramayana is a product of gradual growth it is not easy to assign a definite date to this passage, but it is probably not later than the first or second century A.D. and an early date is rendered probable by the fact that the Alexandrian Geographer Ptolemy (*c.* 130 A.D.) mentions[1] Νῆσος Ἰαβαδίου ἢ Σαβαδίου and by various notices collected from inscriptions and from Chinese historians. The annals of the Liang Dynasty (502–556 A.D.) in speaking of the countries of the Southern Ocean say that in the reign of Hsüan Ti (73–49 B.C.) the Romans and Indians sent envoys to China by that route[2], thus indicating that the Archipelago was frequented by Hindus. The same work describes under the name of Lang-ya-hsiu a country which professed Buddhism and used the Sanskrit language and states that "the people say that their country was established more than 400 years ago[3]." Lang-ya-hsiu has been located by some in Java by others in the Malay Peninsula, but even on the latter supposition this testimony to Indian influence in the Far East is still important. An inscription found at Kedah in the Malay Peninsula is believed to be older than 400 A.D.[4] No more definite accounts are forthcoming before the fifth or sixth century. Fa-Hsien[5] relates how in 418 he returned to China from India by sea and "arrived at a country called Ya-va-di." "In this country" he says "heretics and Brahmans flourish but the law of Buddha hardly deserves mentioning[6]." Three inscriptions found in west Java in the district of Buitenzorg are referred for palæographic reasons to about 400 A.D. They are all in Sanskrit and eulogize a prince named Pûrṇavarman, who appears to have been a Vishnuite. The name of his capital is

[1] Ptolemy's *Geography*, VII. 2. 29 (see also VIII. 27, 10). Ἰαβαδίου (ἢ Σαβαδίου), ὃ σημαίνει κριθῆς, νῆσος. Εὐφορωτάτη δὲ λέγεται ἡ νῆσος εἶναι καὶ ἔτι πλεῖστον χρυσὸν ποιεῖν, ἔχειν τε μητρόπολιν ὄνομα Ἀργυρῆν ἐπὶ τοῖς δυσμικοῖς πέρασιν.

[2] The Milinda Pañhâ of doubtful but not very late date also mentions voyages to China.

[3] Groeneveldt, *Notes on the Malay Archipelago compiled from Chinese sources*, 1876 (cited below as Groeneveldt), p. 10. Confirmed by the statement in the Ming annals book 324 that in 1432 the Javanese said their kingdom had been founded 1376 years before.

[4] Kern in *Versl. en Med. K. Ak. v. W. Afd. Lett.* 3 *Rks.* I. 1884, pp. 5–12.

[5] Chap. XL. Legge, p. 113, and Groeneveldt, pp. 6–9.

[6] He perhaps landed in the present district of Rembang "where according to native tradition the first Hindu settlement was situated at that time" (Groeneveldt, p. 9).

deciphered as Narumâ or Tarumâ. In 435 according to the Liu Sung annals[1] a king of Ja-va-da named Shih-li-pa-da-do-a-la-pa-mo sent tribute to China. The king's name probably represents a Sanskrit title beginning with Śrî-Pâda and it is noticeable that two footprints are carved on the stones which bear Pûrṇavarman's inscriptions. Also Sanskrit inscriptions found at Koetei on the east coast of Borneo and considered to be not later than the fifth century record the piety and gifts to Brahmans of a King Mûlavarman and mention his father and grandfather[2].

It follows from these somewhat disjointed facts that the name of Yava-dvîpa was known in India soon after the Christian era, and that by the fifth century Hindu or hinduized states had been established in Java. The discovery of early Sanskrit inscriptions in Borneo and Champa confirms the presence of Hindus in these seas. The T'ang annals[3] speak definitely of Kaling, otherwise called Java, as lying between Sumatra and Bali and say that the inhabitants have letters and understand a little astronomy. They further mention the presence of Arabs and say that in 674 a queen named Sima ascended the throne and ruled justly.

But the certain data for Javanese history before the eighth century are few. For that period we have some evidence from Java itself. An inscription dated 654 Śaka (= 732 A.D.) discovered in Kĕdoe celebrates the praises of a king named Sanjaya, son of King Sanna. It contains an account of the dedication of a linga, invocations of Śiva, Brahmâ and Vishṇu, a eulogy of the king's virtue and learning, and praise of Java. Thus about 700 A.D. there was a Hindu kingdom in mid Java and this, it would seem, was then the part of the island most important politically. Buddhist inscriptions of a somewhat later date (one is of 778 A.D.) have been found in the neighbourhood of Prambânam. They are written in the Nagari alphabet and record various pious foundations. A little later again (809 and 840 A.D.) are the inscriptions found on the Dieng (Dihyang), a

[1] Groeneveldt, p. 9. The transcriptions of Chinese characters given in the following pages do not represent the modern sound but seem justified (though they cannot be regarded as certain) by the instances collected in Julien's *Méthode pour déchiffrer et transcrire les noms sanscrits.* Possibly the syllables Do-a-lo-pa-mo are partly corrupt and somehow or other represent Pûrṇavarman.

[2] Kern in *Versl. en Meded. Afd. Lett.* 2 *R.* XI. *D.* 1882.

[3] Groeneveldt, pp. 12, 13.

lonely mountain plateau on which are several Brahmanic shrines in fair preservation. There is no record of their builders but the New T'ang Annals say that the royal residence was called Java but "on the mountains is the district Lang-pi-ya where the king frequently goes to look at the sea[1]." This may possibly be a reference to pilgrimages to Dieng. The inscriptions found on the great monument of Boroboedoer throw no light on the circumstances of its foundation, but the character of the writing makes it likely that it was erected about 850 and obviously by a king who could command the services of numerous workmen as well as of skilled artists. The temples of Prambânam are probably to be assigned to the next century. All these buildings indicate the existence from the eighth to the tenth century of a considerable kingdom (or perhaps kingdoms) in middle Java, comprising at least the regions of Mataram, Kĕdoe and the Dieng plateau. From the Arabic geographers also we learn that Java was powerful in the ninth century and attacked Qamar (probably Khmer or Camboja). They place the capital at the mouth of a river, perhaps the Solo or Brantas. If so, there must have been a principality in east Java at this period. This is not improbable for archæological evidence indicates that Hindu civilization moved eastwards and flourished first in the west, then in mid Java and finally from the ninth to the fifteenth centuries in the east.

The evidence at our disposal points to the fact that Java received most of its civilization from Hindu colonists, but who were these colonists and from what part of India did they come? We must not think of any sudden and definite conquest, but rather of a continuous current of immigration starting perhaps from several springs and often merely trickling, but occasionally swelling into a flood. Native traditions collected by Raffles[2] ascribe the introduction of Brahmanism and the Śaka era to the sage Tritresta and represent the invaders as coming from Kalinga or from Gujarat.

The difference of locality may be due to the fact that there was a trade route running from Broach to Masulipatam through Tagara (now Ter). People arriving in the Far East by this route might be described as coming either from Kalinga, where they

[1] Groeneveldt, p. 14.

[2] *History of Java*, vol. II. chap. X.

embarked, or from Gujarat, their country of origin. Dubious as is the authority of these legends, they perhaps preserve the facts in outline. The earliest Javanese inscriptions are written in a variety of the Vengi script and the T'ang annals call the island Kaling as well as Java. It is therefore probable that early tradition represented Kalinga as the home of the Hindu invaders. But later immigrants may have come from other parts. Fa-Hsien could find no Buddhists in Java in 418, but Indian forms of Mahayanism indubitably flourished there in later centuries. The Kalasan inscription dated 778 A.D. and engraved in Nâgari characters records the erection of a temple to Târâ and of a Mahayanist monastery. The change in both alphabet and religion suggests the arrival of new influences from another district and the Javanese traditions about Gujarat are said to find an echo among the bards of western India and in such proverbs as, they who go to Java come not back[1]. In the period of the Hunnish and Arab invasions there may have been many motives for emigration from Gujarat. The land route to Kalinga was probably open and the sea route offers no great difficulties[2].

Another indication of connection with north-western India is found in the Chinese work *Kao Sêng Chuan* (519 A.D.) or *Biographies of Eminent Monks*, if the country there called Shê-p'o can be identified with Java[3]. It is related that Guṇavarman, son of the king of Kashmir, became a monk and, declining the throne, went first to Ceylon and then to the kingdom of Shê-p'o, which he converted to Buddhism. He died at Nanking in 431 B.C.

Târanâtha[4] states that Indo-China which he calls the Koki country[5], was first evangelized in the time of Asoka and that

[1] Jackson, *Java and Cambodja*. App. IV. in *Bombay Gazetteer*, vol. I. part 1, 1896.

[2] It is also possible that when the Javanese traditions speak of Kaling they mean the Malay Peninsula. Indians in those regions were commonly known as Kaling because they came from Kalinga and in time the parts of the Peninsula where they were numerous were also called Kaling.

[3] See for this question Pelliot in *B.E.F.E.O.* 1904, pp. 274 ff. Also Schlegel in *T'oung Pao*, 1899, p. 247, and Chavannes, *ib.* 1904, p. 192.

[4] Chap. XXXIX. Schiefner, p. 262.

[5] Though he expressly includes Camboja and Champa in Koki, it is only right to say that he mentions Nas-gling (= Yava-dvipa) separately in another enumeration together with Ceylon. But if Buddhists passed in any numbers from India to Camboja and *vice versa*, they probably appeared in Java about the same time, or rather later.

Mahayanism was introduced there by the disciples of Vasubandhu, who probably died about 360 A.D., so that the activity of his followers would take place in the fifth century. He also says that many clergy from the Koki country were in Madhyadeśa from the time of Dharmapâla (about 800 A.D.) onwards, and these two statements, if they can be accepted, certainly explain the character of Javanese and Cambojan Buddhism. Târanâtha is a confused and untrustworthy writer, but his statement about the disciples of Vasubandhu is confirmed by the fact that Dignâga, who was one of them, is the only authority cited in the Kamahâyânikan[1].

The fact that the terms connected with rice cultivation are Javanese and not loan-words indicates that the island had some indigenous civilization when the Hindus first settled there. Doubtless they often came with military strength, but on the whole as colonists and teachers rather than as conquerors. The Javanese kings of whom we know most appear to have been not members of Hindu dynasties but native princes who had adopted Hindu culture and religion. Sanskrit did not oust Javanese as the language of epigraphy, poetry and even religious literature. Javanese Buddhism appears to have preserved its powers of growth and to have developed some special doctrines. But Indian influence penetrated almost all institutions and is visible even to-day. Its existence is still testified to by the alphabet in use, by such titles as Arjo, Radja, Praboe, Dipati (= adhipati), and by various superstitions about lucky days and horoscopes. Communal land tenure of the Indian kind still exists and in former times grants of land were given to priests and, as in India, recorded on copper plates. Offerings to old statues are still made and the Tenggerese[2] are not even nominal Mohammedans. The Balinese still profess a species of Hinduism and employ a Hindu Calendar.

From the tenth century onwards the history of Java becomes a little plainer.

Copper plates dating from about 900 A.D. mention Mataram. A certain Mpoe Sindok was vizier of this kingdom in 919, but ten years later we find him an independent king in east Java.

[1] See Kamaha. pp. 9, 10, and Watters, *Yüan Chwang*, II. pp. 200–214.

[2] They preserve to some extent the old civilization of Madjapahit. See the article "Tengereezen" in *Encyclopaedie van Nederlandsch-Indië.*

He lived at least twenty-five years longer and his possessions included Pa_‾eroean, Soerabaja and Kediri. His great-grandson, Er-langga (or Langghya), is an important figure. Er-langga's early life was involved in war, but in 1032 he was able to call himself, though perhaps not with great correctness, king of all Java. His memory has not endured among the Javanese but is still honoured in the traditions of Bali and Javanese literature began in his reign or a little earlier. The poem Arjuna-vivâha is dedicated to him, and one book of the old Javanese prose translation of the Mahabharata bears a date equivalent to 996 A.D.[1]

One of the national heroes of Java is Djajabaja[2] who is supposed to have lived in the ninth century. But tradition must be wrong here, for the free poetic rendering of part of the Mahabharata called Bhârata-Yuddha, composed by Mpoe Sĕdah in 1157 A.D., is dedicated to him, and his reign must therefore be placed later than the traditional date. He is said to have founded the kingdom of Daha in Kediri, but his inscriptions merely indicate that he was a worshipper of Vishṇu. Literature and art flourished in east Java at this period for it would seem that the Kawi Ramayana and an *ars poetica* called Vṛitta-sañcaya[3] were written about 1150 and that the temple of Panataran was built between 1150 and 1175.

In western Java we have an inscription of 1030 found on the river Tjitjatih. It mentions a prince who is styled Lord of the World and native tradition, confirmed by inscriptions, which however give few details, relates that in the twelfth century a kingdom called Padjadjaran was founded in the Soenda country south of Batavia by princes from Toemapĕl in eastern Java.

There is a gap in Javanese history from the reign of Djajabaja till 1222 at which date the Pararaton[4], or Book of the Kings of Toemapĕl and Madjapahit, begins to furnish information. The Sung annals[5] also give some account of the island but it is not

[1] See Kern, *Kawi-studien Arjuna-vivâha*, I. and II. 1871. Juynboll, *Drie Boeken van het oudjavaansche Mahâbhârata*, 1893, and *id. Wirâtaparwwa*, 1912. This last is dated Śaka 918 = 996 A.D.

[2] Or Jayabaya.

[3] See *Râmâyana. Oudjavaansche Heldendicht*, edited Kern, 1900, and *Vṛtta Sañcaya*, edited and translated by the same, 1875.

[4] Composed in 1613 A.D.

[5] Groeneveldt, p. 14.

clear to what years their description refers. They imply, however, that there was an organized government and that commerce was flourishing. They also state that the inhabitants "pray to the gods and Buddha": that Java was at war with eastern Sumatra: that embassies were sent to China in 992 and 1109 and that in 1129 the Emperor gave the ruler of Java (probably Djajabaja) the title of king.

The Pararaton opens with the fall of Daha in 1222 which made Toemapĕl, known later as Singasari, the principal kingdom. Five of its kings are enumerated, of whom Vishṇuvardhana was buried in the celebrated shrine of Tjandi Djago, where he was represented in the guise of Buddha. His successor Śrî Râjasanâgara was praised by the poet Prapantja[1] as a zealous Buddhist but was known by the posthumous name of Śivabuddha. He was the first to use the name of Singasâri and perhaps founded a new city, but the kingdom of Toemapĕl came to an end in his reign for he was slain by Djaja Katong[2], prince of Daha, who restored to that kingdom its previous primacy, but only for a short time, since it was soon supplanted by Madjapahit. The foundation of this state is connected with a Chinese invasion of Java, related at some length in the Yüan annals[3], so that we are fortunate in possessing a double and fairly consistent account of what occurred.

We learn from these sources that some time after Khubilai Khan had conquered China, he sent missions to neighbouring countries to demand tribute. The Javanese had generally accorded a satisfactory reception to Chinese missions, but on this occasion the king (apparently Djaja Katong) maltreated the envoy and sent him back with his face cut or tattooed. Khubilai could not brook this outrage and in 1292 despatched a punitive expedition. At that time Raden Vidjaja, the son-in-law of Kĕrtanagara, had not submitted to Djaja Katong and held out at Madjapahit, a stronghold which he had founded near the river Brantas. He offered his services to the Chinese and after a two months' campaign Daha was captured and Djaja Katong killed. Raden Vidjaja now found that he no longer

[1] In the work commonly called "Nâgarakrĕtâgama" (ed. Brandes, *Verhand. Bataav. Genootschap.* LIV. 1902), but it is stated that its real name is "Deçawarṇnana." See *Tijdschrift*, LVI. 1914, p. 194.

[2] Or Jayakatong.

[3] Groeneveldt, pp. 20–34.

needed his Chinese allies. He treacherously massacred some and prepared to fight the rest. But the Mongol generals, seeing the difficulties of campaigning in an unknown country without guides, prudently returned to their master and reported that they had taken Daha and killed the insolent king.

Madjapahit (or Wilwatikta) now became the premier state of Java, and had some permanency. Eleven sovereigns, including three queens, are enumerated by the Pararaton until its collapse in 1468. We learn from the Ming annals and other Chinese documents[1] that it had considerable commercial relations with China and sent frequent missions: also that Palembang was a vassal of Java. But the general impression left by the Pararaton is that during the greater part of its existence Madjapahit was a distracted and troubled kingdom. In 1403, as we know from both Chinese and Javanese sources, there began a great war between the western and eastern kingdoms, that is between Madjapahit and Balambangan in the extreme east, and in the fifteenth century there was twice an interregnum. Art and literature, though not dead, declined and events were clearly tending towards a break-up or revolution. This appears to have been consummated in 1468, when the Pararaton simply says that King Paṇḍansalas III left the *Kraton*, or royal residence.

It is curious that the native traditions as to the date and circumstances in which Madjapahit fell should be so vague, but perhaps the end of Hindu rule in Java was less sudden and dramatic than we are inclined to think. Islam had been making gradual progress and its last opponents were kings only in title. The Chinese mention the presence of Arabs in the seventh century, and the geography called *Ying-yai Shêng-lan* (published in 1416), which mentions Grissé, Soerabaja and Madjapahit as the principal towns of Java, divides the inhabitants into three classes: (*a*) Mohammedans who have come from the west, "their dress and food is clean and proper"; (*b*) the Chinese, who are also cleanly and many of whom are Mohammedans; (*c*) the natives who are ugly and uncouth, devil-worshippers, filthy in food and habits. As the Chinese do not generally speak so severely of the hinduized Javanese it would appear that Hinduism lasted longest among the lower and more savage

[1] Groeneveldt, pp. 34–53.

classes, and that the Moslims stood on a higher level. As in other countries, the Arabs attempted to spread Islam from the time of their first appearance. At first they confined their propaganda to their native wives and dependents. Later we hear of veritable apostles of Islam such as Malik Ibrahim, and Raden Rahmat, the ruler of a town called Ampel[1] which became the head quarter of Islam. The princes whose territory lay round Madjapahit were gradually converted and the extinction of the last Hindu kingdom became inevitable[2].

3

It is remarkable that the great island of Sumatra, which seems to lie in the way of anyone proceeding from India eastwards and is close to the Malay peninsula, should in all ages have proved less accessible to invaders coming from the west than the more distant Java. Neither Hindus, Arabs nor Europeans have been able to establish their influence there in the same thorough manner. The cause is probably to be found in its unhealthy and impenetrable jungles, but even so its relative isolation remains singular.

It does not appear that any prince ever claimed to be king of all Sumatra. For the Hindu period we have no indigenous literature and our scanty knowledge is derived from a few statues and inscriptions and from notices in Chinese writings. The latter do not refer to the island as a whole but to several states such as Indragiri near the Equator and Kandali (afterwards called San-bo-tsai, the Sabaza of the Arabs) near Palembang. The annals of the Liang dynasty say that the customs of Kandali were much the same as those of Camboja and apparently we are to understand that the country was Buddhist, for one king visited the Emperor Wu-ti in a dream, and his son addressed a letter to His Majesty eulogizing his devotion to Buddhism. Kandali is said to have sent three envoys to China between 454 and 519.

[1] Near Soerabaja. It is said that he married a daughter of the king of Champa, and that the king of Madjapahit married her sister. For the connection between the royal families of Java and Champa at this period see Maspéro in *T'oung Pao*, 1911, pp. 595 ff., and the references to Champa in Nâgarakrĕtagama, 15, 1, and 83, 4.

[2] See Raffles, chap. x, for Javanese traditions respecting the decline and fall of Madjapahit.

The Chinese pilgrim I-Ching[1] visited Sumatra twice, once for two months in 672 and subsequently for some years (about 688–695). He tells us that in the islands of the Southern Sea, "which are more than ten countries," Buddhism flourishes, the school almost universally followed being the Mûlasarvâstivâda, though the Sammitîyas and other schools have a few adherents. He calls the country where he sojourned and to which these statements primarily refer, Bhoja or Śrîbhoja (Fo-shih or Shih-li-fo-shih), adding that its former name was Malayu. It is conjectured that Shih-li-fo-shih is the place later known as San-bo-tsai[2] and Chinese authors seem to consider that both this place and the earlier Kandali were roughly speaking identical with Palembang. I-Ching tells us that the king of Bhoja favoured Buddhism and that there were more than a thousand priests in the city. Gold was abundant and golden flowers were offered to the Buddha. There was communication by ship with both India and China. The Hinayana, he says, was the form of Buddhism adopted "except in Malayu, where there are a few who belong to the Mahayana." This is a surprising statement, but it is impossible to suppose that an expert like I-Ching can have been wrong about what he actually saw in Śrîbhoja. So far as his remarks apply to Java they must be based on hearsay and have less authority, but the sculptures of Boroboedoer appear to show the influence of Mûlasarvâstivâdin literature. It must be remembered that this school, though nominally belonging to the Hinayana, came to be something very different from the Theravâda of Ceylon.

The Sung annals and subsequent Chinese writers know the same district (the modern Palembang) as San-bo-tsai (which may indicate either mere change of name or the rise of a new city) and say that it sent twenty-one envoys between 960 and 1178. The real object of these missions was to foster trade and there was evidently frequent intercourse between eastern Sumatra, Champa and China. Ultimately the Chinese seem to have thought that the entertainment of Sumatran diplomatists cost more than they were worth, for in 1178 the emperor ordered that they should not come to Court but present themselves in

[1] See Takakusu, *A record of the Buddhist religion*, especially pp. xl to xlvi.

[2] In another pronunciation the characters are read San-fo-chai. The meaning appears to be The Three Buddhas.

the province of Fu-kien. The Annals state that Sanskrit writing was in use at San-bo-tsai and lead us to suppose that the country was Buddhist. They mention several kings whose names or titles seem to begin with the Sanskrit word Śrî[1]. In 1003 the envoys reported that a Buddhist temple had been erected in honour of the emperor and they received a present of bells for it. Another envoy asked for dresses to be worn by Buddhist monks. The Ming annals also record missions from San-bo-tsai up to 1376, shortly after which the region was conquered by Java and the town decayed[2]. In the fourteenth century Chinese writers begin to speak of Su-mên-ta-la or Sumatra by which is meant not the whole island but a state in the northern part of it called Samudra and corresponding to Atjeh[3]. It had relations with China and the manners and customs of its inhabitants are said to be the same as in Malacca, which probably means that they were Moslims.

Little light is thrown on the history of Sumatra by indigenous or Javanese monuments. Those found testify, as might be expected, to the existence here and there of both Brahmanism and Buddhism. In 1343 a Sumatran prince named Âdityavarman, who was apparently a vassal of Madjapahit, erected an image of Manjuśrî at Tjandi Djago and in 1375 one of Amoghapâśa.

4

The Liang and T'ang annals both speak of a country called Po-li, described as an island lying to the south-east of Canton. Groeneveldt identified it with Sumatra, but the account of its position suggests that it is rather to be found in Borneo, parts of which were undoubtedly known to the Chinese as Po-lo and Pu-ni[4]. The Liang annals state that Po-li sent an embassy to the Emperor Wu-ti in 518 bearing a letter which described the

[1] *E.g.* Si-li-ma-ha-la-sha (=Śrîmahârâja) Si-li-tieh-hwa (perhaps =Śrîdeva).

[2] The conquest however was incomplete and about 1400 a Chinese adventurer ruled there some time. The name was changed to Ku-Kang, which is said to be still the Chinese name for Palembang.

[3] The Ming annals expressly state that the name was changed to Atjeh about 1600.

[4] For the identification of Po-li see Groeneveldt, p. 80, and Hose and McDougall, *Pagan Tribes of Borneo*, chap. II. It might be identified with Bali, but it is doubtful if Hindu civilization had spread to that island or even to east Java in the sixth century.

country as devoted to Buddhism and frequented by students of the three vehicles. If the letter is an authentic document the statements in it may still be exaggerations, for the piety of Wu-ti was well known and it is clear that foreign princes who addressed him thought it prudent to represent themselves and their subjects as fervent Buddhists. But there certainly was a Hindu period in Borneo, of which some tradition remains among the natives[1], although it ended earlier and left fewer permanent traces than in Java and elsewhere.

The most important records of this period are three Sanskrit inscriptions found at Koetei on the east coast of Borneo[2]. They record the donations made to Brahmans by King Mûlavarman, son of Aśvavarman and grandson of Kuṇḍagga. They are not dated, but Kern considers for palæographical reasons that they are not later than the fifth century. Thus, since three generations are mentioned, it is probable that about 400 A.D. there were Hindu princes in Borneo. The inscriptions testify to the existence of Hinduism there rather than of Buddhism: in fact the statements in the Chinese annals are the only evidence for the latter. But it is most interesting to find that these annals give the family name of the king of Poli as Kauṇḍinya[3] which no doubt corresponds to the Kuṇḍagga of the Koetei inscription. At least one if not two of the Hindu invaders of Camboja bore this name, and we can hardly be wrong in supposing that members of the same great family became princes in different parts of the Far East. One explanation of their presence in Borneo would be that they went thither from Camboja, but we have no record of expeditions from Camboja and if adventurers started thence it is not clear why they went to the *east* coast of Borneo. It would be less strange if Kaundinyas emigrating from Java reached both Camboja and Koetei. It is noticeable that in Java, Koetei, Champa and Camboja alike royal names end in *varman*.

[1] See Hose and McDougall, *l.c.* p. 12.

[2] See Kern, "Over de Opschriften uit Koetei" in *Verslagen Meded. Afd. Lett.* 2 *R.* XI. *D.* Another inscription apparently written in debased Indian characters but not yet deciphered has been found in Sanggau, south-west Borneo.

[3] Groeneveldt, p. 81. The characters may be read Kau-ḍi-nya according to Julien's method. The reference is to Liang annals, book 54.

5

The architectural monuments of Java are remarkable for their size, their number and their beauty. Geographically they fall into two chief groups, the central (Boroboedoer, Prambanan, Dieng plateau, etc.) in or near the kingdom of Mataram and the eastern (Tjandi Djago, Singasari, Panataran, etc.) lying not at the extremity of the island but chiefly to the south of Soerabaja. No relic of antiquity deserving to be called a monument has been found in western Java for the records left by Pûrnavarman (*c.* 400 A.D.) are merely rocks bearing inscriptions and two footprints, as a sign that the monarch's triumphal progress is compared to the three steps of Vishṇu.

The earliest dated (779 A.D.) monument in mid Java, Tjandi Kalasan, is Buddhist and lies in the plain of Prambanan. It is dedicated to Târâ and is of a type common both in Java and Champa, namely a chapel surmounted by a tower. In connection with it was erected the neighbouring building called Tjandi Sari, a two-storied monastery for Mahayanist monks. Not far distant is Tjandi Sevu, which superficially resembles the 450 Pagodas of Mandalay, for it consists of a central cruciform shrine surrounded by about 240 smaller separate chapels, every one of which, apparently, contained the statue of a Dhyâni Buddha. Other Buddhist buildings in the same region are Tjandi Plaosan, and the beautiful chapel known as Tjandi Mendut in which are gigantic seated images of the Buddha, Manjuśrî and Avalokita. The face of the last named is perhaps the most exquisite piece of work ever wrought by the chisel of a Buddhist artist.

It is not far from Mendut to Boroboedoer, which deserves to be included in any list of the wonders of the world. This celebrated stûpa—for in essence it is a highly ornamented stûpa with galleries of sculpture rising one above the other on its sides—has been often described and can be described intelligibly only at considerable length. I will therefore not attempt to detail or criticize its beauties but will merely state some points which are important for our purpose.

It is generally agreed that it must have been built about 850 A.D., but obviously the construction lasted a considerable time and there are indications that the architects altered their original plan. The unknown founder must have been a powerful and prosperous king for no one else could have commanded the necessary labour. The stûpa shows no sign of Brahmanic influence. It is purely Buddhist and built for purposes of edification. The worshippers performed pradakshiṇâ by walking round the galleries, one after the other, and as they did so had an opportunity of inspecting some 2000 reliefs depicting the previous births of Śâkyamuni, his life on earth and finally the mysteries of Mahayanist theology. As in Indian pilgrim cities, temple guides were probably ready to explain the pictures.

The selection of reliefs is not due to the artists' fancy but aims at illustrating certain works. Thus the scenes of the Buddha's life reproduce in stone the story of the Lalita Vistara[1] and the Jâtaka pictures are based on the Divyâvadâna. It is interesting to find that both these works are connected with the school of the Mûlasarvâstivâdins, which according to I-Ching was the form of Buddhism prevalent in the archipelago. In the third gallery the figure of Maitreya is prominent and often seems to be explaining something to a personage who accompanies him. As Maitreya is said to have revealed five important scriptures to Asaṅga, and as there is a tradition that the east of Asia was evangelized by the disciples of Asaṅga or Vasubandhu, it is possible that the delivery and progress of Maitreya's revelation is here depicted. The fourth gallery seems to deal with the five superhuman Buddhas[2], their paradises and other supra-mundane matters, but the key to this series of sculptures has not yet been found. It is probable that the highest storey proved to be too heavy in its original form and that the central dagoba had to be reduced lest it should break the substructure. But it is not known what image or relic was preserved in this dagoba. Possibly it was dedicated to Vairocana who was regarded as the Supreme Being and All-God by some Javanese Buddhists[3].

The creed here depicted in stone seems to be a form of

[1] See Pleyte, *Die Buddhalegende in den Sculpturen von Borobudur*. But he points out that the version of the Lalita Vistara followed by the artist is not quite the same as the one that we possess.

[2] Amitâbha, Amoghasiddhi, Ratnasambhava, Akshobhya, Vairocana, sometimes called Dhyâni Buddhas, but it does not seem that this name was in common use in Java or elsewhere. The Kamahâyânikan calls them the Five Tathâgatas.

[3] So in the Kunjarakarna, for which see below. The Kamahâyânikan teaches an elaborate system of Buddha emanations but for purposes of worship it is not quite clear which should be adored as the highest.

Mahayanism. Śâkyamuni is abundantly honoured but there is no representation of his death. This may be because the Lalita Vistara treats only of his early career, but still the omission is noteworthy. In spite of the importanee of Śâkyamuni, a considerable if mysterious part is played by the five superhuman Buddhas, and several Bodhisattvas, especially Maitreya, Avalokita and Manjuśrî. In the celestial scenes we find numerous Bodhisattvas both male and female, yet the figures are hardly Tantric and there is no sign that any of the personages are Brahmanic deities.

Yet the region was not wholly Buddhist. Not far from Boroboedoer and apparently of about the same age is the Sivaite temple of Banon, and the great temple group of Prambanam is close to Kalasan and to the other Buddhist shrines mentioned above. It consists of eight temples of which four are dedicated to Brahmâ, Śiva, Vishṇu and Nandi respectively, the purpose of the others being uncertain. The largest and most decorated is that dedicated to Śiva, containing four shrines in which are images of the god as Mahâdeva and as Guru, of Ganeśa and of Durgâ. The balustrade is ornamented with a series of reliefs illustrating the Ramayana. These temples, which appear to be entirely Brahmanic, approach in style the architecture of eastern Java and probably date from the tenth century, that is about a century later than the Buddhist monuments. But there is no tradition or other evidence of a religious revolution.

The temples on the Dieng plateau are also purely Brahmanic and probably older, for though we have no record of their foundation, an inscribed stone dated 800 A.D. has been found in this district. The plateau which is 6500 feet high was approached by paved roads or flights of stairs on one of which about 4000 steps still remain. Originally there seem to have been about 40 buildings on the plateau but of these only eight now exist besides several stone foundations which supported wooden structures. The place may have been a temple city analogous to Girnar or Śatrunjaya, but it appears to have been deserted in the thirteenth century, perhaps in consequence of volcanic activity. The Dieng temples are named after the heroes of the Mahabharata (Tjandi Ardjuno, Tjandi Bimo, etc.), but these appear to be late designations. They are rectangular tower-like shrines with porches and a single cellule within. Figures of Brahmâ, Śiva and Vishṇu have been discovered, as well as spouts to carry off the libation water.

Before leaving mid Java I should perhaps mention the relatively modern (1435–1440 A.D.) temples of Suku. I have not seen these buildings, but they are said to be coarse in execution and to indicate that they were used by a debased sect of Vishṇuites. Their interest lies in the extraordinary resemblance which they bear to the temples of Mexico and Yucatan, a resemblance "which no one can fail to observe, though no one has yet suggested any hypothesis to account for it[1]."

The best known and probably the most important monuments of eastern Java are Panataran, Tjandi Djago and Tjandi Singasari[2].

The first is considered to date from about 1150 A.D. It is practically a three-storied pyramid with a flat top. The sides of the lowest storey are ornamented with a series of reliefs illustrating portions of the Ramayana, local legends and perhaps the exploits of Krishna, but this last point is doubtful[3]. This temple seems to indicate the same stage of belief as Prambanam. It shows no trace of Buddhism and though Śiva was probably the principal deity, the scenes represented in its sculptures are chiefly Vishnuite.

Tjandi Djago is in the province of Pasoeroean. According to the Pararaton and the Nâgarakrĕtâgama[4], Vishṇuvardhana, king of Toemapĕl, was buried there. As he died in 1272 or 1273 A.D. and the temple was already in existence, we may infer that it dates from at least 1250. He was represented there in the form of Sugata (that is the Buddha) and at Waleri in the form of Śiva. Here we have the custom known also in Champa and Camboja of a deceased king being represented by a statue with his own features but the attributes of his tutelary deity. It is strange that a king named after Vishṇu should be portrayed in the guise of Śiva and Buddha. But in spite of this impartiality, the cult practised at Tjandi Djago seems to have been not a mixture but Buddhism of a late Mahayanist type. It was

[1] Fergusson, *History of Indian and Eastern Architecture*, ed. 1910, vol. II. p. 439.

[2] See *Archaeologisch Onderzoek op Java en Madura*, I. "Tjandi Djago," 1904; II. "Tj. Singasari en Panataran," 1909.

[3] See Knebel in *Tijds. voor Indische T., L. en Volkenkunde*, 41, 1909, p. 27.

[4] See passages quoted in *Archaeol. Onderzoek*, I. pp. 96–97.

doubtless held that Buddhas and Bodhisattvas are identical with Brahmanic deities, but the fairly numerous pantheon discovered in or near the ruins consists of superhuman Buddhas and Bodhisattvas with their spouses[1].

In form Tjandi Djago has somewhat the appearance of a three-storied pyramid but the steps leading up to the top platform are at one end only and the shrine instead of standing in the centre of the platform is at the end opposite to the stairs. The figures in the reliefs are curiously square and clumsy and recall those of Central America.

Tjandi Singasari, also in the province of Pasoeroean, is of a different form. It is erected on a single low platform and consists of a plain rectangular building surmounted by five towers such as are also found in Cambojan temples. There is every reason to believe that it was erected in 1278 A.D. in the reign of Krĕtanâgara, the last king of Toemapĕl, and that it is the temple known as Śiva-buddhâlaya in which he was commemorated under the name of Śiva-buddha. An inscription found close by relates that in 1351 A.D. a shrine was erected on behalf of the royal family in memory of those who died with the king[2].

The Nâgarakrĕtagama represents this king as a devout Buddhist but his very title Śivabuddha shows how completely Sivaism and Buddhism were fused in his religion. The same work mentions a temple in which the lower storey was dedicated to Śiva and the upper to Akshobhya: it also leads us to suppose that the king was honoured as an incarnation of Akshobhya even during his life and was consecrated as a Jina under the name of Śrîjnânabajreśvara[3]. The Singasari temple is less ornamented with reliefs than the others described but has furnished numerous statues of excellent workmanship which illustrate the fusion of the Buddhist and Sivaite pantheons. On the one side we have Prajnâpâramitâ, Manjuśrî and Târâ, on the other Ganeśa, the Linga, Śiva in various forms (Guru, Nandîsvara, Mahâkâla, etc.), Durgâ and Brahmâ. Not only is

[1] Hayagriva however may be regarded as a Brahmanic god adopted by the Buddhists.

[2] See for reasons and references *Archaeol. Onderzoek*, II. pp. 36–40. The principal members of the king's household probably committed suicide during the funeral ceremonies.

[3] Kern in *Tijds. voor T., L. en Volkenkunde*, Deel LII. 1910, p. 107. Similarly in Burma Alompra was popularly regarded as a Bodhisattva.

the Sivaite element predominant but the Buddhist figures are concerned less with the veneration of the Buddha than with accessory mythology.

Javanese architecture and sculpture are no doubt derived from India, but the imported style, whatever it may have been, was modified by local influences and it seems impossible at present to determine whether its origin should be sought on the eastern or western side of India. The theory that the temples on the Dieng plateau are Chalukyan buildings appears to be abandoned but they and many others in Java show a striking resemblance to the shrines found in Champa. Javanese architecture is remarkable for the complete absence not only of radiating arches but of pillars, and consequently of large halls. This feature is no doubt due to the ever present danger of earthquakes. Many reliefs, particularly those of Panataran, show the influence of a style which is not Indian and may be termed, though not very correctly, Polynesian. The great merit of Javanese sculpture lies in the refinement and beauty of the faces. Among figures executed in India it would be hard to find anything equal in purity and delicacy to the Avalokita of Mendut, the Manjuśri now in the Berlin Museum or the Prajñâpâramitâ now at Leyden.

6

From the eleventh century until the end of the Hindu period Java can show a considerable body of literature, which is in part theological. It is unfortunate that no books dating from an earlier epoch should be extant. The sculptures of Prambanam and Boroboedoer clearly presuppose an acquaintance with the Ramayana, the Lalita Vistara and other Buddhist works but, as in Camboja, this literature was probably known only in the original Sanskrit and only to the learned. But it is not unlikely that the Javanese adaptations of the Indian epics which have come down to us were preceded by earlier attempts which have disappeared.

The old literary language of Java is commonly known as Båså Kawi or Kawi, that is the language of poetry[1]. It is

[1] Sanskrit Kavi, a poet. See for Javanese literature Van der Tuuk in *J.R.A.S.* XIII. 1881, p. 42, and Hinloopen Labberton, *ib.* 1913, p. 1. Also the article "Litteratuur" in the *Encyc. van Nederlandsch-Indië*, and many notices in the writings of Kern and Veth.

however simply the predecessor of modern Javanese and many authorities prefer to describe the language of the island as Old Javanese before the Madjapahit period, Middle-Javanese during that period and New Javanese after the fall of Madjapahit. The greater part of this literature consists of free versions of Sanskrit works or of a substratum in Sanskrit accompanied by a Javanese explanation. Only a few Javanese works are original, that is to say not obviously inspired by an Indian prototype, but on the other hand nearly all of them handle their materials with freedom and adapt rather than translate what they borrow.

One of the earliest works preserved appears to be the Tantoe Panggĕlaran, a treatise on cosmology in which Indian and native ideas are combined. It is supposed to have been written about 1000 A.D. Before the foundation of Madjapahit Javanese literature flourished especially in the reigns of Erlangga and Djajabaja, that is in the eleventh and twelfth centuries respectively. About the time of Erlangga were produced the old prose version of the Mahabharata, in which certain episodes of that poem are rendered with great freedom and the poem called Arjunavivâha, or the marriage of Arjuna.

The Bhâratayuddha[1], which states that it was composed by Mpoe Sedah in 1157 by order of Djajabaja, prince of Kediri, is, even more than the prose version mentioned above, a free rendering of parts of the Mahabharata. It is perhaps based on an older translation preserved in Bali[2]. The Kawi Ramayana was in the opinion of Kern composed about 1200 A.D. It follows in essentials the story of the Ramayana, but it was apparently composed by a poet unacquainted with Sanskrit who drew his knowledge from some native source now unknown[3]. He appears to have been a Sivaite. To the eleventh century are also referred the Smaradahana and the treatise on prosody called Vrittasañcaya. All this literature is based upon classical Sanskrit models and is not distinctly Buddhist although the prose version of the Mahabharata states that it was written for Brahmans, Sivaites and Buddhists[4]. Many other translations

[1] Edited by Gunning, 1903.

[2] A fragment of it is printed in *Notulen. Batav. Gen.* LII. 1914, 108.

[3] Episodes of the Indian epics have also been used as the subjects of Javanese dramas. See Juynboll, *Indonesische en achterindische tooneelvoorstellingen uit het Râmâyana*, and Hinloopen Labberton, *Pepakem Sapanti Sakoentala*, 1912.

[4] Juynboll, *Drie Boeken van het Oudjavaansche Mahâbhârata*, p. 28.

or adaptations of Sanskrit work are mentioned, such as the Nîtiśâstra, the Sârasamuccaya, the Tantri (in several editions), a prose translation of the Brahmândapurâṇa, together with grammars and dictionaries. The absence of dates makes it difficult to use these works for the history of Javanese thought. But it seems clear that during the Madjapahit epoch, or perhaps even before it, a strong current of Buddhism permeated Javanese literature, somewhat in contrast with the tone of the works hitherto cited. Brandes states that the Sutasoma, Vighnotsava, Kuñjarakarna, Sang Hyang Kamahâyânikan, and Buddhapamutus are purely Buddhist works and that the Tjantakaparva, Arjunavijaya, Nâgarakrĕtagama, Wariga and Bubukshah show striking traces of Buddhism[1]. Some of these works are inaccessible to me but two of them deserve examination, the Sang Hyang Kamahâyânikan[2] and the story of Kuñjarakarṇa[3]. The first is tentatively assigned to the Madjapahit epoch or earlier, the second with the same caution to the eleventh century. I do not presume to criticize these dates which depend partly on linguistic considerations. The Kamahâyânikan is a treatise (or perhaps extracts from treatises) on Mahayanism as understood in Java and presumably on the normal form of Mahayanism. The other work is an edifying legend including an exposition of the faith by no one less than the Buddha Vairocana. In essentials it agrees with the Kamahâyânikan but in details it shows either sectarian influence or the idiosyncrasies of the author.

The Kamahâyânikan consists of Sanskrit verses explained by a commentary in old Javanese and is partly in the form of questions and answers. The only authority whom it cites is Dignâga. It professes to teach the Mahâyâna and Mantrâyana, which is apparently a misspelling for Mantrayâna. The emphasis laid on Bajra (that is vajra or dorje), ghantâ, mudrâ, maṇḍala, mystic syllables, and Devîs marks it as an offshoot of Tantrism and it offers many parallels to Nepalese literature. On the other hand it is curious that it uses the form Nibâṇa not Nirvâṇa[4]. Its

[1] *Archaeol. Onderzoek*, I. p. 98. This statement is abundantly confirmed by Krom's index of the proper names in the Nâgarakrĕtâgama in *Tijdschrift*, LVI. 1914, pp. 495 ff.

[2] Edited with transl. and notes by J. Kat, 's Gravenhage, 1910.

[3] Edited with transl. by H. Kern in *Verh. der K. Akademie van Wetenschappen te Amsterdam. Afd. Lett. N.R.* III. 3. 1901.

[4] But this probably represents nizbâṇa and is not a Pali form. Cf. Bajra, Bâyu for Vajra, Vâyu.

object is to teach a neophyte, who has to receive initiation, how to become a Buddha[1]. In the second part the pupil is addressed as Jinaputra, that is son of the Buddha or one of the household of faith. He is to be moderate but not ascetic in food and clothing: he is not to cleave to the Purâṇas and Tantras but to practise the Pâramitâs. These are defined first as six[2] and then four others are added[3]. Under Prajñâpâramitâ is given a somewhat obscure account of the doctrine of Śûnyatâ. Then follows the exposition of Paramaguhya (the highest secret) and Mahâguhya (the great secret). The latter is defined as being Yoga, the bhâvanâs, the four noble truths and the ten pâramitâs. The former explains the embodiment of Bhaṭâra Viśesha, that is to say the way in which Buddhas, gods and the world of phenomena are evolved from a primordial principle, called Advaya and apparently equivalent to the Nepalese Âdibuddha[4]. Advaya is the father of Buddha and Advayajñâna, also called Bharâlî Prajñâpâramitâ, is his mother, but the Buddha principle at this stage is also called Divarûpa. In the next stage this Divarûpa takes form as Śâkyamuni, who is regarded as a superhuman form of Buddhahood rather than as a human teacher, for he produces from his right and left side respectively Lokeśvara and Bajrapâni. These beings produce, the first Akshobhya and Ratnasambhava, the second Amitâbha and Amoghasiddhi, but Vairocana springs directly from the face of Śâkyamuni. The five superhuman Buddhas are thus accounted for. From Vairocana spring Îśvara (Śiva), Brahmâ, and Vishṇu: from them the elements, the human body and the whole world. A considerable part of the treatise is occupied with connecting these various emanations of the Advaya with mystic syllables and in showing how the five Buddhas correspond to the different skandas, elements, senses, etc. Finally we are told that there are five Devîs, or female counterparts corresponding in the same order to the Buddhas named above and called Locanâ, Mâmakî, Pâṇḍaravâsinî, Târâ and Dhâtvîśvarî. But it is declared that

[1] Adyâbhishiktâyushmanta, p. 30. Prâptam buddhatvam bhavadbhir, *ib.* and Esha mârga varaḥ śrîmân mahâyâna mahodayaḥ Yena yûyam gamishyanto bhavishyatha Tathâgatâh.

[2] Dâna, śîla, kshânti, vîrya, dhyâna, prajñâ.

[3] Maitrî, karunâ, muditâ, upekshâ.

[4] The Kâraṇḍavyûha teaches a somewhat similar doctrine of creative emanations. Avalokita, Brahmâ, Śiva, Vishṇu and others all are evolved from the original Buddha spirit and proceed to evolve the world.

the first and last of these are the same and therefore there are really only four Devîs.

The legend of Kuñjarakarṇa relates how a devout Yaksha of that name went to Bodhicitta[1] and asked of Vairocana instruction in the holy law and more especially as to the mysteries of rebirth. Vairocana did not refuse but bade his would-be pupil first visit the realms of Yama, god of the dead. Kuñjarakarṇa did so, saw the punishments of the underworld, including the torments prepared for a friend of his, whom he was able to warn on his return. Yama gave him some explanations respecting the alternation of life and death and he was subsequently privileged to receive a brief but more general exposition of doctrine from Vairocana himself.

This doctrine is essentially a variety of Indian pantheism but peculiar in its terminology inasmuch as Vairocana, like Kṛishṇa in the Bhagavadgîtâ, proclaims himself to be the All-God and not merely the chief of the five Buddhas. He quotes with approval the saying "you are I: I am you" and affirms the identity of Buddhism and Śivaism. Among the monks[2] there are no *muktas* (*i.e.* none who have attained liberation) because they all consider as two what is really one. "The Buddhists say, we are Bauddhas, for the Lord Buddha is our highest deity: we are not the same as the Śivaites, for the Lord Śiva is for them the highest deity." The Śivaites are represented as saying that the five Kuśikas are a development or incarnations of the five Buddhas. "Well, my son" is the conclusion, "These are all one: we are Śiva, we are Buddha."

In this curious exposition the author seems to imply that his doctrine is different from that of ordinary Buddhists, and to reprimand them more decidedly than Śivaites. He several times uses the phrase *Namo Bhaṭâra, namaḥ Śivâya* (Hail, Lord: hail to Śiva) yet he can hardly be said to favour the Śivaites on the whole, for his All-God is Vairocana who once (but only once) receives the title of Buddha. The doctrine attributed to the Śivaites that the five Kusikas are identical with the superhuman Buddhas remains obscure[3]. These five personages are said to be often mentioned in old Javanese literature but to be variously

[1] The use of this word, as a name for the residence of Vairocana, seems to be peculiar to our author.

[2] This term may include Śivaite ascetics as well as Buddhist monks.

[3] See further discussion in Kern's edition, p. 16.

enumerated[1]. They are identified with the five Indras, but these again are said to be the five senses (indriyas). Hence we can find a parallel to this doctrine in the teaching of the Kamahâyânikan that the five Buddhas correspond to the five senses.

Two other special theses are enounced in the story of Kuñjarakarṇa. The first is Vairocana's analysis of a human being, which makes it consist of five Âtmans or souls, called respectively Âtman, Cetanâtman, Parâtman, Nirâtman and Antarâtman, which somehow correspond to the five elements, five senses and five Skandhas. The singular list suggests that the author was imperfectly acquainted with the meaning of the Sanskrit words employed and the whole terminology is strange in a Buddhist writer. Still in the later Upanishads[2] the epithet pancâtmaka is applied to the human body, especially in the Garbha Upanishad which, like the passage here under consideration, gives a psychophysiological explanation of the development of an embryo into a human being.

The second thesis is put in the mouth of Yama. He states that when a being has finished his term in purgatory he returns to life in this world first as a worm or insect, then successively as a higher animal and a human being, first diseased or maimed and finally perfect. No parallel has yet been quoted to this account of metempsychosis.

Thus the Kuñjarakarṇa contains peculiar views which are probably sectarian or individual. On the other hand their apparent singularity may be due to our small knowledge of old Javanese literature. Though other writings are not known to extol Vairocana as being Śiva and Buddha in one, yet they have no scruple in identifying Buddhist and Brahmanic deities or connecting them by some system of emanations, as we have already seen in the Kamahâyânikan. Such an identity is still more definitely proclaimed in the old Javanese version of the Sutasoma Jâtaka[3]. It is called Purushâda-Śânta and was

[1] As are the Panchpirs in modern India.

[2] Garbha. Up. 1 and 3, especially the phrase asmin pancâtmake śarîre. Piṇḍa Up. 2. Bhinne pancâtmake dehe. Mahâ Nâr. Up. 23. Sa vâ esha purushaḥ pancadhâ pancâtmâ.

[3] See Kern, "Over de Vermenging van Civaisme en Buddhisme op Jâva" in *Vers. en Meded. der Kon. Akad. van Wet. Afd. Lett.* 3 *R.* 5 *Deel*, 1888.

For the Sutasomajâtaka see Speyer's translation of the Jâtakamâlâ, pp. 291–313, with his notes and references. It is No. 537 in the Pali Collection of Jâtakas.

composed by Tantular who lived at Madjapahit in the reign of Râjasanagara (1350–1389 A.D.). In the Indian original Sutasoma is one of the previous births of Gotama. But the Javanese writer describes him as an Avatâra of the Buddha who is Brahmâ, Vishṇu and Îśvara, and he states that "The Lord Buddha is not different from Śiva the king of the gods....They are distinct and they are one. In the Law is no dualism." The superhuman Buddhas are identified with various Hindu gods and also with the five senses. Thus Amitâbha is Mahâdeva and Amoghasiddhi is Vishṇu. This is only a slight variation of the teaching in the Kamahâyânikan. There Brahmanic deities emanate from Śâkyamuni through various Bodhisattvas and Buddhas: here the Buddha spirit is regarded as equivalent to the Hindu Trimûrti and the various aspects of this spirit can be described in either Brahmanic or Buddhistic terminology though in reality all Buddhas, Bodhisattvas and gods are one. But like the other authors quoted, Tantular appears to lean to the Buddhist side of these equations, especially for didactic purposes. For instance he says that meditation should be guided "by Lokeśvara's word and Śâkyamuni's spirit."

7

Thus it will be seen that if we take Javanese epigraphy, monuments and literature together with Chinese notices, they to some extent confirm one another and enable us to form an outline picture, though with many gaps, of the history of thought and religion in the island. Fa-Hsien tells us that in 418 A.D. Brahmanism flourished (as is testified by the inscriptions of Pûrṇavarman) but that the Buddhists were not worth mentioning. Immediately afterwards, probably in 423, Guṇavarman is said to have converted Shê-po, if that be Java, to Buddhism, and as he came from Kashmir he was probably a Sarvâstivâdin. Other monks are mentioned as having visited the southern seas[1]. About 690 I-Ching says that Buddhism of the Mûlasarvâstivâdin school was flourishing in Sumatra, which he visited, and in the other islands of the Archipelago. The remarkable series of Buddhist monuments in mid Java ex-

[1] See Nanjio Cat. Nos. 137, 138.

tending from about 779 to 900 A.D. confirms his statement. But two questions arise. Firstly, is there any explanation of this sudden efflorescence of Buddhism in the Archipelago, and next, what was its doctrinal character? If, as Târanâtha says, the disciples of Vasubandhu evangelized the countries of the East, their influence might well have been productive about the time of I-Ching's visit. But in any case during the sixth and seventh centuries religious travellers must have been continually journeying between India and China, in both directions, and some of them must have landed in the Archipelago. At the beginning of the sixth century Buddhism was not yet decadent in India and was all the fashion in China. It is not therefore surprising if it was planted in the islands lying on the route. It may be, as indicated above, that some specially powerful body of Hindus coming from the region of Gujarat and professing Buddhism founded in Java a new state.

As to the character of this early Javanese Buddhism we have the testimony of I-Ching that it was of the Mûlasarvâstivâdin school and Hinayanist. He wrote of what he had seen in Sumatra but of what he knew only by hearsay in Java and his statement offers some difficulties. Probably Hinayanism was introduced by Guṇavarman but was superseded by other teachings which were imported from time to time after they had won for themselves a position in India. For the temple of Kalasan (A.D. 779) is dedicated to Târâ and the inscription found there speaks of the Mahayana with veneration. The later Buddhism of Java has literary records which, so far as I know, are unreservedly Mahayanist but probably the sculptures of Boroboedoer are the most definite expression which we shall ever have of its earlier phases. Since they contain images of the five superhuman Buddhas and of numerous Bodhisattvas, they can hardly be called anything but Mahayanist. But on the other hand the personality of Śâkyamuni is emphasized; his life and previous births are pictured in a long series of sculptures and Maitreya is duly honoured. Similar collections of pictures and images may be seen in Burma which differ doctrinally from those in Java chiefly by substituting the four human Buddhas[1] and Maitreya for the superhuman Buddhas. But Mahayanist teaching declares that these human Buddhas are reflexes of

[1] Gotama, Kassapa, Konâgamana and Kakusandha.

counterparts of the superhuman Buddhas so that the difference is not great.

Mahayanist Buddhism in Camboja and at a later period in Java itself was inextricably combined with Hinduism, Buddha being either directly identified with Śiva or regarded as the primordial spirit from which Śiva and all gods spring. But the sculptures of Boroboedoer do not indicate that the artists knew of any such amalgamation nor have inscriptions been found there, as in Camboja, which explain this compound theology. It would seem that Buddhism and Brahmanism co-existed in the same districts but had not yet begun to fuse doctrinally. The same condition seems to have prevailed in western India during the seventh and eighth centuries, for the Buddhist caves of Ellora, though situated in the neighbourhood of Brahmanic buildings and approximating to them in style, contain sculptures which indicate a purely Buddhist cultus and not a mixed pantheon.

Our meagre knowledge of Javanese history makes it difficult to estimate the spheres and relative strength of the two religions. In the plains the Buddhist monuments are more numerous and also more ancient and we might suppose that the temples of Prambanan indicate the beginning of some change in belief. But the temples on the Dieng plateau seem to be of about the same age as the oldest Buddhist monuments. Thus nothing refutes the supposition that Brahmanism existed in Java from the time of the first Hindu colonists and that Buddhism was introduced after 400 A.D. It may be that Boroboedoer and the Dieng plateau represent the religious centres of two different kingdoms. But this supposition is not necessary for in India, whence the Javanese received their ideas, groups of temples are found of the same age but belonging to different sects. Thus in the Khajraho group[1] some shrines are Jain and of the rest some are dedicated to Śiva and some to Vishṇu.

The earliest records of Javanese Brahmanism, the inscriptions of Pûrnavarman, are Vishnuite but the Brahmanism which prevailed in the eighth and ninth centuries was in the main Śivaite, though not of a strongly sectarian type. Brahmâ, Vishṇu and Śiva were all worshipped both at Prambanan and on the Dieng but Śiva together with Ganeśa, Durgâ, and Nandi

[1] About 950–1050 A.D. Fergusson, *Hist. of Indian Architecture*, II. p. 141.

is evidently the chief deity. An image of Śiva in the form of Bhaṭâra Guru or Mahâguru is installed in one of the shrines at Prambanan. This deity is characteristic of Javanese Hinduism and apparently peculiar to it. He is represented as an elderly bearded man wearing a richly ornamented costume. There is something in the pose and drapery which recalls Chinese art and I think the figure is due to Chinese influence, for at the present day many of the images found in the temples of Bali are clearly imitated from Chinese models (or perhaps made by Chinese artists) and this may have happened in earlier times. The Chinese annals record several instances of religious objects being presented by the Emperors to Javanese princes. Though Bhaṭâra Guru is only an aspect of Śiva he is a sufficiently distinct personality to have a shrine of his own like Ganeśa and Durgâ, in temples where the principal image of Śiva is of another kind.

The same type of Brahmanism lasted at least until the erection of Panataran (*c.* 1150). The temple appears to have been dedicated to Śiva but like Prambanan it is ornamented with scenes from the Ramayana and from Vishnuite Purânas[1]. The literature which can be definitely assigned to the reigns of Djajabaja and Erlangga is Brahmanic in tone but both literature and monuments indicate that somewhat later there was a revival of Buddhism. Something similar appears to have happened in other countries. In Camboja the inscriptions of Jayavarman VII (*c.* 1185 A.D.) are more definitely Buddhist than those of his predecessors and in 1296 Chou Ta-kuan regarded the country as mainly Buddhist. Parakrama Bahu of Ceylon (1153–1186) was zealous for the faith and so were several kings of Siam. I am inclined to think that this movement was a consequence of the flourishing condition of Buddhism at Pagan in Burma from 1050 to 1250. Pagan certainly stimulated religion in both Siam and Ceylon and Siam reacted strongly on Camboja[2]. It is true that the later Buddhism of Java was by no means of the Siamese type, but probably the idea was current that the great kings of the world were pious Buddhists and consequently in

[1] See Knebel, "Recherches préparatoires concernant Krishna et les bas reliefs des temples de Java" in *Tijdschrift*, LI. 1909, pp. 97–174.

[2] In Camboja the result seems to have been double. Pali Buddhism entered from Siam and ultimately conquered all other forms of religion, but for some time Mahayanist Buddhism, which was older in Camboja, revived and received Court patronage.

most countries the local form of Buddhism, whatever it was, began to be held in esteem. Java had constant communication with Camboja and Champa and a king of Madjapahit married a princess of the latter country. It is also possible that a direct stimulus may have been received from India, for the statement of Târanâtha[1] that when Bihar was sacked by the Mohammedans the Buddhist teachers fled to other regions and that some of them went to Camboja is not improbable.

But though the prestige of Buddhism increased in the thirteenth century, no rupture with Brahmanism took place and Pali Buddhism does not appear to have entered Java. The unity of the two religions is proclaimed: Buddha and Śiva are one. But the Kamahâyânikan while admitting the Trimûrti makes it a derivative, and not even a primary derivative, of the original Buddha spirit. It has been stated that the religion of Java in the Madjapahit epoch was Śivaism with a little Buddhism thrown in, on the understanding that it was merely another method of formulating the same doctrine. It is very likely that the bulk of the population worshipped Hindu deities, for they are the gods of this world and dispense its good things. Yet the natives still speak of the old religion as Buddhâgama; the old times are "Buddha times" and even the flights of stairs leading up to the Dieng plateau are called Buddha steps. This would hardly be so if in the Madjapahit epoch Buddha had not seemed to be the most striking figure in the non-Mohammedan religion. Also, the majority of *religious* works which have survived from this period are Buddhist. It is true that we have the Ramayana, the Bhârata Yuddha and many other specimens of Brahmanic literature. But these, especially in their Javanese dress, are *belles lettres* rather than theology, whereas Kamahâyânikan and Kuñjarakarna are dogmatic treatises. Hence it would appear that the religious life of Madjapahit was rooted in Buddhism, but a most tolerant Buddhism which had no desire to repudiate Brahmanism.

I have already briefly analysed the Sang Hyang Kamahâyânikan which seems to be the most authoritative exposition of this creed. The learned editor has collected many parallels from Tibetan and Nepalese works and similar parallels between Javanese and Tibetan iconography have been indicated by

[1] Chap. 37.

Pleyte[1] and others. The explanation must be that the late forms of Buddhist art and doctrine which flourished in Magadha spread to Tibet and Nepal but were also introduced into Java. The Kamahâyânikan appears to be a paraphrase of a Sanskrit original, perhaps distorted and mutilated. This original has not been identified with any work known to exist in India but might well be a Mahayanist catechism composed there about the eleventh century. The terminology of the treatise is peculiar, particularly in calling the ultimate principle Advaya and the more personal manifestation of it Divarûpa. The former term may be paralleled in Hemacandra and the Amarakosha, which give respectively as synonyms for Buddha, advaya (in whom is no duality) and advayavâdin (who preaches no duality), but Divarûpa has not been found in any other work[2]. It is also remarkable that the Kamahâyânikan does not teach the doctrine of the three bodies of Buddha[3]. It clearly states[4] that the Divarûpa is identical with the highest being worshipped by various sects: with Paramaśûnya, Paramaśiva, the Purusha of the followers of Kapila, the Nirguṇa of the Vishnuites, etc. Many names of sects and doctrines are mentioned which remain obscure, but the desire to represent them all as essentially identical is obvious.

The Kamahâyânikan recognizes the theoretical identity of the highest principles in Buddhism and Vishnuism[5] but it does not appear that Vishṇu-Buddha was ever a popular conception like Śiva-Buddha or that the compound deity called Śiva-Vishṇu, Hari-Hara, Śaṅkara-Narâyaṇa, etc., so well known in Camboja, enjoyed much honour in Java. Vishṇu is relegated to a distinctly secondary position and the Javanese version of the Mahabharata is more distinctly Śivaite than the Sanskrit text. Still he has a shrine at Prambanan, the story of the Ramayana is depicted there and at Panataran, and various

[1] "Bijdrage tot de Kennis van het Mahâyâna op Java" in *Bijd. tot de Taal Land en Volkenkunde van Nederlandsch-Indië*, 1901 and 1902.

[2] This use of advaya and advayavâdin strengthens the suspicion that the origins of the Advaita philosophy are to be sought in Buddhism.

[3] It uses the word trikâya but expressly defines it as meaning Kâya, vâk and citta.

[4] In a passage which is not translated from the Sanskrit and may therefore reflect the religious condition of Java.

[5] So too in the Sutasoma Jâtaka Amoghasiddhi is said to be Vishṇu.

unedited manuscripts contain allusions to his worship, more especially to his incarnation as Narasimha and to the Garuḍa on which he rides[1].

8

At present nearly all the inhabitants of Java profess Islam although the religion of a few tribes, such as the Tenggarese, is still a mixture of Hinduism with indigenous beliefs. But even among nominal Moslims some traces of the older creed survive. On festival days such monuments as Boroboedoer and Prambanan are frequented by crowds who, if they offer no worship, at least take pleasure in examining the ancient statues. Some of these however receive more definite honours: they are painted red and modest offerings of flowers and fruit are laid before them. Yet the respect shown to particular images seems due not to old tradition but to modern and wrongheaded interpretations of their meaning. Thus at Boroboedoer the relief which represents the good tortoise saving a shipwrecked crew receives offerings from women because the small figures on the tortoise's back are supposed to be children. The minor forms of Indian mythology still flourish. All classes believe in the existence of raksasas, boetas (bhûtas) and widadaris (vidyâdharîs), who are regarded as spirits similar to the Jinns of the Arabs. Lakshmî survives in the female genius believed even by rigid Mohammedans to preside over the cultivation of rice and the somewhat disreputable sect known as Santri Birahis are said to adore devas and the forces of nature[2]. Less obvious, but more important as more deeply affecting the national character, is the tendency towards mysticism and asceticism. What is known as ngelmoe[3] plays a considerable part in the religious life of the modern Javanese. The word is simply the Arabic 'ilm (or knowledge) used in the sense of secret science. It sometimes signifies mere magic but the higher forms of it, such as the *ngelmoe peling*, are said to teach that the contemplative life is the way to the knowledge of God and the attainment of supernatural powers. With such

[1] See Juynboll in *Bijdragen tot de Taal Land en Volkenkunde van Ned.-Indië*, 1908, pp. 412–420.

[2] Veth, *Java*, vol. IV. p. 154. The whole chapter contains much information about the Hindu elements in modern Javanese religion.

[3] See Veth, *l.c.* and *ngelmoe* in *Encycl. van Nederlandsch-Indië.*

ngelmoe is often connected a belief in metempsychosis, in the illusory nature of the world, and in the efficacy of regulating the breath. Asceticism is still known under the name of tåpå and it is said that there are many recluses who live on alms and spend their time in meditation. The affinity of all this to Indian religion is obvious, although the Javanese have no idea that it is in any way incompatible with orthodox Islam.

Indian religion, which in Java is represented merely by the influence of the past on the present, is not dead in Bali[1] where, though much mixed with aboriginal superstitions, it is still a distinct and national faith, able to hold its own against Mohammedanism and Christianity[2].

The island of Bali is divided from the east coast of Java only by a narrow strait but the inhabitants possess certain characters of their own. They are more robust in build, their language is distinct from Javanese though belonging to the same group, and even the alphabet presents idiosyncrasies. Their laws, social institutions, customs and calendar show many peculiarities, explicable on the supposition that they have preserved the ancient usages of pre-Mohammedan Java. At present the population is divided into the Bali-Agas or aborigines and the Wong Madjapahit who profess to have immigrated from that kingdom. The Chinese references[3] to Bali seem uncertain but, if accepted, indicate that it was known in the middle ages as a religious centre. It was probably a colony and dependency of Madjapahit and when Madjapahit fell it became a refuge for those who were not willing to accept Islam.

Caste is still a social institution in Bali, five classes being recognized, namely Brahmans, Kshatriyas (Satriyas), Vaisyas (Visias), Sudras and Parias. These distinctions are rigidly observed and though intermarriage (which in former times was often punished with death) is now permitted, the offspring are not recognized as belonging to the caste of the superior parent. The bodies of the dead are burned and Sati, which was formerly frequent, is believed still to take place in noble families. Pork

[1] Also to some extent in Lombok. The Balinese were formerly the ruling class in this island and are still found there in considerable numbers.

[2] It has even been suggested that hinduized Malays carried some faint traces of Indian religion to Madagascar. See *T'oung Pao* 1906, p. 93, where Zanahari is explained as Yang (=God in Malay) Hari.

[3] Groeneveldt, pp. 19, 58, 59.

is the only meat used and, as in other Hindu countries, oxen are never slaughtered.

An idea of the Balinese religion may perhaps be given most easily by describing some of the temples. These are very abundant: in the neighbourhood of Boeleling (the capital) alone I have seen more than ten of considerable size. As buildings they are not ancient, for the stone used is soft and does not last much more than fifty years. But when the edifices are rebuilt the ancient shape is preserved and what we see in Bali to-day probably represents the style of the middle ages. The temples consist of two or more courts surrounded by high walls. Worship is performed in the open air: there are various pyramids, seats, and small shrines like dovecots but no halls or rooms. The gates are ornamented with the heads of monsters, especially lions with large ears and winglike expansions at the side. The outermost gate has a characteristic shape. It somewhat resembles an Indian gopuram divided into two parts by a sharp, clean cut in the middle and tradition quotes in explanation the story of a king who was refused entrance to heaven but cleft a passage through the portal with his sword.

In the outer court stand various sheds and hollow wooden cylinders which when struck give a sound like bells. Another ornamented doorway leads to the second court where are found some or all of the following objects: (*a*) Sacred trees, especially *Ficus elastica*. (*b*) Sheds with seats for human beings. It is said that on certain occasions these are used by mediums who become inspired by the gods and then give oracles. (*c*) Seats for the gods, generally under sheds. They are of various kinds. There is usually one conspicuous chair with an ornamental back and a scroll hanging behind it which bears some such inscription as "This is the chair of the Bhatâra." Any deity may be invited to take this seat and receive worship. Sometimes a stone linga is placed upon it. In some temples a stone chair, called padmâsana, is set apart for Sûrya. (*d*) Small shrines two or three feet high, set on posts or pedestals. When well executed they are similar to the cabinets used in Japanese temples as shrines for images but when, as often happens, they are roughly made they are curiously like dovecots. On them are hung strips of dried palm-leaves in bunches like the Japanese *gohei*. As a rule the shrines contain no image but only a small seat and some objects said to be stones which are wrapped up in a cloth and called Artjeh[1]. In some temples (*e.g.* the Bale Agoeng at Singaraja) there are erections called Meru, supposed to represent the sacred mountain where the gods reside. They consist of a stout pedestal or basis of brick on which is erected a cabinet shrine as already described. Above this are large round discs made of straw and wood, which may be described as curved roofs or umbrellas. They are from three to five in number and rise one above the other, with slight intervals between them. (*e*) In many temples (for instance at Sangsit and Sawan) pyramidal erections are found either in addition to the Merus or instead of them. At the end of the second court is a pyramid in four stages or terraces, often with prolongations at the side of the main structure or at right angles to it. It is ascended by several staircases, consisting of about twenty-five steps, and at the top are rows of cabinet shrines.

Daily worship is not performed in these temples but offerings are laid before the shrines from time to time by those who need the help of the gods and there are several annual festivals. The object of the ritual is not to honour any image or object habitually kept in the temple but to induce the gods, who are supposed to be hovering round like birds, to seat themselves in the chair provided or to enter into some sacred object, and then receive homage and offerings. Thus both the ideas and ceremonial are different from those which prevail in Hindu temples and have more affinity with Polynesian beliefs. The deities are called Dewa, but many of them are indigenous nature spirits (especially mountain spirits) such as Dewa Gunung Agung, who are sometimes identified with Indian gods.

Somewhat different are the Durgâ temples. These are dedicated to the spirits of the dead but the images of Durgâ and her attendant Kaliki receive veneration in them, much as in Hindu temples. But on the whole the Malay or Polynesian element seemed to me to be in practice stronger than Hinduism in the religion of the Balinese and this is borne out by the fact that the Pĕmangku or priest of the indigenous gods ranks higher than the Pĕdanda or Brahman priest. But by talking to Balinese one may obtain a different impression, for they are proud of their connection with Madjapahit and Hinduism: they

[1] This word appears to be the Sanskrit arca, an image for worship.

willingly speak of such subjects and Hindu deities are constantly represented in works of art. Ganeśa, Indra, Vishṇu, Kṛishṇa, Sûrya, Garuḍa and Śiva, as well as the heroes of the Mahâbhârata, are well known but I have not heard of worship being offered to any of them except Durgâ and Śiva under the form of the linga. Figures of Vishṇu riding on Garuḍa are very common and a certain class of artificers are able to produce images of all well known Indian gods for those who care to order them. Many Indian works such as the Veda, Mahâbhârata, Râmâyana, Brahmâpurâṇa and Nîtiśâstra are known by name and are said to exist not in the original Sanskrit but in Kawi. I fancy that they are rarely read by the present generation, but any knowledge of them is much respected. The Balinese though confused in their theology are greatly attached to their religion and believe it is the ancient faith of Madjapahit.

I was unable to discover in the neighbourhood of Singarâja even such faint traces of Buddhism as have been reported by previous authors[1], but they may exist elsewhere. The expression Śiva-Buddha was known to the Pĕdandas but seemed to have no living significance, and perhaps certain families have a traditional and purely nominal connection with Buddhism. In Durgâ temples however I have seen figures described as Pusa, the Chinese equivalent of Bodhisattva, and it seems that Chinese artists have reintroduced into this miscellaneous pantheon an element of corrupt Buddhism, though the natives do not recognize it as such.

The art of Bali is more fantastic than that of ancient Java. The carved work, whether in stone or wood, is generally polychromatic. Figures are piled one on the top of another as in the sculptures of Central America and there is a marked tendency to emphasize projections. Leaves and flowers are very deeply carved and such features as ears, tongues and teeth are monstrously prolonged. Thus Balinese statues and reliefs have a curiously bristling and scaly appearance and are apt to seem barbaric, especially if taken separately[2]. Yet the general aspect of the temples is not unpleasing. The brilliant colours and

[1] *E.g.* Van Eerde, "Hindu Javaansche en Balische Eeredienst" in *Bijd. T. L. en Volkenkunde van Nederlandsch-Indië*, 1910. I visited Bali in 1911.

[2] See Pleyte, *Indonesian Art*, 1901, especially the seven-headed figure in plate XVI said to be Krishna.

fantastic outlines harmonize with the tropical vegetation which surrounds them and suggest that the guardian deities take shape as gorgeous insects. Such bizarre figures are not unknown in Indian mythology but in Balinese art Chinese influence is perhaps stronger than Indian. The Chinese probably frequented the island as early as the Hindus and are now found there in abundance. Besides the statues called Pusa already mentioned, Chinese landscapes are often painted behind the seats of the Devas and in the temple on the Volcano Batoer, where a special place is assigned to all the Balinese tribes, the Chinese have their own shrine. It is said that the temples in southern Bali which are older and larger than those in the north show even more decided signs of Chinese influence and are surrounded by stone figures of Chinese as guardians.

CHAPTER XLI

CENTRAL ASIA

1

THE term Central Asia is here used to denote the Tarim basin, without rigidly excluding neighbouring countries such as the Oxus region and Badakshan. This basin is a depression surrounded on three sides by high mountains: only on the east is the barrier dividing it from China relatively low. The water of the whole area discharges through the many branched Tarim river into Lake Lobnor. This so-called lake is now merely a flooded morass and the basin is a desert with occasional oases lying chiefly near its edges. The fertile portions were formerly more considerable but a quarter of a century ago this remote and lonely region interested no one but a few sportsmen and geographers. The results of recent exploration have been important and surprising. The arid sands have yielded not only ruins, statues and frescoes but whole libraries written in a dozen languages. The value of such discoveries for the general history of Asia is clear and they are of capital importance for our special subject, since during many centuries the Tarim region and its neighbouring lands were centres and highways for Buddhism and possibly the scene of many changes whose origin is now obscure. But I am unfortunate in having to discuss Central Asian Buddhism before scholars have had time to publish or even catalogue completely the store of material collected and the reader must remember that the statements in this chapter are at best tentative and incomplete. They will certainly be supplemented and probably corrected as year by year new documents and works of art are made known.

Tarim, in watery metaphor, is not so much a basin as a pool in a tidal river flowing alternately to and from the sea. We can imagine that in such a pool creatures of very different provenance might be found together. So currents both from east to west and from west to east passed through the Tarim, leaving behind whatever could live there: Chinese administration and civilization from the east: Iranians from the west, bearing with them in the stream fragments that had drifted from Asia Minor and Byzantium, while still other currents brought Hindus and Tibetans from the south.

One feature of special interest in the history of the Tarim is that it was in touch with Bactria and the regions conquered by Alexander and through them with western art and thought. Another is that its inhabitants included not only Iranian tribes but the speakers of an Aryan language hitherto unknown, whose presence so far east may oblige us to revise our views about the history of the Aryan race. A third characteristic is that from the dawn of history to the middle ages warlike nomads were continually passing through the country. All these people, whether we call them Iranians, Turks or Mongols had the same peculiarity: they had little culture of their own but they picked up and transported the ideas of others. The most remarkable example of this is the introduction of Islam into Europe and India. Nothing quite so striking happened in earlier ages, yet tribes similar to the Turks brought Manichæism and Nestorian Christianity into China and played no small part in the introduction of Buddhism.

A brief catalogue of the languages represented in the manuscripts and inscriptions discovered will give a safe if only provisional idea of the many influences at work in Central Asia and its importance as a receiving and distributing centre. The number of tongues simultaneously in use for popular or learned purposes was remarkably large. To say nothing of great polyglot libraries like Tun-huang, a small collection at Toyog is reported as containing Indian, Manichæan, Syriac, Sogdian, Uigur and Chinese books. The writing materials employed were various like the idioms and include imported palm leaves, birch bark, plates of wood or bamboo, leather and paper, which last was in use from the first century A.D. onwards. In this dry atmosphere all enjoyed singular longevity.

Numerous Sanskrit writings have been found, all dealing with religious or quasi religious subjects, as medicine and grammar were then considered to be. Relatively modern Mahayanist literature is abundant but greater interest attaches to portions of an otherwise lost Sanskrit canon which agree in substance though not verbally with the corresponding passages in the Pali Canon and are apparently the original text from which much of the Chinese Tripitaka was translated. The manuscripts hitherto published include Sûtras from the Samyukta and Ekottara Âgamas, a considerable part of the Dharmapada, and the Prâtimoksha of the Sarvâstivâdin school. Fa-Hsien states that the monks of Central Asia were all students of the language of India and even in the seventh century Hsüan Chuang tells us the same of Kucha. Portions of a Sanskrit grammar have been found near Turfan and in the earlier period at any rate Sanskrit was probably understood in polite and learned society. Some palm leaves from Ming-Öi contain fragments of two Buddhist religious dramas, one of which is the Sâriputra-prakaraṇa of Aśvaghosha. The handwriting is believed to date from the epoch of Kanishka so that we have here the oldest known Sanskrit manuscripts, as well as the oldest specimens of Indian dramatic art[1]. They are written like the Indian classical dramas in Sanskrit and various forms of Prâkrit. The latter represent hitherto unknown stages in the development of Indian dialects and some of them are closely allied to the language of Aśoka's inscriptions. Another Prâkrit text is the version of the Dharmapada written in Kharoshṭhî characters and discovered by the Dutreuil de Rhins mission near Khotan[2], and numerous official documents in this language and alphabet have been brought home by Stein from the same region. It is probable that they are approximately coeval with the Kushan dynasty in India and the use of an Indian vernacular as well as of Sanskrit in Central Asia shows that the connection between the two countries was not due merely to the introduction of Buddhism.

Besides these hitherto unknown forms of Prâkrit, Central Asia has astonished the learned world with two new languages, both written in a special variety of the Brahmi alphabet called Central Asian Gupta. One is sometimes called Nordarisch and is regarded by some authorities as the language of the Śakas whose incursions into India appear to have begun about the second century B.C. and by others as the language of the Kushans and of Kanishka's Empire. It is stated that the basis of the language is Iranian but strongly influenced by Indian

[1] See Lüders, *Bruchstücke Buddhistischer Dramen*, 1911, and *id.*, *Das Sâriputra-prakarana*, 1911.

[2] See Senart, "Le ms Kharoshṭhî du Dhammapada," in *J.A.*, 1898, II. p. 193.

idioms[1]. Many translations of Mahayanist literature (for instance the Suvarṇaprabhâsa, Vajracchedikâ and Aparimitâyus Sûtras) were made into it and it appears to have been spoken principally in the southern part of the Tarim basin[2]. The other new language was spoken principally on its northern edge and has been called Tokharian, which name implies that it was the tongue of the Tokhars or Indoscyths[3]. But there is no proof of this and it is safer to speak of it as the language of Kucha or Kuchanese. It exists in two different dialects known as A and B whose geographical distribution is uncertain but numerous official documents dated in the first half of the seventh century show that it was the ordinary speech of Kucha and Turfan. It was also a literary language and among the many translations discovered are versions in it of the Dharmapada and Vinaya. It is extremely interesting to find that this language spoken by the early and perhaps original inhabitants of Kucha not only belongs to the Aryan family but is related more nearly to the western than the eastern branch. It cannot be classed in the Indo-Iranian group but shows perplexing affinities to Latin, Greek, Keltic, Slavonic and Armenian[4]. It is possible that it influenced Chinese Buddhist literature[5].

Besides the "Nordarisch" mentioned above which was written in Brahmi, three other Iranian languages have left literary remains in Central Asia, all written in an alphabet of Aramaic origin. Two of them apparently represent the speech of south-western Persia under the Sassanids, and of north-western Persia under the Arsacids. The texts preserved in both are Manichæan but the third Iranian language, or Sogdian, has

[1] Lüders, "Die Śakas und die Nordarische Sprache," *Sitzungsber. der Kön. Preuss. Akad.* 1913. Konow, *Götting. Gel. Anz.* 1912, pp. 551 ff.

[2] See Hoernle in *J.R.A.S.* 1910, pp. 837 ff. and 1283 ff.; 1911, pp. 202 ff., 447 ff.

[3] An old Turkish text about Maitreya states that it was translated from an Indian language into Tokhri and from Tokhri into Turkish. See F. K. W. Müller, *Sitzungsber. der Kön. Preuss. Akad.* 1907, p. 958. But it is not clear what is meant by Tokhri.

[4] The following are some words in this language:

Kant, a hundred; rake, a word; por, fire; soye, son (Greek *υἱός*); suwan, swese, rain (Greek *ὕει ὑετός*); âlyek, another; okso, an ox.

[5] The numerous papers on this language are naturally quickly superseded. But Sieg and Siegling Tokharisch, "Die Sprache der Indoskythen" (*Sitzungsber. der Berl. Ak. Wiss.* 1908, p. 815), may be mentioned and Sylvain Lévi, "Tokharien B, Langue de Koutcha," *J.A.* 1913, II. p. 311.

a more varied literary content and offers Buddhist, Manichæan and Christian texts, apparently in that chronological order. It was originally the language of the region round Samarkand but acquired an international character for it was used by merchants throughout the Tarim basin and spread even to China. Some Christian texts in Syriac have also been found.

The Orkhon inscriptions exhibit an old Turkish dialect written in the characters commonly called Runes and this Runic alphabet is used in manuscripts found at Tun-huang and Miran but those hitherto published are not Buddhist. But another Turkish dialect written in the Uigur alphabet, which is derived from the Syriac, was (like Sogdian) extensively used for Buddhist, Manichæan and Christian literature. The name Uigur is perhaps more correctly applied to the alphabet than the language[1] which appears to have been the literary form of the various Turkish idioms spoken north and south of the Tien-shan. The use of this dialect for Buddhist literature spread considerably when the Uigurs broke the power of Tibet in the Tarim basin about 860 and founded a kingdom themselves: it extended into China and lasted long, for Sûtras in Uigur were printed at Peking in 1330 and Uigur manuscripts copied in the reign of K'ang Hsi (1662–1723) are reported from a monastery near Suchow[2]. I am informed that a variety of this alphabet written in vertical columns is still used in some parts of Kansu where a Turkish dialect is spoken. Though Turkish was used by Buddhists in both the east and west of the Tarim basin, it appears to have been introduced into Khotan only after the Moslim conquest. Another Semitic script, hitherto unknown and found only in a fragmentary form, is believed to be the writing of the White Huns or Hephthalites.

As the Tibetans were the predominant power in the Tarim basin from at least the middle of the eighth until the middle of the ninth century, it is not surprising that great stores of Tibetan manuscripts have been found in the regions of Khotan, Miran and Tun-huang. In Turfan, as lying more to the north, traces of Tibetan influence, though not absent, are fewer. The

[1] See Radloff Tisastvustik (*Bibl. Buddh.* vol. XII.), p. v. This manuscript came from Urumtsi. A translation of a portion of the Saddharma-pundarîka (*Bibl. Buddh.* XIV.) was found at Turfan.

[2] Laufer in *T'oung Pao*, 1907, p. 392; Radloff, *Kuan-si-im Pursar*, p. vii.

documents discovered must be anterior to the ninth century and comprise numerous official and business papers as well as Buddhist translations[1]. They are of great importance for the history of the Tibetan language and also indicate that at the period when they were written Buddhism at most shared with the Bön religion the allegiance of the Tibetans. No Manichæan or Christian translations in Tibetan have yet been discovered.

Vast numbers of Chinese texts both religious and secular are preserved in all the principal centres and offer many points of interest among which two may be noticed. Firstly the posts on the old military frontier near Tun-huang have furnished a series of dated documents ranging from 98 B.C. to 153 A.D.[2] There is therefore no difficulty in admitting that there was intercourse between China and Central Asia at this period. Secondly, some documents of the T'ang dynasty are Manichæan, with an admixture of Buddhist and Taoist ideas[3].

The religious monuments of Central Asia comprise stupas, caves and covered buildings used as temples or vihâras. Buddhist, Manichæan and Christian edifices have been discovered but apparently no shrines of the Zoroastrian religion, though it had many adherents in these regions, and though representations of Hindu deities have been found, Hinduism is not known to have existed apart from Buddhism[4]. Caves decorated for Buddhist worship are found not only in the Tarim basin but at Tun-huang on the frontier of China proper, near Ta-t'ung-fu in northern Shensi, and in the defile of Lung-mên in the province of Ho-nan. The general scheme and style of these caves are similar, but while in the last two, as in most Indian caves, the figures and ornaments are true sculpture, in the caves of Tun-huang and the Tarim not only is the wall prepared for frescoes, but even the figures are executed in stucco. This form of decoration was congenial to Central Asia for the images which embellished the temple walls were moulded in the same fashion. Temples and caves were sometimes combined, for instance at Bäzäklik where many edifices were erected on a terrace in front

[1] See especially Stein's *Ancient Khotan*, app. B, and Francke in *J.R.A.S.* 1914, p. 37.

[2] Chavannes, *Les documents chinois découverts par Aurel Stein*, 1913.

[3] See especially Chavannes and Pelliot, "Traité Manichéen" in *J.A.* 1911 and 1913.

[4] Hsüan Chuang notes its existence however in Kabul and Kapiśa.

of a series of caves excavated in a mountain corner. Few roofed buildings are well preserved but it seems certain that some were high quadrilateral structures, crowned by a dome of a shape found in Persia, and that others had barrel-shaped roofs, apparently resembling the chaityas of Ter and Chezarla[1]. Le Coq states that this type of architecture is also found in Persia[2]. The commonest type of temple was a hall having at its further end a cella, with a passage behind to allow of circumambulation. Such halls were frequently enlarged by the addition of side rooms and sometimes a shrine was enclosed by several rectangular courts[3].

Many stupas have been found either by themselves or in combination with other buildings. The one which is best preserved (or at any rate reproduced in greatest detail)[4] is the Stupa of Rawak. It is set in a quadrangle bounded by a wall which was ornamented on both its inner and outer face by a series of gigantic statues in coloured stucco. The dome is set upon a rectangular base disposed in three stories and this arrangement is said to characterize all the stupas of Turkestan as well as those of the Kabul valley and adjacent regions.

This architecture appears to owe nothing to China but to include both Indian (especially Gandharan) and Persian elements. Many of its remarkable features, if not common elsewhere, are at least widely scattered. Thus some of the caves at Ming-Öi have dome-like roofs ornamented with a pattern composed of squares within squares, set at an angle with each other. A similar ornamentation is reported from Pandrenthan in Kashmir and from Bamian[5].

The antiquities of Central Asia include frescoes executed on the walls of caves and buildings, and paintings on silk paper[6]. The origin and affinities of this art are still the subject of investigation and any discussion of them would lead me too far from my immediate subject. But a few statements can be

[1] See for these Fergusson-Burgess, *History of Indian Architecture*, I. pp. 125–8.

[2] *J.R.A.S.* 1909, p. 313.

[3] *E.g.* Grünwedel, *Altbuddhistische Kultstätten*, fig. 624.

[4] Stein, *Ancient Khotan*, plates xiii–xvii and xl, pp. 83 and 482 ff.

[5] See Grünwedel, *Buddh. Kultstätten*, pp. 129–130 and plate. Foucher, "L'Art Gréco-Bouddhique," p. 145, *J.R.A.S.* 1886, 333 and plate i.

[6] See Wachsberger's "Stil-kritische Studien zur Kunst Chinesisch-Turkestan's" in *Ostasiatische Ztsft.* 1914 and 1915.

made with some confidence. The influence of Gandhara is plain in architecture, sculpture, and painting. The oldest works may be described as simply Gandharan but this early style is followed by another which shows a development both in technique and in mythology. It doubtless represents Indian Buddhist art as modified by local painters and sculptors. Thus in the Turfan frescoes the drapery and composition are Indian but the faces are eastern asiatic. Sometimes however they represent a race with red hair and blue eyes.

On the whole the paintings testify to the invasion of Far Eastern art by the ideas and designs of Indian Buddhism rather than to an equal combination of Indian and Chinese influence but in some forms of decoration, particularly that employed in the Khan's palace at Idiqutshähri[1], Chinese style is predominant. It may be too that the early pre-buddhist styles of painting in China and Central Asia were similar. In the seventh century a Khotan artist called Wei-ch'ih Po-chih-na migrated to China, where both he and his son Wei-ch'ih I-sêng acquired considerable fame.

Persian influence also is manifest in many paintings. A striking instance may be seen in two plates published by Stein[2] apparently representing the same Boddhisattva. In one he is of the familiar Indian type: the other seems at first sight a miniature of some Persian prince, black-bearded and high-booted, but the figure has four arms. As might be expected, it is the Manichæan paintings which are least Indian in character. They represent a "lost late antique school[3]" which often recalls Byzantine art and was perhaps the parent of mediæval Persian miniature painting.

The paintings of Central Asia resemble its manuscripts. It is impossible to look through any collection of them without feeling that currents of art and civilization flowing from neighbouring and even from distant lands have met and mingled in this basin. As the reader turns over the albums of Stein, Grünwedel or Le Coq he is haunted by strange reminiscences and resemblances, and wonders if they are merely coincidences or whether the pedigrees of these pictured gods and men really

[1] See Grünwedel, *Buddh. Kultstätten*, pp. 332 ff.

[2] *Ancient Khotan*, vol. II. plates lx and lxi.

[3] Le Coq in *J.R.A.S.* 1909, pp. 299 ff. See the whole article.

stretch across time and space to far off origins. Here are coins and seals of Hellenic design, nude athletes that might adorn a Greek vase, figures that recall Egypt, Byzantium or the Bayeux tapestry, with others that might pass for Christian ecclesiastics; Chinese sages, Kṛishṇa dancing to the sound of his flute, frescoes that might be copied from Ajanta, winged youths to be styled cupids or cherubs according to our mood[1].

Stein mentions[2] that he discovered a Buddhist monastery in the terminal marshes of the Helmund in the Persian province of Seistan, containing paintings of a Hellenistic type which show "for the first time *in situ* the Iranian link of the chain which connects the Græco-Buddhist art of extreme north-west India with the Buddhist art of Central Asia and the Far East."

Central Asian art is somewhat wanting in spontaneity. Except when painting portraits (which are many) the artists do not seem to go to nature or even their own imagination and visions. They seem concerned to reproduce some religious scene not as they saw it but as it was represented by Indian or other artists.

2

Only one side of Central Asian history can be written with any completeness, namely its relations with China. Of these some account with dates can be given, thanks to the Chinese annals which incidentally supply valuable information about earlier periods. But unfortunately these relations were often interrupted and also the political record does not always furnish the data which are of most importance for the history of Buddhism. Still there is no better framework available for arranging our data. But even were our information much fuller, we should probably find the history of Central Asia scrappy and disconnected. Its cities were united by no bond of common blood or language, nor can any one of them have had a continuous development in institutions, letters or art. These were imported in a mature form and more or less assimilated in a precocious Augustan age, only to be overwhelmed in some catastrophe which, if not merely destructive, at least brought the ideas and baggage of another race.

[1] For some of the more striking drawings referred to see Grünwedel, *Buddh. Kultstätten*, figs. 51, 53, 239, 242, 317, 337, 345–349.

[2] In *Geog. Journal*, May 1916, p. 362.

It was under the Emperor Wu-ti (140–87 B.C.) of the Han dynasty that the Chinese first penetrated into the Tarim basin. They had heard that the Hsiung-nu, of whose growing power they were afraid, had driven the Yüeh-chih westwards and they therefore despatched an envoy named Chang Ch'ien in the hope of inducing the Yüeh-chih to co-operate with them against the common enemy. Chang Ch'ien made two adventurous expeditions, and visited the Yüeh-chih in their new home somewhere on the Oxus. His mission failed to attain its immediate political object but indirectly had important results, for it revealed to China that the nations on the Oxus were in touch with India on one hand and with the more mysterious west on the other. Henceforth it was her aim to keep open the trade route leading westwards from the extremity of the modern Kansu province to Kashgar, Khotan and the countries with which those cities communicated. Far from wishing to isolate herself or exclude foreigners, her chief desire was to keep the road to the west open, and although there were times when the flood of Buddhism which swept along this road alarmed the more conservative classes, yet for many centuries everything that came in the way of merchandize, art, literature, and religion was eagerly received. The chief hindrance to this intercourse was the hostility of the wild tribes who pillaged caravans and blocked the route, and throughout the whole stretch of recorded history the Chinese used the same method to weaken them and keep the door open, namely to create or utilize a quarrel between two tribes. The Empire allied itself with one in order to crush the second and that being done, proceeded to deal with its former ally.

Dated records beginning with the year 98 B.C. testify to the presence of a Chinese garrison near the modern Tun-huang[1]. But at the beginning of the Christian era the Empire was convulsed by internal rebellion and ceased to have influence or interest in Central Asia. With the restoration of order things took another turn. The reign of the Emperor Ming-ti is the traditional date for the introduction of Buddhism and it also witnessed the victorious campaigns of the famous general and adventurer Pan Ch'ao. He conquered Khotan and Kashgar and victoriously repulsed the attacks of the Kushans or Yüeh-chih who were interested in these regions and endeavoured to stop his progress. The Chinese annals do not give the name of their

[1] Chavannes, *Documents chinois découverts par Aurel Stein*, 1913.

king but it must have been Kanishka if he came to the throne in 78. I confess however that this silence makes it difficult for me to accept 78–123 A.D. as the period of Kanishka's reign, for he must have been a monarch of some celebrity and if the Chinese had come into victorious contact with him, would not their historians have mentioned it? It seems to me more probable that he reigned before or after Pan Ch'ao's career in Central Asia which lasted from A.D. 73–102. With the end of that career Chinese activity ceased for some time and perhaps the Kushans conquered Kashgar and Khotan early in the second century. Neither the degenerate Han dynasty nor the stormy Three Kingdoms could grapple with distant political problems and during the fourth, fifth and sixth centuries northern China was divided among Tartar states, short-lived and mutually hostile. The Empire ceased to be a political power in the Tarim basin but intercourse with Central Asia and in particular the influx of Buddhism increased, and there was also a return wave of Chinese influence westwards. Meanwhile two tribes, the Hephthalites (or White Huns) and the Turks[1], successively became masters of Central Asia and founded states sometimes called Empires—that is to say they overran vast tracts within which they took tribute without establishing any definite constitution or frontiers.

When the T'ang dynasty (618–907) re-united the Empire, the Chinese Government with characteristic tenacity reverted to its old policy of keeping the western road open and to its old methods. The Turks were then divided into two branches, the northern and western, at war with one another. The Chinese allied themselves with the latter, defeated the northern Turks and occupied Turfan (640). Then in a series of campaigns, in which they were supported by the Uigurs, they conquered their former allies the western Turks and proceeded to organize the Tarim basin under the name of the Four Garrisons[2]. This was the most glorious period of China's foreign policy and at no other time had she so great a position as a western power. The

[1] These of course are not the Osmanlis or Turks of Constantinople. The Osmanlis are the latest of the many branches of the Turks, who warred and ruled in Central Asia with varying success from the fifth to the eighth centuries.

[2] That is Kashgar, Khotan, Kucha and Tokmak for which last Karashahr was subsequently substituted. The territory was also called An Hsi.

list of her possessions included Bokhara in the west and starting from Semirechinsk and Tashkent in the north extended southwards so as to embrace Afghanistan with the frontier districts of India and Persia[1]. It is true that the Imperial authority in many of these regions was merely nominal: when the Chinese conquered a tribe which claimed sovereignty over them they claimed sovereignty themselves. But for the history of civilization, for the migration of art and ideas, even this nominal claim is important, for China was undoubtedly in touch with India, Bokhara and Persia.

But no sooner did these great vistas open, than new enemies appeared to bar the road. The Tibetans descended into the Tarim basin and after defeating the Chinese in 670 held the Four Garrisons till 692, when the fortunes of war were reversed. But the field was not left clear for China: the power of the northern Turks revived, and Mohammedanism, then a new force but destined to ultimate triumph in politics and religion alike, appeared in the west. The conquests of the Mohammedan general Qutayba (705–715) extended to Ferghana and he attacked Kashgar. In the long reign of Hsüan Tsung China waged a double warfare against the Arabs and Tibetans. For about thirty years (719–751) the struggle was successful. Even Tabaristan is said to have acknowledged China's suzerainty. Her troops crossed the Hindu Kush and reached Gilgit. But in 751 they sustained a crushing defeat near Tashkent. The disaster was aggravated by the internal troubles of the Empire and it was long before Chinese authority recovered from the blow[2]. The Tibetans reaped the advantage. Except in Turfan, they were the dominant power of the Tarim basin for a century, they took tribute from China and when it was refused sacked the capital, Chang-an (763). It would appear however that for a time Chinese garrisons held out in Central Asia and Chinese officials exercised some authority, though they obtained no support from the Empire[3]. But although even late in the tenth century Khotan sent embassies to the Imperial Court, China

[1] See for lists and details Chavannes, *Documents sur les Tou-kiue Occidentaux*, pp. 67 ff. and 270 ff.

[2] The conquest and organization of the present Chinese Turkestan dates only from the reign of Ch'ien Lung.

[3] Thus the pilgrim Wu-K'ung mentions Chinese officials in the Four Garrisons.

gradually ceased to be a Central Asian power. She made a treaty with the Tibetans (783) and an alliance with the Uigurs, who now came to the front and occupied Turfan, where there was a flourishing Uigur kingdom with Manichæism as the state religion from about 750 to 843. In that year the Kirghiz sacked Turfan and it is interesting to note that the Chinese who had hitherto tolerated Manichæism as the religion of their allies, at once began to issue restrictive edicts against it. But except in Turfan it does not appear that the power of the Uigurs was weakened[1]. In 860–817 they broke up Tibetan rule in the Tarim basin and formed a new kingdom of their own which apparently included Kashgar, Urumtsi and Kucha but not Khotan. The prince of Kashgar embraced Islam about 945, but the conversion of Khotan and Turfan was later. With this conversion the connection of the Tarim basin with the history of Buddhism naturally ceases, for it does not appear that the triumphal progress of Lamaism under Khubilai Khan affected these regions.

3

The Tarim basin, though sometimes united under foreign rule, had no indigenous national unity. Cities, or groups of towns, divided by deserts lived their own civic life and enjoyed considerable independence under native sovereigns, although the Chinese, Turks or Tibetans quartered troops in them and appointed residents to supervise the collection of tribute. The chief of these cities or oases were Kashgar in the west: Kucha, Karashahr, Turfan (Idiqutshähri, Chotscho) and Hami lying successively to the north-east: Yarkand, Khotan and Miran to the south-east[2]. It may be well to review briefly the special history of some of them.

The relics found near Kashgar, the most western of these cities, are comparatively few, probably because its position exposed it to the destructive influence of Islam at an early date. Chinese writers reproduce the name as Ch'ia-sha, Chieh-ch'a, etc., but also call the region Su-lê, Shu-lê, or Sha-lê[3]. It is

[1] See for this part of their history, Grenard's article in *J.A.* 1900, I. pp. 1–79.

[2] Pelliot also attributes importance to a Sogdian Colony to the south of Lob Nor, which may have had much to do with the transmission of Buddhism and Nestorianism to China. See *J.A.* Jan. 1916, pp. 111–123.

[3] These words have been connected with the tribe called Sacae, Sakas, or Sök.

mentioned first in the Han annals. After the missions of Chang-Ch'ien trade with Bactria and Sogdiana grew rapidly and Kashgar which was a convenient emporium became a Chinese protected state in the first century B.C. But when the hold of China relaxed about the time of the Christian era it was subdued by the neighbouring kingdom of Khotan. The conquests of Pan-Ch'ao restored Chinese supremacy but early in the second century the Yüeh-chih interfered in the politics of Kashgar and placed on the throne a prince who was their tool. The introduction of Buddhism is ascribed to this epoch[1]. If Kanishka was then reigning the statement that he conquered Kashgar and Khotan is probably correct. It is supported by Hsüan Chuang's story of the hostages and by his assertion that Kanishka's rule extended to the east of the Ts'ung-ling mountains: also by the discovery of Kanishka's coins in the Khotan district. Little is heard of Kashgar until Fa-Hsien visited it in 400[2]. He speaks of the quinquennial religious conferences held by the king, at one of which he was present, of relics of the Buddha and of a monastery containing a thousand monks all students of the Hinayana. About 460 the king sent as a present to the Chinese Court an incombustible robe once worn by the Buddha. Shortly afterwards Kashgar was incorporated in the dominions of the Hephthalites, and when these succumbed to the western Turks about 465, it merely changed masters.

Hsüan Chuang has left an interesting account of Kashgar as he found it on his return journey[3]. The inhabitants were sincere Buddhists and there were more than a thousand monks of the Sarvâstivâdin school. But their knowledge was not in proportion to their zeal for they read the scriptures diligently without understanding them. They used an Indian alphabet into which they had introduced alterations.

[1] See Klaproth, *Tabl. Historique*, p. 166, apparently quoting from Chinese sources. Specht, *J.A.* 1897, II. p. 187. Franke, *Beitr. zur Kenntniss Zentral-Asiens*, p. 83. The passage quoted by Specht from the Later Han Annals clearly states that the Yüeh-chih made a man of their own choosing prince of Kashgar, although, as Franke points out, it makes no reference to Kanishka or the story of the hostages related by Hsüan Chuang.

[2] Fa-Hsien's Chieh-ch'a has been interpreted as Skardo, but Chavannes seems to have proved that it is Kashgar.

[3] About 643 A.D. He mentions that the inhabitants tattooed their bodies, flattened their children's heads and had green eyes. Also that they spoke a peculiar language.

According to Hsüan Chuang's religious conspectus of these regions, Kashgar, Osh and Kucha belonged to the Small Vehicle, Yarkand and Khotan mainly to the Great. The Small Vehicle also flourished at Balkh and at Bamian[1]. In Kapiśa the Great Vehicle was predominant but there were also many Hindu sects: in the Kabul valley too Hinduism and Buddhism seem to have been mixed: in Persia[2] there were several hundred Sarvâstivâdin monks. In Tokhara (roughly equivalent to Badakshan) there was some Buddhism but apparently it did not flourish further north in the regions of Tashkent and Samarkand. In the latter town there were two disused monasteries but when Hsüan Chuang's companions entered them they were mobbed by the populace. He says that these rioters were fire worshippers and that the Turks whom he visited somewhere near Aulieata were of the same religion. This last statement is perhaps inaccurate but the T'ang annals expressly state that the population of Kashgar and Khotan was in part Zoroastrian[3]. No mention of Nestorianism in Kashgar at this date has yet been discovered, although in the thirteenth century it was a Nestorian see. But since Nestorianism had penetrated even to China in the seventh century, it probably also existed in Samarkand and Kashgar.

The pilgrim Wu-K'ung spent five months in Kashgar about 786, but there appear to be no later data of interest for the study of Buddhism.

The town of Kucha[4] lies between Kashgar and Turfan, somewhat to the west of Karashahr. In the second century B.C. it was already a flourishing city. Numerous dated documents show that about 630 A.D. the language of ordinary life was the interesting idiom sometimes called Tokharian B, and, since the Chinese annals record no alien invasion, we may conclude that Kucha existed as an Aryan colony peopled by the speakers of

[1] At Bamian the monks belonged to the Lokottaravâdin School.

[2] Beal, *Records*, II. p. 278. The pilgrim is speaking from hearsay and it is not clear to what part of Persia he refers.

[3] See Chavannes, *Documents sur les Tou-kiue Occidentaux*, pp. 121, 125. The inhabitants of K'ang (Samarkand or Sogdiana) are said to honour both religions. *Ib.* p. 135.

[4] Known to the Chinese by several slightly different names such as Ku-chih, Kiu-tse which are all attempts to represent the same sound. For Kucha see S. Lévi's most interesting article "Le 'Tokharien B' langue de Koutcha" in *J.A.* 1913, II. pp. 311 ff.

this language some centuries before the Christian era. It is mentioned in the Han annals and when brought into contact with China in the reign of Wu-ti (140–87 B.C.) it became a place of considerable importance, as it lay at the junction[1] of the western trade routes leading to Kashgar and Aulieata respectively. Kucha absorbed some Chinese civilization but its doubtful loyalty to the Imperial throne often involved it in trouble. It is not until the Western Tsin dynasty that we find it described as a seat of Buddhism. The Tsin annals say that it was enclosed by a triple wall and contained a thousand stupas and Buddhist temples as well as a magnificent palace for the king[2]. This implies that Buddhism had been established for some time but no evidence has been found to date its introduction.

In 383 Fu-chien, Emperor of the Tsin dynasty, sent his general Lü-Kuang to subdue Kucha[3]. The expedition was successful and among the captives taken was the celebrated Kumârajîva. Lü-Kuang was so pleased with the magnificent and comfortable life of Kucha that he thought of settling there but Kumârajîva prophesied that he was destined to higher things. So they left to try their fortune in China. Lü-Kuang rose to be ruler of the state known as Southern Liang and his captive and adviser became one of the greatest names in Chinese Buddhism.

Kumârajîva is a noticeable figure and his career illustrates several points of importance. First, his father came from India and he himself went as a youth to study in Kipin (Kashmir) and then returned to Kucha. Living in this remote corner of Central Asia he was recognized as an encyclopædia of Indian learning including a knowledge of the Vedas and "heretical śâstras." Secondly after his return to Kucha he was converted to Mahayanism. Thirdly he went from Kucha to China where he had a distinguished career as a translator. Thus we see how

[1] *J.A.* 1913, II. p. 326.

[2] See Chavannes in Stein's *Ancient Khotan*, p. 544. The Western Tsin reigned 265–317.

[3] The circumstances which provoked the expedition are not very clear. It was escorted by the king of Turfan and other small potentates who were the vassals of the Tsin and also on bad terms with Kucha. They probably asked Fu-chien for assistance in subduing their rival which he was delighted to give. Some authorities (*e.g.* Nanjio Cat. p. 406) give Karashahr as the name of Kumârajîva's town, but this seems to be a mistake.

China was brought into intellectual touch with India and how the Mahayana was gaining in Central Asia territory previously occupied by the Hinayana. The monk Dharmagupta who passed through Kucha about 584 says that the king favoured Mahayanism[1]. That Kucha should have been the home of distinguished translators is not strange for a statement[2] has been preserved to the effect that Sanskrit texts were used in the cities lying to the west of it, but that in Kucha itself Indian languages were not understood and translations were made, although such Sanskrit words as were easily intelligible were retained.

In the time of the Wei, Kucha again got into trouble with China and was brought to order by another punitive expedition in 448. After this lesson a long series of tribute-bearing missions is recorded, sent first to the court of Wei, and afterwards to the Liang, Chou and Sui. The notices respecting the country are to a large extent repetitions. They praise its climate, fertility and mineral wealth: the magnificence of the royal palace, the number and splendour of the religious establishments. Peacocks were as common as fowls and the Chinese annalists evidently had a general impression of a brilliant, pleasure-loving and not very moral city. It was specially famous for its music: the songs and dances of Kucha, performed by native artists, were long in favour at the Imperial Court, and a list of twenty airs has been preserved[3].

When the T'ang dynasty came to the throne Kucha sent an embassy to do homage but again supported Karashahr in rebellion and again brought on herself a punitive expedition (648). But the town was peaceful and prosperous when visited by Hsüan Chuang about 630.

His description agrees in substance with other notices, but he praises the honesty of the people. He mentions that the king was a native and that a much modified Indian alphabet was in use. As a churchman, he naturally dwells with pleasure on the many monasteries and great images, the quinquennial

[1] S. Lévi, *J.A.* 1913, II. p. 348, quoting Hsü Kao Sêng Chuan.

[2] Quoted by S. Lévi from the *Sung Kao Sêng Chuan*. See *J.A.* 1913, II. p. 344 and *B.E.F.E.O.* 1904, p. 562.

[3] As a proof of foreign influence in Chinese culture, it is interesting to note that there were seven orchestras for the imperial banquets, including those of Kucha, Bokhara and India and a mixed one in which were musicians from Samarkand, Kashgar, Camboja and Japan.

assemblies and religious processions. There were more than 100 monasteries with upwards of 5000 brethren who all followed the Sarvâstivâda and the "gradual teaching," which probably means the Hinayana as opposed to the sudden illumination caused by Mahayanist revelation. The pilgrim differed from his hosts on the matter of diet and would not join them in eating meat. But he admits that the monks were strict according to their lights and that the monasteries were centres of learning.

In 658 Kucha was made the seat of government for the territory known as the Four Garrisons. During the next century it sent several missions to the Chinese and about 788 was visited by Wu-K'ung, who indicates that music and Buddhism were still flourishing. He mentions an Abbot who spoke with equal fluency the language of the country, Chinese and Sanskrit. Nothing is known about Kucha from this date until the eleventh century when we again hear of missions to the Chinese Court. The annals mention them under the heading of Uigurs, but Buddhism seems not to have been extinct for even in 1096 the Envoy presented to the Emperor a jade Buddha. According to Hsüan Chuang's account the Buddhism of Karashahr (Yenki) was the same as that of Kucha and its monasteries enjoyed the same reputation for strictness and learning.

Turfan is an oasis containing the ruins of several cities and possibly different sites were used as the capital at different periods. But the whole area is so small that such differences can be of little importance. The name Turfan appears to be modern. The Ming Annals[1] state that this city lies in the land of ancient Ch'e-shih (or Kü-shih) called Kao Ch'ang in the time of the Sui. This name was abolished by the T'ang but restored by the Sung.

The principal city now generally known as Chotscho seems to be identical with Kao Ch'ang[2] and Idiqutshähri and is called by Mohammedans Apsus or Ephesus, a curious designation connected with an ancient sacred site renamed the Cave of the Seven Sleepers. Extensive literary remains have been found in the oasis; they include works in Sanskrit, Chinese, and various Iranian and Turkish idioms but also in two dialects of so-called

[1] Quoted by Bretschneider, *Mediaeval Researches*, II. 189.

[2] Pelliot, *J.A.* 1912, I. p. 579, suggests that Chotscho or Qoco is the Turkish equivalent of Kao Ch'ang in T'ang pronunciation, the nasal being omitted.

Tokharian. Blue-eyed, red-haired and red-bearded people are frequently portrayed on the walls of Turfan.

But the early history of this people and of their civilization is chiefly a matter of theory. In the Han period[1] there was a kingdom called Kü-shih or Kiü-shih, with two capitals. It was destroyed in 60 B.C. by the Chinese general Chêng-Chi and eight small principalities were formed in its place. In the fourth and fifth centuries A.D. Turfan had some connection with two ephemeral states which arose in Kansu under the names of Hou Liang and Pei Liang. The former was founded by Lü-Kuang, the general who, as related above, took Kucha. He fell foul of a tribe in his territory called Chü-ch'ü, described as belonging to the Hsiung-nu. Under their chieftain Mêng-hsün, who devoted his later years to literature and Buddhism, this tribe took a good deal of territory from the Hou Liang, in Turkestan as well as in Kansu, and called their state Pei Liang. It was conquered by the Wei dynasty in 439 and two members of the late reigning house determined to try their fortune in Turfan and ruled there successively for about twenty years. An Chou, the second of these princes, died in 480 and his fame survives because nine years after his death a temple to Maitreya was dedicated in his honour with a long inscription in Chinese.

Another line of Chinese rulers, bearing the family name of Ch'iu, established themselves at Kao-ch'ang in 507 and under the Sui dynasty one of them married a Chinese princess. Turfan paid due homage to the T'ang dynasty on its accession but later it was found that tributary missions coming from the west to the Chinese court were stopped there and the close relations of its king with the western Turks inspired alarm. Accordingly it was destroyed by the imperial forces in 640. This is confirmed by the record of Hsüan Chuang. In his biography there is a description of his reception by the king of Kao-ch'ang on his outward journey. But in the account of his travels written after his return he speaks of the city as no longer existent.

Nevertheless the political and intellectual life of the oasis was not annihilated. It was conquered by the Uigurs at an uncertain date, but they were established there in the eighth and ninth centuries and about 750 their Khan adopted Manichæism as the state religion. The many manuscripts in Sogdian and

[1] Chavannes, *Tou-kiue Occidentaux*, p. 101.

other Persian dialects found at Turfan show that it had an old and close connection with the west. It is even possible that Mani may have preached there himself but it does not appear that his teaching became influential until about 700 A.D. The presence of Nestorianism is also attested. Tibetan influence too must have affected Turfan in the eighth and ninth centuries for many Tibetan documents have been found there although it seems to have been outside the political sphere of Tibet. About 843 this Uigur Kingdom was destroyed by the Kirghiz.

Perhaps the massacres of Buddhist priests, clearly indicated by vaults filled with skeletons still wearing fragments of the monastic robe, occurred in this period. But Buddhism was not extinguished and lingered here longer than in other parts of the Tarim basin. Even in 1420 the people of Turfan were Buddhists and the Ming Annals say that at Huo-chou (or Kara-Khojo) there were more Buddhist temples than dwelling houses.

Let us now turn to Khotan[1]. This was the ancient as well as the modern name of the principal city in the southern part of the Tarim basin but was modified in Chinese to Yü-t'ien, in Sanskrit to Kustana[2]. The Tibetan equivalent is Li-yul, the land of Li, but no explanation of this designation is forthcoming.

Traditions respecting the origin of Khotan are preserved in the travels of Hsüan Chuang and also in the Tibetan scriptures, some of which are expressly said to be translations from the language of Li. These traditions are popular legends but they agree in essentials and appear to contain a kernel of important truth namely that Khotan was founded by two streams of colonization coming from China and from India[3], the latter being somehow connected with Asoka. It is remarkable that the introduction of Buddhism is attributed not to these original colonists but to a later missionary who, according to Hsüan Chuang, came from Kashmir[4].

[1] For the history of Khotan see Rémusat, *Ville de Khotan*, 1820, and Stein's great work *Ancient Khotan*, especially chapter VII. For the Tibetan traditions see Rockhill, *Life of the Buddha*, pp. 230 ff.

[2] Ku-stana seems to have been a learned perversion of the name, to make it mean breast of the earth.

[3] The combination is illustrated by the Sino-Kharoshthî coins with a legend in Chinese on the obverse and in Prakrit on the reverse. See Stein, *Ancient Khotan*, p. 204. But the coins are later than 73 A.D.

[4] The Tibetan text gives the date of conversion as the reign of King Vijayasambhava, 170 years after the foundation of Khotan.

This traditional connection with India is confirmed by the discovery of numerous documents written in Kharoshṭhî characters and a Prakrit dialect. Their contents indicate that this Prakrit was the language of common life and they were found in one heap with Chinese documents dated 269 A.D. The presence of this alphabet and language is not adequately explained by the activity of Buddhist missionaries for in Khotan, as in other parts of Asia, the concomitants of Buddhism are Sanskrit and the Brahmi alphabet.

There was also Iranian influence in Khotan. It shows itself in art and has left indubitable traces in the language called by some Nordarisch, but when the speakers of that language reached the oasis or what part they played there, we do not yet know.

As a consequence of Chang Ch'ien's mission mentioned above, Khotan sent an Embassy to the Chinese Court in the reign of Wu-ti (140–87 B.C.) and the T'ang Annals state that its kings handed down the insignia of Imperial investiture from that time onwards. There seems however to have been a dynastic revolution about 60 A.D. and it is possible that the Vijaya line of kings, mentioned in various Tibetan works, then began to reign[1]. Khotan became a powerful state but submitted to the conquering arms of Pan-Ch'ao and perhaps was subsequently subdued by Kanishka. As the later Han dynasty declined, it again became strong but continued to send embassies to the Imperial Court. There is nothing more to mention until the visit of Fa-Hsien in 400. He describes "the pleasant and prosperous kingdom" with evident gusto. There were some tens of thousands of monks mostly followers of the Mahayana and in the country, where the homes of the people were scattered "like stars" about the oases, each house had a small stupa before the door. He stopped in a well ordered convent with 3000 monks and mentions a magnificent establishment called The King's New Monastery. He also describes a great car festival which shows the Indian colour of Khotanese religion. Perhaps Fa-Hsien and Hsüan Chuang unduly emphasize ecclesiastical features, but they also did not hesitate to say when they thought things unsatisfactory and their praise shows that Buddhism was flourishing.

In the fifth and sixth centuries Khotan passed through troublous times and was attacked by the Tanguts, Juan-Juan

[1] See Sten Konow in *J.R.A.S.* 1914, p. 345.

and White Huns. Throughout this stormy period missions were sent at intervals to China to beg for help. The pilgrim Sung Yün[1] traversed the oasis in 519. His account of the numerous banners bearing Chinese inscriptions hung up in the temple of Han-mo proves that though the political influence of China was weak, she was still in touch with the Tarim basin.

When the T'ang effectively asserted their suzerainty in Central Asia, Khotan was included in the Four Garrisons. The T'ang Annals while repeating much which is found in earlier accounts, add some points of interest, for they say that the Khotanese revere the God of Heaven (Hsien shên) and also the Law of Buddha[2]. This undoubtedly means that there were Zoroastrians as well as Buddhists, which is not mentioned in earlier periods. The annals also mention that the king's house was decorated with pictures and that his family name was Wei Ch'ih. This may possibly be a Chinese rendering of Vijaya, the Sanskrit name or title which according to Tibetan sources was borne by all the sovereigns of Khotan.

Hsüan Chuang broke his return journey at Khotan in 644. He mentions the fondness of the people for music and says that their language differed from that of other countries. The Mahâyâna was the prevalent sect but the pilgrim stopped in a monastery of the Sarvâstivâdins[3]. He describes several sites in the neighbourhood, particularly the Gośringa or Cow-horn mountain[4], supposed to have been visited by the Buddha. Though he does not mention Zoroastrians, he notices that the people of P'i-mo near Khotan were not Buddhists.

About 674 the king of Khotan did personal homage at the Chinese Court. The Emperor constituted his territory into a government called P'i-sha after the deity P'i-sha-mên or Vaiśravana and made him responsible for its administration. Another king did homage between 742 and 755 and received an imperial princess as his consort. Chinese political influence was effective until the last decade of the eighth century but after 790 the conquests of the Tibetans put an end to it and there is

[1] See Stein, *Ancient Khotan*, pp. 170, 456.

[2] Chavannes, *Tou-kiue*, p. 125, cf. pp. 121 and 170. For Hsien shên see Giles's *Chinese Dict.* No. 4477.

[3] Beal, *Life*, p. 205.

[4] Identified by Stein with Kohmari Hill which is still revered by Mohammedans as a sacred spot.

no mention of Khotan in the Chinese Annals for about 150 years. Numerous Tibetan manuscripts and inscriptions found at Endere testify to these conquests. The rule of the Uigurs who replaced Tibet as the dominant power in Turfan and the northern Tarim basin does not appear to have extended to Khotan.

It is not till 938 that we hear of renewed diplomatic relations with China. The Imperial Court received an embassy from Khotan and deemed it of sufficient importance to despatch a special mission in return. Eight other embassies were sent to China in the tenth century and at least three of them were accompanied by Buddhist priests. Their object was probably to solicit help against the attacks of Mohammedans. No details are known as to the Mohammedan conquest but it apparently took place between 970 and 1009 after a long struggle.

Another cultural centre of the Tarim basin must have existed in the oases near Lob-nor where Miran and a nameless site to the north of the lake have been investigated by Stein. They have yielded numerous Tibetan documents, but also fine remains of Gandharan art and Prakrit documents written in the Kharoshthî character. Probably the use of this language and alphabet was not common further east, for though a Kharoshthî fragment was found by Stein in an old Chinese frontier post[1] the library of Tun-huang yielded no specimens of them. That library, however, dating apparently from the epoch of the T'ang, contained some Sanskrit Buddhist literature and was rich in Sogdian, Turkish, and Tibetan manuscripts.

4

Ample as are the materials for the study of Buddhism in Central Asia those hitherto published throw little light on the time and manner of its introduction. At present much is hypothetical for we have few historical data—such as the career of Kumârajîva and the inscription on the Temple of Maitreya at Turfan—but a great mass of literary and artistic evidence from which various deductions can be drawn.

It is clear that there was constant intercourse with India and the Oxus region. The use of Prakrit and of various Iranian idioms points to actual colonization from these two quarters and

[1] *Desert Cathay*, II. p. 114.

it is probable that there were two streams of Buddhism, for the Chinese pilgrims agree that Shan-shan (near Lob-nor), Turfan, Kucha and Kashgar were Hînayânist, whereas Yarkand and Khotan were Mahâyânist. Further, much of the architecture, sculpture and painting is simply Gandharan and the older specimens can hardly be separated from the Gandharan art of India by any considerable interval. This art was in part coeval with Kanishka, and if his reign began in 78 A.D. or later the first specimens of it cannot be much anterior to the Christian era. The earliest Chinese notices of the existence of Buddhism in Kashgar and Kucha date from 400 (Fa-Hsien) and the third century (Annals of the Tsin, 265–317) respectively, but they speak of it as the national religion and munificently endowed, so that it may well have been established for some centuries. In Turfan the first definite record is the dedication of a temple to Maitreya in 469 but probably the history of religion there was much the same as in Kucha.

It is only in Khotan that tradition, if not history, gives a more detailed narrative. This is found in the works of the Chinese pilgrims Hsüan Chuang and Sung Yün and also in four Tibetan works which are apparently translated from the language of Khotan[1]. As the story is substantially the same in all, it merits consideration and may be accepted as the account current in the literary circles of Khotan about 500 A.D. It relates that the Indians who were part-founders of that city in the reign of Asoka were not Buddhists[2] and the Tibetan version places the conversion with great apparent accuracy 170 years after the foundation of the kingdom and 404 after the death of the Buddha. At that time a monk named Vairocana, who was an incarnation of Manjuśri, came to Khotan, according to Hsüan Chuang from Kashmir[3]. He is said to have introduced a new language as well as Mahâyânism, and the king, Vijayasambhava, built for him the great monastery of Tsarma outside the capital, which was miraculously supplied with relics. We cannot be sure

[1] See Watters, *Yüan Chwang*, II. p. 296. Beal, *Life*, p. 205. Chavannes, "Voyage de Sung Yun," *B.E.F.E.O.* 1903, 395, and for the Tibetan sources, Rockhill, *Life of the Buddha*, chap. VIII. One of the four Tibetan works is expressly stated to be translated from Khotanese.

[2] The Tibetan Chronicles of Li-Yul say that they worshipped Vaiśravana and Śrîmahâdevî.

[3] A monk from Kashmir called Vairocana was also active in Tibet about 750 A.D.

that the Tibetan dates were intended to have the meaning they would bear for our chronology, that is about 80 B.C., but if they had, there is nothing improbable in the story, for other traditions assert that Buddhism was preached in Kashmir in the time of Asoka. On the other hand, there was a dynastic change in Khotan about 60 A.D. and the monarch who then came to the throne may have been Vijayasambhava.

According to the Tibetan account no more monasteries were built for seven reigns. The eighth king built two, one on the celebrated Gośirsha or Gośringa mountain. In the eleventh reign after Vijayasambhava, more chaityas and viharas were built in connection with the introduction of the silkworm industry. Subsequently, but without any clear indication of date, the introduction of the Mahâsanghika and Sarvâstivâdin schools is mentioned.

The Tibetan annals also mention several persecutions of Buddhism in Khotan as a result of which the monks fled to Tibet and Bruzha. Their chronology is confused but seems to make these troubles coincide with a persecution in Tibet, presumably that of Lang-dar-ma. If so, the persecution in Khotan must have been due to the early attacks of Mohammedans which preceded the final conquest in about 1000 A.D.[1]

Neither the statements of the Chinese annalists about Central Asia nor its own traditions prove that Buddhism flourished there before the Christian era. But they do not disprove it and even if the dream of the Emperor Ming-Ti and the consequent embassy are dismissed as legends, it is admitted that Buddhism penetrated to China by land not later than the early decades of that era. It must therefore have been known in Central Asia previously and perhaps Khotan was the place where it first flourished.

It is fairly certain that about 160 B.C. the Yüeh-chih moved westwards and settled in the lands of the Oxus after ejecting the Sakas, but like many warlike nomads they may have oscillated between the east and west, recoiling if they struck against a powerful adversary in either quarter. Le Coq has put forward an interesting theory of their origin. It is that they were one of the tribes known as Scythians in Europe and at an unknown

[1] It is also possible that Buddhism had a bad time in the fifth and sixth centuries at the hands of the Tanguts, Juan-Juan and White Huns.

period moved eastwards from southern Russia, perhaps leaving traces of their presence in the monuments still existing in the district of Minussinsk. He also identifies them with the red-haired, blue-eyed people of the Chotscho frescoes and the speakers of the Tokharian language. But these interesting hypotheses cannot be regarded as proved. It is, however, certain that the Yüeh-chih invaded India[1], founded the Kushan Empire and were intimately connected (especially in the person of their great king Kanishka) with Gandharan art and the form of Buddhism which finds expression in it. Now the Chinese pilgrim Fa-Hsien (*c.* 400) found the Hînayâna prevalent in Shan-shan, Kucha, Kashgar, Osh, Udyana and Gandhara. Hsüan Chuang also notes its presence in Balkh, Bamian, and Persia. Both notice that the Mahâyâna was predominant in Khotan though not to the exclusion of the other school. It would appear that in modern language the North-West Frontier province of India, Afghanistan, Badakshan (with small adjoining states), the Pamir regions and the Tarim basin all accepted Gandharan Buddhism and at one time formed part of the Kushan Empire.

It is probably to this Gandharan Buddhism that the Chinese pilgrims refer when they speak of the Sarvâstivâdin school of the Hînayâna as prevalent. It is known that this school was closely connected with the Council of Kanishka. Its metaphysics were decidedly not Mahâyânist but there is no reason why it should have objected to the veneration of such Bodhisattvas as are portrayed in the Gandhara sculptures. An interesting passage in the life of Hsüan Chuang relates that he had a dispute in Kucha with a Mahâyânist doctor who maintained that the books called Tsa-hsin, Chü-shê, and P'i-sha were sufficient for salvation, and denounced the Yogaśâstra as heretical, to the great indignation of the pilgrim[2] whose practical definition of Mahâyânism seems to have been the acceptance of this work,

[1] The Later Han Annals say that the Hindus are weaker than the Yüeh-chih and are not accustomed to fight because they are Buddhists. (See *T'oung Pao*, 1910, p. 192.) This seems to imply that the Yüeh-chih were not Buddhists. But even this was the real view of the compiler of the Annals we do not know from what work he took this statement nor to what date it refers.

[2] See Beal, *Life*, p. 39, Julien, p. 50. The books mentioned are apparently the Samyuktâbhidharmahṛidaya (Nanjio, 1287), Abhidharma Kosha (Nanjio, 1267), Abhidharma-Vibhâsha (Nanjio, 1264) and Yogâcâryabhûmi (Nanjio, 1170).

reputed to have been revealed by Maitreya to Asanga. Such a definition and division might leave in the Hînayâna much that we should not expect to find there.

The Mahâyânist Buddhism of Khotan was a separate stream and Hsüan Chuang says that it came from Kashmir. Though Kashmir is not known as a centre of Mahâyânism, yet it would be a natural route for men and ideas passing from any part of India to Khotan.

5

The Tarim basin and the lands of the Oxus[1] were a region where different religions and cultures mingled and there is no difficulty in supposing that Buddhism might have amalgamated there with Zoroastrianism or Christianity. The question is whether there is any evidence for such amalgamation. It is above all in its relations with China that Central Asia appears as an exchange of religions. It passed on to China the art and thought of India, perhaps adding something of its own on the way and then received them back from China with further additions[2]. It certainly received a great deal from Persia: the number of manuscripts in different Iranian languages puts this beyond doubt. Equally undoubted is its debt to India, but it would be of even greater interest to determine whether Indian Buddhism owes a debt to Central Asia and to define that debt. For Tibet the relation was mutual. The Tibetans occupied the Tarim basin during a century and according to their traditions monks went from Khotan to instruct Tibet.

The Buddhist literature discovered in Central Asia represents, like its architecture, several periods. We have first of all the fragments of the Sanskrit Âgamas, found at Turfan, Tun-huang, and in the Khotan district: fragments of the dramas and poems of Aśvaghosha from Turfan: the Prâtimoksha of the Sarvastivâdins from Kucha and numerous versions of the anthology called Dharmapada or Udâna. The most interesting of these is the Prakrit version found in the neighbourhood of Khotan, but fragments in Tokharian and Sanskrit have also been discovered.

[1] The importance of the Tarim basin is due to the excellent preservation of its records and its close connection with China. The Oxus regions suffered more from Mohammedan iconoclasm, but they may have been at least equally important for the history of Buddhism.

[2] *E.g.* see the Maitreya inscription of Turfan.

All this literature probably represents the canon as it existed in the epoch of Kanishka and of the Gandharan sculptures, or at least the older stratum in that canon.

The newer stratum is composed of Mahâyânist sutras of which there is a great abundance, though no complete list has been published[1]. The popularity of the Prajñâ-pâramitâ, the Lotus and the Suvarṇa-prabhâsa is attested. The last was translated into both Uigur (from the Chinese) and into "Iranien Oriental." To a still later epoch[2] belong the Dhâraṇîs or magical formulæ which have been discovered in considerable quantities.

Sylvain Lévi has shown that some Mahâyânist sutras were either written or re-edited in Central Asia[3]. Not only do they contain lists of Central Asian place-names but these receive an importance which can be explained only by the local patriotism of the writer or the public which he addressed. Thus the Sûrya-garbha sutra praises the mountain of Gośringa near Khotan much as the Puranas celebrate in special chapters called Mâhâtmyas the merits of some holy place. Even more remarkable is a list in the Chandragarbha sutra. The Buddha in one of the great transformation scenes common in these works sends forth rays of light which produce innumerable manifestations of Buddhas. India (together with what is called the western region) has a total of 813 manifestations, whereas Central Asia and China have 971. Of these the whole Chinese Empire has 255, the kingdoms of Khotan and Kucha have 180 and 99 respectively, but only 60 are given to Benares and 30 to Magadha. Clearly Central Asia was a very important place for the author of this list[4].

One of the Turkish sutras discovered at Turfan contains a discourse of the Buddha to the merchants Trapusha and Bhallika who are described as Turks and Indra is called Kormusta, that is Hormuzd. In another Brahmâ is called Aṣrua, identified as the Iranian deity Zervan[5]. In these instances no innovation of doctrine is implied but when the world of spirits and men

[1] Or at least is not accessible to me here in Hongkong, 1914.

[2] I do not mean to say that all Dhâraṇîs are late.

[3] It is even probable that apocryphal Sûtras were composed in Central Asia. See Pelliot in *Mélanges d'Indianisme*, Sylvain Lévi, p. 329.

[4] The list of manifestations in Jambudvipa enumerates 56 kingdoms. All cannot be identified with certainty, but apparently less than half are within India proper

[5] See *Bibl. Budd.* XII. pp. 44, 46, XIV. p. 45.

becomes Central Asian instead of Indian, it is only natural that the doctrine too should take on some local colour[1].

Thus the dated inscription of the temple erected in Turfan A.D. 469 is a mixture of Chinese ideas, both Confucian and Taoist, with Indian. It is in honour of Maitreya, a Bodhisattva known to the Hînayâna, but here regarded not merely as the future Buddha but as an active and benevolent deity who manifests himself in many forms[2], a view which also finds expression in the tradition that the works of Asanga were revelations made by him. Âkâśagarbha and the Dharmakâya are mentioned. But the inscription also speaks of heaven (t'ien) as appointing princes, and of the universal law (tao) and it contains several references to Chinese literature.

Even more remarkable is the admixture of Buddhism in Manichæism. The discoveries made in Central Asia make intelligible the Chinese edict of 739 which accuses the Manichæans of falsely taking the name of Buddhism and deceiving the people[3]. This is not surprising for Mani seems to have taught that Zoroaster, Buddha and Christ had preceded him as apostles, and in Buddhist countries his followers naturally adopted words and symbols familiar to the people. Thus Manichæan deities are represented like Bodhisattvas sitting cross-legged on a lotus; Mani receives the epithet Ju-lai or Tathâgata: as in Amida's Paradise, there are holy trees bearing flowers which enclose beings styled Buddha: the construction and phraseology of Manichæan books resemble those of a Buddhist Sutra[4]. In some ways the association of Taoism and Manichæism was even closer, for the Hu-hua-ching identifies Buddha with Lao-tzû and Mani, and two Manichæan books have passed into the Taoist Canon[5].

[1] The Turkish sutras repeatedly style the Buddha God (t'angri) or God of Gods. The expression devâtideva is applied to him in Sanskrit, but the Turkish phrases are more decided and frequent. The Sanskrit phrase may even be due to Iranian influence.

[2] An Chou, the Prince to whose memory the temple was dedicated, seems to be regarded as a manifestation of Maitreya.

[3] *J.A.* 1913, I. p. 154. The series of three articles by Chavannes and Pelliot entitled "Un traité Manichéen retrouvé en Chine" (*J.A.* 1911, 1913) is a most valuable contribution to our knowledge of Manichæism in Central Asia and China.

[4] *E.g.* see *J.A.* 1911, pp. 509 and 589. See also Le Coq, *Sitzb. preuss. Akad. der Wiss.* 48, 1909, 1202–1218.

[5] *J.A.* 1913, I. pp. 116 and 132.

Nestorian Christianity also existed in the Tarim basin and became prominent in the seventh century. This agrees with the record of its introduction into China by A-lo-pen in 635 A.D., almost simultaneously with Zoroastrianism. Fragments of the New Testament have been found at Turfan belonging mostly to the ninth century but one to the fifth. The most interesting document for the history of Nestorianism is still the monument discovered at Si-ngan-fu and commonly called the Nestorian stone[1]. It bears a long inscription partly in Chinese and partly in Syriac composed by a foreign priest called Adam or in Chinese King-Tsing giving a long account of the doctrines and history of Nestorianism. Not only does this inscription contain many Buddhist phrases (such as Sêng and Ssŭ for Christian priests and monasteries) but it deliberately omits all mention of the crucifixion and merely says in speaking of the creation that God arranged the cardinal points in the shape of a cross. This can hardly be explained as due to incomplete statement for it reviews in some detail the life of Christ and its results. The motive of omission must be the feeling that redemption by his death was not an acceptable doctrine[2]. It is interesting to find that King-Tsing consorted with Buddhist priests and even set about translating a sutra from the Hu language. Takakusu quotes a passage from one of the catalogues of the Japanese Tripitaka[3] which states that he was a Persian and collaborated with a monk of Kapiśa called Prajña.

We have thus clear evidence not only of the co-existence of Buddhism and Christianity but of friendly relations between Buddhist and Christian priests. The Emperor's objection to such commixture of religions was unusual and probably due to zeal for pure Buddhism. It is possible that in western China and Central Asia Buddhism, Taoism, Manichæism, Nestorianism and Zoroastrianism all borrowed from one another just as the first two do in China to-day and Buddhism may have become modified by this contact. But proof of it is necessary. In most places Buddhism was in strength and numbers the most im-

[1] See especially Havret, "La stèle chrétienne de Si-ngan-fu" in *Variétés Sinologues*, pp. 7, 12 and 20.

[2] See Havret, *l.c.* III. p. 54, for some interesting remarks respecting the unwillingness of the Nestorians and also of the Jesuits to give publicity to the crucifixion.

[3] See Takakusu, *I-tsing*, pp. 169, 223, and *T'oung Pao*, 1896, p. 589.

portant of all these religions and older than all except Zoroastrianism. Its contact with Manichæism may possibly date from the life of Mani, but apparently the earliest Christian manuscripts found in Central Asia are to be assigned to the fifth century.

On the other hand the Chinese Tripiṭaka contains many translations which bear an earlier date than this and are ascribed to translators connected with the Yüeh-chih. I see no reason to doubt the statements that the Happy Land sutra and Prajñâ-pâramitâ (Nanjio, 25, 5) were translated before 200 A.D. and portions of the Avataṃsaka and Lotus (Nanjio, 100, 103, 138) before 300 A.D. But if so, the principal doctrines of Mahayanist Buddhism must have been known in Khotan[1] and the lands of Oxus before we have definite evidence for the presence of Christianity there.

Zoroastrianism may however have contributed to the development and transformation of Buddhism for the two were certainly in contact. Thus the coins of Kanishka bear figures of Persian deities[2] more frequently than images of the Buddha: we know from Chinese sources that the two religions co-existed at Khotan and Kashgar and possibly there are hostile references to Buddhism (Buiti and Gaotema the heretic) in the Persian scriptures[3].

It is true that we should be cautious in fancying that we detect a foreign origin for the Mahâyâna. Different as it may be from the Buddhism of the Pali Canon, it is an Indian not an exotic growth. Deification, pantheism, the creation of radiant or terrible deities, extreme forms of idealism or nihilism in metaphysics are tendencies manifested in Hinduism as clearly as in Buddhism. Even the doctrine of the Buddha's three bodies, which sounds like an imitation of the Christian Trinity, has roots in the centuries before the Christian era. But late Buddhism indubitably borrowed many personages from the Hindu pantheon, and when we find Buddhas and Bodhisattvas such as Amitâbha, Avalokita, Manjuśrî and Kshitigarbha without clear antecedents in India we may suspect that they are borrowed from some other mythology, and if similar figures were known to Zoroastrianism, that may be their source.

[1] Turfan and Kucha are spoken of as being mainly Hînayânist.

[2] See Stein, *Zoroastrian deities on Indo-Scythian coins*, 1887.

[3] See *S.B.E.* IV. (Vendîdâd) pp. 145, 209; XXIII. p. 184, V. p. III.

The most important of them is Amitâbha. He is strangely obscure in the earlier art and literature of Indian Buddhism. Some of the nameless Buddha figures in the Gandharan sculptures may represent him, but this is not proved and the works of Grünwedel and Foucher suggest that compared with Avalokita and Târâ his images are late and not numerous. In the earlier part of the Lotus[1] he is only just mentioned as if he were of no special importance. He is also mentioned towards the end of the Awakening of Faith ascribed to Aśvaghosha, but the authorship of the work cannot be regarded as certain and, if it were, the passage stands apart from the main argument and might well be an addition. Again in the Mahâyâna-sûtrâlankâra[2] of Asanga, his paradise is just mentioned.

Against these meagre and cursory notices in Indian literature may be set the fact that two translations of the principal Amidist scripture into Chinese were made in the second century A.D. and four in the third, all by natives of Central Asia. The inference that the worship of Amitâbha flourished in Central Asia some time before the earliest of these translations is irresistible.

According to Târanâtha, the Tibetan historian of Buddhism[3], this worship goes back to Saraha or Rahulabhadra. He was reputed to have been the teacher of Nâgârjuna and a great magician. He saw Amitâbha in the land of Dhingkoṭa and died with his face turned towards Sukhâvatî. I have found no explanation of the name Dhingkoṭa but the name Saraha does not sound Indian. He is said to have been a sudra and he is represented in Tibetan pictures with a beard and topknot and holding an arrow[4] in his hand. In all this there is little that can be called history, but still it appears that the first person whom tradition connects with the worship of Amitâbha was of low caste, bore a foreign name, saw the deity in an unknown country, and like many tantric teachers was represented as totally unlike a Buddhist monk. It cannot be proved that he came from the lands of the Oxus or Turkestan, but such an

[1] Chap. VII. The notices in Chaps. XXII. and XXIV. are rather more detailed but also later.

[2] XII. p. 23.

[3] Transl. Schiefner, pp. 93, 105 and 303, and Pander's *Pantheon*, No. 11. But Târanâtha also says that he was Âryadeva's pupil.

[4] Śara in Sanskrit.

origin would explain much in the tradition. On the other hand, there would be no difficulty in accounting for Zoroastrian influence at Peshawar or Takkasila within the frontiers of India.

Somewhat later Vasubandhu is stated to have preached faith in Amitâbha but it does not appear that this doctrine ever had in India a tithe of the importance which it obtained in the Far East.

The essential features of Amidist doctrine are that there is a paradise of light belonging to a benevolent deity and that the good[1] who invoke his name will be led thither. Both features are found in Zoroastrian writings. The highest heaven (following after the paradises of good thoughts, good words and good deeds) is called Boundless Light or Endless Light[2]. Both this region and its master, Ahuramazda, are habitually spoken of in terms implying radiance and glory. Also it is a land of song, just as Amitâbha's paradise re-echoes with music and pleasant sounds[3]. Prayers can win this paradise and Ahura Mazda and the Archangels will come and show the way thither to the pious[4]. Further whoever recites the Ahuna-vairya formula, Ahura Mazda will bring his soul to "the lights of heaven[5]," and although, so far as I know, it is not expressly stated that the repetition of Ahura Mazda's name leads to paradise, yet the general efficacy of his names as invocations is clearly affirmed[6].

Thus all the chief features of Amitâbha's paradise are Persian: only his method of instituting it by making a vow is Buddhist. It is true that Indian imagination had conceived numerous paradises, and that the early Buddhist legend tells of the Tushita heaven. But Sukhâvatî is not like these abodes of bliss. It appears suddenly in the history of Buddhism as something exotic, grafted adroitly on the parent trunk but sometimes overgrowing it[7].

[1] The doctrine of salvation by faith alone seems to be later. The longer and apparently older version of the Sukhâvatî Vyûha insists on good works as a condition of entry into Paradise.

[2] *S.B.E.* IV. p. 293; *ib.* XXXIII. pp. 317 and 344.

[3] It may also be noticed that Ameretât, the Archangel of immortality, presides over vegetation and that Amida's paradise is full of flowers.

[4] *S.B.E.* XXIII. pp. 335–7.

[5] *S.B.E.* XXXI. p. 261.

[6] *S.B.E.* XXIII. pp. 21–31 (the Ormasd Yasht).

[7] Is it possible that there is any connection between Sukhâvatî and the land of Saukavastan, governed by an immortal ruler and located by the Bundehish between

Avalokita is also connected with Amitâbha's paradise. His figure, though its origin is not clear, assumes distinct and conspicuous proportions in India at a fairly early date. There appears to be no reason for associating him specially with Central Asia. On the other hand later works describe him as the spiritual son or reflex of Amitâbha. This certainly recalls the Iranian idea of the Fravashi defined as "a spiritual being conceived as a part of a man's personality but existing before he is born and in independence of him: it can also belong to divine beings[1]." Although India offers in abundance both divine incarnations and explanations thereof yet none of these describe the relationship between a Dhyânî Buddha and his Boddhisattva so well as the Zoroastrian doctrine of the Fravashi.

S. Lévi has suggested that the Bodhisattva Manjuśrî is of Tokharian origin[2]. His worship at Wu-tai-shan in Shan-si is ancient and later Indian tradition connected him with China. Local traditions also connect him with Nepal, Tibet, and Khotan, and he is sometimes represented as the first teacher of civilization or religion. But although his Central Asian origin is eminently probable, I do not at present see any clear proof of it.

The case of the Bodhisattva Kshitigarbha[3] is similar. He appears to have been known but not prominent in India in the fourth century A.D.: by the seventh century if not earlier his cult was flourishing in China and subsequently he became in the Far East a popular deity second only to Kuan-yin. This popularity was connected with his gradual transformation into a god of the dead. It is also certain that he was known in Central Asia[4] but whether he first became important there or in China is hard to decide. The devotion of the Chinese to their dead suggests that it was among them that he acquired his great position, but his rôle as a guide to the next world has a parallel in the similar benevolent activity of the Zoroastrian angel Srosh.

Turkistan and Chinistan? I imagine there is no etymological relationship, but if Saukavastan was well known as a land of the blessed it may have influenced the choice of a significant Sanskrit word with a similar sound.

[1] *E.R.E. sub voce.*

[2] *J.A.* 1912, I. p. 622. Unfortunately only a brief notice of his communication is given with no details. See also S. Lévi, *Le Népâl*, pp. 330 ff.

[3] Ti-tsang in Chinese, Jizo in Japanese. See for his history Visser's elaborate articles in *Ostasiatische Ztsft.* 1913–1915.

[4] He was accepted by the Manichæans as one of the Envoys of Light. *J.A.* 1911, II. p. 549.

One of Central Asia's clearest titles to importance in the history of the East is that it was the earliest and on the whole the principal source of Chinese Buddhism, to which I now turn. Somewhat later, teachers also came to China by sea and still later, under the Yüan dynasty, Lamaism was introduced direct from Tibet. But from at least the beginning of our era onwards, monks went eastwards from Central Asia to preach and translate the scriptures and it was across Central Asia that Chinese pilgrims went to India in search of the truth.

CHAPTER XLII

CHINA

Prefatory note.

FOR the transcription of Chinese words I use the modern Peking pronunciation as represented in Giles's Dictionary. It may be justly objected that of all dialects Pekingese is perhaps the furthest removed from ancient Chinese and therefore unsuited for historical studies and also that Wade's system of transcription employed by Giles is open to serious criticism. But, on the other hand, I am not competent to write according to the pronunciation of Nanking or Canton all the names which appear in these chapters and, if I were, it would not be a convenience to my readers. Almost all English works of reference about China use the forms registered in Giles's Dictionary or near approximations to them, and any variation would produce difficulty and confusion. French and German methods of transcribing Chinese differ widely from Wade's and unfortunately there seems to be no prospect of sinologues agreeing on any international system.

INTRODUCTORY.

THE study of Chinese Buddhism is interesting but difficult[1]. Here more than in other Asiatic countries we feel that the words and phrases natural to a European language fail to render justly the elementary forms of thought, the simplest relationships. But Europeans are prone to exaggerate the mysterious, topsy-turvy character of the Chinese mind. Such epithets are based on the assumption that human thought and conduct normally conform to reason and logic, and that when such conformity is wanting the result must be strange and hardly human, or at least such as no respectable European could expect or approve. But the assumption is wrong. In no country with which I am

[1] For Chinese Buddhism see especially Johnston, *Chinese Buddhism*, 1913 (cited as Johnston). Much information about the popular side of Buddhism and Taoism may be found in *Recherches sur les superstitions en Chine* par le Père Henri Doré, 10 vols. 1911–1916, Shanghai (cited as Doré).

acquainted are logic and co-ordination of ideas more wanting than in the British Isles. This is not altogether a fault, for human systems are imperfect and the rigorous application of any one imperfect system must end in disaster. But the student of Asiatic psychology must begin his task by recognising that in the West and East alike, the thoughts of nations, though not always of individuals, are a confused mosaic where the pattern has been lost and a thousand fancies esteemed at one time or another as pleasing, useful or respectable are crowded into the available space. This is especially true in the matter of religion. An observer fresh to the subject might find it hard to formulate the relations to one another and to the Crown of the various forms of Christianity prevalent in our Empire or to understand how the English Church can be one body, when some sections of it are hardly distinguishable from Roman Catholicism and others from non-conformist sects. In the same way Chinese religion offers startling combinations of incongruous rites and doctrines: the attitude of the laity and of the government to the different churches is not to be defined in ordinary European terms and yet if one examines the practice of Europe, it will often throw light on the oddities of China.

The difficulty of finding a satisfactory equivalent in Chinese for the word God is well known and has caused much discussion among missionaries. Confucius inherited and handed on a worship of Heaven which inspired some noble sayings and may be admitted to be monotheism. But it was a singularly impersonal monotheism and had little to do with popular religion, being regarded as the prerogative and special cult of the Emperor. The people selected their deities from a numerous pantheon of spirits, falling into many classes among which two stand out clearly, namely, nature spirits and spirits of ancestors. All these deities, as we must call them for want of a better word, present odd features, which have had some influence on Chinese Buddhism. The boundary between the human and the spirit worlds is slight. Deification and euhemerism are equally natural to the Chinese. Not only are worthies of every sort made into gods[1], but foreign deities are explained on the same

[1] A curious instance of deification is mentioned in *Muséon*, 1914, p. 61. It appears that several deceased Jesuits have been deified. For a recent instance of deification in 1913 see Doré, x. p. 753.

principle. Thus Yen-lo (Yama), the king of the dead, is said to have been a Chinese official of the sixth century A.D. But there is little mythology. The deities are like the figures on porcelain vases: all know their appearance and some their names, but hardly anyone can give a coherent account of them. A polydæmonism of this kind is even more fluid than Hinduism: you may invent any god you like and neglect gods that don't concern you. The habit of mind which produces sects in India, namely the desire to exalt one's own deity above others and make him the All-God, does not exist. No Chinese god inspires such feelings.

The deities of medieval and modern China, including the spirits recognized by Chinese Buddhism, are curiously mixed and vague personalities[1]. Nature worship is not absent, but it is nature as seen by the fancy of the alchemist and astrologer. The powers that control nature are also identified with ancient heroes, but they are mostly heroes of the type of St George and the Dragon of whom history has little to say, and Chinese respect for the public service and official rank takes the queer form of regarding these spirits as celestial functionaries. Thus the gods have a Ministry of Thunder which supervises the weather and a Board of Medicine which looks after sickness and health.

The characteristic expression of Chinese popular religion is not exactly myth or legend but religious romance. A writer starts from some slender basis of fact and composes an edifying novel. Thus the well-known story called Hsi-Yu-Chi[2] purports to be an account of Hsüan Chuang's journey to India but, except that it represents the hero as going there and returning with copies of the scriptures, it is romance pure and simple, a

[1] The spirits called San Kuan 三官 or San Yüan 三元 are a good instance of Chinese deities. The words mean Three Agents or Principles who strictly speaking have no names: (*a*) Originally they appear to represent Heaven, Earth and Water. (*b*) Then they stand for three periods of the year and the astrological influences which rule each. (*c*) As Agents, and more or less analogous to human personalities, Heaven gives happiness, Earth pardons sins and Water delivers from misfortune. (*d*) They are identified with the ancient Emperors Yao, Shun, Yü. (*e*) They are also identified with three Censors under the Emperor Li-Wang, B.C. 878–841.

[2] 西遊記. Hsüan Chuang's own account of his travels bears the slightly different title of Hsi-Yü-Chi 西域記. The work noticed here is attributed to Chiu Ch'ang Ch'un, a Taoist priest of the thirteenth century. It is said to be the Buddhist book most widely read in Korea where it is printed in the popular script. An abridged English translation has been published by T. Richard under the title of *A Mission to Heaven*.

fantastic Pilgrim's Progress, the scene of which is sometimes on earth and sometimes in the heavens. The traveller is accompanied by allegorical creatures such as a magic monkey, a pig, and a dragon horse, who have each their own significance and may be seen represented in Buddhist and Taoist temples even to-day. So too another writer, starting from the tradition that Avalokita (or Kuan-Yin) was once a benevolent human being, set himself to write the life of Kuan-Yin, represented as a princess endued with every virtue who cheerfully bears cruel persecution for her devotion to Buddhism. It would be a mistake to seek in this story any facts throwing light on the history of Avalokita and his worship. It is a religious novel, important only because it still finds numerous readers.

It is commonly said that the Chinese belong to three religions, Confucianism, Buddhism and Taoism, and the saying is not altogether inaccurate. Popular language speaks of the three creeds and an ordinary person in the course of his life may take part in rites which imply a belief in them all[1]. Indeed the fusion is so complete that one may justly talk of Chinese religion, meaning the jumble of ceremonies and beliefs accepted by the average man. Yet at the same time it is possible to be an enthusiast for any one of the three without becoming unconventional.

Of the three religions, Confucianism has a disputable claim to the title. If the literary classes of China find it sufficient, they do so only by rejecting the emotional and speculative sides of religion. The Emperor Wan-li[2] made a just epigram when he said that Confucianism and Buddhism are like the wings of a bird. Each requires the co-operation of the other. Confucius was an ethical and political philosopher, not a prophet, hierophant or church founder. As a moralist he stands in the first rank, and I doubt if either the Gospels or the Pitakas contain maxims for the life of a good citizen equal to his sayings. But he ignored that unworldly morality which, among Buddhists and Christians, is so much admired and so little practised. In religion he claimed no originality, he brought no revelation, but

[1] I am writing immediately after the abolition of the Imperial Government (1912), and what I say naturally refers to a state of things which is passing away. But it is too soon to say how the new regime will affect religion. There is an old saying that China is supported by the three religions as a tripod by three legs.

[2] 萬曆 strictly speaking the title of his reign 1573–1620.

he accepted the current ideas of his age and time, though perhaps he eliminated many popular superstitions. He commended the worship of Heaven, which, if vague, still connected the deity with the moral law, and he enjoined sacrifice to ancestors and spirits. But all this apparently without any theory. His definition of wisdom is well known: "to devote oneself to human duties and keep aloof from spirits while still respecting them." This is not the utterance of a sceptical statesman, equivalent to "remember the political importance of religion but keep clear of it, so far as you can." The best commentary is the statement in the *Analects* that he seldom spoke about the will of Heaven, yet such of his utterances about it as have been preserved are full of awe and submission[1]. A certain delicacy made him unwilling to define or discuss the things for which he felt the highest reverence, and a similar detached but respectful attitude is still a living constituent of Chinese society. The scholar and gentleman will not engage in theological or metaphysical disputes, but he respectfully takes part in ceremonies performed in honour of such venerated names as Heaven, Earth and Confucius himself. Less willingly, but still without remonstrance, he attends Buddhist or Taoist celebrations.

If it is hard to define the religious element in Confucianism, it is still harder to define Taoism, but for another reason, namely, that the word has more than one meaning. In one sense it is the old popular religion of China, of which Confucius selected the scholarly and gentlemanly features. Taoism, on the contrary, rejected no godlings and no legends however grotesque: it gave its approval to the most extravagant and material superstitions, especially to the belief that physical immortality could be insured by drinking an elixir, which proved fatal to many illustrious dupes. As an organized body it owes its origin to Chang-Ling (*c.* 130 A.D.) and his grandson Chang-Lu[2]. The sect received its baptism of blood but made terms with the Chinese Government, one condition being that a member of the house of Chang should be recognized as its hereditary

[1] Compare *Anal.* IX. 1 and XIV. 38. 2. See also *Doctrine of the Mean*, chap. XVI, for more positive views about spirits.

[2] 張陵 and 張魯. See De Groot, "Origins of the Taoist Church" in *Trans. Third Congress Hist. Relig.* 1908.

Patriarch or Pope[1]. Rivalry with Buddhism also contributed to give Taoism something of that consistency in doctrine and discipline which we associate with the word religion, for in their desire to show that they were as good as their opponents the Taoists copied them in numerous and important particulars, for instance triads of deities, sacred books and monastic institutions.

The power of inventive imitation is characteristic of Taoism[2]. In most countries great gods are children of the popular mind. After long gestation and infancy they emerge as deities bound to humanity by a thousand ties of blood and place. But the Taoists, whenever they thought a new deity needful or ornamental, simply invented him, often with the sanction of an Imperial Edict. Thus Yü-Ti[3], the precious or jade Emperor, who is esteemed the supreme ruler of the world, was created or at least brought into notice about 1012 A.D. by the Emperor Chên Tsung[4] who pretended to have correspondence with him. He is probably an adaptation of Indra and is also identified with a prince of ancient China, but cannot be called a popular hero like Rama or Krishna, and has not the same hold on the affections of the people.

But Taoism is also the name commonly given not only to this fanciful church but also to the philosophic ideas expounded in the Tao-tê-ching and in the works of Chuang-tzŭ. The Taoist priesthood claim this philosophy, but the two have no necessary connection. Taoism as philosophy represents a current of thought opposed to Confucianism, compared with which it is ascetic, mystic and pantheistic, though except in comparison it does not deserve such epithets. My use of pantheistic in particular may raise objection, but it seems to me that Tao, however hard to define, is analogous to Brahman, the impersonal Spirit of Hindu philosophy. The universe is the expression of Tao and in conforming to Tao man finds happiness. For Confucianism, as for Europe, man is the pivot and centre of things,

[1] Chang Yüan-hsü, who held office in 1912, was deprived of his titles by the Republican Government. In 1914 petitions were presented for their restoration, but I do not know with what result. See *Peking Daily News*, September 5th, 1914.

[2] Something similar may be seen in Mormonism where angels and legends have been invented by individual fancy without any background of tradition.

[3] 玉帝. [4] 眞宗.

but less so for Taoism and Buddhism. Philosophie Taoism, being somewhat abstruse and unpractical, might seem to have little chance of becoming a popular superstition. But from early times it was opposed to Confucianism, and as Confucianism became more and more the hall-mark of the official and learned classes, Taoism tended to become popular, at the expense of degrading itself. From early times too it dallied with such fascinating notions as the acquisition of miraculous powers and longevity. But, as an appeal to the emotional and spiritual sides of humanity, it was, if superior to Confucianism, inferior to Buddhism.

Buddhism, unlike Confucianism and Taoism, entered China as a foreign religion, but, in using this phrase, we must ask how far any system of belief prevalent there is accepted as what we call a religion. Even in Ceylon and Burma people follow the observances of two religions or at least of a religion and a superstition, but they would undoubtedly call themselves Buddhists. In China the laity use no such designations and have no sense of exclusive membership. For them a religion is comparable to a club, which they use for special purposes. You may frequent both Buddhist and Taoist temples just as you may belong to both the Geographical and Zoological Societies. Perhaps the position of spiritualism in England offers the nearest analogy to a Chinese religion. There are, I believe, some few persons for whom spiritualism is a definite, sufficient and exclusive creed. These may be compared to the Buddhist clergy with a small minority of the laity. But the majority of those who are interested or even believe in spiritualism, do not identify themselves with it in this way. They attend séanees as their curiosity or affections may prompt, but these beliefs and practices do not prevent them from also belonging to a Christian denomination. Imagine spiritualism to be better organized as an institution and you will have a fairly accurate picture of the average Chinaman's attitude to Buddhism and Taoism. One may also compare the way in which English poets use classical mythology. *Lycidas*, for instance, is an astounding compound of classical and biblical ideas, and Milton does not hesitate to call the Supreme Being Jove in a serious passage. Yet Milton's Christianity has never, so far as I know, been called in question.

There is an obvious historical parallel between the religions of the Chinese and early Roman Empires. In both, the imperial and official worship was political and indifferent to dogma without being hostile, provided no sectary refused to call the Emperor Son of Heaven or sacrifice to his image. In both, ample provision was made outside the state cult for allaying the fears of superstition, as well as for satisfying the soul's thirst for knowledge and emotion. A Roman magistrate of the second century A.D. may have offered official sacrifices, propitiated local genii, and attended the mysteries of Mithra, in the same impartial way as Chinese magistrates took part a few years ago in the ceremonies of Confucianism, Taoism and Buddhism. In both cases there was entire liberty to combine with the official religious routine private beliefs and observances incongruous with it and often with one another: in both there was the same essential feature that no deity demanded exclusive allegiance. The popular polytheism of China is indeed closely analogous to the paganism of the ancient world[1]. Hinduism contains too much personal religion and real spiritual feeling to make the resemblance perfect, but in dealing with Apollo, Mars and Venus a Roman of the early Empire seems to have shown the mixture of respect and scepticism which is characteristic of China.

This attitude implies not only a certain want of conviction but also a utilitarian view of religion. The Chinese visit a temple much as they visit a shop or doctor, for definite material purposes, and if it be asked whether they are a religious people in the better sense of the word, I am afraid the answer must be in the negative. It is with regret that I express this opinion and I by no means imply that there are not many deeply religious persons in China, but whereas in India the obvious manifestations of superstition are a superficial disease and the heart of the people is keenly sensitive to questions of personal salvation and speculative theology, this cannot be said of the masses in China, where religion, as seen, consists of superstitious rites and the substratum of thought and feeling is small.

[1] The sixth Æneid would seem to a Chinese quite a natural description of the next world. In it we have Elysium, Tartarus, transmigration of souls, souls who can find no resting place because their bodies are unburied, and phantoms showing still the wounds which their bodies received in life. Nor is there any attempt to harmonize these discordant ideas.

This struck me forcibly when visiting Siam some years ago. In Bangkok there is a large Chinese population and several Buddhist temples have been made over to them. The temples frequented by Siamese are not unlike catholic churches in Europe: the decoration is roughly similar, the standard of decorum much the same. The visitors come to worship, meditate or hear sermons. But in the temples used by the Chinese, a lower standard is painfully obvious and the atmosphere is different. Visitors are there in plenty, but their object is to "get luck," and the business of religion has become transformed into divination and spiritual gambling. The worshipper, on entering, goes to a counter where he buys tapers and incense-sticks, together with some implements of superstition such as rods or inscribed cards. After burning incense he draws a card or throws the rods up into the air and takes an augury from the result. Though the contrast presented in Siam makes the degradation more glaring, yet these temples in Bangkok are not worse than many which I have seen in China. I gladly set on the other side of the account some beautiful and reverent halls of worship in the larger monasteries, but I fear that the ordinary Chinese temple, whether Taoist or Buddhist, is a ghostly shop where, in return for ceremonies which involve neither moral nor intellectual effort, the customer is promised good luck, offspring, and other material blessings.

It can hardly be denied that the populace in China are grossly superstitious. Superstition is a common failing and were statistics available to show the number and status of Europeans who believe in fortune-telling and luck, the result might be startling. But in most civilized countries such things are furtive and apologetic. In China the strangest forms of magic and divination enjoy public esteem. The ideas which underlie popular practice and ritual are worthy of African savages: there has been a monstrous advance in systematization, yet the ethics and intellect of China, brilliant as are their achievements, have not leavened the lump. The average Chinese, though an excellent citizen, full of common sense and shrewd in business, is in religious matters a victim of fatuous superstition and completely divorced from the moral and intellectual standards which he otherwise employs.

Conspicuous among these superstitions is Fêng Shui or

Geomancy[1], a pseudo-science which is treated as seriously as law or surveying. It is based on the idea that localities have a sort of spiritual climate which brings prosperity or the reverse and depends on the influences of stars and nature spirits, such as the azure dragon and white tiger. But since these agencies find expression in the contours of a locality, they can be affected if its features are modified by artificial means, for instance, the construction of walls and towers. Buddhism did not disdain to patronize these notions. The principal hall of a monastery is usually erected on a specially auspicious site and the appeals issued for the repair of sacred buildings often point out the danger impending if edifices essential to the good Fêng Shui of a district are allowed to decay. The scepticism and laughter of the educated does not clear the air, for superstition can flourish when neither respected nor believed. The worst feature of religion in China is that the decently educated public ridicules its external observances, but continues to practise them, because they are connected with occasions of good fellowship or because their omission might be a sign of disrespect to departed relatives or simply because in dealing with uncanny things it is better to be on the safe side. This is the sum of China's composite religion as visible in public and private rites. Its ethical value is far higher than might be supposed, for its most absurd superstitions also recommend love and respect in family life and a high standard of civic duty. But China has never admitted that public or private morality requires the support of a religious creed.

As might be expected, life and animation are more apparent in sects than in conventional religion. Since the recent revolution it is no longer necessary to confute the idea that the Chinese are a stationary and unemotional race, but its inaccuracy was demonstrated by many previous movements especially the T'ai-p'ing rebellion, which had at first a religious tinge. Yet in China such movements, though they may kindle enthusiasm and provoke persecution, rarely have the religious value at-

[1] 風水. A somewhat similar pseudo-science called vatthu-vijjâ is condemned in the Pali scriptures. *E.g.* Digha N. I. 21. Astrology also has been a great force in Chinese politics. See Bland and Backhouse, *Ann. and Memoirs, passim.* The favour shown at different times to Buddhist, Manichæan and Catholic priests was often due to their supposed knowledge of astrology.

taching to a sect in Christian, Hindu and Mohammedan countries. Viewed as an ecclesiastieal or spiritual movement, the T'ai-p'ing is insignificant: it was a secret society permitted by circumstances to become a formidable rising and in its important phases the political element was paramount. The same is true of many sects which have not achieved such notoriety. They are secret societies which adopt a creed, but it is not in the creed that their real vitality lies.

If it is difficult to say how far the Buddhism of China is a religion, it is equally difficult to define its relation to the State. Students well acquainted with the literature as well as with the actual condition of China have expressed diametrically opposite views as to the religious attitude of the Imperial Government[1], one stating roundly that it was "the most intolerant, the most persecuting of all earthly Governments," and another that it "at no period refused hospitality and consideration to any religion recommended as such[2]."

In considering such questions I would again emphasize the fact that Chinese terms have often not the same extension as their apparent synonyms in European languages, which, of course, means that the provinces of human life and thought have also different boundaries. For most countries the word clergy has a definite meaning and, in spite of great diversities, may be applied to Christian clerics, Mollahs and Brahmans without serious error. It means a class of men who are the superintendents of religion, but also more. On the one side, though they may have serious political differences with the Government, they are usually in touch with it: on the other, though they may dislike reformers and movements from below, they patronize and minister to popular sentiment. They are closely connected with education and learning and sometimes with the law. But in China there is no class which unites all these features. Learning, law and education are represented by the Confucian scholars or literati. Though no one would think of calling them priests, yet they may offer official sacrifices, like Roman magis-

[1] I may again remind the reader that I am not speaking of the Chinese Republic but of the Empire. The long history of its relations to Buddhism, Taoism and Confucianism, though it concerns the past, is of great interest.

[2] De Groot and Parker. For an elaboration of the first thesis see especially De Groot's *Sectarianism and Religious Persecution in China.*

trates. Though they are contemptuous of popular superstition, yet they embody the popular ideal. It is the pride of a village to produce a scholar. But the scholarship of the literati is purely Confucian: Buddhist and Taoist learning have no part in it.

The priest, whether Buddhist or Taoist, is not in the mind of the people the repository of learning and law. He is not in religious matters the counterpart of the secular arm, but rather a private practitioner, duly licensed but of no particular standing. But he is skilful in his own profession: he has access to the powers who help, pity and console, and even the sceptic seeks his assistance when confronted with the dangers of this world and the next.

The student of Chinese history may object that at many periods, notably under the Yüan dynasty, the Buddhist clergy were officially recognized as an educational body and even received the title of Kuo-shih or teacher of the people. This is true. Such recognition by no means annihilated the literati, but it illustrates the decisive influence exercised by the Emperor and the court. We have, on the one side, a learned official class, custodians of the best national ideals but inclined to reject emotion and speculation as well as superstition: on the other, two priesthoods, prone to superstition but legitimately strong in so far as they satisfied the emotional and speculative instincts. The literati held persistently, though respectfully, to the view that the Emperor should be a Confucianist pure and simple, but Buddhism and Taoism had such strong popular support that it was always safe and often politic for an Emperor to patronize them. Hence an Emperor of personal convictions was able to turn the balance, and it must be added that Buddhism often flourished in the courts of weak and dissolute Emperors who were in the hands of women and eunuchs. Some of these latter were among its most distinguished devotees.

All Chinese religions agreed in accepting the Emperor as head of the Church, not merely titular but active. He exercised a strange prerogative of creating, promoting and degrading deities. Even within the Buddhist sphere he regulated the incarnations of Bodhisattvas in the persons of Lamas and from time to time re-edited the canon[1] or added new works to it. This

[1] But it must be remembered that the Chinese canon is not entirely analogous to the collections of the scriptures current in India, Ceylon or Europe.

extreme Erastianism had its roots in Indian as well as Chinese ideas. The Confucianist, while reminding the Emperor that he should imitate the sages and rulers of antiquity, gladly admitted his right to control the worship of all spirits[1] and the popular conscience, while probably unable to define what was meant by the title *Son of Heaven*[2], felt that it gave him a vice-regal right to keep the gods in order, so long as he did not provoke famine or other national calamities by mismanagement. The Buddhists, though tenacious of freedom in the spiritual life, had no objection to the patronage of princes. Asoka permitted himself to regulate the affairs of the Church and the success of Buddhists as missionaries was due in no small measure to their tact in allowing other sovereigns to follow his example.

That Buddhism should have obtained in China a favourable reception and a permanent status is indeed remarkable, for in two ways it was repugnant to the sentiments of the governing classes to say nothing of the differences in temper and outlook which divide Hindus and Chinese. Firstly, its ideal was asceticism and celibacy; it gave family life the lower place and ignored the popular Chinese view that to have a son is not only a duty, but also essential for those sacrifices without which the departed spirit cannot have peace. Secondly, it was not merely a doctrine but an ecclesiastical organization, a congregation of persons who were neither citizens nor subjects, not exactly an *imperium in imperio* nor a secret society, but dangerously capable of becoming either. Such bodies have always incurred the suspicion and persecution of the Chinese Government. Even in the fifth century Buddhist monasteries were accused of organizing armed conspiracies and many later sects suffered from the panic which they inspired in official bosoms. But both difficulties were overcome by the suppleness of the clergy.

[1] The Emperor is the Lord of all spirits and has the right to sacrifice to all spirits, whereas others should sacrifice only to such spirits as concern them. For the Emperor's title "Lord of Spirits," see Shu Ching IV., VI. 2–3, and Shih Ching, III., II. 8, 3.

[2] The title is undoubtedly very ancient and means Son of Heaven or Son of God. See Hirth, *Ancient History of China*, pp. 95–96. But the precise force of *Son* is not clear. The Emperor was Viceregent of Heaven, high priest and responsible for natural phenomena, but he could not in historical times be regarded as sprung (like the Emperor of Japan) from a family of divine descent, because the dynasties, and with them the imperial family, were subject to frequent change.

If they outraged family sentiment they managed to make themselves indispensable at funeral ceremonies[1]. If they had a dangerous resemblance to an *imperium in imperio*, they minimized it by their obvious desire to exercise influence through the Emperor. Though it is true that the majority of anti-dynastic political sects had a Buddhist colour, the most prominent and influential Buddhists never failed in loyalty. To this adroitness must be added a solid psychological advantage. The success of Buddhism in China was due to the fact that it presented religious emotion and speculation in the best form known there, and when it began to spread the intellectual soil was not unpropitious. The higher Taoist philosophy had made familiar the ideas of quietism and the contemplative life: the age was unsettled, harassed alike by foreign invasion and civil strife. In such times when even active natures tire of unsuccessful struggles, the asylum of a monastery has attractions for many.

We have now some idea of the double position of Buddhism in China and can understand how it sometimes appears as almost the established church and sometimes as a persecuted sect. The reader will do well to remember that in Europe the relations of politics to religion have not always been simple: many Catholic sovereigns have quarrelled with Popes and monks. The French Government supports the claims of Catholic missions in China but does not favour the Church in France. The fact that Huxley was made a Privy Councillor does not imply that Queen Victoria approved of his religious views. In China the repeated restrictive edicts concerning monasteries should not be regarded as acts of persecution. Every politician can see the loss to the state if able-bodied men become monks by the thousand. In periods of literary and missionary zeal, large congregations of such monks may have a sufficient sphere of activity but in sleepy, decadent periods they are apt to become a moral or political danger. A devout Buddhist or Catholic may reasonably hold that though the monastic life is the best for the elect, yet for the unworthy it is more dangerous than the temptations of the world. Thus the founder of the Ming dynasty had himself been a bonze, yet he limited the number

[1] Similarly it is a popular tenet that if a man becomes a monk all his ancestors go to Heaven. See *Paraphrase of sacred Edict*, VII.

and age of those who might become monks[1]. On the other hand, he attended Buddhist services and published an edition of the Tripitaka. In this and in the conduct of most Emperors there is little that is inconsistent or mysterious: they regarded religion not in our fashion as a system deserving either allegiance or rejection, but as a modern Colonial Governor might regard education. Some Governors are enthusiastic for education: others mistrust it as a stimulus of disquieting ideas: most accept it as worthy of occasional patronage, like hospitals and races. In the same way some Emperors, like Wu-Ti[2], were enthusiasts for Buddhism and made it practically the state religion: a few others were definitely hostile either from conviction or political circumstances, but probably most sovereigns regarded it as the average British official regards education, as something that one can't help having, that one must belaud on certain public occasions, that may now and then be useful, but still emphatically something to be kept within limits.

Outbursts against Buddhism are easy to understand. I have pointed out its un-Chinese features and the persistent opposition of the literati. These were sufficient reasons for repressive measures whenever the Emperor was unbuddhist in his sympathies, especially if the monasteries had enjoyed a period of prosperity and become crowded and wealthy. What is harder to understand is the occasional favour shown by apparently anti-Buddhist Emperors.

The Sacred Edict of the great K'ang Hsi forbids heterodoxy (i tuan) in which the official explanation clearly includes Buddhism[3]. It was published in his extreme youth, but had his mature approval, and until recently was read in every prefecture twice a month. But the same Emperor gave many gifts to monasteries, and in 1705 he issued a decree to the monks of P'uto in which he said, "we since our boyhood have been earnest students of Confucian lore and have had no time to become minutely acquainted with the sacred books of Buddhism, but we are satisfied that Virtue is the one word

[1] Japanese Emperors did the same, *e.g.* Kwammū Tennō in 793.

[2] 梁武帝.

[3] K'ang Hsi is responsible only for the text of the Edict which merely forbids heterodoxy. But his son Yung Chêng who published the explanation and paraphrase repaired the Buddhist temples at P'uto and the Taoist temple at Lung-hu-shan.

which indicates what is essential in both systems. Let us pray to the compassionate Kuan-yin that she may of her grace send down upon our people the spiritual rain and sweet dew of the good Law: that she may grant them bounteous harvests, seasonable winds and the blessings of peace, harmony and long life and finally that she may lead them to the salvation which she offers to all beings in the Universe[1]." The two edicts are not consistent but such inconsistency is no reproach to a statesman nor wholly illogical. The Emperor reprimands extravagance in doctrine and ceremonial and commends Confucianism to his subjects as all that is necessary for good life and good government, but when he finds that Buddhism conduces to the same end he accords his patronage and politely admits the existence and power of Kuan-yin.

But I must pass on to another question, the relation of Chinese to Indian Buddhism. Chinese Buddhism is often spoken of as a strange and corrupt degeneration, a commixture of Indian and foreign ideas. Now if such phrases mean that the pulse of life is feeble and the old lights dim, we must regretfully admit their truth, but still little is to be found in Chinese Buddhism except the successive phases of later Indian Buddhism, introduced into China from the first century A.D. onwards. In Japan there arose new sects, but in China, when importation ceased, no period of invention supervened. The T'ien-t'ai school has some originality, and native and foreign ideas were combined by the followers of Bodhidharma. But the remaining schools were all founded by members of Indian sects or by Chinese who aimed at scrupulous imitation of Indian models. Until the eighth century, when the formative period came to an end, we have an alternation of Indian or Central Asian teachers arriving in China to meet with respect and acceptance, and of Chinese enquirers who visited India in order to discover the true doctrine and practice and were honoured on their return in proportion as they were believed to have found it. There is this distinction between China and such countries as Java, Camboja and Champa, that whereas in

[1] See Johnston, p. 352. I have not seen the Chinese text of this edict. In Laufer and Francke's *Epigraphische Denkmäler aus China* is a long inscription of Kang Hsi's giving the history both legendary and recent of the celebrated sandal-wood image of the Buddha.

them we find a mixture of Hinduism and Buddhism, in China the traces of Hinduism are slight. The imported ideas, however corrupt, were those of Indian Buddhist scholars, not the mixed ideas of the Indian layman[1].

Of course Buddhist theory and practice felt the influence of their new surroundings. The ornaments and embroidery of the faith are Chinese and sometimes hide the original material. Thus Kuan-yin, considered historically, has grown out of the Indian deity Avalokita, but the goddess worshipped by the populace is the heroine of the Chinese romance mentioned above. And, since many Chinese are only half Buddhists, tales about gods and saints are taken only half-seriously; the Buddha periodically invites the immortals to dine with him in Heaven and the Eighteen Lohan are described as converted brigands.

In every monastery the buildings, images and monks obviously bear the stamp of the country. Yet nearly all the doctrines and most of the usages have Indian parallels. The ritual has its counterpart in what I-Ching describes as seen by himself in his Indian travels. China has added the idea of *fêng-shui*, and has modified architectural forms. For instance the many-storeyed pagoda is an elongation of the stupa[2]. So, too, in ceremonial, the great prominence given to funeral rites and many superstitious details are Chinese, yet, as I have often mentioned in this work, rites on behalf of the dead were tolerated by early Buddhism. The curious mingling of religious services with theatrical pagents which Hsüan Chuang witnessed at Allahabad in the reign of Harsha, has its modest parallel to-day in many popular festivals.

The numerous images which crowd a Chinese temple, the

[1] This indicates that the fusion of Buddhism and Hinduism was less complete than some scholars suppose. Where there was a general immigration of Hindus, the mixture is found, but the Indian visitors to China were mostly professional teachers and their teaching was definitely Buddhist. There are, however, two non-Buddhist books in the Chinese Tripitaka. Nanjio Cat. Nos. 1295 and 1300.

[2] It has been pointed out by Fergusson and others that there were high towers in China before the Buddhist period. Still, the numerous specimens extant date from Buddhist times, many were built over relics, and the accounts of both Fa-hsien and Hsüan Chuang show that the Stupa built by Kanishka at Peshawar had attracted the attention of the Chinese.

I regret that de Groot's interesting work *Der Thūpa: das heiligste Heiligtum des Buddhismus in China*, 1919, reached me too late for me to make use of it.

four kings, Arhats and Bodhisattvas, though of unfamiliar appearance to the Indian student, are Indian in origin. A few Taoist deities may have side chapels, but they are not among the principal objects of worship. The greater part of the Chinese Tripitaka is a translation from the Sanskrit and the Chinese works (only 194 against 1467 translations) are chiefly exegetical. Thus, though Chinese bonzes countenance native superstitions and gladly undertake to deal with all the gods and devils of the land, yet in its doctrine, literature, and even in many externals their Buddhism remains an Indian importation. If we seek in it for anything truly Chinese, it is to be found not in the constituents, but in the atmosphere, which, like a breeze from a mountain monastery sometimes freshens the gilded shrines and libraries of verbose sutras. It is the native spirit of the Far East which finds expression in the hill-side hermit's sense of freedom and in dark sayings such as *Buddhism is the oak-tree in my garden*. Every free and pure heart can become a Buddha, but also is one with the life of birds and flowers. Both the love of nature[1] and the belief that men can become divine can easily be paralleled in Indian texts, but they were not, I think, imported into China, and joy in natural beauty and sympathy with wild life are much more prominent in Chinese than in Indian art.

Is then Buddhist doctrine, as opposed to the superstitions tolerated by Buddhism, something exotic and without influence on the national life? That also is not true. The reader will perceive from what has gone before that if he asks for statistics of Buddhism in China, the answer must be, in the Buddha's own phrase, that the question is not properly put. It is incorrect to describe China as a Buddhist country. We may say that it contains so many million Mohammedans or Christians, because these creeds are definite and exclusive. We cannot quote similar figures for Buddhism or Confucianism. Yet assuredly Buddhism has been a great power in China, as great perhaps as Christianity in Europe, if we remember how much is owed by European art, literature, law and science to non-Christian sources. The Chinese language is full of Buddhist phraseology[2], not only in literature

[1] The love of nature shown in the Pali Pitakas (particularly the Thera and Therî Gâthâ) has often been noticed, but it is also strong in Mahâyânist literature. *E.g.* Bodhicaryâvatâra VIII. 26–39 and 86–88.

[2] See especially Watters, *Essays on the Chinese Language*, chaps. VIII and IX, and Clementi, *Cantonese Love Songs in English*, pp. 9 to 12

but in popular songs and proverbs and an inspection of such entries in a Chinese dictionary as *Fo* (Buddha), *Kuan Yin*, *Ho Shang* (monk)[1] will show how large and not altogether flattering a part they play in popular speech.

Popular literature bears the same testimony. It is true that in what are esteemed the higher walks of letters Buddhism has little place. The quotations and allusions which play there so prominent a part are taken from the classics and Confucianism can claim as its own the historical, lexicographical and critical[2] works which are the solid and somewhat heavy glory of Chinese literature. But its lighter and less cultivated blossoms, such as novels, fairy stories and poetry, are predominantly Buddhist or Taoist in inspiration. This may be easily verified by a perusal of such works as the *Dream of the Red Chamber*, *Strange Stories from a Chinese Studio*, and Wieger's *Folk Lore Chinois Moderne.* The same is true in general of the great Chinese poets, many of whom did not conceal that (in a poetic and unascetic fashion) they were attached to Buddhism.

It may be asked if the inspiration is not Taoist in the main rather than Buddhist. Side by side with ethics and ceremony, a native stream of bold and weird imagination has never ceased to flow in China and there was no need to import tales of the Genii, immortal saints and vampire beauties. But when any coherency unites these ideas of the supernatural, that I think is the work of Buddhism and so far as Taoism itself has any coherency it is an imitation of Buddhism. Thus the idea of metempsychosis as one of many passing fancies may be indigenous to China but its prevalence in popular thought and language is undoubtedly due to Buddhism, for Taoism and Confucianism have nothing definite to say as to the state of the dead.

Much the same story of Buddhist influence is told by Chinese art, especially painting and sculpture. Here too Taoism is by no means excluded: it may be said to represent the artistic side

[1] 佛，觀音，和尙.

[2] I cannot refrain from calling attention to the difference between the Chinese and most other Asiatic peoples (especially the Hindus) as exhibited in their literature. Quite apart from European influence the Chinese produced several centuries ago catalogues of museums and descriptive lists of inscriptions, works which have no parallel in Hindu India.

of the Chinese mind, as Confucianism represents the political. But it is impossible to mistake the significance of chronology. As soon as Buddhism was well established in China, art entered on a new phase which culminated in the masterpieces of the T'ang and Sung[1]. Buddhism did not introduce painting into China or even perfect a rudimentary art. The celebrated roll of Ku K'ai-chih[2] shows no trace of Indian influence and presupposes a long artistic tradition. But Mahayanist Buddhism brought across Central Asia new shapes and motives. Some of its imports were of doubtful artistic value, such as figures with many limbs and eyes, but with them came ideas which enriched Chinese art with new dramatic power, passion and solemnity. Taoism dealt with other worlds but they were gardens of the Hesperides, inhabited by immortal wizards and fairy queens, not those disquieting regions where the soul receives the reward of its deeds. But now the art of Central Asia showed Chinese painters something new; saints preaching the law with a gesture of authority and deities of infinite compassion inviting suppliants to approach their thrones. And with them came the dramatic story of Gotama's life and all the legends of the Jatakas.

This clearly is not Taoism, but when the era of great art and literature begins, any distinction between the two creeds, except for theological purposes, becomes artificial, for Taoism borrowed many externals of Buddhism, and Buddhism, while not abandoning its austere and emaciated saints, also accepted the Taoist ideal of the careless wandering hermit, friend of mountain pines and deer. Wei Hsieh[3] who lived under the Chin dynasty, when the strength of Buddhism was beginning to be felt, is considered by Chinese critics as the earliest of the great painters and is said to have excelled in both Buddhist and Taoist subjects. The same may be said of the most eminent names, such as Ku K'ai-chih and Wu Tao-tzŭ[4], and we may also remember that Italian artists painted the birth of Venus and the origin of the milky way as well as Annunciations and

[1] There are said to have been four great schools of Buddhist painting under the T'ang. See Kokka 294 and 295.

[2] Preserved in the British Museum and published.

[3] 衞協 of the 晉 dynasty.

[4] 顧愷之, 吳道子.

Assumptions, without any hint that one incident was less true than another. Buddhism not only provided subjects like the death of the Buddha and Kuan Yin, the Goddess of Mercy, which hold in Chinese art the same place as the Crucifixion and the Madonna in Europe, and generation after generation have stimulated the noblest efforts of the best painters. It also offered a creed and ideals suited to the artistic temperament: peace and beauty reigned in its monasteries: its doctrine that life is one and continuous is reflected in that love of nature, that sympathetic understanding of plants and animals, that intimate union of sentiment with landscape which marks the best Chinese pictures.

CHAPTER XLIII

CHINA (*continued*)

HISTORY.

THE traditional date for the introduction of Buddhism is 62 A.D., when the chronicles tell how the Emperor Ming-Ti of the Later Han Dynasty dreamt that he saw a golden man fly into his palace[1] and how his courtiers suggested that the figure was Fo-t'o[2] or Buddha, an Indian God. Ming-Ti did not let the matter drop and in 65 sent an embassy to a destination variously described as the kingdom of the Ta Yüeh Chih[3] or India with instructions to bring back Buddhist scriptures and priests. On its return it was accompanied by a monk called Kâśyapa Mâtanga[4], a native of Central India. A second called Chu Fa-Lan[5], who came from Central Asia and found some difficulty in obtaining permission to leave his country, followed shortly afterwards. Both were installed at Loyang, the capital of the dynasty, in the White Horse Monastery[6], so called because the foreign monks rode on white horses or used them for carrying books.

The story has been criticized as an obvious legend, but I see no reason why it should not be true to this extent that Ming-Ti sent an embassy to Central Asia (not India in our sense) with the result that a monastery was for the first time established under imperial patronage. The gravest objection is that before the campaigns of Pan Ch'ao[7], which began about 73 A.D., Central Asia was in rebellion against China. But those

[1] See *B.E.F.E.O.* 1910, Le Songe et l'Ambassade de l'Empereur Ming Ti, par M. H. Maspéro, where the original texts are translated and criticized. It is a curious coincidence that Ptolemy Soter is said to have introduced the worship of Serapis to Egypt from Sinope in consequence of a dream.

[2] 佛陀. No doubt then pronounced something like Vut-tha.

[3] 大月支 or 氏. [4] 迦葉摩騰. [5] 竺法蘭.

[6] 白馬寺. [7] 班超.

campaigns show that the Chinese Court was occupied with Central Asian questions and to send envoys to enquire about religion may have been politically advantageous, for they could obtain information without asserting or abandoning China's claims to sovereignty. The story does not state that there was no Buddhism in China before 62 A.D. On the contrary it implies that though it was not sufficiently conspicuous to be known to the Emperor, yet there was no difficulty in obtaining information about it and other facts support the idea that it began to enter China at least half a century earlier. The negotiations of Chang Ch'ien[1] with the Yüeh Chih (129–119 B.C.) and the documents discovered by Stein in the ancient military posts on the western frontier of Kansu[2] prove that China had communication with Central Asia, but neither the accounts of Chang Ch'ien's journeys nor the documents contain any allusion to Buddhism. In 121 B.C. the Annals relate that "a golden man" was captured from the Hsiung-nu but, even if it was an image of Buddha, the incident had no consequences. More important is a notice in the Wei-lüeh which gives a brief account of the Buddha's birth and states that in the year 2 B.C. an ambassador sent by the Emperor Ai to the court of the Yüeh Chih was instructed in Buddhism by order of their king[3]. Also the Later Han Annals intimate that in 65 A.D. the Prince of Ch'u[4] was a Buddhist and that there were Śramanas and Upâsakas in his territory.

The author of the Wei-lüeh comments on the resemblance of Buddhist writings to the work of Lao-tzŭ, and suggests that the latter left China in order to teach in India. This theory found many advocates among the Taoists, but is not likely to commend itself to European scholars. Less improbable is a view held by

[1] 張騫.

[2] See Chavannes, *Les documents Chinois découverts par Aurel Stein*, 1913, Introduction. The earliest documents are of 98 B.C.

[3] The Wei-lüeh or Wei-lio 魏畧, composed between 239 and 265 A.D., no longer exists as a complete work, but a considerable extract from it dealing with the countries of the West is incorporated in the San Kuo Chih 三國志 of P'ei-Sung-Chih 裴松之 (429 A.D.). See Chavannes, translation and notes in *T'oung Pao*, 1905, pp. 519–571.

[4] 楚. See Chavannes, *l.c.* p. 550.

many Chinese critics[1] and apparently first mentioned in the Sui annals, namely, that Buddhism was introduced into China at an early date but was exterminated by the Emperor Shih Huang Ti (221–206) in the course of his crusade against literature. But this view is not supported by any details and is open to the general objection that intercourse between China and India *viâ* Central Asia before 200 B.C. is not only unproved but improbable.

Still the mystical, quietist philosophy of Lao-tzŭ and Chuang-tzŭ has an undoubted resemblance to Indian thought. No one who is familiar with the Upanishads can read the Tao-Tê-Ching without feeling that if Brahman is substituted for Tao the whole would be intelligible to a Hindu. Its doctrine is not specifically Buddhist, yet it contains passages which sound like echoes of the Pitakas. Compare Tao-Tê-Ching, 33. 1, "He who overcomes others is strong: he who overcomes himself is mighty," with Dhammapada, 103, "If one man overcome a thousand thousand in battle and another overcome himself, this last is the greatest of conquerors"; and 46. 2, "There is no greater sin that to look on what moves desire: there is no greater evil than discontent: there is no greater disaster than covetousness," with Dhammapada, 251, "There is no fire like desire, there is no monster like hatred, there is no snare like folly, there is no torrent like covetousness." And if it be objected that these are the coincidences of obvious ethics, I would call attention to 39. 1, "Hence if we enumerate separately each part that goes to form a cart, we have no cart at all." Here the thought and its illustration cannot be called obvious and the resemblance to well-known passages in the Samyutta Nikâya and Questions of Milinda[2] is striking.

Any discussion of the indebtedness of the Tao-Tê-Ching to India is too complicated for insertion here since it involves the

[1] See Francke, *Zur Frage der Einführung des Buddhismus in China*, 1910, and Maspéro's review in *B.E.F.E.O.* 1910, p. 629. Another Taoist legend is that Dipankara Buddha or Jan Têng, described as the teacher of Śâkyamuni was a Taoist and that Śâkyamuni visited him in China. Giles quotes extracts from a writer of the eleventh century called Shên Kua to the effect that Buddhism had been flourishing before the Ch'in dynasty but disappeared with its advent and also that eighteen priests were imprisoned in 216 B.C. But the story adds that they recited the Prajnâpâramitâ which is hardly possible at that epoch.

[2] Sam. Nik. v. 10. 6. Cf. for a similar illustration in Chuang-tzŭ, *S.B.E.* XL. p. 126.

question of its date or the date of particular passages, if we reject the hypothesis that the work as we have it was composed by Lao-tzŭ in the sixth century B.C.[1] But there is less reason to doubt the genuineness of the essays of Chuang-tzŭ who lived in the fourth century B.C. In them we find mention of trances which give superhuman wisdom and lead to union with the all-pervading spirit, and of magical powers enjoyed by sages, similar to the Indian *iddhi*. He approves the practice of abandoning the world and enunciates the doctrines of evolution and reincarnation. He knows, as does also the Tao-Tê-Ching, methods of regulating the breathing which are conducive to mental culture and long life. He speaks of the six faculties of perception, which recall the Shaḍâyatana, and of name and real existence (nâmarûpam) as being the conditions of a thing[2]. He has also a remarkable comparison of death to the extinction of a fire: "what we can point to are the faggots that have been consumed: but the fire is transmitted and we know not that it is over and ended." Several Buddhist parallels to this might be cited[3].

The list of such resemblances might be made longer and the explanation that Indian ideas reached China sporadically, at least as early as the fourth century B.C., seems natural. I should accept it, if there were any historical evidence besides these literary parallels. But there seems to be none and it may be justly urged that the roots of this quietism lie so deep in the Chinese character, that the plant cannot have sprung from some chance wind-wafted seed. That character has two sides, one seen in the Chinese Empire and the classical philosophy, excellent as ethics but somewhat stiff and formal: the other in revolutions and rebellions, in the free life of hermits and wanderers, in poetry and painting. This second side is very like the temper of Indian Buddhism and easily amalgamated with it[4], but it has a special note of its own.

[1] I may say, however, that I think it is a compilation containing very ancient sayings amplified by later material which shows Buddhist influence. This may be true to some extent of the Essays of Chuang-tzŭ as well.

[2] See Legge's translation in *S.B.E.* Part I. pp. 176, 257, II. 46, 62; *ib.* I. pp. 171, 192, II. 13; *ib.* II. p. 13; *ib.* II. p. 9, I. p. 249; *ib.* pp. 45, 95, 100, 364, II. p. 139; *ib.* II. p. 130; *ib.* II. p. 120.

[3] *Ib.* I. p. 202; cf. the Buddha's conversation with Vaccha in Maj. Nik. 72.

[4] Kumârajîva and other Buddhists actually wrote commentaries on the Tao-Tê-Ching.

The curiosity of Ming-Ti did not lead to any immediate triumph of Buddhism. We read that he was zealous in honouring Confucius but not that he showed devotion to the new faith. Indeed it is possible that his interest was political rather than religious. Buddhism was also discredited by its first convert, the Emperor's brother Chu-Ying, who rebelled unsuccessfully and committed suicide. Still it flourished in a quiet way and the two foreign monks in the White Horse Monastery began that long series of translations which assumed gigantic proportions in the following centuries. To Kâśyapa is ascribed a collection of extracts known as the Sûtra of forty-two sections which is still popular[1]. This little work adheres closely to the teaching of the Pali Tripitaka and shows hardly any traces of the Mahâyâna. According to the Chinese annals the chief doctrines preached by the first Buddhist missionaries were the sanctity of all animal life, metempsychosis, meditation, asceticism and Karma.

It is not until the third century[2] that we hear much of Buddhism as a force at Court or among the people, but meanwhile the task of translation progressed at Lo-yang. The Chinese are a literary race and these quiet labours prepared the soil for the subsequent efflorescence. Twelve[3] translators are named as having worked before the downfall of the Han Dynasty and about 350 books are attributed to them. None of them were Chinese. About half came from India and the rest from Central Asia, the most celebrated of the latter being An Shih-kao, a prince of An-hsi or Parthia[4]. The Later Han Dynasty was

[1] 四十二章經. It speaks, however, in section 36 of being born in the condition or family of a Bodhisattva (P'u-sa-chia), where the word seems to be used in the late sense of a devout member of the Buddhist Church.

[2] But the Emperor Huan is said to have sacrificed to Buddha and Lao-tzŭ. See Hou Han Shu in *T'oung Pao*, 1907, p. 194. For early Buddhism see "Communautés et Moines Bouddhistes Chinois au II et au III siècles," by Maspéro in *B.E.F.E.O.* 1910, p. 222. In the second century lived Mou-tzŭ 牟子 a Buddhist author with a strong spice of Taoism. His work is a collection of questions and answers, somewhat resembling the Questions of Milinda. See translation by Pelliot (in *T'oung Pao*, vol. XIX. 1920) who gives the date provisionally as 195 A.D.

[3] Accounts of these and the later translators are found in the thirteen catalogues of the Chinese Tripitaka (see Nanjio, p. xxvii) and other works such as the Kao Sang-Chuan (Nanjio, No. 1490).

[4] 安世高, 安息. He worked at translations in Loyang 148–170.

followed by the animated and romantic epoch known as the Three Kingdoms (221–265) when China was divided between the States of Wei, Wu and Shu. Loyang became the capital of Wei and the activity of the White Horse Monastery continued. We have the names of five translators who worked there. One of them was the first to translate the Pâtimokkha[1], which argues that previously few followed the monastic life. At Nanking, the capital of Wu, we also hear of five translators and one was tutor of the Crown Prince. This implies that Buddhism was spreading in the south and that monks inspired confidence at Court.

The Three Kingdoms gave place to the Dynasty known as Western Tsin[2] which, for a short time (A.D. 265–316), claimed to unite the Empire, and we now reach the period when Buddhism begins to become prominent. It is also a period of political confusion, of contest between the north and south, of struggles between Chinese and Tartars. Chinese histories, with their long lists of legitimate sovereigns, exaggerate the solidity and continuity of the Empire, for the territory ruled by those sovereigns was often but a small fraction of what we call China. Yet the Tartar states were not an alien and destructive force to the same extent as the conquests made by Mohammedan Turks at the expense of Byzantium. The Tartars were neither fanatical, nor prejudiced against Chinese ideals in politics and religion. On the contrary, they respected the language, literature and institutions of the Empire: they assumed Chinese names and sometimes based their claim to the Imperial title on the marriage of their ancestors with Chinese princesses.

During the fourth century and the first half of the fifth some twenty ephemeral states, governed by Tartar chieftains and perpetually involved in mutual war, rose and fell in northern China. The most permanent of them was Northern Wei which lasted till 535 A.D. But the Later Chao and both the Earlier and Later Ts'in are important for our purpose[3]. Some writers make it a reproach to Buddhism that its progress, which had been

[1] Dharmakâla, see Nanjio, p. 386. The Vinaya used in these early days of Chinese Buddhism was apparently that of the Dharmagupta school. See *J.A.* 1916, II. p. 40. An Shih-kao (c. A.D. 150) translated a work called The 3000 Rules for Monks (Nanjio, 1126), but it is not clear what was the Sanskrit original.

[2] 西晉.

[3] 北魏, 後趙, 前秦, 後秦.

slow among the civilized Chinese, became rapid in the provinces which passed into the hands of these ruder tribes. But the phenomenon is natural and is illustrated by the fact that even now the advance of Christianity is more rapid in Africa than in India. The civilization of China was already old and self-complacent: not devoid of intellectual curiosity and not intolerant, but sceptical of foreign importations and of dealings with the next world. But the Tartars had little of their own in the way of literature and institutions: it was their custom to assimilate the arts and ideas of the civilized nations whom they conquered: the more western tribes had already made the acquaintance of Buddhism in Central Asia and such native notions of religion as they possessed disposed them to treat priests, monks and magicians with respect.

Of the states mentioned, the Later Chao was founded by Shih-Lo[1] (273–332), whose territories extended from the Great Wall to the Han and Huai in the South. He showed favour to an Indian monk and diviner called Fo-t'u-ch'êng[2] who lived at his court and he appears to have been himself a Buddhist. At any rate the most eminent of his successors, Shih Chi-lung[3], was an ardent devotee and gave general permission to the population to enter monasteries, which had not been granted previously. This permission is noticeable, for it implies, even at this early date, the theory that a subject of the Emperor has no right to become a monk without his master's leave.

In 381 we are told that in north-western China nine-tenths of the inhabitants were Buddhists. In 372 Buddhism was introduced into Korea and accepted as the flower of Chinese civilization.

The state known as the Former Ts'in[4] had its nucleus in

[1] 石勒.

[2] 佛圖澄. He was a remarkable man and famous in his time, for he was credited not only with clairvoyance and producing rain, but with raising the dead. Rémusat's account of him, based on the Tsin annals, may still be read with interest. See *Nouv. Mélanges Asiatiques*, II. 1829, pp. 179 ff. His biography is contained in chap. 95 of the Tsin 晉 annals.

[3] 石季龍. Died 363 A.D.

[4] Ts'in 秦 must be distinguished from Tsin 晉, the name of three short but legitimate dynasties.

Shensi, but expanded considerably between 351 and 394 A.D. under the leadership of Fu-Chien[1], who established in it large colonies of Tartars. At first he favoured Confucianism but in 381 became a Buddhist. He was evidently in close touch with the western regions and probably through them with India, for we hear that sixty-two states of Central Asia sent him tribute.

The Later Ts'in dynasty (384–417) had its headquarters in Kansu and was founded by vassals of the Former Ts'in. When the power of Fu-Chien collapsed, they succeeded to his possessions and established themselves in Ch'ang-an. Yao-hsing[2], the second monarch of this line was a devout Buddhist, and deserves mention as the patron of Kumârajîva[3], the most eminent of the earlier translators.

Kumârajîva was born of Indian parents in Kucha and, after following the school of the Sarvâstivâdins for some time, became a Mahayanist. When Kucha was captured in 383 by the General of Fu-Chien, he was carried off to China and from 401 onwards he laboured at Ch'ang-an for about ten years. He was appointed Kuo Shih[4], or Director of Public Instruction, and lectured in a hall specially built for him. He is said to have had 3000 disciples and fifty extant translations are ascribed to him. Probably all the Tartar kingdoms were well disposed towards Buddhism, though their unsettled condition made them precarious residences for monks and scholars. This was doubtless true of Northern Wei, which had been growing during the period described, but appears as a prominent home of Buddhism somewhat later.

Meanwhile in the south the Eastern Tsin Dynasty, which represented the legitimate Empire and ruled at Nanking from 317 to 420, was also favourable to Buddhism and Hsiao Wu-Ti, the ninth sovereign of this line, was the first Emperor of China to become a Buddhist.

The times were troubled, but order was gradually being restored. The Eastern Tsin Dynasty had been much disturbed by the struggles of rival princes. These were brought to an end in 420 by a new dynasty known as Liu Sung which reigned in

[1] 苻堅. [2] 姚興.

[3] See Nanjio, Catalogue, p. 406.

[4] 國師. For this title see Pelliot in *T'oung Pao*, 1911, p. 671.

the south some sixty years. The north was divided among six Tartar kingdoms, which all perished before 440 except Wei. Wei then split into an Eastern and a Western kingdom which lasted about a hundred years. In the south, the Liu Sung gave place to three short dynasties, Ch'i, Liang and Ch'ên, until at last the Sui (589–605) united China.

The Liu Sung Emperor Wên-Ti (424–454) was a patron of Confucian learning, but does not appear to have discouraged Buddhism. The Sung annals record that several embassies were sent from India and Ceylon to offer congratulations on the flourishing condition of religion in his dominions, but they also preserve memorials from Chinese officials asking for imperial interference to prevent the multiplication of monasteries and the growing expenditure on superstitious ceremonies. This marks the beginning of the desire to curb Buddhism by restrictive legislation which the official class displayed so prominently and persistently in subsequent centuries. A similar reaction seems to have been felt in Wei, where the influential statesman Ts'ui Hao[1], a votary of Taoism, conducted an anti-Buddhist campaign. He was helped in this crusade by the discovery of arms in a monastery at Ch'ang-an. The monks were accused of treason and debauchery and in 446 Toba Tao[2], the sovereign of Wei, issued an edict ordering the destruction of Buddhist temples and sacred books as well as the execution of all priests. The Crown Prince, who was a Buddhist, was able to save many lives, but no monasteries or temples were left standing. The persecution, however, was of short duration. Toba Tao was assassinated and almost the first act of his successor was to re-establish Buddhism and allow his subjects to become monks. From this period date the sculptured grottoes of Yün-Kang in northern Shan-si which are probably the oldest specimens of Buddhist art in China. In 471 another ruler of Wei, Toba Hung, had a gigantic image of Buddha constructed and subsequently abdicated in order to devote himself to

[1] 崔浩.

[2] 拓跋燾. He was canonized under the name of Wu 武, and the three great persecutions of Buddhism are sometimes described as the disasters of the three Wu, the others being Wu of the North Chou dynasty (574) and Wu of the T'ang (845).

Buddhist studies. His successor marks a reaction, for he was an ardent Confucianist who changed the family name to Yüan and tried to introduce the Chinese language and dress. But the tide of Buddhism was too strong. It secured the favour of the next Emperor in whose time there are said to have been 13,000 temples in Wei.

In the Sung dominions a conspiracy was discovered in 458 in which a monk was implicated, and restrictive, though not prohibitive, regulations were issued respecting monasteries. The Emperor Ming-Ti, though a cruel ruler was a devout Buddhist and erected a monastery in Hu-nan, at the cost of such heavy taxation that his ministers remonstrated. The fifty-nine years of Liu Sung rule must have been on the whole favourable to Buddhism, for twenty translators flourished, partly natives and partly foreigners from Central Asia, India and Ceylon. In 420 a band of twenty-five Chinese started on a pilgrimage to India. They had been preceded by the celebrated pilgrim Fa-Hsien[1] who travelled in India from 399 to 414.

In the reign of Wu-Ti, the first Emperor of the Ch'i dynasty, one of the imperial princes, named Tzŭ Liang[2], cultivated the society of eminent monks and enjoyed theological discussions. From the specimens of these arguments which have been preserved we see that the explanation of the inequalities of life as the result of Karma had a great attraction for the popular mind and also that it provoked the hostile criticism of the Confucian literati.

The accession of the Liang dynasty and the long reign of its first emperor Wu-Ti (502–549) were important events in the history of Buddhism, for this monarch rivalled Asoka in pious enthusiasm if not in power and prosperity. He obviously set the Church above the state and it was while he was on the throne that Bodhidharma came to China and the first edition of the Tripitaka was prepared.

His reign, though primarily of importance for religion, was not wanting in political interest, and witnessed a long conflict with Wei. Wu-Ti was aided by the dissensions which distracted Wei but failed to achieve his object, probably as a result of his religious preoccupations, for he seemed unable to estimate the

[1] 法顯. For the 25 pilgrims see Nanjio, p. 417. [2] 子良.

power of the various adventurers who from time to time rose to pre-eminence in the north and, holding war to be wrong, he was too ready to accept insincere overtures for peace. Wei split into two states, the Eastern and Western, and Hou-Ching[1], a powerful general who was not satisfied with his position in either, offered his services to Wu-Ti, promising to add a large part of Ho-nan to his dominions. He failed in his promise but Wu-Ti, instead of punishing him, first gave him a post as governor and then listened to the proposals made by the ruler of Eastern Wei for his surrender. On this Hou-Ching conspired with an adopted son of Wu-Ti, who had been set aside as heir to the throne and invested Nanking. The city was captured after the horrors of a prolonged siege and Wu-Ti died miserably.

Wu-Ti was not originally a Buddhist. In fact until about 510, when he was well over forty, he was conspicuous as a patron of Confucianism. The change might be ascribed to personal reasons, but it is noticeable that the same thing occurred in Wei, where a period of Confucianism was succeeded by a strong wave of Buddhism which evidently swept over all China. Hu[2], the Dowager Empress of Wei, was a fervent devotee, though of indifferent morality in both public and private life since she is said to have poisoned her own son. In 518 she sent Sung Yün and Hui Shêng[3] to Udyâna in search of Buddhist books of which they brought back 175.

Wu-Ti's conversion is connected with a wandering monk and magician called Pao-Chih[4], who received the privilege of approaching him at all hours. A monastery was erected in Nanking at great expense and edicts were issued forbidding not only the sacrifice of animals but even the representation of living things in embroidery, on the ground that people might cut up such figures and thus become callous to the sanctity of life. The emperor expounded sûtras in public and wrote a work on Buddhist ritual[5]. The first Chinese edition of the Tripitaka, in manuscript and not printed, was collected in 518.

[1] 侯景. [2] 胡.

[3] 宋雲, 惠生. See Chavannes, "Voyage de Song Yun dans l'Udyâna et le Gandhâra, 518–522," p. E in *B.E.F.E.O.* 1903, pp. 379–441. For an interesting account of the Dowager Empress see pp. 384–5.

[4] 寶誌. [5] 慈悲道場懺.

Although Wu-Ti's edicts, particularly that against animal sacrifices, gave great dissatisfaction, yet the Buddhist movement seems to have been popular and not merely an imperial whim, for many distinguished persons, for instance the authors Liu Hsieh and Yao Ch'a[1], took part in it.

In 520 (or according to others, in 525) Bodhidharma (generally called Ta-mo in Chinese) landed in Canton from India. He is described as the son of a king of a country called Hsiang-chih in southern India, and the twenty-eighth Patriarch[2]. He taught that merit does not lie in good works and that knowledge is not gained by reading the scriptures. The one essential is insight, which comes as illumination after meditation. Though this doctrine had subsequently much success in the Far East, it was not at first appreciated and Bodhidharma's introduction to the devout but literary Emperor in Nanking was a fiasco. He offended his Majesty by curtly saying that he had acquired no merit by causing temples to be built and books to be transcribed. Then, in answer to the question, what is the most important of the holy doctrines, he replied "where all is emptiness, nothing can be called holy." "Who," asked the astonished Emperor, "is he who thus replies to me?" "I do not know," said Bodhidharma.

Not being able to come to any understanding with Wu-Ti, Bodhidharma went northwards, and is said to have crossed the Yang-tse standing on a reed, a subject frequently represented in Chinese art[3]. He retired to Lo-yang where he spent nine years in the Shao-Lin[4] temple gazing silently at a wall, whence he was popularly known as the wall-gazer. One legend says that he sat so long in contemplation that his legs fell off, and

[1] 劉勰 and 姚察.

[2] See chap. XXIII. p. 95, and chap. XLV below (on schools of Chinese Buddhism), for more about Bodhidharma. The earliest Chinese accounts of him seem to be those contained in the Liang and Wei annals. But one of the most popular and fullest accounts is to be found in the Wu Têng Hui Yüan (first volume) printed at Kushan near Fuchow.

[3] His portraits are also frequent both in China and Japan (see *Ostasiat. Ztsft* 1912, p. 226) and the strongly marked features attributed to him may perhaps represent a tradition of his personal appearance, which is entirely un-Chinese. An elaborate study of Bodhidharma written in Japanese is noticed in *B.E.F.E.O.* 1911, p. 457.

[4] 少林.

a kind of legless doll which is a favourite plaything in Japan is still called by his name. But according to another tale he preserved his legs. He wished to return to India but died in China. When Sung Yün, the traveller mentioned above, was returning from India, he met him in a mountain pass barefooted and carrying one sandal in his hand[1]. When this was reported, his coffin was opened and was found to contain nothing but the other sandal which was long preserved as a precious relic in the Shao-Lin temple.

Wu-Ti adopted many of the habits of a bonze. He was a strict vegetarian, expounded the scriptures in public and wrote a work on ritual. He thrice retired into a monastery and wore the dress of a Bhikkhu. These retirements were apparently of short duration and his ministers twice redeemed him by heavy payments.

In 538 a hair of the Buddha was sent by the king of Fu-nan and received with great ceremony. In the next year a mission was despatched to Magadha to obtain Sanskrit texts. It returned in 546 with a large collection of manuscripts and accompanied by the learned Paramârtha who spent twenty years in translating them[2]. Wu-Ti, in his old age, became stricter. All luxury was suppressed at Court, but he himself always wore full dress and showed the utmost politeness, even to the lowest officials. He was so reluctant to inflict the punishment of death that crime increased. In 547 he became a monk for the third time and immediately afterwards the events connected with Hou-Ching (briefly sketched above) began to trouble the peace of his old age. During the siege of Nanking he was obliged to depart from his vegetarian diet and eat eggs. When he was told that his capital was taken he merely said, "I obtained the kingdom through my own efforts and through me it has been lost. So I need not complain."

Hou-Ching proceeded to the palace, but[3], overcome with awe, knelt down before Wu-Ti who merely said, "I am afraid you must be fatigued by the trouble it has cost you to destroy my kingdom." Hou-Ching was ashamed and told his officers that

[1] The legend does not fit in well with chronology since Sung-Yün is said to have returned from India in 522.

[2] See Takakusu in *J.R.A.S.* 1905, p. 33.

[3] Mailla, *Hist. Gén. de la Chine*, p. 369.

he had never felt such fear before and would never dare to see Wu-Ti again. Nevertheless, the aged Emperor was treated with indignity and soon died of starvation. His end, though melancholy, was peaceful compared with that in store for Hou-Ching who, after two years of fighting and murdering, assumed the imperial title, but immediately afterwards was defeated and slain. The people ate his body in the streets of Nanking and his own wife is said to have swallowed mouthfuls of his flesh.

One of Wu-Ti's sons, Yüan-Ti, who reigned from 552 to 555, inherited his father's temper and fate with this difference that he was a Taoist, not a Buddhist. He frequently resided in the temples of that religion, studied its scriptures and expounded them to his people. A great scholar, he had accumulated 140,000 volumes, but when it was announced to him in his library that the troops of Wei were marching on his capital, he yielded without resistance and burnt his books, saying that they had proved of no use in this extremity.

This alternation of imperial patronage in the south may have been the reason why Wên Hsüan Ti, the ruler of Northern Ch'i[1], and for the moment perhaps the most important personage in China, summoned Buddhist and Taoist priests to a discussion in 555. Both religions could not be true, he said, and one must be superfluous. After hearing the arguments of both he decided in favour of Buddhism and ordered the Taoists to become bonzes on pain of death. Only four refused and were executed.

Under the short Ch'ên dynasty (557–589) the position of Buddhism continued favourable. The first Emperor, a mild and intelligent sovereign, though circumstances obliged him to put a great many people out of the way, retired to a monastery after reigning for two years. But in the north there was a temporary reaction. Wu-Ti, of the Northern Chou dynasty[2], first of all defined the precedence of the three religions as Confucianism, Taoism, Buddhism and then, in 575, prohibited the two latter, ordering temples to be destroyed and priests to return to the world. But as usual the persecution was not of long duration. Five years later Wu-Ti's son withdrew his father's edict and in 582, the founder of the Sui dynasty, gave the population permission to become monks. He may be said to have used

[1] 北齊, 文宣. [2] 北周, 武帝.

Buddhism as his basis for restoring the unity of the Empire and in his old age he became devout. The Sui annals observe that Buddhist books had become more numerous under this dynasty than those of the Confucianists, and no less than three collections of the Tripitaka were made between 594 and 616.

With the seventh century began the great T'ang dynasty (620–907). Buddhism had now been known to the rulers of China for about 550 years. It began as a religion tolerated but still regarded as exotic and not quite natural for the sons of Han. It had succeeded in establishing itself as the faith of the majority among both Tartars and Chinese. The rivalry of Taoism was only an instance of that imitation which is the sincerest flattery. Though the opposition of the mandarins assumed serious proportions whenever they could induce an Emperor to share their views, yet the hostile attitude of the Government never lasted long and was not shared by the mass of the people. It is clear that the permissions to practise Buddhism which invariably followed close on the prohibitions were a national relief. Though Buddhism tended to mingle with Taoism and other indigenous ideas, the many translations of Indian works and the increasing intercourse between Chinese and Hindus had diffused a knowledge of its true tenets and practice.

The T'ang dynasty witnessed a triangular war between Confucianism, Buddhism and Taoism. As a rule Confucianism attacked the other two as base superstitions but sometimes, as in the reign of Wu Tsung, Taoism seized a chance of being able to annihilate Buddhism. This war continued under the Northern Sung, though the character of Chinese Buddhism changed, for the Contemplative School, which had considerable affinities to Taoism, became popular at the expense of the T'ien T'ai. After the Northern Sung (except under the foreign Mongol dynasty) we feel that, though Buddhism was by no means dead and from time to time flourished exceedingly, yet Confucianism had established its claim to be the natural code and creed of the scholar and statesman. The Chinese Court remained a strange place to the end but scholarship and good sense had a large measure of success in banishing extravagance from art and literature. Yet, alas, the intellectual life of China lost more in fire and brilliancy than it gained in sanity. Probably the most critical times for literature and indeed for thought were those brief periods under the Sui and T'ang[1] when Buddhist and Taoist books were accepted as texts for the public examinations and the last half century of the Northern Sung, when the educational reforms of Wang An Shih were intermittently in force. The innovations were cancelled in all cases. Had they lasted, Chinese style and mentality might have been different.

The T'ang dynasty, though on the whole favourable to Buddhism, and indeed the period of its greatest prosperity, opened with a period of reaction. To the founder, Kao Tsu, is attributed the saying that Confucianism is as necessary to the Chinese as wings to a bird or water to a fish. The imperial historiographer Fu I[2] presented to his master a memorial blaming Buddhism because it undervalued natural relationships and urging that monks and nuns should be compelled to marry. He was opposed by Hsiao Yü[3], who declared that hell was made for such people as his opponent—an argument common to many religions. The Emperor followed on the whole advice of Fu I. Magistrates were ordered to inquire into the lives of monks and nuns. Those found pure and sincere were collected in the large establishments. The rest were ordered to return to the world and the smaller religious houses were closed. Kao Tsu abdicated in 627 but his son Tai Tsung continued his religious policy, and the new Empress was strongly anti-Buddhist, for when mortally ill she forbade her son to pray for her recovery in Buddhist shrines. Yet the Emperor cannot have shared these sentiments at any rate towards the end of his reign[4]. He issued an edict allowing every monastery to receive five new monks and the

[1] See Biot, *Hist. de l'instruction publique en Chine*, pp. 289, 313.

[2] 傅奕. Is celebrated in Chinese history as one of the greatest opponents of Buddhism. He collected all the objections to it in 10 books and warned his son against it on his death bed. Giles, *Biog. Dict.* 589.

[3] 蕭瑀. An important minister and apparently a man of talent but of ungovernable and changeable temper. In 639 he obtained the Emperor's leave to become a priest but soon left his monastery. The Emperor ordered him to be canonized under the name Pure but Narrow. Giles, *Biog. Dict.* 722. The monk Fa-Lin 法琳 also attacked the views of Fu I in two treatises which have been incorporated in the Chinese Tripitaka. See Nanjio, Cat. Nos. 1500, 1501.

[4] Subsequently a story grew up that his soul had visited hell during a prolonged fainting fit after which he recovered and became a devout Buddhist. See chap. XI of the Romance called Hsi-yu-chi, a fantastic travesty of Hsüan Chuang's travels, and Wieger, *Textes Historiques*, p. 1585.

celebrated journey of Hsüan Chuang[1] was made in his reign. When the pilgrim returned from India, he was received with public honours and a title was conferred on him. Learned monks were appointed to assist him in translating the library he had brought back and the account of his travels was presented to the Emperor who also wrote a laudatory preface to his version of the Prajnâpâramitâ. It was in this reign also that Nestorian missionaries first appeared in China and were allowed to settle in the capital. Diplomatic relations were maintained with India. The Indian Emperor Harsha sent an envoy in 641 and two Chinese missions were despatched in return. The second, led by Wang Hsüan-Ts'ê[2], did not arrive until after the death of Harsha when a usurper had seized the throne. Wang Hsüan-Ts'ê collected a small army in Tibet, dethroned the usurper and brought him as a prisoner to China.

The latter half of the seventh century is dominated by the figure of the Dowager Empress Wu, the prototype of the celebrated lady who took charge of China's fate in our own day and, like her, superhuman in decision and unscrupulousness, yet capable of inspiring loyalty. She was a concubine of the Emperor Tai Tsung and when he died in 649 lived for a short time as a Buddhist nun. The eventful life of Wu Hou, who was at least successful in maintaining order at home and on the frontiers, belongs to the history of China rather than of Buddhism. She was not an ornament of the faith nor an example of its principles, but, mindful of the protection it had once afforded her, she gave it her patronage even to the extent of making a bonze named Huai I[3] the minister of her mature passions when she was nearly

[1] 玄奘. This name has been transliterated in an extraordinary number of ways. See *B.E.F.E.O.* 1905, pp. 424–430. Giles gives Hsüan Chuang in his *Chinese Dictionary*, but Hsüan Tsang in his *Biographical Dictionary*. Probably the latter is more correct. Not only is the pronunciation of the characters variable, but the character 玄 was tabooed as being part of the Emperor K'ang Hsi's personal name and 元 substituted for it. Hence the spelling Yüan Chuang.

[2] 王玄策. See Vincent Smith, *Early History of India*, pp. 326–327, and Giles, *Biog. Dict.*, *s.v.* Wang Hsüan-T'se. This worthy appears to have gone to India again in 657 to offer robes at the holy places.

[3] 懷義. Some of the principal statues in the caves of Lung-men were made at her expense, but other parts of these caves seem to date from at least 500 A.D. Chavannes, *Mission Archéol.* tome I, deuxième partie.

seventy years old. A magnificent temple, at which 10,000 men worked daily, was built for him, but the Empress was warned that he was collecting a body of vigorous monks nominally for its service, but really for political objects. She ordered these persons to be banished. Huai I was angry and burnt the temple. The Empress at first merely ordered it to be rebuilt, but finding that Huai I was growing disrespectful, she had him assassinated.

We hear that the Mahâmegha-sûtra[1] was presented to her and circulated among the people with her approval. About 690 she assumed divine honours and accommodated these pretensions to Buddhism by allowing herself to be styled Maitreya or Kuan-yin. After her death at the age of 80, there does not appear to have been any religious change, for two monks were appointed to high office and orders were issued that Buddhist and Taoist temples should be built in every Department. But the earlier part of the reign of Hsüan Tsung[2] marks a temporary reaction. It was represented to him that rich families wasted their substance on religious edifices and that the inmates were well-to-do persons desirous of escaping the burdens of public service. He accordingly forbade the building of monasteries, making of images and copying of sutras, and 12,000 monks were ordered to return to the world. In 725 he ordered a building known as "Hall of the Assembled Spirits" to be renamed "Hall of Assembled Worthies," because spirits were mere fables.

In the latter part of his life he became devout though addicted to Taoism rather than Buddhism. But he must have outgrown his anti-Buddhist prejudices, for in 730 the seventh collection of the Tripitaka was made under his auspices. Many poets of this period such as Su Chin and the somewhat later Liu Tsung Yüan[3] were Buddhists and the paintings of the great Wu Tao-tzŭ and Wang-wei (painter as well as poet) glowed with the inspiration of the T'ien-t'ai teaching. In 740 there were in the city of Ch'ang-An alone sixty-four monasteries and

[1] 大雲經. Ta-Yün-Ching. See *J.A.* 1913, p. 149. The late Dowager Empress also was fond of masquerading as Kuan-yin but it does not appear that the performance was meant to be taken seriously.

[2] "That romantic Chinese reign of Genso (713–756) which is the real absolu culmination of Chinese genius." Fenollosa, *Epochs of Chinese and Japanese ar* I. 102.

[3] 蘇晉, 柳宗元.

twenty-seven nunneries. A curious light is thrown on the inconsistent and composite character of Chinese religious sentiment—as noticeable to-day as it was twelve hundred years ago —by the will of Yao Ch'ung[1] a statesman who presented a celebrated anti-Buddhist memorial to this Emperor. In his will he warns his children solemnly against the creed which he hated and yet adds the following direction. "When I am dead, on no account perform for me the ceremonies of that mean religion. But if you feel unable to follow orthodoxy in every respect, then yield to popular custom and from the first seventh day after my death until the last (*i.e.* seventh) seventh day, let mass be celebrated by the Buddhist clergy seven times: and when, as these masses require, you must offer gifts to me, use the clothes which I wore in life and do not use other valuable things."

In 751 a mission was sent to the king of Ki-pin[2]. The staff included Wu-K'ung[3], also known as Dharmadhâtu, who remained some time in India, took the vows and ultimately returned to China with many books and relics. It is probable that in this and the following centuries Hindu influence reached the outlying province of Yünnan directly through Burma[4].

Letters, art and pageantry made the Court of Hsüan Tsung brilliant, but the splendour faded and his reign ended tragically in disaster and rebellion. The T'ang dynasty seemed in danger of collapse. But it emerged successfully from these troubles and continued for a century and a half. During the whole of this period the Emperors with one exception[5] were favourable to Buddhism, and the latter half of the eighth century marks in Buddhist history an epoch of increased popularity among the masses but also the spread of ritual and doctrinal corruption, for it is in these years that its connection with ceremonies for the repose and honour of the dead became more intimate.

1 姚崇.

2 罽賓. The meaning of this name appears to vary at different times. At this period it is probably equivalent to Kapisa or N.E. Afghanistan.

3 悟空.

4 See *B.E.F.E.O.* 1904, p. 161. This does not exclude the possibility of an opposite current, *viz.* Chinese Buddhism flowing into Burma.

5 Wu-Tsung, 841–847.

These middle and later T'ang Emperors were not exclusive Buddhists. According to the severe judgment of their own officials, they were inclined to unworthy and outlandish superstitions. Many of them were under the influence of eunuchs, magicians and soothsayers, and many of those who were not assassinated died from taking the Taoist medicine called Elixir of Immortality. Yet it was not a period of decadence and dementia. It was for China the age of Augustus, not of Heliogabalus. Art and literature flourished and against Han-Yü, the brilliant adversary of Buddhism, may be set Liu Tsung Yüan[1], a writer of at least equal genius who found in it his inspiration. A noble school of painting grew up in the Buddhist monasteries and in a long line of artists may be mentioned the great name of Wu Tao-tzŭ, whose religious pictures such as Kuan-yin, Purgatory and the death of the Buddha obtained for him a fame which is still living. Among the streams which watered this paradise of art and letters should doubtless be counted the growing importance of Central and Western Asia in Chinese policy and the consequent influx of their ideas. In the mid T'ang period Manichæism, Nestorianism and Zoroastrianism all were prevalent in China. The first was the religion of the Uigurs. So long as the Chinese had to keep on good terms with this tribe Manichæism was respected, but when they were defeated by the Kirghiz and became unimportant, it was abruptly suppressed (843). In this period, too, Tibet became of great importance for the Chinese. Their object was to keep open the passes leading to Ferghana and India. But the Tibetans sometimes combined with the Arabs, who had conquered Turkestan, to close them and in 763 they actually sacked Chang An. China endeavoured to defend herself by making treaties with the Indian border states, but in 175 the Arabs inflicted a disastrous defeat on her troops. A treaty of peace was subsequently made with Tibet[2].

When Su-Tsung (756–762), the son of Hsüan-Tsung, was safely established on the throne, he began to show his devotion to Buddhism. He installed a chapel in the Palace which was

[1] "Liu-Tsung-Yuan has left behind him much that for purity of style and felicity of expression has rarely been surpassed," Giles, *Chinese Literature*, p. 191.

[2] Apparently in 783 A.D. See Waddell's articles on Ancient Historical Edicts at Lhasa in *J.R.A.S.* 1909, 1910, 1911.

served by several hundred monks and caused his eunuchs and guards to dress up as Bodhisattvas and Genii. His ministers, who were required to worship these maskers, vainly remonstrated as also when he accepted a sort of Sibylline book from a nun who alleged that she had ascended to heaven and received it there.

The next Emperor, Tai-Tsung, was converted to Buddhism by his Minister Wang Chin[1], a man of great abilities who was subsequently sentenced to death for corruption, though the Emperor commuted the sentence to banishment. Tai-Tsung expounded the scriptures in public himself and the sacred books were carried from one temple to another in state carriages with the same pomp as the sovereign. In 768 the eunuch Yü Chao-Ên[2] built a great Buddhist temple dedicated to the memory of the Emperor's deceased mother. In spite of his minister's remonstrances, His Majesty attended the opening and appointed 1000 monks and nuns to perform masses for the dead annually on the fifteenth day of the seventh month. This anniversary became generally observed as an All Souls' Day, and is still one of the most popular festivals in China. Priests both Buddhist and Taoist recite prayers for the departed, rice is scattered abroad to feed hungry ghosts and clothes are burnt to be used by them in the land of shadows. Large sheds are constructed in which are figures representing scenes from the next world and the evening is enlivened by theatricals, music and fireworks[3].

The establishment of this festival was due to the celebrated teacher Amogha (Pu-k'ung), and marks the official recognition by Chinese Buddhism of those services for the dead which have rendered it popular at the cost of forgetting its better aspects. Amogha was a native of Ceylon (or, according to others, of Northern India), who arrived in China in 719 with his teacher Vajrabodhi. After the latter's death he revisited India and Ceylon in search of books and came back in 746. He wished to return to his own country, but permission was refused and until his death in 774 he was a considerable personage at Court,

[1] 王縉. [2] 魚朝恩.

[3] See Eitel, *Handbook of Chinese Buddhism*, p. 185 *s.v.* Ullambana, a somewhat doubtful word, apparently rendered into Chinese as Yü-lan-p'ên.

receiving high rank and titles. The Chinese Tripitaka contains 108 translations[1] ascribed to him, mostly of a tantric character, though to the honour of China it must be said that the erotic mysticism of some Indian tantras never found favour there. Amogha is a considerable, though not auspicious, figure in the history of Chinese Buddhism, and, so far as such changes can be the work of one man, on him rests the responsibility of making it become in popular estimation a religion specially concerned with funeral rites[2].

Some authors[3] try to prove that the influx of Nestorianism under the T'ang dynasty had an important influence on the later development of Buddhism in China and Japan and in particular that it popularized these services for the dead. But this hypothesis seems to me unproved and unnecessary. Such ceremonies were an essential part of Chinese religion and no faith could hope to spread, if it did not countenance them: they are prominent in Hinduism and not unknown to Pali Buddhism[4]. Further the ritual used in China and Japan has often only a superficial resemblance to Christian masses for the departed. Part of it is magical and part of it consists in acquiring merit by the recitation of scriptures which have no special reference to the dead. This merit is then formally transferred to them. Doubtless Nestorianism, in so far as it was associated with Buddhism, tended to promote the worship of Bodhisattvas and prayers addressed directly to them, but this tendency existed independently and the Nestorian monument indicates not that Nestorianism influenced Buddhism but that it abandoned the doctrine of the atonement.

In 819 a celebrated incident occurred. The Emperor Hsien-Tsung had been informed that at the Fa-mên monastery in Shen-si a bone of the Buddha was preserved which every thirty years exhibited miraculous powers. As this was the auspicious year, he ordered the relic to be brought in state to the capital

[1] See Nanjio Catalogue, pp. 445–448.

[2] He is also said to have introduced the images of the Four Kings which are now found in every temple. A portrait of him by Li Chien is reproduced in Tajima's *Masterpieces*, vol. VIII, plate IX. The artist was perhaps his contemporary.

[3] *E.g.* Saeki, *The Nestorian Monument in China*, 1916. See also above, p. 217.

[4] See Khuddaka-Patha, 7; Peta Vatthu, 1, 5 and the commentary; Milinda Panha, IV. 8, 29; and for modern practices my chapter on Siam, and Copleston, *Buddhism*, p. 445.

and lodged in the Imperial Palace, after which it was to make the round of the monasteries in the city. This proceeding called forth an animated protest from Han-Yü[1], one of the best known authors and statesmen then living, who presented a memorial, still celebrated as a masterpiece. The following extract will give an idea of its style. "Your Servant is well aware that your Majesty does not do this (give the bone such a reception) in the vain hope of deriving advantage therefrom but that in the fulness of our present plenty there is a desire to comply with the wishes of the people in the celebration at the capital of this delusive mummery....For Buddha was a barbarian. His language was not the language of China. His clothes were of an alien cut. He did not utter the maxims of our ancient rulers nor conform to the customs which they have handed down. He did not appreciate the bond between prince and minister, the tie between father and son. Had this Buddha come to our capital in the flesh, your Majesty might have received him with a few words of admonition, giving him a banquet and a suit of clothes, before sending him out of the country with an escort of soldiers.

"But what are the facts? The bone of a man long since dead and decomposed is to be admitted within the precincts of the Imperial Palace. Confucius said, 'respect spiritual beings but keep them at a distance.' And so when princes of old paid visits of condolence, it was customary to send a magician in advance with a peach-rod in his hand, to expel all noxious influences before the arrival of his master. Yet now your Majesty is about to introduce without reason a disgusting object, personally taking part in the proceedings without the intervention of the magician or his wand. Of the officials not one has raised his voice against it: of the Censors[2] not one has pointed out the enormity of such an act. Therefore your servant, overwhelmed with shame for the Censors, implores your Majesty that these bones may be handed over for destruction by fire

[1] 韓愈. Some native critics, however, have doubted the authenticity of the received text and the version inserted in the Official History seems to be a summary. See Wieger, *Textes Historiques*, vol. III. pp. 1726 ff., and Giles, *Chinese Literature*, pp. 200 ff.

[2] The officials whose duty it was to remonstrate with the Emperor if he acted wrongly.

or water, whereby the root of this great evil may be exterminated for all time and the people may know how much the wisdom of your Majesty surpasses that of ordinary men[1]."

The Emperor became furious when he read the memorial and wished to execute its author on the spot. But Han-Yü's many friends saved him and the sentence was commuted to honourable banishment as governor of a distant town. Shortly afterwards the Emperor died, not of Buddhism, but of the elixir of immortality which made him so irritable that his eunuchs put him out of the way. Han-Yü was recalled but died the next year. Among his numerous works was one called Yüan Tao, much of which was directed against non-Confucian forms of religion. It is still a thesaurus of arguments for the opponents of Buddhism and, let it be added, of Christianity.

It is not surprising that the prosperity of the Buddhist church should have led to another reaction, but it came not so much from the literary and sceptical class as from Taoism which continued to enjoy the favour of the T'ang Emperors, although they died one after another of drinking the elixir. The Emperor Wu-Tsung was more definitely Taoist than his predecessors. In 843 he suppressed Manichæism and in 845, at the instigation of his Taoist advisers, he dealt Buddhism the severest blow which it had yet received. In a trenchant edict[2] he repeated the now familiar arguments that it is an alien and maleficent superstition, unknown under the ancient and glorious dynasties and injurious to the customs and morality of the nation. Incidentally he testifies to its influence and popularity for he complains of the crowds thronging the temples which eclipse the imperial palaces in splendour and the innumerable monks and nuns supported by the contributions of the people. Then, giving figures, he commands that 4600 great temples and 40,000 smaller rural temples be demolished, that their enormous[3] landed property be confiscated, that 260,500 monks and nuns be secularized and 150,000 temple slaves[4] set free. These statistics are probably exaggerated and in any case the Emperor had barely time to execute his drastic orders,

[1] Giles, *Chinese Literature*, pp. 201, 202—somewhat abbreviated.

[2] See Wieger, *Textes Historiques*, vol. III. pp. 1744 ff.

[3] "Thousands of ten-thousands of Ch'ing." A Ch'ing = 15·13 acres.

[4] Presumably similar to the temple slaves of Camboja, etc.

though all despatch was used on account of the private fortunes which could be amassed incidentally by the executive.

As the Confucian chronicler of his doings observes, he suppressed Buddhism on the ground that it is a superstition but encouraged Taoism which is no better. Indeed the impartial critic must admit that it is much worse, at any rate for Emperors. Undeterred by the fate of his predecessors Wu-Tsung began to take the elixir of immortality. He suffered first from nervous irritability, then from internal pains, which were explained as due to the gradual transformation of his bones, and at the beginning of 846 he became dumb. No further explanation of his symptoms was then given him and his uncle Hsüan Tsung was raised to the throne. His first act was to revoke the anti-Buddhist edict, the Taoist priests who had instigated it were put to death, the Emperor and his ministers vied in the work of reconstruction and very soon things became again much as they were before this great but brief tribulation. Nevertheless, in 852 the Emperor received favourably a memorial complaining of the Buddhist reaction and ordered that all monks and nuns must obtain special permission before taking orders. He was beginning to fall under Taoist influence and it is hard to repress a smile on reading that seven years later he died of the elixir. His successor I-Tsung (860–874), who died at the age of 30, was an ostentatious and dissipated Buddhist. In spite of the remonstrances of his ministers he again sent for the sacred bone from Fa-mên and received it with even more respect than his predecessor had shown, for he met it at the Palace gate and bowed before it.

During the remainder of the T'ang dynasty there is little of importance to recount about Buddhism. It apparently suffered no reverses, but history is occupied with the struggle against the Tartars. The later T'ang Emperors entered into alliance with various frontier tribes, but found it hard to keep them in the position of vassals. The history of China from the tenth to the thirteenth centuries is briefly as follows. The T'ang dynasty collapsed chiefly owing to the incapacity of the later Emperors and was succeeded by a troubled period in which five short dynasties founded by military adventurers, three of whom were of Turkish race, rose and fell in 53 years[1]. In 960 the

[1] One Emperor of this epoch, Shih-Tsung of the later Chou dynasty, suppressed

Sung dynasty united the Chinese elements in the Empire, but had to struggle against the Khitan Tartars in the north-east and against the kingdom of Hsia in the north-west. With the twelfth century appeared the Kins or Golden Tartars, who demolished the power of the Khitans in alliance with the Chinese but turned against their allies and conquered all China north of the Yang-tze and continually harassed, though they did not capture, the provinces to the south of it which constituted the reduced empire of the Sungs. But their power waned in its turn before the Mongols, who, under Chinggiz Khan and Ogotai, conquered the greater part of northern Asia and eastern Europe. In 1232 the Sung Emperor entered into alliance with the Mongols against the Kins, with the ultimate result that though the Kins were swept away, Khubilai, the Khan of the Mongols, became Emperor of all China in 1280.

The dynasties of T'ang and Sung mark two great epochs in the history of Chinese art, literature and thought, but whereas the virtues and vices of the T'ang may be summed up as genius and extravagance, those of the Sung are culture and tameness. But this summary judgment does not do justice to the painters, particularly the landscape painters, of the Sung and it is noticeable that many of the greatest masters, including Li Lung-Mien[1], were obviously inspired by Buddhism. The school which had the greatest influence on art and literature was the Ch'an[2] or contemplative sect better known by its Japanese name Zen. Though founded by Bodhidharma it did not win the sympathy and esteem of the cultivated classes until the Sung period. About this time the method of block-printing was popularized and there began a steady output of comprehensive histories, collected works, encyclopædias and biographies which excelled anything then published in Europe. Antiquarian research and accessible editions of classical writers were favour-

monasteries and coined bronze images into currency, declaring that Buddha, who in so many births had sacrificed himself for mankind, would have no objection to his statues being made useful. But in the South Buddhism flourished in the province of Fukien under the princes of Min 閩 and the dynasty which called itself Southern T'ang.

[1] 李龍眠. See Kokka No. 309, 1916. [2] 禪.

able to Confucianism, which had always been the religion of the literati.

It is not surprising that the Emperors of this literary dynasty were mostly temperate in expressing their religious emotions. T'ai-Tsu, the founder, forbade cremation and remonstrated with the Prince of T'ang, who was a fervent Buddhist. Yet he cannot have objected to religion in moderation, for the first printed edition of the Tripitaka was published in his reign (972) and with a preface of his own. The early and thorough application of printing to this gigantic Canon is a proof—if any were needed—of the popular esteem for Buddhism.

Nor did this edition close the work of translation: 275 later translations, made under the Northern Sung, are still extant and religious intercourse with India continued. The names and writings of many Hindu monks who settled in China are preserved and Chinese continued to go to India. Still on the whole there was a decrease in the volume of religious literature after 900 A.D.[1] In the twelfth century the change was still more remarkable. Nanjio does not record a single translation made under the Southern Sung and it is the only great dynasty which did not revise the Tripitaka.

The second Sung Emperor also, T'ai Tsung, was not hostile, for he erected in the capital, at enormous expense, a stupa 360 feet high to contain relics of the Buddha. The fourth Emperor, Jên-tsung, a distinguished patron of literature, whose reign was ornamented by a galaxy of scholars, is said to have appointed 50 youths to study Sanskrit but showed no particular inclination towards Buddhism. Neither does it appear to have been the motive power in the projects of the celebrated social reformer, Wang An-Shih. But the dynastic history says that he wrote a book full of Buddhist and Taoist fancies and, though there is nothing specifically Buddhist in his political and economic theories, it is clear from the denunciations against him that his system of education introduced Buddhist and Taoist subjects into the public examinations[2]. It is also clear that this system was favoured by those Emperors of the Northern Sung dynasty who were able to think for themselves. In 1087 it was abolished

[1] The decrease in translations is natural for by this time Chinese versions had been made of most works which had any claim to be translated.

[2] See Biot, *L'instruction publique en Chine*, p. 350.

by the Empress Dowager acting as regent for the young Chê Tsung, but as soon as he began to reign in his own right he restored it, and it apparently remained in force until the collapse of the dynasty in 1127.

The Emperor Hui-Tsung (1101–1126) fell under the influence of a Taoist priest named Lin Ling-Su[1]. This young man had been a Buddhist novice in boyhood but, being expelled for misconduct, conceived a hatred for his old religion. Under his influence the Emperor not only reorganized Taoism, sanctioning many innovations and granting many new privileges, but also endeavoured to suppress Buddhism, not by persecution, but by amalgamation. By imperial decree the Buddha and his Arhats were enrolled in the Taoist pantheon: temples and monasteries were allowed to exist only on condition of describing themselves as Taoist and their inmates had the choice of accepting that name or of returning to the world.

But there was hardly time to execute these measures, so rapid was the reaction. In less than a year the insolence of Lin Ling-Su brought about his downfall: the Emperor reversed his edict and, having begun by suppressing Buddhism, ended by oppressing Taoism. He was a painter of merit and perhaps the most remarkable artist who ever filled a throne. In art he probably drew no distinction between creeds and among the pictures ascribed to him and preserved in Japan are some of Buddhist subjects. But like Hsüan Tsung he came to a tragic end, and in 1126 was carried into captivity by the Kin Tartars among whom he died.

Fear of the Tartars now caused the Chinese to retire south of the Yang-tse and Hang-chow was made the seat of Government. The century during which this beautiful city was the capital did not produce the greatest names in Chinese history, but it witnessed the perfection of Chinese culture, and the background of impending doom heightens the brilliancy of this literary and æsthetic life. Such a society was naturally eclectic in religion but Buddhism of the Ch'an school enjoyed consideration and contributed many landscape painters to the roll of fame. But the most eminent and perhaps the most characteristic thinker of the period was Chu-Hsi (1130–1200), the celebrated com-

[1] 林靈素.

mentator on Confucius who reinterpreted the master's writings to the satisfaction of succeeding ages though in his own life he aroused opposition as well as enthusiasm. Chu-Hsi studied Buddhism in his youth and some have detected its influence in his works, although on most important points he expressly condemned it. I do not see that there is much definite Buddhism in his philosophy, but if Mahayanism had never entered China this new Confucianism would probably never have arisen or would have taken another shape. Though the final result may be anti-Buddhist yet the topics chosen and the method of treatment suggest that the author felt it necessary to show that the Classics could satisfy intellectual curiosity and supply spiritual ideals just as well as this Indian religion. Much of his expositions is occupied with cosmology, and he accepts the doctrine of world periods, recurring in an eternal series of growth and decline: also he teaches not exactly transmigration but the transformation of matter into various living forms[1]. His accounts of sages and saints point to ideals which have much in common with Arhats and Buddhas and, in dealing with the retribution of evil, he seems to admit that when the universe is working properly there is a natural *Karma* by which good or bad actions receive even in this life rewards in kind, but that in the present period of decline nature has become vitiated so that vice and virtue no longer produce appropriate results.

Chu-Hsi had a celebrated controversy with Lu Chiu-Yüan[2], a thinker of some importance who, like himself, is commemorated in the tablets of Confucian temples, although he was accused of Buddhist tendencies. He held that learning was not indispensable and that the mind could in meditation rise above the senses and attain to a perception of the truth. Although he strenuously denied the charge of Buddhist leanings, it is clear that his doctrine is near in spirit to the mysticism of Bodhidharma and sets no store on the practical ethics and studious habits which are the essence of Confucianism.

The attitude of the Yüan or Mongol dynasty (1280–1368) towards Buddhism was something new. Hitherto, whatever may have been the religious proclivities of individual Emperors,

[1] See Le Gall, *Variétés Sinologiques*, No. 6 Tchou-Hi: Sa doctrine Son influence. Shanghai, 1894, pp. 90, 122.

[2] 陸九淵. Compare the similar doctrines of Wang Yang-Ming.

the Empire had been a Confucian institution. A body of official and literary opinion always strong and often overwhelmingly strong regarded imperial patronage of Buddhism or Taoism as a concession to the whims of the people, as an excrescence on the Son of Heaven's proper faith or even a perversion of it. But the Mongol Court had not this prejudice and Khubilai, like other members of his house[1] and like Akbar in India, was the patron of all the religions professed by his subjects. His real object was to encourage any faith which would humanize his rude Mongols. Buddhism was more congenial to them than Confucianism and besides, they had made its acquaintance earlier. Even before Khubilai became Emperor, one of his most trusted advisers was a Tibetan lama known as Pagspa, Bashpa or Pa-ssŭ-pa[2]. He received the title of Kuo-Shih, and after his death his brother succeeded to the same honours.

Khubilai also showed favour to Mohammedans, Christians, Jews and Confucianists, but little to Taoists. This prejudice was doubtless due to the suggestions of his Buddhist advisers, for, as we have seen, there was often rivalry between the two religions and on two occasions at least (in the reigns of Hui Tsung and Wu Tsung) the Taoists made determined, if unsuccessful, attempts to destroy or assimilate Buddhism. Khubilai received complaints that the Taoists represented Buddhism as an offshoot of Taoism and that this objectionable perversion of truth and history was found in many of their books, particularly the Hua-Hu-Ching[3]. An edict was issued ordering all Taoist books to be burnt with the sole exception of the Tao-Tê-Ching but it does not appear that the sect was otherwise persecuted.

The Yüan dynasty was consistently favourable to Buddhism. Enormous sums were expended on subventions to monasteries, printing books and performing public ceremonies. Old restrictions were removed and no new ones were imposed. But the sect which was the special recipient of the imperial favour was

[1] *E.g.* his elder brother Mangku who showed favour to Buddhists, Mohammedans and Nestorians alike. He himself wished to obtain Christian teachers from the Pope, by the help of Marco Polo, but probably merely from curiosity.

[2] More accurately hPhags-pa. It is a title rather than a name, being the Tibetan equivalent of Ârya. Khubilai seems to be the correct transcription of the Emperor's name. The Tibetan and Chinese transcriptions are Hvopilai and Hu-pi-lieh.

[3] For this curious work see *B.E.F.E.O.* 1908, p. 515, and *J.A.* 1913, I, pp. 116–132. For the destruction of Taoist books see Chavannes in *T'oung Pao*, 1904, p. 366.

not one of the Chinese schools but Lamaism, the form of Buddhism developed in Tibet, which spread about this time to northern China, and still exists there. It does not appear that in the Yüan period Lamaism and other forms of Buddhism were regarded as different sects[1]. A lamaist ecclesiastic was the hierarchical head of all Buddhists, all other religions being placed under the supervision of a special board.

The Mongol Emperors paid attention to religious literature. Khubilai saw to it that the monasteries in Peking were well supplied with books and ordered the bonzes to recite them on stated days. A new collection of the Tripitaka (the ninth) was published 1285–87. In 1312, the Emperor Jên-tsung ordered further translations to be made into Mongol and later had the whole Tripitaka copied in letters of gold. It is noticeable that another Emperor, Chêng Tsung, had the Book of Filial Piety translated into Mongol and circulated together with a brief preface by himself.

It is possible that the Buddhism of the Yüan dynasty was tainted with Śâktism from which the Lama monasteries of Peking (in contrast to all other Buddhist sects in China) are not wholly free. The last Emperor, Shun-ti, is said to have witnessed indecent plays and dances in the company of Lamas and created a scandal which contributed to the downfall of the dynasty[2]. In its last years we hear of some opposition to Buddhism and of a reaction in favour of Confucianism, in consequence of the growing numbers and pretensions of the Lamas. Whole provinces were under their control and Chinese historians dwell bitterly on their lawlessness. It was a common abuse for wealthy persons to induce a Lama to let their property be registered in his name and thus avoid all payment of taxes on the ground that priests were exempt from taxation by law[3].

The Mongols were driven out by the native Chinese dynasty known as Ming, which reigned from 1368 to 1644. It is not

[1] At the present day an ordinary Chinese regards a Lama as quite different from a Hoshang or Buddhist monk.

[2] The Yüan Emperors were no doubt fond of witnessing religious theatricals in the Palace. See for extracts from Chinese authors, *New China Review*, 1919, pp. 68 ff. Compare the performances of the T'ang Emperor Su Tsung mentioned above.

[3] For the ecclesiastical abuses of the time see Köppen, II. 103, and de Mailla, *Histoire de la Chine*, IX. 475, 538.

easy to point out any salient features in religious activity or thought during this period, but since the Ming claimed to restore Chinese civilization interrupted by a foreign invasion, it was natural that they should encourage Confucianism as interpreted by Chu-Hsi. Yet Buddhism, especially Lamaism, acquired a new political importance. Both for the Mings and for the earlier Manchu Emperors the Mongols were a serious and perpetual danger, and it was not until the eighteenth century that the Chinese Court ceased to be preoccupied by the fear that the tribes might unite and again overrun the Empire. But the Tibetan and Mongolian hierarchy had an extraordinary power over these wild horsemen and the Government of Peking won and used their goodwill by skilful diplomacy, the favours shown being generally commensurate to the gravity of the situation. Thus when the Grand Lama visited Peking in 1652 he was treated as an independent prince: in 1908 he was made to kneel.

Few Ming Emperors showed much personal interest in religion and most of them were obviously guided by political considerations. They wished on the one hand to conciliate the Church and on the other to prevent the clergy from becoming too numerous or influential. Hence very different pictures may be drawn according as we dwell on the favourable or restrictive edicts which were published from time to time. Thus T'ai-Tsu, the founder of the dynasty, is described by one authority as always sympathetic to Buddhists and by another as a crowned persecutor[1]. He had been a bonze himself in his youth but left the cloister for the adventurous career which conducted him to the throne. It is probable that he had an affectionate recollection of the Church which once sheltered him, but also a knowledge of its weaknesses and this knowledge moved him to publish restrictive edicts as to the numbers and qualifications of monks. On the other hand he attended sermons, received monks in audience and appointed them as tutors to his sons. He revised the hierarchy and gave appropriate titles to its various grades. He also published a decree ordering that all monks should study

[1] See Wieger, *Textes Historiques*, III. p. 2013, and De Groot, *Sectarianism and Religious Persecution in China*, I. p. 82. He is often called Hung Wu which is strictly speaking the title of his reign. He was certainly capable of changing his mind, for he degraded Mencius from his position in Confucian temples one year and restored him the next.

three sûtras (Lankâvatâra, Prajnâpâramitâ and Vajracchedikâ), and that three brief commentaries on these works should be compiled (see Nanjio's Catalogue, 1613–15).

It is in this reign that we first hear of the secular clergy, that is to say, persons who acted as priests but married and did not live in monasteries. Decrees against them were issued in 1394 and 1412, but they continued to increase. It is not clear whether their origin should be sought in a desire to combine the profits of the priesthood with the comforts of the world or in an attempt to evade restrictions as to the number of monks. In later times this second motive was certainly prevalent, but the celibacy of the clergy is not strictly insisted on by Lamaists and a lax observance of monastic rules[1] was common under the Mongol dynasty.

The third Ming Emperor, Ch'êng-tsu[2], was educated by a Buddhist priest of literary tastes named Yao Kuang-Hsiao[3], whom he greatly respected and promoted to high office. Nevertheless he enacted restrictions respecting ordination and on one occasion commanded that 1800 young men who presented themselves to take the vows should be enrolled in the army instead. His prefaces and laudatory verses were collected in a small volume and included in the eleventh collection of the Tripitaka[4], called the Northern collection, because it was printed at Peking. It was published with a preface of his own composition and he wrote another to the work called the Liturgy of Kuan-yin[5], and a third introducing selected memoirs of various remarkable monks[6]. His Empress had a vision in which she imagined a sûtra was revealed to her and published the same with an introduction. He was also conspicuously favourable to the Tibetan clergy. In 1403 he sent his head eunuch to Tibet to invite the presence of Tsoṅ-kha-pa, who refused to come himself

[1] See de Mailla, *Histoire de la Chine*, IX. p. 470.

[2] Often called Yung-Lo which is strictly the title of his reign.

[3] 姚廣孝.

[4] See Nanjio, Cat. 1613–16.

[5] See Beal, *Catena of Buddhist Scriptures*, p. 398. The Emperor says: "So we, the Ruler of the Empire...do hereby bring before men a mode for attaining to the condition of supreme Wisdom. We therefore earnestly exhort all men...carefully to study the directions of this work and faithfully to follow them."

[6] Nanjio, Cat. 1620. See also *ib.* 1032 and 1657 for the Empress's sûtra.

but sent a celebrated Lama called Halima[1]. On arriving at the capital Halima was ordered to say masses for the Emperor's relatives. These ceremonies were attended by supernatural manifestations and he received as a recognition of his powers the titles of Prince of the Great Precious Law and Buddha of the Western Paradise[2]. His three principal disciples were styled Kuo Shih, and, agreeably to the precedent established under the Yüan dynasty, were made the chief prelates of the whole Buddhist Church. Since this time the Red or Tibetan Clergy have been recognized as having precedence over the Grey or Chinese.

In this reign the Chinese made a remarkable attempt to assert their authority in Ceylon. In 1405 a mission was sent with offerings to the Sacred Tooth and when it was ill received a second mission despatched in 1407 captured the king of Ceylon and carried him off as a prisoner to China. Ceylon paid tribute for fifty years, but it does not appear that these proceedings had much importance for religion[3].

In the reigns of Ying Tsung and Ching-Ti[4] (1436–64) large numbers of monks were ordained, but, as on previous occasions, the great increase of candidates led to the imposition of restrictions and in 1458 an edict was issued ordering that ordinations should be held only once a year. The influence of the Chief Eunuchs during this period was great, and two successive holders of this post, Wang-Chên and Hsing-An[5], were both devoted Buddhists and induced the Emperors whom they served to expend enormous sums on building monasteries and performing ceremonies at which the Imperial Court were present.

[1] Or Kalima 哈立麻. In Tibetan Karma de bshin gshegs-pa. He was the fifth head of the Karma-pa school. See Chandra Das's dictionary, *s.v.*, where a reference is given to kLong-rdol-gsung-hbum. It is noticeable that the Karma-pa is one of the older and more Tantric sects.

[2] 大寶法王，西天大善自在佛. Yüan Shih K'ai prefixed to this latter the four characters 誠順賛化.

[3] See Yule, *Cathay and the Way Thither*, pp. 75 ff.

[4] When Ying Tsung was carried away by the Mongols in 1449 his brother Ching-Ti was made Emperor. Though Ying Tsung was sent back in 1450, he was not able to oust Ching-Ti from the throne till 1457.

[5] 王振，興安.

The end of the fifteenth century is filled by two reigns, Hsien Tsung and Hsiao Tsung. The former fell under the influence of his favourite concubine Wan and his eunuchs to such an extent that, in the latter part of his life, he ceased to see his ministers and the chief eunuch became the real ruler of China. It is also mentioned both in 1468 and 1483 that he was in the hands of Buddhist priests who instructed him in secret doctrines and received the title of Kuo-Shih and other distinctions. His son Hsiao Tsung reformed these abuses: the Palace was cleansed: the eunuchs and priests were driven out and some were executed: Taoist books were collected and burnt. The celebrated writer Wang Yang Ming[1] lived in this reign. He defended and illustrated the doctrine of Lu Chin-Yüan, namely that truth can be obtained by meditation. To express intuitive knowledge, he used the expression *Liang Chih*[2] (taken from Mencius). *Liang Chih* is inherent in all human minds, but in different degrees, and can be developed or allowed to atrophy. To develop it should be man's constant object, and in its light when pure all things are understood and peace is obtained. The phrases of the Great Learning "to complete knowledge," "investigate things," and "rest in the highest excellence," are explained as referring to the *Liang Chih* and the contemplation of the mind by itself. We cannot here shut our eyes to the influence of Bodhidharma and his school, however fervently Wang Yang Ming may have appealed to the Chinese Classics.

The reign of Wu-tsung (1506–21) was favourable to Buddhism. In 1507 40,000 men became monks, either Buddhist or Taoist. The Emperor is said to have been learned in Buddhist literature and to have known Sanskrit[3] as well as Mongol and Arabic, but he was in the hands of a band of eunuchs, who were known as the eight tigers. In 1515 he sent an embassy to Tibet with the object of inducing the Grand Lama to visit Peking, but the invitation was refused and the Tibetans expelled the mission with force. The next Emperor, Shih-T'sung (1522–

[1] 王陽明. His real name was Wang Shou Jên 王守仁.

[2] 良知.

[3] Though the ecclesiastical study of Sanskrit decayed under the Ming dynasty, Yung-lo founded in 1407 a school of language for training interpreters at which Sanskrit was taught among other tongues.

66), inclined to Taoism rather than Buddhism. He ordered the images of Buddha in the Forbidden City to be destroyed, but still appears to have taken part in Buddhist ceremonies at different periods of his reign. Wan Li (1573–1620), celebrated in the annals of porcelain manufacture, showed some favour to Buddhism. He repaired many buildings at P'u-t'o and distributed copies of the Tripitaka to the monasteries of his Empire. In his edicts occurs the saying that Confucianism and Buddhism are like the two wings of a bird: each requires the co-operation of the other.

European missionaries first arrived during the sixteenth century, and, had the Catholic Church been more flexible, China might perhaps have recognized Christianity, not as the only true religion but as standing on the same footing as Buddhism and Taoism. The polemics of the early missionaries imply that they regarded Buddhism as their chief rival. Thus Ricci had a public controversy with a bonze at Hang-Chou, and his principal pupil Hsü Kuang-Ch'i[1] wrote a tract entitled "The errors of the Buddhists exposed." Replies to these attacks are preserved in the writings of the distinguished Buddhist priest Shen Chu-Hung[2].

In 1644 the Ming dynasty collapsed before the Manchus and China was again under foreign rule. Unlike the Mongols, the Manchus had little inclination to Buddhism. Even before they had conquered China, their prince, T'ai Tsung, ordered an inspection of monasteries and limited the number of monks. But in this edict he inveighs only against the abuse of religion and admits that "Buddha's teaching is at bottom pure and chaste, true and sincere: by serving him with purity and piety, one can obtain happiness[3]." Shun-Chih, the first Manchu Emperor, wrote some prefaces to Buddhist works and entertained the Dalai Lama at Peking in 1652[4]. His son and successor, commonly known as K'ang-Hsi (1662–1723), dallied for a while with Christianity, but the net result of his religious policy was to secure to Confucianism all that imperial favour can give. I have mentioned above his Sacred Edict and the

[1] 徐光啟.   [2] 沈袾宏.

[3] De Groot, *l.c.* p. 93.

[4] Some authorities say that he became a monk before he died, but the evidence is not good. See Johnston in *New China Review*, Nos. 1 and 2, 1920.

partial favour which he showed to Buddhism. He gave donations to the monasteries of P'u-t'o, Hang-chou and elsewhere: he published the Kanjur with a preface of his own[1] and the twelfth and last collection of the Tripitaka was issued under the auspices of his son and grandson. The latter, the Emperor Ch'ien Lung, also received the Teshu Lama not only with honour, but with interest and sympathy, as is clear from the inscription preserved at Peking, in which he extols the Lama as a teacher of spiritual religion[2]. He also wrote a preface to a sutra for producing rain[3] in which he says that he has ordered the old editions to be carefully corrected and prayer and worship to be offered, "so that the old forms which have been so beneficial during former ages might still be blessed to the desired end." Even the late Empress Dowager accepted the ministrations of the present Dalai Lama when he visited Peking in 1908, although, to his great indignation she obliged him to kneel at Court[4]. Her former colleague, the Empress Tzŭ-An was a devout Buddhist. The statutes of the Manchu dynasty (printed in 1818) contain regulations for the celebration of Buddhist festivals at Court, for the periodical reading of sutras to promote the imperial welfare, and for the performance of funeral rites.

Still on the whole the Manchu dynasty showed less favour to Buddhism than any which preceded it and its restrictive edicts limiting the number of monks and prescribing conditions for ordination were followed by no periods of reaction. But the vitality of Buddhism is shown by the fact that these restrictions merely led to an increase of the secular clergy, not legally ordained, who in their turn claimed the imperial attention. Ch'ien Lung began in 1735 by giving them the alternative of becoming ordinary laymen or of entering a monastery but this drastic measure was considerably modified in the next few years. Ultimately the secular clergy were allowed to continue as such, if they could show good reason, and to have one disciple each.

[1] See *T'oung Pao*, 1909, p. 533.

[2] See E. Ludwig, *The visit of the Teshoo Lama to Peking*, Tien Tsin Press, 1904.

[3] The Ta-yün-lung-ch'ing-yü-ching. Nanjio's Catalogue, Nos. 187–8, 970, and see Beal, *Catena of Buddhist Scriptures*, pp. 417–9.

[4] See for an account of his visit "The Dalai Lamas and their relations with the Manchu Emperor of China" in *T'oung Pao*, 1910, p. 774.

CHAPTER XLIV

CHINA (*continued*)

The Canon

The Buddhist scriptures extant in the Chinese language are known collectively as San Tsang[1] or the three store-houses, that is to say, Tripitaka. Though this usage is justified by both eastern and European practice, it is not altogether happy, for the Chinese thesaurus is not analogous to the Pali Canon or to any collection of sacred literature known in India, being in spite of its name arranged in four, not in three, divisions. It is a great *Corpus Scriptorum Sanctorum*, embracing all ages and schools, wherein translations of the most diverse Indian works are supplemented by original compositions in Chinese. Imagine a library comprising Latin translations of the Old and New Testaments with copious additions from the Talmud and Apocryphal literature; the writings of the Fathers, decrees of Councils and Popes, together with the *opera omnia* of the principal schoolmen and the early protestant reformers and you will have some idea of this theological miscellany which has no claim to be called a canon, except that all the works included have at some time or other received a certain literary or doctrinal hall-mark.

1

The collection is described in the catalogue compiled by Bunyiu Nanjio[2]. It enumerates 1662 works which are classified in four great divisions, (*a*) Sûtra, (*b*) Vinaya, (*c*) Abhidharma, (*d*) Miscellaneous. The first three divisions contain translations only; the fourth original Chinese works as well.

The first division called Ching or Sûtras amounts to nearly two-thirds of the whole, for it comprises no less than 1081

[1] 三藏. For an account of some of the scriptures here mentioned see chap. xx.

[2] *A catalogue of the Chinese Translation of the Buddhist Tripitaka.* Oxford, Clarendon Press, 1893. An index to the Tokyo edition has been published by Fujii. Meiji xxxi (1898). See too Forke, *Katalog des Pekinger Tripitaka,* 1916.

works and is subdivided as follows: (*a*) Mahâyâna Sûtras, 541, (*b*) Hînayâna Sûtras, 240, (*c*) Mahâyâna and Hînayâna Sûtras, 300 in number, admitted into the canon under the Sung and Yüan dynasties, A.D. 960–1368. Thus whereas the first two subdivisions differ in doctrine, the third is a supplement containing later translations of both schools. The second subdivision, or Hînayâna Sûtras, which is less numerous and complicated than that containing the Mahâyâna Sûtras, shows clearly the character of the whole collection. It is divided into two classes of which the first is called A-han, that is, Âgama[1]. This comprises translations of four works analogous to the Pali Nikâyas, though not identical with the texts which we possess, and also numerous alternative translations of detached sûtras. All four were translated about the beginning of the fifth century whereas the translations of detached sûtras are for the most part earlier. This class also contains the celebrated Sûtra of Forty-two Sections, and works like the Jâtaka-nidâna. The second class is styled Sûtras of one translation[2]. The title is not used rigorously, but the works bearing it are relatively obscure and it is not always clear to what Sanskrit texts they correspond. It will be seen from the above that the Chinese Tripitaka is a literary and bibliographical collection rather than an ecclesiastical canon. It does not provide an authorized version for the edification of the faithful, but it presents for the use of the learned all translations of Indian works belonging to a particular class which possess a certain age and authority.

The same characteristic marks the much richer collection of Mahâyâna Sûtras, which contains the works most esteemed by Chinese Buddhists. It is divided into seven classes:

1. 般若. Pan-jo (Po-jo) or Prajnâpâramitâ[3].
2. 寶積. Pao-chi or Ratnakûṭa.
3. 大集. Ta-chi or Mahâsannipâta.
4. 華嚴. Hua-yen or Avatamsaka.

[1] 阿含.

[2] Tan-i-ching 單譯經. Some of the works classed under Tan-i-ching appear to exist in more than one form, *e.g.* Nanjio, Nos. 674 and 804.

[3] These characters are commonly read Pojo by Chinese Buddhists but the Japanese reading Hannya shows that the pronunciation of the first character was Pan.

5. 湼槃. Nieh-pan or Parinirvâṇa.
6. 五大部外重譯經. Sûtras in more than one translation but not falling into any of the above five classes.
7. 單譯經. Other sûtras existing in only one translation.

Each of the first five classes probably represents a collection of sûtras analogous to a Nikâya and in one sense a single work but translated into Chinese several times, both in a complete form and in extracts. Thus the first class opens with the majestic Mahâprajnâpâramitâ in 600 fasciculi and equivalent to 200,000 stanzas in Sanskrit. This is followed by several translations of shorter versions including two of the little sûtras called the Heart of the Prajnâpâramitâ, which fills only one leaf. There are also six translations of the celebrated work known as the Diamond-cutter[1], which is the ninth sûtra in the Mahâprajnâpâramitâ and all the works classed under the heading Pan-jo seem to be alternative versions of parts of this great Corpus.

The second and third classes are collections of sûtras which no longer exist as collections in Sanskrit, though the Sanskrit text of some individual sûtras is extant. That called Pao-chi or Ratnakûṭa opens with a collection of forty-nine sûtras which includes the longer version of the Sukhâvatîvyûha. This collection is reckoned as one work, but the other items in the same class are all or nearly all of them duplicate translations of separate sûtras contained in it. This is probably true of the third class also. At least seven of the works included in it are duplicate translations of the first, which is called Mahâsannipâta, and the sûtras called Candragarbha, Kshitig., Sumerug., and Akâśag., appear to be merely sections, not separate compositions, although this is not clear from the remarks of Nanjio and Wassiljew.

The principal works in class 4 are two translations, one fuller than the other, of the Hua-yen or Avatamsaka Sûtra[2], still one of the most widely read among Buddhist works, and at least sixteen of the other items are duplicate renderings of

[1] Vajracchedikâ or 金剛 Chin Kang.

[2] Winternitz (*Gesch. Ind. Lit.* II. i. p. 242) states on the authority of Takakusu that this work is the same as the Gaṇḍavyûha. See also Pelliot in *J.A.* 1914, II. pp. 118–21. The Gaṇḍavyûha is probably an extract of the Avatamsaka.

parts of it. Class 5 consists of thirteen works dealing with the death of the Buddha and his last discourses. The first sûtra, sometimes called the northern text, is imperfect and was revised at Nanking in the form of the southern text[1]. There are two other incomplete versions of the same text. To judge from a specimen translated by Beal[2] it is a collection of late discourses influenced by Vishnuism and does not correspond to the Mahâparinibbânasutta of the Pali Canon.

Class 6 consists of sûtras which exist in several translations, but still do not, like the works just mentioned, form small libraries in themselves. It comprises, however, several books highly esteemed and historically important, such as the Saddharmapuṇḍarîka (six translations), the Suvarṇaprabhâsa, the Lalitavistara, the Lankâvatâra, and the Shorter Sukhâvatîvyûha[3], all extant in three translations. In it are also included many short tracts, the originals of which are not known. Some of them are Jâtakas, but many[4] deal with the ritual of image worship or with spells. These characteristics are still more prominent in the seventh class, consisting of sûtras which exist in a single translation only. The best known among them are the Śûrângama and the Mahâvairocana (Ta-jih-ching), which is the chief text of the Shin-gon or Mantra School[5].

The Lü-tsang or Vinaya-pitaka is divided into Mahâyâna and Hînayâna texts, neither very numerous. Many of the Mahâyâna texts profess to be revelations by Maitreya and are extracts of the Yogâcâryabhûmiśâstra[6] or similar to it. For practical purposes the most important is the Fan-wang-ching[7] or net of Brahmâ. The Indian original of this work is not known, but since the eighth century it has been accepted in China as the standard manual for the monastic life[8].

[1] Nos. 113 and 114 北本 and 南本.

[2] *Catena of Buddhist Scriptures*, pp. 160 ff.

[3] The longer Sukhâvatîvyûha is placed in the Ratnakûta class.

[4] The Sûtra of Kuan-yin with the thousand hands and eyes is very popular and used in most temples. Nanjio, No. 320.

[5] No. 399 首楞嚴 and 530 大日經.

[6] Said to have been revealed to Asanga by Maitreya. No. 1170.

[7] 梵網經. No. 1087. It has nothing to do with the Pali Sûtra of the same name. Digha, I.

[8] See below for an account of it.

The Hînayâna Vinaya comprises five very substantial recensions of the whole code, besides extracts, compendiums, and manuals. The five recensions are: (*a*) Shih-sung-lü in sixty-five fasciculi, translated in A.D. 404. This is said to be a Vinaya of the Sarvâstivâdins, but I-Ching[1] expressly says that it does not belong to the Mûlasarvâstivâdin school, though not unlike it. (*b*) The Vinaya of this latter translated by I-Ching who brought it from India. (*c*) Shih-fen-lü-tsang in sixty fasciculi, translated in 405 and said to represent the Dharmagupta school. (*d*) The Mi-sha-so Wu-fên Lü or Vinaya of the Mahîśâsakas, said to be similar to the Pali Vinaya, though not identical with it[2]. (*e*) Mo-ko-sêng-chi Lü or Mahasanghika Vinaya brought from India by Fa-Hsien and translated 416 A.D. It is noticeable that all five recensions are classed as Hinayanist, although (*b*) is said to be the Vinaya used by the Tibetan Church. Although Chinese Buddhists frequently speak of the five-fold Vinaya[3], this expression does not refer to these five texts, as might be supposed, and I-Ching condemns it, saying that[4] the real number of divisions is four.

The Abhidharma-Pitaka or Lun-tsang is, like the Sûtra Pitaka, divided into Mahayanist and Hinayanist texts and texts of both schools admitted into the Canon after 960 A.D. The Mahayanist texts have no connection with the Pali Canon and their Sanskrit titles do not contain the word Abhidharma[1]. They are philosophical treatises ascribed to Aśvaghosha, Nâgârjuna, Asanga, Vasubandhu and others, including three works supposed to have been revealed by Maitreya to Asanga[5]. The principal of these is the Yogâcârya-bhûmiśâstra, a scripture of capital importance for the Yogâcârya school. It describes the career of a Bodhisattva and hence parts of it are treated as belonging to the Vinaya. Among other important works in this section may be mentioned the Madhyamaka Śâstra of

[1] *Record of Buddhist Practices*, p. 20.

[2] See Oldenberg, *Vinaya*, vol. I. pp. xxiv–xlvi.

[3] See Watters, *Yüan Chwang*, I. p. 227. The five schools are given as Dharmagupta, Mahîs'âsika, Sarvâstivâdin, Kâ'syapîya and Mahâsanghika. For the last Vatsiputra or Sthavira is sometimes substituted.

[4] *Record of Buddhist Practices*, p. 8.

[5] The Chinese word lun occurs frequently in them, but though it is used to translate Abhidharma, it is of much wider application and means discussion of Śâstra.

[6] See Watters, *Yüan Chwang*, I, pp. 355 ff.

Nâgârjuna, the Mahâyânasûtrâlankâra of Asanga, and the Awakening of Faith ascribed to Aśvaghosha[1].

The Hînayâna texts also show no correspondence with the Pali Pitaka but are based on the Abhidharma works of the Sarvâstivâdin school[2]. These are seven in number, namely the Jnânaprasthânasâstra of Kâtyâyanîputra with six accessory treatises or Pâdas[3]. The Mahâvibhâshasâstra, or commentary on the Jnânaprasthâna, and the Abhidharmakósa[4] are also in this section.

The third division of the Abhidharma is of little importance but contains two curious items: a manual of Buddhist terminology composed as late as 1272 by Pagspa for the use of Khubilai's son and the Sânkhyakârikâbhâshya, which is not a Buddhist work but a compendium of Sânkhya philosophy[5].

The fourth division of the whole collection consists of miscellaneous works, partly translated from Sanskrit and partly composed in Chinese. Many of the Indian works appear from their title not to differ much from the later Mahâyâna Sûtras, but it is rather surprising to find in this section four translations[6] of the Dharmapada (or at least of some similar anthology) which are thus placed outside the Sûtra Pitaka. Among the works professing to be translated from Sanskrit are a History of the Patriarchs, the Buddhacarita of Aśvaghosha, a work similar to the Questions of King Milinda, Lives of Aśvaghosha, Nâgârjuna, Vasubandhu and others and the Suhrillekha or Friendly Epistle ascribed to Nâgârjuna.

The Chinese works included in this Tripitaka consist of nearly two hundred books, historical, critical, controversial and homiletic, composed by one hundred and two authors. Excluding late treatises on ceremonial and doctrine, the more interesting may be classified as follows:

(*a*) *Historical.*—Besides general histories of Buddhism, there

[1] Nos. 1179, 1190, 1249.

[2] For a discussion of this literature see Takakusu on the Abhidharma Literature of the Sarvâstivâdins, *J. Pali Text Society*, 1905, pp. 67 ff.

[3] Nanjio, Cat. Nos. 1273, 1275, 1276, 1277, 1292, 1281, 1282, 1296, 1317. This last work was not translated till the eleventh century.

[4] Nanjio, Cat. Nos. 1263, 1267 and 1269.

[5] See Takakusu's study of these translations in *B.E.F.E.O.* 1904, pp. 1 ff. and pp. 978 ff.

[6] Nanjio, Cat. Nos. 1321, 1353, 1365, 1439.

are several collections of ecclesiastical biography. The first is the Kao-sêng-chuan[1], or Memoirs of eminent Monks (not, however, excluding laymen), giving the lives of about five hundred worthies who lived between 67 and 519 A.D. The series is continued in other works dealing with the T'ang and Sung dynasties. For the Contemplative School there are further supplements carrying the record on to the Yüan. There are also several histories of the Chinese patriarchs. Of these the latest and therefore most complete is the Fo-tsu-t'ung-chi[2] composed about 1270 by Chih P'an of the T'ien-T'ai school. The Ching-tê-ch'uan-têng-lu[3] and other treatises give the succession of patriarchs according to the Contemplative School. Among historical works may be reckoned the travels of various pilgrims who visited India.

(*b*) *Critical.*—There are thirteen catalogues of the Tripitaka as it existed at different periods. Several of them contain biographical accounts of the translators and other notes. The work called Chên-chêng-lun criticizes several false sûtras and names. There are also several encyclopædic works containing extracts from the Tripitaka, arranged according to subjects, such as the Fa-yüan-chu-lin[4] in 100 volumes; concordances of numerical categories and a dictionary of Sanskrit terms, Fan-i-ming-i-chi[5], composed in 1151.

(*c*) The literature of several Chinese sects is well represented. Thus there are more than sixty works belonging to the T'ien T'ai school beginning with the San-ta-pu or three great books attributed to the founder and ending with the ecclesiastical history of Chih-p'an, written about 1270. The Hua-yen school is represented by the writings of four patriarchs and five monks: the Lü or Vinaya school by eight works attributed to its founder, and the Contemplative School by a sûtra ascribed to Hui-nêng, the sixth patriarch, by works on the history of the Patriarchs and by several collections of sayings or short compositions.

[1] 高僧傳. No. 1490.

[2] 佛祖統紀, 志磐. No. 1661. For more about the Patriarchs see the next chapter.

[3] 景德傳燈錄. No. 1524, written A.D. 1006.

[4] 法苑珠林. No. 1482.

[5] 翻譯名義集. No. 1640.

(*d*) *Controversial.*—Under this heading may be mentioned polemics against Taoism, including two collections of the controversies which took place between Buddhists and Taoists from A.D. 71 till A.D. 730: replies to the attacks made against Buddhism by Confucian scholars and refutations of the objections raised by sceptics or heretics such as the Chê-i-lun and the Yüan-jên-lun, or Origin of man[1]. This latter is a well-known text-book written by the fifth Patriarch of the Hua-yen school and while criticizing Confucianism, Taoism, and the Hînayâna, treats them as imperfect rather than as wholly erroneous[2]. Still more conciliatory is the Treatise on the three religions composed by Liu Mi of the Yüan dynasty[3], which asserts that all three deserve respect as teaching the practice of virtue. It attacks, however, anti-Buddhist Confucianists such as Han-Yü and Chu-Hsi.

The Chinese section contains three compositions attributed to imperial personages of the Ming, viz., a collection of the prefaces and laudatory verses written by the Emperor T'ai-Tsung, the Shên-Sêng-Chuan or memoirs of remarkable monks with a preface by the Emperor Ch'êng-tsu, and a curious book by his consort the Empress Jên-Hsiao, introducing a sûtra which Her Majesty states was miraculously revealed to her on New Year's day, 1398 (see Nanjio, No. 1657).

Though the Hindus were careful students and guardians of their sacred works, their temperament did not dispose them to define and limit the scriptures. But, as I have mentioned above[4], there is some evidence that there was a loose Mahayanist canon in India which was the origin of the arrangement found in the Chinese Tripitaka, in so far as it (1) accepted Hinayanist as well as Mahayanist works, and (2) included a great number of relatively late sûtras, arranged in classes such as Prajnâpâramitâ and Mahâsannipâta.

2

The Tripitaka analyzed by Nanjio, which contains works assigned to dates ranging from 67 to 1622 A.D., is merely the

[1] 折疑論 and 原人論. Nos. 1634 and 1594.

[2] See for some account of it Masson-Oursel's article in *J.A.* 1915, I. pp. 229–354.

[3] 三教平心論 by 劉謐.

[4] See chap. XX on the Mahayanist canon in India.

best known survivor among several similar thesauri[1]. From 518 A.D. onwards twelve collections of sacred literature were made by imperial order and many of these were published in more than one edition. The validity of this Canon depends entirely on imperial authority, but, though Emperors occasionally inserted the works of writers whom they esteemed[2], it does not appear that they aimed at anything but completeness nor did they favour any school. The Buddhist Church, like every other department of the Empire, received from them its share of protection and supervision and its claims were sufficient to induce the founder, or at least an early Sovereign, of every important dynasty to publish under his patronage a revised collection of the scriptures. The list of these collections is as follows[3]:

1. A.D. 518 in the time of Wu-Ti, founder of the Liang.
2. „ 533–4 Hsiao-Wu of the Northern Wei.
3. „ 594 } Wan-ti, founder of the Sui.
4. „ 602 }
5. „ 605–16 Yang-Ti of the Sui.
6. „ 695 the Empress Wu of the T'ang.
7. „ 730 Hsüan-Tsung of the T'ang.
8. „ 971 T'ai-Tsu, founder of the Sung.
9. „ 1285–7 Khubilai Khan, founder of the Yüan.
10. „ 1368–98 Hung-Wu, founder of the Ming.
11. „ 1403–24 Yung-Lo of the Ming.
12. „ 1735–7 Yung-Ching and Ch'ien-Lung of the Ch'ing[4].

Of these collections, the first seven were in MS. only: the last five were printed. The last three appear to be substantially the same. The tenth and eleventh collections are known as

[1] It is described at the beginning as Ta Ming San Tsang, but strictly speaking it must be No. 12 of the list, as it contains a work said to have been written about 1622 A.D. (p. 468).

[2] Thus the Emperor Jên Tsung ordered the works of Ch'i Sung 契嵩 to be admitted to the Canton in 1062.

[3] Taken from Nanjio's Catalogue, p. xxvii.

[4] Ch'ien-Lung is said to have printed the Tripitaka in four languages, Chinese, Tibetan, Mongol and Manchu, the whole collection filling 1392 vols. See Möllendorf in China Branch, *J.A.S.* XXIV. 1890, p. 28.

southern and northern[1], because they were printed at Nanking and Peking respectively. They differ only in the number of Chinese works admitted and similarly the twelfth collection is merely a revision of the tenth with the addition of fifty-four Chinese works.

As mentioned, the Tripitaka contains thirteen catalogues of the Buddhist scriptures as known at different dates[2]. Of these the most important are (*a*) the earliest published between 506 and 512 A.D., (*b*) three published under the T'ang dynasty and known as Nei-tien-lu, T'u-chi (both about 664 A.D.), and K'ai-yüan-lu (about 720 A.D.), (*c*) Chih-Yüan-lu or catalogue of Yüan dynasty, about 1285, which, besides enumerating the Chinese titles, transliterates the Sanskrit titles and states whether the Indian works translated are also translated into Tibetan. (*d*) The catalogue of the first Ming collection.

The later collections contain new material and differ from the earlier by natural accretion, for a great number of translations were produced under the T'ang and Sung. Thus the seventh catalogue (695 A.D.) records that 859 new works were admitted to the Canon. But this expansion was accompanied by a critical and sifting process, so that whereas the first collection contained 2213 works, the Ming edition contains only 1622. This compression means not that works of importance were rejected as heretical or apocryphal, for, as we have seen, the Tripitaka is most catholic, but that whereas the earlier collections admitted multitudinous extracts or partial translations of Indian works, many of these were discarded when complete versions had been made.

Nanjio considers that of the 2213 works contained in the first collection only 276 are extant. Although the catalogues are preserved, all the earlier collections are lost: copies of the

[1] But according to another statement the southern recension was not the imperial collection begun in 1368 but a private edition now lost. See Nanjio, Cat. p. xxiii.

[2] See for the complete list Nanjio, Cat. p. xxvii. Those named above are (*a*) 內典錄, 圖紀, 開元錄, Nos. 1483, 1485, 1487, and (*b*) 至元錄, No. 1612. For the date of the first see Maspéro in *B.E.F.E.O.* 1910, p. 114. There was a still earlier catalogue composed by Tao-an in 374 of which only fragments have been preserved. See Pelliot in *T'oung Pao*, XIX. 1920, p. 258.

eighth and ninth were preserved in the Zō-jō-ji Library of Tokyo[1] and Chinese and Japanese editions of the tenth, eleventh and twelfth are current. So far as one can judge, when the eighth catalogue, or K'ai-yüan-lu, was composed (between 713 and 741), the older and major part of the Canon had been definitively fixed and the later collections merely add the translations made by Amogha, and by writers of the Sung and Yüan dynasties.

The editions of the Chinese Tripitaka must be distinguished from the collections, for by editions are meant the forms in which each collection was published, the text being or purporting to be the same in all the editions of each collection. It is said[2] that under the Sung and Yüan twenty different editions were produced. These earlier issues were printed on long folding sheets and a nun called Fa-chên[3] is said to have first published an edition in the shape of ordinary Chinese books. In 1586 a monk named Mi-Tsang[4] imitated this procedure and his edition was widely used. About a century later a Japanese priest known as Tetsu-yen[5] reproduced it and his publication, which is not uncommon in Japan, is usually called the Ō-baku edition. There are two modern Japanese editions: (*a*) that of Tokyo, begun in 1880, based on a Korean edition[6] with various readings taken from other Chinese editions. (*b*) That of Kyoto, 1905, which is a reprint of the Ming collection[7]. A Chinese edition has been published at Shanghai (1913) at the expense of Mrs Hardoon, a Chinese lady well known as a munificent patron of the faith, and I believe another at Nanking, but I do not know if it is complete or not[8].

[1] For the Korean copy now in Japan, see Courant, *Bibliographie coréenne*, vol. III. pp. 215–19.

[2] See Nanjio, Cat. p. xxii.

[3] 法珍. [4] 密藏.

[5] Also called Do-ko.

[6] The earlier collections of the Tripitaka seem to have been known in Korea and about 1000 A.D. the king procured from China a copy of the Imperial Edition, presumably the eighth collection (971 A.D.). He then ordered a commission of scholars to revise the text and publish an edition of his own. The copy of this edition, on which the recent Tokyo edition was founded, was brought to Japan in the Bun-mei period 1469–1486.

[7] A supplement to the Tripitaka containing non-canonical works in 750 volumes (Dai Nippon Zoku-Zōkyō) was published in 1911.

[8] The Peking Tripitaka catalogued by Forke appears to be a set of 1223 works represented by copies taken from four editions published in 1578, 1592, 1598 and 1735 A.D., all of which are editions of the collections numbered 11 and 12 above.

3

The translations contained in the Chinese Tripitaka belong to several periods[1]. In the earliest, which extends to the middle of the fourth century, the works produced were chiefly renderings of detached sûtras[2]. Few treatises classified as Vinaya or Abhidharma were translated and those few are mostly extracts or compilations. The sûtras belong to both the Hîna and Mahâyâna. The earliest extant translation or rather compilation, the Sûtra of Forty-two sections, belongs to the former school, and so do the majority of the translations made by An-Shih-Kao (148–170 A.D.), but from the second century onwards the Prajnâpâramitâ and Amitâbha Sûtras make their appearance[3]. Many of the translations made in this period are described as incomplete or incorrect and the fact that most of them were superseded or supplemented by later versions shows that the Chinese recognized their provisional character. Future research will probably show that many of them are paraphrases or compendiums rather than translations in our sense.

The next period, roughly speaking 375–745 A.D., was extraordinarily prolific in extensive and authoritative translations. The translators now attack not detached chapters or discourses but the great monuments of Indian Buddhist literature. Though it is not easy to make any chronological bisection in this period, there is a clear difference in the work done at the beginning and at the end of it. From the end of the fourth century onwards a desire to have complete translations of the great canonical works is apparent. Between 385 and 445 A.D. were translated the four Âgamas, analogous to the Nikâyas of the Pali Canon, three great collections of the Vinaya, and the principal scriptures of the Abhidharma according to the Sarvâstivâdin school. For the Mahâyâna were translated the great sûtras known as Avatamsaka, Lankâvatâra, and many others, as well as works

[1] For two interesting lives of translators see the *T'oung Pao*, 1909, p. 199, and 1905, p. 332, where will be found the biographies of Sêng Hui, a Sogdian who died in 280 and Jinagupta a native of Gandhâra (528–605).

[2] But between 266 and 313 Dharmaraksha translated the Saddharmapundarîka (including the additional chapters 21–26) and the Lalitavistara. His translation of the Prajñâpâramitâ is incomplete.

[3] In the translations of Lokâkshî 147–186, Chih-Ch'ien 223–243, Dharmaraksha 266–313.

ascribed to Aśvaghosha and Nâgârjuna. After 645 A.D. a further development of the critical spirit is perceptible, especially in the labours of Hsüan Chuang and I-Ching. They attempt to give the religious public not only complete works in place of extracts and compendiums, but also to select the most authoritative texts among the many current in India. Thus, though many translations had appeared under the name of Prajnâpâramitâ, Hsüan Chuang filled 600 fasciculi with a new rendering of the gigantic treatise. I-Ching supplemented the already bulky library of Vinaya works with versions of the Mûlasarvâstivâdin recension and many auxiliary texts.

Amogha (Pu-K'ung) whose literary labours extended from 746 to 774 A.D. is a convenient figure to mark the beginning of the next and last period, although some of its characteristics appear a little earlier. They are that no more translations are made from the great Buddhist classics—partly no doubt because they had all been translated already, well or ill—but that renderings of works described as Dhâraṇî or Tantra pullulate and multiply. Though this literature deserves such epithets as decadent and superstitious, yet it would appear that Indian Tantras of the worst class were not palatable to the Chinese.

4

The Chinese Tripitaka is of great importance for the literary history of Buddhism, but the material which it offers for investigation is superabundant and the work yet done is small. We are confronted by such questions as, can we accept the dates assigned to the translators, can we assume that, if the Chinese translations or transliterations correspond with Indian titles, the works are the same, and if the works are professedly the same, can we assume that the Chinese text is a correct presentment of the Indian original?

The dates assigned to the translators offer little ground for scepticism. The exactitude of the Chinese in such matters is well attested, and there is a general agreement between several authorities such as the Catalogues of the Tripitaka, the memoirs known as Kao-Sêng Chuan with their continuations, and the chapter on Buddhist books in the Sui annals. There are no signs of a desire to claim improbable accuracy or improbable antiquity. Many works are said to be by unknown translators, doubtful authorship is frankly discussed, and the movement of literature and thought indicated is what we should expect. We have first fragmentary and incomplete translations belonging to both the Mahâ and Hînayâna: then a series of more complete translations beginning about the fifth century in which the great Hînayâna texts are conspicuous: then a further series of improved translations in which the Hînayâna falls into the background and the works of Asanga and Vasubandhu come to the front. This evidently reflects the condition of Buddhist India about 500–650 A.D., just as the translations of the eighth century reflect its later and tantric phase.

But can Chinese texts be accepted as reasonably faithful reproductions of the Indian originals whose names they bear, and some of which have been lost? This question is really double; firstly, did the translators reproduce with fair accuracy the Indian text before them, and secondly, since Indian texts often exist in several recensions, can we assume that the work which the translators knew under a certain Sanskrit name is the work known to us by that name? In reply it must be said that most Chinese translators fall short of our standards of accuracy. In early times when grammars and dictionaries were unknown the scholarly rendering of foreign books was a difficult business, for professional interpreters would usually be incapable of understanding a philosophic treatise. The method often followed was that an Indian explained the text to a literary Chinese, who recast the explanation in his own language. The many translations of the more important texts and the frequent description of the earlier ones as imperfect indicate a feeling that the results achieved were not satisfactory. Several so-called translators, especially Kumârajîva, gave abstracts of the Indian texts[1]. Others, like Dharmaraksha, who made a Chinese version of Aśvaghosha's Buddhacarita, so amplified and transposed the

[1] But his translation of the Lotus won admiration for its literary style. See Anesaki Nichiren, p. 17. Wieger (*Croyances*, p. 367) says that the works of An-shih-kao illustrate the various methods of translation: absolutely literal renderings which have hardly any meaning in Chinese: word for word translations to which is added a paraphrase of each sentence in Chinese idiom: and elegant renderings by a native in which the original text obviously suffers.

original that the result can hardly be called a translation[1]. Others combined different texts in one. Thus the work called Ta-o-mi-to-ching[2] consists of extracts taken from four previous translations of the Sukhâvatîvyûha and rearranged by the author under the inspiration of Avalokita to whom, as he tells us, he was wont to pray during the execution of his task. Others again, like Dharmagupta, anticipated a method afterwards used in Tibet, and gave a word for word rendering of the Sanskrit which is hardly intelligible to an educated Chinese. The later versions, *e.g.* those of Hsüan Chuang, are more accurate, but still a Chinese rendering of a lost Indian document cannot be accepted as a faithful representation of the original without a critical examination[3].

Often, however, the translator, whatever his weaknesses may have been, had before him a text differing in bulk and arrangement from the Pali and Sanskrit texts which we possess. Thus, there are four Chinese translations of works bearing some relation to the Dhammapada of the Pali Canon. All of these describe the original text as the compilation of Dharmatrâta, to whom is also ascribed the compilation of the Tibetan Udânavarga[4]. His name is not mentioned in connection with the Pali text, yet two of the Chinese translations are closely related to that text. The Fa-chü-ching[5] is a collection of verses translated in 224 A.D. and said to correspond with the Pali except that it has nine additional chapters and some additional stanzas. The Fa-chü-p'i-yü-ching[6] represents another edition of the same

[1] Yet it must have been intended as such. The title expressly describes the work as composed by the Bodhisattva Ma-Ming (Aśvaghosha) and translated by Dharmaraksha. Though his idea of a translation was at best an amplified metrical paraphrase, yet he coincides verbally with the original so often that his work can hardly be described as an independent poem inspired by it.

[2] 大阿彌陀經. No. 203.

[3] See Sukhâvatîvyûha, ed. Max Müller and Bunyiu Nanjio, Oxford, 1883. In the preface, pp. vii–ix, is a detailed comparison of several translations and in an appendix, pp. 79 ff., a rendering of Sanghavarman's Chinese version of verses which occur in the work. Chinese critics say that Tao-an in the third century was the first to introduce a sound style of translation. He made no translations himself which have survived but was a scholar and commentator who influenced others.

[4] This is an anthology (edited by Beckh, 1911: translated by Rockhill, 1892) in which 300 verses are similar to the Pali Dhammapada.

[5] 法句經. No. 1365. [6] 法句譬喻經. No. 1353.

verses, illustrated by a collection of parables. It was translated between 290 and 306. The Ch'u-yao-ching[1], translated in 399, is a similar collection of verses and parables, but founded on another Indian work of much greater length. A revised translation containing only the verses was made between 980 and 1001[2]. They are said to be the same as the Tibetan Udâna, and the characteristics of this book, going back apparently to a Sanskrit original, are that it is divided into thirty-three chapters, and that though it contains about 300 verses found in Pali, yet it is not merely the Pali text plus additions, but an anthology arranged on a different principle and only partly identical in substance[3].

There can be little doubt that the Pali Dhammapada is one among several collections of verses, with or without an explanatory commentary of stories. In all these collections there was much common matter, both prose and verse, but some were longer, some shorter, some were in Pali and some in Sanskrit. Whereas the Chinese Dhammapada is longer than the Indian texts, the Chinese version of Milinda's Questions[4] is much shorter and omits books iv-vii. It was made between 317 and 420 A.D. and the inference is that the original Indian text received later additions.

A more important problem is this: what is the relation to the Pali Canon of the Chinese texts bearing titles corresponding to Dîrgha, Madhyama, Samyukta and Ekottara? These collections of sûtras do not call themselves Nikâya but A-han or Âgama: the titles are translated as Ch'ang (long), Chung (medium), Tsa (miscellaneous) and Tseng-i, representing Ekottara rather than Anguttara[5]. There is hence *prima facie* reason

1 出曜經. No. 1321.

2 法集要頌經. Fa-chi-yao-sung-ching, No. 1439.

3 There seem to be at least two other collections. Firstly a Prâkrit anthology of which Dutreuil de Rhins discovered a fragmentary MS. in Khotan and secondly a much amplified collection preserved in the Korean Tripitaka and reprinted in the Tokyo edition (XXIV.'g). The relation of these to the other recensions is not clear.

4 Nanjio, Cat. 1358. See Pelliot, *J.A.* 1914, II. p. 379.

5 長, 中, 雜, 增壹. For the relations of the Chinese translations to the Pali Tripitaka, and to a Sanskrit Canon now preserved only in a fragmentary state, see *inter alia*, Nanjio, Cat. pp. 127 ff., especially Nos. 542, 543, 545. Anesaki, *J.R.A.S.* 1901, p. 895; *id.* "On some problems of the textual history of the Buddhist scriptures," in *Trans. A. S. Japan*, 1908, p. 81, and more especially his longer article

to suppose that these works represent not the Pali Canon, but a somewhat similar Sanskrit collection. That one or many Sanskrit works may have coexisted with a somewhat similar Pali work is clearly shown by the Vinaya texts, for here we have the Pali Canon and Chinese translations of five Sanskrit versions, belonging to different schools, but apparently covering the same ground and partly identical. For the Sûtra Pitaka no such body of evidence is forthcoming, but the Sanskrit fragments of the Samyuktâgama found near Turfan contain parts of six sûtras which are arranged in the same order as in the Chinese translation and are apparently the original from which it was made. It is noticeable that three of the four great Agamas were translated by monks who came from Tukhara or Kabul. Guṇabhadra, however, the translator of the Samyuktâgama, came from Central India and the text which he translated was brought from Ceylon by Fa-Hsien. It apparently belonged to the Abhayagiri monastery and not to the Mahâvihâra. Nanjio[1], however, states that about half of it is repeated in the Chinese versions of the Madhyama and Ekottara Agamas. It is also certain that though the Chinese Agamas and Pali Nikâyas contain much common matter, it is differently distributed[2].

There was in India a copious collection of sûtras, existing primarily as oral tradition and varying in diction and arrangement, but codified from time to time in a written form. One of such codifications is represented by the Pali Canon, at least one other by the Sanskrit text which was rendered into Chinese. With rare exceptions the Chinese translations were from the Sanskrit[3]. The Sanskrit codification of the sûtra literature, while

entitled, "The Four Buddhist Âgamas in Chinese" in the same year of the *Trans.*; *id.* "Traces of Pali Texts in a Mahâyana Treatise," *Muséon*, 1905. S. Lévi, Le Samyuktâgama Sanskrit, *T'oung Pao*, 1904, p. 297.

[1] No. 544.

[2] Thus seventy sûtras of the Pali Anguttara are found in the Chinese Madhyama and some of them are repeated in the Chinese Ekottara. The Pali Majjhima contains 125 sûtras, the Chinese Madhyamâgama 222, of which 98 are common to both. Also twenty-two Pali Majjhima dialogues are found in the Chinese Ekottara and Samyukta, seventy Chinese Madhyama dialogues in Pali Anguttara, nine in Digha, seven in Samyutta and five in Khuddaka. Anesaki, *Some Problems of the textual history of the Buddhist Scriptures.* See also Anesaki in *Muséon*, 1905, pp. 23 ff. on the Samyutta Nikâya.

[3] Anesaki, "Traces of Pali Texts," *Muséon*, 1905, shows that the Indian author of the Mahâprajnâpâramitâ Sâstra may have known Pali texts, but the only certain translation from the Pali appears to be Nanjio, No. 1125, which is a translation of

differing from the Pali in language and arrangement, is identical in doctrine and almost identical in substance. It is clearly the product of the same or similar schools, but is it earlier or later than the Pali or contemporary with it? The Chinese translations merely fix the latest possible date. A portion of the Samyuktâgama (Nanjio, No. 547) was translated by an unknown author between 220 and 280. This is probably an extract from the complete work which was translated about 440, but it would be difficult to prove that the Indian original was not augmented or rearranged between these dates. The earliest translation of a complete Agama is that of the Ekottarâgama, 384 A.D. But the evidence of inscriptions[1] shows that works known as Nikâyas existed in the third century B.C. The Sanskrit of the Agamas, so far as it is known from the fragments found in Central Asia, does not suggest that they belong to this epoch, but is compatible with the theory that they date from the time of Kanishka of which if we know little, we can at least say that it produced much Buddhist Sanskrit literature. M. Sylvain Lévi has suggested that the later appearance of the complete Vinaya in Chinese is due to the late compilation of the Sanskrit original[2]. It seems to me that other explanations are possible. The early translators were clearly shy of extensive works and until there was a considerable body of Chinese monks, to what public would these theological libraries appeal? Still, if any indication were forthcoming from India or Central Asia that the Sanskrit Agamas were arranged or rearranged in the early centuries of our era, the late date of the Chinese translations would certainly support it. But I am inclined to think that the Nikâyas were rewritten in Sanskrit about the beginning of our era, when it was felt that works claiming a certain position ought to be composed in what had become the general literary language of India[3].

the Introduction to Buddhaghosa's Samanta-pâsâdikâ or commentary on the Vinaya. See Takakusu in *J.R.A.S.* 1896, p. 415. Nanjio's restoration of the title as Sudarśana appears to be incorrect.

[1] See *Epigraphia Indica*, vol. II. p. 93.

[2] In support of this it may be mentioned that Fa-Hsien says that at the time of his visit to India the Vinaya of the Sarvâstivâdins was preserved orally and not committed to writing.

[3] The idea that an important book ought to be in Sanskrit or deserves to be turned into Sanskrit is not dead in India. See Grierson, *J.R.A.S.* 1913, p. 133, who in discussing a Sanskrit version of the Râmâyana of Tulsi Das mentions that translations of vernacular works into Sanskrit are not uncommon.

Perhaps those who wrote them in Sanskrit were hardly conscious of making a translation in our sense, but simply wished to publish them in the best literary form.

It seems probable that the Hinayanist portion of the Chinese Tripitaka is in the main a translation of the Canon of the Sarvastivâdins which must have consisted of:

(1) Four Agamas or Nikâyas only, for the Dhammapada is placed outside the Sutta Pitaka.
(2) A voluminous Vinaya covering the same ground as the Pali recension but more copious in legend and anecdote.
(3) An Abhidharma entirely different from the Pali works bearing this name.

It might seem to follow from this that the whole Pali Abhidharma and some important works such as the Thera-Therîgâthâ were unknown to the Hinayanists of Central Asia and Northern India in the early centuries of our era. But caution is necessary in drawing such inferences, for until recently it might have been said that the Sutta Nipâta also was unknown, whereas fragments of it in a Sanskrit version have now been discovered in Eastern Turkestan[1]. The Chinese editors draw a clear distinction between Hinayanist and Mahayanist scriptures. They exclude from the latter works analogous to the Pali Nikâyas and Vinaya, and also the Abhidharma of the Sarvâstivâdins. But the labours of Hsüan Chuang and I-Ching show that this does not imply the rejection of all these works by Mahayanists.

5

Buddhist literary activity has an interesting side aspect, namely the expedients used to transliterate Indian words, which

[1] *J.R.A.S.* 1916, p. 709. Also, the division into five Nikâyas is ancient. See Bühler in *Epig. Indica*, II. p. 93. Anesaki says (*Trans. A. S. Japan*, 1908, p. 9) that Nanjio, No. 714, Pên Shih is the Itivuttakam, which could not have been guessed from Nanjio's entry. Portions of the works composing the fifth Nikâya (*e.g.* the Sutta Nipata) occur in the Chinese Tripitaka in the other Nikâyas. For mentions of the fifth Nikâya in Chinese, see *J.A.* 1916, II. pp. 32–33, where it is said to be called Tsa-Tsang. This is also the designation of the last section of the Tripitaka, Nanjio, Nos. 1321 to 1662, and as this section contains the Dharmapada, it might be supposed to be an enormously distended version of the Kshudraka Nikâya. But this can hardly be the case, for this Tsa-Tsang is placed as if it was considered as a fourth Piṭaka rather than as a fifth Nikâya.

almost provided the Chinese with an alphabet. To some extent Indian names, particularly proper names possessing an obvious meaning, are translated. Thus Asoka becomes Wu-yu, without sorrow: Aśvaghosha, Ma-ming or horse-voice, and Udyâna simply Yüan or park[1]. But many proper names did not lend themselves to such renderings and it was a delicate business to translate theological terms like Nirvâṇa and Samâdhi. The Buddhists did not perhaps invent the idea of using the Chinese characters so as to spell with moderate precision[2], but they had greater need of this procedure than other writers and they used it extensively[3] and with such variety of detail that though they invented some fifteen different syllabaries, none of them obtained general acceptance and Julien[4] enumerates 3000 Chinese characters used to represent the sounds indicated by 47 Indian letters. Still, they gave currency[5] to the system known as *fan-ch'ieh* which renders a syllable phonetically by two characters, the final of the first and the initial of the second not being pronounced. Thus, in order to indicate the sound Chung, a Chinese dictionary will use the two characters *chu yung*, which are to be read together as *Ch ung*.

The transcriptions of Indian words vary in exactitude and the later are naturally better. Hsüan Chuang was a notable reformer and probably after his time Indian words were rendered in Chinese characters as accurately as Chinese words are now transcribed in Latin letters. It is true that modern pronunciation makes such renderings as Fo seem a strange distortion of the original. But it is an abbreviation of Fo-t'o and these syllables were probably once pronounced something like Vut-tha[6]. Similarly Wên-shu-shih-li[7] seems a parody of Manjuśri.

[1] 無憂, 馬鳴, 苑.

[2] See Watters, *Essays on the Chinese Language*, pp. 36, 51, and, for the whole subject of transcription, Stanislas Julien, *Méthode pour déchiffrer et transcrire les noms Sanscrits qui se rencontrent dans les livres chinois*.

[3] Entire Sanskrit compositions were sometimes transcribed in Chinese characters. See Kien Ch'ui Fan Tsan, *Bibl. Budd.* xv. and Max Müller, *Buddhist Texts from Japan*, III. pp. 35–46.

[4] *L.c.* pp. 83–232.

[5] See *inter alia* the Preface to K'ang Hsi's Dictionary. The *fan-ch'ich* 反切 system is used in the well-known dictionary called Yü-Pien composed 543 A.D.

[6] Even in modern Cantonese Fo is pronounced as Fat.

[7] 文殊師利.

But the evidence of modern dialects shows that the first two syllables may have been pronounced as Man-ju. The pupil was probably taught to eliminate the obscure vowel of *shih*, and *li* was taken as the nearest equivalent of *ri*, just as European authors write *chih* and *tzŭ* without pretending that they are more than conventional signs for Chinese sounds unknown to our languages. It was certainly possible to transcribe not only names but Sanskrit prayers and formulæ in Chinese characters, and though many writers sneer at the gibberish chaunted by Buddhist priests yet I doubt if this ecclesiastical pronunciation, which has changed with that of the spoken language, is further removed from its original than the Latin of Oxford from the speech of Augustus.

Sanskrit learning flourished in China for a considerable period. In the time of the T'ang, the clergy numbered many serious students of Indian literature and the glossaries included in the Tripitaka show that they studied the original texts. Under the Sung dynasty (A.D. 1151) was compiled another dictionary of religious terms[1] and the study of Sanskrit was encouraged under the Yüan. But the ecclesiastics of the Ming produced no new translations and apparently abandoned the study of the original texts which was no longer kept alive by the arrival of learned men from India. It has been stated that Sanskrit manuscripts are still preserved in Chinese monasteries, but no details respecting such works are known to me. The statement is not improbable in itself[2] as is shown by the Library which Stein discovered at Tun-huang and by the Japanese palm-leaf manuscripts which came originally from China. A few copies of Sanskrit sûtras printed in China in the Lanja variety of the Devanâgari alphabet have been brought to Europe[3]. Max Müller published a facsimile of part of the Vajracchedikâ obtained at Peking and printed in Sanskrit from wooden blocks. The place of production is unknown, but the characters are similar to those used for printing Sanskrit in Tibet, as may be seen from

[1] Nanjio, Cat. No. 1640.

[2] History repeats itself. I have seen many modern Burmese and Sinhalese MSS. in Chinese monasteries.

[3] *Buddhist Texts from Japan*, ed. Max Müller in *Anecdota Oxoniensia*, Aryan Series, I, II and III. For the Lanja printed text see the last facsimile in I, also III. p. 34 and *Bibl. Budd.* XIV (Kuan-si-im Pusar), pp. vi, vii. Another copy of this Lanja printed text was bought in Kyoto, 1920.

another facsimile (No. 3) in the same work. Placards and pamphlets containing short invocations in Sanskrit and Tibetan are common in Chinese monasteries, particularly where there is any Lamaistic influence, but they do not imply that the monks who use them have any literary acquaintance with those languages.

CHAPTER XLV

CHINA (*continued*)

SCHOOLS[1] OF CHINESE BUDDHISM

THE Schools (Tsung) of Chinese Buddhism are an intricate subject of little practical importance, for observers agree that at the present day all salient differences of doctrine and practice have been obliterated, although the older monasteries may present variations in details and honour their own line of teachers. A particular Bodhisattva may be singled out for reverence in one locality or some religious observance may be specially enjoined, but there is little aggressiveness or self assertion among the sects, even if they are conscious of having a definite name: they each tolerate the deities, rites and books of all and pay attention to as many items as leisure and inertia permit. There is no clear distinction between Mahâyâna and Hînayâna.

The main division is of course into Lamaism on one side and all remaining sects on the other. Apart from this we find a record of ten schools which deserve notice for various reasons. Some, though obscure in modern China, have flourished after transportation to Japan: some, such as the T'ien-t'ai, are a memorial of a brilliant epoch: some represent doctrines which, if not now held by separate bodies, at least indicate different tendencies, such as magical ceremonies, mystical contemplation, or faith in Amitâbha.

[1] 宗. See especially Hackmann, "Die Schulen des chinesischen Buddhismus" (in the *Mitth. Seminars für Orientalische Sprachen*, Berlin, 1911), which contains the text and translation of an Essay by a modern Chinese Buddhist, Yang Wên Hui. Such a review of Chinese sects from the contemporary Buddhist point of view has great value, but it does not seem to me that Mr Yang explains clearly the dogmatic tenets of each sect, the obvious inference being that such tenets are of little practical importance. Chinese monasteries often seem to combine several schools. Thus the Tz'ŭ-Fu-Ssŭ monastery near Peking professes to belong both to the Lin-Chi and Pure Land schools and its teachers expound the Diamond-cutter, Lotus and Shou-Lêng-Ching. So also in India. See Rhys Davids in article Sects Buddhist, *E.R.E.* Hackmann gives a list of authorities. Edkins, *Chinese Buddhism* (chaps. VII and VIII), may still be consulted, though the account is far from clear.

The more important schools were comparatively late, for they date from the sixth and seventh centuries. For two or three hundred years the Buddhists of China were a colony of strangers, mainly occupied in making translations. By the fifth century the extent and diversity of Indian literature became apparent and Fa-Hsien went to India to ascertain which was the most correct Vinaya and to obtain copies of it. Theology was now sufficiently developed to give rise to two schools both Indian in origin and merely transported to China, known as Ch'êng-shih-tsung and San-lun-tsung[1].

The first is considered as Hinayanist and equivalent to the Sautrântikas[2]. In the seventh century it passed over to Japan where it is known as Ji-jitsu-shu, but neither there nor in China had it much importance. The San-lun-tsung recognizes as three authorities (from which it takes its name) the Mâdhyamika-śâstra and Dvâdasanikâyaśâstra of Nâgârjuna with the Śataśâstra of his pupil Deva. It is simply the school of these two doctors and represents the extreme of Mahayanism. It had some importance in Japan, where it was called San-Ron-Shu.

The arrival of Bodhidharma at Canton in 520 (or 526) was a great event for the history of Buddhist dogma, although his special doctrines did not become popular until much later. He introduced the contemplative school and also the institution of the Patriarchate, which for a time had some importance. He wrote no books himself, but taught that true knowledge is gained in meditation by intuition[3] and communicated by transference of thought. The best account of his teaching is contained in the Chinese treatise which reports the sermon preached by him before the Emperor Wu-Ti in 520[4]. The chief thesis of this discourse is that the only true reality is the Buddha

[1] 成實宗 and 三論宗.

[2] It based itself on the Satyasiddhiśâstra of Harivarman, Nanjio, Cat. 1274.

[3] This meditation however is of a special sort. The six Pâramitâs are, Dâna, Sîla, Kshanti, Vîrya, Dhyâna and Prajñâ. The meditation of Bodhidharma is not the Dhyâna of this list, but meditation on Prajñâ, the highest of the Pâramitâs. See Hackmann's Chinese text, p. 249.

[4] Ta-mo-hsüe-mai-lun, analyzed by Wieger in his *Histoire des Croyances religieuses en Chine*, pp. 520 ff. I could wish for more information about this work, but have not been able to find the original.

nature[1] in the heart of every man. Prayer, asceticism and good works are vain. All that man need do is to turn his gaze inward and see the Buddha in his own heart. This vision, which gives light and deliverance, comes in a moment. It is a simple, natural act like swallowing or dreaming which cannot be taught or learnt, for it is not something imparted but an experience of the soul, and teaching can only prepare the way for it. Some are impeded by their karma and are physically incapable of the vision, whatever their merits or piety may be, but for those to whom it comes it is inevitable and convincing.

We have only to substitute *âtman* for Buddha or Buddha nature to see how closely this teaching resembles certain passages in the Upanishads, and the resemblance is particularly strong in such statements as that the Buddha nature reveals itself in dreams, or that it is so great that it embraces the universe and so small that the point of a needle cannot prick it. The doctrine of Mâyâ is clearly indicated, even if the word was not used in the original, for it is expressly said that all phenomena are unreal. Thus the teaching of Bodhidharma is an anticipation of Śankara's monism, but it is formulated in consistently Buddhist language and is in harmony with the views of the Mâdhyamika school and of the Diamond-cutter. This Chinese sermon confirms other evidence which indicates that the ideas of the Advaita philosophy, though Brahmanic in their origin and severely condemned by Gotama himself, were elaborated in Buddhist circles before they were approved by orthodox Hindus.

Bodhidharma's teaching was Indian but it harmonized marvellously with Taoism and Chinese Buddhists studied Taoist books[2]. A current of Chinese thought which was old and strong, if not the main stream, bade man abstain from action and look for peace and light within. It was, I think, the junction of this native tributary with the river of inflowing Buddhism which gave the Contemplative School its importance. It lost that importance because it abandoned its special doctrines

[1] Also called Fa-shên or dharmakâya in the discourse. Bodhidharma said that he preached the *seal of the heart* (hsinyin). This probably corresponds to some Sanskrit expression, but I have not found the Indian equivalent.

[2] I-Ching, in his *Memoirs of Eminent Monks*, mentions three pilgrims as having studied the works of Chuang-tzŭ and his own style shows that he was well-read in this author.

and adopted the usages of other schools. When Taoism flourished under the Sung Emperors it was also flourishing and influenced art as well as thought, but it probably decayed under the Yüan dynasty which favoured religion of a different stamp. It is remarkable that Bodhidharma appears to be unknown to both Indian and Tibetan[1] writers but his teaching has imparted a special tone and character to a section (though not the whole) of Far Eastern Buddhism. It is called in Chinese Tsung-mên or Ch'an-tsung, but this word Ch'an[2] is perhaps better known to Europe in its Japanese form Zen.

Bodhidharma is also accounted the twenty-eighth Patriarch, a title which represents the Chinese Tsu Shih[3] rather than any Indian designation, for though in Pali literature we hear of the succession of teachers[4], it is not clear that any of them enjoyed a style or position such as is implied in the word Patriarch. Hindus have always attached importance to spiritual lineage and every school has a list of teachers who have transmitted its special lore, but the sense of hierarchy is so weak that it is misleading to describe these personages as Popes, Patriarchs or Bishops, and apart from the personal respect which the talents of individuals may have won, it does not appear that there was any succession of teachers who could be correctly termed heads of the Church. Even in China such a title is of dubious accuracy for whatever position Bodhidharma and his successors may have claimed for themselves, they were not generally accepted as being more than the heads of a school and other schools also gave their chief teachers the title of Tsu-shih. From time to time the Emperor appointed overseers of religion with the title of Kuo-shih[5], instructor of the nation, but these were officials appointed by the Crown, not prelates consecrated by the Church.

Twenty-eight Patriarchs are supposed to have flourished between the death of the Buddha and the arrival of Bodhidharma in China. The Chinese lists[6] do not in the earlier part agree with

[1] He is not mentioned by Târanâtha.

[2] 禪.   [3] 祖師.

[4] Âcâriyaparamparâ. There is a list of such teachers in Mahâvaṃsa, v. 95 ff., Dîpavaṃsa, IV. 27 ff. and v. 69.

[5] 國師.

[6] The succession of Patriarchs is the subject of several works comprised in the Chinese Tripitaka. Of these the Fu-fa-tsang-yin-yüan-ching (Nanjio, 1340) is the

the Singhalese accounts of the apostolic succession and contain few eminent names with the exception of Aśvaghosha, Nâgârjuna, Deva and Vasubandhu.

According to most schools there were only twenty-four Patriarchs. These are said to have been foretold by the Buddha and twenty-four is a usual number in such series[1]. The twenty-fourth Patriarch Simha Bhikshu or Simhâlaputra went to Kashmir and suffered martyrdom there at the hands of Mihirakula[2] without appointing a successor. But the school of Bodhidharma continues the series, reckoning him as the twenty-eighth, and the first of the Chinese Patriarchs. Now since the three Patriarchs between the martyr and Bodhidharma are all described as living in southern India, whereas such travellers as Fa-Hsien obviously thought that the true doctrine was to be found in northern India, and since Bodhidharma left India altogether, it is probable that the later Patriarchs represent the

most important, because it professes to be translated (A.D. 472) from an Indian work, which, however, is not in the Tibetan Canon and is not known in Sanskrit. The Chinese text, as we have it, is probably not a translation from the Sanskrit, but a compilation made in the sixth century which, however, acquired considerable authority. See Maspéro in *Mélanges d'Indianisme*: Sylvain Lévi, pp. 129–149, and *B.E.F.E.O.* 1911, pp. 344–348. Other works are the Fo-tsu-t'ung-chi (Nanjio, 1661), of Chih P'an (c. 1270), belonging to the T'ien-t'ai school, and the Ching-tê-ch'uan-têng-lu together with the Tsung-mên-t'ung-yao-hsü-chi (Nanjio, 1524, 1526) both belonging to the school of Bodhidharma. See also Nanjio, 1528, 1529. The common list of Patriarchs is as follows: 1. Mahâkâśyapa; 2. Ananda; 3. Śanavâsa or Śanakavâsa; 4. Upagupta; 5. Dhṛitaka; 6. Micchaka. Here the name of Vasumitra is inserted by some but omitted by others; 7. Buddhanandi; 8. Buddhamitra; 9. Pârśva; 10. Punyayasas; 11. Aśvaghosha; 12. Kapimala; 13. Nâgârjuna; 14. Deva (Kâṇadeva); 15. Râhulata; 16. Sanghanandi; 17. Sanghayaśas; 18. Kumârata; 19. Jayata; 20. Vasubandhu; 21. Manura; 22. Haklena or Padmaratna; 23. Simha Bhikshu; 24. Basiasita; 25. Putnomita or Punyamitra; 26. Prajnâtara; 27 (or 28, if Vasumitra is reckoned) Bodhidharma. Many of these names are odd and are only conjectural restorations made from the Chinese transcription, for which see Nanjio, 1340. Other lists of Patriarchs vary from that given above, partly because they represent the traditions of other schools. It is not strange, for instance, if the Sarvâstivâdins did not recognize Nâgârjuna as a Patriarch. Two of their lists have been preserved by Sêng-yu (Nanjio, 1476) who wrote about 520. Some notes on the Patriarchs and reproductions of Chinese pictures representing them will be found in Doré, pp. 244 ff. It is extremely curious that Aśvaghosha is represented as a woman.

[1] It is found, for instance, in the lists of the Jain Tirthankaras and in some accounts of the Buddhas and of the Avatâras of Vishnu.

[2] See Watters, *Yüan Chwang*, p. 290. But the dates offer some difficulty, for Mihirakula, the celebrated Hun chieftain, is usually supposed to have reigned about 510–540 A.D. Târanâtha (Schiefner, p. 95) speaks of a martyr called Mâlikabuddhi. See, too, *ib.* p. 306.

spiritual genealogy of some school which was not the Church as established at Nâlandâ[1].

It will be convenient to summarize briefly here the history of Bodhidharma's school. Finding that his doctrines were not altogether acceptable to the Emperor Wu-Ti (who did not relish being told that his pious exertions were vain works of no value) he retired to Lo-yang and before his death designated as his successor Hui-k'o. It is related of Hui-k'o that when he first applied for instruction he could not attract Bodhidharma's attention and therefore stood before the sage's door during a whole winter night until the snow reached his knees. Bodhidharma indicated that he did not think this test of endurance remarkable. Hui-k'o then took a knife, cut off his own arm and presented it to the teacher who accepted him as a pupil and ultimately gave him the insignia of the Patriarchate—a robe and bowl. He taught for thirty-four years and is said to have mixed freely with the lowest and most debauched reprobates. His successors were Sêng-ts'an, Tao-hsin, Hung-jên, and Hui-nêng[2] who died in 713 and declined to nominate a successor, saying that the doctrine was well established. The bowl of Bodhidharma was buried with him. Thus the Patriarch was not willing to be an Erastian head of the Church and thought the Church could get on without him. The object of the Patriarchate was simply to insure the correct transmission from teacher to scholar of certain doctrines, and this precaution was especially necessary in sects which rejected scriptural authority and relied on personal instruction. So soon as there were several competent teachers handing on the tradition such a safeguard was felt to be unnecessary.

That this feeling was just is shown by the fact that the school of Bodhidharma is still practically one in teaching. But its small regard for scripture and insistence on oral instruction caused the principal monasteries to regard themselves as centres with an apostolic succession of their own and to form divisions which were geographical rather than doctrinal. They are often

[1] It is clear that the school of Valabhi was to some extent a rival of Nâlandâ.

[2] For a portrait of Hui-nêng see Kokka, No. 297. The names of Bodhidharma's successors are in Chinese characters 慧可, 僧璨, 道信, 弘忍, 慧能.

called school (tsung), but the term is not correct, if it implies that the difference is similar to that which separates the Ch'an-tsung and Lü-tsung or schools of contemplation and of discipline. Even in the lifetime of Hui-nêng there seems to have been a division, for he is sometimes called the Patriarch of the South, Shên-Hsiu[1] being recognized as Patriarch of the North. But all subsequent divisions of the Ch'an-tsung trace their lineage to Hui-nêng. Two of his disciples founded two schools called Nan Yüeh and Ch'ing Yüan[2] and between the eighth and tenth centuries these produced respectively two and three subdivisions, known together as Wu-tsung or five schools. They take their names from the places where their founders dwelt and are the schools of Wei-Yang, Lin-Chi, Ts'ao-Tung, Yün-Mên and Fa-Yen[3]. This is the chronological order, but the most important school is the Lin-Chi, founded by I-Hsüan[4], who resided on the banks of a river[5] in Chih-li and died in 867. It is not easy to discriminate the special doctrines[6] of the Lin-Chi for it became the dominant form of the school to such an extent that other variants are little more than names. But it appears to have insisted on the transmission of spiritual truths not only by oral instruction but by a species of telepathy between teacher and pupil culminating in sudden illumination. At the present day the majority of Chinese monasteries profess to belong to the Ch'an-tsung and it has encroached on other schools. Thus it is now accepted on the sacred island of P'uto which originally followed the Lü-tsung.

Although the Ch'an school did not value the study of scripture as part of the spiritual life, yet it by no means neglected letters and can point to a goodly array of ecclesiastical authors,

[1] 神秀.

[2] 南嶽, 青原. Much biographical information respecting this and other schools will be found in Doré, vols. VII and VIII. But there is little to record in the way of events or literary and doctrinal movements.

[3] 潙仰, 臨濟, 曹洞, 雲門, 法眼. [4] 義玄.

[5] Lin-Chi means coming to the ford. Is this an allusion to the Pali expression Sotâpanno? The name appears in Japanese as Rinzai. Most educated Chinese monks when asked as to their doctrine say they belong to the Lin-Chi.

[6] They are generally called the three mysteries (Hsüan) and the three important points (Yao), but I have not been able to obtain any clear explanation of what they mean. See Edkins, *Chinese Buddhism*, p. 164, and Hackmann, *l.c.* p. 250.

extending down to modern times[1]. More than twenty of their treatises have been admitted into the Tripitaka. Several of these are historical and discuss the succession of Patriarchs and abbots, but the most characteristic productions of the sect are collections of aphorisms, usually compiled by the disciples of a teacher who himself committed nothing to writing[2].

In opposition to the Contemplative School or Tsung-mên, all the others are sometimes classed together as Chiao-mên. This dichotomy perhaps does no more than justice to the importance of Bodhidharma's school, but is hardly scientific, for, whatever may be the numerical proportion, the other schools differ from one another as much as they differ from it. They all agree in recognizing the authority not only of a founder but of a special sacred book. We may treat first of one which, like the Tsung-mên, belongs specially to the Buddhism of the Far East and is both an offshoot of the Tsung-mên and a protest against it—there being nothing incompatible in this double relationship. This is the T'ien-t'ai[3] school which takes its name from a celebrated monastery in the province of Chê-kiang. The founder of this establishment and of the sect was called Chih-K'ai or Chih-I[4] and followed originally Bodhidharma's teaching, but ultimately rejected the view that contemplation is all-sufficient, while still claiming to derive his doctrine from Nâgârjuna. He had a special veneration for the Lotus Sûtra and paid attention to ceremonial. He held that although the Buddha-mind is present in all living beings, yet they do not of themselves come to the knowledge and use of it, so that instruction is necessary to remove error and establish true ideas. The phrase Chih-kuan[5] is almost the motto of the school: it is a translation of the two words Samatha and Vipassanâ, taken to mean calm and insight.

[1] Wieger, *Bouddhisme Chinois*, p. 108, states that 230 works belonging to this sect were published under the Manchu dynasty.

[2] See *e.g.* Nanjio, Cat. 1527, 1532.

[3] 天台. Tendai in Japanese. It is also called in China 法華 Fa-hua.

[4] 智顗. Also often spoken of as Chih-chê-ta-shih 智者大師. Officially he is often styled the fourth Patriarch of the school. See Doré, p. 449.

[5] 止觀. In Pali Buddhism also, especially in later works, Samatha and Vipassanâ may be taken as a compendium of the higher life as they are respectively the results of the two sets of religious exercises called Adhicitta and Adhipaññâ. (See Ang. Nik. III. 88.)

The T'ien-T'ai is distinguished by its many-sided and almost encyclopaedic character. Chih-I did not like the exclusiveness of the Contemplative School. He approved impartially of ecstasy, literature, ceremonial and discipline: he wished to find a place for everything and a point of view from which every doctrine might be admitted to have some value. Thus he divided the teaching of the Buddha into five periods, regarded as progressive not contradictory, and expounded respectively in (*a*) the Hua-yen Sûtra; (*b*) the Hînayâna Sûtras; (*c*) the Lêng-yen-ching; (*d*) the Prajnâ-pâramitâ; (*e*) the Lotus Sûtra which is the crown, quintessence and plenitude of all Buddhism. He also divided religion into eight parts[1], sometimes counted as four, the latter half of the list being the more important. The names are collection, progress, distinction and completion. These terms indicate different ways of looking at religion, all legitimate but not equally comprehensive or just in perspective. By collection is meant the Hînayâna, the name being apparently due to the variously catalogued phenomena which occupy the disciple in the early stages of his progress: the scriptures, divisions of the universe, states of the human minds and so on. Progress (T'ung, which might also be rendered as transition or communication) is applicable to the Hîna and Mahâyanâ alike and regards the religious life as a series of stages rising from the state of an unconverted man to that of a Buddha. Pieh, or distinction, is applicable only to the Mahâyanâ and means the special excellences of a Bodhisattva. Yüan, completeness or plenitude, is the doctrine of the Lotus which embraces all aspects of religion. In a similar spirit of synthesis and conciliation Chih-I uses Nâgârjuna's view that truth is not of one kind. From the standpoint of absolute truth all phenomena are void or unreal; on the other hand they are indubitably real for practical purposes. More just is the middle view which builds up the religious character. It sees that all phenomena both exist and do not exist and that thought cannot content itself with the hypothesis either of their real existence or of the void. Chih-I's teaching as

[1] In Chinese 頓, 漸, 秘密, 不定, 藏, 通, 別, 圓. Tun, Chien, Pi-mi, Pu-ting, Tsang, T'ung, Pieh, Yüan. See Nanjio, 1568, and for very different explanations of these obscure words, Edkins, *Chinese Buddhism*, p. 182, and Richard's *New Testament of Higher Buddhism*, p. 41. Masson-Oursel in *J.A.* 1915, I. p. 305.

to the nature of the Buddha is almost theistic. It regards the fundamental (pên) Buddhahood as not merely the highest reality but as constant activity exerting itself for the good of all beings. Distinguished from this fundamental Buddhahood is the derivative Buddhahood or trace (chi) left by the Buddha among men to educate them. There has been considerable discussion in the school as to the relative excellence of the *pên* and the *chi*[1].

The T'ien-T'ai school is important, not merely for its doctrines, but as having produced a great monastic establishment and an illustrious line of writers. In spite of the orders of the Emperor who wished to retain him at Nanking, Chih-I retired to the highlands of Chê-Kiang and twelve monasteries still mark various spots where he is said to have resided. He had some repute as an author, but more as a preacher. His words were recorded by his disciple Kuan-Ting[2] and in this way have been preserved two expositions of the Lotus and a treatise on his favourite doctrine of Chih-Kuan which together are termed the San-ta-pu, or Three Great Books. Similar spoken expositions of other sûtras are also preserved. Some smaller treatises on his chief doctrines seem to be works of his own pen[3]. A century later Chan-Jan[4], who is reckoned the ninth Patriarch of the T'ien-t'ai school, composed commentaries on the Three Great Books as well as some short original works. During the troubled period of the Five Dynasties, the T'ien-t'ai monasteries suffered severely and the sacred books were almost lost. But the school had a branch in Korea and a Korean priest called Ti-Kuan[5] re-established it in China. It continued to contribute literature to the Tripitaka until 1270 but after the tenth century its works, though numerous, lose their distinctive character and are largely concerned with magical formulæ and the worship of Amida.

The latter is the special teaching of the Pure Land school, also known as the Lotus school, or the Short Cut[6]. It is indeed

[1] 本 and 蹟. [2] 灌頂. The books are Nanjio, Nos. 1534, 1536, 1538.

[3] Among them is the compendium for beginners called Hsiao-chih-kuan, (Nanjio, 1540), partly translated in Beal's *Catena*, pp. 251 ff.

[4] 湛然. [5] 諦觀.

[6] 淨土宗, 蓮宗, 淨土橫超門.

a short cut to salvation, striking unceremoniously across all systems, for it teaches that simple faith in Amitâbha (Amida) and invocation of his name can take the place of moral and intellectual endeavour. Its popularity is in proportion to its facility: its origin is ancient, its influence universal, but perhaps for this very reason its existence as a corporation is somewhat indistinct. It is also remarkable that though the Chinese Tripitaka contains numerous works dedicated to the honour of Amitâbha, yet they are not described as composed by members of the Pure Land school but appear to be due to authors of all schools[1].

The doctrine, if not the school, was known in China before 186, in which year there died at Lo-yang, a monk of the Yüeh-chih called Lokâkshi, who translated the longer Sukhâvatî-vyûha. So far as I know, there is no reason for doubting these statements[2]. The date is important for the history of doctrine, since it indicates that the sûtra existed in Sanskrit some time previously. Another translation by the Parthian An Shih-Kao, whose activity falls between 148 and 170 A.D. may have been earlier and altogether twelve translations were made before 1000 A.D. of which five are extant[3]. Several of the earlier translators were natives of Central Asia, so it is permissible to suppose that the sûtra was esteemed there. The shorter Sukhâvatî-vyûha was translated by Kumârajîva (*c.* 402) and later by Hsüan Chuang. The Amitâyurdhyânasûtra was translated by Kâlayaśas about 424. These three books[4] are the principal scriptures of the school and copies of the greater Sukhâvatî may still be found in almost every Chinese monastery, whatever principles it professes.

Hui Yüan[5] who lived from 333 to 416 is considered as the founder of the school. He was in his youth an enthusiastic

[1] The list of Chinese authors in Nanjio's Catalogue, App. III, describes many as belonging to the T'ien-t'ai, Avatamsaka or Dhyâna schools, but none as belonging to the Ching-T'u.

[2] For the authorities, see Nanjio, p. 381.

[3] Nanjio, p. 10, note.

[4] They are all translated in *S.B.E.* XLIX. The two former exist in Sanskrit. The Amitâyurdhyâna is known only in the Chinese translation. They are called in Chinese 無量壽經, 阿彌陀經 and 觀無量壽佛經.

[5] 慧遠.

Taoist and after he turned Buddhist is said to have used the writings of Chuang-tzŭ to elucidate his new faith. He founded a brotherhood, and near the monastery where he settled was a pond in which lotus flowers grew, hence the brotherhood was known as the White Lotus school[1]. For several centuries[2] it enjoyed general esteem. Pan-chou, one of its Patriarchs, received the title of Kuo-shih about 770 A.D., and Shan-tao, who flourished about 650 and wrote commentaries, was one of its principal literary men[3]. He popularized the doctrine of the Pai-tao or White Way, that is, the narrow bridge leading to Paradise across which Amitâbha will guide the souls of the faithful. But somehow the name of White Lotus became connected with conspiracy and rebellion until it was dreaded as the title of a formidable secret society, and ceased to be applied to the school as a whole. The teaching and canonical literature of the Pure Land school did not fall into disrepute but since it was admitted by other sects to be, if not the most excellent way, at least a permissible short cut to heaven, it appears in modern times less as a separate school than as an aspect of most schools[4]. The simple and emotional character of Amidism, the directness of its "Come unto me," appeal so strongly to the poor and uneducated, that no monastery or temple could afford to neglect it.

Two important Indian schools were introduced into China in the sixth and seventh centuries respectively and flourished until about 900 A.D. when they began to decay. These are the Chü-shê-tsung and Fa-hsiang-tsung[5]. The first name is merely a Chinese transcription of the Sanskrit Ko'sa and is due to the fact that the chief authority of the school is the Abhidharmakośa-

[1] 白蓮社. The early history of the school is related in a work called Lien-shê-kao-hsien-ch'uan, said to date from the Tsin dynasty. See for some account of the early worthies, Doré, pp. 280 ff. and 457 ff. Their biographies contain many visions and miracles.

[2] Apparently at least until 1042. See De Groot, *Sectarianism*, p. 163. The dated inscriptions in the grottoes of Lung-mên indicate that the cult of Amitâbha flourished especially from 647 to 715. See Chavannes, *Mission. Archéol.* Tome I, deuxième partie, p. 545.

[3] 般舟 and 善導.

[4] See for instance the tract called Hsüan-Fo-P'u 選佛譜 and translated by Richard under the title of *A Guide to Buddhahood*, pp. 97 ff.

[5] 俱舍宗 and 法相宗.

śâstra of Vasubandhu[1]. This work expounds the doctrine of the Sarvâstivâdins, but in a liberal spirit and without ignoring other views. Though the Chü-shê-tsung represented the best scholastic tradition of India more adequately than any other Chinese sect, yet it was too technical and arid to become popular and both in China and Japan (where it is known as Kusha-shu) it was a system of scholastic philosophy rather than a form of religion. In China it did not last many centuries.

The Fa-Hsiang school is similar inasmuch as it represented Indian scholasticism and remained, though much esteemed, somewhat academic. The name is a translation of Dharmalakshaṇa and the school is also known as Tz'ŭ-ên-tsung[2], and also as Wei-shih-hsiang-chiao because its principal text-book is the Ch'êng-wei-shih-lun[3]. This name, equivalent to Vidyâmâtra, or Vijnânamâtra, is the title of a work by Hsüan Chuang which appears to be a digest of ten Sanskrit commentaries on a little tract of thirty verses ascribed to Vasubandhu. As ultimate authorities the school also recognizes the revelations made to Asanga by Maitreya[4] and probably the Mahâyânasûtrâlankâra[5] expresses its views. It claims as its founder Śîlabhadra the teacher of Hsüan Chuang, but the latter was its real parent.

Closely allied to it but reckoned as distinct is the school called the Hua-yen-tsung[6] because it was based on the Hua-yen-ching or Avatamsakasûtra. The doctrines of this work and of Nâgârjuna may be conveniently if not quite correctly contrasted as pantheistic and nihilistic. The real founder and first patriarch was Tu-Fa-Shun who died in 640 but the school sometimes bears the name of Hsien-Shou, the posthumous title of its third Patriarch who contributed seven works to the Tripitaka[7]. It

[1] See Watters, *On Yüan Chwang*, I. 210, and also Takakusu, *Journal of the Pali Text Soc.* 1905, p. 132.

[2] 慈恩宗. The name refers not to the doctrines of the school, but to Tz'ŭ-ên-tai-shih, a title given to Kuei-chi the disciple of Hsüan Chuang who was one of its principal teachers and taught at a monastery called Tz'ŭ-ên.

[3] 成唯識論. See Nanjio, Cat. Nos. 1197 and 1215.

[4] See Watters, *On Yüan Chwang*, I. pp. 355 ff.

[5] Ed. and transl. by Sylvain Lévi, 1911.

[6] 華嚴宗.

[7] His name when alive was Fa-tsang. See Nanjio, Cat. p. 462, and Doré, 450. The Empress Wu patronized him.

began to wane in the tenth century but has a distinguished literary record.

The Lü-tsung or Vinaya school[1] was founded by Tao Hsüan (595–667). It differs from those already mentioned inasmuch as it emphasizes discipline and asceticism as the essential part of the religious life. Like the T'ien-t'ai this school arose in China. It bases itself on Indian authorities, but it does not appear that in thus laying stress on the Vinaya it imitated any Indian sect, although it caught the spirit of the early Hînayâna schools. The numerous works of the founder indicate a practical temperament inclined not to mysticism or doctrinal subtlety but to biography, literary history and church government. Thus he continued the series called Memoirs of Eminent Monks and wrote on the family and country of the Buddha. He compiled a catalogue of the Tripitaka, as it was in his time, and collections of extracts, as well as of documents relating to the controversies between Buddhists and Taoists[2]. Although he took as his chief authority the Dharmagupta Vinaya commonly known as the Code in Four Sections, he held, like most Chinese Buddhists, that there is a complete and perfect doctrine which includes and transcends all the vehicles. But he insisted, probably as a protest against the laxity or extravagance of many monasteries, that morality and discipline are the indispensable foundation of the religious life. He was highly esteemed by his contemporaries and long after his death the Emperor Mu-tsung (821–5) wrote a poem in his honour. The school is still respected and it is said that the monks of its principal monastery, Pao-hua-shan in Kiangsu, are stricter and more learned than any other.

The school called Chên-yen (in Japanese Shin-gon), true word, or Mi-chiao[3], secret teaching, equivalent to the Sanskrit Mantrayâna or Tantrayâna, is the latest among the recognized divisions of Chinese Buddhism since it first made its appearance in the eighth century. The date, like that of the translation of the Amida scriptures is important, for the school was introduced

[1] 律宗. Also called Nan Shan or Southern mountain school from a locality in Shensi.

[2] 道宣. Nanjio, Cat. 1493, 1469, 1470, 1120, 1481, 1483, 1484, 1471.

[3] 眞言 or 密教.

from India and it follows that its theories and practices were openly advocated at this period and probably were not of repute much earlier. It is akin to the Buddhism of Tibet and may be described in its higher aspects as an elaborate and symbolic pantheism, which represents the one spirit manifesting himself in a series of emanations and reflexes. In its popular and unfortunately commoner aspect it is simply polytheism, fetichism and magic. In many respects it resembles the Pure Land school. Its principal deity (the word is not inaccurate) is Vairocana, analogous to Amitâbha, and probably like him a Persian sun god in origin. It is also a short cut to salvation, for, without denying the efficiency of more laborious and ascetic methods, it promises to its followers a similar result by means of formulæ and ceremonies. Like the Pure Land school it has become in China not so much a separate corporation as an aspect, and often the most obvious and popular aspect, of all Buddhist schools.

It claims Vajrabodhi as its first Patriarch. He was a monk of the Brahman caste who arrived in China from southern India[1] in 719 and died in 730 after translating several Tantras and spells. His companion and successor was Amoghavajra of whose career something has already been said. The fourth Patriarch, Hui Kuo, was the instructor of the celebrated Japanese monk Kobo Daishi who established the school in Japan under the name of Shingon[2].

The principal scripture of this sect is the Ta-jih-ching or sûtra of the Sun-Buddha[3]. A distinction is drawn between exoteric and esoteric doctrine (the "true word") and the various phases of Buddhist thought are arranged in ten classes. Of these the first nine are merely preparatory, but in the last or esoteric phase, the adept becomes a living Buddha and receives full intuitive knowledge. In this respect the Tantric school resembles the teaching of Bodhidharma but not in detail. It teaches that Vairocana is the whole world, which is divided into Garbhadhâtu (material) and Vajradhâtu (indestructible), the two together forming Dharmadhâtu. The manifestations of

[1] From Mo-lai-yê, which seems to mean the extreme south of India. Doré gives some Chinese legends about him, p. 299.

[2] For an appreciative criticism of the sect as known in Japan, see Anesaki's *Buddhist Art*, chap. III.

[3] Nanjio, No. 530. Nos. 533, 534 and 1039 are also important texts of this sect.

Vairocana's body to himself—that is Buddhas and Bodhisattvas—are represented symbolically by diagrams of several circles[1]. But it would be out of place to dwell further on the dogmatic theology of the school, for I cannot discover that it was ever of importance in China whatever may have been its influence in Japan. What appealed only too powerfully to Chinese superstition was the use of spells, charms and magical formulæ and the doctrine that since the universe is merely idea, thoughts and facts are equipollent. This doctrine (which need not be the outcome of metaphysics, but underlies the magical practices of many savage tribes) produced surprising results when applied to funeral ceremonies, which in China have always formed the major part of religion, for it was held that ceremonial can represent and control the fortunes of the soul, that is to say that if a ceremony represents figuratively the rescue of a soul from a pool of blood, then the soul which is undergoing that punishment will be delivered. It was not until the latter part of the eighth century that such theories and ceremonies were accepted by Chinese Buddhism, but they now form a large part of it.

Although in Japan Buddhism continued to produce new schools until the thirteenth century, no movement in China attained this status after about 730, and Lamaism, though its introduction produced considerable changes in the north, is not usually reckoned as a Tsung. But numerous societies and brotherhoods arose especially in connection with the Pure Land school and are commonly spoken of as sects. They differ from the schools mentioned above in having more or less the character of secret societies, sometimes merely brotherhoods like the Freemasons but sometimes political in their aims. Among those whose tenets are known that which has most religion and least politics in its composition appears to be the Wu-wei-chiao[2], founded about 1620 by one Lo-tsu[3] who claimed to have received a revelation contained in five books. It is strictly vegetarian

[1] In the T'ien-t'ai and Chên-yen schools, and indeed in Chinese Buddhism generally, Dharma (*Fa* in Chinese) is regarded as cosmic law. Buddhas are the visible expression of Dharma. Hence they are identified with it and the whole process of cosmic evolution is regarded as the manifestation of Buddhahood.

[2] 無爲敎. See the account by Edkins, *Chinese Buddhism*, pp. 271 ff.

[3] 羅祖.

and antiritualistic, objecting to the use of images, incense and candles in worship.

There are many other sects with a political tinge. The proclivity of the Chinese to guilds, corporations and secret societies is well known and many of these latter have a religious basis. All such bodies are under the ban of the Government, for they have always been suspected with more or less justice of favouring anti-social or anti-dynastic ideas. But, mingled with such political aspirations, there is often present the desire for co-operation in leading privately a religious life which, if made public, would be hampered by official restrictions. The most celebrated of these sects is the White Lotus. Under the Yüan dynasty it was anti-Mongol, and prepared the way for the advent of the Ming. When the Ming dynasty in its turn became decadent, we hear again of the White Lotus coupled with rebellion, and similarly after the Manchus had passed their meridian, its beautiful but ill-omened name frequently appears. It seems clear that it is an ancient and persistent society with some idea of creating a millennium, which becomes active when the central government is weak and corrupt. Not unlike the White Lotus is the secret society commonly known as the Triad but called by its members the Heaven and Earth Association. The T'ai-p'ing sect, out of which the celebrated rebellion arose, was similar but its inspiration seems to have come from a perversion of Christianity. The Tsai-Li sect[1] is still prevalent in Peking, Tientsin, and the province of Shantung. I should exceed the scope of my task if I attempted to examine these sects in detail[2], for their relation to Buddhism is often doubtful. Most of them combine with it Taoist and other beliefs and some of them expect a Messiah or King of Righteousness who is usually identified with Maitreya. It is easy to see how at this point hostility to the existing Government arises and provokes not unnatural resentment[3].

[1] 在理. See *China Mission Year Book*, 1896, p. 43.

[2] For some account of them, see Stanton, The Triad Society, White Lotus Society, etc., 1900, reprinted from *China Review*, vols. XXI, XXII, and De Groot, *Sectarianism and religious persecution in China*, vol. I. pp. 149–259.

[3] The Republic of China has not changed much from the ways of the Empire. The Peking newspapers of June 17, 1914, contain a Presidential Edict stating that "the invention of heretical religions by ill-disposed persons is strictly prohibited by law," and that certain religious societies are to be suppressed.

Recently several attempts have been made to infuse life and order into Chinese Buddhism. Japanese influence can be traced in most of them and though they can hardly be said to represent a new school, they attempt to go back to Mahayanism as it was when first introduced into China. The Hinâyâna is considered as a necessary preliminary to the Mahâyâna and the latter is treated as existing in several schools, among which are included the Pure Land school, though the Contemplative and Tantric schools seem not to be regarded with favour. They are probably mistrusted as leading to negligence and superstition[1].

[1] See, for an account of such a reformed sect, O. Francke, "Ein Buddhistischer Reformversuch in China," *T'oung Pao*, 1909, p. 567.

CHAPTER XLVI

CHINA (*continued*)

Chinese Buddhism at the Present Day

The Buddhism treated of in this chapter does not include Lamaism, which being identical with the religion of Tibet and Mongolia is more conveniently described elsewhere. Ordinary Chinese Buddhism and Lamaism are distinct, but are divided not so much by doctrine as by the race, language and usages of the priests. Chinesc Buddhism has acquired some local colour, but it is still based on the teaching and practice imported from India before the Yüan dynasty, whereas Lamaist tradition is not direct: it represents Buddhism as received not from India but from Tibet. Some holy places, such as P'uto and Wu-t'ai-shan are frequented by both Lamas and Chinese monks, and Tibetan prayers and images may sometimes be seen in Chinese temples, but as a rule the two divisions do not coalesce.

Chinese Buddhism has a physiognomy and language of its own. The Paraphrase of the Sacred Edict in a criticism, which, though unfriendly, is not altogether inaccurate, says that Buddhists attend only to the heart, claim that Buddha can be found in the heart, and aim at becoming Buddhas. This sounds strange to those who are acquainted only with the Buddhism of Ceylon and Burma, but is intelligible as a popular statement of Bodhidharma's doctrine. Heart[1] means the spiritual nature of man, essentially identical with the Buddha nature and capable of purification and growth so that all beings can become Buddhas. But in the Far East the doctrine became less pantheistic and more ethical than the corresponding Indian ideas. The Buddha in the heart is the internal light and monitor rather than the universal spirit. Amida, Kuan-yin and Ti-tsang with other radiant and benevolent spirits have risen from humanity and will help man to rise as they have done. Chinese Buddhists do not regard Amida's vows as an isolated achievement. All

[1] 心. For a specimen of devotional literature about the heart see the little tract translated in China Branch, *R.A.S.* XXIII. pp. 9–22.

Boddhisattvas have done the same and carried out their resolution in countless existences. Like the Madonna these gracious figures appeal directly to the emotions and artistic senses and their divinity offers no difficulty, for in China Church and State alike have always recognized deification as a natural process. One other characteristic of all Far Eastern Buddhism may be noticed. The Buddha is supposed to have preached many creeds and codes at different periods of his life and each school supposes its own to be the last, best and all inclusive.

As indicated elsewhere, the essential part of the Buddhist Church is the monkhood and it is often hard to say if a Chinese layman is a Buddhist or not. It will therefore be best to describe briefly the organization and life of a monastery, then the services performed there and to some extent attended by the laity, and thirdly the rites performed by monks on behalf of the laity, especially funeral ceremonies.

The Chinese Tripitaka contains no less than five recensions of the Vinaya, and the later pilgrims who visited India made it their special object to obtain copies of the most correct and approved code. But though the theoretical value of these codes is still admitted, they have for practical purposes been supplemented by other manuals of which the best known are the Fan-wang-ching or Net of Brahmâ[1] and the Pai-chang-ts'ung-lin-ch'ing-kuei or Rules of Purity of the Monasteries of Pai Chang.

The former is said to have been translated in A.D. 406 by Kumârajîva and to be one chapter of a larger Sanskrit work. Some passages of it, particularly the condemnation of legislation which forbids or imposes conditions on the practice of Buddhism[2], read as if they had been composed in China rather than India, and its whole attitude towards the Hinayanist Vinaya as something inadequate and superseded, can hardly have been usual in India or China even in the time of I-Ching (700 A.D.). Nothing is known of the Indian original, but it certainly was not the Brahmajâlasutta of the Pali Canon[3]. Though the translation

[1] 梵網經. For text translation and commentary, see De Groot, *Code du Mahâyâna en Chine*, 1893, see also Nanjio, No. 1087.

[2] De Groot, p. 81.

[3] The identity of name seems due to a similarity of metaphor. The Brahmajâla sutta is a net of many meshes to catch all forms of error. The Fan-wang-ching

is ascribed to so early a date, there is no evidence that the work carried weight as an authority before the eighth century. Students of the Vinaya, like I-Ching, ignore it. But when the scholarly endeavour to discover the most authentic edition of the Vinaya began to flag, this manual superseded the older treatises. Whatever external evidence there may be for attributing it to Kumârajîva, its contents suggest a much later date and there is no guarantee that a popular manual may not have received additions. The rules are not numbered consecutively but as 1–10 and 1–48, and it may be that the first class is older than the second. In many respects it expounds a late and even degenerate form of Buddhism for it contemplates not only a temple ritual (including the veneration of images and sacred books), but also burning the head or limbs as a religious practice. But it makes no allusion to salvation through faith in Amitâbha and says little about services to be celebrated for the dead[1].

Its ethical and disciplinary point of view is dogmatically Mahayanist and similar to that of the Bodhicaryâvatâra. The Hînayâna is several times denounced[2] and called heretical, but, setting aside a little intolerance and superstition, the teaching of this manual is truly admirable and breathes a spirit of active charity—a desire not only to do no harm but to help and rescue.

It contains a code of ten primary and forty-eight secondary commandments, worded as prohibitions, but equivalent to positive injunctions, inasmuch as they blame the neglect of various active duties. The ten primary commandments are called Prâtimoksha and he who breaks them is Pârâjika[3], that is to say, he *ipso facto* leaves the road leading to Buddhahood and is condemned to a long series of inferior births. They prohibit taking life, theft, unchastity, lying, trading in alcoholic liquors, evil speaking, boasting, avarice, hatred and blasphemy. Though infraction of the secondary commandments has less permanently serious consequence, their observance is indispensable for all monks. Many of them are amplifications of the

compares the varieties of Buddhist opinion to the meshes of a net (De Groot, *l.c.* p. 26), but the net is the all-inclusive common body of truth.

[1] See, however, sections 20 and 39.

[2] See especially De Groot, *l.c.* p. 58, where the reading of the Abhidharma is forbidden. Though this name is not confined to the Hînayâna, A-pi-t'an in Chinese seems to be rarely used as a title of Mahayanist books.

[3] The Indian words are transliterated in the Chinese text.

ten major commandments and are directed against indirect and potential sins, such as the possession of weapons. The Bhikshu may not eat flesh, drink alcohol, set forests on fire or be connected with any business injurious to others, such as the slave trade. He is warned against gossip, sins of the eye, foolish practices such as divination and even momentary forgetfulness of his high calling and duties. But it is not sufficient that he should be self-concentrated and without offence. He must labour for the welfare and salvation of others, and it is a sin to neglect such duties as instructing the ignorant, tending the sick, hospitality, saving men or animals from death or slavery, praying[1] for all in danger, exhorting to repentance, sympathy with all living things. A number of disciplinary rules prescribe a similarly high standard for daily monastic life. The monk must be strenuous and intelligent; he must yield obedience to his superiors and set a good example to the laity: he must not teach for money or be selfish in accepting food and gifts. As for creed he is strictly bidden to follow and preach the Mahâyâna: it is a sin to follow or preach the doctrine of the Srâvakas[2] or read their books or not aspire to ultimate Buddhahood. Very remarkable are the injunctions to burn one's limbs in honour of Buddhas: to show great respect to copies of the scriptures and to make vows. From another point of view the first and forty-seventh secondary commandments are equally remarkable: the first bids officials discharge their duties with due respect to the Church and the other protests against improper legislation.

The Fan-wang-ching is the most important and most authoritative statement of the general principles regulating monastic life in China. So far as my own observation goes, it is known and respected in all monasteries. The Pai-chang-ch'ing-kuei[3] deals rather with the details of organization and ritual and has not the same universal currency. It received the

[1] More accurately reading the sûtras on their behalf, but this exercise is practically equivalent to intercessory prayer.

[2] 聲聞.

[3] The full title is 百文叢林淸規. Pai Chang is apparently to be taken as the name of the author, but it is the designation of a monastery used as a personal name. See Hackmann in *T'oung Pao*, 1908, pp. 651–662. It is No. 1642 in Nanjio's Catalogue. He says that it has been revised and altered.

approval of the Yüan dynasty[1] and is still accepted as authoritative in many monasteries and gives a correct account of their general practice. It was composed by a monk of Kiang-si, who died in 814 A.D. He belonged to the Ch'an school, but his rules are approved by others. I will not attempt to summarize them, but they include most points of ritual and discipline mentioned below. The author indicates the relations which should prevail between Church and State by opening his work with an account of the ceremonies to be performed on the Emperor's birthday, and similar occasions.

Large Buddhist temples almost always form part of a monastery, but smaller shrines, especially in towns, are often served by a single priest. The many-storeyed towers called pagodas which are a characteristic beauty of Chinese landscapes, are in their origin stupas erected over relics but at the present day can hardly be called temples or religious buildings, for they are not places of worship and generally owe their construction to the dictates of Fêng-shui or geomancy. Monasteries are usually built outside towns and by preference on high ground, whence *shan* or mountain has come to be the common designation of a convent, whatever its position. The sites of these establishments show the deep feeling of cultivated Chinese for nature and their appreciation of the influence of scenery on temper, an appreciation which connects them spiritually with the psalms of the monks and nuns preserved in the Pali Canon. The architecture is not self-assertive. Its aim is not to produce edifices complete and satisfying in their own proportions but rather to harmonize buildings with landscape, to adjust courts and pavilions to the slope of the hillside and diversify the groves of fir and bamboo with shrines and towers as fantastic and yet as natural as the mountain boulders. The reader who wishes to know more of them should consult Johnston's *Buddhist China*, a work which combines in a rare degree sound knowledge and literary charm.

A monastery[2] is usually a quadrangle surrounded by a wall.

[1] See *T'oung Pao*, 1904, pp. 437 ff.

[2] It is probable that the older Chinese monasteries attempted to reproduce the arrangement of Nâlanda and other Indian establishments. Unfortunately Hsüan Chuang and the other pilgrims give us few details as to the appearance of Indian monasteries: they tell us, however, that they were surrounded by a wall, that the monks' quarters were near this wall, that there were halls where choral services

Before the great gate, which faces south, or in the first court is a tank, spanned by a bridge, wherein grows the red lotus and tame fish await doles of biscuit. The sides of the quadrangle contain dwelling rooms, refectories, guest chambers, store houses, a library, printing press and other premises suitable to a learned and pious foundation. The interior space is divided into two or three courts, bordered by a veranda. In each court is a hall of worship or temple, containing a shelf or alcove on which are set the sacred images: in front of them stands a table, usually of massive wood, bearing vases of flowers, bowls for incense sticks and other vessels. The first temple is called the Hall of the Four Great Kings and the figures in it represent beings who are still in the world of transmigration and have not yet attained Buddhahood. They include gigantic images of the Four Kings, Maitreya, the Buddha designate of the future, and Wei-to[1], a military Bodhisattva sometimes identified with Indra. Kuan-ti, the Chinese God of War, is often represented in this building. The chief temple, called the Precious Hall of the Great Hero[2], is in the second court and contains the principal images. Very commonly there are nine figures on either side representing eighteen disciples of the Buddha and known as the Eighteen Lohan or Arhats[3]. Above the altar are one or more large gilt

were performed and that there were triads of images. But the Indian buildings had three stories. See Chavannes, *Mémoire sur les Religieux Eminents*, 1894, p. 85.

[1] 韋陀 or 馱. For this personage see the article in *B.E.F.E.O.* 1916. No. 3, by Péri who identifies him with Wei, the general of the Heavenly Kings who appeared to Tao Hsüan the founder of the Vinaya school and became popular as a protecting deity of Buddhism. The name is possibly a mistaken transcription of Skandha.

[2] 大雄寶殿.

[3] 羅漢. See Lévi and Chavannes' two articles in *J.A.* 1916, I and II, and Watters in *J.R.A.S.* 1898, p. 329, for an account of these personages. The original number, still found in a few Chinese temples as well as in Korea, Japan and Tibet was sixteen. Several late sûtras contain the idea that the Buddha entrusted the protection of his religion to four or sixteen disciples and bade them not enter Nirvana but tarry until the advent of Maitreya. The Ta-A-lo-han-nan-t'i-mi-to-lo-so-shuo-fa-chu-chi (Nanjio, 1466) is an account of these sixteen disciples and of their spheres of influence. The Buddha assigned to each a region within which it is his duty to guard the faith. They will not pass from this life before the next Buddha comes. Piṇḍola is the chief of them. Nothing is known of the work cited except that it was translated in 654 by Hsüan Chuang, who, according to Watters, used an earlier translation. As the Arhats are Indian personalities, and their spheres are mapped out from the

images. When there is only one it is usually Śâkya-muni, but more often there are three. Such triads are variously composed and the monks often speak of them vaguely as the "three precious ones," without seeming to attach much importance to their identity[1]. The triad is loosely connected with the idea of the three bodies of Buddha but this explanation does not always apply and the central figure is sometimes O-mi-to or Kuan-yin, who are the principal recipients of the worship offered by the laity. The latter deity has usually a special shrine at the back of the main altar and facing the north door of the hall, in which her merciful activity as the saviour of mankind is represented in a series of statuettes or reliefs. Other Bodhisattvas such as Ta-shih-chi (Mahâsthâmaprâpta) and Ti-tsang also have separate shrines in or at the side of the great hall[2]. The third hall contains as a rule only small images. It is used for expounding the scriptures and for sermons, if the monastery has a preacher, but is set apart for the religious exercises of the monks rather than the devotions of the laity. In very large monasteries there is a fourth hall for meditation.

Monasteries are of various sizes and the number of monks is not constant, for the peripatetic habit of early Buddhism is not extinct: at one time many inmates may be absent on their

point of view of Indian geography, there can be no doubt that we have to do with an Indian idea, imported into Tibet as well as into China where it became far more popular than it had ever been in India. The two additional Arhats (who vary in different temples, whereas the sixteen are fixed) appear to have been added during the T'ang dynasty and, according to Watters, in imitation of a very select order of merit instituted by the Emperor T'ai Tsung and comprising eighteen persons. Chavannes and Lévi see in them spirits borrowed from the popular pantheon.

Chinese ideas about the Lohans at the present day are very vague. Their Indian origin has been forgotten and some of them have been provided with Chinese biographies. (See Doré, p. 216.) One popular story says that they were eighteen converted brigands.

In several large temples there are halls containing 500 images of Arhats, which include many Chinese Emperors and one of them is often pointed out as being Marco Polo. But this is very doubtful. See, however, Hackmann, *Buddhismus*, p. 212.

[1] Generally they consist of Śâkya-muni and two superhuman Buddhas or Bodhisattvas, such as O-mi-to (Amitâbha) and Yo-shih-fo (Vaidûrya): Pi-lu-fo (Vairocana) and Lo-shih-fo (Lochana): Wên-shu (Manjuś-ri) and P'u-hsien (Samantabhadra). The common European explanation that they are the Buddhas of the past, present and future is not correct.

[2] 大勢至 and 地藏. For the importance of Ti-tsang in popular Buddhism, which has perhaps been underestimated, see Johnston, chap. VIII.

travels, at another there may be an influx of strangers. There are also wandering monks who have ceased to belong to a particular monastery and spend their time in travelling. A large monastery usually contains from thirty to fifty monks, but a very large one may have as many as three hundred. The majority are dedicated by their parents as children, but some embrace the career from conviction in their maturity and these, if few, are the more interesting. Children who are brought up to be monks receive a religious education in the monastery, wear monastic clothes and have their heads shaved. At the age of about seventeen they are formally admitted as members of the order and undergo three ceremonies of ordination, which in their origin represented stages of the religious life, but are now performed by accumulation in the course of a few days. One reason for this is that only monasteries possessing a licence from the Government[1] are allowed to hold ordinations and that consequently postulants have to go some distance to be received as full brethren and are anxious to complete the reception expeditiously. At the first ordination the candidates are accepted as novices: at the second, which follows a day or two afterwards and corresponds to the upasampadâ, they accept the robes and bowl and promise obedience to the rules of the Prâtimoksha. But these ceremonies are of no importance compared with the third, called Shou Pu-sa-chieh[2] or acceptance of the Bodhisattva precepts, that is to say the fifty-eight precepts enunciated in the Fan-wang-ching. The essential part of this ordination is the burning of the candidate's head in from three to eighteen places. The operation involves considerable pain and is performed by lighting pieces of charcoal set in a paste which is spread over the shaven skull.

Although the Fan-wang-ching does not mention this burning of the head as part of ordination, yet it emphatically enjoins the practice of burning the body or limbs, affirming that those who neglect it are not true Bodhisattvas[3]. The prescription is founded on the twenty-second chapter of the Lotus[4] which, though a later addition, is found in the Chinese transla-

[1] I speak of the Old Imperial Government which came to an end in 1911.

[2] 受菩薩戒.

[3] De Groot, *l.c.* p. 51.

[4] See Kern's translation, especially pp. 379 and 385.

tion made between 265 and 316 A.D.[1] I-Ching discusses and reprobates such practices. Clearly they were known in India when he visited it, but not esteemed by the better Buddhists, and the fact that they form no part of the ordinary Tibetan ritual indicates that they had no place in the decadent Indian Buddhism which in various stages of degeneration was introduced into Tibet[2]. In Korea and Japan branding is practised but on the breast and arms rather than on the head.

It would appear then that burning and branding as part of initiation were known in India in the early centuries of our era but not commonly approved and that their general acceptance in China was subsequent to the death of I-Ching in A.D. 713[3]. This author clearly approved of nothing but the double ordination as novice and full monk. The third ordination as Bodhisattva must be part of the later phase inaugurated by Amogha about 750[4].

This practice is defended as a trial of endurance, but the earlier and better monks were right in rejecting it, for in itself it is an unedifying spectacle and it points to the logical conclusion that, if it is meritorious to cauterize the head, it is still more meritorious to burn the whole body. Cases of suicide by burning appear to have occurred in recent years, especially in the province of Che-Kiang[5]. The true doctrine of the Mahâyâna is that every one should strive for the happiness and salvation of all beings, but this beautiful truth may be sadly perverted

[1] See Nanjio, Nos. 138 and 139. The practice is not entirely unknown in the legends of Pali Buddhism. In the Lokapaññatti, a work existing in Burma but perhaps translated from the Sanskrit, Asoka burns himself in honour of the Buddha, but is miraculously preserved. See *B.E.F.E.O.* 1904, pp. 421 and 427.

[2] See I-Tsing, *Records of the Buddhist Religion*, trans. Takakusu, pp. 195 ff., and for Tibet, Waddell, *Buddhism of Tibet*, p. 178, note 3, from which it appears that it is only in Eastern Tibet and probably under Chinese influence that branding is in vogue. For apparent instances in Central Asian art, see Grünwedel, *Budd. Kultst.* p. 23, note 1.

[3] Branding is common in many Hindu sects, especially the Mâdhvas, but is reprobated by others.

[4] It is condemned as part of the superstition of Buddhism in a memorial of Han Yü, 819 A.D.

[5] See those cited by De Groot, *l.c.* p. 228, and the article of MacGowan (*Chinese Recorder*, 1888) there referred to. See also Hackmann, *Buddhism as a Religion*, p. 228. Chinese sentiment often approves suicide, for instance, if committed by widows or the adherents of defeated princes. For a Confucian instance, see Johnston, p 341

if it is held that the endurance of pain is in itself meritorious and that such acquired merit can be transferred to others. Self-torture seems not to be unknown in the popular forms of Chinese Buddhism[1].

The postulant, after receiving these three ordinations, becomes a full monk or Ho-shang[2] and takes a new name. The inmates of every monastery owe obedience to the abbot and some abbots have an official position, being recognized by the Government as representing the clergy of a prefecture, should there be any business to be transacted with the secular authorities. But there is no real hierarchy outside the monasteries, each of which is an isolated administrative unit. Within each monastery due provision is made for discipline and administration. The monks are divided into two classes, the Western who are concerned with ritual and other purely religious duties and the Eastern who are relatively secular and superintend the business of the establishment[3]. This is often considerable for the income is usually derived from estates, in managing which the monks are assisted by a committee of laymen. Other laymen of humbler status[4] live around the monastery and furnish the labour necessary for agriculture, forestry and whatever industries the character of the property calls into being. As a rule there is a considerable library. Even a sympathetic stranger will often find that the monks deny its existence, because many books have been destroyed in political troubles, but most monasteries possess copies of the principal scriptures and a complete Tripitaka, usually the edition of 1737, is not rare. Whether the books are much read I do not know, but I have observed that after the existence of the library has been ad-

[1] See *e.g.* Du Bose, *The Dragon, Image and Demon*, p. 265. I have never seen such practices myself. See also *Paraphrase of the Sacred Edict*, VII. 8.

[2] 和尙. This word, which has no derivation in Chinese, is thought to be a corruption of some vernacular form of the Sanskrit Upâdhyâya current in Central Asia. See I-tsing, transl. Takakusu, p. 118. Upâdhyâya became Vajjha (as is shown by the modern Indian forms Ojha or Jha and Tamil Vâddyar). See Bloch in *Indo-Germanischen Forschungen*, vol. XXV. 1909, p. 239. Vajjha might become in Chinese Ho-sho or Ho-shang for Ho sometimes represents the Indian syllable *va*. See Julien, *Méthode*, p. 109, and Eitel, *Handbook of Chinese Buddhism*, p. 195.

[3] For details see Hackmann in *T'oung Pao*, 1908.

[4] They apparently correspond to the monastic lay servants or "pure men" described by I-Ching, chap. XXXII, as living as Nâlanda.

mitted, it often proves difficult to find the key. There is also a printing press, where are prepared notices and prayers, as well as copies of popular sûtras.

The food of the monks is strictly vegetarian, but they do not go round with the begging bowl nor, except in a few monasteries, is it forbidden to eat after midday. As a rule there are three meals, the last about 6 p.m., and all must be eaten in silence. The three garments prescribed by Indian Buddhism are still worn, but beneath them are trousers, stockings, and shoes which are necessary in the Chinese climate. There is no idea that it is wrong to sleep on a bed, to receive presents or own property.

Two or three services are performed daily in the principal temple, early in the morning, about 4 p.m., and sometimes in the middle of the day. A specimen of this ritual may be seen in the service called by Beal the Liturgy of Kuan Yin[1]. It consists of versicles, responses and canticles, and, though strangely reminiscent both in structure and externals (such as the wearing of vestments) of the offices of the Roman Church[2], appears to be Indian in origin. I-Ching describes the choral services which he attended in Nalanda and elsewhere—the chanting, bowing, processions—and the Chinese ritual is, I think, only the amplification of these ceremonies. It includes the presentation of offerings, such as tea, rice and other vegetables. The Chinese pilgrims testify that in India flowers, lights and incense were offered to relics and images (as in Christian churches), and the Bodhicaryâvatâra[3], one of the most spiritual of later Mahayanist works, mentions offerings of food and drink as part of worship. Many things in Buddhism lent themselves to such a transformation or parody of earlier teaching. Offerings of food to hungry ghosts were countenanced, and it was easy to include among the recipients other spirits. It was meritorious to present food, raiment and property to living saints: oriental,

[1] *A Catena of Buddhist Scriptures from the Chinese*, pp. 339 ff.

[2] The abbot and several upper priests wear robes, which are generally red and gold, during the service. The abbot also carries a sort of sceptre. The vestments of the clergy are said to be derived from the robes of honour which used to be given to them when they appeared at Court.

[3] II. 16. Cf. the rituals in De la Vallée Poussin's *Bouddhisme et Matériaux*, pp. 214 ff. Târanâtha frequently mentions burnt offerings as part of worship in medieval Magadha.

and especially Chinese, symbolism found it natural to express the same devotion by offerings made before images.

In the course of most ceremonies, the monks make vows on behalf of all beings and take oath to work for their salvation. They are also expected to deliver and hear sermons and to engage in meditation. Some of them superintend the education of novices which consists chiefly in learning to read and repeat religious works. Quite recently elementary schools for the instruction of the laity have been instituted in some monasteries[1].

The regularity of convent life is broken by many festivals. The year is divided into two periods of wandering, two of meditation and one of repose corresponding to the old Vassa. Though this division has become somewhat theoretical, it is usual for monks to set out on excursions in the spring and autumn. In each month there are six fasts, including the two uposatha days. On these latter the 250 rules of the Prâtimoksha are recited in a refectory or side hall and subsequently the fifty-eight rules of the Fan-wang-ching are recited with greater ceremony in the main temple.

Another class of holy days includes the birthdays[2] not only of Sâkya-muni, but of other Buddhas and Bodhisattvas, the anniversaries of events in Sâkya-muni's life and the deaths of Bodhidharma and other Saints, among whom the founder or patron of each monastery has a prominent place. Another important and popular festival is called Yü-lan-pên or All Souls' day, which is an adaptation of Buddhist usages to Chinese ancestral worship. Of many other festivals it may be said that they are purely Chinese but countenanced by Buddhism: such are the days which mark the changes of the seasons, those sacred to Kuan-ti and other native deities, and (before the revolution) imperial birthdays.

The daily services are primarily for the monks, but the laity may attend them, if they please. More frequently they pay their devotions at other hours, light a few tapers and too often have recourse to some form of divination before the images. Some-

[1] I do not refer to the practice of turning disused temples into schools which is frequent. In some monasteries the monks, while retaining possession, have themselves opened schools.

[2] It is not clear to me what is really meant by the *birthdays* of beings like Maitreya and Amitâbha.

times they defray the cost of more elaborate ceremonies to expiate sins or ensure prosperity. But the lay attendance in temples is specially large at seasons of pilgrimage. For an account of this interesting side of Chinese religious life I cannot do better than refer the reader to Mr Johnston's volume already cited.

Though the services of the priesthood may be invoked at every crisis of life, they are most in requisition for funeral ceremonies. A detailed description of these as practised at Amoy has been given by De Groot[1] which is probably true in essentials for all parts of China. These rites unite in incongruous confusion several orders of ideas. Pre-Buddhist Chinese notions of the life after death seem not to have included the idea of hell. The disembodied soul is honoured and comforted but without any clear definition of its status. Some representative—a person, figure, or tablet—is thought capable of giving it a temporary residence and at funeral ceremonies offerings are made to such a representative and plays performed before it. Though Buddhist language may be introduced into this ritual, its spirit is alien to even the most corrupt Buddhism.

Buddhism familiarized China with the idea that the average man stands in danger of purgatory and this doctrine cannot be described as late or Mahayanist[2]. Those epithets are, however, merited by the subsidiary doctrine that such punishment can be abridged by vicarious acts of worship which may take the form of simple prayer addressed to benevolent beings who can release the tortured soul. More often the idea underlying it is that the recitation of certain formulæ acquires merit for the reciter who can then divert this merit to any purpose[3]. This is really a theological refinement of the ancient and widespread notion that words have magic force. Equally ancient and un-Buddhist in origin is the theory of sympathetic magic. Just as by sticking pins into a wax figure you may kill the person represented, so by imitating physical operations of rescue, you may deliver a soul from the furnaces and morasses of hell. Thus

[1] *Actes du Sixième Congres des Orientalistes*, Leide, 1883, sec. IV. pp. 1–120.

[2] *E.g.* in Dipavamsa, XIII; Mahâv. XIV. Mahinda is represented as converting Ceylon by accounts of the terrors of the next world.

[3] The merit of good deeds can be similarly utilized. The surviving relatives feed the poor or buy and maintain for the rest of its life an animal destined to slaughter. The merit then goes to the deceased.

a paper model of hades is made which is knocked to pieces and finally burnt: the spirit is escorted with music and other precautions over a mock bridge, and, most singular of all, the priests place over a receptacle of water a special machine consisting of a cylinder containing a revolving apparatus which might help a creature immersed in the fluid to climb up. This strange mummery is supposed to release those souls who are condemned to sojourn in a pool of blood[1]. This, too, is a superstition countenanced only by Chinese Buddhism, for the punishment is incurred not so much by sinners as by those dying of illnesses which defile with blood. Many other rites are based on the notion that objects—or their paper images—ceremonially burnt are transmitted to the other world for the use of the dead. Thus representations in paper of servants, clothes, furniture, money and all manner of things are burned together with the effigy of the deceased and sometimes also certificates and passports giving him a clean bill of health for the Kingdom of Heaven.

As in funeral rites, so in matters of daily life, Buddhism gives its countenance and help to popular superstition, to every kind of charm for reading the future, securing happiness and driving away evil spirits. In its praise may be said that this patronage, though far too easy going, is not extended to cruel or immoral customs. But the reader will ask, is there no brighter side? I believe that there is, but it is not conspicuous and, as in India, public worship and temple ritual display the lower aspects of religion. But in China a devout Buddhist is generally a good man and the objects of Buddhist associations are praiseworthy and philanthropic. They often include vegetarianism and abstinence from alcohol and drugs. The weakness of the religion to-day is no doubt the want of intelligence and energy among the clergy. There are not a few learned and devout monks, but even devotion is not a characteristic of the majority. On the other hand, those of the laity who take their religion seriously generally attain a high standard of piety and there have been

[1] It may possibly be traceable to Manichæism which taught that souls are transferred from one sphere to another by a sort of cosmic water wheel. See Cumont's article, "La roue à puiser les âmes du Manichéisme" in *Rev. de l'Hist. des Religions*, 1915, p. 384. Chavannes and Pelliot have shown that traces of Manichæism lingered long in Fu-Kien. The metaphor of the endless chain of buckets is also found in the Yüan Jên Lun.

attempts to reform Buddhism, to connect it with education and to spread a knowledge of the more authentic scriptures[1].

When one begins to study Buddhism in China, one fears it may be typified by the neglected temples on the outskirts of Peking, sullen and mouldering memorials of dynasties that have passed away. But later one learns not only that there are great and flourishing monasteries in the south, but that even in Peking one may often step through an archway into courtyards of which the prosaic streets outside give no hint and find there refreshment for the eye and soul, flower gardens and well-kept shrines tended by pious and learned guardians.

[1] See Francke, "Ein Buddhistischer Reformversuch in China," *T'oung Pao*, 1909, pp. 567–602.

CHAPTER XLVII

KOREA[1]

The Buddhism of Korea cannot be sharply distinguished from the Buddhism of China and Japan. Its secluded mountain monasteries have some local colour, and contain halls dedicated to the seven stars and the mountain gods of the land. And travellers are impressed by the columns of rock projecting from the soil and carved into images (miriok), by the painted walls of the temples and by the huge rolled-up pictures which are painted and displayed on festival days. But there is little real originality in art: in literature and doctrine none at all. Buddhism started in Korea with the same advantages as in China and Japan but it lost in moral influence because the monks continually engaged in politics and it did not win temporal power because they were continually on the wrong side. Yet Korea is not without importance in the annals of far-eastern Buddhism for, during the wanderings and vicissitudes of the faith, it served as a rest-house and depot. It was from Korea that Buddhism first entered Japan: when, during the wars of the five dynasties the T'ien-t'ai school was nearly annihilated in China, it was revived by a Korean priest and the earliest extant edition of the Chinese Tripitaka is known only by a single copy preserved in Korea and taken thence to Japan.

For our purposes Korean history may be divided into four periods:

I. The three States (B.C. 57–A.D. 668).
II. The Kingdom of Silla (668–918).
III. The Kingdom of Korye (918–1392).
IV. The Kingdom of Chosen (1392–1910).

The three states were Koguryu in the north, Pakche in the south-west and Silla in the south-east[2]. Buddhism, together

[1] See various articles in the *Trans. of the Korean Branch of the R.A.S.*, and F. Starr, *Korean Buddhism.* Also M. Courant, *Bibliographie coréenne,* especially vol. III. chap. 2.

[2] The orthography of these three names varies considerably. The Japanese equivalents are Koma, Kudara and Shiragi. There are also slight variations in the dates given for the introduction of Buddhism into various states. It seems probable that Mârânanda and Mukocha, the first missionaries to Pakche and Silla were

with Chinese writing, entered Koguryu from the north in 372 and Pakche from the south a few years later. Silla being more distant and at war with the other states did not receive it till about 424. In 552 both Japan and Pakche were at war with Silla and the king of Pakche, wishing to make an alliance with the Emperor of Japan sent him presents which included Buddhist books and images. Thus Korea was the intermediary for introducing Buddhism, writing, and Chinese culture into Japan, and Korean monks played an important part there both in art and religion. But the influence of Korea must not be exaggerated. The Japanese submitted to it believing that they were acquiring the culture of China and as soon as circumstances permitted they went straight to the fountain head. The principal early sects were all imported direct from China.

The kingdom of Silla, which became predominant in the seventh century, had adopted Buddhism in 528, and maintained friendly intercourse with the T'ang dynasty. As in Japan Chinese civilization was imitated wholesale. This tendency strengthened Buddhism at the time, but its formidable rival Confucianism was also introduced early in the eighth century, although it did not become predominant until the thirteenth[1].

In the seventh century the capital of Silla was a centre of Buddhist culture and also of trade. Merchants from India, Tibet and Persia are said to have frequented its markets and several Korean pilgrims visited India.

In 918 the Wang dynasty, originating in a northern family of humble extraction, overthrew the kingdom of Silla and with it the old Korean aristocracy. This was replaced by an official nobility modelled on that of China: the Chinese system of examinations was adopted and a class of scholars grew up. But with this attempt to reconstruct society many abuses appeared. The number of slaves greatly increased[2], and there were many

Hindus or natives of Central Asia who came from China and some of the early art of Silla is distinctly Indian in style. See Starr, *l.c.* plates VIII and IX.

[1] These dates are interesting, as reflecting the changes of thought in China. In the sixth century Chinese influence meant Buddhism. It is not until the latter part of the Southern Sung, when the philosophy of Chu-hsi had received official approval, that Chinese influence meant Confucianism.

[2] The reasons were many, but the upper classes were evidently ready to oppress the lower. Poor men became the slaves of the rich to obtain a livelihood. All children of slave women were declared hereditary slaves and so were the families of criminals.

hereditary low castes, the members of which were little better than slaves. Only the higher castes could compete in examinations or hold office and there were continual struggles and quarrels between the military and civil classes. Buddhism flourished much as it flourished in the Hei-an period of Japan, but its comparative sterility reflected the inferior social conditions of Korea. Festivals were celebrated by the Court with great splendour: magnificent monasteries were founded: the bonzes kept troops and entered the capital armed: the tutor of the heir apparent and the chancellor of the kingdom were often ecclesiastics, and a law is said to have been enacted to the effect that if a man had three sons one of them must become a monk. But about 1250 the influence of the Sung Confucianists began to be felt. The bonzes were held responsible for the evils of the time, for the continual feuds, exactions and massacres, and the civil nobility tended to become Confucianist and to side against the church and the military. The inevitable outburst was delayed but also rendered more disastrous when it came by the action of the Mongols who, as in China, were patrons of Buddhism. The Yüan dynasty invaded Korea, placed regents in the principal towns and forced the Korean princes to marry Mongol wives. It was from Korea that Khubilai despatched his expeditions against Japan, and in revenge the Japanese harried the Korean coast throughout the fourteenth century. But so long as the Yüan dynasty lasted the Korean Court which had become Mongol remained faithful to it and to Buddhism; when it was ousted by the Ming, a similar movement soon followed in Korea. The Mongolized dynasty of Koryc was deposed and another, which professed to trace its lineage back to Silla, mounted the throne and gave the country the name of Chosen.

This revolution was mainly the work of the Confucianist party in the nobility and it was not unnatural that patriots and reformers should see in Buddhism nothing but the religion of the corrupt old regime of the Mongols. During the next century and a half a series of restrictive measures, sometimes amounting to persecution, were applied to it. Two kings who dared to build monasteries and favour bonzes were deposed. Statues were melted down, Buddhist learning was forbidden: marriages and burials were performed according to the rules of Chu-hsi. About the beginning of the sixteenth century (the date is variously given as 1472 and 1512 and perhaps there was more than one edict) the monasteries in the capital and all cities were closed and this is why Korean monasteries are all in the country and often in almost inaccessible mountains. It is only since the Japanese occupation that temples have been built in towns.

At first the results of the revolution were beneficial. The great families were compelled to discharge their body-guards whose collisions had been a frequent cause of bloodshed. The public finances and military forces were put into order. Printing with moveable type and a phonetic alphabet were brought into use and vernacular literature began to flourish. But in time the Confucian literati formed a sort of corporation and became as troublesome as the bonzes had been. The aristocracy split into two hostile camps and Korean politics became again a confused struggle between families and districts in which progress and even public order became impossible. For a moment, however, there was a national cause. This was when Hideyoshi invaded Korea in 1592 as part of his attack on China. The people rose against the Japanese troops and, thanks to the death of Hideyoshi rather than to their own valour, got rid of them. It is said that in this struggle the bonzes took part as soldiers fighting under their abbots and that the treaty of peace was negotiated by a Korean and a Japanese monk[1].

Nevertheless it does not appear that Buddhism enjoyed much consideration in the next three centuries. The Hermit Kingdom, as it has been called, became completely isolated and stagnant nor was there any literary or intellectual life except the mechanical study of the Chinese classics. Since the annexation by Japan (1910) conditions have changed and Buddhism is encouraged. Much good work has been done in collecting and reprinting old books, preserving monuments and copying inscriptions. The monasteries were formerly under the control of thirty head establishments or sees, with somewhat conflicting interests. But about 1912 these thirty sees formed a union under a president who resides in Seoul and holds office for a year. A theological seminary also has been founded and a Buddhist magazine is published.

[1] These statements are taken from Maurice Courant's Epitome of Korean History in Madrolle's *Guide to North China*, p. 428. I have not been successful in verifying them in Chinese or Japanese texts. See, however, Starr, *Korean Buddhism*, pp. 29–30.

CHAPTER XLVIII

ANNAM

THE modern territory called Annam includes the ancient Champa, and it falls within the French political sphere which includes Camboja. Of Champa I have treated elsewhere in connection with Camboja, but Annam cannot be regarded as the heir of this ancient culture. It represents a southward extension of Chinese influence, though it is possible that Buddhism may have entered it in the early centuries of our era either by sea or from Burma.

At the present day that part of the French possessions which occupies the eastern coast of Asia is divided into Tonkin, Annam and Cochin China. The Annamites are predominant in all three provinces and the language and religion of all are the same, except that Cochin China has felt the influence of Europe more strongly than the others. But before the sixteenth century the name Annam meant rather Tonkin and the northern portion of modern Annam, the southern portion being the now vanished kingdom of Champa.

Until the tenth century A.D.[1] Annam in this sense was a part of the Chinese Empire, although it was occasionally successful in asserting its temporary independence. In the troubled period which followed the downfall of the T'ang dynasty this independence became more permanent. An Annamite prince founded a kingdom called Dai-cô-viêt[2] and after a turbulent interval there arose the Li dynasty which reigned for more than two centuries (1009–1226 A.D.). It was under this dynasty that the country was first styled An-nam: previously the official designation of the land or its inhabitants was Giao-Chi[3]. The

[1] The dates given are 111 B.C.–939 A.D.

[2] French scholars use a great number of accents and even new forms of letters to transcribe Annamite, but since this language has nothing to do with the history of Buddhism or Hinduism and the accurate orthography is very difficult to read, I have contented myself with a rough transcription.

[3] This is the common orthography, but Chiao Chih would be the spelling according to the system of transliterating Chinese adopted in this book.

Annamites were at this period a considerable military power, though their internal administration appears to have been chaotic. They were occasionally at war with China, but as a rule were ready to send complimentary embassies to the Emperor. With Champa, which was still a formidable antagonist, there was a continual struggle. Under the Tran dynasty (1225–1400) the foreign policy of Annam followed much the same lines. A serious crisis was created by the expedition of Khubilai Khan in 1285, but though the Annamites suffered severely at the beginning of the invasion, they did not lose their independence and their recognition of Chinese suzerainty remained nominal. In the south the Chams continued hostilities and, after the loss of some territory, invoked the aid of China with the result that the Chinese occupied Annam. They held it, however, only for five years (1414–1418).

In 1428 the Li dynasty came to the throne and ruled Annam at least in name until the end of the eighteenth century. At first they proved vigorous and capable; they organized the kingdom in provinces and crushed the power of Champa. But after the fifteenth century the kings became merely titular sovereigns and Annamite history is occupied entirely with the rivalry of the two great families, Trinh and Nguyen, who founded practically independent kingdoms in Tonkin and Cochin-China respectively. In 1802 a member of the Nguyen family made himself Emperor of all Annam but both he and his successors were careful to profess themselves vassals of China.

Thus it will be seen that Annam was at no time really detached from China. In spite of political independence it always looked towards the Chinese Court and though complimentary missions and nominal vassalage seem unimportant, yet they are significant as indicating admiration for Chinese institutions. Between Champa and Annam on the other hand there was perpetual war: in the later phases of the contest the Annamites appear as invaders and destroyers. They seem to have disliked the Chams and were not disposed to imitate them. Hence it is natural that Champa, so long as it existed as an independent kingdom, should mark the limit of *direct* Indian influence on the mainland of Eastern Asia, though afterwards Camboja became the limit. By direct, I do not mean to exclude the possibility of transmission through Java or elsewhere, but by whatever route Indian civilization came to Champa, it brought its own art, alphabet and language, such institutions as caste and forms of Hinduism and Buddhism which had borrowed practically nothing from non-Indian sources. In Annam, on the other hand, Chinese writing and, for literary purposes, a form of the Chinese language were in use: the arts, customs and institutions were mainly Chinese: whatever Buddhism can be found was imported from China and is imperfectly distinguished from Taoism: of Hinduism there are hardly any traces[1].

The Buddhism of Annam is often described as corrupt and decadent. Certainly it would be vain to claim for it that its doctrine and worship are even moderately pure or primitive, but it cannot be said to be moribund. The temples are better kept and more numerously attended than in China and there are also some considerable monasteries. As in China very few except the monks are exclusive Buddhists and even the monks have no notion that the doctrines of Lao-tzŭ and Confucius are different from Buddhism. The religion of the ordinary layman is a selection made according to taste from a mass of beliefs and observances traceable to several distinct sources, though no Annamite is conscious that there is anything incongruous in this heterogeneous combination. This fusion of religions, which is more complete even than in China, is illustrated by the temples of Annam which are of various kinds[2]. First we have the Chua or Buddhist temples, always served by bonzes or nuns. They consist of several buildings of which the principal contains an altar bearing a series of images arranged on five or six steps, which rise like the tiers of a theatre. In the front row there is usually an image of the infant Śâkyamuni and near him stand figures of At-nan (Ânanda) and Muc-Lien (Maudgalyâyana). On the next stage are Taoist deities (the Jade Emperor, the Polar Star, and the Southern Star) and on the higher stages are images representing (*a*) three Buddhas[3] with attendants,

[1] It is said that the story of the Râmâyana is found in Annamite legends (*B.E.F.E.O.* 1905, p. 77), and in one or two places the Annamites reverence statues of Indian deities.

[2] The most trustworthy account of Annamite religion is perhaps Dumoutier, *Les Cultes Annamites*, Hanoi, 1907. It was published after the author's death and consists of a series of notes rather than a general description. See also Diguet, *Les Annamites*, 1906, especially chap. VI.

[3] Maitreya is called Ri-lac = Chinese Mi-le. The equivalence of the syllables *ri* and *mi* seems strange, but certain. Cf. A-ri-da = Amida or O-mi-to.

(*b*) the Buddhist Triratna and (*c*) the three religions, Buddhism, Confucianism and Taoism. But the arrangement of the images is subject to much variation and the laity hardly know who are the personages represented. At side altars there are generally statues of Quan-Am, guardian deities, eminent bonzes and other worthies. Representations of hell are also common. Part of the temple is generally set apart for women who frequent it in the hope of obtaining children by praying to Quan-Am and other goddesses. Buddhist literature is sometimes printed in these Chua and such works as the Amitâyurdhyânasûtra and collections of Dhâraṇîs are commonly placed on the altars.

Quan-Am (Kuan-Yin) is a popular deity and the name seems to be given to several goddesses. They would probably be described as incarnations of Avalokita, if any Annamite were to define his beliefs (which is not usual), but they are really legendary heroines who have left a reputation for superhuman virtue. One was a daughter of the Emperor Chuang of the Chou dynasty. Another (Quan-Am-Thi-Kinh), represented as sitting on a rock and carrying a child in her arms, was a much persecuted lady who passed part of her life disguised as a bonze. A third form, Quan-Am-Toa-Son, she who dwells on the mountains, has an altar in nearly every temple and is specially worshipped by women who wish for sons. At Hanoi there is a small temple, rising on one column out of the water near the shore of a lake, like a lotus in a tank, and containing a brass image of Quan-Am with eight arms, which is evidently of Indian origin. Sometimes popular heroines such as Cao Tien, a princess who was drowned, are worshipped without (it would seem) being identified with Quan-Am.

But besides the Chua there are at least three other kinds of religious edifices: (i) Dinh. These are municipal temples dedicated to beings commonly called genii by Europeans, that is to say, superhuman personages, often, but not always, departed local worthies, who for one reason or another are supposed to protect and supervise a particular town or village. The Dinh contains a council room as well as a shrine and is served by laymen. The genius is often represented by an empty chair and his name must not be pronounced within the temple. (ii) Taoist deities are sometimes worshipped in special temples, but the Annamites do not seem to think that such worship is antagonistic to Buddhism or even distinct from it. (iii) Temples dedicated to Confucius (Van mien) are to be found in the towns, but are generally open only on certain feast days, when they are visited by officials. Sometimes altars dedicated to the sage may be found in natural grottoes or other picturesque situations. Besides these numerous elements, Annamite religion also includes the veneration of ancestors and ceremonies such as the worship of Heaven and Earth performed in imitation of the Court of Peking. To this must be added many local superstitions in which the worship of animals, especially the tiger, is prominent. But a further analysis of this composite religion does not fall within my province.

There is little to be said about the history of Buddhism in Annam, but native tradition places its introduction as late as the tenth century[1]. Buddhist temples usually contain a statue of Phat To[2] who is reported to have been the first adherent of the faith and to have built the first pagoda. He was the tutor of the Emperor Li-Thai-To who came to the throne in 1009. Phat-To may therefore have been active in the middle of the tenth century and this agrees with the statement that the Emperor Dinh Tien-Hoang Dê (968–979) was a fervent Buddhist who built temples and did his best to make converts[3]. One Emperor, Li Hué-Ton, abdicated and retired to a monastery.

The Annals of Annam[4] record a discussion which took place before the Emperor Thai-Tôn (1433–1442) between a Buddhist and a sorcerer. Both held singularly mixed beliefs but recognized the Buddha as a deity. The king said that he could not decide between the two sects, but gave precedence to the Buddhists.

[1] Pelliot (Meou-Tseu, traduit et annoté, in *T'oung Pao*, vol. XIX. p. 1920) gives reasons for thinking that Buddhism was prevalent in Tonkin in the early centuries of our era, but, if so, it appears to have decayed and been reintroduced. Also at this time Chiao-Chih may have meant Kuang-tung.

[2] Diguet, *Les Annamites*, p. 303.

[3] Maybon et Russier, *L'Histoire d'Annam*, p. 45.

[4] Dumoutier, *Les Cultes Annamites*, p. 58.

CHAPTER XLIX

TIBET

Introductory

The religion of Tibet and Mongolia, often called Lamaism, is probably the most singular form of Buddhism in existence and has long attracted attention in Europe on account of its connection with politics and its curious resemblance to the Roman Church in ritual as well as in statecraft. The pontiffs and curia of Lhasa emulated the authority of the medieval papacy, so that the Mings and Manchus in China as well as the British in India had to recognize them as a considerable power.

Tibet had early relations with Kashmir, Central Asia and China which may all have contributed something to its peculiar civilization, but its religion is in the main tantric Buddhism imported from Bengal and invigorated from time to time by both native and Indian reformers. But though almost every feature of Lamaism finds a parallel somewhere in India, yet too great insistence on its source and historical development hardly does justice to the originality of the Tibetans. They borrowed a foreign faith wholesale, but still the relative emphasis which they laid on its different aspects was something new. They had only a moderate aptitude for asceticism, meditation and metaphysics, although they manfully translated huge tomes of Sanskrit philosophy, but they had a genius for hierarchy, discipline and ecclesiastical polity unknown to the Hindus. Thus taking the common Asiatic idea that great and holy men are somehow divine, they made it the principle of civil and sacerdotal government by declaring the prelates of the church to be deities incarnate. Yet in strange contrast to these practical talents, a certain innate devilry made them exaggerate all the magical, terrifying and demoniac elements to be found in Indian Tantrism.

The extraordinary figures of raging fiends which fill Tibetan shrines suggest at first that the artists simply borrowed and made more horrible the least civilized fancies of Indian sculpture, yet the majesty of Tibetan architecture (for, judging by the photographs of Lhasa and Tashilhumpo, it deserves no less a name) gives another impression. The simplicity of its lines and the solid, spacious walls unadorned by carving recall Egypt rather than India and harmonize not with the many-limbed demons but with the calm and dignified features of the deified priests who are also portrayed in these halls.

An atmosphere of mystery and sorcery has long hung about the mountainous regions which lie to the north of India. Hindus and Chinese alike saw in them the home of spirits and wizards, and the grand but uncanny scenery of these high plateaux has influenced the art and ideas of the natives. The climate made it natural that priests should congregate in roomy strongholds, able to defy the cold and contain the stores necessary for a long winter, and the massive walls seem to imitate the outline of the rocks out of which they grow. But the strange shapes assumed by mists and clouds, often dyed many colours by the rising or setting sun, suggest to the least imaginative mind an aerial world peopled by monstrous and magical figures. At other times, when there is no fog, distant objects seem in the still, clear atmosphere to be very near, until the discovery that they are really far away produces a strange feeling that they are unreal and unattainable.

In discussing this interesting faith, I shall first treat of its history and then of the sacred books on which it professes to be based. In the light of this information it will be easier to understand the doctrines of Lamaism and I shall finally say something about its different sects, particularly as there is reason to think that the strength of the Established Church, of which the Grand Lama is head, has been exaggerated.

CHAPTER L

TIBET (*continued*)

HISTORY

IT is generally stated that Buddhism was first preached in Tibet at the instance of King Srong-tsan-gam-po[1] who came to the throne in 629 A.D. Some legendary notices of its earlier appearance[2] will bear the natural interpretation that the Tibetans (like the Chinese) had heard something about it from either India or Khotan before they invited instructors to visit them[3].

At this time Tibet played some part in the politics of China

[1] Tibetan orthography Sroṅ-btsan-sgam-po. It is hard to decide what is the best method of representing Tibetan words in Latin letters:

(*a*) The orthography differs from the modern pronunciation more than in any other language, except perhaps English, but it apparently represents an older pronunciation and therefore has historical value. Also, a word can be found in a Tibetan dictionary only if the native spelling is faithfully reproduced. On the other hand readers interested in oriental matters know many words in a spelling which is a rough representation of the modern pronunciation. It seems pedantic to write bKaḫ-ḫgyur and ḫBras-spuṅs when the best known authorities speak of Kanjur and Debung. On the whole, I have decided to represent the commoner words by the popular orthography as given by Rockhill, Waddell and others while giving the Tibetan spelling in a foot-note. But when a word cannot be said to be well known even among Orientalists I have reproduced the Tibetan spelling.

(*b*) But it is not easy to reproduce this spelling clearly and consistently. On the whole I have followed the system used by Sarat Chandra Das in his Dictionary. It is open to some objections, as, for instance, that the sign h has more than one value, but the more accurate method used by Grünwedel in his *Mythologie* is extremely hard to read. My transcription is as follows in the order of the Tibetan consonants.

k, kh, g, ṅ, c, ch, j, ny.
t, th, d, n, p, ph, b, m.
ts, ths, ds, w.
zh, z, ḫ, y.
r, l, ś, s, h.

Although tsh is in some respects preferable to represent an aspirated ts, yet it is liable to be pronounced as in the English words *hat shop*, and perhaps ths is on the whole better.

[2] See Waddell, *Buddhism of Tibet*, p. 19.

[3] It has been argued (*e.g.*, *J.R.A.S.*, 1903, p. 11) that discoveries in Central Asia indicate that Tibetan civilization and therefore Tibetan Buddhism are older than is generally supposed. But recent research shows that Central Asian MSS. of even the eighth century say little about Buddhism, whatever testimony they may bear to civilization.

and northern India. The Emperor Harsha and the T'ang Emperor T'ai Tsung exchanged embassies but a second embassy sent from China arrived after Harsha's death and a usurper who had seized the throne refused to receive it. The Chinese with the assistance of the kings of Tibet and Nepal dethroned him and carried him off captive. There is therefore nothing improbable in the story that Srong-tsan-gam-po had two wives, who were princesses of Nepal and China respectively. He was an active ruler, warlike but progressive, and was persuaded by these two ladies that Buddhism was a necessary part of civilization. According to tradition he sent to India a messenger called Thonmi Sanbhota, who studied there for several years, adapted a form of Indian writing to the use of his native language and translated the Karaṇḍa Vyûha. Recent investigators however have advanced the theory that the Tibetan letters are derived from the alphabet of Indian origin used in Khotan and that Sanbhota made its acquaintance in Kashmir[1]. Though the king and his two wives are now regarded as the first patrons of Lamaism and worshipped as incarnations of Avalokita and Târâ, it does not appear that his direct religious activity was great or that he built monasteries. But his reign established the foundations of civilization without which Buddhism could hardly have flourished, he to some extent unified Central Tibet, he chose the site of Lhasa as the capital and introduced the rudiments of literature and art. But after his death in 650 we hear little more of Buddhism for some decades.

About 705 King Khri-gtsug-lde-btsan is said to have built monasteries, caused translations to be made, and summoned monks from Khotan. His efforts bore little fruit, for no Tibetans were willing to take the vows, but the edict of 783 preserved in Lhasa mentions his zeal for religion, and he prepared the way for Khri-sroṅ-lde-btsan in whose reign Padma-Sambhava, the real founder of Lamaism, arrived in Tibet[2].

[1] See Hoernle MS. *Remains found in E. Turkestan*, 1916, pp. xvii ff., and Francke, *Epig. Ind.* XI. 266 ff., and on the other side Laufer in *J.A.O.S.* 1918, pp. 34 ff. There is a considerable difference between the printed and cursive forms of the Tibetan alphabet. Is it possible that they have different origins and that the former came from Bengal, the latter from Khotan?

[2] There were some other streams of Buddhism, for the king had a teacher called Sântarakshita who advised him to send for Padma-Sambhava and Padma-Sambhava was opposed by Chinese bonzes.

This event is said to have occurred in 747 and the epoch is noticeable for two reasons. Firstly Tibet, which had become an important military power, was now brought into contact both in peace and war with China and Central Asia. It was predominant in the Tarim Basin and ruled over parts of Ssŭ-chuan and Yunnan. China was obliged to pay tribute and when it was subsequently refused the Tibetans sacked the capital, Chang-an. In 783 China made a treaty of peace with Tibet. The king was the son of a Chinese princess and thus blood as well as wide experience disposed him to open Tibet to foreign ideas. But in 747 relations with China were bad, so he turned towards India and invited to his Court a celebrated Pandit named Śântarakshita, who advised him to send for Padma-Sambhava.

Secondly this was the epoch when Amogha flourished in China and introduced the Mantrayâna system or Chên Yen. This was the same form of corrupt Buddhism which was brought to Tibet and was obviously the dominant sect in India in the eighth century. It was pliant and amalgamated easily with local observances, in China with funeral rites, in Tibet with demonolatry.

At this time Padma-Sambhava was one of the most celebrated exponents of Tantric Buddhism, and in Tibet is often called simply the Teacher (Guru or Mahâcârya). His portraits represent him as a man of strongly marked and rather angry features, totally unlike a conventional monk. A popular account of his life[1] is still widely read and may contain some grains of history, though the narrative as a whole is fantastic. It describes him as born miraculously in Udyâna but as having studied at Bodhgaya and travelled in many regions with the intention of converting all the world. According to his plan, the conversion of his native land was to be his last labour, and when he had finished his work in Tibet he vanished thither miraculously. Thus Udyâna is not represented as the source and home of Tantric Buddhism but as being like Tibet a land of

[1] The Pad-ma-than-yig. It indicates some acquaintance with Islam and mentions Hulugu Khan. See *T'oung Pao*, 1896, pp. 526 ff. See for a further account Grünwedel, *Mythologie*, p. 47, Waddell, *Buddhism*, p. 380, and the Tibetan text edited and translated by Laufer under the title *Der Roman einer tibetischen Königin*, especially pp. 250 ff. Also E. Schlagintweit, "Die Lebensbeschreibung von Padma-Sambhava," *Abhand. k. bayer. Akad.* I. CL. xxi. Bd. ii. Abth. 419–444, and *ib.* I. CL. xxii. Bd. iii. Abth. 519–576.

magic and mystery but, like Tibet, needing conversion: both are disposed to welcome Tantric ideas but those ideas are elaborated by Padma-Sambhava not in Udyâna but in Bengal which from other sources we know to have been a centre of Tantrism.

Some other points of interest in these legends may be noticed. Padma-Sambhava is not celibate but is accompanied by female companions. He visits many countries which worship various deities and for each he has a new teaching suited to its needs. Thus in Tibet, where the older religion consisted of defensive warfare against the attacks of evil spirits[1], he assumes the congenial character of a victorious exorcist, and in his triumphant progress subdues local demons as methodically as if he were suppressing the guerilla warfare of native tribes. He has new revelations called Terma which he hides in caves to be discovered by his successors. These revelations are said to have been in an unknown language[2]. Those at present existing are in Tibetan but differ from the canonical scriptures in certain orthographical peculiarities. The legend thus admits that Padma-Sambhava preached a non-celibate and magical form of Buddhism, ready to amalgamate with local superstitions and needing new revelations for its justification.

He built the monastery of Samye[3] about thirty miles from Lhasa on the model of Odantapuri in Bengal. Śântarakshita became abbot and from this period dates the foundation of the order of Lamas[4]. Mara (Thse Ma-ra) was worshipped as well as the Buddhas, but however corrupt the cultus may have been, Samye was a literary centre where many translations were made. Among the best known translators was a monk from Kashmir named Vairocana[5]. It would appear however that

[1] Much of Chinese popular religion has the same character. See De Groot, *Religious System of China*, vol. VI. pp. 929, 1187. "The War against Spectres."

[2] Both he and the much later Saskya Pandita are said to have understood the Bru-zha language, for which see *T'oung Pao*, 1908, pp. 1–47.

[3] Or bSam-yas. See Waddell, *Buddhism*, p. 266, for an account of this monastery at the present day.

[4] The Tibetan word bLama means upper and is properly applicable to the higher clergy only though commonly used of all.

[5] He was temporarily banished owing to the intrigues of the Queen, who acted the part of Potiphar's wife, but he was triumphantly restored. A monk called Vairocana is also said to have introduced Buddhism into Khotan from Kashmir, but at a date which though uncertain must be considerably earlier than this.

there was considerable opposition to the new school not only from the priests of the old native religion but from Chinese Buddhists[1].

Numerous Tibetan documents discovered in the Tarim basin[2] date from this period. The absence in them of Buddhist personal names and the rarity of direct references to Buddhism indicate that though known in Tibet it was not yet predominant. Buddhist priests (ban-de) are occasionally mentioned but the title Lama has not been found. The usages of the Bonpo religion seem familiar to the writers and there are allusions to religious struggles.

When Padma-Sambhava vanished from Tibet, the legend says that he left behind him twenty-five disciples, all of them magicians, who propagated his teaching. At any rate it flourished in the reign of Ralpachan (the grandson of Khri-sroṅ-lde-btsan). Monasteries multiplied and received land and the right to collect tithes. To each monk was assigned a small revenue derived from five tenants and the hierarchy was reorganized[3]. Many translators were at work in this period and a considerable part of the present canon was then rendered into Tibetan. The king's devotion to Buddhism was however unpopular and he was murdered[4] apparently at the instigation of his brother and successor Lang-dar-ma[5], who endeavoured to extirpate Lamaism. Monasteries were destroyed, books burnt, Indian monks were driven out of the country and many Lamas were compelled to become hunters or butchers. But the persecution only lasted three years[6], for the wicked king was assassinated by a Lama who has since been canonized by the Church and the incident of his murder or punishment is still acted in the mystery plays performed at Himis and other monasteries.

After the death of Lang-dar-ma Tibet ceased to exist as a

[1] See *Journal of Buddhist Text Society*, 1893, p. 5. I imagine that by Hoshang Mahâyâna the followers of Bodhidharma are meant.

[2] *J.R.A.S.* 1914, pp. 37–59.

[3] See Rockhill, *Life of the Buddha*, p. 225.

[4] Various dates are given for his death, ranging from 838 to 902. See Rockhill (*Life of the Buddha*), p. 225, and Bushell in *J.R.A.S.* 1880, pp. 440 ff. But the treaty of 822 was made in his reign.

[5] g Lan-dar-ma.

[6] But see for other accounts Rockhill (*Life of the Buddha*), p. 226. According to Csoma de Körös's tables the date of the persecution was 899.

united kingdom and was divided among clans and chieftains. This was doubtless connected with the collapse of Tibetan power in the Tarim basin, but whether as effect or cause it is hard to say. The persecution may have had a political motive: Lang-dar-ma may have thought that the rise of monastic corporations, and their right to own land and levy taxes were a menace to unity and military efficiency. But the political confusion which followed on his death was not due to the triumphant restoration of Lamaism. Its recovery was slow. The interval during which Buddhism almost disappeared is estimated by native authorities as from 73 to 108 years, and its subsequent revival is treated as a separate period called phyi-dar or later diffusion in contrast to the sṅa-dar or earlier diffusion. The silence of ecclesiastical history during the tenth century confirms the gravity of the catastrophe[1]. On the other hand the numerous translations made in the ninth century were not lost and this indicates that there were monasteries to preserve them, for instance Samye.

At the beginning of the eleventh century we hear of foreign monks arriving from various countries. The chronicles[2] say that the chief workers in the new diffusion were La-chen, Lo-chen, the royal Lama Yeśes Ḥod and Atîśa. The first appears to have been a Tibetan but the pupil of a teacher who had studied in Nepal. Lo-chen was a Kashmiri and several other Kashmiri Lamas are mentioned as working in Tibet. Yeśes Ḥod was a king or chieftain of mṄa-ris in western Tibet who is said to have been disgusted with the debased Tantrism which passed as Buddhism. He therefore sent young Lamas to study in India and also invited thence learned monks. The eminent Dharmapâla, a monk of Magadha who was on a pilgrimage in Nepal, became his tutor. Yeśes Ḥod came to an unfortunate end. He was taken captive by the Raja of Garlog, an enemy of Buddhism, and died in prison. It is possible that this Raja was the ruler of Garhwal and a Mohammedan. The political history of the period is far from clear, but evidently there were numerous Buddhist schools in Bengal, Kashmir and Nepal and numerous learned monks ready to take up their residence in Tibet. This

[1] See the chronological table in Waddell's *Buddhism*, p. 576. Not a single Tibetan event is mentioned between 899 and 1002.

[2] Pag Som Jon Zang. Ed. Sarat Chandra Das, p. 183.

readiness has been explained as due to fear of the rising tide of Islam, but was more probably the result of the revival of Buddhism in Bengal during the eleventh century. The most illustrious of these pandits was Atîśa[1] (980–1053), a native of Bengal, who was ordained at Odontapuri and studiod in Burma[2]. Subsequently he was appointed head of the monastery of Vikramaśîla and was induced to visit Tibet in 1038[3]. He remained there until his death fifteen years later; introduced a new calendar and inaugurated the second period of Tibetan Buddhism which is marked by the rise of successive sects described as reforms. It may seem a jest to eall the teaching of Atîśa a reform, for he professed the Kâlacakra, the latest and most corrupt form of Indian Buddhism, but it was doubtless superior in discipline and coherency to the native superstitions mixed with debased tantrism, which it replaced.

As in Japan during the eleventh and twelfth centuries many monasteries were founded and grew in importance, and what might have happened in Japan but for the somewhat unscrupulous prescience of Japanese statesmen actually did happen in Tibet. Among the numerous contending chiefs none was pre-eminent: the people were pugnacious but superstitious. They were ready to build and respect when built the substantial structures required to house monastic communities during the rigorous winter. Hence the monasteries became the largest and safest buildings in the land, possessing the double strength of walls and inviolability. The most important was the Sakya monastery. Its abbots were of royal blood and not celibate, and this dynasty of ecclesiastical statesmen practically ruled Tibet at a critical period in the history of eastern Asia and indeed of the world, namely, the conquests of Chinggiz[4] and the rise of the Mongol Empire.

[1] Or Dîpaṅkara Śrîjñâna. See for a life of him *Journal of Buddhist Text Society*, 1893, "Indian Pandits in Tibet," pp. 7 ff.

[2] Suvarṇadvîpa, where he studied, must be Thaton and it is curious to find that it was a centre of tantric learning.

[3] From 1026 onwards see the chronological tables of Sum-pa translated by Sarat Chandra Das in *J.A.S.B.* 1889, pp. 40–82. They contain many details, especially of ecclesiastical biography. The Tibetan system of computing time is based on cycles of sixty years beginning it would seem not in 1026 but 1027, so that in many dates there is an error of a year. See Pelliot, *J.A.* 1913, I. 633, and Laufer, *T'oung Pao*, 1913, 569.

[4] Or Jenghiz Khan. The form in the text seems to be the more correct.

There is no evidence that Chinggiz was specially favourable to Buddhism. His principle was one King and one God[1] and like other princes of his race he thought of religions not as incompatible systems but as different methods of worship of no more importance than the different languages used in prayer. The destruction wrought by the Mongol conquerors has often been noticed, but they had also an ample, unifying temper which deserves recognition. China, Russia and Persia all achieved a unity after the Mongol conquest which they did not possess before, and though this unification may be described as a protest and reaction, yet but for the Mongols and their treatment of large areas as units it would not have been possible. The Mings could not have united China before the Yüan dynasty as they did after it.

In spite of some statements to the contrary there is no proof that the early Mongols invaded or conquered central Tibet, but Khubilai subdued the eastern provinces and through the Lamaist hierarchy established a special connection between Tibet and his dynasty. This connection began even in the time of his predecessor, for the head Lama of the Sakya monastery commonly known as Sakya Pandita (or Sa-skya-pan-cen) was summoned to the Mongol Court in 1246–8, and cured the Emperor of an illness[2]. This Lama was a man of great learning and influence. He had received a double education both secular and religious, and was acquainted with foreign languages. The favourable impression which he created no doubt facilitated the brilliant achievements of his nephew and successor, who is commonly known as Bashpa or Pagspa[3].

Khubilai Khan was not content with the vague theism of Central Asia and wished to give his rude Mongols a definite religion with some accessories of literature and manners. Confucianism was clearly too scholastic for a fighting race and we may surmise that he rejected Christianity as distant and

[1] Tegri or Heaven. This monotheism common to the ancient Chinese, Turks and Mongols did not of course exclude the worship of spirits.

[2] Guyuk was Khagan at this time but the *Mongol History of Sanang Setsen* (Schmidt, p. 3) says that the Lama was summoned by the Khagan Godan. It seems that Godan was never Khagan, but as an influential prince he may have sent the summons.

[3] ḥPhagspa (corrupted in Mongol to Bashpa) is merely a title equivalent to Âyra in Sanskrit. His full style was ḥPhagspa bLo-gros-rgyal-mthsan.

unimportant, Mohammedanism as inconveniently mixed with politics. But why did he prefer Lamaism to Chinese Buddhism? The latter can hardly have been too austerely pure to suit his ends, and Tibetan was as strange as Chinese to the Mongols. But the Mongol Court had already been favourably impressed by Tibetan Lamas and the Emperor probably had a just feeling that the intellectual calibre of the Mongols and Tibetans was similar and also that it was politic to conciliate the uncanny spiritual potentates who ruled in a land which it was difficult to invade. At any rate he summoned the abbot of Sakya to China in 1261 and was initiated by him into the mysteries of Lamaism[1].

It is said that before Pagspa's birth the God Ganeśa showed his father all the land of Tibet and told him that it would be the kingdom of his son. In later life when he had difficulties at the Chinese Court Mahâkâla appeared and helped him, and the mystery which he imparted to Khubilai is called the Hevajravaśitâ[2]. These legends indicate that there was a large proportion of Sivaism in the religion first taught to the Mongols, larger perhaps than in the present Lamaism of Lhasa.

The Mongol historian Sanang Setsen relates[3] that Pagspa took a higher seat than the Emperor when instructing him and on other occasions sat on the same level. This sounds improbable, but it is clear that he enjoyed great power and dignity. In China he received the title of Kuo-Shih or instructor of the nation and was made the head of all Buddhists, Lamaists and other. In Tibet he was recognized as head of the Church and tributary sovereign, though it would appear that the Emperor named a lay council to assist him in the government and also had a commissioner in each of the three provinces. This was a good political bargain and laid the foundations of Chinese influence in a country which he could hardly have subdued by force.

Pagspa was charged by the Emperor to provide the Mongols with an alphabet as well as a religion. For this purpose he used

[1] By abhiśekha or sprinkling with water.

[2] Vaśitâ is a magical formula which compels the obedience of spirits or natural forces. Hevajra (apparently the same as Heruka) is one of the fantastic beings conceived as manifestations of Buddhas and Bodhisattvas made for a special purpose, closely corresponding, as Grünwedel points out, to the manifestations of Śiva.

[3] Schmidt's edition, p. 115.

a square form of the Tibetan letters[1], written not in horizontal but in vertical lines. But the experiment was not successful. The characters were neither easy to write nor graceful, and after Pagspa's death his invention fell into disuse and was replaced by an enlarged and modified form of the Uigur alphabet. This had already been employed for writing Mongol by Sakya Pandita and its definitive form for that purpose was elaborated by the Lama Chos-kyi-ḥod-zer in the reign of Khubilai's successor. This alphabet is of Aramaic origin, and had already been utilized by Buddhists for writing religious works, so its application to Mongol was merely an extension of its general currency in Asia[2].

Pagspa also superintended the preparation of a new edition of the Tripitaka, not in Mongol but in Chinese. Among the learned editors were persons acquainted with Sanskrit, Chinese, Tibetan and Uigur. An interesting but natural feature of this edition is that it notes whether the various Chinese texts are found in the Tibetan Canon or not.

Khubilai further instituted a bureau of fine arts, the head of which was a Lama called Aniko, skilled in both sculpture and painting. He and his Chinese pupil Liu Yüan introduced into Peking various branches of Tibetan art such as Buddhist images of a special type, ornamental ironwork and gold tapestry. The Chinese at this period appear to have regarded Tibetan art as a direct importation from India[3]. And no doubt Tibetan art was founded on that of Nepal which in its turn came from Bengal. Miniature painting is a characteristic of both. But in later times the individuality of Tibet, shown alike in its monstrous deities and its life-like portraits of Lamas, imposed itself on Nepal. Indian and Tibetan temples are not alike. In the former there is little painting but the walls and pillars are covered with a superabundance of figures carved in relief: in Tibet pictures and painted banners are the first thing to strike the eye, but carvings in relief are rare.

It is hard to say to what extent the Mongols beyond such

[1] It is given in Isaac Taylor's *The Alphabet*, vol. II. p. 336. See also *J.R.A.S.* 1910, pp. 1208–1214.

[2] *E.g.* see the Tisastvustik, a sûtra in a Turkish dialect and Uigur characters found at Turfan and published in *Bibliotheca Buddhica*, XII.

[3] See Kokka, No. 311, 1916, *Tibetan Art in China*.

parts of northern China as felt the direct influence of the imperial court were converted to Lamaism. At any rate their conversion was only temporary for, as will be related below, a reconversion was necessary in the sixteenth century. It looks as if the first growth of Mongolian Buddhism was part of a political system and collapsed together with it. But so long as the Yüan dynasty reigned, Lamaist influence was strong and the downfall of the Yüan was partly caused by their subservience to the clergy and extravagant expenditure on religious buildings and ceremonies. After the departure of Pagspa, other Lamas held a high position at the Court of Peking such as Chos-kyi-ḥod-zer and gYuṅ-ston rDo-rje-dpal. The latter was a distinguished exponent of the Kâlacakra system and the teacher of the historian Bu-ston who is said to have arranged the Tibetan Canon.

Although the Yüan dynasty heaped favours upon priests and monasteries, it does not appear that religion flourished in Tibet during the fourteenth century for at the end of that period the grave abuses prevalent provoked the reforming zeal of Tsong-kha-pa. From 1270 to 1340 the abbots of Sakya were rulers of both Church and State, and we hear that in 1320 they burned the rival monastery of Dikung. The language of Sanang Setsen implies that each abbot was appointed or invested by the Emperor[1] and their power declined with the Yüan dynasty. Other monasteries increased in importance and a chief known as Phagmodu[2] succeeded, after many years of fighting, in founding a lay dynasty which ruled parts of Tibet until the seventeenth century.

In 1368 the Ming superseded the Yüan. They were not professed Buddhists to the same extent and they had no preference for Lamaism but they were anxious to maintain good relations with Tibet and to treat it as a friendly but vassal state. They accorded imperial recognition (with an implication of suzerainty) to the dynasty of Phagmodu and also to the abbots of eight monasteries. Though they were doubtless glad to see Tibet a divided and contentious house, it does not appear that they interfered actively in its affairs or did more than recognize

[1] *Sanang Setsen*, p. 121. The succession of the Sakya abbots is not clear but the primacy continued in the family. See Köppen, II. p. 105.

[2] Strictly speaking a place-name.

the *status quo*. In the time of Khubilai the primacy of Sakya was a reality: seventy years later Sakya was only one among several great monasteries.

The advent of the Ming dynasty coincided with the birth of Tsong-kha-pa[1], the last reformer of Lamaism and organizer of the Church as it at present exists. The name means the man of the onion-bank, a valley near the monastery of Kumbum in the district of Amdo, which lies on the western frontiers of the Chinese province of Kansu. He became a monk at the age of seven and from the hair cut off when he received the tonsure is said to have sprung the celebrated tree of Kumbum which bears on its leaves wondrous markings[2]. According to the legend, his birth and infancy were attended by miracles. He absorbed instruction from many teachers and it has been conjectured that among them were Roman Catholic missionaries[3]. In early manhood he proceeded to Tibet and studied at Sakya, Dikung and finally at Lhasa. His reading convinced him that Lamaism as he found it was not in harmony with the scriptures, so with the patronage of the secular rulers and the support of the more earnest clergy he successfully executed a thorough and permanent work of reform. This took visible shape in the Gelugpa, the sect presided over by the Grand Lama, which acquired such paramount importance in both ecclesiastical and secular matters that it is justly termed the Established Church of Tibet. It may also be conveniently termed the Yellow Church, yellow being its special colour particularly for hats and girdles, in opposition to the red or unreformed sects which use red for the same purpose. Tsong-kha-pa's reforms took two principal lines. Firstly he made monastic discipline stricter, insisting on celibacy and frequent services of prayer: secondly he greatly reduced, although he did not annihilate, the tantric and magical element

[1] The Tibetan orthography is bTsoṅ (or Tsoṅ)-kha-pa. He was called rJe-rin-po-che bLo-bzaṅ-grags-pa in Tibetan and Ârya-mahâratna Sumatikîrti in Sanskrit. The Tibetan orthography of the monastery is sKu-ḥbum or hundred thousand pictures. See, for accounts of his life, Sarat Chandra Das in *J.A.S.B.* 1882, pp. 53–57 and 127. Huth, *Buddhismus in der Mongolei*, II. pp. 175 ff.

[2] There is some difference of statement as to whether these markings are images of Tsong-kha-pa or Tibetan characters. Huc, though no Buddhist, thought them miraculous. See his *Travels in Tartary*, vol. II. chap. II. See also Rockhill, *Land of the Lamas*, p. 67, and Filchner, *Das Kloster Kumbum*, chap. VI.

[3] But the tradition mentioned by Huc that he was instructed by a long-nosed stranger from the west, has not been found in any Tibetan biography.

in Lamaism. These principles were perpetuated by an effective organization. He himself founded the great monastery of Gandan near Lhasa and became its first abbot. During his lifetime or shortly afterwards were founded three others, Sera and Depung both near Lhasa and Tashilhunpo[1]. He himself seems to have ruled simply in virtue of his personal authority as founder, but his nephew and successor Geden-dub[2] claimed the same right as an incarnation of the divine head of the Church, and this claim was supported by a hierarchy which became overwhelmingly powerful.

Tsong-kha-pa died in 1417 and is said to have been transfigured and carried up into heaven while predicting to a great crowd the future glories of his church. His mortal remains, however, preserved in a magnificent mausoleum within the Gandan monastery, still receive great veneration.

Among his more eminent disciples were Byams-chen-chos-rje and mKhas-grub-rje who in Tibetan art are often represented as accompanying him. The first played a considerable part in China. The Emperor Yung-Lo sent an embassy to invite Tsong-kha-pa to his capital. Tsong-kha-pa felt unable to go himself but sent his pupil to represent him. Byams-chen-chos-rje was received with great honour[3]. The main object of the Ming Emperors was to obtain political influence in Tibet through the Lamas but in return the Lamas gained considerable prestige. The Kanjur was printed in China (1410) and Byams-chen-chos-rje and his disciples were recognized as prelates of the whole Buddhist Church within the Empire. He returned to Tibet laden with presents and titles and founded the monastery of Serra in 1417. Afterwards he went back to China and died there at the age of eighty-four.

[1] Tibetan orthography writes dGaḥ-ldan, Se-ra, hBras-spuns and bKra-śis-Lhun-po. dGaḥ-ldan, the happy, is a translation of the Sanskrit Tushita or Paradise. Tsong-kha-pa's reformed sect was originally called dGaḥ-lugs-pa or those who follow the way of dGaḥ-ldan. But this possibly suggested those who pursue pleasure and the name was changed to dGe-lugs-pa or those of the virtuous order.

[2] dGe-'dun grub.

[3] He was not the same as Ha-li-ma (see p. 277) of whom more is heard in Chinese accounts. Ha-li-ma or Karma was fifth head of the Karma-pa school and was invited on his own merits to China where he died in 1426 or 1414. See Huth, *l.c.* vol. I. p. 109 and vol. II. p. 171. Also Köppen, *die Rel. des Buddha*, II. 107. Byams-chen-chos-rje was invited as the representative of Tsong-ka-pa. See Huth, *l.c.* vol. I. p. 120, vol. II. p. 129.

mKhas-grub-rje founded the monastery of Tashilhunpo and became its abbot, being accepted as an incarnation of the Buddha Amitâbha. He was eighth in the series of incarnations, which henceforth were localized at Tashilhunpo, but the first is said to have been Subhûti, a disciple of Gotama, and the second Mañjuśrîkirti, king of the country of Śambhala[1].

The abbot of Tashilhunpo became the second personage in the ecclesiastical and political hierarchy. The head of it was the prelate commonly known as the Grand Lama and resident at Lhasa. Geden-dub[2], the nephew of Tsong-kha-pa, is reckoned by common consent as the first Grand Lama (though he seems not to have borne the title) and the first incarnation of Avalokita as head of the Tibetan Church[3]. The Emperor Ch'êng Hua (1365–1488) who had occasion to fight on the borders of Tibet confirmed the position of these two sees as superior to the eight previously recognized and gave the occupants a patent and seal. From this time they bore the title of rGyal-po or king.

It was about this time that the theory of successive incarnations[4] which is characteristic of Lamaism was developed and defined. At least two ideas are combined in it. The first is that divine persons appear in human form. This is common in Asia from India to Japan, especially among the peoples who have accepted some form of Hindu religion. The second is that in a school, sect or church there is real continuity of life. In the unreformed sects of Tibet this was accomplished by the simple principle of heredity so that celibacy, though undeniably correct, seemed to snap the thread. But it was reunited by the theory that a great teacher is reborn in the successive occupants of his chair. Thus the historian Târanâtha is supposed to be reborn in the hierarchs of Urga. But frequently the hereditary soul is identified with a Buddha or Bodhisattva, as in the great

[1] See for a list of the Lamas of Tashilhunpo and their lives *J.A.S.B.* 1882, pp. 15–52. The third incarnation was Abhayakara Gupta, a celebrated Bengali Pandit who flourished in the reign of Râmapâla. This appears to have been about 1075–1115, but there is considerable discrepancy in the dates given.

[2] See for his life *J.A.S.B.* 1882, p. 24.

[3] Tsong-kha-pa is not reckoned in this series of incarnations, for firstly he was regarded as an incarnation of Mañjuśrî and secondly Geden-dub was born before his death and hence could not represent the spirit which dwelt in him.

[4] Tibetan sPrul-pa, Mongol Khubilghan. Both are translations of the Sanskrit Nirmâna and the root idea is not incarnation but transformation in an illusive form.

incarnations of Lhasa and Tashilhunpo. This dogma has obvious advantages. It imparts to a Lamaist see a dignity which the papacy cannot rival but it is to the advantage of the Curia rather than of the Pope for the incarnate deity of necessity succeeds to his high office as an infant, is in the hands of regents and not unfrequently dies when about twenty years of age. These incarnations are not confined to the great sees of Tibet. The heads of most large monasteries in Mongolia claim to be living Buddhas and even in Peking there are said to be six.

The second Grand Lama[1] enjoyed a long reign, and set the hierarchy in good order, for he distinguished strictly clerical posts, filled by incarnations, from administrative posts. He was summoned to Peking by the Emperor, but declined to go and the somewhat imperative embassy sent to invite him was roughly handled. His successor, the third Grand Lama bSod-nams[2], although less noticed by historians than the fifth, perhaps did more solid work for the holy see of Lhasa than any other of his line for he obtained, or at least received, the allegiance of the Mongols who since the time of Khubilai had woefully back-slidden from the true faith.

As mentioned above, the conversion of the Mongols to Buddhism took place when their capital was at Peking and chiefly affected those resident in China. But when the Yüan dynasty had been dethroned and the Mongols, driven back into their wilds, were frequently at war with China, they soon relapsed into their original superstitions. About 1570 Altan[3]

[1] The following list of Grand Lamas is taken from Grünwedel's *Mythologie*, p. 206. Their names are followed by the title rGya-mThso and in many cases the first part of the name is a title.

1. dGe-ḥdun-dub, 1391–1478.
2. dGe-ḥdun, 1479–1541.
3. bSod-nams, 1543–1586.
4. Yon-tan, 1587–1614.
5. Ṅag-dbaṅ bLo-bzaṅ, 1617–1680.
6. Rin-chen Thsaṅs-dbyaṅs, 1693–1703.
7. bLo-bzaṅ sKal-dan, 1705–1758.
8. bLo-bzaṅ ḥJam-dpal, 1759–1805.
9. bLo-bzaṅ Luṅ-rtogs, 1806–1815.
10. bLo-bzaṅ Thsul-khrims, 1817–1837.
11. bLo-bzaṅ dGe-dmu, 1838–1855.
12. bLo-bzaṅ Phrin-las, 1856–1874.
13. Ṅag-dbaṅ bLo-bzaṅ Thub-ldam, 1875.

[2] See for an account of his doings Sanang Setsen, chap. IX. Huth, *Geschichte*, II. pp. 200 ff. Köppen, II. pp. 134 ff. It would appear that about 1545 north-western Tibet was devastated by Mohammedans from Kashgar. See Waddell, *Buddhism*, p. 583.

[3] Also known as Yenta or Anda. See, for some particulars about him, Parker in N. China Branch of *R.A.S.* 1913, pp. 92 ff.

Khagan, the powerful chief of the Tümed, became more nearly acquainted with Tibet, since some Lamas captured in a border fray had been taken to his Court. After causing China much loss and trouble he made an advantageous peace and probably formed the idea (which the Manchus subsequently proved to be reasonable) that if the Mongols were stronger they might repeat the conquests of Khubilai. The Ming dynasty was clearly decadent and these mysterious priests of Tibet appeared to be on the upward grade[1]. They might help him both to become the undisputed chief of all the Mongol tribes and also to reconquer Peking. So he sent an embassy to invite the Grand Lama's presence, and when it was not successful he followed it with a second.

The Grand Lama then accepted and set out on his travels with great pomp. According to the story he appeared to the astonished Mongols in the guise of Avalokita with four arms (of which two remained folded on his breast) and the imprint of his horse's hoofs showed the six mystic syllables *om mani padme hum*. These wonders are so easily explicable that they may be historical.

A great congregation was held near Lake Kokonor and Sanang Setsen records an interesting speech made there by one of his ancestors respecting the relations of Church and State, which he compared with the sun and moon. The Lama bestowed on the Khagan high sounding titles and received himself the epithet Dalai or Talai, the Mongol word for sea, signifying metaphorically vast extent and profundity[2]. This is the origin of the name Dalai Lama by which the Tibetan pontiff is commonly known to Europeans. The hierarchy was divided into four classes parallel to the four ranks of Mongol nobles: the use of meat was restricted and the custom of killing men and horses at funerals forbidden. The observance of Buddhist festivals was made compulsory and native idols were destroyed, but the

[1] Naturally the narrative is not told without miraculous embellishment, including the singular story that Altan who suffered from the gout used to put his feet every month into the ripped up body of a man or horse and bathe them in the warm blood. Avalokita appeared to him when engaged in this inhuman cure and bade him desist and atone for his sins.

[2] In Tibetan rGya-mThso. Compare the Chinese expression hai liang (sea measure) meaning capacious or broad minded. The Khagan received the title of lHai thsaṅs-pa chen-po equivalent to Divyamahâbrahmâ.

deities which they represented were probably identified with others in the new pantheon. The Grand Lama specially recommended to the Mongols the worship of the Blue Mahâkâla, a six armed representation of Śiva standing on a figure of Ganeśa, and he left with them a priest who was esteemed an incarnation of Mañjuśrî, and for whom a temple and monastery were built in Kuku-khoto.

His Holiness then returned to Tibet, but when Altan Khagan died in 1583 he made a second tour in Mongolia in order to make sure of the allegiance of the new chiefs. He also received an embassy from the Chinese Emperor Wan-Li, who conferred on him the same titles that Khubilai had given to Pagspa. The alliance between the Tibetans and Mongols was naturally disquieting to the Ming dynasty and they sought to minimize it by showing extreme civility to the Lamas.

This Grand Lama died at the age of forty-seven, and it is significant that the next incarnation appeared in the Mongol royal house, being a great-grandson of Altan Khagan. Until he was fourteen he lived in Mongolia and when he moved to Lhasa a Lama was appointed to be his vicar and Primate of all Mongolia with residence at Kuren or Urga[1]. The prelates of this line are considered as incarnations of the historian Târanâtha[2]. In common language they bear the name of rJe-btsun-dam-pa but are also called Maidari Khutuktu, that is incarnation of Maitreya. About this time the Emperor of China issued a decree, which has since been respected, that these hierarchs must be reborn in Tibet, or in other words that they must not reappear in a Mongol family for fear of uniting religion and patriotism too closely.

Lozang[3], the fifth Grand Lama, is by common consent the most remarkable of the pontifical line. He established the right of himself and his successors—or, as he might have said, of himself in his successive births—to the temporal and ecclesiastical sovereignty of Tibet: he built the Potala and his dealings with

[1] The correct Mongol names of this place seem to be Örgö and Kürä. The Lama's name was bSam-pa rGya-mThso.

[2] He finished his history in 1608 and lived some time longer so that bSam-pa rGya-mThso cannot have been an incarnation of him.

[3] This is an accepted abbreviation of his full name Ṅag-dbaṅ bLo-zaṅ rGya-mThso. Ṅag-dbaṅ is an epithet meaning eloquent.

the Mongols and the Emperor of China are of importance for general Asiatic history.

From the seventeenth century onwards there were four factors in Tibetan politics.

1. The Gelugpa or Yellow Church, very strong but anxious to become stronger both by increasing its temporal power and by suppressing other sects. Its attitude towards Chinese and Mongols showed no prejudice and was dictated by policy.

2. The Tibetan chiefs and people, on the whole respectful to the Yellow Church but not single-hearted nor forgetful of older sects: averse to Chinese and prone to side with Mongols.

3. The Mongols, conscious of their imperfect civilization and anxious to improve themselves by contact with the Lamas. As a nation they wished to repeat their past victories over China, and individual chiefs wished to make themselves the head of the nation. People and princes alike respected all Lamas.

4. The Chinese, apprehensive of the Mongols and desirous to keep them tranquil, caring little for Lamaism in itself but patiently determined to have a decisive voice in ecclesiastical matters, since the Church of Lhasa had become a political power in their border lands.

Lo-zang was born as the son of a high Tibetan official about 1616 and was educated in the Depung monastery under the supervision of Chos-kyi-Gyal-tsan, abbot of Tashilhunpo and a man of political weight. The country was then divided into Khamdo, Wu and Tsang, or Eastern, Central and Western Tibet, and in each province there ruled a king of the Phagmodu dynasty. In Central Tibet, and specially at Lhasa, the Gelugpa was the established church and accepted by the king but in the other provinces there was much religious strife and the older sects were still predominant. About 1630 the regent of Tsang captured Lhasa and made himself sovereign of all Tibet. He was a follower of the Sakya sect and his rule was a menace to the authority and even to the existence of the Yellow Church, which for some years suffered much tribulation. When the young Grand Lama grew up, he and his preceptor determined to seek foreign aid and appealed to Gushi Khan[1]. This prince

[1] The name is variously written Gushi, Gushri, Gus'ri, etc., and is said to stand for Guruśrī. The name of the tribe also varies: Oirad and Oegeled are both found.

was a former pupil of Chos-kyi-Gyal-tsan and chief of the Oelöt, the ancestors of the Kalmuks and other western tribes, but then living near Kokonor. He was a staunch member of the Yellow Church and had already made it paramount in Khamdo which he invaded in 1638. He promptly responded to the appeal, invaded Tibet, took the regent prisoner, and, after making himself master of the whole country, handed over his authority to the Grand Lama, retaining only the command of his Mongol garrisons. This arrangement was advantageous to both parties. The Grand Lama not only greatly increased his ecclesiastical prestige but became a temporal sovereign of considerable importance. Gushi, who had probably no desire to reside permanently in the Snow Land, received all the favours which a grateful Pope could bestow on a king and among the superstitious Mongols these had a real value. Further the Oelöt garrisons which continued to occupy various points in Tibet gave him a decisive voice in the affairs of the country, if there was ever a question of using force.

The Grand Lamas had hitherto resided in the Depung monastery but Lo-zang now moved to the hill of Marpori, the former royal residence and began to build on it the Potala[1] palace which, judging from photographs, must be one of the most striking edifices in the world, for its stately walls continue the curves of the mountain side and seem to grow out of the living rock. His old teacher was given the title of Panchen Rinpoche, which has since been borne by the abbots of Tashilhunpo, and the doctrine that the Grand Lamas of Lhasa and Tashilhunpo are respectively incarnations of Avalokita and Amitâbha was definitely promulgated[2].

The establishment of the Grand Lama as temporal ruler of Tibet coincided with the advent of the Manchu dynasty (1644). The Emperor and the Lama had everything to gain from friendly relations and their negotiations culminated in a visit which

[1] So called from the sacred hill in India on which Avalokita lives. The origin of the name is doubtful but before the time of Hsüan Chuang it had come to be applied to a mountain in South India.

[2] Some European authorities consider that Lo-zang invented this system of incarnations. Native evidence seems to me to point the other way, but it must be admitted that if he was the first to claim for himself this dignity it would be natural for him to claim it for his predecessors also and cause ecclesiastical history to be written accordingly.

Lo-zang paid to Peking in 1652–3. He was treated as an independent sovereign and received from the Emperor a long title containing the phrase "Self-existent Buddha, Universal Ruler of the Buddhist faith." In return he probably undertook to use his influence with the Mongols to preserve peace and prevent raids on China.

After his return to Tibet, he appears to have been a real as well as a nominal autocrat for his preceptor and Gushi Khan both died, and the new Manchu dynasty had its hands full. His chief adviser was the Desi[1] or Prime Minister, supposed to be his natural son. In 1666 the great Emperor K'ang-hsi succeeded to the throne: and shortly afterwards the restlessness of the Mongol Princes began to inspire the Chinese Court with apprehension. In 1680 Lo-zang died but his death was a state secret. It was apparently known in Tibet and an infant successor was selected but the Desi continued to rule in Lo-zang's name and even the Emperor of China had no certain knowledge of his suspected demise but probably thought that the fiction of his existence was the best means of keeping the Mongols in order. It was not until 1696 that his death and the accession of a youth named Thsang-yang Gya-thso were made public.

But the young Grand Lama, who owing to the fiction that his predecessor was still alive had probably been brought up less strictly than usual, soon began to inspire alarm at Peking for he showed himself wilful and intelligent. He wrote love songs which are still popular and his licentious behaviour was quite out of harmony with the traditions of the holy see. In 1701, under joint pressure from the Chinese and Mongols, he resigned his ecclesiastical rights and handed over the care of the Church to the abbot of Tashilhunpo, while retaining his position as temporal ruler. But the Chinese still felt uneasy and in 1705 succeeded in inducing him to undertake a journey to Peking. When he got as far as Mongolia he died of either dropsy or assassination. The commander of the Oelöt garrisons in Tibet was a friend of the Chinese, and at once produced a new Grand Lama called Yeśes, a man of about twenty-five, who claimed to be the true reincarnation of the fifth Grand Lama, the pretensions of the dissolute youth who had just died being thus set aside. It suited the Chinese to deal with an adult, who

[1] sDe-srid.

could be made to understand that he had received and held his office only through their good will, but the Tibetans would have none of this arrangement. They clung to the memory of the dissolute youth and welcomed with enthusiasm the news that he had reappeared in Li-t'ang as a new-born child, who was ultimately recognized as the seventh Grand Lama named Kalzang. The Chinese imprisoned the infant with his parents in the monastery of Kumbum in Kansu and gave all their support to Yeśes. For the better control of affairs in Lhasa two Chinese Agents were appointed to reside there with the Manchu title of Amban[1].

But the Tibetans would not accept the rule of Yeśes and in 1717 the revolutionary party conspired with the Oelöt tribes of Ili to put Kalzang on the throne by force. The troops sent to take the holy child were defeated by the Chinese but those which attacked Lhasa were completely successful. Yeśes abdicated and the city passed into the possession of the Mongols. The Chinese Government were greatly alarmed and determined to subdue Tibet. Their first expedition was a failure but in 1720 they sent a second and larger, and also decided to install the youthful Kalzang as Grand Lama, thus conciliating the religious feelings of the Tibetans. The expedition met with little difficulty and the result of it was that China became suzerain of the whole country. By imperial edict the young Grand Lama was recognized as temporal ruler, the four ministers or Kalön were given Chinese titles, and garrisons were posted to keep open the road from China. But the Tibetans were still discontented. In 1727 a rebellion, instigated it was said by the family of the Grand Lama, broke out, and the Prime Minister was killed. This rising was not permanently successful and the Chinese removed the Grand Lama to the neighbourhood of their frontier. They felt however that it was unsafe to give ground for suspicion that they were ill-treating him and in 1734 he was reinstated in the Potala. But the dislike of the Tibetans for Chinese supervision was plain. In 1747 there was another rebellion. The population of Lhasa rose and were assisted by Oelöt troops who suddenly arrived on the scene. Chinese rule was saved only by the heroism of the two Chinese Agents, who invited the chief conspirators to a meeting and engaged them in personal combat. They lost their

[1] It is said that all Ambans were Manchus.

own lives but killed the principal rebels. The Chinese then abolished the office of Prime Minister, increased their garrison and gave the Agents larger powers.

About 1758 the Grand Lama died and was succeeded by an infant called Jambal. The real authority was wielded by the Panchen Lama who acted as regent and was so influential that the Emperor Ch'ien-Lung insisted on his visiting Peking[1]. He had a good reception and probably obtained some promise that the government of Tibet would be left more in the hands of the Church but he died of smallpox in Peking and nothing came of his visit except a beautiful tomb and an epitaph written by the Emperor. After his death a new complication appeared. The prelates of the Red Church encouraged an invasion of the Gurkhas of Nepal in the hope of crushing the Yellow Church. The upshot was that the Chinese drove out the Gurkhas but determined to establish a more direct control. The powers of the Agents were greatly increased and not even the Grand Lama was allowed the right of memorializing the throne, but had to report to the Agents and ask their orders.

In 1793 Ch'ien-Lung issued a remarkable edict regulating the appearance of incarnations which, as he observed, had become simply the hereditary perquisites of certain noble Mongol families. He therefore ordered that when there was any question of an incarnation the names of the claimants to the distinction should be written on slips of paper and placed in a golden bowl: that a religious service should be held and at its close a name be drawn from the bowl in the presence of the Chinese Agents and the public. The child whose name should be drawn was to be recognized as the true incarnation but required investiture by an imperial patent.

A period of calm followed, and when the Grand Lama died in 1804 the Tibetans totally neglected this edict and selected a child born in eastern Tibet. The Chinese Court, desirous of avoiding unnecessary trouble, approved[2] the choice on the ground that the infant's precocious ability established his divine

[1] See E. Ludwig, *The visit of the Teshoo Lama to Peking*, Tientsin Press, 1904. See also *J.A.S.B.* 1882, pp. 29–52.

[2] See the curious edict of Chia Ch'ing translated by Waddell in *J.R.A.S.* 1910, pp. 69 ff. The Chinese Government were disposed to discredit the sixth, seventh and eighth incarnations and to pass straight from the fifth Grand Lama to the ninth.

character but when he died in 1815 and an attempt was made to repeat this irregularity, a second edict was published, insisting that the names of at least three candidates must be placed in the golden urn and that he whose name should be first drawn must be Grand Lama. This procedure was followed but the child elected by the oracle of the urn died before he was twenty and another infant was chosen as his successor in 1838. As a result the Lama who was regent acquired great power and also unpopularity. His tyranny caused the Tibetans to petition the Emperor; and His Majesty sent a new Agent to investigate his conduct. Good reason was shown for holding him responsible for the death of the Grand Lama in 1838 and for other misdeeds. The Emperor then degraded and banished him and, what is more singular, forbade him to reappear in a human reincarnation.

The reigns of Grand Lamas in the nineteenth century have mostly been short. Two others were selected in 1858 and 1877 respectively. The latter who is the present occupant of the post was the son of a Tibetan peasant: he was duly chosen by the oracle of the urn and invested by the Emperor. In 1893 he assumed personal control of the administration and terminated a regency which seems to have been oppressive and unpopular. The British Government were anxious to negotiate with him about Sikhim and other matters, but finding it impossible to obtain answers to their communications sent an expedition to Lhasa in 1904. The Grand Lama then fled to Urga, in which region he remained until 1907. In the autumn of 1908 he was induced to visit Peking where he was received with great ceremony but, contrary to the precedent established when the fifth Grand Lama attended Court, he was obliged to kneel and kotow before the Empress Dowager. Neither could he obtain the right to memorialize the throne, but was ordered to report to the Agents. The Court duly recognized his religious position. On the birthday of the Empress he performed a service for her long life, at which Her Majesty was present. It was not wholly successful, for a week or two later he officiated at her funeral. At the end of 1908 he left for Lhasa. He visited India in 1910 but this created dissatisfaction at Peking. In the same year[1]

[1] See for a translation of this curious decree, *North China Herald* of March 4th, 1910.

a decree was issued deposing him from his spiritual as well as his temporal powers and ordering the Agents to seek out a new child by drawing lots from the golden urn. This decree was probably *ultra vires* and certainly illogical, for if the Chinese Government recognized the Lama as an incarnation, they could not, according to the accepted theory, replace him by another incarnation before his death. And if they regarded him as a false incarnation, they should have ordered the Agents to seek out not a child but a man born about the time that the last Grand Lama died. At any rate the Tibetans paid no attention to the decree.

The early deaths of Grand Lamas in the nineteenth century have naturally created a presumption that they were put out of the way and contemporary suspicion accused the regent in 1838. There is no evidence that the deaths of the other three were regarded as unnatural but the earlier Grand Lamas as well as the abbots of Tashilhunpo lived to a good age. On the other hand the Grand Lamas of Urga are said to die young. If the pontiffs of some lines live long and those of others die early, the inference is not that the life of a god incarnate is unhealthy but that in special cases special circumstances interfere with it, and on the whole there are good grounds for suspecting foul play. But it is interesting to note that most Europeans who have made the acquaintance of high Lamas speak in praise of their character and intelligence. So Manning (the friend of Charles Lamb) of the ninth Grand Lama (1811), Bogle of the Tashi Lama about 1778, Sven Hedin of his successor in 1907, and Waddell of the Lama Regent in 1904.

The above pages refer to the history of Lamaism in Tibet and Mongolia. It also spread to China, European Russia, Ladak, Sikhim and Bhutan. In China it is confined to the north and its presence is easily explicable by the genuine enthusiasm of Khubilai and the encouragement given on political grounds by the Ming and Manchu dynasties. Further, several Mongol towns such as Kalgan and Kuku-khoto are within the limits of the eighteen provinces.

The Kalmuks who live in European Russia are the descendants of tribes who moved westwards from Dzungaria in the seventeenth century. Many of them left Russia and returned to the east in 1771, but a considerable number remained behind, chiefly between the Volga and the Don, and the population professing Lamaism there is now reckoned at about 100,000.

Buddhist influences may have been at work in Ladak from an early period. In later times it can be regarded as a dependency of Tibet, at any rate for ecclesiastical purposes, for it formed part of Tibet until the disruption of the kingdom in the tenth century and it subsequently accepted the sovereignty of Lhasa in religious and sometimes in political matters. Concerning the history of Bhutan, I have been able to discover but little. The earliest known inhabitants are called Tephu and the Tibetans are said to have conquered them about 1670. Lamaism probably entered the country at this time, if not earlier[1]. At any rate it must have been predominant in 1774 when the Tashi Lama used his good offices to conclude peace between the Bhutiyas and the East India Company. The established church however is not the Gelugpa but the Dugpa, which is a subdivision of the Kar-gyu-pa. There are two rulers in Bhutan, the Dharmarâja or spiritual and the Debrâja or temporal. The former is regarded as an incarnation of the first class, though it is not clear of what deity[2].

The conversion of Sikhim is ascribed to a saint named Latsün Ch'embo, who visited it about 1650 with two other Lamas. They associated with themselves a native chief whom they ordained as a Lama and made king. All four then governed Sikhim. Though Latsün Ch'embo is represented as a friend of the fifth Grand Lama, the two sects at present found in Sikhim are the Nying-ma-pa, the old unreformed style of Lamaism, and the Karmapa, a branch of the Kar-gyu-pa, analogous to the Dugpa of Bhutan. The principal monasteries are at Pemiongchi (Peme-yang-tse) and Tashiding[3].

[1] In the List of the Bhutan Hierarchs given by Waddell (*Buddhism*, p. 242) it is said that the first was contemporary with the third Grand Lama, 1543–1580.

[2] According to Waddell (*Buddhism*, p. 242) he appears to be a rebirth of Dupgani Sheptun, a Lama greatly respected by the Tibetan invaders of Bhutan. For some account of the religion of Bhutan in the early 19th century, see the article by Davis in *T.R.A.S.* vol. II. 1830, p. 491.

[3] The fullest account of Sikhimese Buddhism is given by Waddell in the *Gazetteer of Sikhim*, 1894. See also Rémy, *Pèlerinage au Monastère de Pemmiontsi*, 1880; Silacara "Buddhism in Sikkim," *Buddhist Review*, 1916, p. 97.

CHAPTER LI

TIBET (*continued*)

The Canon

Tibet is so remote and rude a land that it is a surprise to learn that it has a voluminous literature and further that much of this literature, though not all, is learned and scholastic. The explanation is that the national life was most vigorous in the great monasteries which were in close touch with Indian learning. Moreover Tibetan became to some extent the Latin of the surrounding countries, the language of learning and religion.

For our purpose the principal works are the two great collections of sacred and edifying literature translated into Tibetan and known as the Kanjur and Tanjur[1]. The first contains works esteemed as canonical, including Tantras. The second is composed of exegetical literature and also of many treatises on such subjects as medicine, astronomy and grammar[2]. The two together correspond roughly speaking to the Chinese Tripitaka, but are more bulky. The canonical part is smaller but the commentaries and miscellaneous writings more numerous. There are also other differences due to the fact that the great literary epoch of Tibet was in the ninth century, whereas nearly three-quarters of the Chinese Tripitaka had been translated before that date. Thus the Kanjur appears to contain none[3] of the Abhidhamma works of the Hînayâna and none of the great Nikâyas as such, though single sûtras are entered in the catalogues as separate books. Further there is only one version of the Vinaya whereas the Chinese Tripitaka has five, but there

[1] The Tibetan orthography is bKaḥ-ḥgyur (the translated command) and bsTan-ḥgyur (the translated explanation). Various spellings are used by European writers such as Kah-gyur, Kandjour, Bkahgyur, etc. Waddell writes Kah-gyur and Tän-gyur.

[2] Though this distinction seems to hold good on the whole, yet it is not strictly observed. Thus the work called Udâna and corresponding to the Dhammapada is found in both the Kanjur and Tanjur.

[3] Nanjio's catalogue states that a great many Abhidharma works in Chinese agree with Tibetan, but their titles are not to be found in Csoma's analysis of the Kanjur. They may however be in the Tanjur, which is less fully analyzed.

are several important Tantras which are wanting in Chinese. The Tibetan scriptures reflect the late Buddhism of Magadha when the great books of the Hinayanist Canon were neglected, though not wholly unknown, and a new tantric literature was flourishing exuberantly.

The contents of the Kanjur and Tanjur are chiefly known by analyses and indices[1], although several editions and translations of short treatises have been published[2]. The information obtained may be briefly summarized as follows.

The Kanjur in its different editions consists of one hundred or one hundred and eight volumes, most of which contain several treatises, although sometimes one work, for instance the Vinaya, may fill many volumes. The whole collection is commonly divided into seven parts[3].

I. The Dulva[4], equivalent to the Vinaya. It is stated to be the Mûla-sarvâstivâda Vinaya, and so far as any opinion can be formed from the small portions available for comparison, it agrees with the Chinese translation of Kumârajîva and also (though with some difference in the order of paragraphs) with the Sanskrit Prâtimoksha found at Kucha[5]. It is longer and more mixed with narrative than the corresponding Pali code.

[1] Analysis of the Dulva, etc., four parts in *Asiatic Researches*, vol. xx. 1836, by A. Csoma Körösi. Translated into French by Feer, *Annales du Musée Guimet*, tome 2me, 1881. *Index des Kanjur*, herausgegeben von I. J. Schmidt (in Tibetan), 1845. Huth, *Verzeichnis der in Tibetischen Tanjur, Abtheilung mDo, erhaltenen Werke* in *Sitzungsber. Berlin. Akad.* 1895. P. Cordier, *Catalogue du fonds Tibétain de la Bibliothèque Nationale.* Beckh, *Verzeichnis der tibetischen Handscriften der K. Bibliothek zu Berlin*, 1 Abth., Kanjur, 1914. This is an analysis of the edition in 108 volumes, whereas Csoma de Körös and Feer analyzed the edition in 100 volumes. The arrangement of the two editions is not quite the same. See too Pelliot's review of Beckh's catalogue in *J.A.* 1914, II. pp. 111 ff. See also Waddell, "Tibetan Manuscripts and Books" in *Asiatic Quarterly*, July, 1912, pp. 80–113, which, though not an analysis of the Canon, incidentally gives much information.

[2] *E.g.* Udâna (=Dhammapada) by Rockhill, 1892 (transl.), and Beckh (text 1911) Madhyamakâvatâra: de la Vallée Poussin, 1912, Madyamika-śâstra: Max Walleser, 1911 (transl.), Citralakshana, ed. and trans. Laufer, 1913; Feer, *Fragments extraits du Kanjur*, *Annales du Musée Guimet*, tome 5me, 1883.

[3] It is also sometimes divided into three Pitakas. When this is done, the Dulva is the Vinaya P., the Śer-chin is the Abhidharma P., and all the other works whether Sûtras or Tantras are classed together as the Sûtra P.

[4] ḥDul-ba.

[5] See Nanjio, Nos. 1115–1119, 1122, 1132–4. Rockhill, *Prâtimoksha Sûtra selon la version Tibétaine*, 1884. Huth, *Tibetische Version der Naihsargikaprâyaccittikadharmâs*, 1891. Finot and Hüber, "Le Prâtimoksa des Sarvâstivadins," *J.A.* 1913, II. p. 465.

II. The second division is known as Śer-chin[1], corresponding to the Prajñâ-pâramitâ and in the estimation of the Tibetans to the Abhidharma. It is said to have been first collected by Kâśyapa and to represent the teaching delivered by the Buddha in his fifty-first year. This section appears to contain nothing but versions, longer or shorter, of the Prajñâ-pâramitâ, the limit of concentration being reached by a text in which the Buddha explains that the whole of this teaching is comprised in the letter A. As in China and Japan, the Vajracchedikâ (rDo-rJe-gCod-pa) is very popular and has been printed in many editions.

III. The third division is called Phal-chen, equivalent to Avataṃsaka. Beckh treats it as one work in six volumes without subdivisions. Feer gives forty-five subdivisions, some of which appear as separate treatises in the section of the Chinese Tripitaka called Hua Yen[2].

IV. The fourth division called dKon-brtsegs or Ratnakûṭa agrees closely with the similar section of the Chinese Tripitaka but consists of only forty-eight or forty-five sûtras, according to the edition[3].

V. The fifth section is called mDo, equivalent to Sûtra. In its narrower sense mDo means sûtras which are miscellaneous in so far as they do not fall into special classes, but it also comprises such important works as the Lalita-vistara, Lankâvatâra and Saddharma-puṇḍarîka. Of the 270 works contained in this section about 90 are *prima facie* identical with works in the Ching division of the Chinese Tripitaka and probably the identity of many others is obscured by slight changes of title. An interesting point in the mDo is that it contains several sûtras translated from the Pali[4], viz. Nos. 13–25 of vol. xxx,

[1] Strictly Śer-phyin.

[2] Waddell in *Asiatic Quarterly*, 1912, xxxiv. p. 98, renders the title as Vata sangha, which probably represents Avataṃsaka. Sarat Chandra Das, *sub voce*, says Phal-chen-sde-pa = Mahâsanghika.

[3] The statements of Nanjio as to "deest in Tibetan" are not quite accurate as regards the edition in 108 volumes. Compare his catalogue with Beckh's.

[4] This statement made by such scholars as Feer (*Anal. du Kanjour*, p. 288) and Rockhill (*Udâna*, p. x) is of great weight, but I have not found in their works any quotation from the Tibetan translation saying that the original language was not Sanskrit and the titles given by Feer are in Sanskrit not in Pali. I presume it is not meant that the Tibetan text is a translation from a Sanskrit text which corresponds with the Pali text known to us. In Beckh's catalogue of the edition in

nine of which are taken from the collection known as Paritta. The names and dates of the translators are not given but the existence of these translations probably indicates that a knowledge of Pali lingered on in Magadha later than is generally supposed. It will also be remembered that about A.D. 1000, Atîśa though a Tantrist, studied in Burma and presumably came in contact with Pali literature. Rockhill notes that the Tanjur contains a commentary on the Lotus Sûtra written by Prithivibandhu, a monk from Ceylon, and Pali manuscripts have been found in Nepal[1]. It is possible that Sinhalese may have brought Pali books to northern India and given them to Tibetans whom they met there.

VI. The sixth division is called Myaṅg-ḥdas or Nirvâṇa, meaning the description of the death of the Buddha which also forms a special section in the Chinese Tripitaka. Here it consists of only one work, apparently corresponding to Nanjio 113[2].

VII. The seventh and last section is called rGyud[3] or Tantra. It consists of twenty-two volumes containing about 300 treatises. Between thirty and forty are *prima facie* identical with treatises comprised in the Chinese Tripitaka and perhaps further examination might greatly increase the number, for the titles of these books are often long and capable of modification. Still it is probable that the major part of this literature was either deliberately rejected by the Chinese or was composed at a period when religious intercourse had become languid between India and China but was still active between India and Tibet. From the titles it appears that many of these works are Brahmanic in spirit rather than Buddhist; thus we have the Mahâgaṅapati-tantra, the Mahâkâla-tantra, and many others. Among the better known Tantras may be mentioned the Ârya-mañjuśrî-mûla-tantra and the Śrî-Guhya Samaja[4], both highly praised by Csoma de Körös: but perhaps more important is the Tantra

108 volumes the same titles occur in the Prajñâ-pâramitâ section, but without any statement that the works are translated from Pali. See Beckh, p. 12, and Feer, pp. 288 ff.

[1] *Life of the Buddha*, p. 224, and *J.R.A.S.* 1899, p. 422.

[2] There is another shorter sûtra on the same subject in the mDo section of the Kanjur. Feer, p. 247. In the edition of 108 volumes, the whole section is incorporated in the mDo, Beckh, p. 33.

[3] The word seems originally to mean string or chain.

[4] Apparently not the same as the Tathâgata-Guhyaka *alias* Guhya Samagha described by R. Mitra, *Sk. Bud. Lit.* p. 261.

on which the Kâlacakra system is founded. It is styled Paramâdibuddha-uddhṛita-śrî-kâlacakra and there is also a compendium giving its essence or Hṛidaya.

The Tanjur is a considerably larger collection than the Kanjur for it consists of 225 volumes but its contents are imperfectly known. A portion has been catalogued by Palmyr Cordier. It is known to contain a great deal of relatively late Indian theology such as the works of Aśvaghosha, Nâgârjuna, Asanga, Vasubandhu, and other Mahayanist doctors, and also secular literature such as the Meghadûta of Kâlidâsa, together with a multitude of works on logic, rhetoric, grammar and medicine[1]. Some treatises, such as the Udâna[2] occur in both collections but on the whole the Tanjur is clearly intended as a thesaurus of exegetical and scientific literature, science being considered, as in the middle ages of Europe, to be the handmaid of the Church. Grammar and lexicography help the understanding of scripture: medicine has been of great use in establishing the influence of the Lamas: secular law is or should be an amplification of the Church's code: history compiled by sound theologians shows how the true faith is progressive and triumphant: art and ritual are so near together that their boundaries can hardly be delimitated. Taking this view of the world, we find in the Tanjur all that a learned man need know[3].

It is divided into two parts, mDo (Sûtra) and rGyud (Tantra), besides a volume of hymns and an index. The same method of division is really applicable to the Kanjur, for the Tibetan Dulva is little more than a combination of Sûtras and Jâtakas and sections two, three, four and six of the Kanjur are collections of special sûtras. In both compilations the tantric section appears to consist of later books expounding ideas which are further from the teaching of Gotama than the Mahayanist sûtras.

[1] See notices of these in four articles by Satiścandra Vidyâbhûshana in *J.A.S. Beng.* 1907.

[2] *I.e.* the Dhammapada.

[3] Huth's analysis of vols. 117–124 of the Tanjur (*Sitzungsber. Kön. Preuss. Akad. Wiss. Berlin*, 1895) shows that they contain *inter alia* eight works on Sanskrit literature and philology besides the Meghadûta, nine on medicine and alchemy with commentaries, fourteen on astrology and divination, three on chemistry (the composition of incense), eight on gnomic poetry and ethics, one encyclopædia, six lives of the Saints, six works on the Tibetan language and five on painting and fine art. Cordier gives further particulars of the medical works in *B.E.F.E.O.* 1903, p. 604. They include a veterinary treatise.

To the great majority of works in both collections is prefixed a title which gives the Sanskrit name first in transcription and then in translation, for instance "In Sanskrit Citralakshana: in Tibetan Ri-moi-mthsan-ñid[1]." Hence there is usually no doubt as to what the Tibetan translations profess to be. Sometimes however the headings are regrettably brief. The Vinaya for instance appears to be introduced with that simple superscription and with no indication of the school or locality to which the text belonged.

Although the titles of books are given in Sanskrit, yet all Indian proper names which have a meaning (as most have) are translated. Thus the name Droṇa (signifying a measure and roughly equivalent to such an English name as Dr Bushell) is rendered by Bre-bo, a similar measure in Tibetan. This habit greatly increases the difficulty of reading Tibetan texts. The translators apparently desired to give a Tibetan equivalent for every word and even for every part of a word, so as to make clear the etymology as well as the meaning of the sacred original. The learned language thus produced must have varied greatly from the vernacular of every period but its slavish fidelity makes it possible to reconstruct the original Sanskrit with tolerable certainty.

I have already mentioned the presence of translations from the Pali. There are also a few from the Chinese[2] which appear to be of no special importance. One work is translated from the Bru-za language which was perhaps spoken in the modern Gilgit[3] and another from the language of Khotan[4]. Some works in the Kanjur have no Sanskrit titles and are perhaps original compositions in Tibetan. The Tanjur appears to contain many such.

But the Kanjur and Tanjur as a whole represent the literature approved by the late Buddhism of Bengal and certain resemblances to the arrangement of the Chinese Tripitaka

[1] See title in Laufer's edition.

[2] See Feer, *l.c.* for instance, pp. 287, 248.

[3] See Feer, *l.c.* p. 344, and Laufer, "Die Bruza Sprache" in *T'oung Pao*, 1908. It is said that King Ru-che-tsan of Brusha or Dusha translated (? what date) the Mûla-Tantra and Vyâkhyâ-Tantra into the language of his country See *J.A.S.B.* 1882, p. 12. Beckh states that four works have titles in Chinese, one in Bruža and one in Tartar (Hor-gyi-skad-du).

[4] Laufer, *ibid.* p. 4.

suggest that not only new sûtras but new classifications of sûtras had replaced the old Pitakas and Âgamas. The Tibetan Canon being later than the Chinese has lost the Abhidharma and added a large section of Tantras. But both canons recognize the divisions known as Prajñâ-pâramitâ, Ratnakûṭa, Avatamsaka, and Mahâparinirvâṇa as separate sections. The Ratnakûṭa is clearly a collection of sûtras equivalent to a small Nikâya[1]. This is probably also true of the voluminous Prajñâ-pâramitâ in its various editions, but the divisions are not commonly treated as separate works except the Vajracchedikâ. The imperfectly known Avatamsaka Sûtra appears to be a similar collection, since it is described as discourses of the Buddha pronounced at eight assemblies[2]. The Mahâparinirvâṇa Sûtra though not nominally a collection of sûtras (at least in its Pali form) is unique both in subject and structure, and it is easy to understand why it was put in a class by itself.

The translation of all this literature falls into three periods, (i) from the seventh century until the reign of Ralpachan in the ninth, (ii) the reign of Ralpachan, and (iii) some decades following the arrival of Atîśa in 1038. In the first period work was sporadic and the translations made were not always those preserved in the Kanjur. Thonmi Sanbhota, the envoy sent to India in 616 is said to have made renderings of the Karaṇḍa Vyûha and other works (but not those now extant) and three items in the Tanjur are attributed to him[1]. The existence of early translations has been confirmed by Stein who discovered at Endere a Tibetan manuscript of the Śalistambhasûtra which is said not to be later than about 740 A.D.[3] The version now found in the Kanjur appears to be a revision and expansion of this earlier text.

A few translations from Chinese texts are attributed to the reign of Khri-gtsug-lde-btsan (705–755) and Rockhill calls attention to the interesting statement that he sent envoys to India who learned Sanskrit books by heart and on their return reproduced them in Tibetan. If this was a common habit, it may be one of the reasons why Tibetan translations sometimes

[1] See Nanjio, No. 87, and Feer, *l.c.* pp. 208–212, but the two works may not be the same. The Tibetan seems to be a collection of 45 sûtras.

[2] Rockhill, *l.c.* p. 212.

[3] Stein, *Ancient Khotan*, pp. 426–9 and App. B. See also Pelliot in *B.E.F.E.O.* 1908, pp. 507 ff.

show differences in length, arrangement and even subject matter when compared with Sanskrit and Chinese versions bearing the same name. During the reign of Khri-sroṅ-lde-btsan and the visit of Padma-Sambhava (which began in A.D. 747 according to the traditional chronology) the number of translations began to increase. Two works ascribed to the king and one to the saint are included in the canon, but the most prolific writer and translator of this period was Kamalaśîla. Seventeen of his original works are preserved in the Tanjur and he translated part of the Ratnakûṭa. The great period of translation—the Augustan age of Tibet as it is often called—was beginning and a solid foundation was laid by composing two dictionaries containing a collection of Sanskrit Buddhist terms[1].

The Augustus of Tibet was Ralpachan who ruled in the ninth century, though Tibetan and Chinese chronicles are not in accord as to his exact date. He summoned from Kashmir and India many celebrated doctors who with the help of native assistants took seriously in hand the business of rendering the canon into Tibetan. They revised the existing translations and added many more of their own. It is probable that at least half of the works now contained in the Kanjur and Tanjur were translated or revised at this time and that the additions made later were chiefly Tantras (rGyud). On the other hand it is also probable that many tantric translations ascribed to this epoch are really later[2]. The most prolific of Ralpachan's translators was Jinamitra, a pandit of Kashmir described as belonging to the Vaibhâshika school, who translated a large part of the Vinaya and many sûtras[3]. Among the many Tibetan assistants Ye'ses-sde and Dpal-brTsegs are perhaps those most frequently mentioned. These Tibetan translators are commonly described by the title of Lo-tsa-va. As in China the usual procedure seems to have been that an Indian pandit explained the sacred text to a native. The latter then wrote it down, but whereas in China he generally paraphrased whatever he understood, in Tibet he endeavoured to reproduce it with laborious fidelity.

[1] The Mahâvyutpatti edited by Minayeff in *Bibl. Buddhica* and an abridgement.

[2] According to Feer (*Analyse*, p. 325) Tibetan historians state that at this epoch kings prohibited the translation of more than a few tantric works.

[3] Numerous works are also ascribed to Sarvajñâdeva and Dharmaka, both of Kashmir, and to the Indian Vidyâkaraprabhâ and Surendrabodhi.

The language of the translations, which is now the accepted form of literary Tibetan, appears to have been an archaic and classical dialect even in the early days of Tibetan Buddhism, for it is not the same as the language of the secular documents dating from the eighth century, which have been found in Turkestan, and it remains unchanged in the earliest and later translations. It may possibly have been the sacred language of the Bonpo[1] priests.

As narrated in the historical section Buddhism suffered a severe reverse with the death of Ralpachan and it was nearly a century before a revival began. This revival was distinctly tantric and the most celebrated name connected with it is Atîśa. According to Csoma de Körös's chronology the Kâlacakra system was introduced in 1025 and the eminent translator bLo-ldan-shes-rab[2], a follower of Atîśa, was born in 1057. It is thus easy to understand how during the eleventh century a great number of tantric works were translated and the published catalogues of the Kanjur and Tanjur confirm the fact, although the authors of the translations are not mentioned so often as in the other divisions. To Atîśa is ascribed the revision of many works in the Tantra section of the Kanjur and twenty others composed by him are found in the Tanjur[3]. It is said that the definitive arrangement of the two collections as we know them was made by Bu-ston early in the thirteenth century[4]. The Kanjur (but not the Tanjur) was translated into Mongol by order of Khutuktu Khagan (1604–1634) the last prince of the Chakhar Mongols but a printed edition was first published by the Emperor K'ang-Hsi. Though it is said that the Tanjur was translated and printed by order of Ch'ien-Lung, the statement is doubtful. If such a translation was made it was probably partial and in manuscript[5].

[1] See Francke in *J.R.A.S.* 1914, pp. 56–7.

[2] See Pander, *Pantheon*, No. 30.

[3] Waddell, *Buddhism*, p. 36, gives a list of them.

[4] It appears to me that there is some confusion between Brom-ston, a disciple of Atîśa, who must have flourished about 1060 and Bu-ston, who was born in 1288. Grünwedel says that the latter is credited with the compilations of the Kanjur and Tanjur, but Rockhill (*Life of the Buddha*, p. 227) describes Bu-ston as a disciple of Atîśa.

[5] See Huth, *Geschichte des Budd. in der Mongolei*, 291, and Laufer, "Skizze der Mongolischen Literatur" (in *Keleti Szemle*, 1907), p. 219. Also Pelliot in *J.A.* 1914, II. pp. 112–3.

Manuscripts are still extensively copied and used in Tibet but the Kanjur has been printed from wooden blocks for the last 200 years. There are said to be two printing presses, the older at Narthang near Tashilhunpo where an edition in 100 volumes is produced and another at Derge in the eastern province. This edition is in 108 volumes. An edition was also printed at Peking by order of K'ang-Hsi in red type and with a preface by the Emperor himself[1].

Besides the canon the Tibetans possess many religious or edifying works composed in their own language[2]. Such are the Padma-than-yig, or life of Padma-Sambhava, the works of Tsong-kha-pa, and several histories such as those of Bu-ston, Târanâtha, Sum-pa, and hJigs-med-nam-mkha[3], biographies of Lamas without number, accounts of holy places, works of private devotion, medical treatises and grammars.

There are also numerous works called Terma which profess to be revelations composed by Padma-Sambhava. They are said to be popular, though apparently not accepted by the Yellow Church.

Although it hardly comes within the scope of the present study, I may mention that there is also some non-Buddhist literature in Tibet, sometimes described as scriptures of the Bön religion and sometimes as folklore. As samples may be cited Laufer's edition and translation of the *Hundred Thousand Nâgas*[4] and Francke's of parts of the *Kesar-saga*[5].

[1] See Laufer in *Bull. de l'Acad. de S. Pétersbourg*, 1909, pp. 567–574. There are some differences in the editions. That of Narthang is said to contain a series of sûtras translated from the Pali and wanting in the Red Edition, but not to contain two translations from Chinese which are found in the Red Edition. See the preface to Beckh's catalogue. The MS. analyzed by him was obtained at Peking, but it is not known whence it came. An edition by Ch'ien Lung is mentioned by some authors. It is also said that an edition is printed at Punakha in Bhutan, and another in Mongolian at Kumbum.

[2] Some of these are probably included in the Tanjur, which has not been fully catalogued. See *J.A.S. Beng.* 1904, for a list of 85 printed books bought in Lhasa, 1902, and Waddell's article in *Asiatic Quarterly*, July, 1912, already referred to.

[3] Edited and translated by Huth as *Geschichte des Buddhismus in der Mongolei*, 1892.

[4] Finno Ugrian Society of Helsingfors, 1898.

[5] Same Society, 1900 and 1902, and *J.A.S.B.* 1906–7.

CHAPTER LII

TIBET (*continued*)

Doctrines of Lamaism

Lamaism may be defined as a mixture of late Indian Buddhism (which is itself a mixture of Buddhism and Hinduism) with various Tibetan practices and beliefs. The principal of these are demonophobia and the worship of human beings as incarnate deities. Demonophobia is a compendious expression for an obsession which victimizes Chinese and Hindus to some extent as well as Tibetans, namely, the conviction that they are at all times surrounded by fierce and terrible beings against whom they must protect themselves by all the methods that religion and magic can supply. This is merely an acute form of the world-wide belief that all nature is animated by good and bad spirits, of which the latter being more aggressive require more attention, but it assumes startlingly conspicuous forms in Tibet because the Church has enlisted all the forces of art, theology and philosophy to aid in this war against demons. The externals of Tibetan worship suffer much from the idea that benevolent deities assume a terrible guise in order to strike fear into the hosts of evil[1]. The helpers and saviours of mankind such as Avalokita and Târâ are often depicted in the shape of raging fiends, as hideous and revolting as a fanciful brush and distorted brain can paint them. The idea inspiring these monstrous images is not the worship of cruelty and terror, but the hope that evil spirits may be kept away when they see how awful are the powers which the Church can summon. Nevertheless the result is that a Lama temple often looks like a pandemonium and meeting house for devil-worship, an Olympus tenanted by Gorgons, Hydras and Furies. It is only fair to say that Tibetan art sometimes represents with success gods and saints in attitudes of repose and authority, and has produced some striking

[1] The Shingon sect in Japan depict benevolent deities in a raging form, Funnu. See Kokka, No. 292, p. 58. The idea goes back to India where the canons of sacred art recognize that deities can be represented in a pacific (śânta or saumya) or in a terrific (ugra or raudra) form. See Gopinath Rao, *Hindu Iconography*, vol. I. p. 19, and vol. II of the same for a lengthy description of the aspects of Śiva.

portraits[1], but its most marked feature (which it shares with literature) is a morbid love of the monstrous and terrible, a perpetual endeavour to portray fiends surrounded with every circumstance of horror, and still more appalling deities, all eyes, heads and limbs, wreathed with fire, drinking blood from skulls and trampling prostrate creatures to death beneath their feet. Probably the wild and fantastic landscapes of Tibet, the awful suggestions of the spectral mists, the real terrors of precipice, desert and storm have wrought for ages upon the minds of those who live among them.

Like demonophobia, the worship of incarnate deities is common in eastern Asia but here it acquires an extent and intensity unknown elsewhere. The Tibetans show a strange power of organization in dealing with the supernatural. In India incarnations have usually been recognized post-mortem and as incalculable manifestations of the spirit[2]. But at least since the seventeenth century, the Lamas have accepted them as part of the Church's daily round and administrative work. The practices of Shamanism probably prepared the way, for in his mystic frenzies the Shaman is temporarily inhabited by a god and the extreme ease with which distinguished persons are turned into gods or Bodhisattvas in China and Japan is another manifestation of the same spirit. An ancient inscription[3] applies to the kings of Tibet the word *ḥphrul* which is also used of the Grand Lamas and means that a deity is transformed, or as we say, incarnate in a human person. The Yellow Church officially recognized[4] the Emperor of China as an incarnation of Mañjuśrî and the Mongols believed the Tsar of Russia to be an incarnation of the White Târâ.

The admixtures received by Buddhism in Tibet are not alien to Indian thought. They received an unusual emphasis but India provided terrible deities, like Kâlî with her attendant fiends, and also the idea that the divine embodies itself in human personalities or special manifestations. Thus Tibetan Buddhism is not so much an amalgam, as a phase of medieval Hindu

[1] *E.g.* Grünwedel, *Buddhist art in India*, fig. 149, *id. Mythologie*, fig. 54.

[2] But there is still a hereditary incarnation of Ganeśa near Poona, which began in the seventeenth century. See *Asiatic Researches*, VII. 381.

[3] See Waddell in *J.R.A.S.* 1909, p. 941.

[4] See *e.g. J.A.S.B.* 1882, p. 41. The Svayambhû Purâna also states that Mañjuśrî lives in China. See *J. Buddhist Text Society*, 1894, vol. II. part II. p. 33.

religion disproportionately developed in some directions. The Lamas have acquired much the same status as the Brahmans. If they could not make themselves a hereditary caste, they at least enforced the principle that they are the necessary intermediaries between gods and men. Though they adopted the monastic system of Buddhism, they are not so much monks as priests and ghostly warriors who understand the art of fighting with demons.

Yet Tibet like Japan could assimilate and transform as well as borrow. The national and original element in Lamaism becomes plain when we compare Tibet with the neighbouring land of Nepal. There late Indian Buddhism simply decayed under an overgrowth of Brahmanism. In Tibet it acquired more life and character than it had in its native Bengal. This new character has something monstrous and fantastic in government as well as art: the magic fortresses of the Snowland, peopled by priests and demons, seem uncanny homes for plain mortals, yet Lamaism has the strength belonging to all genuine expressions of national character and it clearly suits the Tibetans and Mongols. The oldest known form of Tibetan religion had some of the same characteristics. It is called Bön or Pön. It would be outside my province to discuss it here, but even when first heard of it was more than a rude form of animism. In the eighth century its hierarchy was sufficiently strong to oppose the introduction of Buddhism and it possibly contained a pre-buddhist stratum of Iranian ideas[1]. In later times it adopted or travestied Buddhist dogma, ritual and literature, much as Taoism did in China, but still remained a repository of necromancy, magic, animal sacrifices, devil-dancing, and such like practices, which have in all ages corrupted Tibetan Buddhism though theoretically disapproved.

Of Tibetan Buddhism anterior to 747 there is little to be said. It consisted in the sporadic introduction of books and images from India and did not assume any national character, for it is clear that in this period Tibet was not regarded as a Buddhist country. The first phase deserving the name of Lamaism begins with the arrival of Padma-Sambhava in 747.

[1] See *T'oung Pao*, 1908, p. 13. For the Bön generally see also *J.A.S. Bengal*, 1881, p. 187; Rockhill, *Land of the Lamas*, pp. 217–218; and *T'oung Pao*, 1901, pp. 24–44.

The Nying-ma-pa or Old School claims to represent his teaching, but, as already mentioned, the various sects have interacted on one another so much that their tenets are hardly distinctive. Still it is pretty clear that what Padma-Sambhava brought with him was the late form of India Buddhism called Mantrayâna, closely allied to the Chên Yen of China, and transported to Japan under the name of Shingon and also to the Buddhism of Java as represented in the sculptures of Boroboedoer. The Far East felt shy of the tantric element in this teaching, whereas the Tibetans exaggerated it, but the doctrinal basis is everywhere the same, namely, that there are five celestial Buddhas, of whom Vairocana is the principal and in some sense the origin. These give rise to celestial emanations, female as well as male, and to terrestrial reflexes such as Śâkyamuni. Among the other features of Padma-Sambhava's teaching the following may be enumerated with more or less certainty: (*a*) A readiness to tolerate and incorporate the local cults of the countries where he preached. (*b*) A free use of spells (dhâraṇî) and magical figures (maṇḍala) for the purpose of subduing demons and acquiring supernatural powers. (*c*) The belief that by such methods an adept can not only summon a deity but assume his form and in fact become the deity. (*d*) The worship of Amitâbha, among other deities, and a belief in his paradise. (*e*) The presentation of offerings, though not of flesh, in sacrifice[1] and the performance of ceremonies on behalf of departed souls. (*f*) The worship of departed and perhaps of living teachers. His image is a conspicuous object of veneration in the Nying-ma-pa sect but he does not appear to have taught the doctrine of hierarchical succession by incarnation. Grünwedel[2] has pointed out that the later corruptions of Buddhism in northern India, Tibet and Central Asia are connected with the personages known as the eighty-four Mahâsiddhas, or great magicians. Their appearance as shown in pictures is that of Brahmanic ascetics rather than of Buddhist Bhikshus, but many of them bear names which are not Indian. Their dates cannot be fixed at present and appear

[1] The Lamas offer burnt sacrifices but it is not quite clear whether these are derived from the Indian *homa* adopted by Tantric Buddhism or from Tibetan and Mongol ceremonies. See, for a description of this ceremony, *My Life in Mongolia*, by the Bishop of Norwich, pp. 108–114.

[2] *Mythologie des Buddhismus*, p. 40.

to cover a period from the early centuries of our era up to about 1200, so that they represent not a special movement but a continuous tendency to import into Buddhism very various currents of thought, north Indian, Iranian, Central Asian and even Mohammedan.

The visit of Padma-Sambhava was followed by a period of religious activity which culminated in the ninth century under King Ralpachan, but it does not appear that the numerous translations from Indian works made in this reign did more than supplement and amplify the doctrine already preached. But when after a lengthy eclipse Buddhism was reinstated in the eleventh century under the auspices of Atîśa and other foreign teachers we hear of something new, called the Kâlacakra[1] system also known as the Vajrayâna. Pending the publication of the Kâlacakra Tantra[2], it is not easy to make definite statements about this school which presumably marks the extreme point of development or degeneration in Buddhism, but a persistent tradition connects it with a country called Śambhala or Zhambhala, translated in Tibetan as bDe-ḥbyuṅ or source of happiness. This country is seen only through a haze of myth: it may have been in India or it may have been somewhere in Central Asia, where Buddhism mingled with Turkish ideas[3]. Its kings were called Kulika and the Tibetan calendar introduced by Atîśa is said to have come from it. This fact and the meaning of the word Kâlacakra (wheel of time) suggest that the system has some connection with the Turkish cycle of twelve animals used for expressing dates[4]. A legend[5] states that Śâkyamuni promulgated the Kâlacakra system in Orissa (Dhânyakaṭaka) and that Sucandra, king of Śambhala, having miraculously received this teaching wrote the Kâlacakra Tantra in a prophetic spirit, although it was not published until

[1] In Tibetan Dus-kyi-hkhor-lo. Mongol, Tsagun kürdün.

[2] Announced in the *Bibliotheca Buddhica*.

[3] See Pelliot, *Quelques transcriptions apparentées à Cambhala dans les textes Chinois* (in *T'oung Pao*, vol. XX. 1920, p. 73) for some conjectures. Kulika is translated into Tibetan as Rigs-Ldan. Tibetan texts speak of books coming from Sambhala, see Laufer in *T'oung Pao*, 1913, p. 596.

[4] See Laufer in *T'oung Pao*, 1907, p. 402. In Sumpa's chronology, *J.A.S. Beng.* p. 46, the reign of a Kulika Emperor seems to be simply a designation for a century.

[5] See *J.A.S.B.* 82, p. 225. The king is also (but apparently incorrectly) called Candra-Bhadra.

965 A.D. This is really the approximate date of its compilation and I can only add the following disjointed data[1].

Tibetan authorities state that it was introduced into Nâlandâ by a Pandit called Tsilu or Chilu and accepted by Narotapa who was then head of the University. From Nâlandâ it spread to Tibet. Manjuśrîkîrti, king of Śambhala, is said to have been an exponent of it and to have begun his reign 674 years after the death of the Buddha. But since he is also the second incarnation of the Panchen Lama and since the fourth (Abhayakara) lived about 1075, he may really have been a historical character in the latter part of the tenth century. Its promulgation is also ascribed to a personage called Siddha Pito. It must be late for it is said to mention Islam and Mohammed. It is perhaps connected with anti-mohammedan movements which looked to Kalkî, the future incarnation of Vishnu, as their Messiah, for Hindu tradition says that Kalkî will be born in Śambhalagrâma[2]. We hear also of a Siddha called Telopa or Tailopa, who was a vigorous opponent of Islam. The mythology of the school is Vishnuite, not Sivaitic, and it is noticeable that the Pâncarâtra system which had some connection with Kashmir lays stress on the wheel or discus (*cakra* or *sudarśana*) of Vishnu which is said to be the support of the Universe and the manifestation of Creative will. The Kâlacakra is mentioned as a special form of this cosmic wheel having six spokes[3].

The peculiar doctrine of the Buddhist Kâlacakra is that there is an Âdi-Buddha[4], or primordial Buddha God, from whom all other Buddhas are derived. It is possible that it represents a last effort of Central Asian Buddhism to contend with Moslims, which instead of denying the bases of Mohammed's teaching tried to show that monotheism (like everything else) could be found in Buddhism—a method of argument frequent in India. The doctrine of the Âdi-Buddha was not however new or really

[1] See Grünwedel, *Mythologie*, p. 41. Sarat Chandra Das in *J.A.S. Beng.* 1882, p. 15, and *J.A.S. Beng.* 1912, p. 21, being reprints of earlier articles by Csoma de Körös.

[2] See Kalkî Purâna. Vishnu Purâna, IV. xxiv, Bhâg. Pur, XII. ii. 18, and Norman in *Trans. III, Int. Congress Religions*, vol. II. p. 85. Also Aufrecht, *Cat. Cod. Sansk.* 73A, 84B.

[3] See Schrader, *Introd. to the Pâncarâtra*, pp. 100–106 and 96.

[4] See the article "Âdi Buddha" by De la Vallée Poussin in Hastings' *Encyc. of Religion and Ethics*.

important. For the Indian mind it is implied in the dogma of the three bodies of Buddha, for the Sambhogakâya is practically an Indian Deva and the Dharmakâya is the pantheos or Brahmâ. Under the influence of the Kâlacakra the Lamas did not become theists in the sense of worshipping one supreme God but they identified with the Âdi-Buddha some particular deity, varying according to the sects. Thus Samantabhadra, who usually ranks as a Bodhisattva—that is as inferior to a Buddha—was selected by some for the honour. The logic of this is hard to explain but it is clearly analogous to the procedure, common to the oldest and newest phases of Hindu religion, by which a special deity is declared to be not only all the other gods but also the universal spirit[1]. It does not appear that the Kâlacakra Tantra met with general acceptance. It is unknown in China and Japan and not well known in Nepal[2].

The Kâlacakra adopted all the extravagances of the Tantras and provided the principal Buddhas and Bodhisattvas with spouses, even giving one to the Âdi-Buddha himself[3]. Extraordinary as this is from a Buddhist point of view, it is little more than the Hindu idea that the Supreme Being became male and female for the purpose of producing the universe. But the general effect of the system on monastic and religious life was bad. Celibacy was not observed; morals, discipline and doctrine alike deteriorated. A striking instance is afforded by the ceremonies used by Pagspa when receiving Kublai into the Church. The Tibetan prelate presumably wished to give the Emperor what was best and most important in his creed and selected a formula for invoking a demoniac Buddha.

The latest phase of Lamaism was inaugurated by Tsong-kha-pa's reformation and is still vigorous. Politically and socially it was of capital importance, for it disciplined the priesthood

[1] See, for a modern example of this, the Gaṇeśâtharvaśîrshopanishad (Anândâsrama edition, pp. 11 and 16) Tvam eva sarvam khalvidam Brahmâsi...Tvam Brahmâ Tvam Vishnus Tvam Rudras Tvam Indras Tvam Agnis Tvam Vâyus Tvam Sûryas Tvam Candramâs Tvam *Brahma*. Here Gaṇeśa includes all the deities and the Pantheos. There is also a book called Gaṇeśadarśanam in which the Vedanta sûtras are rewritten and Gaṇeśa made equivalent to Brahma. See Madras, *Cat. of Sk. MSS.* 1910–1913, p. 1030.

[2] It is just mentioned in S. Lévi's *Nepal II*, p. 385, but is not in Rajendralal Mitra's *Catalogue*.

[3] Waddell, *Buddhism*, p. 131. Pander, *Pantheon*, p. 59, No. 56.

and enabled the heads of the Church to rule Tibet. In doctrine it was not marked by the importation of new ideas, but it emphasized the worship of Avalokita as the patron of Tibet, it systematized the existing beliefs about reincarnation, thereby creating a powerful hierarchy, and it restricted Tantrism, without abolishing it. But many monasteries persistently refused to accept these reforms.

Tibetan mythology and ceremonial have been described in detail by Grünwedel, Waddell and others. The pantheon is probably the largest in the world. All heaven and hell seem to meet in it. The originals of the deities are nearly all to be found in Nepalese Buddhism[1] and the perplexing multiplicity of Tibet is chiefly due to the habit of representing one deity in many forms and aspects, thus making him a dozen or more personages both for art and for popular worship. The adoration of saints and their images is also more developed than in Nepal and forms some counterpoise to the prevalent demonolatry.

I will not attempt to catalogue this fantastic host but will merely notice the principal elements in it.

The first of these may be called early Buddhist. The figure of Śâkyamuni is frequent in poses which illustrate the familiar story of his life and the statue in the cathedral of Lhasa representing him as a young man is the most venerated image in all Tibet. The human Buddhas anterior to him also receive recognition together with Maitreya. The Pratimoksha is still known, the Uposatha days are observed and the details of the ordination services recall the prescriptions of the Pali Vinaya; formulæ such as the four truths, the eightfold path and the chain of causation are still in use and form the basis of ethics.

The later (but still not tantric) doctrines of Indian Mahayanism are naturally prominent. The three bodies of Buddha are well known and also the series of five Celestial Buddhas with corresponding Bodhisattvas and other manifestations. I feel doubtful whether the table given by Waddell[2] can be accepted

[1] Nepalese Buddhism knows not only the Dhyâni Buddhas, Śaktis and Bodhisattvas including Vajrasattva and Vajradhara, but also deities like Hayagrîva, Yamântaka, Bhṛikuṭî, Marîcî, Kurukullâ. In both Nepal and Tibet are found pictures called Thsogs-śiṅ in which the deities of the Pantheon (or at least the principal of them) are grouped according to rank. See for an example containing 138 deities the frontispiece of Getty's *Gods of Northern Buddhism.*

[2] *Buddhism*, pp. 350–1.

as a compendium of the Lamaist creed. The symmetry is spoiled by the existence of other groups such as the Thirty Buddhas, the Thousand Buddhas, and the Buddhas of Healing, and also by the habit just mentioned of representing deities in various forms. For instance Amoghapâśa, theoretically a form of Avalokita, is in practice distinct. The fact is that Lamaism accepted the whole host of Indian Buddhas and Bodhisattvas, with additions of its own. The classifications made by various sûtras and tantras were not sufficiently dogmatic to become articles of faith: chance and fancy determined the prominence and popularity of a given figure. Among the Buddhas those most worshipped are Amitâbha, Śâkya and Bhaishajyaguru or the Buddha of Healing: among the Bodhisattvas, Avalokita, Maitreya and Mañjuśrî.

There is nothing in the above differing materially from Chinese or Japanese Buddhism. The peculiarities of Tibet are brought out by the tantric phase which those countries eschewed. Three characteristics of Tibetan Tantrism, which are all more or less Indian, may be mentioned. Firstly, all deities, even the most august, become familiar spirits, who are not so much worshipped as coerced by spells. The neophyte is initiated into their mysteries by a special ceremonial[1]: the adept can summon them, assume their attributes and attain union with them. Secondly, great prominence is given to goddesses, either as the counterparts of male deities or as independent. Thirdly, deities appear in various forms, described as mild, angry or fiendish. It is specially characteristic of Lamaism that naturally benevolent deities are represented as raging in furious frenzy.

Whether the superhuman beings of Tantrism are Buddhas, Bodhisattvas, or Hindu gods like Mahâkala, it is correct to describe them as deities, for they behave and are treated like Indian Devas. Besides the relatively old and simple forms of the various Buddhas and Bodhisattvas, there are many others which are usually accommodated to the system by being described as protecting spirits, that is virtuous and religious fiends who expend their ferocity on the enemies of the Church.

Of these Protectors there are two classes, which are not mutually exclusive, namely, the tutelary deities of individuals,

[1] For an outline of the method followed by Tibetans in studying the Tantras, see *Journal Buddhist Text Society*, 1893, vol. I. part III. pp. 25–6.

and the defenders of the faith or tutelaries of the whole Church. The former, who are extremely important in the religious life of the Lamas, are called Yi-dam and may be compared with the Ishṭa-devatâs of the Hindus: the latter or Chos Skyoṅ correspond to the Dharmapâlas. Every Lama selects a Yi-dam either for life or for a period. His choice must remain a secret but he himself has no doubts, as after fasting and meditation the deity will appear to him[1]. Henceforth he every morning repeats formulæ which are supposed to give him the appearance of his tutelary and thus scare away hostile demons. The most efficacious tutelaries are tantric forms of the Dhyâni Buddhas, especially Vajrasattva, Vajradhara and Amitâyus. The deity is represented not in the guise of a Buddha but crowned, robed, and holding a thunderbolt, and his attributes appear to be derived from those of Indra[2]. In his arms he always clasps a Śakti.

A second class of tutelaries is composed of so-called Buddhas, accompanied by Śaktis and terrific in aspect, who are manifestations of the Buddhahood for special purposes. I do not know if this description is theologically correct, for these fantastic figures have no relation to anything deserving the name of Buddhism, but Grünwedel[3] has shown that they are comparable with the various forms of Śiva. This god does not become incarnate like Vishnu but manifests himself from time to time in many shapes accompanied by a retinue who are sometimes merely attendants and sometimes alternative forms of the Lord. Vîrabhadra, the terrible being created by Śiva from himself in order to confound Daksha's sacrifice, is a close parallel to the demoniac Buddhas of Lamaism. Some of them, such as Mahâkâla and Samvara, show their origin in their names and the rest, such as Hevajra, Buddhakapâla and Yamântaka, are similar. This last is a common subject for art, a many headed and many limbed minotaur, convulsed by a paroxysm of devilish passion. Among his heads the most conspicuous is the face of an ox, yet this grotesque demon is regarded as a manifestation of the benign and intellectual Mañjuśri whose images in other lands are among the most gracious products of Buddhist sculpture.

[1] The deity may appear in an unusual form, so the worshipper can easily persuade himself that he has received the desired revelation.

[2] A figure identified with Indra or Vajrapâni is found in Gandhara sculptures.

[3] *Mythologie*, p. 97.

Most tutelary deities of this class act as defenders of the faith and each sect has one or two as its special guardians[1]. The idea is ancient for even in the Pitakas, Sakka and other spirits respectfully protect the Buddha's disciples, and the Dharmapâlas of Gandharan art are the ancestors of the Chos Skyoṅ. But in Tibet these assume monstrous and manifold disguises. The oldest is Vajrapâṇi and nearly all the others are forms of Śiva (such as Acala or Mi-gyo-ba who reappears in Japan as Fudo) or personages of his retinue. Eight of them are often adored collectively under the name of the Eight Terrible Ones. Several of these are well-known figures in Hindu mythology, for though the Lamas usually give Buddhist titles to their principal deities, yet they also venerate Hindu gods, without any explanation of their status. Thus hJigs-med-nam-mkha says that he composed his history with the help of Śiva[2]. The members of this group vary in different enumerations but the following usually form part of it.

(*a*) Hayagrîva[3], the horse-necked god. In India he appears to be connected with Vishnu rather than Śiva. The magic dagger with which Lamas believe they can stab demons is said to be a form of him. The Mongols regard him as the protector of horses. (*b*) Yama, the Indian god of the dead, accompanied by a hellish retinue including living skeletons. (*c*) Mahâkâla, the form of Śiva already mentioned. It was by his inspiration that Pagspa was able to convert Khubilai Khan. (*d*) Lha-mo, the goddess, that is Devî, the spouse of Śiva. (*e*) lCam-sraṅ, a war god of somewhat uncertain origin but perhaps a Tibetan form of Kârtikeya. Other deities frequently included in this group are Yamântaka, mentioned above, Kubera or Vaiśravana, the Hindu god of wealth, and a deity called the White Brahmâ (Thsangspa dKarpo). This last is an ordinary human figure riding on a white horse and brandishing a sword. He wears white clothes and a crown or turban. He is perhaps Kalkî who, as suggested above, had some connection with the Kâlacakra. The Eight Terrible Ones and their attendants are represented by grotesquely masked figures in the dances and mystery plays enacted by Lamas. These performances are said to be still

[1] The Dhyâni Buddhas however seem to be the Yi-dam of individuals only.
[2] Huth's edition, p. 1.
[3] See *Buddhist Text Society*, vol. II. part II. appendix II. 1904, p. 6.

known among the vulgar as dances of the Red Tiger Devil, but in the hands of the Yellow Church have become a historical drama representing the persecution of Buddhism under King Lang-dar-ma and its ultimate triumph after he has been slain by the help of these ghostly champions.

Lamaist books mention numerous other Indian divinities, such as Brahmâ, the thirty-three Devas, the Kings of the four quarters, etc. These have no particular place in the system but their appearance in art and literature is natural, since they are decorative though not essential parts of early Buddhism. The same may be said of all the host of Nâgas, Yakshas, Rakshasas, etc. But though these multitudinous spirits have been rearranged and classified in conformity with Hindu ideas they are not an importation but rather part of the old folklore of Tibet, in many ways identical with the same stratum of thought in India. Thus the snake demigods or Nâgas[1] occupy in both countries a large place in the popular imagination. In the higher ranks of the Lamaist pantheon all the figures seem to be imported, but some indigenous godlings have retained a place in the lower classes. Such are rDo-rje-legs, at first an opponent of Buddhism as preached by Padma-Sambhava but honoured as a deity after making due submission, and the Five Kings[2], a group of fierce spirits, under the presidency of dPe-dkar.

It remains to say a word of the numerous goddesses who play an important part in Tibetan Buddhism, as in Hindu Tantrism. They are usually represented as the female counterparts or better halves of male deities, but some are self-sufficient. The greatest of these goddesses is Târâ[3]. Though Lamaist theology describes her as the spouse of Avalokita she is not a single personality but a generic name applied to a whole class of female deities and, as in many other cases, no clear distinction is drawn between her attendants and the forms which she herself assumes. Originally benevolent and depicted with the attributes of Lakshmî she is transformed by a turn of Tibetan

[1] See Laufer, "Hundert Tausend Nâgas" in *Memoirs of Finno-Ugrian Society*, 1898.

[2] Or Five Bodies, sKu-Lṅa. dPe-dKar or Pe-har is by some authorities identified with the Chinese deity Wei-to. This latter is represented in the outer court of most Chinese temples.

[3] In Tibetan sGrol-ma, in Mongol Dara äkä. For the early history of Târâ see Blonay, *Matériaux pour servir à l'histoire de...Târâ*, 1895.

imagination, with which the reader is now familiar, into various terrible shapes and is practically the same as the spouse of Śiva, celebrated in the Tantras under countless names. Twenty-one Târâs are often enumerated in a list said to be well known even to the laity[1] and there are others. Among them are (*a*) the Green Târâ, the commonest form in Tibet. (*b*) The White Târâ, much worshipped by Mongols and supposed to be incarnate in the Tsar of Russia. (*c*) Bhṛikuṭî, a dark blue, angry, frowning form. (*d*) Ushṇîshavijayâ[2], a graceful and benevolent form known to the Japanese. She is mentioned in the Horiuji palm-leaf manuscript which dates from at least 609 A.D. (*e*) Parṇa-śavarî, represented as wearing a girdle of leaves and also called Gandhârî, Piśâcî and Sarva-Śavarâṇâm Bhagavatî[3]. She is apparently the goddess of an aboriginal tribe in India. (*f*) Kurukullâ, a goddess of riches, inhabiting caves. She is said to have given great wealth to the fifth Grand Lama, and though she might be suspected of being a native deity was known in Nepal and India[4].

The Goddess Marîcî, often depicted with Târâ, appears to be distinct and in one form is represented with a sow's head and known as Vajravarâhî. As such she is incarnate in the abbesses of several monasteries, particularly Samding on lake Yamdok[5].

A notice of Tibetan Buddhism can hardly avoid referring to the use of praying wheels and the celebrated formula Om maṇi padme hum. Though these are among the most conspicuous and ubiquitous features of Lamaism their origin is strangely obscure[6]. Attempts to connect the praying wheel with the wheel of the law, the cakravartin and other uses of the wheel in Indian symbolism, are irrelevant, for the object to be explained is not really a wheel but a barrel, large or small, containing written prayers, or even a whole library. Those who turn the barrel

[1] Waddell, *Buddhism*, p. 360.

[2] Tibetan gTsug-tor-rnam-par-rgyal-ma.

[3] Cf. Whitehead's statement (*Village Gods of S. India*, p. 79) that women worshipping certain goddesses are clad only in the twigs of the mimosa tree.

[4] See Foucher, *Icon. Bouddhique*, 1900, p. 142, and Târanâtha tr. Schiefner, p. 102.

[5] See Waddell. Grünwedel seems to regard Vajra-Varâhî as distinct from Marîcî.

[6] As for instance is also the origin of Linga worship in India.

acquire all the merit arising from repeating the prayers or reading the books. In Tibet this form of devotion is a national mania. People carry small prayer wheels in their hands as they walk and place large ones in rivers to be turned by the current. In China, Japan and Korea we find revolving libraries and occasional praying machines, though not of quite the same form as in Tibet[1], but, so far as I know, there is nothing to show that these were not introduced from Tibet into China and thence found their way further East. The hypothesis that they were known in India and thence exported to Tibet on one side and China on the other naturally suggests itself, but the total absence of praying machines in India as well as in the ruined cities of Central Asia and the general Hindu habit of regarding scriptures and spells as words rather than written documents lend it no support. It may be that when the illiterate Tibetans first became acquainted with written prayers, they invented this singular method of utilizing them without reading them.

Equally obscure is the origin of the formula Om maṇi padme[2] hum, which permeates Tibet, uttered by every human voice, revolved in countless machines, graven on the rocks, printed on flags. It is obviously a Dhâraṇî[3] and there is no reason to doubt that it came to Tibet with the first introduction of Buddhism, but also no record. The earliest passage hitherto quoted for its occurrence is a Chinese translation made between 980 and 1001 A.D.[4] and said to correspond with the Kanjur and the earliest historical mention of its use is found in Willelm de Rubruk (1254) and in the writings of Bu-ston[5]. The first legend of its origin is contained in the Manikambum, a work of doubtful age and

[1] See Steiner in *Mitth. der Deutsch. Gesellsch. Natur- u. Völkerkunde Ost-Asiens*, 1909–10, p. 35.

[2] Padme is said to be commonly pronounced peme.

[3] Waddell quotes a similar spell known in both Tibet and Japan, but addressed to Vairocana. Om Amogha Vairocanamahâmudra mani padma jvalapravarthtaya hūm. *Buddhism*, p. 149.

[4] *Divyâvadâna* (Cowell and Neil), pp. 613–4, and Raj. Mitra, *Nepalese Bud. Lit.* p. 98. See also the learned note of Chavannes and Pelliot, based on Japanese sources in *J.A.* 1913, I. 314. The text referred to is Nanjio, No. 782. It is not plain if it is the same as earlier translations with similar titles. A mantra of six syllables not further defined is extolled in the Divyâvadâna and the Guṇakâraṇḍavyûha.

[5] Bu-ston was born in 1288 and the summary of his writings contained in the *Journal of the Buddhist Text Society*, vol. I. 1893, represents the formula as used in the times of Atîśa, c. 1030.

authorship but perhaps as old as the fifteenth century[1]. The popularity of the prayer may date from the time when the pontiffs of Lhasa were recognized as incarnations of Avalokita. The first and last words are mystic syllables such as often occur in these formulæ. Maṇi padme is generally interpreted to mean the jewel in the lotus[2], but Thomas has pointed out that it is more consonant with grammar and usage to regard the syllables as one word and the vocative of a feminine title similar to Padmapâṇi, one of Avalokita's many names. The analogy of similar spells supports this interpretation and it seems probable that the formula was originally an invocation of the Śakti under the title of Maṇipadmâ, although so far as I know it is now regarded by the Tibetans as an address to the male Avalokita. It has also been suggested that the prominence of this prayer may be due to Manichæan influence and the idea that it contained the name of Mani. The suggestion is not absurd for in many instances Manichæism and Buddhism were mixed together, but if it were true we should expect to find the formula frequently used in the Tarim basin, but of such use there is no proof.

[1] See for this legend, which is long but not very illuminating, Rockhill's *Land of the Lamas*, pp. 326–334.

[2] *J.R.A.S.* 1906, p. 464, and Francke, *ib.* 1915, pp. 397–404. He points out the parallel between the three formulæ: *Om vagîśvari mum: Om maṇipadme hum: Om vajrapâṇi hum.* The hymn to Durgâ in Mahâbhâr. Bhîshmapar, 796 (like many other hymns) contains a long string of feminine vocatives ending in *e* or *i*.

CHAPTER LIII

TIBET (*continued*)

SECTS

LAMAISM is divided into various sects, which concern the clergy rather than the laity. The differences in doctrine are not very important. Each sect has special tutelary deities, scriptures and practices of its own but they all tend to borrow from one another whatever inspires respect or attracts worshippers. The baser sort try to maintain their dignity by imitating the institutions of the superior sects, but the superior cannot afford to neglect popular superstitions. So the general level is much the same. Nevertheless, these sectarian differences are not without practical importance for each sect has monasteries and a hierarchy of its own and is outwardly distinguished by peculiarities of costume, especially by the hat. Further, though the subject has received little investigation, it is probable that different sects possess different editions of the Kanjur or at any rate respect different books[1]. Since the seventeenth century the Gelugpa has been recognized as the established church and the divinity of the Grand Lama is not disputed, but in earlier times there were many monastic quarrels and forced conversions. In the eighteenth century the Red clergy intrigued with the Gurkhas in the hope of supplanting their Yellow brethren and even now they are so powerful in eastern Tibet that this hope may not be unreasonable, should political troubles shake the hierarchy of Lhasa. In spite of the tendency to borrow both what is good and what is bad, some sects are on a higher grade intellectually and morally than others. Thus the older sects do not insist on celibacy or abstinence from alcohol, and Tantrism and magic form the major part of religion, whereas the Gelugpa or established church maintains strict discipline, and tantric and magical rites, though by no means prohibited, are at least practised in moderation.

Setting aside the earliest period, the history of Buddhism in Tibet is briefly that it was established by Padma-Sambhava

[1] See for instance the particulars given as to various branches of the Nying-ma pa sect in *J.A.S.B.* 1882, pp. 6–14.

about 750, reformed by Atîśa about 1040 and again reformed by Tsong-kha-pa about 1400. The sects correspond to these epochs. The oldest claims to preserve the teaching of Padma-Sambhava, those of middle date are offshoots of the movement started by Atîśa, and the newest represents Atîśa's principal sect corrected by the second reformation. The oldest sect is known as Nying-ma-pa or rNyiṅ-ma-pa, signifying the old ones, and also as the Red Church from the colour of the hats worn by the clergy. Among its subdivisions one called the sect of Udyâna[1], in reference to Padma-Sambhava's birthplace, appears to be the most ancient and still exists in the Himalayas and eastern Tibet. The Nying-ma Lamas are said to have kept the necromancy of the old Tibetan religion more fully than any of the reformed sects. They pay special worship to Padma-Sambhava and accept the revelations ascribed to him. Celibacy and abstinence are rarely observed in their monasteries but these are by no means of low repute. Among the more celebrated are Dorje-dag and Mindolling: the great monastery of Pemiongchi[2] in Sikhim is a branch establishment of the latter.

Of the sects originating in Atîśa's reformation the principal was the Kadampa[3], but it has lost much of its importance because it was remodelled by Tsong-kha-pa and hence hardly exists to-day as an independent body. The Sakya sect is connected with the great monastery of the same name situated about fifty miles to the north of Mount Everest and founded in 1071 by Sakya, a royal prince. It acquired great political importance, for from 1270 to 1340 its abbots were the rulers of Tibet. The historian Târanâtha belonged to one of its sub-sects, and about 1600 settled in Mongolia where he founded the monastery of Urga and established the line of reincarnate Lamas which still rules there. But shortly after his death this monastery was forcibly taken over by the Yellow Church and is still the centre of its influence in Mongolia. In theology the Sakya offers nothing specially distinctive but it mixes the Tantras of the old and new sects and according to Waddell[4] is practically indistinguishable from the Nying-ma-pa. The same is probably true of the Kar-gyu-pa[5] said to have been founded by Marpa and

[1] Urgyen-pa or Dzok-chen-pa.

[2] Or Pemayangtse.

[3] bKah-gDams-pa.

[4] *Buddhism*, p. 70.

[5] bKah-brGyud-pa.

his follower Milarāpa, who set an example of solitary and wandering lives. It is sometimes described as a Nying-ma sect[1] but appears to date from after Atîśa's reforms, although it has a strong tendency to revert to older practices. It has several important sub-sects, such as the Karmapa found in Sikhim and Darjiling, as well as in Tibet, the Dugpa which is predominant in Bhotan and perhaps in Ladak[2], and the Dikung-pa, which owns a large monastery one hundred miles north-east of Lhasa. Milarāpa (or Mila), the cotton-clad saint who wandered over the Snow-land in the light garments of an Indian ascetic, is perhaps the post picturesque figure in Lamaism and in some ways reminds us of St Francis of Assisi[3]. He was a worker of miracles and, what is rarer in Tibet, a poet. His compositions known as the Hundred Thousand Songs are still popular and show the same delicately sensitive love of nature as the Psalms of the Theragâthâ.

The main distinction is between the Gelugpa or Yellow Church and all the other sects. This is merely another way of saying that Atîśa reformed the corrupt superstitions which he found but that his reformed church in its turn became corrupt and required correction. This was given by Tsong-kha-pa who belonged originally to the Kadampa. He collected the scattered members of this sect, remodelled its discipline, and laid the foundations of the system which made the Grand Lamas rulers of Tibet. In externals the Gelugpa is characterized by the use of the yellow cap and the veneration paid to Tsong-kha-pa's image. Its Lamas are all celibate and hereditary succession is not recognized. Among the many great establishments which belong to it are the four royal monasteries or Ling in Lhasa; Gandan, Depung and Serra near Lhasa; and Tashilhunpo.

It has often been noticed that the services performed by the Gelugpa[4] and by the Roman Catholic Church are strangely

[1] Sandberg, *Handbook of Tibetan*, p. 207.

[2] Authorities differ as to the name of the sect which owns Himis and other monasteries in Ladak.

[3] See for some account of him and specimens of his poems, Sandberg, *Tibet and the Tibetans*, chap. XIII.

[4] I do not know whether the ceremonies of the other sects offer the same resemblance. Probably they have all imitated the Gelugpa. Some authors attribute the resemblance to contact with Nestorian Christianity in early times but the resemblance is definitely to Roman costumes and ceremonies not to those of the

similar in appearance. Is this an instance of borrowing or of convergence? On the one hand it is stated that there were Roman missions in Amdo in Tsong-kha-pa's youth, and the resemblances are such as would be natural if he had seen great celebrations of the mass and taken hints. In essentials the similarity is small but in externals such as the vestments and head-dresses of the officiants, the arrangement of the choir, and the general *mise-en-scène*, it is striking. On the other hand many points of resemblance in ceremonial, though not all, are also found in the older Japanese sects, where there can hardly be any question of imitating Christianity, and it would seem that a ritual common to Tibet and Japan can be explained only as borrowed from India. Further, although Tsong-kha-pa may have come in contact with missionaries, is it likely that he had an opportunity of seeing Roman rites performed with any pomp? It is in the great choral services of the two religions that the resemblance is visible, not in their simpler ritual. For these reasons, I think that the debt of Lamaism to the Catholic Church must be regarded as not proven, while admitting the resemblance to be so striking that we should be justified in concluding that Tsong-kha-pa copied Roman ceremonial, could it be shown that he was acquainted with it.

The life and ritual of the Lamas have often been described, and I need not do more than refer the reader to the detailed account given by Waddell in his *Buddhism of Tibet*[1], but it is noticeable that the monastic system is organized on a larger scale and inspired by more energy than in any other country. The monasteries of Tibet, if inferior to those of Japan in the middle ages, are the greatest Buddhist establishments now existing. For instance Depung has 7000 monks, Serra 5500 and Tashilhunpo 3800: at Urga in Mongolia there are said to be 14,000. One is not surprised to hear that these institutions are veritable towns with their own police and doubtless the spirit of discipline learned in managing such large bodies of monks has helped the Lamaist Church in the government of the country. Also these monasteries are universities. Candidates for ordination study a course of theology and are not received

Eastern church. Is there any reason to believe that the Nestorian ritual resembled that of western catholics?

[1] See also Filchner, *Das Kloster Kumbum*, 1906.

as novices or full monks unless they pass successive examina tions. In every monastery there is a central temple in which the monks assemble several times a day to chant lengthy choral offices. Of these there are at least five, the first before dawn and the last at 7 p.m. Though the value of Lamas' learning and ritual may be questioned, it is clear that many of them lead strenuous lives in the service of a religion which, if fantastic, still expresses with peculiar intensity the beliefs and emotions of the Tibetans and Mongols and has forced men of violence to believe that a power higher than their own is wielded by intellect and asceticism.

There seems to be no difference between Tibetan and Mongolian Lamaism in deities, doctrines or observances[1]. Mongolian Lamas imitate the usages of Tibet, study there when they can and recite their services in Tibetan, although they have translations of the scriptures in their own language. Well read priests in Peking have told me that it is better to study the canon in Tibetan than in Mongol, because complete copies in Mongol, if extant, are practically unobtainable.

The political and military decadence of the Mongols has been ascribed by some authors to Lamaism and to the substitution of priestly for warlike ideals. But such a substitution is not likely to have taken place except in minds prepared for it by other causes and it does not appear that the Moslims of Central Asia are more virile and vigorous than the Buddhists. The collapse of the Mongols can be easily illustrated if not explained by the fate of Turks and Tartars in the Balkan Peninsula and Russia. Wherever the Turks are the ruling race they endeavour to assert their superiority over all Christians, often by violent methods. But when the positions are reversed and the Christians become rulers as in Bulgaria, the Turks make no resistance but either retire or acquiesce meekly in the new regime.

[1] Almost the only difference that I have noticed is that whereas Tibetans habitually translate Indian proper names, Mongols frequently use Sanskrit words, such as Manjuśrî, or slightly modified forms such as Dara, Maidari (=Târâ, Maitreya). The same practice is found in the old Uigur translations. See *Bibl. Buddh.* XII. Tisastvustik. For an interesting account of contemporary Lamaism in Mongolia see Binstead, "Life in a Khalkha Steppe Monastery," *J.R.A.S.* 1914, 847–900.

CHAPTER LIV

JAPAN

This work as originally planned contained a section on Japanese Buddhism consisting of three chapters, but after it had been sent to the publishers I was appointed H.M. Ambassador in Tokyo and I decided to omit this section. Let not any Japanese suppose that it contained disparaging criticism of his country or its religions. It would, I hope, have given no offence to either Buddhists or Shintoists, but an ambassador had better err on the side of discretion and refrain from public comments on the institutions of the country to which he is accredited.

The omission is regrettable in so far as it prevents me from noticing some of the most interesting and beautiful developments of Buddhism, but for historical purposes and the investigation of the past the loss is not great, for Japanese Buddhism throws little light on ancient India or even on ancient China. It has not influenced other countries. Its interest lies not in the relics of antiquity which it has preserved but in the new shape and setting which a race at once assimilative and inventive has given to old ideas.

Though the doctrine of the Buddha reached Japan from China through Korea[1], Chinese and Japanese Buddhism differ in several respects. Lamaism never gained a footing in Japan, probably because it was the religion of the hated Mongols. There was hardly any direct intercourse with India. Whereas the state religion of China was frequently hostile to Buddhism, in Japan such relations were generally friendly and from the seventh century until the Meiji era an arrangement known as Ryō-bu Shintō or two-fold Shintō was in force, by which Shintō shrines were with few exceptions handed over to the custody of Buddhist priests, native deities and historical personages being declared to be manifestations of various Buddhas and Bodhisattvas. Again, Buddhism in Japan has had a more intimate connection with social, political and even military matters in various periods than in China. This is one

[1] The accepted date is A.D. 552.

reason for its chief characteristic, namely, the large number and distinct character of its sects. They are not merely schools like the religious divisions of India and China, but real sects with divergent doctrines and sometimes antagonistic to one another.

It became the fashion in Japan to talk of the twelve sects, but the names given are not always the same.

One of the commonest lists is as follows[1]:

1. Kusha.	5. Hossō.	9. Jōdo.
2. Jo-jitsu.	6. Kegon.	10. Zen.
3. Ritsu-shu or Risshu	7. Tendai.	11. Shin.
4. Sanron.	8. Shingon.	12. Nichiren.

This list is historically correct, but Nos. 1–4 are almost or quite extinct, and the number twelve is therefore sometimes made up as follows:

1. Hossō.	5. Yūzū Nembutsu.	9. Ōbaku.
2. Kegon.	6. Jōdo.	10. Shin.
3. Tendai.	7. Rinzai.	11. Nichiren.
4. Shingon.	8. Sōdō.	12. Ji.

Here Nos. 7, 8, 9 are subdivisions of the Zen and 5 and 12 are two small sects.

Taking the first list, we may easily distinguish two classes. The first eight, called by the Japanese Hasshū, are all old and all imported from China. They represent the Buddhism of the Nara and Hei-an periods. The other four all arose after 1170 and were all remodelled, if not created, in Japan. Chronologically the sects may be arranged as follows, the dates marking the foundation or introduction of each:

(i) Seventh century: Sanron, 625; Jo-jitsu, 625; Hossō, 657; Kusha, 660.

(ii) Eighth century: Kegon, 735; Ritsu, 745.

(iii) Ninth century: Tendai, 805; Shingon, 806.

(iv) Twelfth and thirteenth centuries: Yūzū Nembutsu, 1123; Jōdo, 1174; Zen, 1202; Shin, 1224; Nichiren, 1253; Ji, 1275.

[1] These names are mostly borrowed from the Chinese and represent: 1. Chü-shê; 2. Ch'êng-shih; 3. Lü; 4. San-lun; 5. Fa-hsiang; 6. Hua-yen; 7. T'ien-t'ai; 8. Chên-yen; 9. Ching-t'u; 10. Ch'an. See my remarks on these sects in the section on Chinese Buddhism. See Haas, *Die Sekten des Japanischen Buddhismus*, 1905: many notices in the same author's *Annalen des Jap. Bud.* cited above and Ryauon Fujishima, *Le Buddhisme Japonais*, 1889.

All Japanese sects of importance are Mahayanist. The Hinayana is represented only by the Kusha, Jo-jitsu and Risshu. The two former are both extinct: the third still numbers a few adherents, but is not anti-Mahayanist. It merely insists on the importance of discipline.

Though the Hossō and Kegon sects are not extinct, their survival is due to their monastic possessions rather than to the vitality of their doctrines, but the great sects of the ninth century, the Tendai and Shingon, are still flourishing. For some seven hundred years, especially in the Fujiwara period, they had great influence not only in art and literature, but in political and even in military matters, for they maintained large bodies of troops consisting of soldier monks or mercenaries and were a considerable menace to the secular authority. So serious was the danger felt to be that in the sixteenth century Nobunaga and Hideyoshi destroyed the great monasteries of Hieizan and Negoro and the pretensions of the Buddhist Church to temporal power were brought to an end.

But apart from this political activity, new sects which appeared in the twelfth and thirteenth centuries suited the popular needs of the time and were a sign of true religious life. Two of these sects, the Jōdo and Shinshū[1], are Amidist—that is to say they teach that the only or at least the best way of winning salvation is to appeal to the mercy of Amida, who will give his worshippers a place in his paradise after death. The Jōdo is relatively old fashioned, and does not differ much in practice from the worship of Amida as seen in China, but the Shinshū has no exact parallel elsewhere. Though it has not introduced many innovations in theology, its abandonment of monastic discipline, its progressive and popular spirit and its conspicuous success make it a distinct and remarkable type. Its priests marry and eat meat: it has no endowments and relies on voluntary subscription, yet its temples are among the largest and most conspicuous in Japan. But the hierarchical spirit is not absent and since Shinshū priests can marry, there arose the institution of hereditary abbots who were even more like barons than the celibate prelates of the older sects.

The Nichiren sect is a purely Japanese growth, without any prototype in China, and is a protest against Amidism and an

[1] As well as the smaller sects called Ji and Yūzūnembutsu.

attempt to restore Shaka—the historical Buddha—to his proper position from which he has been ousted. Nichiren, the founder, is one of the most picturesque figures of Japanese history. His teaching, which was based on the Lotus Sûtra, was remarkable for its combative spirit and he himself played a considerable part in the politics of his age. His followers form one of the most influential and conspicuous sects at the present day, although not so numerous as the Amidists.

Zen is the Japanese equivalent of Ch'an or Dhyâna and is the name given to the sect founded in China by Bodhidharma. It is said to have been introduced into Japan in the seventh century, but died out. Later, under the Hōjō Regents, and especially during the Ashikaga period, it flourished exceedingly. Zen ecclesiastics managed politics like the French cardinals of the seventeenth century and profoundly influenced art and literature, since they produced a long line of painters and writers. But the most interesting feature in the history of this sect in Japan is that, though it preserves the teaching of Bodhidharma without much change, yet it underwent a curious social metamorphosis, for it became the chosen creed of the military class and contributed not a little to the Bushido or code of chivalry. It is strange that this mystical doctrine should have spread among warriors, but its insistence on simplicity of life, discipline of mind and body, and concentration of thought harmonized with their ideals.

Apart from differences of doctrine such as divide the Shinshu, Nichiren and Zen, Japanese sects show a remarkable tendency to multiply subdivisions, due chiefly to disputes as to the proper succession of abbots. Thus the Jōdo sect has four subsects, and the first and second of these are again subdivided into six and four respectively. And so with many others. Even the little Ji sect, which is credited with only 509 temples in all Japan, includes thirteen subdivisions.

BOOK VII

MUTUAL INFLUENCE OF EASTERN AND WESTERN RELIGIONS

CHAPTER LV

INFLUENCE OF CHRISTIANITY IN INDIA.

In phrases like the above title, the word influence is easy and convenient. When we hesitate to describe a belief or usage as borrowed or derived, it comes pat to say that it shows traces of external influence. But in what circumstances is such influence exercised? It is not the necessary result of contact, for in the east of Europe the Christian Church has not become mohammedanized nor in Poland and Roumania has it contracted any taint of Judaism. In these cases there is difference of race as well as of religion. In business the Turk and Jew have some common ground with the oriental Christian: in social life but little and in religion none at all. Europe has sometimes shown an interest in Asiatic religions, but on the whole an antipathy to them. Christianity originated in Palestine, which is a Mediterranean rather than an Asiatic country, and its most important forms, particularly the Roman Catholic Church, took shape on European soil. Such cults as the worship of Isis and Mithra were prevalent in Europe but they gained their first footing among Asiatic slaves and soldiers and would perhaps not have maintained themselves among European converts only. And Buddhism, though it may have attracted individual minds, has never produced any general impression west of India. Both in Spain and in south-eastern Europe Islam was the religion of invaders and made surprisingly few converts. Christian heretics, such as the Nestorians and Monophysites, who were expelled from Constantinople and had their home in Asia, left the west alone and proselytized in the east. The peculiar detestation felt by the Church for the doctrines of the Manichæans was perhaps partly due to the fact that they were in spirit Asiatic. And the converse of this antipathy is also true: the progress of Christianity in Asia has been insignificant.

But when people of the same race profess different creeds, these creeds do influence one another and tend to approximate. This is specially remarkable in India, where Islam, in theory the uncompromising opponent of image worship and polytheism, is sometimes in practice undistinguishable from the lower superstitions of Hinduism. In the middle ages Buddhism and Hinduism converged until they coincided so completely that Buddhism disappeared. In China it often needs an expert to distinguish the manifestations of Taoism and Buddhism: in Japan Buddhism and the old national religion were combined in the mixed worship known as Ryōbu Shintō. In the British Isles an impartial observer would probably notice that Anglicans and English Roman Catholics (not Irish perhaps) have more in common than they think.

There are clearly two sets of causes which may divide a race between religions: internal movements, such as the rise of Buddhism, and external impulses, such as missions or conquest. Conquest pure and simple is best illustrated by the history of Islam, also by the conversion of Mexico and South America to Roman Catholicism. But even when conversion is pacific, it will generally be found that, if it is successful on a large scale, it means the introduction of more than a creed. The religious leader in his own country can trust to his eloquence and power over his hearers. The real support of the missionary, however little he may like the idea, is usually that he represents a superior type of civilization. At one time in their career Buddhism and Christianity were the greatest agencies for spreading civilization in Asia and Europe respectively. They brought with them art and literature: they had the encouragement of the most enlightened princes: those who did not accept them in many cases remained obviously on a lower level. Much the same thing happens in Africa to-day. The natives who accept Mohammedanism or Christianity are moved, not by the arguments of the Koran or Bible, but by the idea that it is a fine thing to be like an Arab or a European. A pagan in Uganda is literally a pagan; an uninstructed rustic from a distant village.

Now if we consider the relations of India with the west, we find on neither side the conditions which usually render propaganda successful. Before the Mohammedan invasions and the Portuguese conquest of Goa, no faith can have presented itself to the Hindus with anything like the prestige which marked the advent of Buddhism in China and Japan. Alexander opened a road to India for Hellenic culture and with it came some religious ideas, but the Greeks had no missionary spirit and if there were any early Christian missions they must have been on a small scale. The same is true of the west: if Asoka's missions reached their destination, they failed to inspire any record of their doings. Still there was traffic by land and sea. The Hindus, if self-complacent, were not averse to new ideas, and before the establishment of Christianity there was not much bigotry in the west, for organized religion was unknown in Europe: practices might be forbidden as immoral or anti-social but such expressions as contrary to the Bible or Koran had no equivalent. Old worships were felt to be unsatisfying: new ones were freely adopted: mysteries were relished. There was no invasion, nothing that suggested foreign conquest or alarmed national jealousy, but the way was open to ideas, though they ran some risk of suffering transformation on their long journey.

As I have repeatedly pointed out, Hinduism and Buddhism are essentially religions of central and eastern, not of western Asia, but they came in contact with the west in several regions and an enquiry into the influence which they exercised or felt can be subdivided. There is the question whether they owe anything to Christianity in their later developments and also the question whether Christianity has borrowed anything from them[1]. Other questions to be considered are the relations of Indian religions to Zoroastrianism in ancient and to Islam in more recent times, which, if of less general interest than problems involving Christianity, are easier to investigate and of considerable importance.

Let us begin with the influence of Christianity on Indian religion. For earlier periods the record of contact between Hindus and Christians is fragmentary, but the evidence of the last two centuries may give a significant indication as to the effect of early Christian influence. In these two centuries Christianity has been presented to the Hindus in the most favourable circumstances: it has come as the religion of the

[1] The most learned and lucid discussion of these questions, which includes an account of earlier literature on the subject, is to be found in Garbe's *Indien und das Christentum*, 1914. But I am not able to accept all his conclusions. The work, to which I am much indebted, is cited below as Garbe. See also Carpenter, *Theism in Medieval India*, 1921, pp. 521–524.

governing power and associated with European civilization: it has not, like Mohammedanism, been propagated by force or accompanied by any intolerance which could awaken repugnance, but its doctrines have been preached and expounded by private missionaries, if not always with skill and sympathy, at least with zeal and a desire to persuade. The result is that according to the census of 1911 there are now 3,876,000 Christians including Europeans, that is to say, a sect a little stronger than the Sikhs as against more than sixty-six million Mohammedans. Of these 3,876,000 many are drawn from the lowest castes or from tribes that are hardly considered as Hindus. Some religious associations, generally known as Somaj, have been founded under the influence of European philosophy as much as of Christianity: imitation of European civilization (which is quite a different thing from Christianity) is visible in the objects and methods of religious and philanthropic institutions: some curious mixed sects of small numerical strength have been formed by the fusion of Christian with Hindu or Mohammedan elements or of all three together. Yet the religious thought and customs of India in general seem hardly conscious of contact with Christianity: there is no sign that they have felt any fancy for the theology of the Athanasian Creed or the ceremonics of the Roman Catholic Church which might have interested speculative and ritualistic minds. Similarly, though intellectual intercourse between India and China was long and fairly intimate and though the influence of Indian thought on China was very great, yet the influence of China on Indian thought is negligible. This being so, it would be rash to believe without good evidence that, in the past, doctrines which have penetrated Indian literature during centuries and have found acceptance with untold millions owe their origin to obscure foreign colonists or missions.

Writers who wish to prove that Indian religions are indebted to Christianity often approach their task with a certain misconception. They assume that if at some remote epoch a few stray Christians reached India, they could overcome without difficulty the barriers of language and social usage and further that their doctrine would be accepted as something new and striking which would straightway influence popular superstition and philosophic thought. But Lyall gives a juster perspective in his poem about the Meditations of a Hindu Prince who, grown sceptical in the quest of truth, listens to the "word of the English," and finds it:

"Naught but the world wide story how the earth and the heavens began,
How the gods were glad and angry and a deity once was man."

Many doctrines preached by Christianity such as the love of God, salvation by faith, and the incarnation, had been thought out in India before the Christian era, and when Christian missionaries preached them they probably seemed to thoughtful Hindus a new and not very adequate version of a very old tale. On the other hand the central and peculiar doctrine of dogmatic Christianity is that the world has been saved by the death of Christ. If this doctrine of the atonement or the sacrifice of a divine being had appeared in India as an importation from the west, we might justly talk of the influence of Christianity on Indian religion. But it is unknown in Hinduism and Buddhism or (since it is rash to make absolute statements about these vast and multifarious growths of speculation) it is at any rate exceedingly rare. These facts create a presumption that the resemblances between Christianity and Indian religion are due to coincidence rather than borrowing, unless borrowing can be clearly proved, and this conclusion, though it may seem tame, is surely a source of satisfaction. The divagations of human thought are manifold and its conclusions often contradictory, but if there is anything that can be called truth it is but natural that logic, intuition, philosophy, poetry, learning and saintship should in different countries sometimes attain similar results.

Christianity, like other western ideas, may have reached India both by land and by sea. After the conquests of Alexander had once opened the route to the Indus and established Hellenistic kingdoms in its vicinity, the ideas and art of Greece and Rome journeyed without difficulty to the Panjab, arriving perhaps as somewhat wayworn and cosmopolitan travellers but still clearly European. A certain amount of Christianity *may* have come along this track, but for any historical investigation clearly the first question is, what is the earliest period at which we have any record of its presence in India? It would appear[1]

[1] See Garbe and Harnack, *Mission und Ausbreitung des Christentums*, II. Chrysostom (Hom. in Joh. 2. 2) writing at the end of the fourth century speaks of Syrians,

that the first allusions to the presence of Christians in Parthia, Bactria and the border lands of India date from the third century and that the oldest account[1] of Christian communities in southern India is the narrative of Cosmas Indicopleustes (*c.* 525 A.D.). These latter Christians probably came to India by sea from Persia in consequence of the persecutions which raged there in 343 and 414, exactly as at a later date the Parsees escaped the violence of the Moslims by emigrating to Gujarat and Bombay.

The story that the Apostle Thomas preached in some part of India has often been used as an argument for the early introduction and influence of Christianity, but recent authorities agree in thinking that it is legendary or at best not provable. The tale occurs first in the Acts of St Thomas[2], the Syriac text of which is considered to date from about 250. It relates how the apostle was sold as a slave skilled in architecture and coming to the Court of Gundaphar, king of India, undertook to build a palace but expended the moneys given to him in charity and, when called to account, explained that he was building for the king a palace in heaven, not made with hands. This sounds more like an echo of some Buddhist Jâtaka written in praise of liberality than an embellishment of any real biography. Other legends make southern India the sphere of Thomas's activity, though he can hardly have taught in both Madras and Parthia, and a similar uncertainty is indicated by the tradition that his relics were transported to Edessa, which doubtless means that according to other accounts he died there. Tradition connects Thomas with Parthians quite as much as with Indians, and, if he really contributed to the diffusion of Christianity, it is more

Egyptians, Persians and ten thousand other nations learning Christianity from translations into their languages, but one cannot expect geographical accuracy in so rhetorical a passage.

[1] Eusebius (*Ecc. Hist.* v. 10), supported by notices in Jerome and others, states that Pantænus went from Alexandria to preach in India and found there Christians using the Gospel according to Matthew written in Hebrew characters. It had been left there by the Apostle Bartholomew. But many scholars are of opinion that by India in this passage is meant southern Arabia. In these early notices India is used vaguely for Eastern Parthia, Southern Arabia and even Ethiopia. It requires considerable evidence to make it probable that at the time of Pantænus (second century A.D.) any one in India used the Gospel in a Semitic language.

[2] See, for the Thomas legend, Garbe, Vincent Smith, *Early History of India*, 3rd ed. pp. 231 ff., and Philipps in *I.A.* 1903, pp. 1–15 and 145–160.

likely that he laboured in the western part of Parthia than on its extreme eastern frontiers. The fact that there really was an Indo-Parthian king with a name something like Gondophares no more makes the legend of St Thomas historical than the fact that there was a Bohemian king with a name something like Wenceslas makes the Christmas carol containing that name historical.

On the other hand it is clear that during the early centuries of our era no definite frontier in the religious and intellectual sphere can be drawn between India and Persia. Christianity reached Persia early: it formed part of the composite creed of Mani, who was born about 216, and Christians were persecuted in 343. From at least the third century onwards Christian ideas *may* have entered India, but this does not authorize the assumption that they came with sufficient prestige and following to exercise any lively influence, or in sufficient purity to be clearly distinguished from Zoroastrianism and Manichæism.

By water there was an ancient connection between the west coast of India and both the Red Sea and Persian Gulf. Traffic by the former route was specially active, from the time of Augustus to that of Nero. Pliny[1] complains that every year India and the East took from Italy a hundred million sesterces in return for spices, perfumes and ornaments. Strabo[2] who visited Egypt tells how 120 ships sailed from Myos Hormos (on the Red Sea) to India "although in the time of the Ptolemies scarcely any one would undertake this voyage." Muziris (Cranganore) was the chief depot of western trade and even seems to have been the seat of a Roman commercial colony. Roman coins have been found in northern and even more abundantly in southern India, and Hindu mints used Roman models. But only rarely can any one except sailors and merchants, who made a speciality of eastern trade, have undertaken the long and arduous journey. Certainly ideas travel with mysterious rapidity. The debt of Indian astronomy to Greece is undeniable[3] and if the same cannot be affirmed of Indian mathematics and medicine yet the resemblance between Greek and Indian treatises on these sciences is remarkable. Early

[1] *Nat. Hist.* XII. 18 (41).

[2] II. iv. 12. Strabo died soon after 21 A.D.

[3] It is seen even in borrowed words, *e.g.* hora = ὥρα: Jyau = Ζεύς: Heli = ἥλιος.

Tamil poems[1] speak of Greek wines and dumb (that is unintelligible) Roman soldiers in the service of Indian kings, but do not mention philosophers, teachers or missionaries. After 70 A.D. this trade declined, perhaps because the Flavian Emperors and their successors were averse to the oriental luxuries which formed its staple, and in 215 the massacre ordered by Caracalla dealt a blow to the commercial importance of Alexandria from which it did not recover for a long time. Thus the period when intercourse between Egypt and India was most active is anterior to the period when Christianity began to spread: it is hardly likely that in 70 or 80 A.D. there were many Christians in Egypt.

As already mentioned, colonies of Christians from Persia settled on the west coast of India, where there are also Jewish colonies of considerable antiquity. The story that this Church was founded by St Thomas and that his relics are preserved in south India has not been found in any work older than Marco Polo[2]. Cosmas Indicopleustes states that the Bishop of Kalliana was appointed from Persia, and this explains the connection of Nestorianism with southern India, for at that time the Nestorian Catholicos of Ctesiphon was the only Christian prelate tolerated by the Persian Government.

This Church may have had a considerable number of adherents for it was not confined to Malabar, its home and centre, but had branches on the east coast near Madras. But it was isolated and became corrupt. It is said that in 660 it had no regular ministry and in the fourteenth century even baptism had fallen into disuse. Like the popular forms of Mohammedanism it adopted many Hindu doctrines and rites. This implies on the one hand a considerable exchange of ideas: on the other hand, if such reformers as Râmânuja and Râmânanda were in touch with these Nestorians we may doubt if they would have imbibed from them the teaching of the New Testament. There is evidence that Roman Catholic missions on their way to or from China landed in Malabar during the thirteenth and fourteenth centuries and made some converts. In 1330 the

[1] See Kanakasabhai's book, *The Tamils 1800 years ago.*

[2] Harnack (*Mission und Ausbreitung des Christentums*, II. 126) says "Dass die Thomas-Christen welche man im 16 Jahrhundert in Indien wieder entdeckte bis ins 3 Jahrhundert hinaufgehen lässt sich nicht erweisen."

Pope sent a Bishop to Quilon with the object of bringing the Nestorians into communion with the see of Rome. But the definite establishment of Roman Catholicism dates from the Portuguese conquest of Goa in 1510, followed by the appointment of an Archbishop and the introduction of the Inquisition. Henceforth there is no difficulty in accounting for Christian influence, but it is generally admitted that the intolerance of the Portuguese made them and their religion distasteful to Hindus and Moslims alike. We hear, however, that Akbar, desiring to hear Christian doctrines represented in a disputation held at his Court, sent for Christian priests from Goa, and his Minister Abul Fazl is quoted as having written poetry in which mosques, churches and temples are classed together as places where people seek for God[1].

Such being the opportunities and approximate dates for Christian influence in India, we may now examine the features in Hinduism which have been attributed to it. They may be classified under three principal heads. (i) The monotheistic Sivaism of the south. (ii) Various doctrines of Vaishnavism such as *bhakti*, grace, the love and fatherhood of God, the Word, and incarnation. (iii) Particular ceremonies or traditions such as the sacred meal known as Prasâda and the stories of Krishna's infancy.

In southern India we have a seaboard in communication with Egypt, Arabia and the Persian Gulf. The reality of intercourse with the west is attested by Roman, Jewish, Nestorian and Mohammedan settlements, but on the other hand the Brahmans of Malabar are remarkable even according to Hindu standards for their strictness and aloofness. As I have pointed out elsewhere, the want of chronology in south Indian literature makes it difficult to sketch with any precision even the outlines of its religious history, but it is probable that Aryan religion came first in the form of Buddhism and Jainism and that Sivaism made its appearance only when the ground had been prepared by them. They were less exposed than the Buddhism of the north to the influences which created the Mahâyâna, but they no doubt mingled with the indigenous beliefs of the Dravidians. There is no record of what these may have been before

[1] For Akbar and Christianity, see *Cathay and the Way Thither* (Hakluyt Society), vol. IV. 172–3.

contact with Hindu civilization; in historical times they comprise the propitiation of spirits, mostly malignant and hence often called devils, but also a strong tendency to monotheism and ethical poetry of a high moral standard. These latter characteristics are noticeable in most, if not all, Dravidian races, even those which are in the lower stages of civilization[1]. This temperament, educated by Buddhism and finally selecting Sivaism, might spontaneously produce such poems as the Tiruvâçagam. Such ideas as God's love for human souls and the soul's struggle to be worthy of that love are found in other Indian religions besides Tamil Sivaism and in their earlier forms cannot be ascribed to Christian influence, but it must be admitted that the poems of the Sittars show an extraordinary approximation to the language of devotional literature in Europe. If, as Caldwell thinks, these compositions are as recent as the sixteenth or seventeenth century, there is no chronological difficulty in supposing their contents to be inspired by Christian ideas. But the question rather is, would Portuguese Catholicism or corrupt Nestorianism have inspired poems denouncing idolatry and inculcating the purest theism? Scepticism on this point is permissible. I am inclined to think that the influence of Christianity as well as the much greater influence of Mohammedanism was mostly indirect. They imported little in the way of custom and dogma but they strengthened the idea which naturally accompanies sectarianism, namely, that it is reasonable and proper for a religion to inculcate the worship of one all-sufficient power. But that this idea can flourish in surroundings repugnant to both Christianity and Islam is shown by the sect of Lingâyats.

The resemblances to Christianity in Vishnuism are on a larger scale than the corresponding phenomena in Sivaism. In most parts of India, from Assam to Madras, the worship of Vishnu and his incarnations has assumed the form of a monotheism which, if frequently turning into pantheism, still persistently inculcates loving devotion to a deity who is himself moved by love for mankind. The corresponding phase of Sivaism is restricted to certain periods and districts of southern India. The doctrine of *bhakti*, or devotional faith, is common to Vishnuites and Sivaites, but is more prominent among the

[1] See Gover, *Folk Songs of Southern India*, 1871.

former. It has often been conjectured to be due to Christian influence but the conjecture is, I think, wrong, for the doctrine is probably pre-Christian. Pâṇini[1] appears to allude to it, and the idea of loving devotion to God is fully developed in the Śvetâśvatara Upanishad and the Bhagavad-gîtâ, works of doubtful date it is true, but in my opinion anterior to the Christian era and on any hypothesis not much posterior to it. Some time must have elapsed after the death of Christ before Christianity could present itself in India as an influential doctrine. Also *bhakti* does not make its first appearance as something new and full grown. The seed, the young plant and the flower can all be found on Indian soil. So, too, the idea that God became man for the sake of mankind is a gradual Indian growth. In the Veda Vishnu takes three steps for the good of men. It is probable that his avatâras were recognized some centuries before Christ and, if this is regarded as not demonstrable, it cannot be denied that the analogous conception of Buddhas who visit the world to save and instruct mankind is pre-Christian[2]. Similarly though passages may be found in the writings of Kabir and others in which the doctrine of Śabda or the Word is stated in language recalling the fourth Gospel, and though in this case the hypothesis of imitation offers no chronological difficulties, yet it is unnecessary. For Śabda, in the sense of the Veda conceived as an eternal self-existent sound, is an old Indian notion and when stated in these terms does not appear very Christian. It is found in Zoroastrianism, where Manthra Spenta the holy word is said to be the very soul of God[3], and it is perhaps connected with the still more primitive notion that words and names have a mysterious potency and are in themselves spells. But even if the idea of Śabda were derived from the idea of Logos it need not be an instance of specifically Christian influence, for this Logos idea was only utilized by Christianity and was part of the common stock of religious thought prevalent about the time of Christ in Egypt, Syria and Asia Minor, and it is even possible that its earlier forms may owe something to India. And were it proved that

[1] IV. 3. 95, 98.

[2] Cf. the Pali verses in the Therîgâthâ, 157: "Hail to thee, Buddha, who savest me and many others from suffering."

[3] See Yasht, 13. 81 and Vendidad, 19. 14.

the teaching of Kabir, which clearly owes much to Islam, also owes much to Christianity, the fact would not be very important, for the followers of Kabir form a small and eccentric though interesting sect, in no way typical of Hinduism as a whole.

The form of Vishnuism known as Pancarâtra appears to have had its origin, or at least to have flourished very early, in Kashmir and the extreme north-west, and perhaps a direct connection may be traced between central Asia and some aspects of the worship of Krishna at Muttra. The passage of Greek and Persian influence through the frontier districts is attested by statuary and coins, but no such memorials of Christianity have been discovered. But the leaders of the Vishnuite movement in the twelfth and subsequent centuries were mostly Brahmans of southern extraction who migrated to Hindustan. Stress is sometimes laid on the fact that they lived in the neighbourhood of ancient Nestorian churches and even Garbe thinks that Râmânuja, who studied for some time at Conjevaram, was in touch with the Christians of Mailapur near Madras. I find it hard to believe that such contact can have had much result. For Râmânuja was a Brahman of the straitest sect who probably thought it contamination to be within speaking distance of a Christian[1]. He was undoubtedly a remarkable scholar and knew by heart all the principal Hindu scriptures, including those that teach *bhakti*. Why then suppose that he took his ideas not from works like the Bhagavad-gîtâ on which he wrote a commentary or from the Pancarâtra which he eulogizes, but from persons whom he must have regarded as obscure heretics? And lastly is there any proof that such ideas as the love of God and salvation by faith flourished among the Christians of Mailapur? In remote branches of the oriental Church Christianity is generally reduced to legends and superstitions, and this Church was so corrupt that it had even lost the rite of

[1] The liberal ideas as to caste held by some Vishnuites are due to Râmânand (c. 1400) who was excommunicated by his coreligionists. I find it hard to agree with Garbe that Râmânuja admitted the theoretical equality of all castes. He says himself (Sri-Bhâshya, II. 3. 46, 47) that souls are of the same nature in so far as they are all parts of Brahman (a proposition which follows from his fundamental principles and is not at all due to Christian influence), but that some men are entitled to read the Veda while others are debarred from the privilege. All fire, he adds, is of the same nature, but fire taken from the house of a Brahman is pure, whereas fire taken from a cremation ground is impure. Even so the soul is defiled by being associated with a low-caste body.

baptism and is said to have held that the third person of the Trinity was the Madonna[1] and not the Holy Ghost. Surely this doctrine is an extraordinary heresy in Christianity and far from having inspired Hindu theories as to the position of Vishnu's spouse is borrowed from those theories or from some of the innumerable Indian doctrines about the Śakti.

It is clear that the Advaita philosophy of Śankara was influential in India from the ninth century to the twelfth and then lost some of its prestige owing to the rise of a more personal theism. It does not seem to me that any introduction or reinforcement of Christianity, to which this theistic movement might be attributed, can be proved to have taken place about 1100, and it is not always safe to seek for a political or social explanation of such movements. But if we must have an external explanation, the obvious one is the progress of Mohammedanism. One may even suggest a parallel between the epochs of Śankara and of Râmânuja. The former, though the avowed enemy of Buddhism, introduced into Hinduism the doctrine of Mâyâ described by Indian critics as crypto-Buddhism. Râmânuja probably did not come into direct contact with Islam[2], which was the chief enemy of Hinduism in his time, but his theism (which, however, was semi-pantheistic) may have been similarly due to the impression produced by that enemy on Indian thought[3].

It is easy to see superficial parallels between Hindu and Christian ceremonies, but on examination they are generally not found to prove that there has been direct borrowing from Christianity. For instance, the superior castes are commonly styled twice born in virtue of certain initiatory ceremonies performed on them in youth, and it is natural to compare this second birth with baptismal regeneration. But, though there is here a real similarity of ideas, it would be hard to deny that these ideas as well as the practices which express them have arisen

[1] See Grieson and Garbe. But I have not found a quotation from any original authority. Mohammed, however, had the same notion of the Trinity.

[2] But the Mappilahs or Moplahs appear to have settled on the Malabar coast about 900 A.D.

[3] Similarly the neo-Confucianism of the Sung dynasty was influenced by Mahâyânist Buddhism. Chu-hsi and his disciples condemned Buddhism, but the new problems and new solutions which they brought forward would not have been heard of but for Buddhism.

independently[1]. And though a practice of sprinkling the forehead with water similar to baptism is in use among Hindus, it is only a variety of the world-wide ceremony of purification with sacred water. Several authors have seen a resemblance between the communion and a sacred meal often eaten in Hindu temples and called *prasâd* (favour) or mahâprasâd. The usual forms of this observance do not resemble the Mass in externals (as do certain ceremonies in Lamaism) and the analogy, if any, resides in the eating of a common religious meal. Such a meal in Indian temples has its origin in the necessity and advantage of disposing of sacrificial food. It cannot be maintained that the deities eat the substance of it and, if it is not consumed by fire, the obvious method of disposal is for mankind to eat it. The practice is probably world-wide and the consumers may be either the priests or the worshippers. Both varieties of the rite are found in India. In the ancient Soma sacrifices the officiants drank the residue of the sacred drink: in modern temples, where ample meals are set before the god more than once a day, it is the custom, perhaps because it is more advantageous, to sell them to the devout. From this point of view the *prasâd* is by no means the equivalent of the Lord's Supper, but rather of the things offered to idols which many early Christians scrupled to eat. It has, however, another and special significance due to the regulations imposed by caste. As a rule a Hindu of respectable social status cannot eat with his inferiors without incurring defilement. But in many temples members of all castes can eat the *prasâd* together as a sign that before the deity all his worshippers are equal. From this point of view the *prasâd* is really analogous to the communion inasmuch as it is the sign of religious community, but it is clearly distinct in origin and though the sacred food may be eaten with great reverence, we are not told that it is associated with the ideas of commemoration, sacrifice or transubstantiation which cling to the Christian sacrament[2].

[1] The idea of the second birth is found in the Majjhima Nikâya, where in Sutta 86 the converted brigand Angulimâla speaks of his regenerate life as *Yato aham ariyâya jâtiyâ jâto*, "Since I was born by this noble (or holy) birth." Brahmanic parallels are numerous, *e.g.* Manu, 2. 146.

[2] It is said, however, that the celebration of the Prasâd by the Kabirpanthis bears an extraordinary resemblance to the Holy Communion of Christians. This may be so, but, as already mentioned, this late and admittedly composite sect is not typical of Hinduism as a whole.

The most curious coincidences between Indian and Christian legend are afforded by the stories and representations of the birth and infancy of Krishna. These have been elaborately discussed by Weber in a well-known monograph[1]. Krishna is represented with his mother, much as the infant Christ with the Madonna; he is born in a stable[2], and other well-known incidents such as the appearance of a star are reproduced. Two things strike us in these resemblances. Firstly, they are not found in the usual literary version of the Indian legend[3], and it is therefore probable that they represent an independent and borrowed story: secondly, they are almost entirely concerned with the mythological aspects of Christianity. Many Christians would admit that the adoration of the Virgin and Child is unscriptural and borrowed from the worship of pagan goddesses who were represented as holding their divine offspring in their arms. If this is admitted, it is possible that Devakî and her son may be a replica not of the Madonna but of a pagan prototype. But there is no difficulty in admitting that Christian legends and Christian art may have entered northern India from Bactria and Persia, and have found a home in Muttra. Only it does not follow from this that any penetrating influence transformed Hindu thought and is responsible for Krishna's divinity, for the idea of *bhakti*, or for the theology of the Bhagavad-gîtâ. The borrowed features in the Krishna story are superficial and also late. They do not occur in the Mahâbhârata and the earliest authority cited by Weber is Hemâdri, a writer of the thirteenth century. Allowing that what he describes may have existed several centuries before his own date, we have still no ground for tracing the main ideas of Vaishnavism to Christianity and the later vagaries of Krishnaism are precisely the aspects of Indian religion which most outrage Christian sentiment.

One edition of the Bhavishya Purana contains a summary

[1] Krishṇajanmâshṭamî, *Memoirs of Academy of Berlin*, 1867.

[2] In spite of making enquiry I have never seen or heard of these representations of a stable myself. As Senart points out (*Légende*, p. 336) all the personages who play a part in Krishna's early life are shown in these tableaux in one group, but this does not imply that shepherds and their flocks are supposed to be present at his birth.

[3] Though the ordinary legend does not say that Krishna was born in a stable yet it does associate him with cattle.

of the book of Genesis from Adam to Abraham[1]. Though it is a late interpolation, it shows conclusively that the editors of Puranas had no objection to borrowing from Christian sources and it may be that some incidents in the life of Krishna as related by the Vishnu, Bhâgavata and other Puranas are borrowed from the Gospels, such as Kamsa's orders to massacre all male infants when Krishna is born, the journey of Nanda, Krishna's foster-father, to Mathurâ in order to pay taxes and the presentation of a pot of ointment to Krishna by a hunchback woman whom he miraculously makes straight. In estimating the importance of such coincidences we must remember that they are merely casual details in a long story of adventures which, in their general outline, bear no relation to the life of Christ. The most striking of these is the "massacre of the Innocents." The Harivaṃsa, which is not later than the fifth century A.D., relates that Kamsa killed all the other children of Devakî, though it does not mention a general massacre, and Pâtanjali (*c.* 150 B.C.) knew the legend of the hostility between Krishna and Kamsa and the latter's death[2]. So if anything has been borrowed from the Gospel account it is only the general slaughter of children. The mention of a pot of ointment strikes Europeans because such an object is not familiar to us, but it was an ordinary form of luxury in India and Judæa alike, and the fact that a woman honoured both Krishna and Christ in the same way but in totally different circumstances is hardly more than a chance coincidence. The fact that both Nanda and Joseph leave their homes in order to pay their taxes is certainly curious and I will leave the reader to form his own opinion about it. The instance of the Bhavishya Purana shows that Hindus had no scruples about borrowing from the Bible and in some Indian dialects the name Krishna appears as Krishto or Kushto. On the other hand, whatever borrowing there may have been is concerned exclusively with trivial details: the principal episodes of the Krishna legend were known before the Christian era.

This is perhaps the place to examine a curious episode of the Mahâbhârata which narrates the visit of certain sages to

[1] Pargiter, *Dynasties of the Kali age*, p. xviii.

[2] Commentary on Pânini, 2. 3. 36, 3. 1. 36 and 3. 2. 111. It seems probable that Pâtanjali knew the story of Krishna and Kamsa substantially as it is recounted in the Harivaṃsa.

a region called Śvetadvîpa, the white island or continent, identified by some with Alexandria or a Christian settlement in central Asia. The episode occurs in the Śantiparvan[1] of the Mahâbhârata and is introduced by the story of a royal sacrifice, at which most of the gods appeared in visible shape but Hari (Vishnu or Krishna) took his offerings unseen. The king and his priests were angry, but three sages called Ekata, Dvita and Trita, who are described as the miraculous offspring of Brahmâ, interposed explaining that none of those present were worthy to see Hari. They related how they had once desired to behold him in his own form and after protracted austerities repaired under divine guidance to an island called Śvetadvîpa on the northern shores of the Sea of Milk[2]. It was inhabited by beings white and shining like the moon who followed the rules of the Pancarâtra, took no food and were continually engaged in silent prayer. So great was the effulgence that at first the visitors were blinded. It was only after another century of penance that they began to have hopes of beholding the deity. Then there suddenly arose a great light. The inhabitants of the island ran towards it with joined hands and, as if they were making an offering, cried, "Victory to thee, O thou of the lotus eyes, reverence to thee, producer of all things: reverence to thee,

[1] Section 337. A journey to Śvetadvîpa is also related in the Kathâsarit sâgara, LIV.

[2] The most accessible statement of the geographical fancies here referred to is in Vishnu Purâna, Book II, chap. IV. The Sea of Milk is the sixth of the seven concentric seas which surround Jambudvîpa and Mt Meru. It divides the sixth of the concentric continents or Śâkadvîpa from the seventh or Pushkara-dvîpa. The inhabitants of Śâkadvîpa worship Vishnu as the Sun and have this much reality that at any rate, according to the Vishnu and Bhavishya Purânas, they are clearly Iranian Sun-worshippers whose priests are called Magas or Mṛigas. Pushkara-dvîpa is a terrestrial paradise: the inhabitants live a thousand years, are of the same nature as the gods and free from sorrow and sin. "The three Vedas, the Purânas, Ethics and Polity are unknown" among them and "there are no distinctions of caste or order: there are no fixed institutes." The turn of fancy which located this non-Brahmanic Utopia in the north seems akin to that which led the Greeks to talk of Hyperboreans. Fairly early in the history of India it must have been discovered that the western, southern, and eastern coasts were washed by the sea so that the earthly paradise was naturally placed in the north. Thus we hear of an abode of the blessed called the country of the holy Uttara Kurus or northern Kurus. Here nothing can be perceived with human senses (Mahâbh. Sabhâ, 1045), and it is mentioned in the same breath as Heaven and the city of Indra (*ib.* Anusâs. 2841).

It is not quite clear (neither is it of much moment), whether the Mahâbhârata intends by Śvetadvîpa one of these concentric world divisions or a separate island. The Kûrma and Padma Purânas also mention it as the shining abode of Vishnu and his saintly servants.

Hṛishikeśa, great Purusha, the first-born." The three sages saw nothing but were conscious that a wind laden with perfumes blew past them. They were convinced, however, that the deity had appeared to his worshippers. A voice from heaven told them that this was so and that no one without faith (abhakta) could see Nârâyaṇa.

A subsequent section of the same book tells us that Nârada visited Śvetadvîpa and received from Nârâyaṇa the Pancarâtra, which is thus definitely associated with the locality.

Some writers have seen in this legend a poetical account of contact with Christianity, but wrongly, as I think. We have here no mythicized version of a real journey but a voyage of the imagination. The sea of milk, the white land and its white shining inhabitants are an attempt to express the pure radiance proper to the courts of God, much as the Book of Revelation tells of a sea of glass, elders in white raiment and a deity whose head and hair were white like wool and snow. Nor need we suppose, as some have done, that the worship of the white sages is an attempt to describe the Mass. The story does not say that whenever the White Islanders held a religious service the deity appeared, but that on a particular occasion when the deity appeared they ran to meet him and saluted him with a hymn. The idea that prayer and meditation are the sacrifice to be offered by perfected saints is thoroughly Indian and ancient. The account testifies to the non-Brahmanic character of this worship of Vishnu, which was patronized by the Brahmans though not originated by them, but there is nothing exotic in the hymn to Nârâyaṇa and the epithet first-born (pûrvaja), in which some have detected a Christian flavour, is as old as the Rig Veda. The reason for laying the scene of the story in the north (if indeed the points of the compass have any place in this mythical geography) is no doubt the early connection of the Pancarâtra with Kashmir and north-western India[1]. The facts that some Puranas people the regions near Śvetadvîpa with Iranian sun-worshippers[2] and that some details of the Pancarâtra (though not the system as a whole) show a resemblance to Zoroastrianism suggest interesting hypotheses as to origin of this form of Vishnuism, but more facts are needed to confirm them. Chronology gives us little help, for though the

[1] Garbe thinks that the Sea of Milk is Lake Balkash. For the Pancarâtra see book v. iii. 3.

[2] See note 2 on last page.

Mahâbhârata was substantially complete in the fourth century, it cannot be denied that additions may have been made to it later and that the story of Śvetadvîpa may be one of them. There were Nestorian Bishops at Merv and Herat in the fifth century, but there appears to be no evidence that Christianity reached Transoxiana before the fall of the Sassanids in the first half of the seventh century.

Thus there is little reason to regard Christianity as an important factor in the evolution of Hinduism, because (*a*) there is no evidence that it appeared in an influential form before the sixteenth century and (*b*) there is strong evidence that most of the doctrines and practices resembling Christianity have an Indian origin. On the other hand abundant instances show that the Hindus had no objection to borrowing from a foreign religion anything great or small which took their fancy. But the interesting point is that the principal Christian doctrines were either indigenous in India—such as *bhakti* and *avatâras*—or repugnant to the vast majority of Hindus, such as the crucifixion and atonement. I do not think that Nestorianism had any appreciable effect on the history of religious thought in southern India. Hellenic and Zoroastrian ideas undoubtedly entered north-western India, but, though Christian ideas may have come with them, few of the instances cited seem even probable except some details in the life of Krishna which affect neither the legend as a whole nor the doctrines associated with it. Some later sects, such as the Kabirpanthis, show remarkable resemblances to Christianity, but then the teaching of Kabir was admittedly a blend of Hinduism and Islam, and since Islam accepted many Christian doctrines, it remains to be proved that any further explanation is needed. Barth observed that criticism is generally on the look out for the least trace of Christian influence on Hinduism but does not pay sufficient attention to the extent of Moslim influence. Every student of Indian religion should bear in mind this dictum of the great French savant. After the sixteenth century there is no difficulty in supposing direct contact with Roman Catholicism. Tukaram, the Maratha poet who lived comparatively near to Goa, may have imitated the diction of the Gospels.

Some authors[1] are disposed to see Christian influence in Chinese and Japanese Buddhism, particularly in the Amidist

[1] *E.g.* several works of Lloyd and Saeki, *The Nestorian Monument in China.*

sects. I have touched on this subject in several places but it may be well to summarize my conclusions here.

The chief Amidist doctrines are clearly defined in the Sukhâvatî-vyûha which was translated from Sanskrit into Chinese in the latter half of the second century A.D. It must therefore have existed in Sanskrit at least in the first century of our era, at which period dogmatic Christianity could hardly have penetrated to India or any part of Central Asia where a Sanskrit treatise was likely to be written. Its doctrines must therefore be independent of Christianity and indeed their resemblance to Christianity is often exaggerated, for though salvation by faith in Amida is remarkably like justification by faith, yet Amida is not a Saviour who died for the world and faith in him is coupled with the use of certain invocations. The whole theory has close parallels in Zoroastrianism and is also a natural development of ideas already existing in India.

Nor can I think that the common use of rites on behalf of the dead in Buddhist China is traceable to Christianity. In this case too the parallel is superficial, for the rites are in most cases not prayers *for* the dead: the officiants recite formulæ by which they acquire merit and they then formally transfer this merit to the dead. Seeing how great was the importance assigned to the cult of the dead in China, it is not necessary to seek for explanations why a religion trying to win its way in those countries invented ceremonies to satisfy the popular craving, and Buddhism had no need to imitate Christianity, for from an early period it had countenanced offerings intended to comfort and help the departed.

Under the T'ang dynasty Manichæism, Nestorianism and new streams of Buddhism all entered China. These religions had some similarity to one another, their clergy may have co-operated and Manichæism certainly adopted Buddhist ideas. There is no reason why Buddhism should not have adopted Nestorian ideas and, in so far as the Nestorians familiarized China with the idea of salvation by faith in a divine personage, they may have helped the spread of Amidism. But the evidence that we possess seems to show not that the Nestorians introduced the story of Christ's life and sacrifice into Buddhism but that they suppressed the idea of atonement by his death, possibly under Buddhist influence.

CHAPTER LVI

INDIAN INFLUENCE IN THE WESTERN WORLD

The influence of Indian religion on Christianity is part of the wider question of its influence on the west generally. It is clear that from 200 B.C. until 300 A.D. oriental religion played a considerable part in the countries round the Mediterranean. The worship of the Magna Mater was known in Rome by 200 B.C. and that of Isis and Serapis in the time of Sulla. In the early centuries of the Christian era the cultus of Mithra prevailed not only in Rome but in most parts of Europe where there were Roman legions, even in Britain. These religions may be appropriately labelled with the vague word oriental, for they are not so much the special creeds of Egypt and Persia transplanted into Roman soil as fragments, combinations and adaptations of the most various eastern beliefs. They differed from the forms of worship indigenous to Greece and Italy in being personal, not national: they were often emotional and professed to reveal the nature and destinies of the soul. If we ask whether there are any definitely Indian elements in all this orientalism, the answer must be that there is no clear case of direct borrowing, nothing Indian analogous to the migrations of Isis and Mithra. If Indian thought had any influence on the Mediterranean it was not immediate, but through Persia, Babylonia and Egypt. But it is possible that the doctrine of metempsychosis and the ideal of the ascetic life are echoes of India. Though the former is found in an incomplete shape among savages in many parts of the world, there is no indication that it was indigenous in Egypt, Syria, Babylonia, Asia Minor, Greece or Italy. It crops up now and again as a tenet held by philosophers or communities of cosmopolitan tastes such as the Orphic Societies, but usually in circumstances which suggest a foreign origin. It is said, however, to have formed part of the doctrines taught by the Druids in Gaul. Similarly though occasional fasts and other mortifications may have been usual in the worship of various deities and though the rigorous Spartan discipline was a sort of military asceticism, still the idea that the religious life consists in suppressing the passions, which plays such a large part in Christian monasticism, can be traced not to any Jewish or European institution but to Egypt. Although monasticism spread quickly thence to Syria, it is admitted that the first Christian hermits and monasteries were Egyptian and there is some evidence for the existence there of pagan hermits[1]. Egypt was a most religious country, but it does not appear that asceticism, celibacy or meditation formed part of its older religious life, and their appearance in Hellenistic times may be due to a wave of Asiatic influence starting originally from India.

Looking westwards from India and considering what were the circumstances favouring the diffusion of Indian ideas, we must note first that Hindus have not only been in all ages preoccupied by religious questions but have also had a larger portion of the missionary spirit than is generally supposed. It is true that in wide tracts and long periods this spirit has been suppressed by Brahmanic exclusiveness, but phenomena like the spread of Buddhism and the establishment of Hinduism in Indo-China and Java speak for themselves. The spiritual tide flowed eastwards rather than westwards; still it is probable that its movement was felt, though on a smaller scale, in the accessible parts of the west. By land, our record tells us mainly of what came into India from Persia and Bactria, but something must have gone out. By water we know that at least after about 700 B.C. there was communication with the Persian Gulf, Arabia and probably the Red Sea. Semitic alphabets were borrowed: in the Jâtakas we hear of merchants going to Baveru or Babylon: Solomon's commercial ventures brought him Indian products. But the strongest testimony to the dissemination of religious ideas is found in Asoka's celebrated edict (probably 256 B.C.) in which he claims to have spread the Dhamma as far as the dominions of Antiochus "and beyond that Antiochus to where dwell the four kings named Ptolemy, Antigonus, Magas and Alexander." The kings mentioned are identified as the rulers of Syria, Egypt, Macedonia, Cyrene and Epirus. Asoka compares his missionary triumphs to the military conquests of other monarchs. It may be that the comparison is only too just

[1] See Scott Moncrieff, *Paganism and Christianity in Egypt*, p. 199. Petrie, *Personal Religion in Egypt*, p. 62. But for a contrary view see Preuschen, *Mönchtum und Serapiskult*, 1903.

and that like them he claimed to have extended his law to regions where his name was unknown. No record of the arrival of Buddhist missions in any Hellenistic kingdom has reached us and the language of the edict, if examined critically, is not precise. On the other hand, however vague it may be, it testifies to two things. Firstly, Egypt, Syria and the other Hellenistic states were realities to the Indians of this period, distant but not fabulous regions. Secondly, the king desired to spread the knowledge of the law in these countries and this desire was shared, or inspired, by the monks whom he patronized. It is therefore probable that, though the difficulties of travelling were great and the linguistic difficulties of preaching an Indian religion even greater, missionaries set out for the west and reached if not Macedonia and Epirus, at least Babylon and Alexandria. We may imagine that they would frequent the temples and the company of the priests and not show much talent for public preaching. If no record of them remains, it is not more wonderful than the corresponding silence in the east about Greek visitors to India.

It is only after the Christian era that we find Apollonius and Plotinus looking towards India as the home of wisdom. In earlier periods the definite instances of connection with India are few. Indian figures found at Memphis perhaps indicate the existence there of an Indian colony[1], and a Ptolemaic gravestone has been discovered bearing the signs of the wheel and trident[2]. The infant deity Horus is represented in Indian attitudes and as sitting on a lotus. Some fragments of the Kanarese language have been found on a papyrus, but it appears not to be earlier than the second century A.D.[3] In 21 A.D. Augustus while at Athens received an embassy from India which came *viâ* Antioch.

It was accompanied by a person described as Zarmanochegas, an Indian from Bargosa who astonished the Athenians by publicly burning himself alive[4]. We also hear of the movement of an Indian tribe from the Panjab to Parthia and thence to

[1] Flinders Petrie, *Man*, 1908, p. 129.

[2] *J.R.A.S.* 1898, p. 875.

[3] Hultzsch, *Hermes*, XXXIX. p. 307, and *J.R.A.S.* 1904, p. 399.

[4] Nicolaus Damascenus, quoted by Strabo, XV. 73. See also Dion Cassius, IX. 58, who calls the Indian Zarmaros. Zarmanochegas perhaps contains the two words Śramana and Âcârya.

Armenia (149–127 B.C.)[1], and of an Indian colony at Alexandria in the time of Trajan. Doubtless there were other tribal movements and other mercantile colonies which have left no record, but they were all on a small scale and there was no general outpouring of India westwards.

The early relations of India were with Babylon rather than with Egypt, but if Indian ideas reached Babylon they may easily have spread further. Communication between Egypt and Babylon existed from an early period and the tablets of Tel-el-Amarna testify to the antiquity and intimacy of this intercourse. At a later date Necho invaded Babylonia but was repulsed. The Jews returned from the Babylonian captivity (538 B.C.) with their religious horizon enlarged and modified. They were chiefly affected by Zoroastrian ideas but they may have become acquainted with any views and practices then known in Babylon, and not necessarily with those identified with the state worship, for the exiles may have been led to associate with other strangers. After about 535 B.C. the Persian empire extended from the valley of the Indus to the valley of the Nile and from Macedonia to Babylon. We hear that in the army which Xerxes led against Greece there were Indian soldiers, which is interesting as showing how the Persians transported subject races from one end of their empire to the other. After the career of Alexander, Hellenistic kingdoms took the place of this empire and, apart from inroads on the north-west frontier of India, maintained friendly relations with her. Seleucus Nicator sent Megasthenes as envoy about 300 B.C. and Ptolemy Philadelphus (285–247 B.C.) a representative named Dionysius. Bindusâra, the father of Asoka, exchanged missions with Antiochus, and, according to a well-known anecdote[2], expressed a wish to buy a professor (σοφιστήν). But Antiochus replied that Greek professors were not for sale.

Egyptologists consider that metempsychosis is not part of the earlier strata of Egyptian religion but appears first about 500 B.C., and Flinders Petrie refers to this period the originals of the earliest Hermetic literature. But other authorities regard these works as being both in substance and language consider-

[1] See *J.R.A.S.* 1907, p. 968.

[2] See Vincent Smith, *Early History of India*, edition III. p. 147. The original source of the anecdote is Hegesandros in Athenæus, 14. 652.

ably posterior to the Christian era and as presenting a jumble of Christianity, Neoplatonism and Egyptian ideas.

I have neither space nor competence to discuss the date of the Hermetic writings, but it is of importance for the question which we are considering. They contain addresses to the deity like I am Thou and Thou art I (*ἐγώ εἰμι σὺ καὶ σὺ ἐγώ*). If such words could be used in Egypt several centuries before Christ, the probability of Indian influence seems to me strong, for they would not grow naturally out of Egyptian or Hellenistic religion. Five hundred years later they would be less remarkable. Whatever may be the date of the Hermetic literature, it is certain that the Book of Wisdom and the writings of Philo are pre-Christian and show a mixture of ideas drawn from many sources, Jewish, Neoplatonic and Neopythagorean. If these hospitable systems made the acquaintance of Indian philosophy, we may be sure that they gave it an unprejudiced and even friendly hearing. In the centuries just before the Christian era Egypt was a centre of growth for personal and private religious ideas[1], hardly possessing sufficient organization to form what we call a religion, yet still, inasmuch as they aspired to teach individual souls right conduct as well as true knowledge, implicitly containing the same scheme of teaching as the Buddhist and Christian Churches. But it is characteristic of all this movement that it never attempted to form a national or universal religion and remained in all its manifestations individual and personal, connected neither with the secular government nor with any national cultus. Among these religious ideas were monotheism mingled with pantheism to the extent of saying that God is all and all is one: the idea of the Logos or Divine Wisdom, which ultimately assumes the form that the Word is an emanation or Son of God; asceticism, or at least the desire to free the soul from the bondage of the senses; metempsychosis and the doctrine of conversion or the new birth of the soul, which fits in well with metempsychosis, though it frequently exists apart from it. I doubt if there is sufficient reason for attributing the doctrine of the Logos[2] to India, but it is possible that asceticism and the belief in metempsychosis received their first impulse thence.

[1] See Flinders Petrie, *Personal Religion in Egypt before Christianity*, 1909.

[2] As I have pointed out elsewhere there is little real analogy between the ideas of Logos and Śabda.

They appear late and, like the phraseology of the Hermetic books, they do not grow naturally out of antecedent ideas and practices in Egypt and Palestine. The life followed by such communities as the Therapeutæ and Essenes is just such as might have been evolved by seekers after truth who were trying to put into practice in another country the religious ideals of India. There are differences: for instance these communities laboured with their hands and observed the seventh day, but their main ideas, retirement from the world and suppression of the passions, are those of Indian monks and foreign to Egyptian and Jewish thought.

The character of Pythagoras's teaching and its relation to Egypt have been much discussed and the name of the master was clearly extended by later (and perhaps also by early) disciples to doctrines which he never held. But it seems indisputable that there were widely spread both in Greece and Italy societies called Pythagorean or Orphic which inculcated a common rule of life and believed in metempsychosis. The rule of life did not as a rule amount to asceticism in the Indian sense, which was most uncongenial to Hellenic ideas, but it comprised great self-restraint. The belief in metempsychosis finds remarkably clear expression: we hear in the Orphic fragments of the circle of birth and of escape from it, language strikingly parallel to many Indian utterances and strikingly unlike the usual turns of Greek speech and thought. Thus the soul is addressed as "Hail thou who hast suffered the suffering" and is made to declare "I have flown out of the sorrowful weary wheel[1]." I see no reason for discrediting the story that Pythagoras visited Egypt[2]. He is said to have been a Samian and during his life (*c.* 500 B.C.) Samos had a special connection with Egypt, for Polycrates was the ally of Amasis and assisted him with troops. The date, if somewhat early, is not far removed from the time when metempsychosis became part of Egyptian religion. The general opinion of antiquity connected the Orphic

[1] *Κύκλου δ' ἐξέπταν βαθυπένθεος ἀργαλέοιο.* From the tablet found at Compagno. Cf. Proclus in Plat. *Tim.* v. 330, *ἧς καὶ οἱ παρ' Ὀρφεῖ τῷ Διονύσῳ καὶ τῇ κόρῃ τελούμενοι τυχεῖν εὔχονται Κύκλου τ' αὖ λῆξαι καὶ ἀναπνεῦσαι κακότητος.* See J. E. Harrison, *Proleg. to the study of Greek Religion*, 1908, cap. XI. and appendix.

[2] Burnet, *Early Greek Philosophy*, p. 94, says that it first occurs in the Busiris of Isocrates and does not believe that the account in Herodotus implies that Pythagoras visited Egypt.

doctrines with Thrace but so little is known of the Thracians and their origin that this connection does not carry us much further. They appear, however, to have had relations with Asia Minor and that region must have been in touch with India[1]. But Orphism was also connected with Crete, and Cretan civilization had oriental affinities[2].

The point of greatest interest naturally is to determine what were the religious influences among which Christ grew up. Whatever they may have been, his originality is not called in question. Mohammed was an enquirer: in estimating his work we have often to ask what he had heard about Christianity and Judaism and how far he had understood it correctly. But neither the Buddha nor Christ were enquirers in this sense: they accepted the best thought of their time and country: with a genius which transcends comparison and eludes definition they gave it an expression which has become immortal. Neither the substance nor the form of their teaching can reasonably be regarded as identical, for the Buddha did not treat of God or the divine government of the world, whereas Christ's chief thesis is that God loves the world and that therefore man should love God and his fellow men. But though their basic principles differ, the two doctrines agree in maintaining that happiness is obtainable not by pleasure or success or philosophy or rites but by an unselfish life, culminating in the state called Nirvana or the kingdom of heaven. "The kingdom of heaven is within you."

In the Gospels Christ teaches neither asceticism nor metempsychosis. The absence of the former is remarkable: he eats flesh and allows himself to be anointed: he drinks wine, prescribes its use in religion and is credited with producing it miraculously when human cellars run short. But he praises poverty and the poor: the Sermon on the Mount and the instructions to the Seventy can be put in practice only by those who, like the members of a religious community, have severed all worldly ties and though the extirpation of desire is not in

[1] Whatever may have been the true character and history of the enigmatic people of Mitanni it appears certain that they adored deities with Indian names about 1400 B.C. But they may have been Iranians, and it may be doubted if the Aryan Indians of this date believed in metempsychosis.

[2] J. E. Harrison, *l.c.* pp. 459 and 564, seems to think that Orphism migrated from Crete to Thrace.

the Gospels held up as an end, the detachment, the freedom from care, lust and enmity prescribed by the law of the Buddha find their nearest counterpart in the lives of the Essenes and Therapeutæ. Though we have no record of Christ being brought into contact with these communities (for John the Baptist appears to have been a solitary and erratic preacher) it is probable that their ideals were known to him and influenced his own. Their rule of life may have been a faint reflex of Indian monasticism. But the debt to India must not be exaggerated: much of the oriental element in the Essenes, such as their frequent purifications and their prayers uttered towards the sun, may be due to Persian influence. They seem to have believed in the pre-existence of the soul and to have held that it was imprisoned in the body, but this hardly amounts to metempsychosis, and metempsychosis cannot be found in the New Testament[1]. The old Jewish outlook, preserved by the Sadducees, appears not to have included a belief in any life after death, and the supplements to this materialistic view admitted by the Pharisees hardly amounted to the doctrine of the natural immortality of the soul but rather to a belief that the just would somehow acquire new bodies and live again. Thus people were ready to accept John the Baptist as being Elias in a new form. Perhaps these rather fragmentary ideas of the Jews are traceable to Egyptian and ultimately to Indian teaching about transmigration. That belief is said to crop up occasionally in rabbinical writings but was given no place in orthodox Christianity[2].

With regard to the teaching of Christ then, the conclusion must be that it owes no direct debt to Indian, Egyptian, Persian or other oriental sources. But inasmuch as he was in sympathy with the more spiritual elements of Judaism, largely borrowed during the Babylonian captivity, and with the unworldly and self-denying lives of the Essenes, the tone of his teaching is

[1] The question of the Disciples in John ix. 2. Who did sin, this man or his parents, that he was born blind? must if taken strictly imply some form of pre-existence. But it is a popular question, not a theological statement, and I doubt if severely logical deductions from it are warranted.

[2] The pre-existence of the soul seems to be implied in the Book of Wisdom viii. 20. The remarkable expression in the Epistle of James iii. 6 *τρόχος τῆς γενήσεως* suggests a comparison with the Orphic expressions quoted above and Saṃsâra, but it is difficult to believe it can mean more than "the course of nature."

nearer to these newer and imported doctrines than to the old law of Israel[1].

Some striking parallels have been pointed out between the Gospels and Indian texts of such undoubted antiquity that if imitation is admitted, the Evangelists must have been the imitators. Before considering these instances I invite the reader's attention to two parallel passages from Shakespeare and the Indian poet Bhartrihari. The latter is thus translated by Monier Williams[2]:

> Now for a little while a child, and now
> An amorous youth; then for a season turned
> Into the wealthy householder: then stripped
> Of all his riches, with decrepit limbs
> And wrinkled frame man creeps towards the end
> Of life's erratic course and like an actor
> Passes behind Death's curtain out of view.

The resemblance of this to the well-known lines in *As You Like It*, "All the world's a stage," etc., is obvious, and it is a real resemblance, although the point emphasized by Bhartrihari is that man leaves the world like an actor who at the end of the piece slips behind the curtain, which formed the background of an Indian stage. But, great as is the resemblance, I imagine that no one would maintain that it has any other origin than that a fairly obvious thought occurred to two writers in different times and countries and suggested similar expressions.

Now many parallels between the Buddhist and Christian scriptures—the majority as it seems to me of those collected by Edmunds and Anesaki—belong to this class[3]. One of the most striking is the passage in the Vinaya relating how the

[1] As in their legends, so in their doctrines, the uncanonical writings are more oriental than the canonical and contain more pantheistic and ascetic sayings. *E.g.* "Where there is one alone, I am with him. Raise the stone and thou shalt find me: cleave the wood and I am there" (*Oxyrhynchus Logia*). "I am thou and thou art I and wheresoever thou art I am also: and in all things I am distributed and wheresoever thou wilt thou gatherest me and in gathering me thou gatherest thyself" (Gospel of Eve in Epiph. *Haer.* XXVI. 3). "When the Lord was asked, when should his kingdom come, he said: When two shall be one and the without as the within and the male with the female, neither male nor female" (*Logia*).

[2] *Hinduism*, p. 549. The original is to be found in Bhartrihari's Vairogyaśatakam, 112.

[3] *The Buddhist and Christian Gospels*, 4th ed. 1909.

Buddha himself cared for a sick monk who was neglected by his colleagues and said to these latter, "Whosoever would wait upon me let him wait on the sick[1]." Here the resemblance to Matthew xxv. 40 and 45 is remarkable, but I do not imagine that the writer of the Gospel had ever heard or read of the Buddha's words. The sentiment which prompted them, if none too common, is at least widespread and is the same that made Confucius show respect and courtesy to the blind. The setting of the saying in the Vinaya and in the Gospel is quite different: the common point is that one whom all are anxious to honour sees that those around him show no consideration to the sick and unhappy and reproves them in the words of the text, words which admit of many interpretations, the simplest perhaps being "I bid you care for the sick: you neglect me if you neglect those whom I bid you to cherish."

But many passages in Buddhist and Christian writings have been compared where there is no real parallel but only some word or detail which catches the attention and receives an importance which it does not possess. An instance of this is the so-called parable of the prodigal son in the Lotus Sûtra, Chapter IV, which has often been compared with Luke xv. 11 ff. But neither in moral nor in plot are the two parables really similar. The Lotus maintains that there are many varieties of doctrine of which the less profound are not necessarily wrong, and it attempts to illustrate this by not very convincing stories of how a father may withhold the whole truth from his children for their good. In one story a father and son are separated for fifty years and *both* move about: the father becomes very rich, the son poor. The son in his wanderings comes upon his father's palace and recognizes no one. The father, now a very old man, knows his son, but instead of welcoming him at once as his heir puts him through a gradual discipline and explains the real position only on his deathbed. These incidents have nothing in common with the parable related in the Gospel except that a son is lost and found, an event which occurs in a hundred oriental tales. What is much more remarkable, though hardly a case of borrowing, is that in both versions the chief personage, that is Buddha or God, is likened to a father as he also is in the parable of the carriages[2].

[1] Mahâvagga, VIII. 26.

[2] *Lotus*, chap. V.

One of the Jain scriptures called Uttarâdyayana[1] contains the following remarkable passage, "Three merchants set out on their travels each with his capital; one of them gained much, the second returned with his capital and the third merchant came home after having lost his capital. The parable is taken from common life; learn to apply it to the Law. The capital is human life, the gain is heaven," etc. It is impossible to fix the date of this passage: the Jain Canon in which it occurs was edited in 454 A.D. but the component parts of it are much older. It clearly gives a rough sketch of the idea which is elaborated in the parable of the talents. Need we suppose that there has been borrowing on either side? Only in a very restricted sense, I think, if at all. The parable is taken from common life, as the Indian text truly says. It occurred to some teacher, perhaps to many teachers independently, that the spiritual life may be represented as a matter of profit and loss and illustrated by the conduct of those who employ their money profitably or not. The idea is natural and probably far older than the Gospels, but the parable of the talents is an original and detailed treatment of a metaphor which may have been known to the theological schools of both India and Palestine. The parable of the sower bears the same relation to the much older Buddhist comparison of instruction to agriculture[2] in which different classes of hearers correspond to different classes of fields.

I feel considerable hesitation about two other parallels. What relation does the story of the girl who gives two copper coins to the Sangha bear to the parable of the widow's mite? It occurs in Aśvaghosa's Sûtrâlankâra, but though he was a learned poet, it is very unlikely that he had seen the Gospels. Although his poem ends like a fairy tale, for the poor girl marries the king's son as the reward of her piety, yet there is an extraordinary resemblance in the moral and the detail of the *two* mites. Can the origin be some proverb which was current in many countries and worked up differently?

The other parallel is between Christ's meeting with the woman of Samaria and a story in the Divyâvadâna[3] telling how Ânanda asked an outcast maiden for water. Here the Indian work, which is probably not earlier than the third century A.D.,

[1] VII. 15–21 in *S.B.E.* XLV. p. 29.

[2] Sam. Nik. XLII. VII.

[3] Ed. Cowell, p. 611.

might well be the borrower. Yet the incident is thoroughly Indian. The resemblance is not in the conversation but in the fact that both in India and Palestine water given by the impure is held to defile and that in both countries spiritual teachers rise above such rules. Perhaps Europeans, to whom such notions of defilement are unknown, exaggerate the similarity of the narratives, because the similarity of customs on which it depends seems remarkable.

There are, however, some incidents in the Gospels which bear so great a likeness to earlier stories found in the Pitakas that the two narratives can hardly be wholly independent. These are (*a*) the testimony of Asita and Simeon to the future careers of the infant Buddha and Christ: (*b*) the temptation of Buddha and Christ: (*c*) their transfiguration: (*d*) the miracle of walking on the water and its dependence on faith: (*e*) the miracle of feeding a multitude with a little bread. The first three parallels relate to events directly concerning the life of a superhuman teacher, Buddha or Christ. In saying that the two narratives can hardly be independent, I do not mean that one is necessarily unhistorical or that the writers of the Gospels had read the Pitakas. That a great man should have a mental crisis in his early life and feel that the powers of evil are trying to divert him from his high destiny is eminently likely. But in the East superhuman teachers were many and there grew up a tradition, fluctuating indeed but still not entirely without consistency, as to what they may be expected to do. Angelic voices at their birth and earthquakes at their death are coincidences in embellishment on which no stress can be laid, but when we find that Zoroaster, the Buddha and Christ were all tempted by the Evil One and all at the same period of their careers, it is impossible to avoid the suspicion that some of their biographers were influenced by the idea that such an incident was to be expected at that point, unless indeed we regard these so-called temptations as mental crises natural in the development of a religious genius. Similarly it is most remarkable that all accounts of the transfiguration of the Buddha and of Christ agree not only in describing the shining body but in adding a reference to impending death. The resemblance between the stories of Asita and Simeon seems to me less striking but I think that they owe their place in both biographies to the tradition that the superman is recognized and saluted by an aged Saint soon after birth.

The two stories about miracles are of less importance in substance but the curious coincidences in detail suggest that they are pieces of folklore which circulated in Asia and Eastern Europe. The Buddhist versions occur in the introductions to Jâtakas 190 and 78, which are of uncertain date, though they may be very ancient[1]. The idea that saints can walk on the water is found in the Majjhima-nikâya[2], but the Jâtaka adds the following particulars. A disciple desirous of seeing the Buddha begins to walk across a river in an ecstasy of faith. In the middle, his ecstasy fails and he feels himself sinking but by an effort of will he regains his former confidence and meets the Buddha safely on the further bank. In Jâtaka 90 the Buddha miraculously feeds 500 disciples with a single cake and it is expressly mentioned that, after all had been satisfied, the remnants were so numerous that they had to be collected and disposed of.

Still all the parallels cited amount to little more than this, that there was a vague and fluid tradition about the superman's life of which fragments have received a consecration in literature. The Canonical Gospels show great caution in drawing on this fund of tradition, but a number of Buddhist legends make their appearance in the Apocryphal Gospels and are so obviously Indian in character that it can hardly be maintained that they were invented in Palestine or Egypt and spread thence eastwards. Trees bend down before the young Christ and dragons (nâgas) adore him: when he goes to school to learn the alphabet he convicts his teacher of ignorance and the good man faints[3]. When he enters a temple in Egypt the images prostrate themselves before him just as they do before the young Gotama in the temple of Kapilavastu[4]. Mary is luminous before the birth of Christ which takes place without pain or impurity[5]. But the parallel which is most curious, because the incident related is unusual in both Indian and European literature, is

[1] See Rhys Davids, *Buddhist India*, p. 206, and Winternitz, *Ges. Ind. Lit.* II. 91.

[2] Maj. Nik. VI.

[3] Gospel of Thomas: longer version, chaps. VI. XIV. See also the Arabic and Syriac Gospels of the Infancy, cf. Lalita-vistara, chap. X.

[4] Pseudo-Matthew, chap. XXII.–XXIV. and Lal. Vist. chap. VIII.

[5] Pseudo-Matthew, XIII. Cf. Dig. Nik. 14 and Maj. Nik. 123. Neumann's notes on the latter give many curious medieval parallels.

the detailed narrative in the Gospel of James, and also in the Lalita-vistara relating how all activity of mankind and nature was suddenly interrupted at the moment of the nativity[1]. Winds, stars and rivers stayed their motion and labourers stood still in the attitude in which each was surprised. The same Gospel of James also relates that Mary when six months old took seven steps, which must surely be an echo of the legend which attributes the same feat to the infant Buddha.

Several learned authors have discussed the debt of medieval Christian legend to India. The most remarkable instance of this is the canonization by both the Eastern and the Western Church of St Joasaph or Josaphat. It seems to be established that this name is merely a corruption of Bodhisat and that the story in its Christian form goes back to the religious romance called Barlaam and Joasaph which appears to date from the seventh century[2]. It contains the history of an Indian prince who was converted by the preaching of Barlaam and became a hermit, and it introduces some of the well-known stories of Gotama's early life, such as the attempt to hide from him the existence of sickness and old age, and his meetings with a cripple and an old man. The legends of St Placidus (or Hubert) and St Christopher have also been identified with the Nigrodha and Sutasoma Jâtakas[3]. The identification is not to my mind conclusive nor, if it is admitted, of much importance. For who doubts that Indian fables reappear in Aesop or Kalilah and Dimnah? Little is added to this fact if they also appear in legends which may have some connection with the Church but which most Christians feel no obligation to believe.

But the occurrence of Indian legends in the Apocryphal Gospels is more important for it shows that, though in the early centuries of Christianity the Church was shy of this oriental exuberance, yet the materials were at hand for those who chose to use them. Many wonders attending the superman's birth were deliberately rejected but some were accepted and oriental practices, such as asceticism, appear with a suddenness that makes the suspicion of foreign influence legitimate.

Not only was monasticism adopted by Christianity but

[1] See Gospel of James, XVIII. and Lal. Vist. VII. *ad init.*

[2] See Rhys Davids, *Buddhist Birth stories*, 1880, introduction; and Joseph Jacobs, *Barlaam and Josaphat*, 1896.

[3] Nos. 12 and 537.

many practices common to Indian and to Christian worship obtained the approval of the Church at about the same time. Some of these, such as incense and the tonsure, may have been legacies from the Jewish and Egyptian priesthoods. Many coincidences also are due to the fact that both Buddhism and Christianity, while abolishing animal sacrifices, were ready to sanction old religious customs: both countenanced the performance before an image or altar of a ritual including incense, flowers, lights and singing. This recognition of old and widespread rites goes far to explain the extraordinary similarity of Buddhist services in Tibet and Japan (both of which derived their ritual ultimately from India) to Roman Catholic ceremonial. Yet when all allowance is made for similar causes and coincidences, it is hard to believe that a collection of such practices as clerical celibacy, confession, the veneration of relics, the use of the rosary and bells can have originated independently in both religions. The difficulty no doubt is to point out any occasion in the third and fourth centuries A.D. when oriental Christians other than casual travellers had an opportunity of becoming acquainted with Buddhist institutions. But the number of resemblances remains remarkable and some of them—such as clerical celibacy, relics, and confession—are old institutions in Buddhism but appear to have no parallels in Jewish, Syrian, or Egyptian antiquity. Up to a certain point, it is a sound principle not to admit that resemblances prove borrowing, unless it can be shown that there was contact between two nations, but it is also certain that all record of such contact may disappear. For instance, it is indisputable that Hindu civilization was introduced into Camboja, but there is hardly any evidence as to how or when Hindu colonists arrived there, and none whatever as to how or when they left India.

It is in Christian or quasi-Christian heresies—that is, the sects which were rejected by the majority—that Indian influence is plainest. This is natural, for if there is one thing obvious in the history of religion it is that Indian speculation and the Indian view of life were not congenial to the people of Europe and western Asia. But some spirits, from the time of Pythagoras onwards, had a greater affinity for oriental ways of thinking, and such sympathy was specially common among the Gnostics. Gnosticism consisted in the combination of Christianity with the already mixed religion which prevailed in Alexandria, Antioch and other centres, and which was an uncertain and varying compound of Judaism, Hellenistic thought and the ideas of oriental countries such as Egypt, Persia and Babylonia. Its fundamental idea, the knowledge of God or Gnosis, is clearly similar to the Jñânakâṇḍa of the Hindus[1], but the emphasis laid on dualism and redemption is not Indian and the resemblances suggest little more than that hints may have been taken and worked up independently. Thus the idea of the Demiurgus is related to the idea of Îśvara in so far as both imply a distinction not generally recognized in Europe between the creator of the world and the Highest Deity, but the Gnostic developments of the Demiurgus idea are independent. Similarly though the Aeons or emanations of the Gnostics have to some extent a parallel in the beings produced by Brahmâ, Prajâpati or Vâsudeva, yet these latter are not characteristic of Hinduism and still less of Buddhism, for the celestial Buddhas and Bodhisattvas of the Mahâyâna are justly suspected of being additions due to Persian influence.

Bardesanes, one of the latest Gnostic teachers (155–233), wrote a book on Indian religion, quoted by Porphyry. This is important for it shows that he turned towards India for truth, but though his teaching included the pre-existence of the soul and some doctrine of Karma, it was not specially impregnated with Indian ideas. This, however, may be said without exaggeration of Carpocrates and Basilides who both taught at Alexandria about 120–130 A.D. Unfortunately we know the views of these interesting men only from the accounts of their opponents. Carpocrates[2] is said to have claimed the power of coercing by magic the spirits who rule the world and to have taught metempsychosis in the form that the soul is imprisoned in the body again and again until it has performed all possible actions, good and evil. Therefore the only way to escape reincarnation (which is the object of religion) and to rise to a superior sphere of peace is to perform as much action as possible, good and evil, for the distinction between the two depends on intention, not on the nature of deeds. It is only through faith and love that a man

[1] As is also the idea that γνῶσις implies a special ascetic mode of life, the *βίος γνωστικός*.

[2] Irenæus, I. XXV.

can obtain blessedness. Much of the above sounds like a caricature, but it may be a misrepresentation of something analogous to the Indian doctrine that the acts of a Yogi are neither black nor white and that a Yogi in order to get rid of his Karma creates and animates many bodies to work it off for him.

In Basilides we find the doctrines not only of reincarnation, which seems to have been common in Gnostic schools[1], but of Karma, of the suffering inherent in existence and perhaps the composite nature of the soul. He is said to have taught that the martyrs suffered for their sins, that is to say that souls came into the world tainted with the guilt of evil deeds done in another existence. This guilt must be expiated by commonplace misfortune or, for the nobler sort, by martyrdom. He considered the world process to consist in sorting out confused things and the gradual establishment of order. This is to some extent true of the soul as well: it is not an entity but a compound (compare the Buddhist doctrine of the Skandhas) and the passions are appendages. He called God *οὐκ ὢν θεός* which seems an attempt to express the same idea as Brahman devoid of all qualities and attributes (nirguṇa). It is significant that the system of Basilides died out[2].

A more important sect of decidedly oriental affinities was Manichæism, or rather it was a truly oriental religion which succeeded in penetrating to Europe and there took on considerably more Christianity than it had possessed in its original form. Mani himself (215–276) is said to have been a native of Ecbatana but visited Afghanistan, Bactria and India, and his followers carried his faith across Asia to China, while in the west it was the parent inspiration of the Bogomils and Albigenses. The nature and sources of his creed have been the subject of considerable discussion but new light is now pouring in from the Manichæan manuscripts discovered in Central Asia, some of which have already been published. These show that about the seventh century and probably considerably earlier the Manichæism

[1] It appears in the Pistis Sophia which perhaps represents the school of Valentinus. Basilides taught that "unto the third and fourth generation" refers to transmigration (see Clem. Al. fragm. sect. 28 Op., ed. Klotz, IV. 14), and Paul's saying "I was alive without the law once" (Rom. vii. 9), to former life as an animal (Orig. in Ep. ad Rom. v. Op. iv. 549).

[2] For Gnosticism, see *Buddhist Gnosticism*, J. Kennedy in *J.R.A.S.* 1902, and Mead, *Fragments of a Faith Forgotten*.

of those regions had much in common with Buddhism. A Manichæan treatise discovered at Tun-huang[1] has the form of a Buddhist Sûtra: it speaks of Mani as the Tathâgata, it mentions Buddhas of Transformation (Hua-fo) and the Bodhisattva Ti-tsang. Even more important is the confessional formula called Khuastuanift[2] found in the same locality. It is clearly similar to the Pâtimokkha and besides using much Buddhist terminology it reckons killing or injuring animals as a serious sin. It is true that many of these resemblances may be due to association with Buddhism and not to the original teaching of Mani, which was strongly dualistic and contained many Zoroastrian and Babylonian ideas. But it was eclectic and held up an ascetic ideal of celibacy, poverty and fasting unknown to Persia and Babylon. To take life was counted a sin and the adepts formed an order apart who lived on the food given to them by the laity. The more western accounts of the Manichæans testify to these features as strongly as do the records from Central Asia and China. Cyril of Jerusalem in his polemic against them[3] charges them with believing in retributive metempsychosis, he who kills an animal being changed into that animal after death. The Persian king Hormizd is said to have accused Mani of bidding people destroy the world, that is, to retire from social life and not have children. Alberuni[4] states definitely that Mani wrote a book called Shâburkân in which he said that God sent different messengers to mankind in different ages, Buddha to India, Zarâdusht to Persia and Jesus to the west. According to Cyril the Manichæan scriptures were written by one Scythianus and revised by his disciple Terebinthus who changed his name to Boddas. This may be a jumble, but it is hard to stifle the suspicion that it contains some allusion to the Buddha, Śâkya-muni and the Bo tree.

I think therefore that primitive Manichæism, though it contained less Buddhism than did its later and eastern forms, still owed to India its asceticism, its order of celibate adepts and its regard for animal life. When it spread to Africa and

[1] Chavannes et Pelliot, "Un traité Manichéen retrouvé en Chine," *J.A.* 1911, I, and 1913, II.

[2] Le Coq in *J.R.A.S.* 1911, p. 277.

[3] Catechetic Lectures, VI. 20 ff. The whole polemic is curious and worth reading.

[4] Alberuni, *Chronology of ancient nations*, trans. Sachau, p. 190.

Europe it became more Christian, just as it became more Buddhist in China, but it is exceedingly curious to see how this Asiatic religion, like the widely different religion of Mohammed, was even in its latest phrases the subject of bitter hatred and persistent misrepresentation.

Finally, do the Neoplatonists, Neopythagoreans and other pagan philosophers of the early centuries after Christ owe any debt to India? Many of them were consciously endeavouring to arrest the progress of Christianity by transforming philosophy into a non-Christian religion. They gladly welcomed every proof that the higher life was not to be found exclusively or most perfectly in Christianity. Hence bias, if not accurate knowledge, led them to respect all forms of eastern mysticism. Apollonius is said to have travelled in India[1]: in the hope of so doing Plotinus accompanied the unfortunate expedition of Gordian but turned back when it failed. We may surmise that for Plotinus the Indian origin of an idea would have been a point in its favour, although his writings show no special hostility to Christianity[2]. So far as I can judge, his system presents those features which might be expected to come from sympathy with the Indian temperament, aided perhaps not by reading but by conversation with thoughtful orientals at Alexandria and elsewhere. The direct parallels are not striking. Plato himself had entertained the idea of metempsychosis and much that seems oriental in Plotinus may be not a new importation but the elaboration of Plato's views in a form congenial to the age[3]. Affirmations that God is τὸ ὄν and τὸ ἕν are not so much borrowings from the Vedânta philosophy as a re-statement of Hellenic ideas in a mystic and quictist spirit, which may owe something to India. But Plotinus seems to me nearer to India than were the Gnostics and Manichæans, because his teaching is not dualistic to the same extent. He finds the world unsatisfying not because it is the creation of the Evil One, but because it is transitory, imperfect and unreal.

[1] The account in Philostratus (books II. and III.) reads like a romance and hardly proves that Apollonius went to India, but still there is no reason why he should not have done so.

[2] He wrote, however, against certain Gnostics.

[3] Similarly Sallustius (c. 360 A.D.), whose object was to revive Hellenism, includes metempsychosis in his creed and thinks it can be proved. See translation in Murray, *Four Stages of Greek Religion*, p. 213.

His system has been called dynamic pantheism and this description applies also to much Indian theology which regards God in himself as devoid of all qualities and yet the source of the forces which move the universe. He held that there are four stages of being: primæval being, the ideal world, the soul and phenomena. This, if not exactly parallel to anything in Indian philosophy, is similar in idea to the evolutionary theories of the Sânkhya and the phases of conditioned spirit taught by many Vishnuite sects.

For Plotinus neither moral good nor evil is ultimate: the highest principle, like Brahman, transcends both and is beyond good (*ὑπεράγαθον*). The highest morality is a morality of inaction and detachment: fasting and abstinence from pleasure are good and so is meditation, but happiness comes in the form of ecstasy and union with God. In human life such union cannot be permanent, though while the ecstasy lasts it affords a resting place on the weary journey, but after death it can be permanent: the divine within us can then return to the universal divine. In these ideas there is the real spirit of India.

CHAPTER LVII

PERSIAN INFLUENCE IN INDIA

Our geographical and political phraseology about India and Persia obscures the fact that in many periods the frontier between the two countries was uncertain or not drawn as now. North-western India and eastern Persia must not be regarded as water-tight or even merely leaky compartments. Even now there are more Zoroastrians in India than in Persia and the Persian sect of Shiite Mohammedans is powerful and conspicuous there. In former times it is probable that there was often not more difference between Indian and Iranian religion than between different Indian sects.

Yet the religious temperaments of India and Iran are not the same. Zoroastrianism has little sympathy for pantheism or asceticism: it does not teach metempsychosis or the sinfulness of taking life. Images are not used in worship[1], God and his angels being thought of as pure and shining spirits. The foundation of the system is an uncompromising dualism of good and evil, purity and impurity, light and darkness. Good and evil are different in origin and duality will be abolished only by the ultimate and complete victory of the good. In the next world the distinction between heaven and hell is equally sharp but hell is not eternal[2].

The pantheon and even the ritual of the early Iranians resembled those of the Veda and we can only suppose that the two peoples once lived and worshipped together. Subsequently came the reform of Zoroaster which substituted theism and dualism for this nature worship. For about two centuries, from 530 B.C. onwards, Gandhara and other parts of north-western India were a Persian province. Between the time of Zoroaster (whatever that may be) and this period we cannot say what

[1] They are forbidden by strict theology, but in practice there are exceptions, for instance, the winged figure believed to represent Ahura Mazda, found on Achæmenian reliefs.

[2] Though the principles of Zoroastrianism sound excellent to Europeans, I cannot discover that ancient Persia was socially or politically superior to India.

were the relations of Indian and Iranian religions, but after the seventh century they must have flourished in the same region. Aristobulus[1], speaking of Taxila in the time of Alexander the Great, describes a marriage market and how the dead were devoured by vultures. These are Babylonian and Persian customs, and doubtless were accompanied by many others less striking to a foreign tourist. Some hold that the Zoroastrian scriptures allude to disputes with Buddhists[2].

Experts on the whole agree that the most ancient Indian architecture which has been preserved—that of the Maurya dynasty—has no known antecedents in India, but both in structure (especially the pillars) and in decoration is reminiscent of Persepolis, just as Asoka's habit of lecturing his subjects in stone sermons and the very turns of his phrases recall the inscriptions of Darius[3]. And though the king's creed is in some respects—such as his tenderness for animal life—thoroughly Indian, yet this cannot be said of his style and choice of themes as a whole. His marked avoidance of theology and philosophy, his insistence on ethical principles such as truth, and his frank argument that men should do good in order that they may fare happily in the next world, suggest that he may have become familiar with the simple and practical Zoroastrian outlook[4], perhaps when he was viceroy of Taxila in his youth. But still he shows no trace of theism or dualism: morality is his one concern, but it means for him doing good rather than suppressing evil.

[1] See Strabo, xv. 62. So, too, the Pitakas seem to regard cemeteries as places where ordinary corpses are thrown away rather than buried or burnt. In Dig. Nik. III. the Buddha says that the ancient Sakyas married their sisters. Such marriages are said to have been permitted in Persia.

[2] "He who returns victorious from discussions with Gaotama the heretic," Farvadin Yasht in *S.B.E.* XXIII. p. 184. The reference of this passage to Buddhism has been much disputed and I am quite incompetent to express any opinion about it. But who is Gaotama if not the Buddha? It is true that there were many other Gautamas of moderate eminence in India, but would any of them have been known in Persia?

[3] The inscriptions near the tomb of Darius at Nakshi-Rustam appear to be hortatory like those of Asoka. See Williams Jackson, *Persia*, p. 298 and references. The use of the Kharoshtri script and of the word *dipi* has also been noted as indicating connection with Persia.

[4] Perhaps the marked absence of figures representing the Buddha in the oldest Indian sculptures, which seems to imply that the holiest things must not be represented, is due to Persian sentiment.

After the death of Asoka his Empire broke up and races who were Iranian in culture, if not always in blood, advanced at its expense. Dependencies of the Persian or Parthian empire extended into India or like the Satrapies of Mathurâ and Saurâshṭra lay wholly within it. The mixed civilization which the Kushans brought with them included Zoroastrianism, as is shown by the coins of Kanishka, and late Kushan coins indicate that Sassanian influence had become very strong in northern India when the dynasty collapsed in the third century A.D.

I see no reason to suppose that Gotama himself was influenced by Iranian thought. His fundamental ideas, his view of life and his scheme of salvation are truly Hindu and not Iranian. But if the childhood of Buddhism was Indian, it grew to adolescence in a motley bazaar where Persians and their ways were familiar. Though the Buddhism exported to Ceylon escaped this phase, not merely Mahayanism but schools like the Sarvâstivadins must have passed through it. The share of Zoroastrianism must not be exaggerated. The metaphysical and ritualistic tendencies of Indian Buddhism are purely Hindu, and if its free use of images was due to any foreign stimulus, that stimulus was perhaps Hellenistic. But the altruistic morality of Mahayanism, though not borrowed from Zoroastrianism, marks a change and this change may well have occurred among races accustomed to the preaching of active charity and dissatisfied with the ideals of self-training and lonely perfection. And Zoroastrian influence is I think indubitable in the figures of the great Bodhisattvas, even Maitreya[1], and above all in Amitâbha and his paradise. These personalities have been adroitly fitted into Indian theology but they have no Indian lineage and, in spite of all explanations, Amitâbha and the salvation which he offers remain in strange contradiction with the teaching of Gotama. I have shown elsewhere[2] what close parallels may be found in the Avesta to these radiant and benevolent genii and to the heaven of boundless light which is entered by those who repeat the name of its master. Also there is good evidence to connect the early worship of Amitâbha with

[1] Strictly speaking there is nothing final about Maitreya who is merely the next in an infinite series of Buddhas, but practically his figure has many analogies to Soshyos or Saoshant, the Parsi saviour and renovator of the world.

[2] See chap. XLI. p. 220.

Central Asia. Later Iranian influence may have meant Mithraism and Manichæism as well as Zoroastrianism and the school of Asanga perhaps owes something to these systems[1]. They may have brought with them fragments of Christianity or doctrines similar to Christianity but I think that all attempts to derive Amitâbhist teaching from Christianity are fanciful. The only point which the two have in common is salvation by faith, and that doctrine is certainly older than Christianity. Otherwise the efforts of Amitâbha to save humanity have no resemblance to the Christian atonement. Nor do the relations between the various Buddhas and Bodhisattvas recall the Trinity but rather the Persian Fravashis.

Persian influences worked more strongly on Buddhism than on Hinduism, for Buddhism not only flourished in the frontier districts but penetrated into the Tarim basin and the region of the Oxus which lay outside the Indian and within the Iranian sphere. But they affected Hinduism also, especially in the matter of sun-worship. This of course is part of the oldest Vedic religion, but a special form of it, introduced about the beginning of our era, was a new importation and not a descendant of the ancient Indian cult[2].

The Brihatsaṃhita[3] says that the Magas, that is Magi, are the priests of the sun and the proper persons to superintend the consecration of temples and images dedicated to that deity, but the clearest statements about this foreign cult are to be found in the Bhavishya Purana[4] which contains a legend as to its introduction obviously based upon history. Sâmba, the son of Krishna, desiring to be cured of leprosy from which he suffered owing to his father's curse, dedicated a temple to the sun on the river Candrabhâgâ, but could find no Brahmans willing to officiate in it. By the advice of Gauramukha, priest of King Ugrasena, confirmed by the sun himself, he imported some Magas from Śâkadvîpa[5], whither he flew on the bird

[1] See chap. on Mahâyâna, VI.

[2] A convenient statement of what is known about this cult will be found in Bhandarkar, *Vaishṇavism and Saivism*, part II. chap. XVI.

[3] Chap. 60. 19. The work probably dates from about 650 A.D.

[4] Chap. 139. See, for extracts from the text, Aufrecht. Cat. Cod. Sansc. p. 30.

[5] For Śâkadvîpa see Vishnu, p. II. IV. where it is said that Brahmans are called there Mriga or Maga and Kshattriyas Mâgadha. The name clearly means the country of the Śâkas who were regarded as Zoroastrians, whether they were Iranian by

Garuḍa[1]. That this refers to the importation of Zoroastrian priests from the country of the Śâkas (Persia or the Oxus regions) is made clear by the account of their customs—such as the wearing of a girdle called Avyaṅga[2]—given by the Purana. It also says that they were descended from a child of the sun called Jaraśabda or Jaraśasta, which no doubt represents Zarathustra.

The river Candrabhâgâ is the modern Chenab and the town founded by Sâmba is Mûlasthâna or Multan, called Mu-la-san-pu-lu by the Chinese pilgrim Hsüan Chuang. The Bhavishya Purana calls the place Sâmbapuri and the Chinese name is an attempt to represent Mûlasâmba-puri. Hsüan Chuang speaks enthusiastically of the magnificent temple[3], which was also seen by Alberuni but was destroyed by Aurungzeb. Târanâtha[4] relates how in earlier times a king called Śrî Harsha burnt alive near Multan 12,000 adherents of the Mleccha sect with their books and thereby greatly weakened the religion of Persians and Sakas for a century. This legend offers difficulties but it shows that Multan was regarded as a centre of Zoroastrianism.

Multan is in the extreme west of India, but sun temples are found in many other parts, such as Gujarat, Gwalior and the district of Gaya, where an inscription has been discovered at Govindapur referring to the legend of Sâmba. This same legend is also related in the Kapila Saṃhitâ, a religious guide-book for Orissa, in connection with the great Sun temple of Konarak[5].

In these temples the sun was represented by images, Hindu convention thus getting the better of Zoroastrian prejudices, but the costume of the images shows their origin, for the Brihat-saṃhitâ[6] directs that Sûrya is to be represented in the dress of

race or not. But the topography is imaginary, for in this fanciful geography India is the central continent and Śakadvîpa the sixth, whereas if it means Persia or the countries of the Oxus it ought to be near India.

[1] The Garuḍa may itself be of Persian provenance, for birds play a considerable part in Persian mythology.

[2] The Aivyâonghen of the Avesta.

[3] Watters, vol. II. 254, and *Life*, chap. IV.

[4] Târanâtha, tr. Schiefner, p. 128, and Vincent Smith's remarks in *Early History*, p. 347, note 2.

[5] See Râjendralâla Mitra, *Antiquities of Orissa*, vol. II. p. 145. He also quotes the Sâmba Purâṇa. The temple is said to have been built between 1240 and 1280 but the beauty of its architecture suggests an earlier date.

[6] 58. 47.

the northerners, covered from the feet upwards and wearing the girdle called avyaṅga or viyaṅga. In Rajputana I have seen several statues of him in high boots and they are probably to be found elsewhere.

Fortuitously or otherwise, the cult of the sun was often associated with Buddhism, as is indicated by these temples in Gaya and Orissa and by the fact that the Emperor Harsha styles his father, grandfather and great-grandfather *paramâditya-bhakta*, great devotees of the sun[1]. He himself, though a devout Buddhist, also showed honour to the image of Sûrya, as we hear from Hsüang Chuang.

[1] See Epig. Ind. 72–73.

CHAPTER LVIII

MOHAMMEDANISM IN INDIA

Let us now turn to Mohammedanism. This is different from the cases which we have been considering and we need not trouble ourselves with any enquiry into opportunities and possibilities. The presence and strength of the Prophet's religion in India are patent facts and it is surprising that the result has not been greater.

The chief and most obvious method by which Islam influenced India was the series of invasions, culminating in the Mughal conquest, which poured through the mountain passes of the north-west frontier. But there was also long established communication and to some extent intermigration between the west coast and Mohammedan countries such as Arabia and Persia. Compared with the enormous political and social changes wrought by the land invasions, the results of this maritime intercourse may seem unworthy of mention. Yet for the interchange of ideas it was not without importance, the more so as it was unaccompanied by violence and hostility. Thus the Mappilas or Moplahs of Malabar appear to be the descendants of Arab immigrants who arrived by sea about 900 A.D., and the sects known as Khojas and Bohras owe their conversion to the zeal of Arab and Persian missionaries who preached in the eleventh century. Apart from Mohammedan conquests there must have been at this time in Gujarat, Bombay, and on the west coast generally some knowledge of the teaching of Islam.

In the annals of invasions and conquests several stages can be distinguished. First we have the Arab conquest of Sind in 712, which had little effect. In 1021 Mahmud of Ghazni annexed the Panjab. He conducted three campaigns against other kingdoms of India but, though he sacked Muttra, Somnath and other religious centres, he did not attempt to conquer these regions, still less to convert thom to Islam. The period of conquests as distinguished from raids did not begin until the end of the twelfth century when Muhammad Ghori began his campaigns and succeeded in making himself master of northern India, which from 1193 to 1526 was ruled by Mohammedan dynasties, mostly of Afghan or Turki descent. In the south the frontiers of Vijayanagar marked the limits of Islam. To the north of them Rajputana and Orissa still remained Hindu states, but with these exceptions the Government was Mohammedan. In 1526 came the Mughal invasion, after which all northern India was united under one Mohammedan Emperor for about two centuries. Aurungzeb (1659–1707) was a fanatical Mohammedan: his intolerant reign marked the beginning of disintegration in the Empire and aroused the opposition of the Mahrattas and Sikhs. But until this period Mohammedan rule was not marked by special bigotry or by any persistent attempt to proselytize. A woeful chronicle of selected outrages can indeed be drawn up. In the great towns of the north hardly a temple remained unsacked and most were utterly destroyed. At different periods individuals, such as Sikander Lodi of Delhi and Jeladdin (1414–1430) in Bengal, raged against Hinduism and made converts by force. But such acts are scattered over a long period and a great area; they are not characteristic of Islam in India. Neither the earlier Mughal Emperors nor the preceding Sultans were of irreproachable orthodoxy. Two of them at least, Ala-ud-Din and Akbar, contemplated founding new religions of their own. Many of them were connected with Hindu sovereigns by marriage or political alliances.

The works of Alberuni and Mohsin Fani show that educated Mohammedans felt an interest not only in Indian science but in Indian religion. In the Panjab and Hindustan Islam was strengthened by immigrations of Mohammedan tribes from the north-west extending over many centuries. Mohammedan sultans and governors held their court in the chief cities, which thus tended to become Mohammedan not only by natural attraction but because high caste Hindus preferred to live in the country and would not frequent the company of those whom they considered as outcasts. Still, Hindus were often employed as accountants and revenue officers. All non-Moslims had to pay the jiziya or poll tax, and the remission of this impost accorded to converts was naturally a powerful incentive to change of faith. Yet Mohammedanism cannot record any wholesale triumph in India such as it has won in Persia, Egypt and Java. At the present day about one-fifth of the population are Moslim. The strength of Islam in the Panjab is due to immigration as well as conversion[1], but it was embraced by large numbers in Kashmir and made rapid progress in Oudh and Eastern Bengal. The number of Mohammedans in Bengal (twenty-five millions out of a total of sixty-two in all India) is striking, seeing that the province is out of touch with the chief Mohammedan centres, but is explicable by the fact that Islam had to deal here not with an educated and organized Hindu community but with imperfectly hinduized aboriginal races, who welcomed a creed with no caste distinctions. Yet, apart from the districts named, which lie on the natural line of march from the Panjab down the Ganges to the sea, it made little progress. It has not even conquered the slopes of the Himalayas or the country south of the Jumna. If we deduct from the Mohammedan population the descendants of Mohammedan immigrants and of those who, like the inhabitants of Eastern Bengal, were not Hindus when they embraced the faith, the impression produced by Islam on the religious thought of India is not great, considering that for at least five centuries its temporal supremacy was hardly contested.

It is not until the time of Kabir that we meet with a sect in which Hindu and Mohammedan ideas are clearly blended, but it may be that the theology of Râmânuja and Madhva, of the Lingayats and Sivaite sects of the south, owes something to Islam. Its insistence on the unity and personality of God may have vivified similar ideas existing within Hinduism, but the expression which they found for themselves is not Moslim in tone, just as nowadays the Arya Samaj is not European in tone. Yet I think that the Arya Samaj would never have come into being had not Hindus become conscious of certain strong points in European religion. In the north it is natural that Moslim influence should not have made itself felt at once. Islam came first as an enemy and a raider and was no more sympathetic to the Brahmans than it was to the Greek Church in Europe. Though Indian theism may sometimes seem practically equivalent to Islam, yet it has a different and gentler tone, and it often rests on the idea that God, the soul and matter are all separate and eternal, an idea foreign to Mohammed's doctrine of creation.

[1] But see on this point *Census of India*, 1911, vol. I. part I. p. 128.

But from the fifteenth century onwards we find a series of sects which are obviously compromises and blends. Advances are made from both sides. Thoughtful Mohammedans see the profundity of Hindu theology: liberal Hindus declare that no caste or condition, including birth in a Moslim family, disqualifies man for access to God.

The fusion of Islam with Hinduism exhibited in these sects has for its basis the unity and omnipresence of God in the light of which minor differences have no existence. But fusion also arises from an opposite tendency, namely the toleration by Indian Moslims of Hindu ideas and practices, especially respect for religious teachers and their deification after death. While known by some such title as saint, which does not shock unitarian susceptibility, they are in practice honoured as godlings. The bare simplicity of the Arabian faith has not proved satisfying to other nations, and Turks, Persians and Indians, even when professing orthodoxy, have allowed embellishments and accretions. Such supplementary beliefs thrive with special luxuriance in India, where a considerable portion of the Moslim population are descended from persons who accepted the new faith unwillingly or from interested motives. They brought with them a plentiful baggage of superstitions and did not attempt to sever the ties which bound them to their Hindu neighbours. In the last century the efforts of the Wahabis and other reformers are said to have been partly successful in purifying Islam from Hindu observances, but even now the mixture is noticeable, especially in the lower classes. Brahmans are employed to cast horoscopes, Hindu ceremonies are observed in connection with marriages and funerals, and the idea of pollution by eating with unbelievers is derived from caste rules, for Mohammedans in other countries have no objection to eating with Christians. Numerous sacred sites, such as the shrine of Sheikh Chisti at Ajmere and of Bhairav Nath at Muttra[1], are frequented by both Moslims and Hindus, and it is an interesting parallel to find that the chief Moslim shrines of Turkestan are erected on spots which were once Buddhist sanctuaries. Sometimes the opposite happens: even Brahmans are known to adopt the observances

[1] Another instance is the shrine of Saiyad Salar Masud at Bahraich. He was a nephew of Mahmud of Ghazni and was slain by Hindus, but is now worshipped by them. See Grierson, *J.R.A.S.* 1911, p. 195.

of Shiahs[1]. But on the whole it is chiefly the Mohammedans who borrow, not the main doctrines of Hinduism, but popular magic and demonology. Ignorant Mohammedans in Bengal worship Sitalâ, Kâlî, Dharmarâj, Baidyanath and other Hindu deities and also respect certain mythical beings who seem to have a Moslim origin, but to have acquired strange characters in the course of time. Such are Khwaja Khizr who lives in rivers, Zindah Ghazi who rides on a tiger in the Sandarbans, and Sultan Shahid who is said to be the bodyguard and lover of Devî. But it is in the adoration of Pirs that this fusion of the two religions is most apparent. A Pir is the Moslim equivalent of a Guru and distinct from the Mollahs or official hierarchy. Just as Hindus receive initiation from their Guru so most Moslims, except the Wahabis and other purists, make a profession of faith before their Pir, accept his guidance and promise him obedience. When an eminent Pir dies his tomb becomes a place of prayer and pilgrimage. Even educated Mohammedans admit that Pirs can intercede with the Almighty and the uneducated offer to them not only direct supplications but even sacrifices. The Shrine of an important Pir, such as Hazrat Moin-ud-Din Chisti at Ajmere, is an edifice dedicated to a superhuman being as much as any Hindu temple.

This veneration of saints attains its strangest development in the sect of the Panchpiriyas or worshippers of the five Pirs. They are treated by the last census of India as "Hindus whose religion has a strong Mohammedan flavour[2]." There is no agreement as to who the five saints or deities are, but though the names vary from place to place they usually comprise five of the best known semi-mythical Pirs[3]. Whoever they may be, they are worshipped under the form of a small tomb with five domes or of a simple mound of clay set in the corner of a room. Every Wednesday the mound is washed and offerings of flowers and incense are made. A somewhat similar sect are the Mâlkânas of the Panjab. These appear to be Hindus formerly converted to Islam and now in process of reverting to Hinduism.

[1] See for examples, *Census of India*, 1901, Panjab, p. 151, *e.g.* the Brahmans of a village near Rawal Pindi are said to be Murids of Abdul-Kadir-Jilani.

[2] *Census of India*, 1911, vol. I. part I. p. 195. The Mâlkânas are described on the same page.

[3] Such as Ghazi Miyan, Pir Badar, Zindha Ghazi, Sheikh Farid, Sheikh Sadu and Khwaja Khizr.

The influence of Hinduism on Indian Mohammedanism is thus obvious. It is responsible for the addition to the Prophet's creed of much superstition but also for rendering it less arid and more human. It is harder to say how far Moslim mysticism and Sufiism are due to the same influence. History and geography raise no difficulties to such an origin. Arabia was in touch with the western coast of India for centuries before the time of Mohammed: the same is true of the Persian Gulf and Bagdad, and of Balkh and other districts near the frontiers of India. But recent writers on Sufiism[1] have shown a disposition to seek its origin in Neoplatonism rather than in the east. This hypothesis, like the other, presents no geographical difficulties. Many Arab authors, such as Avicenna (Ibn Sina) and Averroes (Ibn Rushd) were influenced by Greek Philosophy: Neoplatonists are said to have taken refuge in Persia at the Court of Nushirwan (*c.* A.D. 532): the Fihrist (*c.* 988) mentions Porphyry and Plotinus. If, therefore, Sufiism, early or late, presents distinct resemblances to Neoplatonism, we need not hesitate to ascribe them to direct borrowing, remembering that Neoplatonism itself contains echoes of India. But, admitting that much in the doctrine of the Sufis can be found to the west as well as to the east of the countries where they flourished, can it be said that their general tone is Neoplatonic? Amongst their characteristics are pantheism; the institution of religious orders and monasteries; the conception of the religious life as a path or journey; a bold use of language in which metaphors drawn from love, wine and music are freely used in speaking of divine things and, although the doctrine of metempsychosis may be repudiated as too obviously repugnant to Islam, a tendency to believe in successive existences or states of the soul. Some of these features, such as the use of erotic language, may be paralleled in other ancient religions as well as Hinduism but the pantheism which, not content with speaking of the soul's union with God, boldly identifies the soul with the divinity and says I am God, does not seem traceable in Neoplatonism. And though a distinction may justly be drawn between early and later Sufiism and Indian influence be admitted as stronger in the later developments, still an early Sufi, Al-Hallaj, was executed in 922 A.D. for saying

[1] E. G. Browne, *Literary History of Persia*: R. A. Nicholson, *Selected Poems from the Divan of Shems-i-Tabriz.*

Ana 'l-Haqq, I am the Truth or God, and we are expressly told that he visited India to study magic. Many important Sufis made the same journey or at least came within the geographical sphere of Indian influence. Faridu-'d-Din Attar travelled in India and Turkestan; Jalalu-'d-Din er-Rumi was born at Balkh, once a centre of Buddhism: Sa'di visited Balkh, Ghazna, the Panjab, and Gujarat, and investigated Hindu temples[1]. Hafiz was invited to the Deccan by Sultan Muhammad Bahmani and, though shipwreck prevented the completion of the visit, he was probably in touch with Indian ideas. These journeys indicate that there was a prevalent notion that wisdom was to be found in India and those who could not go there must have had open ears for such Indian doctrines as might reach them by oral teaching or in books. After the establishment of the Caliphate at Bagdad in the eighth century translations of Indian authors became accessible. Arabic versions were made of many works on astronomy, mathematics and medicine and the example of Alberuni shows how easily such treatises might be flavoured with a relish of theology. His book and still more the Fihrist testify to the existence among Moslims, especially in Bagdad and Persia, of an interest in all forms of thought very different from the self-satisfied bigotry which too often characterizes them. The Caliph Ma'mun was so fond of religious speculation and discussion that he was suspected of being a Manichee and nicknamed Amiru-'l-Kafirin, Commander of the Unbelievers. Everything warrants the supposition that in the centuries preceding Mohammed, Indian ideas were widely disseminated in western Asia, partly as a direct overflow from India, for instance in Turkestan and Afghanistan, and partly as entering, together with much other matter, into the doctrines of Neoplatonists and Manichæans. Amid the intolerant victories of early Islam such ideas would naturally retreat, but they soon recovered and effected an entrance into the later phases of the faith and were strengthened by the visits of Sufi pilgrims to Turkestan and India.

The form of Jewish mysticism known as Kabbala, which in Indian terminology might be described as Jewish Tantrism, has a historical connection with Sufiism and a real analogy to it,

[1] He describes how he discovered the mechanism by which the priests made miraculous images move. See Browne, *Lit. Hist. Persia*, II. 529.

for both arise from the desire to temper an austere and regal deism with concessions to the common human craving for the interesting and picturesque, such as mysticism and magic. If the accent of India can sometimes be heard in the poems of the Sufis we may also admit that the Kabbala is its last echo.

Experts do not assign any one region as the origin of the Kabbala but it grew on parallel lines in both Egypt and Babylonia, in both of which it was naturally in touch with the various oriental influences which we have been discussing. It is said to have been introduced to Europe about 900 A.D. but received important additions and modifications at the hands of Isaac Luria (1534–72) who lived in Palestine, although his disciples soon spread his doctrines among the European Jews.

Many features of the Kabbala, such as the marvellous powers assigned to letters, the use of charms and amulets, the emanations or phases of the deity and the theory of the correspondence between macrocosm and microcosm, are amazingly like Indian Tantrism but no doubt are more justly regarded as belonging to the religious ideas common to most of Asia[1]. But in two points we seem able to discern definite Hindu influence. These are metempsychosis and pantheism, which we have so often found to have some connection with India when they exist in an extreme form. Their presence here is specially remarkable because they are alien to the spirit of orthodox Judaism. Yet the pre-existence and repeated embodiment of the soul is taught in the Zohar and even more systematically by Luria, in whose school were composed works called Gilgûlim, or lists of transmigrations. The ultimate Godhead is called En soph or the infinite and is declared to be unknowable, not to be described by positive epithets, and therefore in a sense non-existent, since nothing which is predicated of existing beings can be truly predicated of it. These are crumbs from the table of Plotinus and the Upanishads.

[1] But there is something very Indian in the reluctance of the Kabbalists to accept creation *ex nihilo* and to explain it away by emanations, or by the doctrine of limitation, that is God's self-withdrawal in order that the world might be created, or even by the eternity of matter.

INDEX